VIKINGS

About the Author

W. B. Bartlett has worked across the globe in almost twenty countries and has spent time in over fifty. He is the author of many history books for Amberley including titles on King Cnut, the Crusades and the Mongols. He lives in Bournemouth.

VIKINGS
A HISTORY OF
THE NORTHMEN

W. B. BARTLETT

AMBERLEY

Then the Lord said unto me, out of the north an evil shall break forth
upon all the inhabitants of the land.

Jeremiah 1:14

This edition published 2021

Amberley Publishing
The Hill, Stroud
Gloucestershire, GL5 4EP

www.amberley-books.com

British Library Cataloguing in Publication Data.
A catalogue record for this book is available from the British Library.

ISBN 978 1 3981 0908 7 (paperback)
ISBN 978 1 4456 6595 5 (ebook)

Typeset in 10.5pt on 13pt Sabon.
Typesetting by Aura Technology and Software Services, India.
Printed in the UK.

Contents

Introduction

Vikings: that one word summons up many images. Maybe it is of dragon ships carving their way across the waters, descending on isolated, unprotected monasteries and unleashing terror in their wake. Or perhaps it is an image of Viking explorers, heading out across unknown oceans and facing unfathomable terrors which grips the imagination. It could even be their craftsmanship which draws the reader in. All these views are equally valid and therein lies the attraction of the Vikings; they were multi-dimensional, unpredictable.

They had a decisive impact on the shaping of medieval Europe, and through that on the modern world. They were integral to the development of nation states, not just in their own Scandinavian homelands but in territories further afield such as Britain, Ireland, Francia (modern France and Germany), and Russia. Intriguing in a different way, they created settlements in Iceland, the Faroes and Greenland, not to mention their incursions into North America in their role as frontiersmen and women. Theirs is a fascinating and multi-faceted story.

I make no claim to be writing a definitive history of the Vikings, indeed, I am not even sure that such a thing is possible given the vast sweep of the subject. What I have tried to do in this book is to tell the story of some of the key events and the major characters who bestrode the world of Western Europe and beyond for 250 years. I have arranged the story chronologically. There is a tendency among some modern historians to look at the Viking story thematically. While this approach undoubtedly has its merits, it runs the risk of not seeing the Viking saga as an interconnected tale. For example, that quasi-legendary character Ivarr the Boneless was active in England, Scotland and Ireland as well as probably on the mainland of Europe in a series of more or less sequential actions. In my view it is important that the reader understands how these activities are inter-connected. We will find a number of relevant examples in the story that follows.

Not only did the Vikings shape medieval Europe, equally, medieval Europe shaped them. Another interesting aspect of the saga is how the Vikings transmuted from pagan raiders to devout Christians. Equally interestingly, this did not necessarily make them any less violent, but it did shape the way they acted. Therein lies a tale in itself; violence was not the exclusive preserve of pagan Vikings at the time. However, in the eyes of contemporary observers somehow violence committed by Christians against non-Christians (viz. the soon-to-follow epic of the Crusades and the *Reconquista* in Spain) was far more acceptable.

Although there is a tendency to think of the Viking Age as belonging to the latter part of the so-called Dark Ages, there are a number of sources telling us about the course of events that provide some illumination. These range from annals and chronicles, normally written by monastic observers who potentially had an axe to grind, to later saga writers who had their own perspective on 'the truth'. There are potential difficulties with all of these sources. However, we cannot afford to be overly restrictive in the ones we use, particularly when Viking culture prided itself on its tradition of oral storytelling, which in its own way was a form of record-keeping. Of course in the process many details were subject to interpretation and, over time, to change and elaboration; but I do not think we should ignore them completely even if we are naturally cautious in using them.

This is the story of great warriors and remarkable women, of intrepid adventurers and canny and unscrupulous traders. It is also a tale of many ordinary people, both Scandinavians and those on the wrong end of their unwelcome attentions. Many of the latter are not known to us, nameless shadows from the past. Yet all of them played a part in this remarkable if sometimes harrowing story. The saga deserves to be retold if only for them.

Prologue

The Vikings and their World

Above the prow, the dragon rears its glowing head.

King Harald's Saga

Who were the Vikings?

At the very outset of our journey back into the world of the Vikings, an important question needs to be addressed; what do we mean by a 'Viking'? Academics propose a range of origins for the word, including the Scandinavian term *vik*, which in Norse means 'bay', a convenient gathering point for pirates to assemble before setting out on their raids; or from 'Viken', a region in the south of modern Norway around Oslofjord, the point of origin for some (though not all) of the raiders. *Vikingr* in Old Norse means someone away from home, usually raiding, while *Viking* is the group name for a party of such individuals. There are several contemporary monuments in Scandinavia that record the word 'Viking'.[1] There may also be a link to the Old English *wicing*, loosely meaning a pirate, a word used on five occasions in the *Anglo-Saxon Chronicles (ASC)*, always with reference to a raiding party rather than a larger army. Properly speaking, the term 'Viking' only applies when these Scandinavians are travelling overseas, often raiding, rather than being applied to any Scandinavian of the early Middle Ages – and academics might insist that we should strictly adhere to this line of reasoning when we discuss them.[2] Good luck with winning that particular argument; 'Viking' has rightly or wrongly become shorthand for a Scandinavian of the period.

One expert on the Viking Age said that 'we can refer to Viking-Age society, but not all Scandinavians were Vikings. They themselves used the term to refer to raiders from the region, but it certainly didn't describe the local farmers who were back on the land.'[3] This is pedantically correct; but the situation becomes distinctly blurred when a man might be a Viking one day and then become a farmer on another. Neatly pigeonholing individuals into one category or another is not straightforward and arguably not very useful.

Early medieval chroniclers would rarely call such men, even when raiding, Vikings. In the *ASC,* they are often referred to as 'Danes', even though we know that the raiders who caused such chaos also came from elsewhere. They are sometimes referred to as 'Northmen' or *normanni* from which the later term 'Norman' derives. Adam of Bremen noted that 'the Danes and the other people who live beyond Denmark are all called Northmen by the historians of the Franks'.[4] On other occasions they would merely be named, in dismissive terms, 'pagans', 'heathens' or 'gentiles', something 'other'. The terms 'black' or 'white' foreigners ('Gaills') were often used in Ireland, with in some interpretations 'black foreigners' originating in Norway and 'white' in Denmark.[5] The Muslims of Cordoba, who were briefly on the Vikings' itinerary, called them *majus,* loosely translated as 'heathen wizards'.[6] All these terms come back to much the same thing, generically 'Vikings'. In other words, everything is as clear as mud. Broadly speaking in my simple view of the world a 'Viking' is a Scandinavian of the late eighth to eleventh centuries (with a date range covering 789 to 1103) who was operating overseas. The year 789 is the date of the first recorded Scandinavian raid overseas (though there may well be unrecorded ones pre-dating this) while 1103 saw the death of the Norwegian king, Magnus Barelegs, in Ireland. I freely admit that these dates are rather arbitrary and for that reason even I do not stick slavishly to them in the analysis that follows. But activities during this general time period are the primary focus of my own particular voyage of discovery.

The Vikings and Scandinavia

Scandinavia had a particular point of reference 1,000 years ago that is different from what it has today. Some historians limit their discussions to those activities of the Vikings that were taking place outside of Scandinavia.[7] However, my personal take on the Viking story is that it cannot be fully understood without referring to Scandinavia itself, both to explain the origins of the Vikings and their later development. During this period great changes took place in Norway, Sweden and Denmark, which impacted on Viking activities overseas. Equally some of those distant events affected Scandinavia greatly too. For this reason, I will regularly refer back to events in the Viking 'homelands'.

Scandinavia and its culture is and always has been defined to a significant extent by its geographical location, and this in turn helped to define the peoples who lived there. In the case of the Viking world, when we mention Scandinavia we include not only Norway and Sweden but also Denmark. There are also close cultural links between the south-west of Finland and this wider Scandinavia, and men from other regions would often join Scandinavians on their expeditions: for example, Finns would journey alongside Swedes into the lands of the Rūs. Warriors from other parts of the Baltic region, from what are now Latvia, Lithuania, Estonia, Poland and Belarus, were also engaged as participants in Viking expeditions. Meanwhile, inhabitants from the far north of Scandinavia, such as the Sáami people, are not regarded as Vikings regardless of the modern countries where they are now found. In other words, both the appellation Viking and that of Scandinavia is loosely defined.

The very shape of the landscape helped define the nature and direction of Viking activities. Geographically, Scandinavia is far from one homogeneous whole. Norway has a long, mainly westward-facing coastline that is ripped open by the jagged fingers of fjords clawing into the interior. They gouge out drowned valleys reaching far into the mountain ranges, which form a largely impregnable natural inner barrier preventing most permanent human habitation beyond the coastal zone. These fjords can be extremely long but at the same time they are often narrow, framed by towering rock walls on either side, a source of stunning natural beauty as many an awed modern cruise traveller to the country would confirm.

One could do worse than quote the words of the twelfth/thirteenth century Danish writer Saxo Grammaticus when describing Norway. He talked of it in the following terms:

> Craggy and barren, it is beset all around by cliffs, and the huge desolate boulders give it the aspect of a rugged and gloomy land; in its furthest part the day-star is not hidden even by night; so that the sun, scorning the vicissitudes of day and night, ministers in unbroken presence an equal share of his radiance in either season.[8]

As far as the Viking Age is concerned, Norway can be simplistically divided into three separate regions, though there were many sub-divisions. Firstly, there was Ostland, the eastern region. This comprised the settlements lying along either side of the Oslofjord, which provided some of the best agricultural land in Norway. Significant trading settlements such as Kaupang developed there, acting as a regional centre of trade, much as Helgö and later Birka would in Sweden or Hedeby and Ribe did in Denmark. Vestfold, one of Ostland's sub-divisions which was on the western shores of Oslofjord, became particularly affluent and was well placed to play a key role in the development of a royal dynasty, which later expanded its control over a wider area of Norway.

The Ostland region, centred around modern Oslo, Kristiansand and Gothenburg, was known as the Viken – a name which, as noted above, is a possible point of origin for the term 'Viking'. The area was split up into smaller tribal territories known as *fylki*. It has been suggested that each of these *fylki* would at one stage have had its own king, though he would govern over a very limited area when compared to the national polities that later developed in Scandinavia.[9] Ostland was perfectly situated to provide a link between Sweden and Norway.

More remote was the south-west corner of Norway, the Jaeder and the southern Trøndelag, which formed Vestland. Here regional sub-divisions such as Rogaland and Hordaland were important. This area was defined by steep mountains and fjords that bisected the land like sharp arrowheads. Nowadays this is a prime spot for cruise ships to penetrate inland through breathtaking scenery to remote towns, in some cases scores of miles from the coast. No such luxury attended life here a thousand years ago. Workable land is in short supply. Only small pockets of agriculturally productive terrain are available as steep, rocky mountains hem in the coastal region. Any surplus population is likely to create difficulties, as there is little spare land to expand into. It is notable that many Viking raiders departed from here, perhaps pushed out by shortages and inspired by the prospect of rich pickings to compensate for harsh lives and limited prospects back home. This might also explain why activities that initially took the shape of raids later became far more ambitious attempts at conquest and settlement overseas. Vestland was always likely to produce a fiercely independent and hard-living population who were adventurous risk-takers given their constrained options; those who lived there only had a limited amount to lose.[10]

Further north along the western coast of Norway is the northern Trøndelag where Trondheim later developed. Although closer to the Arctic Circle than Vestland, it provided more agricultural land. Here the mountain range that separates Norway from Sweden, a formation known as the Keel as it mimics the shape of an upturned ship, is situated further inland than it is to the south, giving a greater area available for farming. Trade links from the Trøndelag to the Frisian coast of continental Europe developed from quite early on, and it is notable that one of the earliest phases of Viking settlement in the Viking Age proper was in Frisia. A strong group of independent landowners with supporting laws to protect their interests would develop in the northern Trøndelag, and later aspiring kings of the polity we now call Norway often found themselves faced by fierce resistance here.

Farming opportunities in Norway are therefore limited in scope to relatively narrow strips of land. The coast is protected from the worst of the Atlantic weather by a string of some 1,500 islands, the Lofoten, patrolling the approaches to it like rocky sentries, a great, extended natural windbreak. Inside this outer layer of islands there are some well-protected natural harbours, perfect for Viking ships to moor safely sheltered from the weather. Here, the impact of the Gulf Stream mitigates the worst effects of the regions' proximity to the Arctic; coastal waters do not become icebound in the winter as they do in other parts of the world at the same latitude.

Sea, mountains and forests are writ large in the history of Scandinavia. The mountains, with the dense forests that blanketed the landscape, made overland connection between the different parts of Scandinavia very difficult and sometimes totally impossible; therefore, the best way to travel was by sea. From early in their history, the peoples of Scandinavia were wedded to it. Its surface was their highway, their way of moving from one place to another in the shortest possible time. There is a certain inevitability around the development of superb seafaring skills among the inhabitants of this rugged, isolated area that is embraced and defined by the ocean.

Both Norway and Sweden reach up towards the Far North. During the summer months, virtually permanent daylight is the norm, the more so the further north one travels, while in the winter the opposite is true. Significant parts of both Norway and Sweden lie above the Arctic Circle and the climate changes significantly and becomes harsher the further north the voyager travels. It takes a hardy breed of people to survive, let alone thrive, in such regions given the harshness and longevity of the winter months. A by-product of this meant that summer was a time for raiding and winter for staying at home.

On the Atlantic-facing coast of Scandinavia, weather and current conditions encourage sea journeys from east to west, for example from Norway or Denmark to Britain or France. Thus when Scandinavian seafarers became more adventurous, they tended to look west. They forayed across the Atlantic, first to Scotland and Ireland, then to the Faroes, the 'Sheep Islands' (where the name of the capital Torshavn – 'Thor's Harbour' – eloquently betrays its origins) and Iceland. They went beyond that to Greenland and finally made landfall in Newfoundland, probably visiting the mainland of North America too. This was a 'stepping stone' strategy by which the Vikings expanded westwards 'island hopping' bit by bit.

These were epic voyages in an age when ships rarely sailed out of sight of land and the wild Atlantic was a vast, almost insurmountable barrier. It is difficult to overstate the risks inherent in these extraordinary undertakings. Nature could help to a limited extent in establishing the exact location of a ship at sea; for example, between the Faroes and Iceland, whales could be followed as they fed on the vast stocks of plankton that lived around the undersea mountain range known as the Iceland Ridge; when the saga writers formulaically describe the sea as the 'whale's path' they are being more literal than we might think.[11] But this must have been of limited comfort when sailing uncharted waters.

It is likely that even in remoter places such as the Faroes and Iceland the Viking explorers already found human beings living there. There is evidence of this from the Irish monk Dicuil who wrote a geography of the early medieval world, stating that Irish hermits were living there before the Vikings intruded, such places being much loved by those of a contemplative mind who sought to find God in out-of-the-way locations.[12] Dicuil spent much of his career in Francia, just like the more famous Alcuin of York. His work *De Mensura Orbis Terrae* ('On the Measurement of the World') is a revealing insight into the state of geographical knowledge at the start of the Viking Age (he was active in the early years of the ninth century).

In contrast to Norway and Denmark, Sweden as a general rule tended to look east (though some Swedish Vikings certainly took part in raids on Britain and elsewhere), travelling across the Baltic, a relatively recent relic of melting glaciers after the last Ice Age. When the mood takes it, the Baltic can be perilous and subject to sudden, unexpected squalls; within living memory the sinking of the ferry *Estonia* in 1994, with shocking loss of life, is a painful reminder of this. The Baltic is frequently cloaked in blankets of heavy fog; the saga writers often mention mists as an ill omen, something with which seafarers in any age can empathise. The seas here are renowned for their propensity to generate short but sharp waves. Currents and wind directions in the Baltic encourage journeys from west to east, explaining why Swedes, in alliance with Finns, regularly made the journey eastwards into what is now Russia. The 50,000 islands in the Baltic Sea made for convenient stopping-off points for sailors making their way across.

Geographically, Sweden is to a large extent sectioned off from Norway by the mountain ranges in the west, while the northern part is generously covered by thick carpets of forest. The southern part of Sweden, Scania (Skåne), is more fertile than the lands to the north; it was described in the eleventh century as being 'well provided with men, opulent of crops, rich in merchandise'.[13] It therefore assumed great importance in Viking history. Though it is now in Sweden, for much of its past – and certainly for a good part of the Viking Age – Skåne was part of Denmark. To the north, the infertile plateau of Småland acted as a natural border with the north. Vast forests isolated Skåne and encouraged it to look towards Denmark across the narrow straits that separated the two.

Denmark is in a significantly different geographical spot compared to Norway and Sweden in a metaphorical, if not a literal, sense. Only a few miles separate it from Sweden at its narrowest point and at such places it is easy to see one from the other on all but a misty morning (the two countries are these days connected by a combination of a bridge and a tunnel). But Denmark is joined to the main portion of continental Europe; and the further south in the country that one travels, the more obvious this becomes. On the extreme southern borders of Denmark, historically territory has frequently changed from Danish to German (or in earlier times Frankish) hands and back again, the region of Schleswig being a prime example. Having a strong neighbour just to the south has frequently affected Danish history even, and notably, back in Viking times. On the other hand, Norway and Sweden in a geographical sense are more peripheral and isolated. This makes them better protected and hidden from the eyes – and the unwelcome attentions – of acquisitive neighbours.

Denmark is also geographically distinct in other ways. Its structure is complicated with a mainland portion, Jutland, and a number of islands, some called 'The Belt', just off it. Zealand is the biggest, with Funen in between it and Jutland. There are also more than 400 named smaller islands, though only 74 of them are currently inhabited.[14] Nowadays Denmark has a reputation for efficient and effective agriculture, but this was not always the case. In former times, the boggy nature of much of the land limited farming potential, even though there was no mountainous territory acting as a constraint. Adam of Bremen, writing in the eleventh century, suggests that 'the soil in Denmark is sterile; except for places close to a river, nearly everything looks like a desert'. He also wrote that '[Jutland] is avoided because of the scarcity of crops, and the sea because it is infested by pirates'.[15]

Complicated geography and wide regional variations in Scandinavia mitigated against centralised authority. Deep into the Viking Age, Norway and Sweden were loosely confederated regions at best; and even Denmark was too for much of the time. But for all that there were unifying features between the Scandinavians, most strongly evidenced by shared language – though in Viking times this would evolve and 'West Norse' would become the language of Norway and the Atlantic islands while 'East Norse' would be used in Denmark and Sweden. They were the northernmost representatives of Germanic languages that also included English and Dutch. There was also a common Scandinavian heritage in terms of mythology. The Vikings' religious framework was distinctive and, centuries after most of Western Europe had adopted Christianity, they remained wedded to their pagan belief system, which at one time had also been shared with other Germanic peoples. There were also shared views of the law and a similar social hierarchy across Scandinavia. And there were shared influences on art too, though certainly not in a suffocating monotone way that held back the development of more individualistic regional styles.

Scandinavia was the cradle of the Vikings, and as such it is important to understand something of the region from which they came to make more sense of how they originated and developed; they did not emerge out of thin air but came about as a result of centuries, indeed millennia, of evolution. It was the coincidence of the combination of various factors that led to the timing of their appearance and the impact they had. Some of these factors were technological, in particular developments in shipbuilding. Others were societal, yet more were responses to opportunities that presented themselves as a way of making profit in one form or another. These opportunities derived from the state of the world in which the Vikings operated. In Western Europe in particular, but also in Russia, the current state of affairs played into Viking hands. The Vikings perceived weaknesses in the structure of the wider world and took full advantage of them. It is important to understand both how the Scandinavian region had developed and where it was at on the cusp of the Viking Age. We also need to comprehend the condition of the wider world at the time; and it is to these issues that we now turn.

I

The Dawn of the Viking Age

There's woe in the world, wantonness rampant

The Poetic Edda

Scandinavia in Prehistory

Being far to the north, Norway and Sweden were among the last European territories to emerge from the latest Ice Age. After this ended, hunter-gatherers began to populate the area. These peoples transitioned, like others in Europe, through a Bronze and eventually into an Iron Age, though later than other parts of the Continent. They constructed boat-shaped graves for their prominent dead; ships were required in ancient Scandinavia for more than just terrestrial journeys, an ancient tradition and way of life that continued for millennia, well into the Viking Age.

By about 4,000BC, agriculture had arrived in Scandinavia, crops were being grown and animals domesticated. Small villages were established. Cattle were especially important and became a prime measure of wealth, as they remained into the Viking Age. By about 2,300BC, the Bronze Age had arrived in Scandinavia, accompanied by a new influx of people with a Germanic language. Their technology allowed improved tools to be made. Pottery also developed, invaluable for the storage of perishable items such as food.

These developments gave impetus to trade. Tin and copper, crucial for the making of bronze, were not available in Scandinavia and needed to be imported from other regions such as Central Europe. In return, furs were exchanged along with walrus ivory and whalebone. Even Britain was involved in this extended trading network; hand-axes from the period 4000–2200 BC, which were found locally and are exhibited in the Museum of London, are said by experts to show Scandinavian influence. Some of the goods that flowed out of Scandinavia originated with the

Sáami in the Far North, able to move cross-country with the aid of skis, sleighs and skates and establishing trading links with the more southerly Scandinavians. Amber, prized as a precious stone, was also traded south from the Baltic. Evidence of the wealth that was starting to come into Scandinavia in return can be found in the grave goods buried across the region in the period.

This culture peaked between 1500 and 1100BC, a time known as the Northern Bronze Age and a period of relative plenty for Scandinavia. Although settlements were scattered and no such thing as a town existed, these were good times when trade with parts of Europe further south enabled a degree of prosperity. Rock paintings of the period suggest that later beliefs concerning Viking gods were already developing. Examples have been found in a number of places and are particularly fine at Tanum, Bohuslän, Sweden, where there are petroglyphs of objects including boats, a chariot and a whale. One carving at Bohuslän, the Vitlycke Flat Rock, shows a flotilla of ships with a larger vessel surrounded by smaller ones though there is not a sail to be seen anywhere. Ships are also carved on the walls of the so-called King's Grave near Kivik in Sweden. Religious beliefs were evolving too: the development of large gravesites in the form of barrows strongly suggests a major concentration on burial rites, especially the veneration of ancestors, something else that lived on into the Viking Age.

Then the general European economy declined. This was probably linked to major political upheavals in regions as far afield as Egypt, the Hittite Empire and Greece, leading to a retreat in cross-Continental trade with Scandinavia. For some time, the Far North receded into the twilight as trading routes seized up. The Iron Age that followed was initially harsh for Scandinavia. Climatic conditions contributed to this situation but while a harsher climate made life even tougher for the Scandinavian peoples, the emergence of the Celts as the dominant force in much of continental Europe also hid the northern region from view for a time. Only later in the Iron Age with the emergence of the Celtic La Tene culture did trade between mainland Europe and Scandinavia return. Iron began to be worked in Scandinavia in about 800BC but not for perhaps 400 years after that did quality iron, and maybe even foreign smiths, begin to arrive from further south.

There were important developments in funerary practices in the region during these years with the emergence of massive boat-shaped graves, their outlines traced out by large megaliths (particularly on the islands of Gotland and Bornholm): the abstract paintings on the rocks which we see in the Bronze Age had morphed into something far more recognisable and substantial. At either end of the graves a larger stone was placed to mark the prow and stern of the vessel. The deceased was clearly journeying across an otherworldly sea to another existence.

Other forms of art developed too, and there is evidence of Celtic influence on some of it. One example is the Gundestrup Cauldron, found in Denmark but with metalwork displaying human heads removed from dead bodies, a common Celtic practice.

In the absence of written records, we must make what we can of the Scandinavia of early times from archaeological evidence. However, this changes with several references to the peoples of the Far North in the Classical record. In around 325BC, a Greek geographer, Pytheas, made an astonishing voyage of discovery from Massalia (Marseilles). Journeying around Britain, he sailed up to Scandinavia. He returned with reports of polar ice and the Arctic region. He told how the inhabitants of that far-off region used honey to make mead and how, despite being so far north, they were able to grow barley. He also noted with awe that dazzling lightshow known as the *Aurora Borealis*. Pytheas also mentioned amber, one of the most valuable trade products originating in Scandinavia. It has been suggested that he may even have reached Iceland. Unfortunately, his account of this epic voyage does not survive, and we only know of his travels second-hand through references made by other writers in Antiquity. Therefore, we have to take at face value the words of Strabo who wrote that 'Pytheas asserts that he explored in person the whole northern region of Europe as far as the ends of the world'.

With the subjugation of many of the Celtic territories by Rome, more conduits between north and south were opened. The lands of the north piqued Rome's interest. A naval expedition was despatched by the Emperor Augustus and reached as far as the Kattegat, the narrow strait between Denmark and Sweden. Then in 60AD during Nero's reign, another maritime Roman foray penetrated further into the Baltic. Tacitus wrote shortly afterwards in his *Germania* of a people in the region called the Suiones whose unusual ships had a prow at each end. These people have been identified with the Swedes from Uppland in central Sweden.[1]

The evolution of the Roman Empire had a dramatic economic impact on Europe, including in those areas beyond its borders such as Scandinavia. Trade between them was two-way. High-status Roman goods such as glass, ceramics and silver objects have been found in significant quantities in both Denmark and Skåne; Roman wine was also a much sought-after commodity for the upper classes. Other more mundane objects appear from time to time; for example, the skeleton of a woman buried in Lolland, Denmark, appears to be clutching a Roman sieve.[2] There were more exotic Roman-origin grave goods found in Lolland, too, such as a bronze jug superbly decorated with vine motifs.

Goods also flowed the other way; cattle from Denmark were driven south to feed the tens of thousands of Roman soldiers who garrisoned the frontier of the Empire. In addition, there were trade links between Scandinavian merchants and territories further to the east during the Roman period; the Vistula River was a prominent artery for such movements. Roman weaponry made its way north and swords became highly valued in parts of Scandinavia. Such weapons are referred to in Norse mythology where they are objects that were prized by the gods. Yet Rome never sought to add Scandinavia to her Empire; her nose had been bloodied by Germanic tribes and their very effective guerrilla tactics; this deterred her from pushing into the lands beyond.

As trade continued to expand, petty chieftains in parts of Scandinavia grew more powerful, allowing an upper echelon of strong warlords to emerge. As was common among most peoples of Germanic origin, success in battle was crucial to maintaining the position of these warlords; not only did it enhance their status, it gave them access to new stores of loot with which to practice patronage. With limited land resources, loot was the only available source of wealth to buy support. War bands developed, composed of fraternities of men who served their chosen lord and in return shared in the spoils of peace and war. Standards of behaviour were expected of both parties to the bargain. The warlords were expected to be generous, 'ring-givers' and 'bestowers of gold'; in return, their men were required to be loyal.

The concept of loot as a form of patronage was certainly not unique to Scandinavians of the period. It also happened on a much larger scale in cases of what might be called state-sponsored bounty hunting. The rulers of the eighth/ninth-century Carolingian Empire, and tenth-century Anglo-Saxon England, were able to practise patronage by conquest, giving access to vast stores of new land and portable plunder. Once that expansion stopped, then those rulers were in trouble because their ability to operate a system of patronage was limited. For early medieval states it was a case of 'expand or die'.[3]

As the Roman Empire grew old, it began to unravel. With her decline, the legions were less able to defend her borders. In Britannia, coastal regions were exposed to pirate raids from Anglo-Saxons, precursors of later Viking assaults. During the last centuries of Rome there came the age of the Great Migrations when the fabric of Europe was torn apart by devastating migratory movements from the north and east into the south of the Continent and even beyond into North Africa. One early group from Scandinavia, mentioned as far back as the third century AD, were the Eruli. They were raiding as far away from home as the Black Sea and they gained a reputation for their acts of ferocious piracy. They were accused of all sorts of barbaric behaviour, including making sure that the trials of old age did not affect their elderly folk too much by thoughtfully stabbing them to death before they endured them. The Eruli eventually made their way back to southern Sweden.[4] Other migrations saw peoples come to Britain from Schleswig, on the southern extremities of Denmark; these were the Angles and the Jutes. Bede suggested that the Jutes lived to the north of the Angles in Denmark. The Saxons from north Germany, which is to the south of the other groups, were also involved. Therefore, even before the Viking Age, there was a long tradition of migrations from the north.

There were almost certainly pirate raids from Scandinavia on adjacent parts of Europe at the time. One is obliquely referred to in the epic Anglo-Saxon work *Beowulf*. Although it was not written up until perhaps the ninth or tenth centuries, it probably originates in oral traditions from a time long before then. In it we are told that a warlord called Hygelac, king of the Geats, attacked Frisia. For him, it was a personal disaster as he and all but one of his army were killed in the battle that followed. That this was an actual historical event seems probable because it is also referred to in other sources such as the works of Gregory of Tours, dated to around 521. Hygelac's skeleton was preserved and shown to a curious public at the mouth of the Rhine for some time afterwards. He was such a large man that no horse could carry him (an attribute also claimed for the tenth-century Viking founder of Normandy, Rollo). The Geats, also known as the Gautar, were the traditional great enemies of the Swedes, but where exactly they came from is unclear; it may have been Denmark but it was certainly somewhere in Scandinavia.[5]

Unfortunately, with the decline of the Roman Empire there is also a sharp drop in our documentary evidence concerning Scandinavia. Scandinavian trade significantly tailed off if the scarcity of archaeological remains of imported items is anything to go by. However, a fifth-century writer, Cassiodorus, revived interest in Scandinavia when he wrote *The Origin and Exploits of the Goths*, partly because the Goths – who had created so much chaos in continental Europe for the previous two centuries – had originated in Sweden.

The writer Jordanes, whose work the *Gettica* arrived shortly after that of Cassiodorus and may have been based on it (Cassiodorus's original works have also not survived), wrote of a region in the far north inhabited by the Adogit where, for forty days in the summer, there was unbroken daylight and, in the winter, an equal and opposite duration of perpetual night. So tough were conditions up there, said Jordanes, that no grain could be grown, and the locals survived on a diet of animal flesh and birds' eggs. Jordanes also spoke of a race called the Dani from the region. He was impressed by the superb physical specimens of humanity that were found there, as many later historians would be too.

The Byzantine writer Procopius wrote of Denmark in 550 and of the island, as it was perceived to be, of Thule. The exact location of where Thule was has confusingly moved around throughout history but when spoken of during the time of Procopius, it is believed to have been a part of Scandinavia. He also spoke of the Sáami who relied on animals for virtually every aspect of everyday life. He remarked that it was believed that their children never tasted milk but, from birth, were fed on bone marrow from butchered animals. As soon as they were born, babes in arms were wrapped in a fur cloak and suspended from a tree so that the mother could return to hunting duties as quickly as possible; hunting was important not just for survival but also for trading, especially with neighbours to the south.

Some surviving accounts of pre-Viking Age Scandinavia tell of wars between different groups in the region. The *Ynglinga Saga* suggests that the Swede Ottar (Ohthere) invaded Jutland but was defeated and killed there in a naval battle in the great natural canal across the north of that region called the Limfjord. The Danes, euphoric at their success, exposed his corpse on the top of a mound to be ravaged by the birds and wild beasts. This is further evidence that violence was common in Scandinavia long before the Vikings emerged, as indeed it was across much of Europe during the post-Roman period.

Post-Roman developments

For some time after the collapse of Rome, great migratory tides ebbed and flowed across Europe, swathes of humanity washing across the Continent. A dark veil was once more drawn across the Far North, however, it is clear from archaeology that this was not necessarily a time of extreme hardship in Scandinavia. Items of gold work have been found in Sweden dated to the fifth and sixth centuries including many fine examples of gold neck rings. A gold collar from Färjestaden in Sweden is a magnificent example of simple yet dazzling filigree work. Much of the gold that survives comes from items buried in hoards, leading to speculation that they were deposited in times of trouble and never recovered. Hoards continued to be buried into the Viking Age: so many examples have been found that it has been suggested that the reason for them concerns ritual as well as pragmatic security measures.

Impressive cemeteries in Sweden are a sign of the wealth that was present in the pre-Viking Age. Massive tombs, megalithic edifices in the shape of ships, were constructed; Skåne is particularly well provided with examples. As time moved on, styles changed. Grave mounds erected at Uppsala have been linked with the pre-Viking Yngling dynasty – though archaeological remains to confirm this definitively are in frustratingly short supply. The reference to this dynasty is an important pointer that parts of Sweden had been under the rule of some form of a king for some time before the Viking Age. However, some of the Yngling moved to Norway where they founded a dynasty in the Vik region, close to modern-day Oslo. From them, Harald Fairhair and ultimately the medieval, and modern, Norwegian royal house descended.[6]

When we can start to talk about a Viking Age is a moot point. There is a tendency to want to delimit precise intersections for historical periods, as if one morning with the rising of the sun the Viking Age began when it had not been there the night before. That well-known raconteur of Viking history, the Icelandic-born Magnus Magnusson, wrote that the dates for the Viking Age are clear-cut: 793 to 1066.[7] It is understandable that one might pick as a start date the sacking of Lindisfarne and suggest that a terminus is arrived at in the year of Stamford Bridge and the death of the quasi-legendary Harald Hardrada; but it is an approach that has its problems. History rarely works in such a neat fashion. The Vikings may have appeared to have struck out of the blue when they attacked Lindisfarne in 793 but it is unlikely that they really did. For one thing, the possibility that the raiders happened upon a rich but undefended monastery on a remote island by chance without prior knowledge of it is stretching coincidence beyond breaking point. They surely knew of it beforehand, perhaps had even visited it as traders, so they probably knew exactly where they were headed. Neither is it likely that a group of previously pacific Scandinavian farmers, fishers and hunters suddenly woke up one morning and decided without any forethought to take up arms against unsuspecting distant lands. Indeed, we know they were in England several years before they pillaged Lindisfarne, attacking Portland in the south; and their ancestors were involved in localised raiding long before that.

The Vikings were as much about trading as raiding, a process that must have opened their eyes to the existence of the wider world and the opportunities it offered. Trading settlements existed in Scandinavia long before the Viking Age began. One of the most significant was at Helgö, Sweden. Its origins may date back as far as 200AD. It was situated on Lake Mälar (nowadays Mälaren, in the region of Stockholm) where the settlement of Birka was later sited. Evidence of trading from Helgö includes a very exotic artefact in the form of a fifth- to sixth-century Buddha. This is a small but evocative statue, probably originating from Kashmir on the modern Pakistan/India border. It has a third eye, a classic Buddhist motif. The figure sits cross-legged in meditative pose, as far removed from the stereotypical image of a Viking warrior as you can get. Other exotic finds from Helgö include an Egyptian Coptic ladle and a bishop's crozier from Ireland that dates to the late eighth century, possibly the spoils of an early Viking raid; the latter appears to have a fanciful depiction of Jonah's adventures with a whale carved on it, perhaps a story that the Vikings were attracted to. More mundane archaeological evidence has been found such as furs from beavers, winter squirrels and marten pelts. Ivory from walrus tusks and amber from the Baltic has also been discovered along with the remains of falcons from the Far North. The settlement was icebound in the winter, when rivers and lakes became frozen thoroughfares over which sledges were pulled by men on skis or wearing skates.

The Vikings developed their trading contacts partly because of the range of goods they dealt in. There was very little that they would not trade given the chance; as one historian remarked 'they were particularly well placed to meet the inexhaustible European and Muslim demand for fur and slaves, but turned their hand to any saleable commodity: grain, fish, timber, hides, salt, wine, glass, glue, horses and cattle, white bears and falcons, walrus ivory and seal oil, honey, wax, malt, silks and woollens, amber and hazel nuts, soapstone dishes and basalt millstones, wrought weapons, ornaments, and silver'.[8] This ability to turn their hand to the selling of such a wide range of merchandise was very likely inherited by the Vikings from their forefathers.

But alongside this talent for trade, further evidence of internal violence has been discovered. The end of the fifth and the beginning of the sixth century was seemingly one when coastal raids on Scandinavian settlements were a serious problem. Evidence of settlements that were burned on Öland, an island off the south-east coast of Sweden, and Gotland can cautiously be linked with raiding activities. In addition, a number of fortifications were constructed during the same period, suggesting a need to take significant defensive measures. Those on Öland are particularly striking. Several massive circular structures, such as examples at Ismantorp and Groborg, suggest a desperate need for the local population to defend itself. While Viking raids in the late eighth century and beyond may have come as a shock to Western Europe when they arrived, the people of Scandinavia and the Baltic had already been suffering from violent confrontations for several centuries.

Further reminders that these were tumultuous times are provided by the many hillforts that appeared in Norway and Sweden between 400 and 600. Local aristocrats became more powerful, effectively becoming regional kings. Below them were a number of lesser chieftains, the *hersirs*. But even in these chaotic days a form of law existed, regulated by an assembly called the *Thing*. These assemblies made decisions on the implementation of customary law and protected the rights of free men (which, as there were many slaves around, was far from everybody).

Occasionally in the later Viking sagas, we come across the names of some of these small-scale kings ('kinglets' they might be called, though that might be considered a little patronising: the Norse *smákonungar* or 'small king' seems slightly more respectful). For example, in Norway we read of Halfdan Whiteleg who lived to a very old age before he was buried in a barrow in the Vestfold. Then there was Eystein Fart (Halfdansson) who died while leading a raid up the Oslofjord, allegedly when a powerful warlock on the shore caused his ship's boom to swing and hit him, knocking him into the water and drowning him. Closer to the Viking era proper, in the latter half of the eighth century, there was Halfdan II, nicknamed rather wonderfully 'Halfdan the Generous in Gold and Stingy of Food'. These attributes were important; in the context of the times 'a successful king gave: a bad king hoarded'.[9] Being a 'bracelet-giver' was certainly an important characteristic for the man who would be king.

In the pre-Viking age the impressive ships for which Scandinavian shipwrights were later famed had not yet fully developed. Traders were limited to short-distance travel up and down the fjords or short crossings across the Baltic. Not until the keel was developed did longer-distance travel become possible; the new technology married perfectly with the adventurism and spirit of exploration among the Scandinavian seamen at this moment in history in an unplanned coincidence.

Mention of Sweden, Denmark and Norway requires explanation; in the story that follows these are regions rather than countries. It is important to note that 'the Scandinavian states were small, and the potential resources restricted'; this situation may well have been a significant motivation for Viking expansion.[10] That said, during the Viking Age the initial conceptions of these modern nation states took root but even then these first steps were hesitant and impermanent: what we call the kingdom of Denmark took several attempts before it firmly took hold and even after that there was an ebb and flow to its development. To compound this complication, even when nations began to emerge, their boundaries were fluid. Only as time went on did kings at a national level begin to emerge. Before then, we are looking at smaller territories ruled by warlords or chiefs. Men bound themselves to each other, in Christian as well as in Viking society, through an exchange of patronage and reciprocal obligation;[11] in the latter, loyalty was initially to chief (or 'kinglet') rather than to a national king. These chiefs did not take kindly to someone else claiming sovereignty over them. Even when national kings did emerge, they had to be careful to stay on good terms with their most powerful subjects, who could be dangerous enemies.

The ship gave birth to the Viking. Even if relatively undeveloped, such vessels had long played a part in Scandinavian life. Early carvings of boats from as far back as 3,000BC are liberally dotted across southern Norway, etched into rock surfaces. It has been suggested that the boats depicted are skin-covered craft. The oldest Scandinavian craft yet found, the Als boat from south-west Denmark, dates to about 350BC and has as its base a hollowed-out lime tree with planks for sides. A vessel discovered near Stockholm, the Björke boat, dates from a few hundred years later but is essentially a development based on earlier craft like the Als boat. As time passed, such vessels evolved. The Nydam boat, from southern Jutland and dating to around 400AD, is a relatively large craft, around 25 metres long, made of pine. With rowlocks for thirty oars, it was able to carry a significant human cargo. Although it did not have a keel, it did have the high prow that was typical of the later Viking longship. In common with the ships of the later Viking era the Nydam boat was clinker-built, with the planks from which it was constructed overlapping each other. It was steered by a large detachable steering oar at the stern on the right-hand side (or 'starboard' to give it its correct nautical term: *strybord* is Old Norse for 'steering side'). Captain Magnus Andersen, who sailed across the Atlantic in 1893 in a replica of a later Viking ship, said that the side rudder worked very well and was very easy for one man to handle.

Pagan Viking religion

The Vikings became famous, or rather infamous, as terrifying pagan raiders and their religion was a core part of their legend and their very being. They were warriors from their early days, shaped by their harsh environment and their tough way of life, and this undoubtedly impacted on, and was impacted by, their religion. They lived life at the margins of the world and their belief system mirrored the challenges they faced in eking out an existence. Life hung by a slender thread, which could very easily be cut. The tales of their gods reflected this. Death was a constant companion and explanations needed to be given to deal with this reality; death in battle particularly, as this was a core part of their life as raiders.

And so, we come face-to-face with the Valkyries, the 'choosers of the slain', whose role was to select from those who were killed in battle and take them to the heavenly hall in Valhalla, the 'hall of the slain'. Here they act as the handmaidens of these chosen men, serving them with copious amounts of mead from huge horns that served as goblets. Connections between Viking and Anglo-Saxon lore are quickly apparent when we scratch the surface, of which the Valkyries are one example; in Norse they are called *valkyrja*, in Saxon *wælcryge*. We know of them first and foremost from later written poems that, centuries afterwards, recorded oral traditions. There have also been archaeological artefacts unearthed depicting what looks suspiciously like Valkyries and these unnerving harpies are referred to occasionally in runic inscriptions. While the Valkyries have become somewhat romanticised, particularly through the works of the nineteenth-century composer Richard Wagner, initially they were portrayed as wild figures who roamed the battlefield looking for corpses as if they were carrion, devouring them wholesale – not such a romantic picture.[12]

The world was, in the end, doomed. Ragnarök, 'the twilight of the gods', was the name given to the terrifying end-time of the Viking deities. Its description in the *Völuspá,* part of a collection of oral tales known as the *Poetic Edda* written up by that later paragon of saga writers

Snorri Sturluson, employs words that, even when translated into English, summon up terrifying images of the end of the world:

> Brothers will battle to bloody end
> And sister's kin commit foul acts.
> There's woe in the world, wantonness rampant,
> An axe-age, a sword age, shields are sundered;
> A storm-age, a wolf-age, before the world crumbles.
> No mercy or quarter will man give to man.
> The sun grows dark, earth sinks in the sea,
> The bright stars fall from the skies;
> Flames rage and fires leap high,
> Heaven itself is seared by heat.

Snorri's work, known as the *Prose Edda* was based on the earlier *Poetic Edda*, a collection of Old Norse poems. In this world view, there was a consolation in the shape of a better world to come, of '... a hall more fair than the sun, thatched with gold, at Gimlé; there shall the gods in innocence dwell, live for ever a life of bliss'; the hall, unlike many real-life wooden Viking halls, could not be burned. Just when we might think a happy ending is coming, a life eternal of everlasting joy, the image is demolished by a shattering end-piece where 'the dragon of darkness, a glittering serpent from Nidafell' soars high above. 'It flies over fields and bears on its wings a naked corpse'; a finale that would do Beowulf or, nearer our own time J. R. R. Tolkien, proud.[13]

Given the fact that there was no hope for men, even if they were gifted the prize of riotous feasting in Valhalla for a time, it probably seemed to those who were Vikings that life should be lived a day at a time – and lived to the full. This in its own way must have been an inspiration and a comfort to men who emerged silently from the seas and fell on unsuspecting coastlines, while facing the prospect of their own death in battle; or those who, fired by some spirit of adventure that it is almost impossible for twenty-first century mortals to comprehend (possibly astronauts or deep-sea explorers would be the closest equivalent), sailed into the great unknown across hundreds and thousands of miles of uncharted, dangerous seas.

The Vikings had many gods. They were similar to those of the Angles and Saxons in their pre-Christian era, showing that they shared a common Germanic origin. There were three who towered above all others in the Norse pantheon, a kind of Viking trinity: Odin, Thor and Freyr. Chief of them was Odin (Germanic Woden or Wotan: hence 'Woden's Day' or Wednesday), famously associated with ravens, one of which was perched on each shoulder – these harbingers of death were called Huginn and Muninn, Mind and Memory, and they were sent out every morning to spy on the world and report back. Often depicted wearing a cape and a broad hat, Odin has a wizard-like appearance (Gandalf from the *Lord of the Rings* prompts suitable mental images, though in the *Prose Edda* he is a dwarf rather than a wizard). The Roman writer Tacitus, seeking a suitable counterpart for the Saxon Woden in his own pantheon of gods, equated him with Mercury (hence the French name for Wednesday, Mercredi). Odin, who was sometimes given alternative names emphasising his status such as 'All-Father' or 'High One', lived in a land called Asgard where could be found his great hall, Valhöll; Magnusson bemoans the fact that it is normally incorrectly transliterated into English as Valhalla; but changing that perception would require a turning of the tide that Cnut the Great could not have managed, so in this book Valhalla it will remain. The god travelled around on his eight-legged horse, Sleipnir. Odin is effectively the chief of the gods, the Æsir as they are collectively known, a deity with a reputation for being both dangerous and fickle. The world he was part of had three distinct regions; in addition to Asgard, there was Midgard, the middle region, and Utgard, the outer place. The last of these was populated by giants and separated from Midgard by a sea in which a great serpent lay that encircled the world.

Odin was an aristocratic god, fanatically committed to the search for wisdom, so much so that he lost one eye in the search for it (he surrendered it in return from a drink from the well of Mimmir, the source of knowledge) and even hung himself for nine nights from the great ash tree, Yggdrasil, beneath which sat the three norns, Urd, Vervandi and Skuld; one each for the past, the present and the future, spinning out the destiny of man. Destiny was unavoidable, whatever a man might do. A tenth-century Viking ruler of Kiev, Oleg, was told that his horse would be the death of him. Forewarned, he never rode it again. When the horse died five years later, he visited its skeleton and kicked its skull in delight at avoiding fate. When he did so, a venomous serpent emerged from its bones and delivered him a fatal bite.

Odin's voluntary hanging was undertaken in the hope that in the process he would see things that would not otherwise be visible (he was also associated with the gallows for obvious reasons). Odin happily paid the price of an eye in return for an increase in his knowledge; a sharper contrast with the omnipotent, all-seeing Christian God cannot be imagined, especially when it is remembered that in addition Odin is mortal. While he was in a near-death state he saw the magic markings, the runes, or as Norse poetry put it:

> Into the depths I peered
> I grasped the runes,
> Screaming I grasped them
> And then fell back.[14]

He was a god full of contradiction and paradox; wisdom and cruelty, poetry as well as death. The one-eyed Odin, resplendent with a long, flowing beard, and his attendant ravens along with two wolves, Geri and Freki, wandered body-strewn battlefields after a fight. While the mighty warrior who gave up his life in battle could hope for a hero's welcome in Valhalla, where he could feast and carouse himself to his heart's content until the cataclysmic denouement of Ragnarök, for the rest only oblivion and decay awaited. How a man died truly mattered. To paraphrase the immortal words of Thomas Mordaunt, one crowded hour of glorious life was worth an age without a name.

Even when the Christian God later claimed His exclusive place in the affections of the Scandinavian people, jealously excluding all other gods who sought to rival Him, they still clung on tenaciously to old beliefs beneath their Christianised exterior. Odin continued to play a part in Scandinavian traditions up until modern times. He and his group of fierce animal attendants lived on in English and wider European folklore in the stories of the Wild Hunt, a group of supernatural horsemen who stormed across the sky at night, more often heard than seen, presaging death for those unfortunate enough to witness their passing. These probably reflect older Germanic legends of Wode, the Storm God, who led his wild army, the souls of the dead, across the night sky. Such supernatural chases are a core staple of old Germanic mythology, such as when the Sun and Moon are pulled across the sky by chariots, pursued by wolves.

The West Saxon dynasty in England traced their descent from Woden (as did all other Anglo-Saxon dynasties in the country except for that of Essex)[15] and through them, albeit in a very diluted form, the currently reigning royal dynasty in the United Kingdom can also claim him as an ancestor, though whether they ever actually would is highly doubtful. One interesting suggestion is that Woden, who delivered gifts to the deserving at the time of the Winter Solstice, may be linked to Santa Claus, a Christianised version of a much older Germanic god.[16]

Thor, whose mother was Jörd, 'Earth', was a far more approachable figure than his father Odin. He was the companion through life of the ordinary man, the farmer, the sailor. He roared across the sky in a chariot pulled by two goats, Tanngnoist and Tanngrisnir ('Tooth Gnasher' and 'Snarl Tooth'); it was the movement of his wheeled chariot across the sky that generated the noise of thunder. He too was a fierce figure, red-haired, red-bearded, red-eyed, quick to turn to wrath but just as quick to be appeased. He was associated with storms and tempests and his thunderbolts, Thor's 'hammers', were linked with small items of jewellery of the same name that were almost ubiquitous in Viking society. He wielded his hammer, Mjöllnir, against the Giants who threatened the pantheon of Norse gods and against whom the great battles of Ragnarök would be fought. He also had his Belt of Strength; when he put it on, his strength doubled. He had another treasured possession, his Gloves of Iron, without which he could not grasp his hammer.

The Romans also knew of Thor and equated him with either Hercules or Jupiter. The association lived on for centuries; Adam of Bremen, a primary if negatively biased chronicler of the Viking world of his times, linked Thor with Jupiter and described him as the god who ruled the sky; this being the case it is not surprising that Viking seafarers who were so reliant on good weather respected and worshipped him more than any other. Thor gave his name to the day of the week we call Thursday.

He was renowned for his conflict with the World Serpent, Jǫrmungandr, a monstrous creature so large that it could encompass the whole world and grasp its own tail; when it releases this, the great end-time, Ragnarök, will be at hand. The massive serpent will poison the sky and when Thor goes into battle against it, he will be bitten and die of the venomous bite. It has been suggested that this battle between Thor and the World Serpent was later adopted by Christianity and represented as Christ fighting against Satan who is of course sometimes represented by a snake.[17]

The third of the Viking trinity of major gods was Freyr, the son of Njord, the god of wealth and an ancient and venerated deity, mentioned by Tacitus who said that he was worshipped on an island in the Baltic. Freyr was particularly linked with the Swedes and was the mythical antecedent of the Uppsala dynasty. Typically sculpted with an enormous phallus, fertility and abundance were linked with him and his twin sister and female counterpart, Freyja. Freyr's day of course is Friday. Freyr had a magical ship, *Skíðblaðnir,* which literally means 'made of thin strips of wood'. It had been built by the dwarves (readers who are not totally familiar with Viking mythology may again find themselves comfortably at home if they have read Tolkien's works.) Many centuries later that remarkable saga writer and Icelandic nobleman of the twelfth/thirteenth centuries, Snorri Sturluson, who we will come across frequently, wrote about Freyr and his ship. The most remarkable quality of Freyr's magical ship was that the wind was always behind it wherever it wanted to go; a sailor's dream in the age of sail. Another invaluable magical feature was that it was large enough to take all the gods anywhere that they wanted to go but when it was not needed it could be folded up and put into a pouch.[18]

A good deal of what we know of Viking myth and legend comes from several epic works that Snorri produced, especially two remarkable pieces known as *The Prose Edda* and *The Heimskringla.*[19] Of course, mythology is not history, but it informs our understanding of the latter for it lets us see into the minds of the historical Vikings. We must recognise at once that a man writing in the thirteenth century, using oral tradition as his source, may not represent the mythology of the seventh century accurately; in the same way, the final flowering of the stories of King Arthur written by Thomas Malory in the fifteenth century have come a long way from the works of Geoffrey of Monmouth in the twelfth and further still from any now lost epics from the Celtic regions of earlier times which mentioned Arthur in one form or another. But in both cases, we have a distant memory, a long-lost seed from which later stories flower, in which these later writings are rooted. We will never know every aspect of what seventh-century Scandinavians believed but the writings of epic storytellers like Snorri and many contemporary *skalds* are as close as we are likely to get.[20]

That said, there is a world of difference between the *Prose Edda* and the *Hiemskringla,* even though they were both written by Snorri. The *Prose Edda* is our ultimate surviving source of information on Norse mythology, even though it was written well into the Christian age, as is evidenced by is opening references not to Odin and Thor but to Adam and Eve; while that might seem surprising enough, references to classical mythology going back to Troy might seem equally so.[21] Snorri was concerned that with the advent of Christianity the meaning of Norse poetry would be lost. He took the work known as the *Poetic Edda,* which said much about Norse mythology, and converted it into what has been called a manual about the subject of *skaldic* poetry. A copy of the *Poetic Edda* was found in the seventeenth century so it is still to Snorri that we owe much of what we know about Norse mythology and poetry.[22] In thirteenth-century Icelandic, *edda* means great-grandmother, suggesting links with the ancient past and the roots of Icelandic/Norse mythology in a traditional world which was much faded by the time that it was written up. However, references to the Bible and classical mythology give the impression that, rather than a so-called 'accurate' account of Norse mythology, elements of the *Prose Edda* are an attempt to establish credentials of such to the later world in which Snorri lived and wrote. The *Hiemskringla,* or 'History of the Kings of Norway', on the other hand, is presented very much as a work of history, even though there are strong elements of mythology in it too. Written around the end of the twelfth century, this is the ultimate saga of the Viking kings. It was originally called *kringla heimsins* – 'the circle of the world' – the first two words of one of the manuscripts included in it. Unfortunately, the original work was lost in a disastrous fire in Copenhagen in 1728 though not before copies of it had been made. A great deal of information can be gleaned from studying what survives.

There were many other gods in play in the Viking world, such as Baldr, 'the Beautiful' (wise and merciful but ineffective), Tyr (Tiw in Old English), Bragi and Odin's wife Frig. Tyr was at one stage seemingly among the most important Viking gods. While initially being an all-powerful being, he later became a god of war, in which capacity his runic symbol was often carved on weapons and was linked with victory. Several place names in England such as the parish of Tysoe are linked with him, as is the day of the week known as Tuesday.[23]

There was also the evil trickster Loki, clever, tricky, duplicitous, always a cause of trouble and difficulties and the mastermind behind Ragnarök; he also has an uncanny ability to change shape. He is 'pleasing, even beautiful to look at, but his nature is evil and he is undependable. More than others, he has the kind of wisdom known as cunning, and is treacherous in all matters'.[24] He had a daughter, Hel, cruel and gloomy, who ruled over the Viking underworld of the same name where those who die of disease or old age go. She was half-blue in colour and the kingdom of death, which was her domain, was feared for its intense cold, in stark contrast to Christian views of Hell and its fiery furnaces.

Loki is something of an alter ego for Odin. There is a strange connection between the two: when Loki changes sex and becomes a mare, he gives birth to Odin's horse Sleipnir. He helps the gods to obtain some of their greatest treasures, such as Thor's hammer or the All-Father's magical ring, Draopnir. This ring had great power; every ninth night it would drip and from it eight rings of equal weight would be formed.

Loki had a prodigious appetite and in one of his journeys he consumed vast quantities of food when involved in an eating contest. His children, such as the dark Hel and the wolf Fenrir who will swallow the sun at the time of Ragnarök, play a sinister role in the affairs of the world. Loki was responsible for the death of Baldr, tricking the blind god Hod into shooting him with an arrow made of mistletoe, the only material that could hurt him as he was magically protected from everything else. For this betrayal the gods exerted a bitter vengeance. Loki was chained to a rock, a snake's poison dripping onto his face, doomed to remain there until Ragnarök, convulsing in agony each time the poison splashed him, so much so that each time he did so an earthquake shook the earth. Once Ragnarök arrives he would lead the fight against his rival gods and would die in the process fighting against Heimdallr though nearly every other god – Odin, Thor and Heimdallr included – would perish with him.

There was limited organisation in the religion of the Vikings. Each man and woman made their own decision as to which god to adopt. Even when later Vikings formally adopted Christianity, many would hedge their bets. One such was a man called Helgi the Lean who 'believed in Christ and yet made vows to Thor for sea voyages or in tight corners, and for everything which struck him as of real importance'.[25] The ninth-century chronicler Rimbert who wrote the *Vita Anskarii* ('The Life of Ansgar') mentioned a ceremony which allowed Vikings to associate with the Christian religion without being baptised (which they would often put off until their very last days; in fairness, so too did the first Christian Roman Emperor, Constantine the Great). This strange ceremony was known as primsigning.[26]

The later Vikings were often linked with various forms of sacrifice as ways of propitiating their gods or seeking their help in various ventures. Such practices go a long way back into the dim, distant past in Scandinavia. At Ginderup in the north of Jutland excavations of a pre-Viking house revealed that a dog had been buried beneath the threshold, presumably as an offering to seek the blessing of the gods over the inhabitants. The threshold, the entry and exit point of the dwelling, had clear magical associations and was therefore an especially important location in ritual terms.

In Viking mythology, there were mortal heroes as well as gods. Some of them, like Gunnar and Sigurd, appear on Viking Age carvings. Sigurd appears on a carved stone at Kirk Andreas on the Isle of Man. He was famed for killing the fierce dragon Fafnir (in heroic Germanic literature, Sigurd became Siegfried, the hero of Wagner's Ring Cycle); the carving on Man shows him roasting the dragon's heart over a fire. Viking heroes were expected to undertake extraordinary acts of bravery, and this no doubt inspired some Viking warriors to fight in the same way. When looking for motivation to explain why the Vikings emerged as such a threat to those who came within their orbit, this cultural heroic element should not be overlooked.

The Vikings had a runic alphabet, which may have started out as nothing more than an everyday communication form. Runic letters were carved on memorial stones but were also used for curses and magic charms (though this does not in itself mean that the letters were regarded as possessing magical qualities, any more than using the everyday language for writing curses and leaving them at the baths of Roman *Aquae Sulis* – Bath – would imply that Latin was regarded as a language specifically associated with magic). Letters in the runic alphabet were always composed of variants of straight lines, easier to carve on stone, wood or bone. Runes evolved over time; the oldest-known ones date to the second or third centuries AD, with early examples from Norway (near modern Oslo) and Gotland. The first known version of the runic alphabet had twenty-four letters and is known as the *futhark* after the first six of them ('th' was one letter); a later Scandinavian variant, the so-called 'younger futhark', only had sixteen.[27] The younger alphabet had the virtue of being simpler, easier to use maybe for administrative purposes. For some reason, many more runestones are known from Sweden than anywhere else and it is perhaps surprising that runestones appear to have arrived later in Denmark than in Sweden or Norway.[28]

The runic alphabet was Germanic in origin and old variants of it are found in northern Germany and Denmark. It was also used by Anglo-Saxons in England, and the Frisians in the Low Countries (now part of the Netherlands), though to an extent they later developed there in their own distinctive way. About thirty later examples have even been found in distant Greenland.[29] The underlying inspiration seems to be Italic and it is possible that the language evolved through interfaces between Roman legionaries and Germanic tribesmen and then spread.

Viking social structures

Each god had their own hall in Valhalla and this is significant for it seems to replicate, or have been replicated by, common practice among mortal men, or at least the wealthier sections of society. The epic Anglo-Saxon work *Beowulf* emphasises the importance of the hall as a place of community and feasting where a leader was expected to show his generosity and largesse in as exaggerated a fashion as he could afford. In Scandinavia, very large great halls pre-date the Viking Age, for example that excavated at Tissø in Denmark was a massive 36 metres long and 11.5 metres wide. The space itself became somehow sacred: when a hall deteriorated, as a wooden building inevitably would with age, it was renovated and seemingly never rebuilt elsewhere. It was often also associated with specialist manufacturing such as goldsmithing, a socially important function which a lord would want to control and show off.[30]

Heimdallr, the father of mankind, sometimes referred to as Rig, was an important mythological figure who was assigned a role in the development of social structures. He was the watchman of the gods who could hear grass growing on the earth and wool on sheep. As well as being the guardian of a rainbow bridge between Asgard and Midgard, the golden-toothed Heimdallr established social classes. In mythology, as preserved in later Viking sagas, he entered the home of a poor couple, Great-Grandfather and Great-Grandmother. They treated him as any good host would by feeding him the best of their humble food in the form of a coarse type of bread. He then lay three nights in their bed before leaving. Nine months later the woman, Edda, gave birth to an ill-formed son, dark-skinned, ugly and with coarse, thick features; and so, the class of the slaves was born. Heimdallr next introduced himself to a wealthier couple, Afi and Amma, Grandfather and Grandmother. The man was making a loom and the woman was weaving. Again, Heimdallr lay between them for three nights and nine months later a son was born to Amma, a boy with a red complexion and sparkling eyes. He was called Freedman – and as a result that social class was also born. Heimdallr finally visited another house where Father and Mother lived. The man was sorting out his bow in readiness for hunting while the woman was dressed in elegant attire made from the finest fabrics. They gave him a fantastic feast with the table spread with bountiful quantities of game. Heimdallr also lay between them for three nights. Nine months later, a son duly arrived, a boy who had fine hair, bright cheeks and piercing eyes. They called him *Jarl*, and the class of the earls was born.

Early on then, the Viking world had a tightly defined social structure, and this would continue into the Viking Age. Although boundaries might become more flexible over time, there would always be difficulties in moving from one class to the other. It was important for men and women to know their place. The lot of a slave would always be a harsh one. Some would be so because their parents were slaves, others because of economic hardship or debt. Many slaves were there because of war or piracy. Although they were valuable – in Anglo-Saxon England one slave had the equivalent value of eight cows – they were also expendable. In later years, Viking slaves would come in great numbers from Britain and Ireland. However, many also came from the states to the south and east of the Baltic – the word 'slave' has its origins in 'Slav'. In Norway, it was suggested that the proper establishment for a farm with twelve cattle and two horses was three slaves.[31]

The freedman's rights were limited but he was still essentially, as the name suggests, to an extent his own man. He was normally connected to a greater man whom he served in times of war. In return he could take part in the local assemblies, the *Things*, which decided on matters of law. There was a strong legal code and even the great men of Viking society were expected to observe it, otherwise they could find themselves in difficulties. There were limits to the freedman's rights; he could not, for example, bring a legal case against his social superior and that could leave the system open to abuse.

The *jarls,* or the aristocracy as we might call them, were at the top of the social tree. They enjoyed power and wealth and could bind men to them by the giving of arm rings. Most of them, as one eminent historian observed, were either 'king-allied or god-descended'.[32] Eventually, some grew more ambitious and called themselves kings. Some, more ambitious still, sought to become kings of evolving nation states such as Norway, Denmark and Sweden. As ambition grew, so inevitably did resistance from those who a would-be king sought to rule. This meant that being a Viking king in any region was always a hazardous and frequently a short-term career.

Beneath this upper echelon, a group of more localised chieftains emerged, the *hersirs*. They had power over smaller groups though it was likely that they were capable of launching smaller-scale raids early in the Viking era on their own, or perhaps in temporary alliance with other *hersirs*. Reading the sagas, there is a sense of alliances mutating over time as the various leaders sought to further their self-interests on an opportunistic basis; what was a good alliance during one year or raiding season might not seem so attractive during the next. A suitable analogy might be to think of politics and alliance-building among Scottish clans where, although some alliances might develop on a long-term basis, others might change direction from time to time.

Scandinavia on the Eve of the Viking Age

There is strong circumstantial evidence that the sixth century in particular was tough for the peoples of Scandinavia. Not only do we know that people were migrating from the region, but we also have intimations as to why. In 536, there was a massive volcanic eruption somewhere, which sent a massive black cloud across the Mediterranean. This was no minor incident; it was written about by the Byzantine historian Procopius in terms of terrified awe: 'a remarkable wonder was observed, for throughout this whole year the sun shone like the moon, with no radiance, as though in perpetual eclipse, its light feeble and not at all normal'. A few years after, a plague struck down the population of Constantinople on a scale that approached the later catastrophic levels of the Black Death. There was widespread cold and darkness across the globe in a period known, slightly clunkily, as the Late Antique Little Ice Age, which lasted until the second-half of the seventh century. In Sweden there is evidence that many villages in the Uppland region were abandoned. Once thought to be the result of a volcanic eruption at Ilopango in El Salvador, the latest thinking is that there were massive events in different parts of the globe within a few years of each other.[33] The fall-out of these distant events appears to have been far-reaching. It has even been suggested that there is a link between them and the development of the myth concerning the beginning of Ragnarök, a period when the sun turned black and the weather was atrocious, a time known as Fimbulwinter (Old Norse for 'the great winter'). There would then be three successive winters, unbroken by summer, following which a period of perpetual war would break out. The story forms part of *The Poetic Edda*.

There is continuity in the story of these pre-Viking peoples and their later ancestors. We can see this in Denmark for example, where there is a large cemetery close to the Limfjord, a natural waterway that forms a very useful passageway, effectively acting as a canal across the north of the modern country from the Baltic to the North Sea (at least in those periods when it did not silt up, which it did from time to time). The cemetery at Lindholm Høje has interments dating back to around 500AD, definitively in what we would regard as the pre-Viking Age. But there are burials that can be clearly dated to around 800 though their style is different than those of earlier times and many of these graves were in the shape of boats.

A similar mix of continuity and evolution can be seen in the shape of an earthwork in Schleswig-Holstein, the Danevirke. About 30 kilometres in length, it is not even clear what the Danevirke was for; some have argued that it was not defensive in nature and may have been a form of boundary marker or even linked with canals for ships. It was once thought that the Danevirke was built by an early Danish king, Godfrid, as a defensive measure against the threat posed by the great Frankish ruler, Charlemagne (dating it to around the beginning of the ninth century). However, dendrochronology tests in the early 1970s pushed the date back to around 750 and more recent work has taken it back even earlier, to around 500. So, while in the Viking Age it may have been added to – and the latest thinking is that the last stage of development may be in the mid-tenth century – this was certainly building on what was already there before. This is suggestive. In the past Godfrid was considered the first king of Denmark but at least two other men before him might have a claim to this honour, one called Sigfred and the other Ongendus. But if men were around in the country who were capable of organising such extensive construction schemes even before then, then they must have been at least very powerful chieftains who were ruling over more than a village and a small group of local followers.

Scandinavians also journeyed to other places around the Baltic. In 2008, a group of construction workers were digging near Salme, a town on the island of Saaremaa, off Estonia. What they found was to rewrite our understanding of Viking history. They came across a buried ship, leading to the commencement of a formal archaeological dig, which found another in 2010. Inside were around forty skeletons, all male, many of whom had clearly died violently. Some were decapitated, others had damage to their skeletal structure that suggested a great deal of hacking (some had multiple, horrific cuts), probably from swords.

The men came from central Sweden. They were buried with many swords; more indeed than there were bodies. Gaming pieces made from whale- and cattle-bone were also discovered. They appear to be from a well-known Viking game known as *hnefatafl*. In this chess-like pastime, the most important piece is the king; and a king-piece was found in the mouth of one individual, who was perhaps the leader of this expedition that had somehow gone wrong. Arrowheads were scattered liberally around, possibly the cause of some of the deaths. There was evidence of a ceremonial burial; two hawks were found decapitated along with bones from pigs, sheep, cattle and goats, as if a funeral feast had been held. Enamel from teeth revealed a point of origin in the Stockholm region while swords pommels were similar to Vendel and Valsgärde burials in the region of Uppsala.[34]

The existence of forty slaughtered men from Scandinavia might suggest a Viking raid but current opinion veers towards a diplomatic mission gone wrong. The date of the burials though is interesting: 750, about half a century before the first Viking raids on Britain. Scandinavian sailors were clearly not uncomfortable in journeying around the Baltic back then, though one of the boats found was only equipped for rowing rather than sailing. Given the nature of these finds in Estonia, it is a reminder that travellers from places like Sweden were making their presence known further afield long before what we might think of as the first Viking raids took place.

Ship burials have been found in the Vendel area north of Stockholm dating from the period 500–800AD; other graves have been discovered at Valsgärde. The finds in some of them were breathtaking. They included helmets, double-edged swords with pommels, hilts inlaid with gems and luxury goods from far away. There was even a Byzantine coin that can be dated to around 500. It is perhaps significant that the period in which these splendid interments were made coincided with the famous ship burial in East Anglia discovered at Sutton Hoo in 1939 with items that look decidedly Swedish in origin buried there. Indeed, this may be evidence of a Scandinavian origin for the kings of East Anglia who were known as the Wuffing Dynasty; the great epic *Beowulf* refers to the similarly named Wulffings back in Scandinavia.

Three of the most striking burials from the period were found at Old Uppsala and appear to be the last resting places of three kings from the sixth century-Ynglinga dynasty, Aun, Egill and Adils; though their mighty ridgetop mounds were ascribed at one time to Odin, Thor and Freyr. Snorri Sturluson writes of these kings as roistering, rumbustious men who liked nothing more than a good hunt, a good party or a good battle. When the burial mounds were excavated not only weapons and helmets were found but also a quantity of gold, a rare commodity that was not found in other contemporary graves in the region. This has led some archaeologists to conclude that this was indeed a resting place for royalty.

The Vendel years take their name from a series of impressive graves found at a place of that name in Sweden. Some impressive artefacts have been unearthed there. These included impressive examples of contemporary helmets. One of them could be mistaken as an example from Ancient Greece complete with cheek and neck guards. Another has spectacle-shaped protection around the eyes: a helmet of very similar type was found at Sutton Hoo while similar headpieces have been noted from the later Viking Age.

It is a commonly quoted 'fact' that Vikings did not wear horned helmets; intriguingly though there are images from the period that show the wearing of horns on the head as part of ritual practices, such as those shown on the Golden Horns of Gallehus that have been dated to around 425. There are other examples too, such as the figure of a man carved as an amulet and buried in a woman's grave in Uppland, Sweden, which also shows what look like horns being worn on the head.[35] These are clearly ritual representations – wearing a horned helmet in battle would be cumbersome and ran the risk that the wearer could soon find himself deprived of it just when he needed it most – but it is interesting that there are at least some suggestions that the horned helmet in some form or another is not a complete figment of an overactive imagination, even if its use has been misconstrued.

Another feature that Sutton Hoo and the Vendel graves have in common is the burial of ships. At Sutton Hoo, the wood of the ship has disappeared (along with the body that was once buried there) but its outline remained preserved in the ground, like a 3-D photograph in terms of its clarity. Other finds shed light on the richness of the world in which the deceased had existed. Richly ornamented swords were there, as was evidence of sacrifices, such as the bones of horses. Given the extent of the items consigned to the ground, we can only assume that those who were being celebrated were extremely wealthy members of society. The most commonly held view is that the man buried at Sutton Hoo was Raedwald, a seventh-century king of East Anglia. While this cannot be definitively proven, if this is true then this pagan burial site is linked to a man who had once been baptised; and the suspicion that Raedwald was a lukewarm convert is amply confirmed by uncomplimentary comments made about him by Bede.[36] This hedging of bets in a spiritual sense would be a feature of later Vikings whose conversion to Christianity sometimes appeared to be non-committal.

While archaeology has uncovered less widespread evidence of such grandiose burials in Norway and Denmark, they are not without their own sites of interest. A grave found on the Danish island of Bornholm seems to commemorate a rich local family and includes what appear to be the remains of a slave girl who had been buried alongside them. Graves found at Snartemo in Norway included valuable objects such as weapons, gold rings and items of glass. The presence of the body of the slave girl is a disturbing reminder of how little value was placed on the life of someone unfortunate enough to be in that position in pre-Viking and Viking society (though slavery was by no means exclusive to them and it was also present in Christian societies such as that of the Anglo-Saxons in England and the Celtic kingdoms of Ireland).

There is also evidence of Swedish activity in Kurland (now western Latvia) for some time pre-dating the Viking Age. Cemeteries excavated around Grobin in the twentieth century have marked connections with Vendel Age sites in Sweden and can be dated from 650–800. The island of Gotland, off the coast of Sweden but for a time a separate entity from it though often working in partnership with Swedes, also assumed particular significance. Just when Gotland and Sweden started working in cooperation is currently unclear. However, the *Guta Saga* credits an early king of Gotland, Awair Strabain, with making the first moves (the work was written sometime in the thirteenth or fourteenth centuries but shows evidence of being based on older oral traditions).[37] The *Saga* describes how Gotland was first inhabited and how its people became too numerous for the island to support them all. Some of them then left to seek their fortune elsewhere and ended up in the lands of the Byzantine Emperor.

There were stories of Gotland in its early days being a land of sacred groves and magical graves, of widespread human sacrifice during alcohol-fuelled feasts and festivities. There was a sliding scale of sacrifices: human sacrifices were made on behalf of the island as a whole, while animals were offered to the gods for the different 'thirds' or regions of the island. After many wars with their pagan neighbours, Awair was sent to Sweden on a mission to obtain support from there, in return for which Gotland was required to pay an annual tribute of sixty silver marks. As their reward, the Gotlanders would have tax-free access to Swedish markets and, naturally enough, in return the Swedes would have the same in Gotland.

Sweden plays a critical part in our understanding of this period in that far more runic inscriptions have been found there than anywhere else. They do not generally go into detail concerning great historical events, but they do act as a window into the lives of those that they commemorate. They give flashes of insight into everyday life and death for those who lived in the Viking world and in the years and centuries that led up to it. They also enable us to glean other information about the Viking Age: for example, men would often put up runic carvings in commemoration of their part in funding or building roads and other public works such as bridges. Later carvings would state how so-and-so visited Jerusalem and died in Greece or how such-and-such took part, and died, in a raid on England.

That runes came to have some kind of magical significance is clear enough from what we can translate of them. One seventh-century example from the Björketorp Runestone from Blekinge, in Sweden, states that 'incessantly plagued by maleficence, doomed to insidious death, is he who breaks this monument'. Just what the purpose of such monuments was is often unclear; suggestions include graves, cenotaphs to memorialise someone who is buried far away, or even fertility offerings to the gods. Some might be as prosaic as a boundary marker between two different clans.

As the Viking Age crept up on an unsuspecting world, it went about its business unaware of what was coming. England, like most of southern and western Europe, had once been a part of the Roman Empire. Some parts of the Continent had however remained stubbornly outside Rome's borders; Scandinavia and Ireland for all of the time, Germany for most of the time, most of Scotland for a good part of the time. After the demise of the centralised power of Rome in the West, much of Europe went to the other extreme, with a massive fragmentation in authority the typical scenario. In the longer term, this made it easier for the Vikings to intrude into wider European affairs, as much of Western Europe was about to find out to its cost.

Anglo-Saxon England

Anglo-Saxon England was significantly affected by Viking raids. In the Roman province of Britannia, Saxons had been hired in by the Romans to help defend the fragile borders of the territory before eventually taking it over in a process that took centuries to reach completion. This context is important; the Anglo-Saxon English and the Scandinavian Vikings were cousins, although over time they would drift apart – the onset of Christianity in the Anglo-Saxon world distinguished it from Scandinavian culture and their languages would go their own ways to an extent, though there were enough similarities left to make them to some extent mutually intelligible.

Cultural links between the two were undoubtedly strong in the post-Roman world. An early gem of Anglo-Saxon art, the Finglesham Buckle, is an unmistakable representation of the god Odin/Woden, birds adorning his helmet in the same manner as the ravens which flocked around him in mythological stories; or 'the soot-black blood-seekers', the 'slash-gulls' or the 'wound-falcons' as the sagas describe them.[38] He stands with a spear in either hand. Wrought in gold, the Buckle is a priceless treasure in terms of artistic merit but also an insight into the pagan beliefs that lived on in England for a time and linked the Anglo-Saxons to the peoples of the North.

Much had changed in England since those first incursions during the closing scenes of the Roman Empire in Britain. At the end of the eighth century a well-organised society was developing in England. By this time all those who held land as a gift from the king, including monasteries, had a minimum of three 'common burdens', namely the duty to build bridges, to defend fortifications and to provide men for the *fyrd*, the local militia. This did not mean that churchmen would be in the front line of battle (though some of them were certainly present in such conflicts) but rather that they were required to provide or pay for men to do so. This was an important development; at one time the monasteries were exempted from the last 'burden', but Offa of Mercia (757–796) had stipulated that they must do their part.[39]

There was no standing army to resist any attacks from overseas but there were three layers of defence available. At the top was the king who would provide his own force, essentially a bodyguard but also in times of war much more than this. Below this in the hierarchy were the ealdormen, one for each shire, who commanded the local militia, the *fyrd*, for their own region but who might fight alongside neighbouring shires in larger forces should they have time to assemble at a pre-arranged rallying point, often near the borders of two or more shires. Below the ealdormen were thegns who led smaller war bands. At times of crisis these forces might combine into a larger army – but it was not easy to assemble it quickly, nor to keep the forces together once the army was formed.

While Wessex would eventually emerge as the dominant Anglo-Saxon kingdom in England, it was Offa of Mercia who initially came closest to bringing it together as a unified polity; unified it must be admitted by conquest and strong-arm tactics rather than free will. Offa claimed to be 'king of the English' as far back as 774. He also forged links with the Continent as part of the wider opening-up of politics and trade in Western Europe and was frequently involved in diplomatic exchanges with the court of Charlemagne. But following Offa's death in 796 – the year in which Mercia entered into a commercial treaty with Francia, the first such example that is known – England again began to fragment. Territories that had been subsumed into Offa's Mercian kingdom, such as East Anglia and Kent, started to draw themselves apart. Wessex in the south of England then grew in power and its own strongman, Ecgbert, would rise to challenge and overturn Mercia's former dominance.

In the north, Northumbria on the whole stayed aloof from affairs further south. At one stage, Northumbria had been the strongest of all English kingdoms, but its situation had deteriorated alarmingly in the eighth century. As the century drew to a close, Northumbria appeared to be in meltdown. There were vicious and frequent succession disputes, linked to the expulsion or assassination of reigning kings. England was not quite back at the stage that was reached by the sixth century, when the country we now call England was a heptarchy (divided into seven smaller kingdoms) but it was certainly starting to revert towards it. Such fragmentation would soon afterwards prove of considerable benefit to the Vikings when they launched their attacks on England.

As well as the strong suggestions of Swedish connections at Sutton Hoo there are other archaeological hints of early Scandinavian links elsewhere in England. A fifth- to early sixth-century cemetery at West Heslerton in Yorkshire where the expectation would be that all those remains found there would be of first-generation Anglian settlers surprisingly turned up the skeletons of four women of Scandinavian origin.[40] This shows that there was a degree of integration across different geographical areas including Scandinavia and England from very early on in the Anglo-Saxon period.

Celtic Britain and Ireland

Ireland held an important place in Europe at the time, particularly through its Christian missionary activities. It was a land without a town of note, but it had in the recent past exerted an enormous influence on continental Europe. After the efforts of St Patrick in the fifth century, it became a bastion for Christianity, which was for a while on the back foot in Europe after Rome collapsed. Ireland was stippled with monasteries, powerhouses of evangelism, characterised by humble beehive huts in which the monks lived. One extraordinary benefit of this from a historian's perspective is that the monasteries as centres of learning produced a group of annals that provide evidence of Viking activity in Ireland, and sometimes beyond, with ten principal sources surviving, richer than anywhere else.⁴¹ These annals are priceless but frustratingly laconic. They occasionally refer to national or international events as well as those wherever it was the annalist worked. They are short of detail and it can feel as if one is trying to complete a jigsaw puzzle with two-thirds of the pieces missing; but one-third of the pieces is, after all, better than none.

From their island base, protected from the barbarian tribes that flooded into the Roman Empire, the faith had been preserved by the monks in Ireland, like a nearly extinguished flame with just a glowing ember left alive. On the eve of the Viking Age, Ireland was very rural with a landscape that was strewn with remarkable round stone ringforts. Cattle were highly prized but there is also evidence of widespread pig and sheep farming too. The island was renowned for its 'dense herds of fat deer', its 'boars and wild pigs' and 'wild cats and wolves ... rapacious and voracious, [tearing] to pieces cattle and sheep'. There may even have been the last vestige of a bear population left on the island.⁴² The absence of any major towns in Ireland is somewhat misleading. There are several near-contemporary references which suggest that, as in England, some of the monasteries in the country were home to large communities rather than being the small, hermetical institutions of earlier times.⁴³

Away from the coast much of the countryside was boggy, mountainous or forested, which did not help in terms of creating political cohesion. Ireland, a prime target for early Viking raiders, was very fragmented, so much so that it has been argued that by the time that the Viking Age loomed, it was in 'a precarious political state'.⁴⁴ There was notionally a high-king, the *ard-ri*, based in Tara but this was normally more of an honorific position rather than one with real power. There were six major kingdoms, Connacht, Munster, Leinster, Ulster and the northern and southern Uí Néill. The Uí Néill were the most symbolically significant and the king of one of the two branches would traditionally be the high king of Ireland. They took their name from the quasi-mythical founder of their dynastic fortunes, Niall Naoighiallach, 'Niall of the Nine Hostages', who died in 405. This was a period when Irish rulers like Niall had access to considerable resources in terms of sea power, if reports of raids on Wales and the west of England are a guide, though these were much diminished by the time the Vikings with their longships appeared on the scene. Lower down the pyramid were at least 150 smaller sub-kingdoms (*tuatha*), a statistical demonstration of just how disunited Ireland was. This fragmentation was both a weakness and a strength for Ireland; a weakness because in theory it made it easier for the Vikings to divide and conquer, a strength because it made complete conquest and subjugation of the island in the absence of centralised forms of government (such as those which existed in England) that much harder.

Eventually the flame of Christianity was passed further afield from Ireland. Columba, who came from a powerful dynasty in the north of Ireland and was forced into exile after a bitter civil war, set up a monastery on Iona, tucked within a bay off the Scottish island of Mull. From here, Columba spread the word through the Scottish sub-kingdom of Dál Riata and beyond into Pictland. Christianity later spread from there into the north of England where another spiritual powerhouse developed at Lindisfarne, the home for a time of the seventh-century cleric Cuthbert, who became Anglo-Saxon England's greatest saint, along with other important establishments such as those at Jarrow and Whitby. Hugging the coast of England, they were a prime target for any opportunistic maritime attackers, for they had no defences to speak of to resist any assault.

When its missionaries moved down through England, the Celtic church collided with that of Rome, which had been re-established in the south-east of the country following the arrival of Augustine at Canterbury in 597. But though the Roman church won that particular war, the evangelical spirit of the Irish (latterly joined by the Anglo-Saxon English) would not be extinguished and monks from both areas journeyed to the Continent and attempted to convert the often-violent tribes of Frisia (at the mouth of the Rhine on the North Sea) and Germany to the faith. Some would eventually carry the word to Scandinavia.

Scotland at this stage did not exist as a political entity in its modern form. In the south-west was the kingdom of the Scots, based on Dál Riata (which extended into the north-east of Ireland). Further north, the Picts were still the dominant force. In the southern parts of what is now Scotland there was further division. On the western side was the British kingdom of Strathclyde, the land of the North Britons, a survival of a time when Celtic Britons had been the most powerful influence in England before the Roman legions arrived. The people of Strathclyde were closely related to the Welsh and the Cornish and also, to the north, the Picts. The Strathclyde 'Welsh' held a territory that extended north beyond modern Glasgow with the great fort at Dumbarton as their most significant citadel. These were a different Celtic people, with a different strain of language, than the Gaelic-speaking Irish and Scots.

To the east of Strathclyde, in what is now the north of England and the south of Scotland, much of the territory was under the control of Northumbrian Bernicia. Northumbria had within it two distinct regions, Bernicia in the north and Deira in the south, which were geographically and often politically distinct from each other. This extreme fragmentation across Britain played into the hands of Viking raiders but, ironically, ultimately the Viking raids were to do much to encourage greater unity and centralisation through efforts to resist their attacks.

Continental Europe on the eve of the Viking Age

On the mainland of Europe, much of what is now Germany up to the Elbe, then held by continental Saxons, fell into the hands of Charlemagne, Charles the Great, as the eighth century ended, in campaigns that would in modern times be considered as verging on genocide.[45] These wars were described as being the longest and most savage ever fought; at the end of them, the continental Saxons were forcibly Christianised. It was said by Christian writers of the continental Saxons that 'like almost all the peoples inhabiting Germany, [they] were by nature fierce and given over to the worship of demons and were opposed to our religion and did not think it shameful to violate either human or divine laws'.[46] Such descriptions sum up the spirit of the age and similar observations apply to West European views held of the contemporary inhabitants of Scandinavia and especially Viking raiders.

While the Vikings have a reputation for being a martial society, they were certainly not alone in glorifying warfare in contemporary society; 'warfare was not a Viking monopoly; Vikings were a Scandinavian manifestation of a universal scourge'.[47] Christian culture was equally militaristic as evidenced by the violent acts of Charlemagne and the wars fought within Christian Europe that ultimately resulted, after many twists and turns, in the great historical drama of the Crusades. Frankish, Anglo-Saxon and contemporary Christian culture all had militant militaristic elements to them. After his annual raids, Charlemagne would share the spoils among his supporters, rewarding them with 'gold and silver and silks and other gifts' as the *Annals of Lorsch* for 793 report;[48] not so very different than Viking practices after all. The contemporary commentator Alcuin, in a letter to an Irish monk, noted ominously that the Emperor 'urges some by rewards and others by threats'.[49]

In the process of these violent campaigns, the borders of Christianity expanded. This impacted on Scandinavia, Denmark especially as it was on the periphery of the continental battleground between Christianity and paganism. As one example, the Saxon chieftain, Widukind, who was forced to be baptised in 785, sought and found sanctuary in Denmark. Charlemagne also waged war against the Lombards who were based in the north of Italy after the decline of the imperial power of Rome. They were far more quickly overwhelmed than the continental Saxons had been. Charlemagne subsequently forged increasingly close relationships to the Papacy, then a struggling institution in need of powerful friends. His Frankish Empire was expanding in nearly all directions. This was a dangerous neighbour for the Danes to have on their southern borders.

However, this was not a period typified by violence alone. There was a major economic boom in the latter decades of the eighth century. Charlemagne's Francia became immensely rich but others also benefitted. Across the narrow Channel, the kingdoms of Anglia grew economically. To the north, Scandinavia also began to prosper. As in all ages, there were winners and losers from this; and those excluded from the benefits of economic expansion began to feel that they were missing out. If peaceful ways of profiting were not easily available to them, then they would find other ways of benefitting from the boom. It is also likely that less scrupulous traders who had travelled around the *emporia* of Europe began to notice how weakly they were defended and how susceptible to raids they might be.

To the south of Francia, then composed of much of modern France, the Low Countries, western Germany and northern Italy, a good deal of what is now Spain was in Muslim hands. The Umayyad dynasty based in Al-Andalus in the south of the peninsula was resilient in facing up to Charlemagne, though the most famous defeat he suffered was at the hands of Basques at the Pass of Roncesvalles, which gave birth to the later literary epic the *Song of Roland*. The Umayyad dynasty produced some wonderful architecture and art in cities such as Seville, Cordoba and Granada and they too would be impacted by Viking raiders.

On the far side of Europe, Byzantium – the successor of Rome – was in a mess. It was true that Constantinople was still by far the greatest city in Christendom, dwarfing its West European counterparts and containing breathtaking monuments such as the awesome Hagia Sofia and several magnificent imperial palaces. As Miklagard, the city would assume an almost mythical status in Viking lore; but it was currently at war with itself. To make matters worse, at the close of the eighth century Byzantium found itself ruled by an emperor who was – horror of horrors – a woman. 'Emperor' Irene was appointed to the position after ruling as co-empress for a time with her child Constantine.[50] When Constantine not unnaturally wished to assume dominance, he was deprived of the ability to do so when his mother had his eyes removed, a standard technique for making someone ineligible to rule in Byzantium. Many in the West, including the Pope, were shocked to the core at the possibility that a woman could be left to rule in her own right, particularly one who could demonstrate such ruthlessness.

Byzantium found itself bogged down during the eighth century when Emperor Leo III instituted a policy of iconoclasm (the destruction of icons). This infuriated many of his own people and also the Western Church. Although Leo died in 741, the wound he had opened would take decades to heal. The issue would run and run throughout the century; an apparent resolution at the Council of Nicaea in 787 was subsequently rejected by the Carolingian Church at the Council of Frankfurt shortly afterwards. Such doctrinal niceties would soon pale into insignificance in parts of Europe; the Western Church would find itself faced by much greater threats from the north.

Yet Byzantium had a grandeur and a magnificence outshining anything in the West. She was the inheritor at the same time of both Ancient Greece and of Rome. She had heritage and she also had wealth that the rest of the Christian world could only dream of. The emergence of the Arab/ Islamic threat in the seventh century for a time appeared to threaten the extinction of Byzantium but it proved to be a false alarm. The Byzantine Empire still had another seven centuries to run before it breathed its last. And the Vikings had a fascinating part to play in its subsequent history.

This, in summary, was the state of the world on the eve of the Viking Age. It was seemingly oblivious to the threat that loomed on the threshold. The continent of Europe, and the West in particular, was sleepwalking towards disaster. Its worst and most unlikely nightmares were about to become horrifically real.

2

The Great Suffering
(789–800)

From the North evil breaks forth, and a terrible glory will come from
the Lord
> Alcuin in his letter to the monks of Monkwearmouth-Jarrow

The Lindisfarne raid

Lindisfarne is an otherworldly place. It changes not just by the season
but by the hour. For some of the day it is an island, marooned off the
coast of Northumbria with the great medieval fortress of Bamburgh,
whose origins can be traced back to the earliest Angle colonists in
the sixth century, visible in the distance; unless the sea mists roll in
and blot it out. For the other part, it is attached to the mainland by
a narrow and vulnerable causeway, a fragile umbilical cord where it
seems that the sea might come in and deluge unsuspecting travellers
without warning at any moment. Sometimes it does, and the modern
causeway has raised refuges dotted along its length so that motorists
who have miscalculated the impact of the tides can seek safety even if
their vehicle is doomed.

First and foremost, Lindisfarne was the place where the great abbot
and saint, Cuthbert, earned his reputation. He died in 687, though his
body when exhumed later was found to be uncorrupted, leading along
with talk of miracles to his canonisation. The monastery there had
also been the home of dedicated and brilliant scribes and the work of
some of them, preserved in the renowned *Lindisfarne Gospels,* remains
one of the treasures of not only England but of the world. Crafted in
brilliant, vibrant colours, the scrolling patterns seem to move around
the page as if they are alive, supernatural serpents about to leap off
the parchment; they are a wonderful fusion of Anglo-Saxon and Celtic
art forms; and in the process they present a strong argument in favour

of cultural fusion rather than differentiation. Lindisfarne was famous both for its learning and its sacred connections and pilgrims came from near and far to pay their respects to the remains of Cuthbert and perhaps vicariously obtain some of his saintliness merely by being in the presence of his mortal remains. In some cases, they came no doubt to seek a cure for physical ailments. It was an iconic and holy place, known far and wide.

But there was something sinister in the air in 793. The *Anglo-Saxon Chronicles (ASC)* tell of flashes of lightning (surely not so uncommon) being seen, along with fiery dragons (far rarer one would assume), while the scholar Alcuin wrote how blood-red rain had fallen on the roof of York Minster out of a clear sky, something which he described as a premonition that a punishment from the north was about to fall on the people. These were times of famine, a regular occurrence in a period when men were far more at the mercy of the vagaries of nature than we like to think we are now. These portents suggested that something dreadful was about to happen (though the omens in the *ASC* were written up after the event with the gift of hindsight, the writer already knew what was coming). On 8 June, this premonition of impending doom turned into an awful reality. The hammer of Thor crashed down on the Christian temple on Lindisfarne and smashed it to pieces.[1]

The raiders came unannounced and unsuspected, Viking ships beached on the pebbly shore with their crews charging up towards the monastery that they could see not far off. At the time of the attack, Northumbria was a kingdom in turmoil; a state of affairs that often coincided with Viking raids, as if the marauders were in possession of well-attuned political antennae that enabled them to detect internal instability from afar. The buildings were undefended and quickly broken into. The raiders battered the life out of some of the monks with their swinging axes or ran them through with their swords. Some of the younger brethren were dragged to the beach in chains to be taken off into a harsh half-life of slavery; others were drowned in the sea. It has been suggested that this last action may be a violent parody of the baptism ceremony, and it is by no means inconceivable that those committing these acts of violence did so in part as a religious statement against Christianity, particularly given the violent conversion activities undertaken by Charlemagne in recent years.[2] The buildings were ransacked and all that was of value was taken. It was an outrage made worse because it was so unexpected.

Viking ghosts still seem to haunt the environs of the ruined abbey on Lindisfarne even now. Historical purists might rightly point out that the shattered stump of the priory that we see today was built some centuries after the Vikings struck and that the damage we see was done by that much later pillager of the monasteries, Henry VIII. Similarly, the brooding castle on the hill overlooking the bay at Lindisfarne is a later construction. All this is true; but it does nothing to diminish the sense of melancholy that still haunts the place, particularly when the east wind blows in from the North Sea.

It was not so much melancholy that England and Europe felt after the news came; it was shock and awe. In Francia, Alcuin, formerly deacon at York, had been working for some time as a teacher in the court of Charlemagne. He was a widely respected scholar, hence his invitation to work at the court. Now he wrote letters back home to Northumbria, suggesting that the Vikings were a punishment from God; a typical reaction to any horrific event experienced in those far-off days. This was a *flagellum,* a chastisement from God; the destruction of such a sacred spot with apparent impunity could only have been allowed to happen if it was a punishment for the sins of the people who lived there.

Alcuin's letter to Bishop Higbald of Lindisfarne after the attack had taken place reveals the sense of disbelief that the sack of the monastery generated. Alcuin knew the bishop and, as a Northumbrian and a cleric, he would have been proud of Lindisfarne (he also wrote in similar vein to Æthelred, king of Northumbria, commenting on the terrible way in which fornication, adultery and incest had become far too common in his realm – even nuns apparently were not exempt).[3] He lamented the fact that the raiders had 'trampled the bodies of the saints like dung in the streets'. He also lamented the precedent: if St Cuthbert could not defend the place where he was buried, what hope was there for anyone or anywhere else? He feared that this might be 'the beginning of the great suffering'. To him the Northmen were certainly a scourge sent by God; it was 'the sign of some great guilt'. Although it was customary at this time to make such critiques after a shocking event had taken place, Alcuin made some very specific comments in his letters. He encouraged the monks to disdain the 'vanity of dress' (he was particularly harsh about the over-the-top fashion consciousness of the Northumbrian elite and the way that their long hair emulated pagan styles), to avoid blurring the words of their prayers through drunkenness and to beware 'the indulgences of the flesh' (though in fairness he regularly adjured the monks at York to do the same in his letters to them, so this sounds like a wider problem that was not limited to the Lindisfarne brethren). Above all, the collection of Alcuin's many letters that survive shows frequent concern for the decline of monastic life in England. But they also show something else; if Alcuin was condemning the people of Northumbria for dressing like pagans, then the people of Northumbria clearly knew how pagans dressed. In other words, there was already a familiarity between the people of England and pagans from overseas; what was new was the violence.[4]

Of course, these words may have been uttered by Alcuin formulaically, but it is tempting to speculate that as a man with very specific local knowledge he had inside information to go on regarding the morality and activities of Northumbrian monks, who perhaps were not always practising what they preached. He was also familiar with secular Northumbrian high-fliers, especially those who were close to King Æthelred. He insisted that the brethren of Lindisfarne should not be overwhelmed by their grief but learn from the lessons handed out by the raiders and put their house in order; though his suggestion that God has 'chastised you more because he loves you more' probably rang hollow. He concluded with a practical offer to approach his lord Charles (Charlemagne) and do what he could to recover the monks who had been taken away as captives.[5] Shortly afterwards, he wrote to Æthelhard, the recently appointed Archbishop of Canterbury, reminding him how the sixth-century Romano-British writer, Gildas, had lamented that his fellow Christians had lost their country to the pagan Anglo-Saxons because of their sin; he hoped that the now-Christianised Anglo-Saxons were not destined to lose their country to the pagan Vikings for the same reason.[6]

It is very significant, though not unexpected, that this account of the first major Viking raid emphasised the pagan nature of the attackers. In the accounts that followed in succeeding years, it is almost a given that the raiding was indirectly (and sometimes directly) referred to as a battle between Christianity and paganism. The words that were used from across Britain, Ireland and Francia to label the Vikings routinely include 'heathen, 'pagan' or 'gentile', emphasising the otherness of the raiders and the sharp distinction with 'Christian' armies. So, the confrontation between the Viking and Christian worlds inevitably came to be seen (in the West at least) as one between different religions and world views.

Much would happen because of this clash of religions. Many Vikings would ultimately become Christians, although it would take some time for that to happen. But there would be rarer instances of the reverse happening. Pippin II of Aquitaine would transmute from a monk into a Viking in 864. In 869, a monk was captured and executed after he had abandoned his religion and had become 'extremely dangerous to Christians'.[7] There are accounts of Irish warriors too adopting heathen ways, so the process of conversion was not all one-way traffic.

For all the unexpected nature of the attack on Lindisfarne, it is difficult to believe that the Vikings chanced upon it by accident.

Given its fame they must have heard of it, and even been there before. It was on the right side of England for sailors from Scandinavia and given the development of their ships during the eighth century it was well within their reach. The emergence of important trading centres in Scandinavia at around this time would have brought with it not just the opportunity to create wealth in the region but also enhanced knowledge of the wider world. For all that, the horror of the attack on Lindisfarne rings down through the ages when we read the words of Alcuin as a 9/11 of its day, in its way a defining moment in history (at least in England; there is much less evidence of shock and horror from elsewhere – and curiously enough the well-known later chronicler Florence of Worcester, while clearly aware of Northumbrian affairs at the time, does not even mention the raid). But it announced the coming of the Northmen to the world.

Alcuin's letter to Higbald is an 'industry standard' for historians discussing the attack on Lindisfarne, but there is another source less frequently referred to that gives enlightening additional information. This work, the *Historia Regum Anglorum* ('History of the Kings of England'), was compiled at York by Symeon of Durham around 1110. It was once thought to have been his own work, but historians now believe that his part in its creation has been overstated. Currently, he is perceived as the compiler of a set of older records rather than the creator of the *Historia*. In any event, his work is important as it gives details of the Viking Age in Northumbria that are not available from other sources.[8]

Alcuin was now an old man. He had been in voluntary exile from Northumbria for a while and he was not in good health so was very aware that he had not long for this world. It is therefore understandable that there is an overwhelming sense of nostalgia in his lament for Lindisfarne. Yet there was something else too. His words suggest an attempt to capture 'a wistful sense of lost security and apprehension about the future'.[9] Both of these perceptions are well merited. The old world was indeed about to pass away and would be replaced by something altogether more frightening, impermanent and uncertain. Chaos was imminent. A few years later Alcuin wrote to the court in Kent, which had been in disarray since the death of Offa; after that it had regained its independence even though its position was still very vulnerable. One of the repercussions of this state of affairs was that the Archbishop of Canterbury had fled his see, leaving it vacant, something which predictably filled Alcuin with horror. Nevertheless, he is an invaluable and unique detailed source for the period, even though his regular injunctions on the theme of 'the end of the world is nigh' can get a little tiresome and probably did not reflect the views of many of the more worldly-wise of his contemporaries. However, he was surely right when he referred to the biblical text in

Luke (11:17) which said that 'every nation divided against itself shall not stand'. This was completely relevant; the disunity of so many parts of Western Europe played straight into Viking hands, especially when some factions within the various states in Britain, Ireland and Francia would attempt to employ them as mercenaries at a later stage with sometimes tragic outcomes.[10]

One reference made by Symeon (or his original source) concerns a noble (*dux*), Sicga, who was implicated in the assassination of a near-contemporary, King Ælfwold of Northumbria. He then took his own life and after that was buried on Lindisfarne. The burial of a man who was both a suicide and a king-slayer in such sacred ground would have horrified some contemporary commentators and would to more fundamentalist minds have invited divine retribution, which duly arrived in a terrifying form.

Such views may well have been encouraged by the fact that that great biblical pessimist, Jeremiah, had predicted that divine punishment for God's chosen people would ultimately come from the North, as referred to by Alcuin.[11] Interestingly, Islam also had a very dark view of the lands of the north, seeing them as inhabited by the descendants of Gog and Magog, mythical characters whose violent activities would herald in the end of time.[12] Christianity and Islam therefore had a somewhat eschatological view of the Far North. Just as modern-day millenarian sects look for the playing out of such prophecies in everyday life and events, so too did spiritual commentators of times past, especially when religion played such a crucial part in day-to-day existence.

Symeon's *Historia* refers to a further battle with the interlopers in 794. On this occasion, the Viking raiders got the worst of it as the Northumbrians had now had time to organise their forces to fight back. We are told that 'their chief was, in fact, slain by the English, a cruel death, and after a short space of time the violence of a storm battered, destroyed and broke into pieces and the sea overwhelmed many of them. Some were cast on the shore and soon killed without mercy. And these things befell them rightly, for they had gravely injured those who had not injured them'. St Cuthbert, understandably in the context of the times, was the man given credit for this turnaround in fortunes after his resting place had been defiled in 793.[13]

Despite these earth-shattering events, Lindisfarne recovered, after a fashion at least. In about 796, the exiled Northumbrian king, Osbald, sought refuge there after being ejected from his throne. It is often overlooked how resilient monasteries could be and how quickly after a raid they could return to some kind of normality. Unfortunately, this meant that in some cases they were destined to be raided time and time again. Gradually though, the inhabitants of some places decided that their only option was to remove their foundations to other, supposedly safer, places in more secure locations away from the coast.

Early raids on Scotland and Ireland

The *Annals of Ulster* note for 793 'the devastation of all the islands of Britain by gentiles', an event that is often overlooked because of concentration on the raid on Lindisfarne.[14] This suggests far more widespread raiding – and in the eyes of some historians possibly something more, for this may mean the occupation of some of the outlying islands of Britain, specifically those off the Scottish coast. We have no written evidence for when this took place; but the 790s is as good an estimate of the time that this occupation began as any other that we have.[15] Such statements as those made in the *Annals,* allied to archaeological finds, have enabled some historians to suggest with confidence that the decade before 800 saw the first incursions into islands such as those of Shetland.[16] But contemporary documentary evidence of Viking settlement in Scotland is very thin on the ground.

In 798, Inis-Patrick off the coast of Dublin was burned, again by the 'gentiles' who also broke up a shrine to St Dochonna.[17] The raiders also attacked other parts of Ireland and Scotland, though we are short on details. The raid on Inis-Patrick is referred to in the *Annals of Clonmacnoise*. Not only were items we might regard as treasure taken by the raiders but also cattle: this is a significant detail as it implies they were after sustenance as well as more valuable and portable lucre; such a raid for supplies and profit was known as a *strandhogg*. The raiders may have had a temporary base not far off where they intended to stay for a while. It is possible that they even stayed on Inis-Patrick which, with its offshore location, would be a perfect spot to use as a base as the Vikings, while there, would effectively be safe from counter-attack. These were ferocious raiders, 'merciless, soure and hardie, from their very cradles dissentious', as the later writer of the *Annals of the Four Masters* put it.[18]

It is worth noting that raids on isolated island communities with Christian establishments were nothing new. In 617, the *Annals of Ulster* recorded a raid on Eigg in the Hebrides in which over 100 Christian 'martyrs' were made. This long pre-dates the Viking era and it is unlikely that there was any Scandinavian involvement in this event at all. Rather this was more likely a raid involving men from Ireland; attachment to Christian beliefs should not be seen as automatically meaning that adherents to the faith would avoid raiding such spots, however sacred they might theoretically be.

The Northern and Western Isles of Scotland were a natural stopping point for the Viking seafarers as they made their way further afield from Scandinavia into the Atlantic and they reached them early on in the Viking Age. They left their mark in the DNA of these places and it is still there for those attuned to look for it. An assortment of suggestive place names call out to us of a Viking past. Skye is probably named from the Norse *ski,* meaning mist. Anyone who has been fortunate enough to visit the island but unfortunate enough to witness its weather extremes will fully understand where this suggestion comes from.

Skye provides other place-name evidence too. The island is split into smaller regions such as Waternish, Trotternish, Minginish and Duirinish. Again, this is a tell-tale sign; *nish* is Norse for 'promontory' of which Skye has a number. Norse sailors liked to give prominent geographical features meaningful names, as if the world were a giant's map that they could navigate by. This also explains the origin of the name of the most north-westerly point of mainland Scotland, Cape Wrath; it comes from the Norse *hvarth* which means 'turning point' for here the sailors would know to turn their ships to the south and head for the Western Isles and beyond to Ireland.

It was only a matter of time given its position on the far-most tip of the Western Isles before the great monastic establishment of Iona fell prey to Viking attack. It was dangerously exposed to assault from passing longships as it sat on the extreme edge of Mull, an easy stopping-off point for any passing ship whose crew knew it was there. It was also, like Lindisfarne, immensely rich in contemporary terms and was right on the route from the Northern Isles to Ireland. An attack duly came in 795 but it was just a foreshadowing of even worse to come.

These raiders would eventually leave their mark in other ways. Modern DNA research has matched the genetic make-up of males from various parts of Britain with Norwegians. The results have been fascinating: very strong connections between males in the Western and Northern Isles of Scotland as well as northern and western parts of the mainland, north-west England and the Isle of Man with Norway; there appears to be much less of a link between the DNA of males from Ireland and Norway. This suggests much deeper assimilation in parts of Britain than in much of Ireland.[19]

The Irish Sea would be an area of major activity for these raiders. It is far more sensible to talk about this as a region, rather than a collection of nation states gathered around this sea as we might now think of it. All the modern countries round it – England, Ireland, Scotland, Wales – back then were a collection of smaller territories with no such thing as a supreme overlord or king, though from time to time men might aspire to such a thing, such as when someone became *Bretwalda* in England or the high king in Ireland. However, such arrangements usually did not long survive the death of the man who held the title; often even in their lifetime the title came to mean very little in anything other than a symbolic sense.

The Irish Sea, rather than acting as a barrier (as residents of England might see the English Channel when faced with an Armada, a Bonaparte or a Hitler for example), was a highway. The fact that on a clear day men might see one land from another merely added to the temptation, an enticing glimpse of rich opportunity on the horizon.[20] The Viking settlements that developed around the rim of the Irish Sea exhibited cultural similarities. A movement in the 1960s came up with the name 'the Irish Sea Province' for this phenomenon and, while this seems to be pushing the evidence too far (there is little indication of any over-arching political domination of even the strongest Viking leaders over the whole area), it is certainly sensible to think of this as an Irish Sea Viking region. Such trans-ocean connections across the Irish Sea were nothing new; even in prehistory, thousands of years before the Vikings appeared, cultural interchanges took place across the Sea, evidenced by similarities in great early tombs like Newgrange and Dowth in Ireland and Bryn Celli Ddu in Anglesey.

Yet there was an element of deception here. The fact that the Irish Sea is enclosed, and one is rarely out of sight of land when crossing it, can lead to a false sense of security on the part of the complacent sailor. For the Irish Sea, rather like its Scandinavian counterpart the Baltic, is capable of stormy and unpredictable weather. It may be relatively shallow, but that shallowness contributes to the difficulties that can be experienced in sailing close to shore, whipping up waves that can drive a vessel around as if it is nothing more than a flimsy cork. In living memory ships have been wrecked, such as the passenger ferry *Princess Victoria* that was overwhelmed when sailing from Stranraer in Scotland to Larne in Ireland, a distance as the crow flies of about 30 miles, with the loss of over 100 lives in 1953.

Further south, off the western coast of Britain, there are clues that remote places once figured high in Viking raiding activities. In the Bristol Channel, there is for example Steep Holm and further north, off Penmon, Anglesey, Priestholm ('holm' being Scandinavian for island). Then there is Lundy Island, also in the Bristol Channel (emanating from the Norse name for 'Puffin Island'). All of these places are likely at one stage to have been offshore bases for Viking raiding flotillas, favoured sites for their ships to safely moor.

Further raids on England

There are only a few references to raids on England over the course of the next few decades, though those that took place certainly made an impression. Monkwearmouth-Jarrow, the dual monastery forever associated with a former resident, the 'Venerable' Bede, the founder of English history (or at least the writing-up of it), was one of the few other places we know of that was attacked in England at this time.[21] In its case, this was not so much a bolt from the blue as the raid on Lindisfarne had been; Alcuin had written to the monks there before the attack and noted their exposed position on the coast. He included words based on the Old Testament books of Jeremiah and Job that 'from the North evil breaks forth, and a terrible glory will come from the Lord'. Naturally enough, he then went on to warn the monks that they should amend their sinful ways before it was too late and look to the example of their former brother Bede.[22] Also attacked according to Roger of Wendover were the establishments at Tynemouth and Hartness; he places these last two raids in the year 800, although he wrote several centuries after the event and his general reliability has been doubted in some quarters.[23]

Alcuin held strong views on the state of England, writing in 796 that he did not wish to return there. This was partly because of Viking raids but there were other reasons too. To quote his own words, 'the holiest places have been ravaged by the pagans, altars desecrated by perjury, monasteries fouled by adultery, the earth stained with the blood of lords and princes. What could I do but lament with the Prophet: Woe to the sinful nation, a people laden with iniquity, wicked sons; they have forsaken God and blasphemed the holy saviour of the world in their wickedness'.[24] The raids were part of a much bigger picture for Alcuin. He had previously written to a cleric in Ireland that 'the times are now clearly more dangerous and many have turned from the path of truth, as the apostles prophesised'. He complained of false teachers and heretics and thought that the 'disastrous end of a passing world' was at hand. To him, the Vikings were part of a wider malaise, a moral meltdown caused by heresy and secularism. They became a self-fulfilling prophecy, a punishment from God. This gave him an excellent chance to get on his soap box and he did not disappoint.[25]

The attack on Lindisfarne was not quite as out of the blue as its shock factor might suggest. Several years before, probably in 789, the reeve of King Beorhtric of Wessex, a man named Beaduheard, was in residence at Dorchester, Dorset, a few miles away from the coast, when he received information that some unknown seafarers had landed in three ships at nearby Portland. William of Malmesbury, probably wrongly, said that they were an advanced guard for a larger occupation force (no such force would appear for another half a century), who had come to 'ascertain the fruitfulness of the soil and the courage of the inhabitants'. Unsure of who they were, the reeve quickly covered the short distance on horseback with a few trusted followers and approached them; the chronicler Æthelweard says that he was 'admonishing them in an authoritarian manner', which did not go down too well. The strangers, who apparently came from Hordaland in Norway, were having none of this; soon Beaduheard and his companions lay dead on the sand, the first known English victims of Viking raiders, though William says that they fled without their booty when they were counter-attacked.[26]

The reference to Hordaland is a reminder of how much confusion there was in the minds of the chroniclers as to where these terrifying apparitions came from. The *ASC* later recorded that this was the first time the 'Danes' raided England. Probably the original reference was to Hordaland only and the reference to 'Danes' was added by later scribes when the term had entered more common usage in the vernacular (writing up the *ASC* only started in the reign of King Alfred, nearly a century on and with the benefit of hindsight).[27] The surviving versions of the *ASC* do not give a location for these events: the link with Portland comes from the later *Annals of St Neots* which may have been based on another, now lost, copy of the *Chronicles*. The reference to Hordaland is not in the oldest surviving 'A' (or Winchester) version of the *ASC* so there is a considerable amount of uncertainty surrounding the reliability of the evidence.

The killing of the king's reeve at Portland, while it will have attracted local comment, would probably not have created much of a long-term impression. These were violent times, even in the relatively well-ordered kingdoms of England, and attacks by pirates were far from unknown. It was only with the benefit of hindsight, having seen how extensive and far-reaching the Viking raids would eventually become, turning eventually into active acts of conquest, that the full significance of this early foray into English affairs became apparent.

The suggested point of origin of Hordaland for these raiders may well be accurate. Stuck away in a corner on the south-west coast of Norway, it was well away from the main regional trade routes which tended to go through Denmark or Sweden. It is a tough part of the world climate-wise; on a visit to Bergen (which is in the region) during my research, a guide claimed that it rains for 375 days per year! Opportunities to make a profit locally were in short supply and in their absence those in this isolated corner of Norway sought and found other ways of enriching themselves; even William of Malmesbury suggested that over-population was a driving force for Viking expansionism.[28] From Hordaland they were well-placed to launch raids on Scotland and, sailing down past Cape Wrath and into the Irish Sea, on to the Isle of Man and Ireland too. The man who owned a farm in places such as Hordaland was also likely to have a *naust* – a boathouse. He was not generally just a farmer or a sailor, a raider or a trader; he was often several or all of these things. A Viking was often a chameleon-like figure, capable of changing with the alteration of circumstances and the emergence of opportunities. Profit was clearly a key driver for these men, but Viking activities also gave a chance to obtain other things, particularly status. The sense of adventure and risk can only have added to the motivation for some of them. These were no national undertakings, launched for the good of the country; they were first, foremost and exclusively exercises in self-aggrandisement. One early explanation for the Viking raids proposed by Adam of Bremen was a very simple one: poverty in the Viking homelands.[29]

Historians have in the past attempted to find demographic reasons for the Vikings' descent on Western Europe, land-hunger, *Lebensraum,* even the actions of fanatical pagans fighting back against Christian missionaries: a kind of Crusading movement in reverse. Yet most likely it was uncomplicated opportunism that was the main driver, a coincidence of technological developments in shipbuilding allied to wealthy but weakly defended kingdoms that were open to raiding and that were well-known from trading activities. The monasteries played into their hands; in their search for remote places in which to find their God they made the situation that much easier for their attackers.

But such sites, though they might appear remote to us, were often surrounded by large estates that generated a generous supply of provisions as well as a reservoir of labour that would make for ideal slaves and this added to the attraction from the Vikings' perspective. Such estates were the norm in Anglo-Saxon England. They covered a wide area and a number of villages might come within their orbit. They might be under the control of a royal figure, an aristocrat or a church establishment (in the seventh and eighth centuries such estates gathered around minsters, for example, were very common). Families were spread across the estate working the land. It has been suggested that some of the larger British and Irish religious establishments could have numbers of people counted in the hundreds, even thousands, attached to them.[30]

There are tantalising clues from the reign of King Offa of Mercia that a Scandinavian threat to England was emerging before the attack on Lindisfarne took place. Offa ordered defensive measures to be taken by strengthening coastal fortifications against possible seaborne assault;[31] levies were to be provided to guard against 'marauding heathens'.[32] As more evidence emerges about the eighth century it is becoming clear that England was not at all isolated from Scandinavia. Barbara Yorke has suggested that an eighth-century coin found in West Saxon *Hamwic* (Southampton) may have come from Ribe in Denmark, so earlier pre-raid contacts between England and Scandinavia are entirely plausible.[33] This is completely consistent with the view now generally held that there was a massive increase in trading activity in England in the eighth century, both domestically and internationally.[34] This made the kingdoms there very attractive targets for any would-be raiders.

Early raids on Francia

These events were not limited to Britain and Ireland. Generally, the eighth century had been one of significant economic expansion in Western Europe. *Emporia,* trading settlements, grew up along the coasts, both stimulating and benefiting from increases in trade. Some were on the mainland of continental Europe, such as at Dorestad (now in the Netherlands) and Quentovic near Boulogne. In England, places such as Hamwic (Southampton) and Gipeswic (Ipswich) boomed. There was a similar scenario in Scandinavia with Ribe, Hedeby, Birka and Kaupang emerging as well as Staraja Ladoga in what is now Russia. No doubt much of the trading that took place was entirely lawful, including that involving Scandinavians. But inevitably the emergence of a 'nouveau riche' as we might now call them was an irresistible temptation to those of a more piratical tendency, especially if they were conversant with state-of-the-art shipbuilding technology.

The early Viking raids were probably sporadic and seasonal (limited mainly to the summer months when sea travel was less risky) and the numbers of ships and men involved was relatively small.[35] Such seasonal raiding was not the sole preserve of Vikings; Charlemagne launched a campaign every year for almost thirty years after a spring assembly had been held.[36] In the Vikings' case, such attacks were made possible by the seafaring skills of the raiders. A key development which led to the Coming of the Northmen was the evolution of shipbuilding in Scandinavia. The Kvalsund boat from the west of Norway had a basic keel, a crucial step forward that allowed the deployment of larger sails and in turn gave Viking seamen the ability to range much further afield, beyond the Baltic. Dating from around 700, the ship was an important evolutionary step in shipbuilding development. Ships were now emerging with a very shallow draft (rarely more than 3½ feet) and were equally adept at crossing oceans or sailing up rivers, arteries going to the heart of kingdoms enabling Viking raiders to penetrate deep inland. There were further developments and modifications to design which helped improve the sailing abilities of these ships, for example the shape of the bow enabled the vessel to be raised out of the water when travelling at speed, reducing drag in a way that is similar to that of a modern hydrofoil.[37]

Some twentieth-century historians such as Peter Sawyer postulated that the negative impacts of the Vikings have been exaggerated. They pointed out that Viking history is invariably written by their victims; an accusation that certainly has a basis in fact. The chroniclers and annalists of the time were normally churchmen of one stamp or another. Religious institutions were rich, often relatively accessible from the sea, and poorly guarded, certainly in the early days of Viking activity. This was a potentially disastrous combination which made them ripe for the picking. Critics of stereotypical views of pagan raiders will point out that so-called Vikings were also non-violent traders and that their mercantile activities, alongside their voyages of exploration, mean that their other enterprises should not be ignored. Yet there is a danger that these apologists protest too much. To read through the *ASC* or the ninth-century Frankish *Annals of St Bertin* is to be forcibly reminded of the terror that the Northmen generated in the eye of the beholder. It is much easier to urge us to remember the Vikings for their other achievements from the comfort of a twenty-first century armchair than it would have been a thousand years ago.

One historian, publishing in 1970, opined that 'the Vikings were pagans, and it was perhaps to some extent for that reason that the accounts of them that have been left by the early writers of Britain and Western Europe are so unflattering, for the writers were Christians: in any case their raids were described as wholly disastrous, and only fire, pillage and universal destruction is attributed to them'.[38] It is naïve to expect Christian chroniclers who have witnessed events or heard accounts of monasteries, churches and towns being pillaged to then remind their readers that the Vikings were not all bad and had a softer side to them; and therefore a blind eye should be turned to their excesses. If one wants to find a balanced opinion, one is unlikely to find it in a victim.

But there is an irony in this. The raids on Lindisfarne and other great institutions came to be seen with hindsight as the apocalyptic announcement of a terrible new age. However, these early events, dramatic though they were, appear to have been occasional – if dreadful – happenings. This was not yet an all-out assault on Western Europe. They were, some have suggested, something of a false beginning.[39] There are occasional ongoing glimpses of incursions from Scandinavia, but they were an imperfect portent of the far more coordinated attempts at conquest that were to have a greater long-term impact on the mid-medieval period. Most of the early raids were relatively small-scale, possibly needing no more involvement than that of the *hersir*, the local war chief.

Yet there were those who already apprehended the full extent and danger of the threat from the North. Charlemagne was an extraordinary man; indeed, so extraordinary that his example proved far too great for his successors to emulate. From places like Aachen he oversaw the day-to-day management of a cumbersome and unwieldy empire which extended across a territory of well over a million square kilometres. Among his acts was the preparation of defences against the depredations of Scandinavian raiders. He foresaw that, terrible though the sacking of monasteries was, these raids were not as great a threat as possible attacks against the trading *emporia* that were now dotting the coasts of north-west Europe. This was the driving force behind the naval flotilla that he now established to patrol the approaches to the Scheldt. Ports like Dorestad were vulnerable targets upon which opportunistic raiders might fall creating chaos and he needed to guard against them.

Charlemagne's biographer, Notker the Stammerer, also credits the Emperor with premonitory powers regarding the Vikings. He says Charlemagne was looking out of a window overlooking the port of Narbonne in the south of France when a Viking fleet hove into view. They exited the harbour quickly when they knew that Charlemagne was in residence. However, the Emperor was inconsolable when he saw them; 'he shed tears beyond price. And none dared to speak a word to him; but at last he explained his actions and his tears to his nobles in these words: "Do you know why I weep so bitterly, my true servants? I have no fear of these worthless jokers doing any harm to me; but I am sad at heart to think that even during my lifetime they have dared to touch this shore; and I am torn by a great sorrow because I foresee what evil things they will do to my descendants and their subjects."'[40]

This is a classic case of writing with the benefit of hindsight; Notker wrote some three-quarters of a century after Charlemagne's supposed speech was made, by which point the 'prophecy' had been duly fulfilled; and his biography is a eulogistic assessment of the Emperor's reign where he is painted as a paragon of contemporary Christian kingship, and quasi-supernatural powers are routinely attributed to him. The location for this incident also appears highly dubious as there is no other account putting the Vikings this far into the Mediterranean by this time; though the raids of Hæsten and Björn Ironside in the 850s do specifically mention an attack on Narbonne. But it shows how the Vikings very quickly entered into the legendary corpus of the time.

In reality, few observers can initially have seen just how profound the effect of the Viking attacks would be, or how ferocious and threatening they would eventually become. The year 800 is widely remembered as being that in which Charlemagne gave new life to the long-defunct Western Roman Empire when he was crowned its head by Pope Leo III. Less widely remembered is a hidden-away entry in the *Royal Frankish Annals* which talks of the North Sea being infested with pirates, so much so that even Charlemagne was forced to build up his naval forces to respond to the threat.[41] That said, it is easy to overlook the fact that the Carolingian navy of the time was a formidable enough force in its own right, as victories over Muslim and Byzantine forces during Charlemagne's reign evidence.[42]

Through what remained of Charlemagne's reign, the threat would never quite go away. Einhard, the emperor's chronicler (who as a young man had been a pupil of the famed Alcuin), wrote that 'he caused watch and ward to be kept in all the harbours, and at the mouths of rivers large enough to permit the entrance of vessels, to prevent the enemy from disembarking'. He also fitted out ships to take on Viking vessels in an effort to reduce the threat; for by now too much of the French and German coast had been exposed to raids.[43] If even Charlemagne was forced to recognise the extent of the challenge from the North, then how much more would his less capable successors struggle to cope with it? Only time would tell and even he, with all his alleged powers of premonition, could never have foreseen just how terrifying the Viking threat would become.

3

The Shadow of Terror
(801–825)

Blood rains from the cloudy web of the broad loom of slaughter.

Njal's Saga

The intensification of raids on the Celtic west

Britain and Ireland were very fragmented with Anglo-Saxons, Britons ('Welsh'), Scots, Picts and Irish ethnic groups present; and among these there were many small kingdoms with no more than local dominance. Although some of the region was influenced by what went on in Carolingian Francia, these small kingdoms did not have access to the collective wealth, resources and consequently power needed to resist the raiders effectively so they could not copy Charlemagne's initiative in creating a defensive network to fight them off. There were also many sea routes leading from Scandinavia to Britain and Ireland, enabling Vikings with their superior sea power to gain ingress virtually at will in the absence of strong naval defences to resist them. There were a number of different entrance ways around the coast through which the Vikings could gain access, and many of them were weakly guarded.

There were marked regional differences in terms of simple economics between various parts of Britain and Ireland. In Britain, the island could very simplistically be divided between highland and lowland areas (the former mainly in the north and west, the latter in the south and east). Agriculture in lowland areas, most of which was occupied by the Anglo-Saxons, was by the standards of time very productive with large tracts of arable land where crops could be grown, a surplus achieved as a result, and wealth thereby created. A strong kingship supported by a rich and tightly organised Church was able to flourish and grow wealthy in such conditions.[1]

In the highland areas, those that collectively formed what we might, again simplistically, call the Celtic region, in which we should also for convenience include Ireland (though the island was completely politically independent from Britain), the institutions in place did not enjoy such centralised authority and the population was more likely to be comprise herders rather than arable farmers, making it more difficult to create an economic surplus. It is no accident that the Anglo-Saxon economy was one that knew coins from the early seventh century but the Celtic region did not;[2] in the former, silver coins of a 'startlingly high quality' were produced, in the main the silver pennies that formed the basis of English coinage for the next 500 years.[3]

It was the Celtic region, more vulnerable to attack and initially offering easier pickings for the raiders due to its fragmented organisation, which was to feel the blows of Viking attacks the keenest in those early decades. Judging from surviving records, it was the remoter areas which suffered the most from early attacks, Scotland and Ireland especially. The attack on Iona in 795 was just a taster of something worse. In 801, another attack on the monastic community there was launched, and the situation was already, in the eyes of the resident brethren, becoming impossible.[4] In 804, Cellach, abbot of Iona, started discussions about the development of another community at Kells in Ireland, a relative safe haven and a bolthole if it were needed. Like Iona, Kells was one of Columba's most famous establishments but it had one great virtue to recommend it: it was far from the coast and therefore it was more difficult to launch a surprise attack on it.

The Iona community dithered regarding implementing its move to Kells. In 806 another attack on Iona came: the worst yet, in which sixty-eight people died. That was that: the year after, building at Kells finally began. Iona eventually became a pale shadow of what it had once been and it would be several centuries into the future before, with Viking raids no longer a threat, a renewal of its fortunes occurred. In contrast, the community at Kells thrived, though for many years the two monasteries operated as a joint establishment.[5] But in the long run, Kells would not prove to be immune from Viking attacks either. Within a few years of the migration from Iona, the masterpiece known as the *Book of Kells* came into being.[6] Perhaps predictably, a scholarly debate continues to be fought over whether the *Book of Kells* was produced at Iona or Kells. Wherever it was crafted, it is a work of timeless genius and a fascinating insight into the age. Certainly, Kells grew in status. Although the monks originally had to make do with timber buildings, by about 814 a stone church had been constructed there.

There were many raids on Ireland in those early years. In 806/7 Inishmurray, a monastic foundation in the north-west of the island, was sacked, and Ross Com was also raided.[7] These attacks may well have been launched by the same group of raiders who had attacked Iona in the previous year. The attack on 'Ross Com' suggested to some historians that Roscommon was the target, an intriguing development as it was far from the coast and therefore supposedly less vulnerable to attack; if accurate, previous assumptions about safe havens inland might have to be reassessed. But in 1972 it was suggested that 'Ross Com' was in fact Roscam near Galway Bay, leading to a very different (and more logical) interpretation.[8] These opening blows were an ominous introduction to the events that were 'to make the ninth century one of the unhappiest in Ireland's history'.[9]

Not all such incidents are recorded but some can be tantalisingly glimpsed from other evidence. In Bute Museum, on an island off the west coast of Scotland, is a slate carving known as 'The Hostage Stone'. On it can be seen an oared ship, its prow raised high above the rest of the vessel. There is to the left of this a man with flowing long hair moving determinedly towards the ship. He is dragging an object in tow at the end of a chain; the object looks very like a human being. The style dates the stone to around the year 800: and it seems that here we have an early illustration of the Viking slave trade in operation. Not everybody agrees with this interpretation of what is portrayed on the slate and the carvings are rather abstract and open to other explanations; in this case, as with many others involving the Vikings, as the old saying goes, 'you pays your money and you takes your choice'. But if this interpretation is accurate, it is an insight into the Vikings dark *tour de force*. It was not that the Vikings were unique in practising slavery, which was widespread in Britain and Ireland before and during the Viking period, it was rather that they turned it into a global operation.

There are other contemporary signs uncovered by archaeology that suggest possible Viking violence. On the other side of Scotland, at Portmahomack on the tip of the Tarbat Peninsula in Easter Ross, there was once a Pictish monastery. It was built in 550 and came to a dramatic end when it was burned down, most probably in the 800s. It has been argued that at its peak this was an important monastic foundation, possibly founded by St Columba though more likely linked to Saint Colman, a former abbot of Lindisfarne from the seventh century. It was once a thriving stone-sculpture manufacturing site as well as producing manuscripts; there is archaeological evidence of a facility for making vellum. Large stone crosses were smashed into small pieces in what appears to be an attack and the skeletons of two monks were found with blade cuts to the head. The effort put into the smashing of the crosses in particular suggests a violent aversion to Christianity and a determination on the part of the attackers to make this clear to all and sundry. The sculpture production stopped abruptly and, although the site came back into use, it now only produced mundane items like belts and buckles.

While life went on, after a fashion, it seems that Portmahomack never recovered from this bitter blow.

The Vikings are the prime suspects for Portmahomack's destruction, given its timing. The positioning of several massive cross-slabs nearby, probably sited to be prominent markers from the sea, would have been a handy notification to any passing raider that there was a place of importance (and wealth) close by. There are several prominent marker stones along the Tarbat Peninsula at Shandwick and Nigg, which would have advertised from out at sea the presence of something important nearby. What makes Portmahomack particularly interesting was that there is no contemporary reference to its end in any documentary evidence such as the *Annals of Ulster*, which does refer to other attacks on parts of Scotland. It is a salient reminder that chroniclers did not write up every single significant event of the time and were in the main focused on those which affected their locality; even the *ASC* is guilty of such a failing.[10] Out of sight was often out of mind.

Early on, Viking incursions into Ireland and Scotland took similar forms. These were hit-and-run raids directed against establishments on the coast on a seemingly opportunistic basis. However, later in the Viking history of Britain and Ireland the approach diverged. Whereas in Ireland significant Viking settlements, Dublin and others, were established and grew into important trading sites, there is limited evidence that any such development took place in Scotland. There was also a much clearer dividing line between Scandinavian and Gaelic territories in Scotland and less direct evidence of any significant cultural hybrid such as the Hiberno-Norse in Ireland taking place on the other side of the Irish Sea; that said, there is some indirect evidence to be found in the shape of artistic crossovers that occurred in some regions of Scotland which hint that something along similar lines may have taken place.

Details of raids in the western part of Ireland are initially in short supply. This does not mean that they did not happen; merely that chroniclers did not record them or, if they did, their work has not survived. The west was relatively isolated, and this may also be a case of out of sight being out of mind. But we have enough evidence to believe that raids on the west coast of Ireland were indeed taking place. In recent times historians have started to argue with increasing confidence that there may have been a Viking base, or bases, there from as early as the beginning of the ninth century, perhaps around Eyrephort, Galway and Beginish in Kerry, where Viking burials and middens have been found.[12]

In 812, there were battles against secular dynasties in Ireland as opposed to raids on isolated monastic settlements. A reference in the *Annals* to a 'slaughter of the heathens in Mumu (Munster)' by 'Cobthach son of Mael Duin' attests a defeat at the hands of a dynasty that is traditionally associated with Killarney, a little way inland from the west coast of Ireland. Such incursions require more than just opportunistic hit-and-run raids but a degree of forward planning and well-thought-out implementation.[13] There are references to other Viking raids in succeeding years, for example Howth near Dublin was attacked in 821 and a number of women were taken away, presumably more additions to the slave trade.

Even though many of the monks had relocated to Kells from Iona, there were still enough remaining on the Scottish island to attract the unwelcome attention of more passing pillagers. A raid there in 824 left the abbot, Blathmac, dead. He was tortured to death because he refused to reveal the hiding place of the shrine of St Colum Cille (Columba). These horrific events were recalled in a poem written by Walafrid Strabo, a scholar connected to the Carolingian court and the abbot of Reichenau on Lake Constance. According to his account, Blathmac foresaw in a vision what was coming but refused to flee, instead welcoming his impending martyrdom; it duly came, with him being 'torn limb from limb'.[14] Somewhat surprisingly in the light of this ongoing Viking activity, relics were taken back to Iona from Kells in 829, only to make the return journey two years later. This was not the end of the toing and froing of these precious items. The *Annals of Ulster* record that Colum Cille's shrine and other relics were brought to Kells in 878 in a hurry after yet another Viking attack.

The year 824 saw a great deal of Viking activity in Ireland. The *Annals of Ulster* tell us of oratories (small, private chapels) being ransacked and several confrontations between 'gentiles' and Irish in various parts of the island. Again, it is notable that while the raiders won some of these battles, they lost others; there was an ebb and flow to the confrontations. Watching modern interpretations of the Vikings in Hollywood movies and the like, an impression that they were invincible comes across. Such was clearly not the case, especially if the locals had a chance to prepare themselves against an imminent assault or catch the raiders by surprise on their way back from a raid.

While many of the establishments attacked would most likely have been relatively wealthy and well stocked with potential slave labour, this could probably not be said of the remote community on Skellig Michael, that amazing rocky outcrop off the coast of Kerry. Even today this is a hard place to get to. In 824, it was raided and its abbot taken off as a hostage, a tactic that did not work very well as he subsequently died of hunger and thirst. Given the poor pickings that were likely to be available in this remote ascetic community, the motivations for this raid are hard to establish; possibly they were political given the symbolic significance of the site or maybe on this occasion this raid had a definitive anti-Christian agenda. Alongside the slaughter of the abbot of Iona, this may be evidence there were some hard-line supporters of the Norse gods sailing the Irish Sea at the time.

The impact of early Viking raids

How much overall impact the raids had across Ireland and the wider Irish Sea region is a moot point. On a case-by-case basis they were devastating to the individual communities affected; but even many of these proved resilient. Iona for example would rise from the ashes on a number of occasions though it would never return to its former heights during the Viking era. It is also important to consider what the Vikings were after. It has been suggested by the historian A. T. Lucas that the gold and silver present in these monastic communities would not have been in large quantities. Gold in his view was only used in 'microscopic quantities in things like gilding and filigree work and silver would not have been much more common'.

Possibly the main targets of these raids would be something that was valuable in a different way – human beings to use or sell on as slaves. Other mundane items such as food and cattle would also be targeted but these cannot have been the main purpose of the raids beyond immediate sustenance; if the raiders were not settling in Ireland and it is unlikely that they took the cattle away with them, then we are left with the conclusion that these raids must have been primarily to feed the slave trade.[15]

A number of Irish religious establishments were raided in the 820s such as those at Bangor, Downpatrick and Movilla (in the north-east). Lusk and Clonmore on the east coast were also raided later in the decade. Some places such as Armagh, Kildare and Glendalough were attacked on several occasions, sometimes more than once in a year. If nothing else, such places show remarkable resilience. It is notable that the writers of the *Annals of Ulster* changed their description of the raiders from 'gentiles' to 'foreigners', hinting that an ethnic perspective was coming into play. During the following decade raids would also start to move inland, away from the coast. The raiders were clearly encouraged by their successes to become more ambitious.[16]

The resilience of some of the Viking targets has been commented on by some modern historians. To some, the Viking attacks were indeed devastating; to others their impact has been overplayed. There is certainly a danger that later writers, in particular chroniclers of the twelfth and thirteenth centuries, have talked up the extent of the devastation wrought as a result of these attacks; yet it might also be true that they had access to records which are no longer available to us. One view, developed by the eminent twentieth-century historian of the period,

Sir Frank Stenton, was that 'the Danish invasions of the ninth century shattered the organisation of the English church', threatening the very fabric of English society.[17] In considering the extent and impact of Viking raids on the Church, it is important to note that in a number of cases statements that such-and-such an establishment was destroyed often come from speculation by antiquarians which has been accepted, sometimes uncritically, by later historians. This does not mean that their speculation is wrong; merely that it is often unproven.[18]

The occasional shocking and dramatic raid excepted, England seems to have been relatively unaffected for a while. There are nevertheless hints that a climate of fear was abroad, especially among members of the Church. For example, in 804 Selethryth, the Abbess of Lyminge in Kent, sought and obtained permission to move her establishment away from the coast and into the relative security of the walls of Canterbury.[19] Given the violent Viking raids that had been launched on monastic establishments near the coast during the previous decade (not just those at Lindisfarne, Jarrow and Hartness but possibly others which have gone unrecorded) it is an obvious conclusion that this was a move prompted by a desire for greater security under the threat of future raids. Other suggestive references of the time include the granting of land by Ceolwulf, king of Mercia, at Sevenoaks in Kent free of burdens apart from the need to provide military service against 'pagan enemies', which presumably means Vikings.[20]

All this talk of monasteries and monks might give the impression that the regions raided were peace-loving territories filled with nothing except people at prayer. Nothing could be further than the truth. Frankish, Celtic and Anglo-Saxon societies were essentially governed by a warrior elite who, even if they did not spend their whole lives fighting, were expected to step up to the mark in battle whenever the occasion demanded. King Alfred later said that society could be divided into three estates; those who worked, those who prayed and those who fought. It was undoubtedly the job of the aristocracy to take the lead in the last of these three categories, though men from the other two estates (including those who prayed) were often heavily involved in fighting too.

This meant that Viking raiders did not always have it all their own way during the centuries in which they were active. But these early raids were characterised by surprise attacks where local forces were either non-existent or caught off-guard. When, over the course of a very long time, the areas being raided improved their defences and their general state of preparedness, the raiders would often be on the wrong end of a defeat; but that situation would take time to come about in many regions.

England was potentially far more vulnerable to extensive penetration than most other parts of Britain. As well as its extensive coastline, populated with rich and largely undefended monastic institutions, it was criss-crossed by multiple river systems – ideal for a raider with shallow-draft ships to sail up with ease – and a still-functioning legacy of Roman road systems and even older prehistoric paths (the roads in particular exposed England to problems to a greater extent than elsewhere in the British Isles and Ireland). To compound the threat, few towns were well fortified. Even those that were did not always have strong defences on the riverside as no attack from this direction had previously been expected.

Developments in Sweden and lands to the east

There was evidence of significant change in Sweden at around this time. The port at Helgö was being outgrown. This was a pity because its location was in many ways ideal. It was situated on Lake Mälar in the south-east of Sweden, not far from modern Stockholm. The lake's modern name though is deceptive, for in the heyday of the Viking Age it was not an isolated lake but a harbour connected to the Baltic. This made it perfect for trading purposes. Lake Mälar was surrounded by fertile land, making it as attractive to farmers as to traders. During the Viking period, there were perhaps 2,000 farms dotted around the shoreline.[21] The area was therefore generally attractive but Helgö was no longer sufficient. A new settlement was established at nearby Birka on Björkö ('Birch Island'). It was strongly defended, being surrounded by walls and earth ramparts. Archaeology has revealed how the people there lived and thrived during the Viking era. Even more has been found concerning how they were treated in death.

The houses excavated on the site were humble structures made of wattle and daub, or timber. A layer of soil over much of it contains high levels of ash deposits from an occupation layer, giving it a colour that has therefore been called 'black earth'. Cattle, pigs, goats/sheep (infuriatingly similar in terms of their biological structure and therefore hard to identify from skeletal remains) and fish formed the main part of the diet. The bones of many foxes in the area suggest that they were often killed for their fur. Residual traces of wheat also demonstrate that arable farming was taking place in the area.

Round about Birka, outside its ramparts, are dotted a number of Viking cemeteries. The grave goods found here include artefacts from many different parts of the globe including silver and silks from the Middle East, pottery and glass from the Rhine region, and ornaments and weapons from England and Ireland. Clearly Viking men and women, or at least those from the elite levels of the social hierarchy, liked to be well dressed in death. The graves were part of an extensive dig in the nineteenth century by Hjalmar Stolpe; in a quarter of a century he found 1,800 graves. In more recent times (the 1970s and 1990s) further archaeological searches were carried out by Björn Ambrosiani: the latter helped pushed back the foundation of Birka to around 750.

There are now known to be at least 2,300 graves in the area, of which currently over 1,100 have been examined.[22] There is wide variation in the types of graves, with about half containing cremations and the remainder inhumations including some individuals who were buried in coffins. The cremations are linked with paganism, although it should be noted that some Viking sagas suggest that ashes from cremations were not always buried but were sometimes deposited at sea. As well as pagan symbols, such as the Thor's Hammers which were found, mundane items such as a large number of combs were uncovered. This suggests a concentration on personal hygiene which is backed up by various written references to bathing and the discovery of archaeological evidence from several sites such as tweezers for plucking out unwanted hair and small spoons that are believed to have been used for scooping out ear wax. Some surviving pictorial evidence shows Viking warriors with splendid handlebar moustaches.[23]

The more elaborate burials at Birka were interred in chamber graves, some with rich grave goods and others with none, though it has been suggested by experts that the absence of such does not imply relative poverty on the part of the inhumed individual, as the style of the grave itself is sophisticated. Chamber graves were by no means a new phenomenon; some wonderful examples of similarly styled tombs have been found in Britain in the shape of Neolithic passage graves; these are 4,000 years older than those found at Birka. More relevantly they are also found in Scandinavian countries from the Bronze Age onwards.

This suggests that the builders of such graves were inspired as much by tradition as anything else, an essential conservatism that contrasts with some of the innovation and adventurism typifying the Viking Age; there was a 'proper' way to perform such rituals. Similar graves have been found in Denmark with examples near Hedeby and at Jelling. Some of a like vintage have been found in regions where Viking traders were active, including Poland and Russia. At Birka, jewellery and beads were found in abundance and some graves included evidence of horse sacrifice; examples of the latter are especially significant as this constitutes the destruction of a valuable, high-status object. Items of equestrian equipment were also found in some of the graves.

Among the twenty excavated chamber graves that are considered high-ranking in status, thirteen contained female remains; one was a double burial with two females interred in it and a number of women were buried with high-status objects. This suggests that the Vikings had a certain gender equality in their view of the world. A number of the graves contained weapons. Some of the graves can be dated to the ninth but most to the tenth century, helping us to follow the development of Birka as a trading emporium. The chamber graves appear to experts to be reserved for high-status individuals, implying a degree of social differentiation in Viking society. It has been hypothesised that those buried may be kings, chieftains or their close retainers.[24] This contrasts with earlier interpretations that argued that the tomb styles were so different from earlier Viking graves that they must have been constructed for foreign merchants and their families.

However, Birka was living on borrowed time even when it was first built. There were some things that even Vikings struggled to conquer, specifically nature. The entrances to the lake began to silt up and by the eleventh century Birka was no longer viable, as it was increasingly cut off from the Baltic. The drying-up of trade to Russia in about 970 also hit home. Even locally, Birka lost influence to nearby Sigtuna, a town that was closely linked to Odin.[25] By modern standards Birka was never large: the town is estimated to have supported about 1,000 people. No wonder the Vikings were staggered when they visited Constantinople – *Miklagard,* 'The Great City' as they called it. With a population of perhaps a quarter of a million people at the time, Constantinople would have dwarfed any Viking town and surely seemed to exist on another planet.

The Vikings developed strong trading links to Constantinople through Russia. Several routes developed over time, all involving major journeys that were adventures in their own right. The Western Dvina River formed part of one of them. This flows out into the Baltic through the Gulf of Riga, ideally placed in terms of access for traders from Sweden and neighbouring lands. From the Western Dvina, the Dnieper could then be accessed. This was a major river system passing through what is now Belarus and Ukraine before emptying into the Black Sea from where ships could sail on to Constantinople.

Another important access point to this river network, which cut across much of the Russian steppe from north to south, was at its northern end where it entered the Baltic. On Lake Ladoga, an important Viking settlement, Staraja Ladoga, was established some 75 miles to the east of modern St Petersburg (though excavations here have not conclusively proved a Viking presence with some of the buildings that have been excavated appearing to be more Finnish in nature).[26] To further confuse the issue, archaeology dates the earliest remains uncovered to as far back as 753, before the 'classic' Viking Age began, demonstrating just how imperfect reliance on traditional dating systems with black-and-white start and end points actually is. It is highly probable that given its location a massive proportion of Islamic silver flowed through Staraja Ladoga far into the Viking Age, as suggested, for example, by a large hoard of silver Islamic coins found there dating to around 790.[27]

A major challenge on the Dnieper was the presence at certain parts of the river of unnavigable rapids. The Vikings' answer to this problem involved carrying their ships across land, portage as it is known, thereby bypassing the obstacle. This was no doubt strenuous work but the relatively streamlined design of Viking ships made it at least possible. There were seven major rapids to be bypassed on the Dnieper (the names of many of them are of Scandinavian origin) and over time trading centres would develop at points where portage was required. These probably had a defensive function, too, as the region was renowned for its unruliness and the existence of hostile Pecheneg tribes who frequently sensed an opportunity for profit. Portage was a well-known Viking method and in Ireland and Scotland the place name Tarbert reveals where such an expedient was routinely followed (the name is Gaelic for 'carry across' suggesting that it was not just Vikings who used such spots for portage).[28]

Further east, the Volga river route was also important. The lands around the Volga were in the sphere of influence of tough tribesmen, the Bulgar and the Khazar, who charged tolls for traders wishing to cross their territories. There was little in the way of permanent 'civilisation' in this part of the world and the tribes, such as those mentioned above and the Pechenegs, were typically nomadic or semi-nomadic. However, the opportunities beyond this region, particularly those arising from the Silk Road from Baghdad to China in one direction and the Byzantine Empire in the other, made the cost and the risk worthwhile to those with an appropriate sense of adventure.

Viking traders would use both river routes, though in later times the Dnieper seems to have become the more commonly used. Effectively, they were roads linking Scandinavia to the waters of the Caspian and Black Seas. Viking ships would sail along them and, when necessary, were dragged across land to reach the desired destinations far away to the south and east. When the traders returned they would bring with them precious goods and exotic items but, most importantly of all to them, vast amounts of silver, often in the form of coins. These routes were mentioned in an Islamic work called the *Book of Roads and Kingdoms*, which appeared in 885. It was written by Ibn Khurradādhbih, director of the Abbasid Bureau of Posts and Intelligence, but is believed to contain information that dates back to a time far earlier in the ninth century. During their journeys, these travellers came into contact with various local middlemen, for example the Judeo-Turkic Khazars operating from their capital Itil in the Volga Delta, on the northern shores of the Caspian Sea, or the Bulgars; two groups who were traditionally at each other's throats. Very different worlds started to come into frequent contact with each other, which must have been a source of confusion and questioning but also wonderment for all parties concerned.

Runes dateable to the ninth century and after give powerful evidence of links between Scandinavia and 'Greece' as Byzantium was then known. One such found at Ed near Stockholm mentions a man, Ragnall, who erected a memorial in memory of his mother Fastvi. The inscription tells us that Ragnall 'had the runes cut, he was in Greece, he was the leader of the host'. This is an early sign that Scandinavian warriors were beginning to be recruited to serve a Byzantine master, though it was a long time before the famous Varangian Guard was formally established in 988.

Godfrid – the first Danish king?

By 810 a settlement had been established at Hedeby in the south of Denmark which became a major cog in the Viking trading machine. It was in Schleswig, ideally placed for trading purposes, near the Baltic on the one hand, connected to it by a navigable channel called the Schlei, and also on a major north-south land route known as the Army Road on the other; this led up to the north of Jutland, meaning that Hedeby was perfectly located for both sea and land routes. It was developed by Godfrid, king of part of Denmark since the death of Sigfred in about 800, though he probably built on an already existing settlement that had been founded a few decades before. There was a mention of it in the biography of Charlemagne written by Einhard, placing it early in the ninth century (this account was one of the most influential works of the period and no less than 123 copies of it have survived; it would be a role model for later biographies of secular figures such as that written by Bishop Asser on Alfred the Great in England).[29] Godfrid adopted a strong military strategy for several reasons; partly to gain wealth from taxation and from plundering neighbouring territories but also to secure income from trade by protecting ports such as Hedeby, particularly necessary given the assertive Carolingian Empire right on his southern borders.[30]

Godfrid jump-started Hedeby's further evolution when he destroyed the competing Slavic settlement at nearby Rerik in Germany, though exactly what is meant by 'nearby' is speculative as its site has not been definitively identified. Rerik had the misfortune to be right on the borders of two competing power blocs, never a good position to be in. It was at the extremes of the sphere of influence of Charlemagne on the one hand but on the other inconveniently close to Godfrid to whom, from time to time, it paid tribute. In 808 Godfrid fell on it, destroyed the settlement and forced its traders to relocate to Hedeby. This was in response to an alliance between the Franks and the Slavic Abodrit residents of Rerik, which angered Godfrid who understandably viewed it as a threat on Charlemagne's part. The great emperor had used Abodrit support to keep recalcitrant Saxons in the region under control; but such strategic considerations would have meant little to Godfrid. In fact, tensions between Denmark and Francia went back much further and even in Merovingian times, several centuries before, occasional flare-ups on the frontier and beyond had occurred.[31]

The aggressive (in every sense of the word) policy of expansionism undertaken by Charlemagne inevitably put the Danes on their guard. As Frankish power increased, it set off alarm bells over the northern border. While this aggression was certainly not uniquely directed towards the Saxons (Lombards, Avars, Bavarians, Bohemians and Muslim powers in Spain were also on the wrong end of it), the proximity of Saxon lands to those of the Danes would have increased the sense of alarm. Military conquest was accompanied by what amounted to forced conversion of conquered pagans to Christianity; and when Charlemagne founded bishoprics at first Bremen and then Hamburg, close to the borders of Denmark, the alarm bells became deafening.

So, there were important and compelling political reasons for Godfrid's interventions. There were also sound economic reasons for replacing Rerik with Hedeby as it gave the latter the opportunity to benefit from lucrative international trade between north and south, east and west. Ribe on the west coast of Jutland was one regional town that had already profited from a growth in trade and the development of Hedeby further boosted its economy. Recent archaeological excavations at Ribe have unearthed some interesting information. The town was a hive of urban activity with houses closely packed together and evidence of trading activities in abundance that can be traced back to the eighth and ninth centuries. The finds include a number of items that clearly formed part of a trading network. From Norway, these included whetstones, iron, and reindeer antlers, while from the Rhine region to the south imported objects included glass, metal and wine pitchers. The lead seal of a Byzantine envoy, along with glass beads and dirhams (Islamic coins), show a connection to the Mediterranean farther afield. Manufacturing activities at Ribe included the production of iron knives, antler combs, amber amulets, glass beads, bronze and silver jewellery and locks and keys. This was clearly a busy and cosmopolitan trading centre.[32]

The development of such trading towns was a feature of Viking Scandinavia. Regional *emporia* that evolved at places such as Hedeby and Ribe (Denmark), Birka (Sweden) and Kaupang (Norway) met several important objectives. They served as a meeting place to bring traders together to exchange their goods. This was not only for the purposes of international trade, exotic and interesting though that might be, but also for more localised economic purposes such as the buying and selling of local agricultural products. But developing such *emporia* brought risks: by bringing together concentrated amalgamations of wealth they also made very attractive targets to any opportunistic raider. If not properly protected, they could prove irresistible to pirates as the very exposed Frisian emporium of Dorestad found out to its great cost. It is also noticeable that Adam of Bremen, who wrote in the second-half of the eleventh century, waxed indignant at the frequency of pirate raids in the Baltic region. Clearly, Viking activity was not only prevalent in places far distant from Scandinavia.

As a result of this high risk of attack, the Viking *emporia* were built in easily defended places. Hedeby was on a narrow fjord (as was the later Danish town of Roskilde, built in the latter years of the Viking Age), Helgö and then Birka were on a lake which, although accessible from the sea, could be easily defended from the land (it was in fact miles from the ocean, linked by a channel) and Kaupang was in a bay where the approaches were not easy to navigate. To further strengthen these natural defences, fortifications were added at places such as Hedeby and Birka and in the form of earthworks erected around Grobin (now in Latvia). Thus, Vikings had a view to the defensive as well as the offensive. This was all part of an increasing urbanisation process (though this would remain relatively small-scale even by the end of the Viking Age). Other towns developed later, for example Bergen and Trondheim in Norway. It has been suggested that such towns also formed assembly points where merchant ships could arrange themselves into some kind of basic convoy formation as a means of increasing their collective protection.[33]

Hedeby was extensively excavated in the twentieth century, producing a huge array of finds. These revealed that it was defended on three sides by a semi-circular rampart, enclosing an area about 24 hectares in extent; on its fourth side lay the sea, easily accessible from the port with well-protected channels; a 'D-shape' design that would become a feature of Viking forts overseas. These ramparts were developed substantially over time, and the tenth century defences dwarfed those of the ninth. We would regard the houses inside the ramparts as humble: doors were normally low; the walls were of wood, or wattle and daub; and the roofs were made of reed thatch. When a house started to fall apart, the site was levelled and it was replaced by another one built over the top in more or less the same place.

Charlemagne, ageing and distracted by a daunting range of challenges, did not respond aggressively to the attack on Rerik. This emboldened Godfrid, who soon after raided the coast of Frisia, extracting a healthy amount of tribute in the process. But he would have little time to enjoy his success for soon after he was murdered by one of his close associates. The late ninth-century biographer of Charlemagne, Notker the Stammerer, says that the act was done by

Godfrid's own son, shortly after the king had abandoned his mother for a new wife. Notker says that the son caught Godfrid unawares just as he was pulling his hawk off a heron, an interesting insight into hunting practices in the Viking world.[34]

Any semblance of unity Godfrid developed proved illusory but his reign was extremely significant nevertheless. He felt confident enough to take on Charlemagne and at other times to negotiate with him. These were not the actions of a petty chieftain but of someone with real power. Charlemagne, slowing down physically, considered a retaliatory strike for the attack on Rerik but it fizzled out, if indeed it ever really began. Perhaps the most remarkable feature of his response was the accompaniment of his abortive expeditionary force by an elephant, a gift from the famous Baghdad caliph Harun al-Rashid a few years earlier.[35] The elephant, who was called Abul Abaz, died at Lippeham on the Rhine. What the Vikings would have made of such an animal if they had seen it is anyone's guess.

Godfrid is the first Danish king who made a significant impact on wider international affairs; or to be more accurate the first that we know of, though various sagas refer to an earlier powerful king of Denmark, Hrólfr Kraki, who, if he lived, can probably be dated to the sixth century. Because Godfrid's 'kingdom' did not long survive his demise, he is rather overshadowed by the generation that came over a hundred years later of Gorm, Harald Bluetooth, Sveinn Forkbeard ('Tjúguskeg') and Cnut. This rather unfairly ignores his notable achievements and impact. It was even suggested by the *Frankish Royal Annals* that he governed the Vestfold in southern Norway as well as Denmark.

Godfrid's departure stage left resulted in a predictable plot-line which saw his family battling each other to take his place. It was a timely release for Charlemagne, for Godfrid had assembled an army with which he proposed to march on Aachen.[36] Einhard, probably drawing on the *Frankish Royal Annals,* suggests that Viking raids were already becoming more than a nuisance; he says that 'the Northmen continually overran and laid waste the Gallic and German coasts'. He also makes specific mention of them harrying the Frisian Islands.[37]

At first, Godfrid's nephew Hemming emerged triumphant in Denmark but he only lasted two years, from 810 to 812. However, in that short time there was the significant event of a treaty between the Danes and the Franks, the first such formal bargain involving a political entity that could be considered a country in Scandinavia; such treaties had not traditionally been used in Scandinavia and these actions had the effect of drawing Scandinavians more closely into the mainstream of European affairs.[38]

There was a bitter succession dispute following the death of Hemming. Two of Godfrid's relatives, Sigefrid and Anulo, sought to gain power but both men lost their lives in the war that followed, along with 11,000 others. One of those who emerged in the aftermath was Reginfrid, but he was unsuccessful in his bid for power and took to piracy instead.[39] Hemming's place was ultimately taken by King Horik I, a son of Godfrid. He was in opposition to Harald Klak, a rival for the throne, a struggle for supremacy that would last for a decade. Perhaps here we have a clue as to another factor that drove some men to become Vikings, namely frustrated ambition and complex power politics.

The raids from Scandinavia no doubt made a great impact on much of western and northern Europe. They were at the moment more of an irritant than a massive global threat. Of course, there was shock and alarm when attacks came and some regions felt particularly vulnerable. However, there was soon to be a ratcheting up of the pressure as, emboldened by the successes that they had enjoyed so far, the scale of the incursions made by forces from Scandinavia was about to increase. The threat they posed would move from being just a nuisance, albeit sometimes a major one, to something far more disturbing.

4

Breakout (826–850)

Out of the North a scourge shall break forth on all the inhabitants of
the earth.

Ermentarius of Noirmoutier

Early Christian evangelism in Scandinavia

An uneasy decade followed in Denmark. With his position in the country
vulnerable, in 826 Harald Klak sought help from the Frankish ruler,
Charlemagne's successor Louis the Pious. Several times before, Harald
had tried to gain the assistance of his Frankish neighbours, having
suffered frequent reverses in his attempts to gain control over lands in
the south of Denmark, sometimes gaining the upper hand, at others
forced to flee. Due to his precarious situation, Harald decided it was time
to make a personal sacrifice to improve his prospects, so at Mainz he was
baptised along with 400 of his followers. Among the congregation was
probably a very uninterested three-year-old boy, Charles; several decades
later, as Charles the Bald, the Vikings would very much be his problem.[1]
From Harald's perspective it was a move that was probably motivated
by pragmatism, not by any deeply felt religious feeling, but that does
not alter the fact that the long-term consequences of these actions were
enormous for Scandinavia.

The baptism of pagans was by no means new. There were precedents
involving both Byzantines and Franks and their non-Christian
adversaries; indeed, the Franks themselves were first cajoled to become
Christians when their emperor Clovis was baptised as long ago as 498.
No doubt there was an element of spiritual reasoning behind such
measures, fuelled by a desire to Christianise as many pagans as possible;
but it would be naïve to overlook the political angle of such actions, as
they gave the Christian ruler acting as a sponsor a kind of moral and

practical superiority over the convert. Viking converts seemed happy enough to go along with the ceremony as long as it conveyed significant political benefits with it.[2] Louis stood godfather for Harald, and his wife Judith as godmother for Harald's spouse.

However, not everyone was fooled by such ceremonies. A few decades earlier Alcuin had commented on similar events to Charlemagne (on this occasion, talking about Saxons rather than Vikings). Alcuin noted that 'careful thought must also be given to the right method of preaching and baptising, that the washing of the body be not made useless by lack in the soul of an understanding of the faith'. He went on to intimate that Charlemagne's motive in converting the Saxons to Christianity was to extort high levels of tax from them through tithing. He understood that the process of baptism risked being nothing more than a cosmetic sham, which is what he tactfully inferred to his royal master.[3]

Underlying these religious tensions were some fundamental intrinsic differences between paganism and Christianity. Paganism was to a large degree random; individuals made up their own minds about their chosen gods and how best to worship them with little in the way of what we might now call 'organised religion'. It was essentially a religion of the countryside, of the trees and the hills, the seas and the sky; the word *paganus* means rustic or country dweller. On the other hand, Christianity was rigidly structured; the Church told people what to do and when and how to do it. Christianity was essentially urban in nature; unsurprisingly pagan practices proved more durable in the countryside than in the towns.[4]

In response to this convenient conversion, a missionary, Ansgar, 'The Apostle of the North', set out for Denmark, a country which was according to Christian propagandists of the time renowned for the 'barbarous cruelty' of its people. It was suggested that Ansgar took on the task because he desired martyrdom.[5] He was associated with the monastery of Corvey, a young, well-connected Carolingian establishment on the northern borders of the Francian empire (now in north-west Germany) on the cusp of territories that were still pagan; an ideal launchpad from which to commence a proselytising initiative into Scandinavia. Ansgar's story was written up by his successor Rimbert, a protégé of his who was considered a saintly man in his own right – Rimbert merited his own hagiographical *Life* and later proselytised in Denmark himself. A near-contemporary copy of Rimbert's biography of Ansgar from the tenth century survives in the *Codex Stuttgardiensis*. It is more of a hagiography than a work of history but, though health warnings about the likely reliability of some of its content should be noted, it is an important source of information about the turbulent times in which Ansgar lived and worked.

The region of Denmark was now on the frontline in attempts to spread Christianity in Europe. Early attempts to spread the faith there, especially by the English missionary Willibrord in the eighth century when he visited King Ongendus of Denmark, had mainly fallen on stony ground, though when he later left he took thirty Danish boys with him to educate, presumably intending to use them as missionaries.

It proved much easier to convert Harald Klak than it did to convince his people to adopt the new faith alongside him. Harald was not universally popular in Denmark and, when he was subsequently ejected from his territories by his prospective subjects, Ansgar went with him. The Emperor then gave Harald a fief in Frisia and members of his family later exerted significant influence there, particularly his probable nephew. There would be no overnight conversion in Denmark and the story of Scandinavia for the next several hundred years was one of an ongoing battle between Christianity on the one hand and the traditional pagan gods of the Vikings on the other. Like the sea, the tide of Christian advancement would ebb and flow. But ultimately the surge of the new faith would overwhelm traditional belief systems and largely submerge them.

The earliest Christian missions in Scandinavia were based in towns like Hedeby, Ribe and Birka, where one might expect some existing adherents of the faith among foreign traders (not to mention slaves, though whether they were given an opportunity to practise their faith is a moot point). The early converts were often pragmatic. Even in later times, many Vikings underwent baptism as a way of becoming acceptable Christians but at the same time carried on practising their pagan rituals and worshipping their Viking gods. This hedging of bets in a spiritual sense, keeping options open so to speak, became the norm in many parts of Scandinavia where old beliefs proved stubbornly hard to eradicate.

The survival of pagan practices even when Christianity eventually became widely established across Scandinavia (a process which accelerated from the mid-tenth century onwards) was probably helped by several factors. Firstly, religion seems to have been a matter of individual choice, though later kings such as Óláfr Tryggvason and Óláfr Haraldsson of Norway attempted to enforce Christianity, with very unfortunate personal results for both of them. Another point in favour of pagan survivals was that, despite the later writings of those like Thietmar of Merseburg and Adam of Bremen who gave evocative descriptions of pagan temples, many Viking rituals were associated with outdoor places such as groves of trees, ancient burial mounds and the shores of lakes or the sea.[6] Therefore, grandiose and spectacular buildings were not required by the pagans; such edifices would offer irrefutable evidence that their practices lived on and could lead to countermeasures being taken to obliterate them. In the absence of identifiable temples, pagan worship could carry on largely unobserved by prying and critical eyes. The geographical remoteness of some parts of Scandinavia, especially in Sweden and Norway, was probably also a factor in the stubborn resistance of paganism.

The foray of Ansgar in 829 was not the first to be made to the Far North by a Christian missionary. Earlier attempts to Christianise parts of Scandinavia had been made by Ebo of Rheims, a remarkable man who had been born the son of a peasant but rose to be Archbishop of Rheims. He journeyed to Scandinavia at the behest of Louis the Pious, but his efforts had largely foundered on the hard rock of pagan resistance, though he had managed to convert a few of the local population along the way. When Ansgar went later, he took with him a loyal lieutenant, Autbert. Ansgar was also invited to Sweden where the first Christian church was founded in 832. Sweden was then inhabited by people known as the Svear, or Swedes, in the north and the Goths in the south. The Swedish king, who claimed descent from Odin, had his court at Uppsala, which had become a byword for pagan practices and would remain so for several centuries yet; it was said to be 'the most eminent in the cult of their gods'.[7]

Ansgar visited Birka on several occasions. His first journey there was in 829 and he almost failed to arrive at all. On the way across the Baltic, his ship was seized by pirates who deprived him of all he was carrying including gifts to make a good first impression on the ruler of Birka, Björn (among them were forty books, a large library for the time). He was lucky to escape with his life. Ansgar returned to Francia several years later but came back to Birka again in about 850. However, the Christian community in Birka had been having a tough time in the interim and at least one missionary, Nithard, had been killed (or 'crowned with martyrdom' as Adam of Bremen eloquently put it)[8] while others had been expelled.

Ansgar's later return to Sweden was announced in advance and led to some confusion as to what to do on the part of the people of Birka. A man came to speak to the king saying that the old gods were angered by the thought that a new god was arriving who would effectively obliterate their pantheon. The king held a meeting with his people at which discussions were held as to what steps to take. He threw lots, a common Viking practice, and they were favourable for Ansgar's mission. Then another man spoke up on behalf of Christianity, saying that the old gods appeared to be of little use. The people finally decided to accept the Christian priests who were on their way. It was a very democratic way of dealing with the situation.

The pope, grateful for Ansgar's earlier efforts, had appointed him as bishop of Hamburg in 831. This became the launchpad for ongoing efforts to cement the position of Christianity in the lands of the Vikings. In 847, Hamburg was joined to the bishopric of Bremen, probably as a way of coping with the heavy blow that the former had suffered when the Vikings fell on it just before, and the new see became the local centre of Christianity not just in the immediate vicinity but also across all of Scandinavia and later the more distant lands of Iceland and Greenland. Hamburg was in a dangerous position, being exposed at this time to raids from Denmark and also, slightly later on, to attacks from the Slavs, which led to the building of vastly strengthened defences in the eleventh century.[9] While back in Hamburg, Ansgar may have been away from the Vikings' homelands but he was certainly not immune from their impact.

Viking opportunity – the fracturing of Charlemagne's empire

Viking raids were about to intensify. It was not just their growing strength that fed this trend but also the increasing weakness of their potential targets, creating a sense of enhanced opportunities for the raiders. Charlemagne died in 814 and it did not take long for the structure he left behind him to start to crumble. He was the greatest figure to bestride the affairs of Western Europe since the fall of the Roman Empire nearly half a millennium before; his successors were incapable of protecting his inheritance, though the supposed incompetence of some of them has been overstated. He left a long shadow, which loomed over them all. The extent of his huge empire and the internecine rivalry of his successors proved a fatal combination.

On Charlemagne's death, his son Louis 'the Pious' took over. He fathered a number of sons, an ambitious and ruthless brood with little room for fraternal sentiment. Louis divided the empire among them but this did not satisfy any of them and they continued to jostle for position at the expense of each other and, most of all, their father. Walafrid Strabo, in his introduction to Einhard's biography of Charlemagne, wrote that 'the republic of the Franks was battered by many different disturbances'.[10] The Vikings were very quick to pick up on, and benefit from, such internal conflicts. One of the quarrelsome brood, Lothar, sought help from Danish mercenaries in his efforts to displace Louis. They fell on the town of Dorestad in 834. It was a prime spot for cross-border trading activities; from here Rhenish wine was shipped abroad, alongside ceramics from Cologne and Bonn, glass from Trier and millstones from the Eifel region.[11] But already Dorestad was in decline as other regional ports chipped away at its dominance. In its prime it was massive, encompassing an area ten times greater than that of Hedeby; but now it was fading, and the Vikings would pick away at its dying body like a venue of hungry vultures.

The raid of 834 accelerated Dorestad's decline, though ironically by then Lothar had already been beaten and forced back to Italy. Passing through Utrecht on their way to Dorestad, the Vikings launched a night of terror. According to the *Annals of St Bertin*, they killed some of the inhabitants of Dorestad, led off others into a life of slavery and burned the town before departing. From surviving records, we can piece together a story of an upsurge in Viking activity, presaging a true reign of terror that was made more frightening by its widespread nature; Antwerp in 836, the south-east of England the year before, and Noirmoutier at the entrance of the Loire during the same period. Permission had been given for the latter, which was in a desperately exposed position, to be fortified in 830 but this measure made little practical difference. The monastery there was finally abandoned after frequent attacks had made its position untenable. The monks took the relics of Saint Philibert with them, afraid that they would be thrown into the sea by the raiders as had happened in other attacks in the region. This was more evidence of Viking behaviour being specifically anti-Christian in nature.

While not as well-known as the *ASC*, the *Annals of St Bertin* among other surviving Frankish records perform a similarly valuable role in enabling us to understand events in Francia during the ninth century. In the entry for the year 835, they tell us that Louis the Pious was enraged by a second Viking attack on Dorestad and set up coastal defences to guard against a repetition in the future. However, this precaution did little to discourage further raids. This was also a significant year in England, as raiders are recorded as laying waste Sheppey in Kent, a return to activity in the country after many years of annalistic silence; Vikings were now operating on both sides of the Channel.

According to Notker, Louis encouraged the mass conversion of Vikings to Christianity in an attempt to secure their good behaviour. Nobles from his court adopted some of them and the new converts were given white robes and Frankish costume and arms from his own stores. This was a process frequently carried out, normally on Easter Eve, when as many as fifty Vikings were baptised. On one occasion, so many came that there were not enough clothes of linen for them all, so some were given hastily assembled garments made from humble everyday shirts that had been cut up and made into something more or less suitable. One of the recipients took umbrage. He said that 'I have gone through this washing business twenty times already, and I have been dressed in excellent clothes of perfect whiteness; but a sack like this is more fit for swineherds than for soldiers'. While this may be a story told (many years later) by Notker for effect, it intimates well enough how superficial some of the baptisms that took place may have been; though this should not blind us to the fact that on other occasions Vikings did become enthusiastic and energetic Christian converts.[12]

Details of raiding on England up to this point are in short supply. By 830, there had only been mention of three attacks on English targets in surviving sources compared to six in western Scotland. Ireland, based on surviving records, was taking much more of a battering with twenty-five raids recorded over the same period.[13] A caveat is again necessary: contemporary chroniclers as mentioned previously tended to be interested only in what happened locally, especially as it affected their own establishments (for they were nearly all connected to religious foundations in one way or another) or at best regionally; references to events further afield appear much more rarely. Therefore, an absence of evidence is not necessarily tantamount to evidence of absence in parts of Britain where no raids are recorded.

However, the *Annals of Ulster* provide evidence of ongoing incursions in Ireland. In 826 the camp of the men from Leinster was attacked and destroyed and their king, Conall, and 'innumerable' others were killed. But in the following year, two more successes in battle over the raiders are recorded. The *Annals* also refer in 827 to one of the more unusual atrocities attributed to the Vikings when they were responsible for killing a great number of porpoises off the coast, as well as, more conventionally, an anchorite called Temhnen. Success returned to the Vikings in 830 with several battles won and some important captives taken, including sub-kings. This presaged a very difficult year for the Irish in 831. There was widespread plundering when a number of religious sites were looted. Such events would become virtually an annual occurrence over the course of most of the next two decades. Worryingly for the Irish it appears that due to the breakdown of law and order, which occurred as a result, there were copycat raids involving Irish raiding parties taking place, modelled on those of the Vikings; one such was recorded in the *Annals of Ulster* in 846.

The establishment of a base in Dublin, known as a *longphort* (plural *longphuirt)*, took place in 841 and this has been seen as the beginning of a more permanent Viking presence in Ireland.[14] Attacks before that have been seen by most historians as 'hit-and-run' raids after the work of Peter Sawyer in the 1960s. However, this view is being re-assessed by some. Archaeological finds in Dublin, which have been radiocarbon dated, revealed settlement from before 841 and, although this is still not an exact science, questions are starting to be asked as to whether there were earlier semi-permanent bases either in Ireland or on offshore locations. Finds that can be dated to early in the Viking period in Dublin include those of elderly women and newborns, suggesting that there were not just active warriors present in these groups.[15] The presence of females is significant, though they are in the minority compared to the remains of males. Radiocarbon testing gives dates in the first half of the ninth century, around the time that the first *longphort* in Dublin was established.[16] The bodies were possibly buried in an earlier Christian graveyard, which may have been associated with a monastery formerly on the site.

These skeletal remains are important for what they tell us about those who were involved in these early incursions. One grave found was that of a young man. The context of his burial suggests someone of reasonably high status; yet the evidence from his bones was that he lived a hard life. His skeletal development suggests someone used to heavy labour, possibly as a farmer working his lands or a rower helping to propel a Viking ship; more than likely at different times in his life he had played both roles. These men and women were of hardy stock, their toughness honed by the challenging environment that they had grown up in. It was an era when every Viking was expected to pull his or her weight. Evidence of early Viking involvement in Dublin has only emerged in piecemeal fashion, meaning that there is a strong chance of more being uncovered in the future, which may force a reassessment as to the origins of the settlement there. In the past it was assumed that the scope of Viking settlement expanded significantly in the tenth century but recent finds have tended to progressively push that date back. Discoveries of houses in Dublin suggest a ninth-century origin with strong design similarities to Kaupang, the important trading centre in Norway which was very active at around that time.[17]

There was another devastating attack on Dorestad in 836, suggesting that the *emporium* had a strong resilient streak and had managed to resurrect itself since the last outbreak of destruction; though at the same time it does not say much for Louis's coastal defences and their effectiveness. However, this was followed by a message from Horik, the king of Denmark, to Louis disclaiming responsibility for these actions while at the same time complaining that some envoys he had sent to Francia had recently been massacred near Cologne.[18] These were violent times not just in the Viking world.

The Vikings also descended on the south-west of England in 836, raiding the estate of the West Saxon king, Ecgbert, at Carhampton in Somerset. The north Somerset coast had many convenient landing places and there were frequent Viking raids on it during the ninth and tenth centuries.[19] A large force of thirty-five ships was involved in the 836 raid. The local Saxon *fyrd* was assembled to fight off the attack on the king's property; such an assault was an affront to his dignity and a threat to his supremacy – but the Saxon army was badly mauled in the fight that followed. Two ealdormen and two bishops were among the dead. It was a painful reverse for Ecgbert and a reminder to him that the Viking threat, small-scale in his kingdom in recent years, had not gone away. The king had good reason to be worried, for he had enemies very close to home. When the Vikings landed in Cornwall in 838 they found not opponents but allies. Cornwall had only recently been finally grasped by Ecgbert. With the tenacious and independent spirit for which Celtic peoples are so often noted, the Cornish had no desire to stay under Anglo-Saxon control; in this case an alliance with pagan partners was definitely the lesser of two evils.

This time Ecgbert was better prepared than he had been when Carhampton was attacked. He routed the Viking-Cornish forces at Hingston Down, near the Tamar. Ecgbert though was living on borrowed time. He was ageing and had had a tough life, which became increasingly challenging in his final years. Within two years of his victory at Hingston Down he was dying. At the end of his life, he saw the Vikings as a punishment from God for the sins of his people, much as Alcuin perceived the destroyers of Lindisfarne. Ecgbert wrote to his counterpart Louis the Pious in Francia warning him that he foresaw bitter days ahead for Christendom if God's people did not repent of their sinful ways. In his letter, Ecgbert related how a priest had had visions in which boys were seen meticulously recording the sins of the people for which God would surely send punishment. If things did not improve, the priest was warned, 'a great and crushing disaster will swiftly come upon them; for three days and nights a very dense fog will spread over their land, and then all of a sudden pagan men will lay waste with fire and sword most of the people and land of the Christians along with all they possess'.[20]

The role of the Vikings was therefore laid out for all to see by Ecgbert; God's avengers, the punishers of fallen Christian men and women for their sins, not so much agents of the devil but the instruments of God and His awful vengeance. The Vikings were presumably unaware of their part in all this as the huge majority of them were still confirmed pagans. But 'visions' such as this are important in terms of understanding the impact of the Vikings on their world. Whether they actually happened or not is not the only issue; such stories formed a part in developing the myth of the Vikings and helped to establish their stereotype.

This warning must have resonated with Louis, given the problems he was already facing. In 837 the exposed island of Walcheren suffered a Viking assault in which many locals were killed and the area was thoroughly plundered. The raiders set up a temporary home there and then proceeded to yet again ransack Dorestad, for whose residents life must now have been thoroughly miserable. Louis, who was planning to visit Rome, postponed his trip and moved instead to nearby Nijmegen. The raiders, learning of his presence with his army, escaped with impunity. Louis, questioning his local officials, discovered that the coastal defences in the area that he had ordered to be built appeared to be completely useless; he resolved to establish a fleet in the region to improve matters, emulating Charlemagne's earlier example. The chronicler who wrote up the *Annals of St Bertin* expressed the clear opinion that the scale of the Viking attacks was so large that it was by now impossible to fight them off.

The raids on the north-west coast of Francia were not just symptomatic of opportunistic piracy but also of wider geopolitical regional tensions involving the Danes. In 839, King Horik sent another mission to Louis. He was experiencing frontier tensions with the Frisians and sought an alliance with the Franks in support of which he sent gifts to Louis that were well received. Louis agreed to send his representatives to Frisia to ensure that tensions there were reduced. He sent ambassadors to Horik to agree what he hoped would be a permanent peace. However, permanence for Louis was an illusion for in 840, perhaps exhausted by the actions of his troublesome sons, he died. A bitter succession dispute quickly followed; with the wolves at the door, those inside the house argued and battled among themselves. While Louis's three sons, Louis, Lothar II and Charles (later known as 'The Bald'),[21] their much younger half-brother, struggled for prominence a Viking fleet sailed down the Seine and set Rouen ablaze. The monasteries there were plundered, large payments were extorted and the population was understandably terrified.

In the internecine dispute that ripped at the fabric of Francia threatening to tear it apart, Lothar was losing the battle, so he turned again to Vikings for help. One of them, a veteran raider in the region named Harald, was given Walcheren (possibly this was Harald Klak whose conversion to Christianity may have proved short-lived: Saxo Grammaticus describes him as 'a notorious apostate'); no longer were the wolves outside the door, they were now being invited in.[22] Another Frankish trading *emporium* of contemporary importance was that of Quentovic. The port had been around for centuries, having been established by a Neustrian king (Neustria is in the region of what is now north-west France) in the sixth century. Its location in Francia opposite Kent made it a vibrant trading hub for a while in much the same way that Dorestad slightly to the north was. Its exposed location also made it an attractive target for Viking raiders, possibly under a leader called Oskar,[23] who duly fell on it in 842. It was significant that it was at the terminus of several important roads; such *emporia* often formed an intersection point between busy sea routes and major road networks. The raid was again reported by the *Annals of St Bertin* as having catastrophic consequences for the local inhabitants, many of whom were captured or killed. The town was put to the torch except for a few buildings which the Vikings were bought off to preserve. Again, reading between the lines in the *Annals* one gets the strong impression of a Frankish kingdom too self-obsessed with its own internal problems fomented by ambitious and short-sighted politics among its fractured leadership to face up to the scale of the external threat. The events at Walcheren particularly attracted the ire of the writer of the *Annals of St Bertin* (though it should be noted that these chroniclers were in the camp of Charles the Bald, so were hardly neutral). He castigated Lothar for his part in what occurred there. He told how Walcheren and the surrounding territories were given to the raiders as their 'benefice'. This he described as 'an utterly detestable crime'. The reason for this opprobrium was made very obvious in his words; it was the handing over of Christian sites to pagans, 'so that the persecutors of the Christian faith should be set up as lords over Christians', an unforgiveable sin in the context of the times.

Adam of Bremen looked back on these times as particularly dark days. He wrote that after the death of Louis, 'wild barbarism ruled without restraint'. According to him, Saxony was laid waste by the Danes and Northmen and Duke Bruno was killed with twelve other counts and several bishops. Frisia was depopulated and Utrecht pillaged. Cologne and Trier were burned and the 'pirates' stabled their horses in Aachen.[24] From Adam's perspective, two centuries on, Francia was falling apart, though whether this is, in the light of subsequent events, exaggeration for effect, is debatable.

Raids on Francia: a quantum leap

These attacks had been launched by raiders who had been invited, or at least encouraged, by the warring factions in Francia who were driven first and last by their own personal ambitions. Dorestad was not the only example of a town to suffer from this unfortunate and blinkered self-centredness. Count Lambert, an ambitious Frankish warlord who had been caught up in the fallout of the conflicts between the sons of Louis the Pious, thought that the town of Nantes would be a worthy addition to his territories. At his request, raiders (this time possibly Norwegians)[25] fell on the town on 24 June 842. The timing of the raid was perfect; so perfect in fact that it is impossible to believe it was an accident. Again, we are faced with the suspicion – which in this case seems to be a virtual certainty – that the raiders were in possession of inside information, probably provided to them by the unscrupulous Lambert; indeed, stories would emerge that the raiders had been guided through the shallows by knowledgeable local pilots helpfully provided by him.

It was on St John's Day when the hammer blow fell. Nantes was packed with visitors for what was an important religious festival. This was a frequent Viking tactic, attacking at times when the citizens were off their guard. The raiders' intelligence service was on top form and their triumph was total. After they left at nightfall, laden with huge amounts of plunder, Lambert duly became lord of Nantes; though whether it was still worth having was perhaps debatable. Certainly, he would be needing a new bishop to provide for the needs of the local flock, as the previous incumbent had been killed by the raiders while he was saying Mass.[26]

But in many ways, it was what the raiders did next which was the most terrifying thing of all. They did not sail away, sated with their winnings, into the far distance. Instead they set up a base on the island of Noirmoutier where, with their naval dominance, they would be impervious against any counterattack. The *Annals of St Bertin* note that the raiders brought their households with them and established something like a permanent settlement, suggesting that this was far more than a hit-and-run raid with an eye only on short-term profit. Noirmoutier also had lucrative trading connections, both with regards to salt, and as a port for wines from the Loire region, so there was an economic incentive too. Occupying such offshore safe havens would become another standard Viking tactic, emulated frequently in the future. The cuckoo, once invited into the nest in Francia, had no intention of departing but would stay in the region, looking for other nests to occupy. Noirmoutier was also close to various frontiers including that with Aquitaine in the south and this may have enabled the Vikings to take advantage of internal political tensions by selectively entering into alliances in much the same way as they also did in Ireland, or as they had done in England when forming an alliance with the Cornish against the Anglo-Saxons.[27] Again, Vikings were exploiting a divided kingdom and in 844 they sailed up the Garonne as far as Toulouse and the following year they wintered in the Saintogne after attacking Saintes.

This was only a prelude to one of the most audacious moves that the Vikings had yet made. In 845, when Francia was suffering a particularly harsh winter, they sailed up the Seine and fell on Paris. At a time when Vikings 'contemplated arduous upstream journeys but quick getaways',[28] the great river was like an arrow pointed at the very heart of Francia. At the head of these raiders was (according to sagas at least) one of the most famous Vikings of them all. The irony is that Ragnar Lodbrok ('Hairy Breeches') might never have existed at all. However, he would become one of the most renowned of all Vikings, mythical or otherwise, who ever (or never) lived.

References to a heroic figure called Ragnar occur early on in *skaldic* poetry. He is referred to in the *Ragnarsdrápa*, which dates back to the ninth century. This was written by Bragi, the first named *skald* we know of. However, the Lodbrok element of Ragnar's name does not appear until two centuries later. Ragnar was a man of enormous size and strength, who supposedly wrestled with and killed giant snakes (against whose venom he was protected by his hirsute trousers). He was also a formidable raider and 'wherever he went, he won victory'.[29] But as some evidence that he may not have been a completely made-up figure the *Vita Anskarii* mentions a Ragnar who was at Turholt in Flanders in 840. This Ragnar was apparently in cahoots with Charles the Bald, who presumably expected mercenary help in return. Not long after, however, the two men fell out. It is tempting to speculate that this Ragnar was the man who was now attacking Paris.[30]

To face up to the threat, Charles, the latest unfortunate to reign in the still-prominent shadow of Charlemagne, divided his army into two and positioned his forces either side of the river. It was a gift, which enabled Ragnar to pick off each force individually. He attacked the smaller of the two first and thoroughly destroyed it. A total of 111 prisoners were taken and hanged on an island in the river to discourage the remaining Frankish soldiers. The other Frankish force, their morale destroyed by the sight of their comrades swinging at the end of a rope, melted away without a fight.

It left Paris wide open and Charles, unable to offer any further military resistance after this desultory fight, paid Ragnar 7,000 lbs of silver to encourage his men, already laden with booty, to go away. They duly sailed off but, as would happen repeatedly over the years, made a note of Charles's weakness and resolved to come back again a few years later when Paris had had the opportunity to rebuild its denuded stores of wealth. As usual, contemporary commentators, in this case a monk from St Germain, blamed the attack on the sins of the Franks and saw it as 'God chastising us as he chastised the Israelites in Babylon'.[31] Raids such as this created huge stores of treasure for the raiders and as a result the situation became self-perpetuating. It meant that Viking warlords obtained significant resources, which they could then use to build more ships and hire more men. For those on the receiving end of these attacks, it was the nastiest of vicious circles.

There are regular mentions of silver being extorted as part of these schemes. The system of currency involving coins was less developed in Scandinavia at the time than it was elsewhere, for example in England, Francia or the Arab world. The most widely traded commodity in the absence of sophisticated currency systems in the Viking world was silver. Small portable scales are a commonly found artefact that Viking traders carried with them to ensure that they were receiving adequate payment (the Franks were also very particular in ensuring that the value of money they received in exchange for goods and services was of the right weight).[32] It was not the coins that the Vikings were interested in, it was their silver content.

Over time, coins would become more important in their own right; the Vikings came to realise that they offered more than just economic benefits, they also brought status. The idea that a man's head could be shown on the obverse and circulate from pocket to pocket and purse to purse meant more than just buying power, it represetned quite another type of power altogether. Having also seen the practical utility of coinage in Carolingian Francia, where even the poorer elements of society seem to have routinely used coins,[33] as well as in Anglo-Saxon England, they undoubtedly came to realise that practical economic benefits come could from their use too. Vikings would eventually come to fully appreciate the advantages of coinage and Scandinavian examples would be found even from the early ninth century, though normally limited to trading sites such as Hedeby and Ribe. Later on, they would adopt monetary currency far more widely.

It would take time for the Scandinavians to reach this stage though. The initial use of silver, rather than coins, as the prime facilitator of exchange is reinforced by the discovery of broken-up items of jewellery and cut-up pieces of metal known as hacksilver, though it was also cast into large ingots. Silver was the main currency of the Vikings; the principal value of coins was not their face value for trading purposes but rather the fact that they could be melted down, turned back into silver and then crafted into something else or just used as bullion. Bullion effectively became a surrogate for hard currency: Arab writers noted that when the Rūs traded with their people, the Arab merchants seemed to consider the transaction as being one that essentially involved hard currency in the form of dirhams, whereas the Vikings were more interested in the silver content.[34]

Early mention of such Viking traders was made by Ibn Khurradādhbih. Writing in 844, he told how the *saqalibah*, a term normally used for fair-haired Europeans, came with their beaver skins and their black fox furs down the Black Sea; other accounts mention sable, Siberian squirrel, ermine, marten, weasel, mink and hare – as well as amber. Then they travelled by camel from Jurjan, on the southern coast of the Caspian, down to Baghdad. The city was surrounded by walls 12 miles in diameter and housed wonderful palaces, mosques, gardens, parks and public buildings; all this must have been mind-boggling to men who came from small villages in the land of the Rūs or from Scandinavia.

Bullion was what Vikings sought more than most other things in return for their furs and other items for sale. In addition to scales, weights have been found, some apparently of Islamic origin while others may be native to Britain and are typically made of lead. Historians detect an upsurge in the use of bullion from the mid-ninth century onwards when Islamic dirhams started to reach Scandinavia in large numbers.[35]

Arm rings and neck rings are also often associated with Vikings. They were given by Viking warlords as a gift in return for which the recipient was expected to pledge their loyalty. The arm or neck rings sometimes had an alternative use. Plain versions of them appear to have been regarded as a form of currency, given the generic name of 'ring money'. While such arm rings were often made of silver, examples of gold ones have also been found; one was allegedly given to the later Viking Egil by King Æthelstan after the Battle of Brunanburh. They served a double purpose: they reflected generosity on the part of the giver and conferred status on the recipient. They were also a highly visible sign that the recipient was bound to their lord.

A great deal of the metalwork that was plundered from Western Europe and made its way back to Scandinavia came from Britain and Ireland. Some of it was of relatively low value and was converted into jewellery, particularly brooches, which are called 'insular' in style. Many of these have been found in graves, the majority of them those of women. This has led to suggestions that one reason for raiding was to provide a 'bride price' to allow a marriage agreement to be entered into; the wives were subsequently buried with their prized mementoes of such arrangements.[36]

Francia in turmoil

The chronicler of the Abbey of St-Germain-des-Prés opposite the Ile de la Cité says that the siege of Paris ended because Ragnar's army was decimated by disease and it was in their interests to leave; though the fact that he does not mention the payment of 7,000 lbs of silver when other sources do is suspiciously kind to Charles the Bald. The suggestion that disease had attacked Ragnar's force is not at all incredible; such circumstances were a regular occurrence in medieval warfare given the insanitary and harsh living conditions in which besieging forces often found themselves, and dysentery was one common decimator of contemporary armies.

Where the story of this chronicler becomes less credible is in its suggestion that it was St Germain himself who had intervened when his abbey was ransacked by the Vikings. The same chronicler then has Ragnar returning to Denmark where he boasted of his deeds to King Horik, telling him that Francia was a land 'full of riches of all kinds, such as he had never seen'. In addition, he said the people of this 'good and fertile land' were 'fearful and cowardly'. Despite the evidence of plentiful stocks of gold and silver, King Horik was not convinced, so Ragnar produced items taken from the Abbey of St Germain in an attempt to prove his case. The shade of St Germain was most unimpressed at this arrogant display and struck Ragnar dead within a few days.[37] Such saintly interventions from beyond the grave were not unique to Ragnar; a future example involving St Edmund would allegedly remove the later Viking giant, Sveinn Forkbeard, from the scene.

As we shall see, there are other equally unlikely ends postulated for Ragnar, though if we ignore the supernatural element in the shape of St Germain it is not impossible that a returning Viking leader may subsequently have succumbed to a disease which had already taken many of his men at the end of a long and potentially debilitating campaign. Perhaps the most interesting aspect of this story though is the light it sheds on the relationship between these Viking warlords and aspiring kings back home. Ragnar is clearly trying to impress Horik in this version of events, suggesting that even for free spirits like him there was still a place for a figurehead who is somehow superior in status. If there is any truth in this version – and it was reported back by a Frankish envoy to Horik's court so elements may well be accurate – then it suggests that men like Ragnar were still trying to position themselves strategically within the Viking world.

These raids into Francia opened the floodgates for other cities in France, from north to south. Able to sail their shallow-draft ships up the rivers that helpfully criss-crossed the region, city after city was attacked by the Vikings. Bordeaux, Bayeux, Périgeux, Limoges, Rouen, Angoulême, Toulouse, Angers, Tours and Orléans felt the bite of their axes; the latter three were, according to Ermentarius of Noirmoutier, 'made deserts'. Like Alcuin, he mournfully recalled the words of that Old Testament pessimist Jeremiah that 'out of the North a scourge shall break forth on all the inhabitants of the earth'.[38] It seemed to some that the End Days were indeed coming.

Yet to blame the Vikings for all this chaos is overegging the pudding. In Francia, as elsewhere, internal disruption was creating conditions that the raiders could take advantage of. A more coordinated response was needed to resist them and that meant all too often internal transfers of power that many with vested interests would not accept. Basic human weaknesses were at the heart of the problem, which was to some extent a self-created one. Undoubtedly the raiders caused chaos; but they also took advantage of internal chaos that was already there.

Ermentarius was one of those who had good reason to appreciate just how harsh the Vikings attacks were, for he was a monk who was forced to leave the exposed island monastery of Noirmoutier behind in the shadow of their impending attack; he eventually found sanctuary of sorts in Burgundy where he wrote the *History of the Miracles and Translations of St Philibert* under which innocuous title he penned a despairing account of just what it was like to live through those bitter decades during the first half of the ninth century. His words are resonant of the terror unleashed across widely dispersed parts of Francia; 'the number of ships increases, the endless flood of Vikings never ceases to grow bigger. Everywhere Christ's people are the victims of massacre, burning and plunder'.[39]

The internecine struggles in Francia encouraged others to intervene to seek personal benefit. In the same year that Ragnar attacked Paris, King Horik sent a force of 600 ships (a quite incredible number) up the Elbe to the heart of Germany where another of the competing brothers, Louis, sometimes known as 'the German' to distinguish him from all the other Louises that were around at the time, was notionally in charge. Fortunately, he found allies in the form of the local Saxons and their combined forces put those of Horik to flight, though Hamburg was sacked by his men and the church, monastery and library were all destroyed. Ansgar was in residence at the time and escaped virtually naked though he did manage to take some holy relics with him. Adam of Bremen says that Cologne was also attacked, though this is not mentioned in any other contemporary sources.[40]

Horik's attitude towards the Franks was ambivalent and in 845 he sought a peace deal with them. The *Annals of St Bertin* suggest that divine intervention was responsible for this. The annalist suggests that this was because when the Viking raiders had been retreating down the Seine, they had attacked a monastery. So incensed was God that he struck down the raiders, some with blindness, others with insanity (this is presumably a repeat of the story of the epidemic that ran through Ragnar's army), creating a strong impression on Horik of His power. Quite why God had done this when He had not intervened in other similar cases is not explained. More plausibly, Horik wanted a breathing space and, like all effective Viking leaders, was able to employ tactics of diplomacy to achieve this when military options seemed unattractive in comparison.

In the aftermath of these upheavals, Ansgar once more proved himself a rock for his religion. Now peace had broken out between Horik and the Franks, Ansgar's attempted to proselytise anew among the Danes. His efforts proved successful and permission was given in 850 for him to build a church in Hedeby. Horik was won over by the efforts of this bishop who became famous, at least in the hagiographical stories that grew up about him, for his abstemiousness and high morals. But any success Ansgar had was temporary; the new faith did not yet have deep roots and its outposts were scattered by the strong winds of resistant paganism, at least for a time.

In the meantime, further raids on Dorestad took place, eating away at its terminally sick body. By 850, the Danes were not only raiding, they had also established a more permanent presence along the coast of Frisia. The Frisians had tried to buy the Vikings off with tribute but, as in so many other cases both before and after, all this tactic did was to buy a very brief respite and encourage others to come back for more. Dorestad had not long left now: by 863, its fate was finally sealed, not by Viking raiders but by a change in direction of the Rhine. It must have seemed to some of the residents as an almost welcome release from several decades of horror.

The mention of Viking raids during these years is a recurrent theme in the *Annals of St Bertin*. At the beginning of the 840s there were frequent raids on Francia. One in 841 led by a Norwegian named Asgeir resulted in a bloody battle, the subsequent burning of Rouen by the raiders and the sacking of the important monastery of Jumièges. Attacks were related by the annalist in 847 on Brittany and Aquitaine, as well as on Dorestad and the surrounding area. The writer makes clear that there were several different groups raiding at the time. This was not a coordinated attack on Western Europe with one controlling brain at the strategic centre of the campaign, but a series of raids launched by opportunist warlords across a wide area. Certainly, by the end of the ninth century the coastal *emporia* of Francia in particular were in terminal decline and there was a marked shift towards inland trading centres such as Magdeburg on the Elbe.[41] Other towns like Liège, Cologne, Mainz, Angers, Ghent and Bruges also grew in importance in different parts of Francia.[42] Whether this was solely due to Viking raids or was part of a longer-term economic evolution is a moot point; but they certainly encouraged the trend.

The Vikings were launching assaults on a number of fronts by now. Charles the Bald was credited by the annalist with launching a determined attack against Vikings besieging Bordeaux in 848 but he relates that nevertheless the city fell to them soon after; in an early example of scapegoating he blames treacherous Jews for this. Nevertheless, Charles's efforts had at least succeeded in winning him some positive recognition in a region where his rule was far from secure, given the fact that it was also claimed by his nephew Pippin. And attacks on Brittany forced one of the main men there, a potential opponent of Charles called Nominoë, to abandon his plans to attack Charles's territories. Despite this, Bordeaux was duly lost and Périgeux was also taken by Vikings in the following year; after they had sacked it, they were able to return unscathed to their ships. These Viking successes, with other examples such as the capture of York in 866 or Bonn and Cologne in 881, show that they were very capable of successfully prosecuting siege warfare.

It was not just the Christian world that felt the sting of Viking attacks. The Moors in Iberia, with its long and vulnerable coastline, were also exposed to their raids.[43] However, they were no pushover. In one raid up the Guadalquivir on Seville, part of the rich Umayyad Caliphate then based on Cordoba, the Vikings (or the *al-majus,* the 'fire-worshippers' as they were known to the Muslims due to their pagan practices – the word has the same root as the biblical Magi) got decidedly the worst of it. The contemporary Islamic writer al-Ya'qūbi wrote that 'the majus who are called al-Rūs entered it in the year 844 and looted, pillaged, burned and killed'[44] (this is a very early use of the term 'Rūs'). It all started well enough when they took the city except for its citadel. But the Emir of Cordoba, Abd al-Rahman II, sent a strong relieving force to win it back. At the end of the battle for Seville that followed, the Moors were triumphant. They left 1,000 Viking dead on the field with hundreds of others swinging from the gallows to discourage any potential future raiders. It was said that so many raiders were hanged that there was not enough gallows space in Seville and many of them were strung up on palm trees.

This discouragement was reinforced by the development of powerful Muslim naval forces to act as a deterrent to further raids. The response to the Viking assault on Seville had been swift and the ongoing development of naval forces proved very effective. Indeed, the immediacy and impact of the Muslim response to the Viking threat has been contrasted by some historians with the relatively ineffective actions taken along similar lines by the governing classes in England and Francia.[45] But it must also be remembered that for the Vikings, Seville was a long way from home and in a largely unknown region. This potentially increased the risks facing them exponentially and the challenge posed to them was therefore much greater. That said, even in the tenth and eleventh centuries there were occasional Viking excursions into Iberia, though it does not appear that they established any permanent settlements there.

Ireland and Britain: the danger increases

In 839, the *Annals of Ulster* record details of an event that may be one of the most significant in British history, though it is largely forgotten now. The Picts remained dominant in Scotland at the time, with their main centre at Fortrui.[46] The Scotti of Dál Riata were seemingly junior partners in Scotland and were allied to the king of the Picts, Wen, who led an army against Viking forces, possibly meeting them on the shores of the Moray Firth. This particular location has a lot to recommend it as the site of a major confrontation. It was at the head of the major loch system that runs through the Great Glen which cuts its way across from the west to the east coast of Scotland like a deep gash. With a fairly small amount of portage involved, Viking forces could traverse their way to or from Ireland to the east coast of Scotland and avoid the longer and more hazardous route around the north of the country by sailing up Loch Oich and Loch Ness. The Glen was therefore a major strategic prize.

The reference in the *Annals* describing what happened is laconic but hard to misinterpret: 'the heathens won a battle over the men of Fortrui and Wen son of Onuist and Bran son of Onuist and Aed son of Boanta [the king of Dál Riata] and others almost innumerable fell there'. Within a century the Picts would disappear without trace and the Scotti would eventually become the dominant force in the country that would take their name. This cataclysmic defeat for the Picts may have accelerated their downfall.[47] Within sixty years, they would disappear from the historical record and while there are almost certainly additional contributory reasons for this, the defeat suffered at the hands of Viking forces may well be a critical factor.

The impact of these Viking incursions on some areas, especially in the north of Scotland, was devastating. While the evidence is far from complete, it is sufficient for one historian to consider that 'between the ninth and eleventh centuries the whole area from Muckle Flugga to the Dornoch Firth and Ardnamurchan became entirely Scandanavianised in as clear-cut a case of ethnic cleansing as can be found in the entirety of British history'.[48]

Remarkable archaeological evidence of Viking settlements on the western island of Barra has long been known. In 1862, a grave was uncovered near a prehistoric standing stone containing the remains of a wealthy woman. The collection of grave goods buried with her included a pair of oval brooches, a ringed-pin, an iron buckle, a comb and a drinking horn. There were also several tools linked to textile production. Traces of clothing suggest that the woman was of Scandinavian origin. Some of the items though suggest a more local origin, intimating that there may have been a degree of assimilation going on in this part of Scotland.[49]

England by now was seeing an increased number of attacks. Although they were occasionally driven off such as one on Hamwic (Southampton) there were simply too many raids too geographically far apart for local defence forces to be everywhere at once. Ealdorman Æthelhelm was killed in a skirmish at Portland and ealdorman Hereberht of Kent also perished in 841. These were important men that the Saxon king could ill afford to lose. There were also Viking attacks on Lundenwic (London) and Rochester, a renewed assault on Carhampton and another on Quentovic on the coast of Francia. Not all Viking attacks were successes though. An attack on a West Saxon army near the mouth of the Parrett in Somerset was beaten back by the *fyrds* of Somerset and Dorset under their ealdormen Eanwulf and Osric.

The St Bertin's annalist notes that by this time the Vikings had set up a ring of bases around the periphery of Ireland and were able to extort tribute from the people there on a regular basis. In these accounts of Viking incursions into Ireland, the name of a Norwegian called Turgéis figures prominently. Hard facts about him are hard to find and it does not help that we have no mention of him back in Scandinavia. Turgéis is associated with raids in Ireland as far back as 820 but in 837 he returned leading a raid on his own account. His fleet was allegedly 120 ships strong; half of it entered the Liffey and the other half the Boyne. He found a community already existing at what is now Dublin and took it over for himself, possibly building a fortress on the site where Dublin Castle now stands (his approach downriver probably made easier by the fact that the Liffey was much wider and shallower than it is now, and the sea came much further in).[50] This became his base from which he raided deeper into the island and also eastwards across the sea into Wales.

He was successful too in the north of Ireland, capturing Armagh, the foremost of all religious sites in Ireland at the time given its connections to St Patrick. Other raids on Christian property followed, notably on Clonmacnoise and Clonfert; at the former, Christian chroniclers state that Turgéis expelled the abbot and then installed himself as a pagan high priest while his wife started to utter all kinds of heathen incantations and spells over the place. These lurid allegations should probably be treated with a generous pinch of salt but Turgéis was a determined and persistent raider. He set up several forts inland, including one on an island in Lough Ree, and claimed some kind of leadership of the Vikings then in Ireland. However, his star waned and he was taken prisoner by the king of Meath, Máel Sechnaill I, and soon after, if the most popular version of his end is to be believed, was executed by drowning in Lough Owel.[51]

A view emerged in the twentieth century that the impact of Turgéis, and the acts attributed to him, were much exaggerated.[52] Alongside this came a perspective that argued that the overwhelming horror of the Viking raids on Ireland was also blown up out of all proportion, especially in the early years of such activity with raiding limited to coastal areas. These averaged out, in records that have survived, at about one a year, consistent perhaps with a cyclical approach from Viking war bands that saw them engaging for part of the year in conventional activities 'back home' wherever that might be (possibly Norway and perhaps bases closer to hand such as islands off the north and west of Scotland).[53]

The year 837 was when the intensity of Viking attacks in Ireland increased. Whereas the earlier part of the century was punctuated by hit-and-run raids, there was now an upsurge in the level of activity on the island. Fleets of sixty-odd ships on both the Boyne and the Liffey constituted more than a small raiding party. Apart from anything else, the size of these fleets suggests a substantial financial investment on the part of those building them. We are told that the approximate cost of building a ship in Anglo-Saxon England during the period was about £345, equivalent to the cost of over 4,000 cows.[54] To construct fleets with sixty ships in them suggest that there was a significant amount of resource available to finance their construction. During this raid, a Viking leader with the name of 'Saxolb' was killed but a battle against the southern Uí Néill was won. As would also happen elsewhere, initial raids involving a handful of ships and a small number of raiders gradually increased in scale and intensity, perhaps as Vikings saw the success arising from these early strikes and more and more of them tried to emulate it. There is evidence that Norwegian raiders were the main beneficiaries of these raids. Large numbers of items of British and Irish origin deposited as grave goods in Scandinavia have been found in Norway, especially in the south-west corner of the country and to a lesser extent further up the west coast. Some such finds have been made around Birka and others in Skåne. Apart from a small concentration around Hedeby there are comparatively few in Denmark.[55]

A *longphort* was set up at Dublin in 841, a fortified camp which would both protect the Viking ships and also serve as a base for raiding and possibly for trading too. This was a semi-permanent camp for overwintering where probably the Vikings had only previously occupied the site on a temporary seasonal basis (though as referred to above recent archaeological finds are throwing some doubt on this assessment). It was an ideal place to moor their ships on the southern side of the river, having sailed up from the sea. Dublin had been the site of a significant monastery previously so it probably had a well-developed infrastructure which would also have been advantageous.

Other *longphuirt* were established on Lough Neagh and at Linn Duachaill (probably Annagassan), County Louth. This is evidenced both by references in the Irish annals and also by archaeology. Linn Duachaill seems to have been closely linked with Dublin and three distinct references are made to it by the annalists: in 841/2, 851/2 and 926/7. It appears to have been a raiding base from which attacks were launched, especially against Church properties and indeed against churchmen themselves. The argument has been made that the location of both Annagassan and Dublin was not just to facilitate raiding. Both places were on or close to frontiers of territories ruled by various Irish sub-kings. There may therefore be an argument that the reason for their location was to a significant extent political, a hypothesis that is borne out by alliances between some sub-kings and Vikings shortly afterwards.[56]

Archaeological finds suggest the presence of a number of other *longphuirt* in Ireland. One, at Dunrally Fort on the banks of the River Barrow, was about 80 kilometres (50 miles) inland from the sea suggesting that the Vikings took full advantage of the river network to push far inland, as they did in England and Francia. In 2003, archaeological investigations in advance of a new road-building scheme at Woodstown near Waterford uncovered evidence of an important site. The discovery of hundreds of ships' nails suggests that vessels were being built, or at least repaired, there. The latest thinking is that some of these *longphuirt* such as that at Dublin formed the nucleus of future towns that developed from them, while others were never anything more than temporary bases. While they certainly served a military purpose, the presence at some sites of significant numbers of weights and quantities of hacksilver suggest that they may also have had a trading purpose. A number reveal evidence of manufacturing there too. They may also have been used as a transit and collection point for slaves.

The Viking base at Dublin became especially important and it appears that other settlements in Ireland did not emerge until later. Dublin formed a link in the trading network from north to south as well as a strategically useful place from which to launch attacks across the Irish Sea on Wales or England. It became a core part of the slave trade in particular. One of the exhibits in the National Museum of Ireland in Dublin brings home just how tough a life the slave would suffer. It is a long chain with massive links that would do Jacob Marley proud. At the end of this heavy, dragging chain is a collar that would be placed around the neck of a slave and restrict movement, as if the human being on the end of it was no better than a dog.

However, the *Annals of Ulster* record several major victories over the Vikings in Ireland in 847/8 – though the *Annals of St Bertin* for 847 state that the raiders took control of the islands around Ireland, so the evidence is contradictory. That said, the latter source also mentions that a delegation from Ireland attended the Carolingian court of Charles the Bald in 848, telling of a great victory their king had won over the interlopers and seeking an alliance, a sure sign that wider international diplomatic efforts were now being made by the victims of Viking attacks, a policy also notable between Francia and Wessex in the 850s. Viking efforts, strenuous though they were, failed to secure a wider territorial advantage on the island. In one battle against Tigernach, king of Brega in modern County Meath, the writer of the *Annals of Ulster* tells us that 1,200 of the enemy were killed and in another a further 500 perished. The Vikings were certainly not having everything their own way in Ireland and perhaps the raiders there, some of whom had been active for a number of years, were tiring by now and losing some of their essential energy. Sadly, for the Irish, a new injection of it was not far away.

The annals make mention of specific bases across Ireland at this time in places that would become associated with Viking activity over an extended period. For example, there are mentions of them at Cork in 848 and 867, at Lough Swilly in Donegal in 842, and at Carlingford in 852 among others. When added to other places already mentioned, this was a wide geographical range over which to be operating. There was also an attack noted in 842 by a band jointly composed of Vikings and Irish allies that ended with the death of Comán, the abbot of Linns (near Dundalk Bay).

Despite establishing towns which sometimes had a small surrounding area under Viking control, no extended Viking kingdom was ever carved out in Ireland as was later the case in England or Normandy, or over a chain of island territories across the North Atlantic and down the west coast of Scotland. It was not for want of trying; but the fragmented political nature of Ireland and the lack of centralised authority, not to mention the determination and ferocity of opposing Irish warlords, always militated against it.

Ships and ship burials

Remarkable discoveries have been made in Norway providing evidence of the ships which gave the Vikings their great power and freedom of movement. In 1880, some farmers were digging in frozen fields near Sandefjord, already well known for its Viking associations and located on the western side of Oslo Fjord. They lived at Gokstad Farm and they were excavating a mound that was linked with a number of Viking legends called *Kongshausen,* 'the king's mound'. What they found staggered them; a ship, beautifully preserved in the blue clay that had fortuitously protected it for over 1,000 years. It was later dated to around 850 when Viking raids were reaching previously unprecedented levels (though it may not have been buried until around the year 900).

As well as providing striking and incontrovertible evidence of what a Viking vessel of the time looked like, the Gokstad ship also told archaeologists much about the rituals of contemporary ceremonial burials. The skeleton of a man of around fifty years of age was found laid out on a bed in the ship. He was around 6 feet tall and accompanied by grave goods including small boats, a tent, a sledge and riding equipment such as a beautifully worked bridle, as well as iron nails to attach to the hooves of a horse for winter travel. There were also animal remains interred including those of twelve horses, six dogs and a peacock. Although the identity of the man so honoured is unknown, he was clearly someone of importance; a ship was no small or inexpensive item so the man who was buried in it must have been a major player in local terms at least. However, his skeletal remains suggest very strongly that he died in battle; there were cuts to his left knee, his right calf and his right thigh bone which had not started to heal, so these were inflicted at or very close to the time of death.

The Gokstad ship was built mainly of oak, though some components such as the decking and mast were of pine. The keel was made of a single T-shaped piece of timber. As is invariably the case, the planks used in the ship were assembled in clinker fashion, overlapping each other. They were lashed to the ribs of the ship by flexible lengths of spruce. Iron rivets with washers were used to hammer them into place. Cross-beams held the whole structure together. The ship's design allowed it to be flexible when in the water so that it could rise and fall with the waves without being damaged. It was a perfect combination of strength and elasticity. Even today, close up to the Gokstad Ship in its purpose-built hall in Oslo it does not take too much imagination to visualise it ploughing its way through the waves.

The mast was probably about 10 metres in length and was held in place by substantial blocks of wood. It seems as if it would be easy to raise or lower it quickly. The sail was hoisted on a single yard, about 11 metres high; the sail was probably made of white wool with red stripes possibly sewn onto it. The Gokstad ship's design reveals that by the ninth century the age of sail had truly arrived in Scandinavia, though it had been evolving for some time before this. It could carry about thirty-two to thirty-five people on board and weighed just over 20 metric tons.[57] Another less feted discovery, of a Viking ship at Tune, set the scene in 1867 but the finding of first the Gokstad and later the Oseberg ship (both of which are much more intact than the vessel from Tune) improved understanding of Viking shipbuilding immeasurably. As in older ships, such as the Nydam Boat, steering was by means of a large steering oar at the stern of the vessel. There were holes in the gunwales three planks down for oars. These would normally only be used either when in inland waters or when the weather was unfavourable to sail. Other items of equipment found included anchors (probably attached to ropes rather than iron chains), a gangplank and bailers.

Another magnificent ship burial dating back to a similar period was found at Oseberg in Norway and excavated by Hákon Shetileg in 1904–5. Evidence derived from the dig suggests that the ship itself was buried around 834 but that it was actually constructed in 800 or possibly even earlier. It was also built of oak and like the Gokstad ship had provision for a sail, which could have propelled it at a rate of around 10 knots. Several replicas of it were later built but unfortunately sank; this appears to have been due to an error in initial calculations for, when measurements were subsequently corrected, a later copy sailed very well. That said, it has been suggested that, beautiful though she is, the Oseberg ship was only built for fairly sheltered waters and taking such a vessel on a longer trans-Atlantic crossing would have been equivalent to sailing in a floating coffin.[58]

Two women were buried in the ship grave at Oseberg. One of them, in her sixties to seventies, was suffering badly from arthritis; she also appears to have had cancer, two neck vertebrae were fused together and there was evidence of a knee injury – given all this it is unsurprising that she probably walked with a stoop and a limp. There was also a younger woman and suggestions have been made that one woman was sacrificed to accompany the other into the Afterlife, though this cannot be definitively proved (this need not necessarily mean that the younger woman was the sacrifice; her teeth were in very good condition as if she had enjoyed a good diet in life). Almost miraculously, some textiles also survived with the burial, including fragments of silk, woollen items and pieces of tapestry. Other objects such as a wooden cart, magnificently ornamented with carvings in the wood, and a bedpost give us further insights into Scandinavian life at this time, as do three sleighs also interred.

The identity of the women is unknown. Some suggest that the more senior figure is a *völva*, a female shaman. Another suggestion is that she is Queen Asa, a woman whose name brings us to the verge of a historical Norwegian period as opposed to one that is legendary or even semi-mythical. Asa is mentioned in the *Ynglinga Saga* as being the daughter of Harald Granraude, king of Agder in the south of Norway. She was famed for her great beauty, so much so that a neighbouring king, Gudrød the Hunter, sought to marry her. However, his attentions were rebuffed.

This did little to put him off though and he launched a raid on Agder, killed Harald and his son and took off Asa as his prize. She was forcibly married to him and a year later a son called Halfdan arrived.

Evidence of ships has been found in burials elsewhere. One find made in 2011 in Ardnamurchan, on the west coast of Scotland, was a Viking boat burial in an area where no previous examples had been found. At Swordle Bay, very close to a Neolithic chambered cairn which may have been an attraction for those responsible for the burials (association with older and presumably sacred monuments is a regular feature in the choice of Viking burial sites), was a boat-shaped cut some 4.9 metres by 1.5 metres. This is not large (the near-contemporary Gokstad ship is nearly 24 metres long) and the dimensions of the boat shape plus the fact that it appears to have been raised at the prow and stern makes it sound suspiciously like a *færing* (Old Norse 'four-oaring'), a small vessel with typically two rows of oars that is still used in Norway. Examples of these were found with the Gokstad ship burial.

The boat itself had decayed but a number of grave goods survived. As well as human remains, other finds ranged from everyday items such as saucepans, sickles and whetstones, flints and strike-a-lights while other more exotic items included a sword and an axe. After the body was buried in the boat, stones were laid around and in it, probably above ground level to mark out its shape. While some of the stones collapsed into the boat-shaped hole as the organic material of the vessel decayed, others were probably taken away and re-used by medieval and later farmers. The whetstone was made of Norwegian schist. Also included were the fragmentary remains of a drinking horn with a top made of copper alloy. Work is ongoing to interpret these finds further. A ring pin of Scandinavian origin was also found, possibly it was used to bind a shroud or alternatively was originally attached to the deceased's clothing; rings had a sacral significance, as evidenced by the importance of arm or neck rings in oath-taking or even something as apparently mundane as door rings which seem to be mainly associated with cultic sites; door rings are often found in later medieval churches in Scandinavia, normally linked with apotropaic designs (that is, to frighten away evil spirits).[59]

Exactly who was buried is a matter of conjecture. Virtually nothing remained of the body; two teeth and two fragments of bone, so opportunities to gain information from these about the identity of the person buried are extremely limited. The presence of a sword and an axe suggests that the owner was not unused to warfare while whetstones and sickles intimate farming activities; the owner was presumably expected to be adept at using all of them so needed to be an adaptable individual, as is likely to be the case for many Vikings. The fact that weapons were present might superficially suggest that the remains were of a male. However, this would be a dangerous assumption to make as there are graves found in other parts of the Viking world where weapons were buried with females, suggesting that they were possibly sometimes engaged in fighting.

Halfdan and the growth of Viking expansionism

The birth of Halfdan was far from the end of the story of Queen Asa. A year after she was abducted, Gudrød was run through with a spear by a servant of Asa during a drunken carousal in his hall. Asa pointedly never denied responsibility for planning the act. Halfdan had a much older half-brother, Óláfr, but he does not appear to have been a strong personality and when he grew up, Halfdan became the dominant figure of the two. Much of this story is not backed up by conclusive evidence but with the arrival of Halfdan on the scene we can at least be confident that we have found an identifiable historical character. After inheriting Agder he took part of the Vestfold for himself, but this was not enough for him for he was soon after acquiring neighbouring territories as well.

Halfdan has his own saga, which is included in Snorri Sturluson's epic work the *Heimskringla,* which draws us back again into what sounds the realm of make-believe. Halfdan took as his second wife Ragnhild, the daughter of Sigurd Hart, the king of Ringerike, a territory to the north-west of modern Oslo. Unfortunately, she was in the hands of Haki, a berserker who had killed her father and then abducted her. The berserkers (or 'berserks') are a regular feature of the sagas. They are renowned warriors who fight, as if in a trance, with no fear and usually no armour. It has been suggested that they were devoted to a bear cult and maybe emulated this notoriously fierce and dangerous animal on the battlefield.

Sigurd fought a good fight before he fell and severely wounded Haki, cutting off an arm. Haki spent the winter recuperating. Halfdan commanded one of his men, Harek, to go and release Ragnhild. Harek surrounded Haki's hall, managed to free Ragnhild and then set fire to the building. Haki may have been down but he was not yet out. He chased after the rescue party, but his pursuit was in vain. The rescued prisoners sped to freedom in a magnificent covered wagon. When they reached a frozen lake, Haki saw that the game was up. In samurai fashion, rather than bear the shame of losing everything, his arm, his wife-to-be and his hall, he fell on his sword. Halfdan, who was given the name 'the Black', married Ragnhild and they had a son, Harald Fairhair, who would become one of the greatest names of early Norwegian history. Halfdan would not live to old age, accidentally drowning when he was about forty years of age.

The events of the previous decades had seen the intensity and regularity of Viking raiding increasing. Encouraged by the decline of states in Western Europe, especially Francia, there was a clear opportunity for

Viking raiders to plunder and enrich themselves across a wide area. There was clearly a mood of opportunism abroad in Scandinavia encouraging a number of disparate groups to set out on raiding activities, or to go a-Viking as they would call it. Different groups were associated with different areas. We cannot be sure that it was the same group involved in all the actions in Aquitaine, for example, but it does not seem unlikely. But we are told by chroniclers that it was not the same group or groups that were, for example, active around Dorestad further north. Given the wide range of activity across a vast geographical area we can be confident that there was little coordination between them.

Something was driving this expansionism, probably a combination of what was happening in Scandinavia allied to fundamental political and military weaknesses in Western Europe. The combination of the two soon led to a significant change of direction where raiding activities translated into campaigns that were designed to lead to ongoing exploitation and settlement on a long-term basis. The nature of Viking attacks was about to change with massive repercussions for the development of Europe.

5

The Great Heathen Army
(851–875)

Their burning zeal has been amply repaid; the ravens have gorged on a
surfeit of raw flesh.

Njal's Saga

The Viking break-out

Based on archaeological finds, some historians now take the view that
the second-half of the ninth century was one of major expansion in the
Scandinavian homelands. This assessment is based on both an increase
in the quantity of Islamic dirhams found and the volume of bullion
discovered. While long-distance trade predates the Viking Age, the
contention based on the evidence is that there was a major upsurge from
about the midpoint of the ninth century onwards.[1] Raids overseas also
increased in intensity, allowing more bullion to be brought in, including
ongoing tribute payments. One explanation of what led to the traumatic
events of the next few decades is that in the Scandinavian homelands men
were emerging who were seeking to consolidate their power over others.
Whereas in the past there had been room for a number of independent
chieftains who might ally with each other from time to time but go their
own way at others, there was now a move towards the emergence of
kings. This had already happened with mixed results in Denmark and
was also about to occur in Norway. This drove men out: those who had
previously acted as independent leaders presumably had no wish to be
subservient to someone else. As a result, overseas Viking expansionism
reached unprecedented levels and movements away from one-off raids
towards longer-term settlement accelerated.

Viking ships were at the heart of this. How they were navigated is not
completely clear. Viking seafarers would by preference sail within sight
of land and they gave names to prominent landmarks such as mountains

visible from the sea as an aid to working out where exactly they were at any given time, as was the case for example on Skye. But as time went on and they became more adventurous, leaping into the dark, sailing across vast unknown stretches of the North Atlantic, that would no longer be a feasible option. Viking sailors attempted to stay on course by choosing a starting and end point on the same latitude and then trying to sail a straight course between the two. So, a sailor might take as his point of origin the well-known landmark of Stad in Norway, about 30 miles north of Bergen. From there he would aim due west for Greenland, many days sailing away. It would be reasonable to assume an understanding of how to read positions from the sun, and from stars at night, to help with navigation.

There is conclusive evidence that Norse seafarers employed bearing dials to work out where they were (these measured the position of the sun at sunrise and sunset); and some, not yet conclusive, that they used sunstones, *sólarsteinn*, to see where the sun was when it was partly obscured by cloud or had dipped just below the horizon.[2] They also used sun boards, primitive indicators of where the sun was positioned at the middle of the day and as a result the navigator could work out if the vessel was too far north or south of where it should be; adjustments to the direction of travel could then be made accordingly. Research into this aspect of Viking navigation continues.

The understandable focus on the Vikings as seafarers has overshadowed their ability to travel efficiently over land. As one example, although the mountain ranges between Norway and Sweden cut off much of the overland route between the two regions, there was a viable route between Uppland in Sweden and Trøndelag in the centre of Norway. Further south, much of the trading between Jutland and Germany took place across overland routes. Evidence from archaeology, and the sagas and chronicles, suggest that the horse was in widespread use in Viking society. Horses were employed as draught animals but also as a form of rapid transport when the Vikings were raiding, a tactic that was about to come into its own in England. Evidence of carts has been found, most notably in the shape of the wonderfully carved vehicle that was buried at Oseberg, though this object appears to be for ceremonial purposes and of limited practical use. Unsurprisingly given the terrain that many Vikings lived in and the winter conditions that they regularly experienced, there is also evidence of sledges being used (again, for example, from finds at Oseberg) which would have been invaluable during the winter months.

The Vikings became increasingly active in Britain. In the Welsh chronicle the *Brut y Tywysogíon* under the year 850 it is said that 'Cyngen was strangled by the pagans'. There is a king of Powys from this period with this name, but he is believed to have died in 855 during a pilgrimage to Rome, so either the tradition is incorrect or there was another man of the same name active at around the same time. Either way, this was clearly a very unpleasant end. Cyngen stands as an example of the many now largely unknown victims of the reign of terror that was about to be unleashed on the British Isles.

The confidence of the raiders was up. A massive naval assault was launched against England in 851, sacking both London and Canterbury with a force that was allegedly 350 ships strong. They attacked both Wessex and the still-independent (if by now precariously so) Mercia. But they overstepped the mark. Æthelwulf of Wessex was ready for them with an army, and won a great victory at Aclea in Surrey (possibly Oakley). Asser, the biographer of King Alfred, exulted over the victory saying that 'we have never heard of a greater slaughter of them [i.e. the Vikings] in any region, on any day, before or since', which is very similar to what Æthelweard says; the latter also gives the detail that it was fought near a wood.[3] Even the Frankish annalists made a rare reference to it in their works, so this must have been a very significant triumph.[4] There was even a victory at sea when Æthelstan (the son of Æthelwulf) and Ealdorman Elfhere captured nine ships at Sandwich. Nevertheless, in 851 the raiders over-wintered in England for the first time, setting up camp at Thanet, a hugely symbolic event that presaged a significant heightening of the threat to England from the Vikings.[5]

Perhaps the triumph at Aclea created a false sense of confidence for the evidence suggests that the true extent of the danger from the Vikings was under-estimated. When Burgred, the king of Mercia, soon after sought an alliance with the West Saxon king, it was to face up to the threat from the Welsh rather than the Northmen.[6] Meanwhile Æthelwulf went on pilgrimage to Rome – a very risky move in the light of increasing Viking activity – and in his long absence was almost unseated by his ambitious son Æthelbald, who launched a coup. A rather shocking wake-up call for the English was not far off. Other parts of England were attacked by Vikings during these years; though in the case of Northumbria the records are particularly sketchy for this period. However, there is a reference by the later chronicler Roger of Wendover to a usurper king of Northumbria by the name of Rædwald being killed in battle against 'pagans' in 844, though numismatic evidence now suggests that this date is at least a decade too early.[7]

Not only in England was the effect of such raids felt. Ireland suffered an unwelcome visit from so-called Danish Vikings in 851. The Viking settlements of Ireland were limited in scope but created ongoing difficulties for their indigenous Celtic neighbours. The Scandinavian elements on the island were not at peace with each other. The *Annals of Ulster* tell how at about this time 'Amlaib [Óláfr], son of the king of Laithland, came to Ireland and the Gaill [the name used to refer in contemporary Irish to 'foreigners'] of Ireland submitted to him and he took tribute from the Irish'.[8] The new Viking arrivals in Ireland were termed 'dark foreigners' by the chroniclers; they were often mentioned in tandem with reference to a region called Laithland, normally construed to mean part of Norway, though alternative suggestions have been made that it may be the northern islands of Scotland and the Hebrides.[9] Their Scandinavian opponents in Ireland were called 'fair Vikings'. Historians have sometimes tied themselves up in knots trying to explain these terms away. The 'dark foreigners' and the 'fair foreigners', it has been suggested, refers to their colouring; other interpretations suggest that the new arrivals were Danes while the existing Viking residents were Norwegians. All this is somewhat nebulous; the terms Dane and Norwegian did not mean very much in 851 as the modern countries to which those names apply did not yet exist.

More recent suggestions are that 'dark' foreigners was a nickname for the new arrivals who were led by Óláfr the White, and a man whose name would resonate in the history of Viking Britain and Ireland, Ivarr.[10] The latter began a dynasty, the ua Ímair, which played a key role in Viking activities in the Irish Sea region over the succeeding century. He is often linked to the legendary Ivarr the Boneless, son of the equally legendary Ragnar Lodbrok, but as this is largely based on twefth/thirteenth-century saga accounts this claim should be treated with caution. However, there are some earlier references suggesting the connection; Adam of Bremen talks of an 'Ingvar, the son of Lodbrok, who everywhere tortured Christians to death'.[11]

The sons of Ragnar Lodbrok

The saga story of Ivarr's conception is intriguing. Ragnar insisted on sleeping with his wife and ignored her pleas that they desist from sex for three nights. She then told him that if he persisted then a child would be born without bones. Their son Ivarr was later born with gristle where there should be skeleton: one of the more fabulous elements contained in the later sagas.[12] Other sons appear in the saga stories such as *The Saga of Ragnar Lodbrok and his Sons*, the *Tale of Ragnar's Sons* and the *Krákumál*: Björn Ironside, Hvitserk the Swift, Sigurd Snake-in-the-Eye and Rognvald to go with Erik and Agnar, born of a previous wife who had died. Among their marvellous exploits was a raid on Sweden when they killed the king, Eystein, after having overcome his secret weapon, a horned cow that bellowed so loudly that men could not withstand its noise.

Moving beyond the fabulous elements of the story of this Ivarr, in 851 the Northmen who had settled in Ireland found themselves on the wrong end of the new group, the 'dark foreigners', who launched an attack at Linn Duachaill, probably Annagassan, but were defeated. In the following year a Viking attack was launched from there and devastated Armagh. This battle for supremacy between the longer-established 'fair foreigners' and the newcomers, the 'dark foreigners', was a violent one and historians do not agree on the identity of the ultimate victors.[13]

Wales was in a dangerous position and fell foul of Viking attacks. In one such in 852 the raiders got as far as the Wrekin in Shropshire, the borderlands of Mercia and the Welsh kingdoms, making use of the deep penetration of the Severn to do so – the region was many miles from the sea. They did not have it all their own way though. Gwynedd was the strongest Welsh kingdom at the time and in 856 the army of one of its most significant kings, Rhodri Mawr ('the Great') who reigned from 844 to 878, killed a Viking leader, Ormr, in battle. However, Rhodri would eventually be driven into exile in 877 as a result of the depredations of the Viking 'foreigners', having lost a battle against them in Anglesey that year.[14]

Scotland too was under attack. The *Chronicles of the Kings of Alba,* a fourteenth-century copy of a twelfth-century compilation, discusses the reign of *Kinadius,* son of Alpin (better known as Kenneth McAlpin, or Cináed mac Ailpin), 'first of the Scots' (though there is strong evidence of Pictish antecedents in his bloodline). He died in 858 and we are told that during his reign the *Danari,* i.e. the Danes, wasted Pictavia including Clunie, later an important royal site, and Dunkeld, where there was an important church. The later chronicle, the Irish *Annals of the Four Masters*, told how in 839, the same year as a heavy Pictish defeat against the Vikings, an Irish chief journeyed to Dál Riata. He gave his support to Cináed mac Ailpin, traditionally regarded as the first king of Alba, a combination of Dál Riata and Pictland. While this claim is treated with some scepticism, clearly the chaos unleashed by Viking attacks created a vacuum into which opportunists like Cináed and not just Vikings attempted to step.[15] Significantly, both Clunie and Dunkeld were far from the coast, so Viking raiders were now confident enough to push inland in Scotland. We are also informed that the Britons of Strathclyde burned Dunblane at around this time. The significance of this latter attack was that the Strathclyde 'Welsh' had disappeared from the historical record for about a century before this.[16] Something had clearly happened to cause their resurgence, including the serious decline of the Picts brought about by defeat at the hands of Viking raiders.

Viking raids also continued along the coast of Francia, and Rouen fell victim to them again in 851. The monastery at Ghent was burned, as was Beauvais further south. From time to time, the raiders were caught as they retreated, perhaps slowed down with plunder, but it was very difficult for the Frankish authorities to coordinate a timely and effective response. Historians are divided as to whether these raids over a wide area in Francia were launched by the same groups or not, and we will probably never know the answer with any confidence.[17] However, it seems most likely that there were several groups in play here. These groups were probably flexible in terms of their composition. Runic inscriptions from Scandinavia suggest that men could, over time, raid with several different groups so while there might have been a hard core of veterans attached to one specific leader, it is likely that others might come and go on a more or less mercenary basis upon which they would be rewarded by a share in the plunder taken on a specific mission. One innovative theory postulated by the late Danish historian Klavs Randsborg as to the cause of these raids was that the loss to the caliphate in Baghdad of mines in Tajikistan seriously interfered with the flow of silver to the Middle East and from there on to Scandinavia. Short of ways of making money from trading with the Middle East, as they had done in the past, something needed to be done to replace this lost source of revenue.[18]

A Viking fleet, said to be composed of the surprisingly precise figure of 252 ships, returned to the coast of Frisia in 852 but was bought off. Francia was in a difficult situation as it had to cope with threats from several directions at once. To the south the Moors had sacked Barcelona – allegedly once more with the active assistance of Jewish sympathisers – and Rome itself had been assaulted by Muslim 'Saracen' pirates. There was also an enemy within to worry about. A probable son of Harald Klak called Godfrid had been baptised at Mainz (as his supposed father had, along with 'a great multitude of Danes')[19] and allied himself to Lothar. Unfortunately for the latter, adopting outwardly Christian appearances did not completely suppress the Viking within. In 852, Godfrid assembled a force and returned to his old ways, raiding first along the Scheldt and then the Seine. Old habits clearly died hard for some.

There was the semblance of a unified response from Lothar and Charles to this new threat as they combined forces and blockaded the raiders on the Seine. However, their men did not want to fight. Charles struck a deal with Godfrid but many of the Vikings refused to budge, showing that sometimes control by their supposed leaders was nominal. Internal Frankish affairs then intervened yet again. For over a decade Charles had worked closely with his brother Louis 'the German', presenting a united front against Lothar. Although this had not been a period of all-out war, Lothar was constantly plotting, manoeuvring and manipulating in an attempt to gain the upper hand. Now though, Charles and Lothar came to terms; Lothar even stood as godfather for Charles's daughter, which was rather unusual as he was already Charles's godfather. Inevitably Louis had taken offence at these new-found expressions of brotherly love and fell out with Charles. Perhaps in this case accidentally, once again Viking interference in Frankish affairs had further muddied already murky waters.

Godfrid's men stayed where they were until March, burning, ravaging and taking many locals captive.[20] Later in 853, they plundered Nantes and then did the same to Tours, the former home of Alcuin, abbot there during his last years. Tours had clearly received advanced warning of what was to come. The venerated remains of St Martin had been interred in the church named after him there, but the monks had time to spirit his body away to the monastery of Cormery while their treasures were moved to Orléans for safe keeping. These raids were conscientiously recorded by chroniclers and annalists who were connected to them; as they were more interested in writing up attacks on their monasteries than they would those on secular sites, the list of specific Viking targets may be substantially understated.

There was now a heightened international response to the threat and political measures were being taken to guard against the Viking menace. Such a strategy may be behind a marriage alliance forged in 856 between Francia and Wessex when Charles the Bald's daughter Judith was given as a bride to Æthelwulf of Wessex. Charles had just beaten back a new Viking force which had set up an overwintering base near Paris, 'with very great slaughter' involved, we are told by the *Annales of Fontanelle*. An alliance with Wessex held many attractions in the face of a common enemy.

The king of the West Saxons was returning from a pilgrimage to Rome when he married Judith. The age difference between the two was marked, even for those days: Æthelwulf was over sixty while Judith was probably in her early teens. She was to lead a hectic life while in Wessex. Unsurprisingly she would outlive her much older husband and when he died would marry her step-son, Æthelbald, much to the fury of some churchmen including Alfred's biographer, Asser (this second marriage did not last long either; by 860 the bride was a widow again and soon back in Francia). This marriage alliance may well have been a response to the Viking challenge faced by both countries.[21] Judith was consecrated as queen, the first West Saxon consort to be so honoured, suggesting that this was a highly significant political match to which the West Saxons in particular attached great importance.[22] The Viking threat was having an indirect but very important effect on the political geography of Western Europe.

Factional infighting

In Ireland, the longer-term resident Vikings found themselves under attack. It is revealing that the main threat at the time came not from the native Irish but from 'Danes' who wanted a share of the available plunder. They seized Dublin in 851 and the following year won a crushing victory over their Viking rivals at Carlingford. But then a fleet from Norway led by Óláfr 'The White' and supported by Ivarr arrived and a bitter battle for supremacy followed. Óláfr found himself in opposition to a group of mixed Irish-Viking heritage, the *Gallgoidil*, the 'Foreigner Gaels'. Confrontations between the two groups are recorded in 856, 857 and 858 but not thereafter. These *Gallgoidil* were in alliance with an Irish king, Máel Sechnaill I, who ruled lands not far from Dublin.

Churches sometimes bore the brunt of Viking raids led by Óláfr. In 856, Slade and Lusk, close to Dublin, were attacked; their proximity to the major Viking port in Ireland suggests that this is where the raids were launched from. Secular targets were attacked too; in the same year Lough Cend, a royal centre in County Limerick, was raided. This was further away from Dublin but it may have still been the men of Óláfr and Ivarr who were involved as they are known to have been active in Munster at around this time. Dublin was becoming a major Viking settlement. Important finds in cemetery sites at Islandbridge and Kilmainham (where the graves of fifty-two Viking warriors have been found)[23] reveal much about the settlers there. At both places the settlers seem to have taken advantage of cemeteries which were previously used for Christian burials. It may be, as has been suggested, that this was a symbolic statement to the indigenous population that the Vikings were there to stay; claiming symbolically significant sites was a way of asserting cultural dominance and emphasising the supremacy of pagan Viking gods.[24] A similar situation would occur in other places such as at Repton in England.

Indigenous rulers in both Ireland and Scotland were concerned enough about the Viking threat by now to enter into alliances with each other. There were strong historical connections between the two regions; the modern situation, where two discrete countries exist, was not the case at this time. The 'Scots' had originated in Ireland and, since settling in Dál Riata in the south-west of Scotland, those historical links had remained strong. Even Columba had a foot in both Irish and Scottish camps. It would be wrong to see the narrow waters that lay between them as a barrier; again, they were a highway that linked the two regions together.

However, alliances were not just made against Vikings but also with them. Ivarr, allied to an Irish king Cerball of Osraige, defeated the *Gallgoidil* at Ara Tire in County Tipperary, on the borders of Munster and the kingdom of the Southern Uí Néill. Cerball became famous as the subject of a saga which is preserved in the *Fragmentary Annals of Ireland*. He later joined attacks involving both Ivarr and Óláfr against Meath, another part of Southern Uí Néill territory. However, he then switched sides and allied himself with Máel Sechnaill, overking of the Southern Uí Néill, against Ivarr and Óláfr. The need to forge alliances lay behind the marriage of Máel Múire, the daughter of Cináed mac Ailpín, and Áed Findlaith, overking of the Northern Uí Neill, a man who 'no spearpoint could conquer'; though presumably he was not convinced of his own propaganda, otherwise no alliance would be necessary. A common Viking enemy no doubt encouraged this alliance.

A little later, in 866, Áed attacked Viking bases along the northern Irish coast (these may have housed Viking groups that were not allied with those in Dublin), potentially loosening their grip on the seaways around the Irish Sea and possibly for a time the Viking insurgents there were forced to retreat to bases in the Western Isles of Scotland. By this time, Ivarr, Óláfr and another brother, Ásl, had left Ireland to seek out opportunities in Britain and in the same year they attacked Fortrui, taking a number of hostages as a result of their campaign; another hammer blow for a Pictish kingdom that was still trying to come to terms with the disastrous defeat at the hands of the Norsemen in 839. Constantin had become king of the Picts in 862 and now had to submit to the indignity of paying over tribute to the Vikings.

Óláfr and Ásl were given hostages by the Picts when they left Scotland on St Patrick's Day (17 March) 867. After Óláfr's departure from Ireland, Viking fortunes on the island had taken a significant dip and they had been defeated in Kerry, Cork and Leinster in 866 and 867. Even Óláfr's fort at Clondalkin near Dublin was ransacked and the heads of 100 prominent Vikings were taken as trophies by the victors.[25] As the *Annals of Ulster* put it, 'he [Áed Findlaith] took away their heads, their flocks and their herds'. This prompted Óláfr to return to Ireland with retribution in his heart. According to the *Annals of Inisfallen* he committed an outrage against the church at Lismore, though exactly what form this took is unclear. In a battle at Killineer on the River Boyne in 868 the son of Óláfr was killed. Soon after, Óláfr plundered the holy site of Armagh; rather than an overtly anti-Christian act, this was more likely a political gesture against an establishment that was closely linked with the kings of the Northern Uí Néill. By now, Óláfr's position had become more complicated; his long-time ally Ivarr was preoccupied with English affairs and his brother Ásl was dead; in some accounts the two men had fallen out and Óláfr had killed Ásl in a fit of rage because of jealousy around the latter's sexual attraction to the former's wife.

It would be repetitive to carry on developing an ever-longer list of Viking attacks in Francia during these years, but they continued to fall with regularity, helped no end by the infighting between the brothers among whom Charlemagne's old empire had been divided. Just as factional infighting divided the Vikings in Ireland, it also helped them in Francia; but it was about to divide them in Denmark too. King Horik had ruled as sole king of the Danes since 827. He had striven to achieve a delicate equilibrium with his ostensibly powerful neighbours in Francia; as we have seen, he on occasion took steps to distance himself from raids that had been launched by Vikings there, though from time to time he was also involved in campaigns against the Franks.

Horik perished in 854 at the hands of his own kin. He ejected a nephew from his lands, but the exile built up a strong following and returned to fight him. A brief but violent confrontation followed, at the end of which Horik lay dead along with many of his nobility. The vacuum that was created encouraged Godfrid to return to Denmark from Francia to try to profit from the chaos; but he was unsuccessful in this and returned to Dorestad. In the end, it was the late king's son who became Horik II and was to hold the kingship until 860. The two Horiks were kings rather than warlords. A king claimed leadership over a group of people based, for example, on ethnicity or a shared cultural heritage: this was more than just being a warlord with a loose and flexible (and often changing and evolving) party behind him. It also implied a special elevated status in times of war or other great periods of upheaval, which must include in these times the decision to undertake some profound move, such as the adoption of Christianity as the chosen religion of a group of people.[26]

Horik II was prevailed upon to close the church in Hedeby which had been opened in his father's reign for a short time but it was reopened soon afterwards following pressure from Ansgar. This time a bell was installed and rung, which had not been the case before; a small sign of acceptance perhaps, but a sign nevertheless. When soon after a church was also opened in the town of Ribe in south-west Jutland, it was another positive step forward for the Christian religion and its prospects in Denmark.

Frankish countermeasures and the Mediterranean voyage

It was perhaps in vessels like the Gokstad Ship that two Viking leaders, Björn Ironside and Hæsten, undertook one of the most daring Viking expeditions yet. An old target was an early stopping-off point for them: Paris. Remembering how profitable the visit there had been a decade previously, in 857 they again fell on the city. Paris was renowned, according to the contemporary writer Abbo of Saint-Germain-des-Prés, for 'the splendour of your bearing'. It was also the key to an important part of Francia and, belatedly perhaps, the Franks had come to understand this. It was now surrounded by battlements and towers, perched on an island in the middle of the Seine – it was a strongly fortified position but for a Viking raider the river presented an open roadway right up to the front door.

Björn was, according to the sagas, the son of the legendary Ragnar Lodbrok and his raid was every bit as successful as his father's had been earlier. When Björn left, once more glutted with riches, most of Paris was a smouldering wreck. Only a few places survived the destruction; these included the churches of St Stephen, St Denis and St Germain, who paid the raiders protection money so that they would leave these establishments intact.[27] At around the same time, Dorestad was again attacked and ransacked, something that was now in danger of almost becoming an annual event. The *emporium* was on its last legs, though there may also have been local reasons such as the silting up of the river to explain this; similar sites such as Quentovic continued to prosper into the second half of the ninth century. The latter was seen as a place of refuge and security, for example monks from St Wandrille, too close to the mouth of the Seine for its own good, fled there for safety in 858.[28]

The Viking raiders were adept hostage takers and knew how to gain maximum advantage from prestigious captives. They must have been delighted when they took prisoner two important individuals in the form of Louis, abbot of St Denis, and his half-brother Gauzlin, in the raid on Paris. Louis was a great prize, being a grandson of Charlemagne. The Vikings charged a heavy price for his release (688 lbs of gold and 3,250 lbs of silver) and a number of church treasuries in the realm of Charles the Bald 'were drained dry at the king's command'. Even this was not enough and the king, some bishops and other men of note were required to top up the ransom fund to an acceptable level; we are told by the annalist that they did this 'eagerly' but one wonders whether or not this is an over-enthusiastic interpretation on his part, especially as the king was deserted by a number of his counts soon after.[29] These were times of 'unprecedented pressure' from the Vikings on Charles's kingdom for previously it had been mainly his domestic opponents who had suffered from such attacks.[30] It is worth re-emphasising that this was not one band of Vikings in action but a number of different groups, capable of shifting allegiances, always searching out the points of weakness with the greatest current opportunities for profit. This was perfectly illustrated in 862 when two rivals, the Breton lord Salomon and Robert, count of Anjou, faced off in battle, each with hired Viking hands supporting them (the latter would be killed fighting Vikings in 866).

There is, however, an alternative and superficially slightly odd explanation for these heavy levels of taxation. Charles was later accused by some of his own people of profiteering and certainly there are signs, such as the increased purity of coins in circulation, that the Frankish economy continued to boom in the 860s. There is then a chance that Charles was overstating the onerous nature of Viking demands and siphoning off some of the money collected for himself.[31] Certainly, there are unmistakable signs of aristocratic revolt at around this period, which manifested themselves when several important men in Francia changed allegiance from Charles the Bald to his rival, Louis the German. Even the normally loyal Hincmar, Archbishop of Rheims, expressed his dissatisfaction at the levels of fiscal exactions that were being demanded.[32]

These were bad times to be a cleric. The abbot of St Denis was fortunate to be valued high enough to be worth the massive ransom. Others were not so lucky. A particularly violent outbreak of raiding took place in 858/9. Ermenfrid, the bishop of Beauvais, was killed during the fighting that took place, as was Baltfrid, bishop of Bayeux. An especially heavy headcount was suffered when raiders took Noyon, about 100 kilometres north of Paris. This was a surprise attack, requiring a substantial overland journey on the part of the raiders, who took Noyon's bishop, Immo, prisoner along with several other important men. They began to march them off to captivity and probable ransom, but something went wrong *en route* for all the captives were subsequently slaughtered; possibly the prisoners attempted to escape or resist in some other way and were overwhelmed by their captors.

However, there were occasional glimpses that the raiders were not invulnerable. In 862, a Viking fleet made its way up the Marne, in the process burning a bridge at Trilbardou. It then sailed further up the river to unleash chaos. But in the meantime, it had been suggested to Charles the Bald that the bridge should be rebuilt and fortified, essentially catching the Vikings in a trap. This very smart move may come as a surprise to those who have come across Charles before and have been told by historians that he was a man who was out of his depth. He was, in fact, a king who was faced with a huge task in maintaining the vitality and supremacy of the Carolingian legacy and did his best to live up to the great responsibility this entailed in difficult circumstances. The measures that he took at Trilbardou were astute and show a keen understanding of what gave the Vikings their strategic advantages and how they could best be countered. Fortification building projects elsewhere at places as far afield as Le Mans, Tours, Dijon and Angoulême show that these were not isolated initiatives.

The bridge-building plan worked a treat and the raiders were forced to sue for peace. Two years later, Charles followed this up in an assembly at Pîtres where a number of edicts were issued, one of them concerning the building of more fortified bridges; though there were other important domestic matters attended to, such as reform of the Frankish coinage. River defences in both Francia and England had been weak up until now, but it was dawning on those responsible for taking defensive measures that they needed to up their game if they were to survive. The construction of the fortifications at Pîtres were seminal and Charles expended significant resources on them. They were at a crucial point in Normandy where two rivers, the Andelle and the Eure, flow into the Seine, and by building fortifications, Charles blocked Viking progress further up the great river. They took years to complete and Charles took pains to ensure that they were adequately garrisoned by assigning a certain number of men to each stretch of wall, much as Alfred would do in England a quarter of a century later; indeed, the king of Wessex may well have been inspired by this earlier example.

Having extracted maximum profit from these lucrative targets, Björn and Hæsten decided to travel further afield. They took their sixty ships, crewed by opportunists who looked death in the eye and laughed at it, on a voyage the like of which had never been seen before. They sailed down the Atlantic coast of Francia and on through the stormy seas of Biscay. They unfurled their sails and raced past the rocky headlands of Iberia. Then they approached the gates of the Mediterranean, the Pillars of Hercules, beyond which lay a whole new ocean, the one that the Roman Empire had called *Mare Nostrum,* 'Our Sea'. It had long since ceased to be that in recent years, mainly due to the activities of pirates who made journeying across it very hazardous; but the pirates responsible were Muslim rather than Scandinavian in origin.

The glories of Rome were far in the past now and there was little to stop Björn and Hæsten as they launched their raids on an unsuspecting region. There is evidence of Viking incursions in Galicia in the northwest of Spain including D-shaped camps that look very similar to those erected in Ireland and England. They attacked the invaluable prize of Santiago de Compostela, managing to extract tribute rather than sacking it, took Algeciras and then raided Cabo Tres Forcas on the North African coast. They took many prisoners here who were sent back to Ireland to be duly processed as part of the human trafficking of slaves (the later *Fragmentary Annals of Ireland* provides details of black slaves being brought over as part of this trade). The Balearic Islands were attacked, as were Narbonne and the Camargue. Then, hugging the coast of what is now north-west Italy, possibly even attacking Pisa, they came to the greatest prize of all, Rome.

As they looked on the walls of the Eternal City, the raiders gulped. It was beyond their siege warfare skills to take such a place, so another time-honoured tactic was employed instead; subterfuge. Hæsten sent word into the city that he was ill, in fact he was dying; and recognising the power of the Christian faith and wishing to protect his immortal soul as it went on its perilous way into another world he wanted to be baptised. The authorities in the city rejoiced at such a gesture and the prestige it brought to their religion. The night following his baptism, news came that Hæsten had been summoned to meet his Maker. All that remained was to give him the Christian burial that his actions surely deserved. And so, the gates of the city were opened to receive his body. As the bells tolled, and the monks in their vestments welcomed him into eternal rest, the people of the city looked on in their finest apparel. It was a day such as the city had not seen for centuries.

Except that Hæsten was far from dead. As the climax of the burial rites was reached, Hæsten jumped up from his bier and struck the officiating bishop dead. The mourners in his cortege then revealed that they were carrying weapons and laid about them, falling on the unsuspecting audience so that they were soon overpowered. The men were hacked down and the women taken off into a life of drudgery to eke out their days as slaves.

Was this story true? Almost certainly not; such stories were employed as frequent *topos* of Viking superheroes in the sagas that write their names into history or, at least, into mythology. Later Norman adventurers such as Bohemond of Taranto and Robert Guiscard allegedly employed similar tactics in their own campaigns.[33] There was also another problem concerning the raid, which suggested that the Vikings' knowledge of Mediterranean geography was as yet rudimentary, for it was not Rome that they had captured but the port of Luna, 300 kilometres to the north. To make the situation more confusing still, no archaeological evidence has yet been found for such a raid. Historians think that it probably did take place, but it is generally conceded that the Vikings, however limited their prior knowledge of the Mediterranean was, would probably never have mistaken Luna for Rome. It was essentially an unprepossessing place, already in decline and well past its peak, and therefore the whole saga has the feel of a Viking tall story.

Though the Mediterranean raid is a fascinating tale, it perhaps revealed to the raiders that the region as a whole was not for them. They may have made it as far as Alexandria, then the greatest port in the world, before turning for home. They were forced to run the gauntlet of the Straits of Gibraltar on the way back where, this time, a Moorish fleet was ready and waiting. It was only with difficulty and after much loss that the Vikings extricated themselves and made their way north back to more familiar waters, though they could not resist falling on Pamplona on the way and holding its prince for ransom. By the time they reached what they might call home territory, the mouth of the Loire, only a third of the original fleet survived. While no doubt the raid had been rewarding in several senses of the word, the cost had been enormous.

Harald Fairhair and Iceland

Events in Norway were about to take a significant turn. Harald Fairhair became king of the country in *c.* 870 when about ten years of age. His reign would be extraordinary, not least for its longevity – he reigned until 933. His efforts to become the undisputed ruler of a united country had profound consequences but were not universally popular; there are no winners in such a contest without a corresponding set of losers. One consequence of his unstinting quest for power was that some high-ranking Norwegians left the country rather than submit to a centralised power. Ari the Wise, the later writer of the *Landnámabók*, talks of 'the tyranny of King Harald Fairhair' and of how it forced men like An

Redfell, son of Grim Shaggy-Cheek, to leave Norway.[34] Another man, Onund Treefoot, son of Ofeig Clubfoot, left Norway having lost his leg in battle at Hafrsfjord fighting against Harald Fairhair. As a result of the *wanderlust* unleashed, the first Viking settlers reached Iceland. Some of them may have emulated An Redfell, who is said to have raided Ireland and seized a wife for himself on the way out. The *Landnámabók* suggests that Thord, a son of Harald, was one of those who eventually settled on the island.[35]

The accounts of those early days sound eerily similar to the opening up of the American West, though for the Vikings in Iceland at least there would be no hostile indigenous tribes to attack them (ultimately as the land filled up they would end up fighting each other instead). This was a land for pioneers, for the staking of claims or 'landtaking'. One touching tale in the *Landnámabók* tells how a slave, Raungud, was sent by his master, Erik, to venture into the mountains that spread across the centre of the island to discover more about them. Erik was so impressed when Raungud became the first man to discover that the mountains could be crossed from north to south that he promptly gave him his freedom when receiving the news.[36]

Legends would accrete to Harald Fairhair like barnacles to a ship. One which gained currency was that there were romantic reasons behind his quest for power. He wanted to marry Gyda, daughter of King Erik of Hordaland, but she would not agree to be his wife until he was ruler of all Norway. This account is fraught with difficulties and it seems unlikely that someone like Harald would need any romantic rationale to explain away his ambition. But the story grew that this was his driving force, as did the legend that he would not have his hair cut (or even combed) until his quest had been fulfilled.[37]

Norway had changed as it entered the Viking era. Farming practices developed, and ways of life adapted. Grave sites are found further up the mountains than in previous eras, suggesting that farmers were taking their stock up to higher pastures in the summer months than had previously been the case. Breeding practices also became more selective with the better or stronger animals kept for procreating superior quality livestock.[38] But not everybody was happy at Harald's ambitious plans, hence the emigration to Iceland. Historical records concerning the island were written up by Ari the Wise in 1130, several hundred years after the events described. Ari stated that Iceland had already been inhabited by Irish monks some time before it was 'discovered' by Viking explorers, though very little archaeological evidence has been found as yet to confirm this; and there are several other statements in Ari's work that suggest the island was uninhabited when the Viking settlers arrived there. Nevertheless, it is certainly the kind of place that Irish monks, with their reputation for hermit lifestyles, would have enjoyed.

Genetic science has given us a fascinating insight into the racial origins of those who settled in Iceland. Research suggests that up to 80 per cent of the early female population and 20 per cent of the males in Iceland were of Celtic-British origin. The most likely explanation for this is that they were largely composed of slaves who had been forcibly brought over to the island rather than having settled there; though Scandinavian intermarrying with British women may also have been a contributory cause.[39] Ari suggests that early on in the Viking settlement some slaves rebelled against their masters and killed them, but they were later caught and massacred by other settlers on the island.[40]

The first Viking expeditions to the island are usually assumed to have taken place in about 860. The main characters on these early voyages were a Swede, Gardar Svavarson, and two Norwegians, Naddod and Flóki Vilgerdarson. Their exploits were recorded in the *Landnámabók*, 'The Book of the Settlements', '*landnám*' meaning 'the taking of the land'. Naddod landed at Reydar on the eastern side of Iceland. He climbed a high hill to see if the land was inhabited but found no trace of settlement. He did not stop but sailed back to the Faroes. Gardar the Swede explored further and sailed around Iceland, establishing that it was an island. He was so pleased with his achievement that he called it Gardarsholm after himself.

Flóki Vilgerdarson (also called Hrafnaflóki, 'Flóki of the Ravens') was described by Ari as a great Viking. He sailed from Norway, stopping first in Shetland in a bay named Flóki's Bight where his daughter, Geirhild, was drowned. Not knowing what lay to the west, he sailed with three ravens on board, reckoning that they would sense land before he saw it. When after two abortive efforts the third bird was released and did not return, he felt sure that he was close to land. He landed on the east coast of Iceland and sailed onwards round its southern shore before travelling up the western side of the island. The autumn weather that greeted them was mild; deceptively so. The winter was the opposite and the party was unprepared; most of the sheep and cattle with them died due to the harsh conditions. The coming of spring was therefore a relief. Climbing a hill to observe the terrain in the distance, Flóki saw a bay to the north full of glaciers and named the place 'Iceland' as a result; in contrast to when 'Greenland' was discovered and named, the title he gave the island would not encourage anyone to go there under false pretences. When he returned to Norway after a year or so, an unenamoured Flóki was dismissive of what he had seen. But one of his party, Thorolf, reported that the land was so fertile that every blade of grass dripped with butter (he was ever after known sarcastically as 'Thorolf Butter' as a result). This may have been slightly less of an exaggeration then that it currently is; later over-farming on the island had significant negative impacts. Flóki had been unlucky; he arrived in a freak cold snap in the middle of what was one of the warmest spells for a long time, known as the Medieval Warm Period or Little Optimum. It has been estimated that while about 20 per cent of modern Iceland is farmable, in the Viking Age the figure was at least 40 per cent and possibly as much as 75 per cent.[41]

About a decade later, the settlement of Iceland began when a party led by two Norwegians, Ingólf Arnarson and his foster brother Leif, journeyed there, though Leif soon took himself off to Ireland (about five days' sail from the south of Iceland according to the *Landnámabók*: it was a seven-day voyage from Stad on the west coast of Norway to Horn in the east of Iceland according to the same source).[42] When he arrived off Iceland with a view to settling there (Ari suggests this was in about 874), Ingólf threw some wooden pillars he had brought from Norway with him overboard and determined that, wherever they might come ashore, then that is where he would set up home.

A settlement was established at a place called the 'smoky bay'; in Old Norse 'Reykjavik'. The island quickly filled up. Within half a century, most of the workable land had been taken (rapid settlement after 871 has been proved by archaeological evidence that widespread building construction took place on top of an ash layer that can scientifically be shown to have been deposited by a volcanic eruption in this year). When the first settlers arrived, there were a number of trees on the island, many of them stunted but there nevertheless. During the next few centuries, an ecological disaster occurred. Deforestation followed on from the settlement and the soil was depleted by overgrazing.

The evidence from Iceland and the later settlements in Greenland was that many of the farms that were established there were very isolated. Towns did not develop on either island. Architecture in Iceland went down a different path than it did back in Scandinavia. The great halls that came to typify the latter are much rarer in Iceland, though they do exist. Houses were typically built of turf, laid over a base of stone. Farm buildings were clustered together with only the smithy (for obvious fire protection reasons) and the byres kept away from the main buildings. By the middle of the tenth century there were perhaps 3–4,000 families resident on Iceland, some 50–60,000 people in total.[43] Many of them originated from the region of Bergen, though there were others from different parts of Scandinavia and also later on from the Viking-held parts of the British Isles.

It would be several hundred years before any Scandinavian king came to assert his authority over Iceland; it was too far off the beaten track and anyway they had greater problems nearer home to worry about. In their place, local chieftains, the *godar*, became powerful in a way that had been the norm in Scandinavia in times past. They had local authority across the four quarters, or *várthing*, into which the island was administratively divided (the quarters were further sub-divided into thirteen local 'things'). Below them were an important group of retainers, or *thingmenn,* who might own land from and serve under more than one *godar,* which could become complicated if disputes broke out.

There was a kind of equality between these men which was increasingly lacking in Norway where a king was attempting to build up his own centralised power. This is hinted at by archaeological evidence. Before this period, in the west of Norway in particular were unique kinds of structures known as 'courtyard sites'. With such sites, a series of houses was built around a central courtyard; each of them very similar in size and structure, as if no man had precedence there. The evidence suggests that they were only temporarily occupied, as if they were some kind of assembly place where a group of important men could meet together to hold discussions. However, at around this time they started to go into decline in Norway, as if a new social structure was emerging to make them redundant; the limited equality that they suggest was no longer the norm.[44]

It was not just to the west that Scandinavians were travelling. In the twelfth century a monk called Nestor wrote a work of history from his monastery near Kiev. In it, he told how some 'Varangians from beyond the sea' took over the area and imposed tribute on it in the years 860–862. They were initially ejected by the locals but, when law and order broke down soon after, they were invited back in again. Just who these 'Varangians' were is a question that has greatly exercised historians. A group known as the *Rūs,* with whom these Varangians are often linked, are first referred to in the *Annals of St Bertin* in 839 as being among a delegation that visited the Frankish court of Louis the Pious while in residence at Ingelheim. The delegation came from the Byzantine Emperor, Theophilus. The *Rūs* with them had journeyed all the way to Constantinople and now sought permission for a safe conduct across Louis' territories back home.

It was determined that these men were of Swedish origin but were no longer, as one twentieth-century historian put it, 'of Sweden itself'.[45] This accords nicely with the later writings of Nestor, which were incorporated into a work known as *The Russian Primary Chronicle.* Nestor tells us that 'these Varangians [a party of which was invited into territory in Russia in 860–862] are called Rūs as others were called Swedes, others again Norwegians or Angles or Goths'; in other words, these Rūs are to be differentiated in some way from Swedes, even if other sources insist that they are of Swedish origin. In Finnish (which is not a Scandinavian language), *Ruotsi* means 'Swede', suggesting nevertheless that those adventurers named the Rūs originally had a Swedish origin.[46]

Louis was suspicious of these men, thinking they were spies, suggesting that relations between Franks and Scandinavians were at the time based on mutual distrust. Nationalist historians have bitterly disagreed on the impact of these Rūs immigrants on the future development of Russia. One party, referred to as the Normanists, suggest they were fundamental to the foundation of the major European cities of western Russia. Others, the anti-Normanists, insist that the Russian State is of mainly Slavic origin. These arguments sometimes seem to be based more on modern nationalist rhetoric than any reasoned historical argument.

In Nestor's account three brothers were with the party. The eldest, Rurik, settled in Novgorod (Holmgarðr in Norse) while the other two, Sineus and Truvor, settled in Beloozero and Izborsk respectively. The death of the latter two in the years following left Rurik as the sole survivor. These Varangians played a key part in the foundation or at least the development of important settlements such as Novgorod, Smolensk and Kiev but how long they retained their underlying Scandinavian character is a matter of conjecture. However, delegations to Constantinople during the tenth century still show a majority of the delegates with Scandinavian names. Further, the existence of an eleventh-century church dedicated to the archetypal Viking saint, Óláfr, in Novgorod suggests that attachments to 'home' Viking territories remained strong.

In Russia, Scandinavians showed an aptitude for assimilating themselves with the local population when they moved in, as they would later in areas like the 'Danelaw' in England or Normandy in Francia. One thing that is of significance though is that the Vikings in Russia were essentially acting in a different way than those involved in the raids on Western Europe. There were no monasteries to ransack and pillage there, rather the activities of the Vikings in this area were in the nature of trading, though a significant part of that was in the harsh world of slave trading. That said, the threat posed by the Vikings was still very real in the east. In 860, a Rūs raiding force attacked Constantinople and devastated its suburbs, though the city's massive walls, which had successfully resisted every attack launched against them for centuries, yet again proved impervious. The city's patriarch, Photios, emulated Alcuin and reasoned that they were a punishment sent by God as chastisement for his sinful flock. God was not so angry though according to the *Russian Primary Chronicle* as He sent a storm to scatter the Viking fleet, driving a number of ships ashore where their crews were promptly killed.

The following year, the Slavic apostles Cyril and his brother Methodius tried to convert the Rūs to the Christian faith. They did not succeed in fulfilling this objective, but their mission did help to establish commercial relationships between the Rūs and Constantinople. In the following century, trade agreements were set up between the Byzantines and the Rūs. Ultimately the Rūs would become assimilated by the Slavic-speaking

Russians, in the process giving their name to the country and the people that ultimately absorbed them; but that appears to have been a process that took some time.

Weland and the Franks

A raider named Weland provided Charles the Bald in Francia with a formidable challenge. Charles was faced with a double threat. As well as Weland's forays along the Somme he also had to contend with another band of raiders who used the isle of Oissel upstream from Rouen on the Seine as their base. He attempted with limited success to play the two war bands off against each other.

This took place in 860, a very disturbing year for Francia. In one extraordinary incident, one of the competing Frankish kings who now ruled different parts of Charlemagne's empire, Lothar II, forced his wife Theutberga to enter a convent after she confessed to having had sodomite intercourse with her brother; a totally trumped-up charge made so that he could escape from a marriage he had entered into for political reasons, and which was now no longer necessary. The wronged woman's plea that 'I will say whatever they want – not because it's true but because I fear for my life' still has the capacity to generate empathy to the point of outrage well over a millennium later.[47] At least in this case, the aggrieved party had the last say as a few years later Lothar was forced to take her back and subsequently died before he was able to bring his continuing plans to divorce her to a successful conclusion. Eclipses of both the sun and moon were also mentioned by the annalist as adding to the strange atmosphere that seemed to cloak the land, an ominous portent for the period ahead and a typical chroniclers' device to build the tension when monumental events were about to happen.

Charles induced Weland to take on the opposing Viking band on the Seine with a promised gift of 3,000 lbs of silver. He imposed taxes widely in Francia in his efforts to raise money to deal with the Viking threat, even very small-scale traders being subject to assessment and payment of dues which they had escaped from in the past. He was unable to make good on the payment in a timely fashion though and, growing frustrated, Weland made the short hop over the English Channel, landing on the Hampshire coast. This announced increased danger for the Anglo-Saxon kingdoms. Winchester, the major city of Wessex, was unprepared and was sacked. Heavily laden with the plunder to which they had helped themselves, the Viking force lumbered back from Winchester towards their ships. The Vikings made a habit of launching quick hit-and-run raids, retreating before their victims could coordinate a response. This time, however, something went wrong. Weland and his men were unprepared when local *fyrds,* led by the ealdormen Osric of Hampshire and Æthelwulf of

Berkshire, fell on them. Weland escaped the slaughter that followed but his booty and many of his men did not. Those who survived were said to have '[taken] to flight like women'.[48]

If Weland was chastened by this reverse he did not show it. He made his way back to Francia where he took on the Seine raiders who were still there and managed to obtain money from them too; he received 6,000 lbs of silver from them and the threat to Charles increased rather than diminished. Paris was burned again in 861 and the churches of Saints Vincent and Germain were destroyed, as was Thérrouane. The Frankish annalists of these bitter times imply that their kings were largely powerless to predict and stop the attacks.

This story had an unexpected ending; Weland ended up as Charles's liegeman. He converted to Christianity with his wife and sons, as many other Vikings would do; a required sign of conformity if such a war chieftain were to gain acceptance. Perhaps he was tiring of wandering or merely saw the opportunity for short-term gain. However, he did not enjoy this relative stability for long. He was accused of duplicity by two of his own men to Charles; an accusation that may not have been without merit given his past history. Weland angrily rebuffed his accusers and demanded satisfaction by single combat. In the duel that followed with one of them, Weland was killed.[49]

Attacks from Viking raiders in Francia continued and caused great distress, especially when launched against venerated Christian sites. King Charles was aghast when he received news in 863 that Poitiers had been attacked. The city paid a ransom to be spared but it did not save the church of St Hilaire, which was outside its walls. Charles ordered the Aquitanians to launch a vigorous response against the raiders who were responsible for this outrage (they were lukewarm subjects so he probably enjoyed the opportunity to criticise them). Another Viking attack on Angoulême left its count dead, though a number of the attackers were also killed in the bitter fight.

Reading the *Annals of St Bertin,* this period in Frankish history was one of seemingly relentless chaos. The annalist paints a picture of a country at war with itself. The Vikings do not seem to have been the prime creators of the chaos – the Franks with their several competing kings and opportunistic warlords did a very good job of causing this on their own – but they were certainly prime beneficiaries of it. During a large raid up the Loire in 865, the important monastic establishments at Fleury and at Orléans were ransacked. The raiders tried to set the church of the Holy Cross ablaze but were unable to do so, not because the citizens stopped them but simply because the building stubbornly refused to go up in smoke.

The Loire Vikings returned to Poitiers later that year, causing more damage there. But in what was presumably an attack that caught the raiders by surprise, 500 of these men were later killed when a force led by Count Robert of Angers fell on them, allegedly without him losing one single man in the battle. The banners and weapons of the dead Vikings were sent to Charles, rare trophies of victory in these difficult times. It was notable how the fighting was now increasingly done on behalf of the Carolingians by the counts rather than the men being led into battle by their kings, a subtle but important change in the way that things were done in the empire.

However, there was further bad news from elsewhere to offset these rare glad tidings. While Charles was visiting his brother Louis, king of the Germans, in Cologne, Viking raiders fell on the hallowed monastery of St Denis near Paris, a site so sacred to the Franks that this action caused particular angst and led to the dismissal of those who were ostensibly responsible for its defence. Swooping down on it on 18 October, the raiders stayed there for twenty days, systematically looting it over that period and methodically carrying their booty to their ships, anchored nearby. They were completely unmolested as they did so and were ultimately bought off by Charles with a payment of 4,000 lbs of silver. Defensive measures put in place by Charles were clearly not working. In recognition of this, soon afterwards Charles made provision for the erection of stone defences around the abbey.

While Charles was powerless to prevent this latest insult, or even avenge it, the annalist of St Bertin suggests that the perpetrators of this heinous act received punishment from a higher authority. He wrote that 'the Northmen who had sacked St Denis became ill with various ailments. Some went mad, some were covered in sores, some discharged their guts with a watery flow through their arses: and so they died'.[50] Despite the vicious vividness of this punishment as described by the writer, it seemed Charles could do little, without divine intervention, to right the wrong that had been committed.

The Loire Vikings were still receiving help from local allies. Brittany at that time was a frequent source of tension for the Frankish kings. An alliance of 400 Loire Vikings and Breton warriors fell on Le Mans, moving on the city on horseback, and sacked it without resistance. However, another group of raiders further south led by a chief called Sigfred was badly mauled by an Aquitanian force on the River Charente, the St Bertin annalist saying that 400 of them were killed in the fight while the rest fled back to their ships. The Franks were being gradually ground down by these frequent raids. The negotiations between the Vikings and Charles were not between two parties in an equal bargaining position; the raiders could pretty much extract what they wanted at this stage. Charles was forced to agree that any slave that had escaped from the Vikings should either be handed back or ransomed. In addition, a price was agreed by which the Vikings would be compensated for any of their number that had been killed. But then there was a change in direction. For the next few years, the annalist of St Bertin, who for the preceding period makes frequent mentions of Viking raids, makes noticeably fewer references to them. There were, it is true, some mentions from time to time in the period between 867 and 870, for example of the 'Loire Northmen' or of an apostate monk who had abandoned the faith and gone to live with them who was beheaded as punishment for his crime when he was captured. But such references are markedly less frequent.

Perhaps, after all, the bridge fortifications constructed on Charles's orders were having a deterrent effect and encouraging the raiders to shift their attention elsewhere. Gradually, and against stiff odds, Charles was introducing a much greater degree of order into Frankish affairs though continuing dynastic squabbling and plotting meant that it remained an uphill struggle for him. The legacy of his grandfather Charlemagne was proving hard to live up to.

The Great Heathen Army arrives

In 865 there was a quantum leap forward in terms of the scale of the Viking attack on England.[51] Hundreds of ships descended on Kent, apparently under the command of three sons of Ragnar Lodbrok: Halfdan, Ubba and Ivarr; writing about a century later, the chronicler Æthelweard intimates that the latter (whom he calls Inwaer) was the principal leader.[52] England was about to find itself under a sustained attack that would threaten the very existence of all the Anglo-Saxon kingdoms.

It is likely that economic and political reasons underlay this change in direction. Land brought long-term wealth in a way that booty did not. It produced financial benefits on an ongoing basis. Rents could be charged, and produce and labour taken as tax by those fortunate enough to be landlords; and if a man owned a great deal of land then he was financially secure for life, which was not the case when he was reliant on occasional inflows of loot from raiding. Politically, men may have been forced to seek their fortunes outside of Scandinavia by the increasingly assertive actions of power-hungry leaders such as Harald Fairhair; but this might not have been a purely negative example to follow – those on the receiving end of these actions may have been inspired to emulate them elsewhere.

The relative decline in activity in Francia suggests that the Vikings had diverted their efforts from there to England. However, Ivarr had been active in Ireland for at least a decade in tandem with his brother Amlaib/ Óláfr, so there may well have been some combining of forces from both Francia and Ireland taking place in the attacks on England. If Ivarr was indeed the 'Boneless' – and that is not certain – then if ever a man lived up to the stereotype of a Viking raider, it was him. There was his exotic nickname for one thing, associated as it was with a suggestion of a horrific deformity, which would no doubt have added to the sense of terror his name generated. For another, he had been involved in a life of almost constant raiding for a decade and more. His involvement in England was just the latest in a series of escapades in which he had played a leading part.

The *Historia de Sancto Cuthberto,* a near-contemporary account of the times in the region and diocese in which the saint had been active (written down in its current surviving version in the tenth or eleventh century), calls these Viking raiders *Scaldingi,* which it has been suggested refers to a point of origin for the raiders of the River Scheldt – *Scaldis* in Latin.[53] This again implies that there were several Viking forces acting simultaneously in Francia, for while the *Scaldingi* turned their attention to England, the Loire force remained active on the other side of the English Channel.

Kent, which was plundered even though a tribute payment had been made by the locals to stop such an occurrence (the first recorded payment of what later became generically known as 'Danegeld' in England), was just a stopping-off point. The raiders moved on to East Anglia, then ruled by King Edmund. Little is known about his early career, though legends would later develop to fill in a few of the gaps; but he had probably been king for about a decade when the terrifying phenomenon of this Viking force appeared. There was initially no conflict. The leaders of what became known as the Great Heathen Army – *se mycel hæpen here* – made their way confidently to Edmund's court; they knew that they were in a dominant military position and the East Anglians had no viable way of resisting them.[54] They demanded horses, food and general provisions and before long they were joined by reinforcements from Francia who had heard that their compatriots had arrived in East Anglia.

There was something ominously different about this Viking host when compared to previous expeditions to England. This one had an air of permanence about it, as if determined to stay for the long term. Bishop Asser, King Alfred's later biographer, tells us that the Vikings were provided with many horses from the well-stocked royal studs of East Anglia. In the process, he hints at something that is often overlooked when discussing the Vikings; they were fine horsemen as well as seafarers. The force that was building up its strength in East Anglia was substantially a mounted one. This did not mean that the Viking army would fight as cavalry in a pitched battle; but with their horses they would be able to move swiftly around England, enabling them to launch surprise attacks inland just as surely as their ships allowed them to do on the coast.[55]

East Anglia, it transpired, was not primarily what this large army was here for – at least not for now. It was adjacent to the rich kingdom of Mercia. The attractiveness of Mercia's wealth to the Vikings was magnified by the declining state of the kingdom. Its king, Burgred, had enjoyed a mixed record militarily and the Vikings scented blood. Mercia seemed ripe for the taking; but Mercia was also not the immediate target. Further north was the kingdom of Northumbria, at the time claimed by a usurper, Ælle. Legend asserts that he was responsible for the death of the enigmatic Ragnar Lodbrok by having him thrown into a pit of snakes. Faced with this unpleasant death, Ragnar defiantly declaimed that 'the piglets would grunt now if they knew what the old pig suffers'.[56] The 'piglets', his sons, would indeed soon be seeking revenge if the saga writers are to be believed.

Northumbria covered a large territory stretching from the Humber to the Firth of Forth, though the northern segment, 'Bernicia', operated in an autonomous fashion. The main city of the southern segment, 'Deira', was York. As autumnal winds descended on the city on Friday 1 November 866, it was crowded for the important religious festival of All Saints' Day. It was packed with people, and therefore wealth. Probably it was weakly guarded given the distraction of the holy festival; predatory Viking forces closing in on the city were very likely well aware of this fact. Inside the city at the time was not only Ælle but the rival king of Northumbria with whom he remained in competition, Osbert (the *Historia de Sancto Cuthberto* says that the two men were actually brothers). Northumbria had descended into political chaos because of the fighting between the two factions; or, as Asser put it, it was in 'a great dispute, fomented by the devil'.[57] Out of the blue, a Viking army shipped up the east coast of England and then up the River Humber, and descended on York. The blow was an overwhelming one. The streets were made slippery by the blood of slaughtered residents and visitors.

In the confusion, the two rival kings of Northumbria both managed to escape. They were so stunned by the descent of Ivarr and his Viking army that they subsequently put aside their differences and combined their forces.[58] Falling on York, they forced the Viking warriors who faced up to them outside the city walls back inside. It was Palm Sunday 867 – another important Christian festival – when they returned, and a wonderful victory seemed to be close at hand for the Northumbrians (other accounts give a slightly different date, suggesting the battle was fought on the Friday before Palm Sunday).[59] It was, though, a mirage. Inside, the streets were crowded, and it was difficult for the Northumbrian soldiers to maintain their cohesion. The Vikings in the city fought back ferociously and in the close quarter scrimmaging that followed in the tightly packed streets they hacked and slashed their way on top. By the end of the day, the Northumbrian army had been obliterated. Both of the rival kings were dead as well as eight ealdormen. According to the account of Asser, this was a crushing Viking victory.

And so, the Viking city of Jorvik was born, although the victors appointed a local man, Ecgbert, as the next king of Northumbria, perhaps thinking that it should be easier to govern that way (a strategy they later repeated in Mercia and probably in East Anglia too). Conceivably the Vikings were taking full advantage of a succession dispute and hoped to gain by supporting Ecgbert;[60] certainly, they played that card on other occasions, not only in England but also in Ireland, Francia and even Scandinavia. The later account of these events written up by Symeon of Durham in the early twelfth century suggests that Northumbria was now split into two with Deira, based around York, becoming a Danish kingdom and the northern segment, Bernicia, remaining Northumbrian. However, some historians are sceptical of this interpretation, suggesting that Symeon interpolated this for his own ulterior motives.[61] But what cannot be disputed is that the fall of York started a chain reaction at the end of which the Anglo-Saxon kingdom of Northumbria had largely disintegrated.

The death of Ælle became a core part of Viking legend. In some accounts, he was captured alive and, in revenge for his killing of Ragnar Lodbrok, he was put to death by the semi-mythical Viking leader's sons in one of the most painful and brutal ways imaginable. He was subjected to the ordeal of the blood eagle; his body was slashed open, his ribcage smashed apart and his lungs were pulled out and splayed across his torso in a macabre symbolic representation of an eagle. Unfortunately (or perhaps from Ælle's perspective very fortunately indeed) there is much about this story that does not ring true. The idea that Ragnar was in the first instance done to death in a pit of venomous snakes seems hugely improbable; Britain has no very venomous snakes to deliver such a dramatic demise. Then there was Ælle's brief reign to consider, hardly long enough to make an enemy of Ragnar and his sons. The whole account has the smell of a very tall tale, the 'blood-eagling' of Ælle included. That said, this violent method of execution is referred to elsewhere in the sagas, such as when Earl Einar of Orkney used it against his rival Halfdan Long-Leg.[62]

Mercia was the next kingdom in the sights of Ivarr and his men. The blow soon fell, and it was Nottingham that felt it. It stands on the River Trent, which eventually flows out into the Humber Estuary, a perfect site for Viking raiders. King Burgred was aware he was vulnerable and had already sought to strengthen himself politically through marriage. He had married a West Saxon princess and had then tied himself still more closely to that dynasty by arranging for the marriage of a Mercian noblewoman, Ealhswith, to a young prince of the royal house of Wessex called Alfred. So, when Nottingham was attacked, an Anglo-Saxon army was raised containing warriors from both Mercia and Wessex and it moved on the town. Ivarr however had no intention of risking his position in open battle. He stayed secure behind the defences of Nottingham, fully prepared to wait out the storm. Eventually Ivarr was bought off by tribute from Mercia. He got what he wanted, a handsome share of the riches of Mercia without having to fight very hard for it. He then returned to Jorvik for a while, allowing him to secure the Viking position there.

The *ASC* is silent on the price paid to persuade the Vikings to move on from Nottingham. It is not difficult to understand why. It was compiled in the later reign of King Alfred; it did not fit with its storyline to explain in detail how Alfred, the hero of the piece, had participated, even indirectly, in such a demeaning experience. However, the cost was probably exorbitant. Payments in gold and silver ranging from 2,000 to 12,000 lbs have been recorded from Francia at around the same period, all humiliatingly counted out under the watchful eyes of Viking supervisors with their ubiquitous scales for weighing out the precious metals. There would also likely be substantial amounts of food that would need to be handed over to provide the raiders with provisions to sustain them through the winter (payments made in wine and cider are sometimes mentioned in Continental accounts).[63]

The Vikings then returned to East Anglia. There were some rich religious foundations to attract them there, such as at Peterborough (*Medehamstede*) which was thoroughly plundered – with a number of monks slaughtered in the process. Inside the magnificent twelfth-century (and later) walls of Peterborough Cathedral is a stone box with twelve carved figures on its sides. Known as the Hedda Stone after an abbot of that name, it was long believed to mark the burial site of the monks slaughtered in the Viking raid. Recent research now suggests it predates any such raid by about seventy years (though this does not prevent some internet sites continuing to perpetuate the Viking link). It is nevertheless a mute witness to the atrocities committed by the Vikings on their way back to East Anglia.

They then made their way to the court of King Edmund. The Vikings set up camp at Thetford, an ideal place for a base as it was both close to the Wash and the sea and also a major road network as it was on the Icknield Way, the ancient track which moved west towards both Mercia and Wessex. Ivarr sent a message to Edmund. The story is picked up by a tenth-century chronicler, Abbo, abbot of Fleury, a religious house near Orléans. Though Abbo's words, in significant part hagiographical, dress the story up quite a bit, the substance of what he says suggests that the Vikings were again after tribute. For whatever reason, it was not forthcoming. Shortly thereafter, Edmund was dead. Asser gives him a straightforward, uncomplicated end, dying in battle at Hoxne with many of his men. However, this was clearly not good enough for Abbo. He makes Edmund a champion of his faith, refusing to kowtow to pagan Vikings and being shot through with arrows for his pains. It was the death of a Christian martyr, modelled on the painful demise of St Sebastian as Abbo intimates it to be.[64] Abbo also suggests that the death throes of Edmund mirrored those of Christ himself. He put responsibility for Edmund's death at Ivarr's feet, as does the chronicler Æthelweard who wrote his account at approximately the same time, a hundred years or so after the event.[65] The saga called the *Tale of Ragnar's Sons* also makes Ivarr the prime motivator of the king's death, though he did not personally do the killing.[66]

In Abbo's account, Edmund's head was roughly cut off and thrown into a wood. Here it gained the protection of a guardian wolf (perhaps evidencing a supernatural link to the old 'Wulffing' royal dynasty of East Anglia). Eventually, Edmund's followers were led to his remains by a voice calling out to them from the trees. Abbo says that it emanated from the decapitated head itself. They found it between the paws of the wolf. They carried their precious if gruesome relic away in solemn procession, being followed dolefully by the wolf until they reached their destination. Once there, the animal sentinel turned around and made its way back into the wood.

It was Abbo's rather more flamboyant version that seized the imaginations of later generations. Among these were none other than the Vikings themselves. When in the future they themselves began to adopt Christianity in large numbers, they regularly contributed to the Abbey of St Edmund's, as if possessed by an enormous guilty conscience over their part in the death of the martyr king. Traditions would even grow up that the ghost of Edmund was responsible for the death of the later Viking warlord Sveinn Forkbeard, something that came to be regarded as the martyred king's 'defining miracle' and which helped to establish him as one of medieval England's foremost saints.[67] The killing of King Edmund had a profound effect on future English culture and developed its own particular martyrology that resonated down the centuries. Over half a century later, Dunstan, one of the greatest English clerics and saints of the Middle Ages, would be moved by hearing the account of the king's death related by Edmund's own armour bearer, presumably by then a very old man.[68] It also affected later Viking thinking. The later Danish king of England and Denmark, Cnut the Great, made large gifts to the abbey at Bury St Edmunds, possibly in atonement for the sins of his Viking forefathers. Long before then, coins were issued in Viking East Anglia in 895 with the legend 'St Edmund the King' on them. These 'memorial pennies' circulated as far north as York and were produced in very large numbers. Remarkably, within twenty-five years of killing him, it was as if the Vikings were claiming Edmund as one of their own.[69]

What happened next in East Anglia is unfortunately obscure. There is nothing in the narrative historical record to tell us more but numismatic evidence from recovered coins is intriguing. Coins have been found with the very Anglo-Saxon names of Æthelred and Oswald on them. These items have design similarities to some found relating to Edmund's reign and also to coins issued in areas under Viking rule. The most likely scenario is that these men were appointees of the successful Scandinavian army that removed Edmund from the scene; it is after all unlikely that the conquerors would meekly allow East Anglia to revert to independent English rule after their victory.[70]

Ivarr's attention was then distracted northward. Óláfr the White and Ivarr had worked in collaboration before and would do so again. In 870, they laid siege to the great British fortress that stood on Dumbarton Rock, 'The Rock of Clyde', dominating the entrance to the river and standing sentinel over the northern gateway to the Irish Sea. It took them four months but at the end of that period, when the defenders had run out of water, they took and ransacked it. The long duration of the siege and its determined prosecution suggests that the aim of the attack was the neutralisation of Dumbarton, the seat of Strathclyde power, rather than plunder alone. It certainly weakened Strathclyde; two years later, Constantin of the Picts apparently had Arthal, king of Strathclyde, murdered, even though the two families were related by marriage and it does not seem unreasonable to assume that the Picts were taking advantage of the reversal suffered by their neighbours. This was the first recorded Viking attack on the then-independent kingdom of Strathclyde. However, given the proximity of the region to Viking sea lanes off the west coast of Scotland and the presence of monasteries potentially attracting avaricious Scandinavians, it would be a surprise if the Britons living there had not previously been on the sharp end of Viking raids.[71] Probably the Vikings saw Strathclyde as a block to further expansion and sought to undermine it as a regional power.

When the raiders returned to Dublin, they had with them 200 ships, full to the gunwales with English, Strathclyde 'Welsh', Scottish and Pictish slaves, many of them probably destined for resale on the lucrative international market. It was a major victory and a serious setback for the ruling regime in Strathclyde. However, a kingdom of Strathclyde did continue to live on, though it was much weakened by this setback and was no longer ruled from the totemic site of Dumbarton but further up the Clyde at Govan. With the move from *Alt Clut,* the Rock of Clyde, the symbolic seat of the region was now in the Lower Valley of the Clyde, *Strat Clut,* hence the name Strathclyde.[72]

The attack on Wessex

Despite Ivarr's northern foray, the Vikings were far from finished in England, where now only Wessex remained unconquered by them.

The fighting that broke out in Wessex in late 870 and reached its climax in 871 was perhaps the most ferocious that had been seen in England since the Roman invasion of nearly a millennium before, and it came close to bringing Wessex, and what was left of Anglo-Saxon England, to its knees. The Danish army was led by Halfdan, a possible brother of that same Ivarr who had made his name in Ireland and therefore another supposed son of the semi-mythical Ragnar Lodbrok, alongside another Danish 'king', Bagsecg.

This huge raid into Wessex began when Halfdan and Bagsecg made their way to one of the royal estates – the *villae regiae* – at Reading, probably arriving from East Anglia. As Christmas was approaching, and winter was not normally a season for warfare, perhaps the defenders were caught off guard and certainly it was quickly enough in Viking hands. Halfdan set up defensive ramparts and waited for reinforcements to join him by river; the raiders were located at the confluence of the Kennet and the Thames, perfectly positioned for Viking longships to sail up and link with other forces launching a pincer movement overland. The Danes dug a ditch between the two rivers, which was possibly also moated. Its site was later identified by local historians as being at the Plummery Ditch; if this is correct then it has been estimated, based on the ground potentially enclosed, that it would hold 1,000 men.[73]

Reading, as a royal estate, was well stocked with supplies for the winter months that lay ahead as the food renders, the *feorm,* for the local district would probably have been stored there. Nearby was the important abbey at Abingdon, very likely similarly well supplied and also a tempting target. But Halfdan was soon forced back on the defensive. One of his compatriots, Jarl Sidroc, went out on New Years' Eve on a foraging mission and was caught by surprise when a local defence force led by Æthelwulf, the ealdorman of Berkshire, fell on him at Englefield. Æthelwulf was a man of great reputation, having fought Vikings for a number of years with some success. Jarl Sidroc and many of his men were cut down. The survivors from among them fled back to Reading, no doubt alarming those inside the Viking camp and giving added energy to their attempts to strengthen their fortifications. Their fears were confirmed when a few days later a larger West Saxon force appeared at the gates, presumably having received news of the success at Englefield and keen to finish off the job.

The West Saxon position appeared still stronger when some Vikings caught outside the camp were killed. However, those Vikings inside reacted: 'like wolves they burst out of all the gates and joined battle with all their might'.[74] Ealdorman Æthelwulf was among those who died in the battle that followed; his body was taken back to Northworthy (later Derby) for honourable Christian burial. The Saxon forces were forced to flee and were able to make good their escape only because their knowledge of local topography exceeded that of the Vikings. The Saxons, led by their king Æthelred and his younger brother Alfred, forded a river crossing at Twyford near Reading and the Vikings, unaware of the existence of it, did not follow them; a lucky escape for the Wessex men. Both forces however were still largely intact, meaning that these were likely to be just the opening sorties of a longer campaign.

On 8 January 871, Halfdan and his men left Reading, moving north-west. They may have been headed for either Wallingford, a crucial crossing point of the Thames, or Abingdon with its wealthy abbey. They had gone about 12 miles when they saw in front of them a substantial Saxon army, blocking their way in a strong position. However, the Vikings held the higher ground. Between the two forces was a solitary thorn tree, which would be the focal point of the battle that followed.

Halfdan divided his force into two. There was a small gap between the Saxon force and the nearby river, which one force probed in an attempt to outflank the Saxon shield wall. King Æthelred, a devout man, was allegedly at his prayers leaving the initial defence to his younger brother Alfred. Alfred was faced with a predicament. One wing of the Viking army, that in which the leading jarls were present, was advancing down the hill towards him. His brother was as yet nowhere to be seen. He could not stand still and must either retreat or go on to the offensive. Alfred was by Asser's account often ill and of a delicate disposition. Yet these exterior weaknesses concealed the heart of a lion (at least according to his chronicler supporters). Against the odds, Alfred charged up the hill against the enemy. It was a brave move, especially as Alfred and the king represented the last surviving senior members of the royal Wessex bloodline. But on that day, fortune favoured the bold. When Æthelred then committed his men to battle, the Vikings were overwhelmed. The Saxon reinforcements crashed into the exposed flanks of the Viking army which was busy trying to engulf Alfred's smaller force. It was the Viking force that broke and fled.

Asser, whose main objective was to emphasise Alfred's achievements, says that he fought 'like a wild boar'. He was also, he intimates, the man who was responsible for the tactical organisation of the troops. Although Halfdan managed to escape to fight another day, Bagsecg and a number of Danish jarls did not: these were presumably in the right wing of the army that moved against Alfred. Halfdan and his reduced force returned to Reading to consider their next move, enthusiastically pursued by the triumphant Saxon forces. That next move was a bold one as they marched further west into Wessex; either the Saxon army had by now gone home, or they were bypassed. The Battle of Ashdown ('the hill of the ash', named after the tree at the epicentre of the battlefield) was clearly not decisive whatever Anglo-Saxon chroniclers might suggest. The Vikings moved to Basing, dangerously near Winchester and its riches. This time, the Vikings held the 'place of slaughter' and Æthelred and Alfred were forced to regroup again.[75] To compound the difficulty, Asser mentions that more warriors now arrived from overseas to reinforce the Viking force in England.[76]

There was a short breathing space while both sides regathered their strength. During this interlude, Æthelred and Alfred reached a crucial agreement: if either man should die in the near future then his surviving brother would inherit all, including if relevant the kingship. Æthelred had young children but it would be a disaster if they should accede to the crown at such a tender age. If he should die, Alfred would become king of Wessex.[77] He was of suitable age and had already cut his teeth in battle; and his marriage to Ealhswith was already bearing fruit, though it was a daughter rather than a son who had been born to them. Her name was Æthelflaed and her part in the Viking story was to be an unexpectedly prominent one.

Towards the end of March 871, a further battle was fought at 'Meretun' (Asser does not mention this battle at all, perhaps as the ultimate outcome did not fit into his scheme of bolstering the reputation of his subject though it would effectively make him king).[78] It was a hard-fought battle, with first one side, then the other, holding the upper hand. But at the end of it all, it was the Vikings who held the advantage. There were great losses on both sides. The Battle of 'Meretun' was possibly fought on Martin Down, on the borders of Hampshire, Wiltshire and Dorset: such intersection points often being a place of assembly for the Anglo-Saxon militias or *fyrds*. Its position on downland was also the type of spot commonly used by Anglo-Saxon forces between 800 and 1066: one survey suggested that of fifty-two battles known to have been fought in this period, sixteen, or around 30 per cent, were in such places.[79] This potential location for the Battle of 'Meretun' was adjacent to an old Roman road, the Ackling Dyke, which existed well into Saxon times, again adding credence to its identification as the site of the battle. Æthelred may well have been mortally wounded in the battle and died shortly after, possibly through his injuries (though this is not specifically stated in the sources). He was buried in Wimborne, at the far end of the Roman road where there was a double monastery, an establishment composed of monks and nuns headed by an abbess and often associated with royal patronage, as was certainly the case here.

Soon after his brother's burial, terrible news reached Alfred. The Vikings were back and moving on Wilton, another royal estate in Wiltshire. It was not far off the Ackling Dyke and he was able to gather together his forces and march quickly up it to face the threat. But at Wilton the Vikings again won the battle. The ASC mentions that nine battles were fought that year but only six of those were named and of those only two were victories for the West Saxons; as has been stated by a modern historian, it would be very surprising if the three others that were not mentioned were not Viking triumphs.[80]

Among the other prominent West Saxon casualties at Meretun was Heahmund, bishop of Sherborne. The presence of a prominent churchman in the battle lines was by no means unique at the time and may have been justified in part by the fact that this was presented as a fight in an ongoing war between Christendom and paganism. But even then, not all churchmen thought the involvement of their brethren in battle was justifiable; Hincmar, Archbishop of Rheims, was one prominent figure who objected to his bishops taking part in such events.[81] However, he had a short memory as he had previously been on such expeditions himself.[82]

The *ASC* also implies that there were other skirmishes in which Alfred took part. It is at its most frustrating here as it implies that a major war was taking place but only hints at the details, perhaps because they were not favourable in their outcomes as far as their hero, Alfred, was concerned. Asser suggests that the final fight at Wilton was a close-run thing and that the Vikings only won the battle when they fled and were followed by such a small force of pursuers that they realised what a numerical advantage they enjoyed. They were able to turn defeat into victory by turning around and overwhelming their pursuers. But again, this could be a case of special pleading on behalf of the tale's hero, Alfred.

At some time in the first half of 871, a 'summer fleet' of Vikings arrived, reinforcements for Halfdan. The late tenth-century chronicler Æthelweard makes an important reference to a battle against these new arrivals which no other account talks of.[83] It was apparently fought by a small force while the new king was absent, possibly attending to the funeral arrangements for his brother. This new action was hard-fought but indecisive. Most significantly perhaps, a new war leader had arrived on the Vikings' side. His name was Guthrum and he would almost prove to be Alfred's nemesis.

This campaign eventually ended in a truce between Wessex and the raiders. In this instance, the silence in Anglo-Saxon sources as to the background to this situation is deafening. Given the resources available to them and the fact that they were more often than not winning against Saxon forces, it seems certain that the raiders were being bought off, an early instance in England of what in much later times became known as *Danegeld*. Certainly, by the following year the Vikings were wintering in London, in Mercia rather than Wessex. They may have developed a healthy respect for the doggedness of their adversaries in Wessex and were happy to turn their attentions to potentially easier targets. However, the progress that the Vikings had made could not be ignored; that winter Halfdan was issuing coins in his own name in London. That said, their losses had also been significant; Æthelweard states that they had lost eleven earls and one king in the campaign.[84]

These events only bought time for Alfred, nothing more. He was heavy-handed in raising money to buy off the Vikings, as a result of which he incurred the enmity of the Church. But Halfdan and his new co-leader Guthrum had for now scented blood elsewhere. Mercia had been the prominent kingdom in England but was now perceived to be weak. Its king, Burgred, seemed overwhelmed at the size of the challenge facing his people and powerless to do anything about the presence of the Vikings; he was forced to buy them off too. In the meantime, Halfdan and Guthrum were perfectly placed in Lundenwic to keep an eye on what was happening in both Mercia and Wessex.

The Great Heathen Army divides

Some of the Viking force in England spent the winter of 872/873 in Lindsey in what is now Lincolnshire and was then part of Mercia. Burgred of Mercia, whose power and spirit seemed to be completely broken, fled and died in exile in Rome. The alliance with Wessex was no longer functional; both Mercia and Wessex were powerless to support each other and had to rely on their own resources to survive. Poor Burgred, a largely forgotten victim of the Vikings, was buried in the Church of the Sancto Spirito in Sassia on the west bank of the Tiber in the Saxon Quarter, a place founded by King Ine of Wessex when he abdicated and went to Rome to live out his last days a century and a half before.

A puppet ruler, Ceolwulf, was installed by the Vikings in Burgred's place; he apparently swore oaths to support his Scandinavian masters and handed over hostages as surety for his good, or at least compliant, behaviour, though the *ASC* seems to have taken umbrage at Ceolwulf's assumption of power from the outset and as a result may have exaggerated his status as a turncoat. His name was the same as that of a former Mercian king and very similar to another called Cenwulf. At the time, members of a ruling Mercian dynasty were conventionally given names that were identifiable with those of their ancestors. The deposed Burgred, his name suggests, was not of that same bloodline as Cenwulf. Again, it appears that the Vikings were siding with a rival claimant in a succession dispute to gain advantage from the situation.

The effective acquisition of Mercia, even if it retained a nominal Mercian ruler, was very important to the Vikings in England as it secured a safe land passage from their territories in East Anglia right the way up to Northumbria. There was a significant impact on the everyday life of the Mercian people. A document from 872 made out on behalf of Wærferth, bishop of Worcester, involving the renting out of land, noted that this was needed because of the 'pressing affliction and immense tribute of the barbarians' and without these actions he would be unable to pay.[85] It was a precursor of things to come.

The Vikings then moved up the Trent to Repton where they set up their base for the winter of 873/4. This was a site of great symbolic significance to the Mercians as a royal mausoleum was located there, as well as an important double monastery. Archaeology has helped immensely in interpreting what took place there. It has revealed evidence of the Viking camp at Repton as well as mass graves of Viking warriors. A major dig took place at Repton between 1974 and 1988. This concluded that a D-shaped set of ramparts were set up as a defensive measure, a feature typical of many contemporary Viking fortifications, such as some found in Ireland in the shape of the *longphuirt*. The shape is the result of one side being anchored on the relatively straight banks of a river, lake or seafront where the Viking ships were moored while the other three sides were to landward and were surrounded by ramparts. It has been suggested that the size of the site indicates a force of hundreds rather than thousands.[86] The church at Repton formed an integral part of these defences, possibly as a strongpoint.

The overall style of defensive enclosure echoes other examples found in Scandinavia, such as that at Hedeby. A stone cross at Repton had been broken up and buried, as if someone there no longer had much time for it (echoing the treatment of Christian monuments at Portmahomack). Viking weapons such as swords and axes were also found.

The remains of one of those buried there were prosaically designated as skeleton number 511. A man of around thirty-five to forty years of age, he had died extremely violently. He had been severely wounded by a hack across the top of his legs, probably when he had already been grounded. The most probable explanation of the injuries he suffered was that he had been castrated when prone; this was a particularly gruesome death or dismemberment soon afterwards. Significantly, when he was buried a boar's tusk was placed between his legs as if replacing part of his anatomy that was no longer there (there was also the humerus of a jackdaw present). To give a clear sign of his cultural affiliations, the dead man had been buried with a Thor's Hammer, a tell-tale sign of Viking connections and beliefs as surely as a crucifix is for a Christian. Also buried with him was a Viking sword of 'Peterson Type M' in the jargon attached to such objects.[87]

As remarkable in its own way, a mass grave was found in the nearby vicarage garden as long ago as 1686. At the centre was a stone coffin, containing a skeleton allegedly 9 feet long. Later digs found many more human remains but the huge skeleton has since disappeared. Beneath the mass grave were the remains of a building from the seventh or eighth century, which had been built over and of which only the foundations remained. The later excavations in the 1980s found the remains of at least 249 skeletons.[88] There were both men and women interred there, though the archaeologists concluded that many of the latter were probably of

Anglo-Saxon rather than Viking origin. Four coins from 872 and one from 873 were critical to dating the site.

Some of the bones had been reburied after being initially put somewhere else. Radiocarbon dating of the bones places them to between the seventh and the ninth centuries; the range in dating strongly suggests that there are Mercian as well as Viking folk. However, more recent testing suggests that some of the remains were of women from Scandinavia and dated to the late ninth century, so there were not just male warriors present in the camp at Repton.[89] Speculation about who the great 9-foot skeleton might have belonged to has centred, perhaps inevitably, around the legendary Ivarr 'the Boneless'. It is also noteworthy that another contemporary cemetery found not far away at Heath Wood, Ingleby, (about 3 miles off) contained cremations, a burial practice that would have never been used by Christians at the time. However, some historians are unconvinced that Ivarr is buried there, arguing that as such conclusions rely on the mention of him in the later sagas of Ragnar Lodbrok, they should be discounted; in addition, as the seemingly preposterous proportions of the skeleton can no longer be proved, as it has long since disappeared, there is no physical evidence remaining to examine either. They also point out that Ivarr is not mentioned in the *ASC* until after his death and that other contemporary records say little about his career in England.

Some historians suggest that Ivarr returned to Ireland before he died;[90] a view that is supported by reference to such a man in Irish records dying in 873, an Ivarr who was extraordinarily and uniquely described as being *rex Nordmannorum totius Hiberniae et Britanniae* ('king of all the Northmen in Ireland and Britain'). Ivarr's role in the Viking attacks in England in the 870s seems to have been much exaggerated, though it is likely he was prominent in the attacks on England in the previous decade.[91] That said, the saga known as the *Tale of Ragnar's Sons* insists that Ivarr died of old age in England and that he was buried there in a 'howe' (a barrow). The same saga also noted that he had no children for 'he had no lust nor love in him', hence perhaps the unusual nickname, which could crudely imply that he was impotent.[92]

A parting of the ways took place at Repton. By now the Great Army had been campaigning for almost a decade and some had decided that it was time to settle down. Many of Halfdan's men moved to Northumbria where they started to put down roots or, as the *ASC* put it, they 'shared out the land of the Northumbrians and they proceeded to plough and to support themselves'; an excellent example of how a man might be a Viking one day and a farmer the next. But they were not yet prepared to concentrate solely on farming and domestic matters: the *ASC* tells us that from their new base they launched raids against the Picts and the Strathclyde Britons. It is likely that rather than ploughing the land themselves they relied to some extent on the previous tenants of the lands that they had taken over to carry on doing their work.

It is easy for these events to overshadow raids that were taking place elsewhere at the time, particularly as the data for other regions is patchy in comparison with what is available regarding England. The Viking position was still strengthening in Ireland. An early *longphort* had been established at Athlunkard near Limerick by now, though during the tenth century the Vikings would move downriver and set up a settlement on King's Island. As yet archaeological finds relating to this later settlement are in short supply and the main evidence of their involvement in Limerick is from annalistic sources.[93]

Between 865 and 870, raiders from Ireland had been making the short hop across the Irish Sea and attacking areas of Pictland and Strathclyde. Óláfr the White was the main cause of these raids. The important foundation of Coldingham, Berwickshire, dating back to 660 and called by Bede 'the Monastery of Virgins' was destroyed in a raid in 870. It would be defunct as a religious organisation until the late eleventh century when it was finally reconstituted. Roger of Wendover, who wrote his *Flores Historiarum* ('The Flowers of History') in the thirteenth century, told how the nuns of Coldingham cut off their noses so that the raiders would kill rather than ravage them. It is a spine-tingling story but it might be no more than that; such accounts are a standard *topos* of thirteenth-century writing. Another story of the time (i.e. the time that the account was written down, the thirteenth century) told how Richard the Lionheart desired a nun and particularly loved her eyes; when she heard this, she cut them out and sent them to him so that he would leave her alone. This is a reminder of one of our classic challenges in interpreting written accounts of the Vikings and their acts when they were not recorded in some cases until centuries afterwards.

There was a battle at Dollar near Stirling, variously dated to 874 or 875, in which the Vikings triumphed against Constantin, king of the Picts, though Óláfr was by now seemingly already dead, having been killed in obscure circumstances by King Constantin. There are several clues that might help to throw more light on these events. The recent demise of Óláfr may mean that this was a revenge attack; and mention in the *ASC* of Halfdan's foray to Scotland may mean that he and his men were involved in the campaign.

The victorious Viking army stayed in Scotland for a year, making the most of their success. There are later accounts that Constantin was subsequently killed by Vikings, and again one is tempted to speculate that this was in revenge for the death of Óláfr. The event was recorded in the *ASC,* the last time that these records mention the Picts, who faded completely from history shortly afterwards. The sacred relics of Columba

The church at Aller, on the site where the Viking Guthrum was baptised.

Alfred's place of refuge on Athelney on a low hill, marked by a Victorian era monument.

The tomb of Æthelstan in Malmesbury Abbey.

The Brough of Birsay on Orkney, a classic Viking site in an exposed coastal location.

The tenth-century mosque at Cordoba; the city was one of the more exotic locations for a Viking raid.

Right: Dacre, the possible site of where Æthelstan met the kings of Britain at a time of great Viking threat.

Below right: Dingwall in north-east Scotland: this nondescript site in a modern car-park marks the location of the *'Thing'* in one of the most important Viking settlements in the country. The *'Thing'* was an assembly that made decisions on implementing customary law.

Below: Dumbarton Rock: the former capital of Strathclyde and the site of a Viking siege during the time of Ivarr the Boneless.

Above left: A statue of Emma of Normandy, wife of both Æthelred 'the Unready' and Cnut the Great, in Winchester Cathedral.

Left: A later medieval period brass commemorates the burial of Æthelred I in Wimborne Minster: the king possibly died of wounds inflicted at the Battle of Martin.

Below: According to local legend 'The Giant's Grave', a set of hogsback markers at Penrith, marks the burial place of Owain of Strathclyde, who probably fought at Brunanburh.

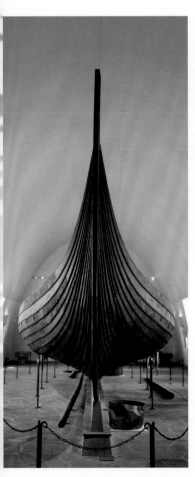

Above left and right: The Gokstad ship in Oslo, an amazing archeological survival from the ninth century which tells us much about Viking shipbuilding techniques and burial customs. (Courtesy of Mal Booth on Flickr)

Above: The opulence and size of Hagia Sofia in Constantinople (now Istanbul) overwhelmed Viking visitors, one of whom (probably named Halfdan) carved graffiti when he visited, which can still be seen today.

Left: A picture of Harald Bluetooth in Roskilde Cathedral, the site of his burial – though the precise whereabouts of his remains is unknown.

The sacred site of Iona off the west coast of Scotland, subject to unwelcome visits from Viking raiders on several occasions.

The rugged coast of Kerry in the west of Ireland, raided by Vikings from very early in the ninth century.

Lindisfarne, the site of the earliest-known significant raid, which took place in 793.

Loch Ness, a watery thoroughfare across Scotland.

A reconstruction of a Viking longhouse at Trelleborg, Denmark.

Martin Down in Dorset, possible location of a crucial battle in Wessex in 871.

Although it is a stunning reminder of the Viking Age, the Oseberg Ship was probably only suitable for sailing in coastal waters.

This later church at Portmahomack, Scotland, is built on the site of a brutal Viking raid where the remains of slaughtered monks and shattered Christian monuments were found.

These prehistoric carvings of ships at Stavanger, Norway, demonstrate that shipbuilding traditions in Scandinavia predate the Vikings by several thousand years.

A Victorian-era statue of Rollo, the founder of Viking Normandy, at Alesund, in Norway (he is also claimed by Denmark).

The author aboard a reconstructed Viking ship at Roskilde, Denmark.

The church of Santa Sabina in Rome is similar in style to what Cnut the Great would have seen when visiting St Peter's in the city in 1027.

Inside the modern protective shell at Shandwick, north-east Scotland, is a marker from the age of the Picts. This stone, advertising the wealth of the monastery at Portmahomack, would attract the unwelcome attention of Viking ships.

A modern statue of monks carrying the coffin of St Cuthbert; Viking raids on Northumbria would force them to carry his remains around in search of a safe resting place.

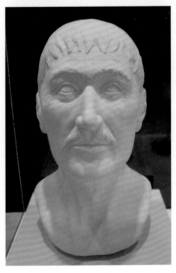

Above left: A statue of Óláfr Haraldsson in Kirkwall Cathedral; the Viking ruler was canonised and became far more successful in death than he was in life.

Above right: These giant swords commemorate the Battle of Hafrsfjord, a crucial event in the formation of Norway.

Right: Face to face with a Viking ruler: the discovery of the remains of Sweyn Estrithsson at Roskilde allowed the details of his face to be reconstructed.

The Seine below Rouen at Les Andelys; the river was a highway down which waves of Viking raiders could sail towards Paris.

The otherworldly landscape of Trotternish, Skye: both these names are based on Viking Age Norse.

The shallow impression in the foreground marks the resting place of a Viking woman who was buried next to a much older Iron Age broch at Gurness, Orkney.

The priory at Wareham, Dorset, by the River Frome; the river was a conduit for Viking raiders on several recorded occasions.

The shrine of St Wite at Whitchurch Canonicorum. According to local legend, the anchoress was killed by Viking raiders.

The assassination of King Edward 'the Martyr' marked the opening of a new and terrifyingly intensive series of raids on Anglo-Saxon England.

Above left: The modern Icelandic flag flies above the spot where the first Viking *Althing* (representative assembly) met in 930 in the dramatic valley of Thingvellir.

Above right: The Icelandic horse, small but strong, is a direct descendant of the animal that the Viking Age settlers brought to the island with them from Norway.

Above: This turf-covered longhouse and tiny stave church are a replica of those excavated at Stöng in Iceland.

Below left: Leif Eriksson, an early explorer of America.

Below right: 'Snorri's Pool', on the site of the home and last resting place of the great saga-writer Snorri Sturluson.

were at last taken over to Ireland for safe keeping; they were clearly no longer secure in Scotland, though whether they had remained in Iona until then or, as was suggested by the *Chronicles of the Kings of Alba*, had already been removed to Dunkeld, is unclear.[94] Possibly the relics had been split up between the two places.[95]

At about the same time back in England a large fortification, over 100 acres in extent, was erected by a Viking army at Torksey near Lincoln. The site at Torksey was in a classic Viking *longphort* location, defended on one side by a river, the Trent, and on another by marshland. Significant archaeological activity has unearthed a vast range of finds with evidence of trading, minting, smithing, textile manufacturing and gaming. The size of Torksey suggests a population in the thousands; clearly no mere raiding force but something far more significant.[96]

Evidence of another Viking camp in England was also found recently in Yorkshire. It was discovered by metal detectorists but, due to concerns over illegal exploitation of the finds on the site, remains anonymous, known only by the acronym ARSNY – 'A Riverine Site in North Yorkshire'. However, details of some of the finds there have been made public. They include weapons and hacksilver and a number of coins, including dirhams, silver pennies and Northumbrian stycas.[97] A significant number of weights have also been found. The site appears to be broadly contemporary with those at Repton and Torksey.[98]

As for Halfdan himself, his efforts to assume the responsibilities of domesticity were short-lived and he died not long afterwards while involved in a raid in Ireland. The *Historia de Sancto Cuthberto* suggests that he had been ejected from Northumbria by his own men, allegedly because he smelt bad, a bizarre explanation.[99] He died in a skirmish in Strangford Lough on the north-east coast of the island in a Viking-on-Viking fight with men of the 'Fair Foreigners', the longer-established Viking element in Ireland. The *Annals of Ulster* for the year 875 says that Oistin, son of Amlaib (Óláfr, who had himself died not long before in Pictland) was 'slain through treachery by Alband'. It has been suggested that the 'Alband' referred to here is an early Irish writer's attempt at 'Halfdan'.[100] If this is so, then Halfdan's death not long after at the hands of Irish Vikings makes a lot of sense as another revenge killing.

The chaos that Halfdan and his men had unleashed in Northumbria continued to reverberate. In 875, the monks of Lindisfarne reasoned that the sacred remains of Cuthbert were no longer safe on the island and, nearly a century after the apocalyptic raid on the abbey, his remains were finally evacuated. So began a peripatetic journey before Cuthbert found a new home at Chester-le-Street, passing through Melrose before arriving there. The *Historia de Sancto Cuthberto* suggests that at one stage the plan was to transfer his body to Ireland, possibly inspired by the similar scheme with the remains of Saint Columba from Iona. However, as the party set off to sail across the sea a great storm blew up and three giant waves the colour of blood forced their vessel back to shore.[101] Even then, Cuthbert's post-mortem wanderings were not quite over for they were moved one final time to the cathedral at Durham towards the end of the tenth century, having initially spent some time at Ripon on the way. These frequent movements, and the difficulty involved in finding a spot where his relics could find security, are in microcosm a summary of the challenges faced by the great Christian establishments in the Viking Age. But at the same time the challenges posed should not be overplayed, nor should the resilience of the community of monks that had originally been based on Lindisfarne be underestimated. The community that established itself at Chester-le-Street proved to be a remarkably influential, indeed powerful, institution – even playing a role in establishing a new Viking dynasty at York.[102]

A Viking army set up camp at Cambridge with unfinished business to attend to in Wessex. The names of three leaders ('kings') of the force there are given by the chroniclers: Oscytel, Guthrum and Anwend; the use of the term 'kings' as applied to three different men suggests that we should be careful before reading too much into such grand titles. Those still at Cambridge in 875 made ready to relaunch the attack on Wessex when the following year's campaigning season began. A new wave of invasions was about to hit Alfred and his West Saxon subjects bringing his kingdom to the verge of extinction.

Charles the Bald and his Viking allies

Charles the Bald was by now seeking support from Viking leaders in Francia. He was again faced with internal dissent, this time led by his son, Carloman. In 872, he met with two Viking warlords, Roric and Rodulf. This followed negotiations held with Roric a couple of years earlier in Nijmegen. Charles's actions may have been a pre-emptive strike as the warlords might instead have sided with Carloman. Later in the year, these discussions were taken a step further at Maastricht on the Meuse but were unsuccessful. While relations between Charles and Roric were cordial, Charles cold-shouldered Rodulf. Rodulf may have been plotting against Charles, perhaps in consort with Carloman, and he was also demanding an excessively high price for his collaboration with the king. By 873, Viking elements in Francia were again creating problems for Charles. He did not need further enemies; not long before, he had ordered that Carloman be blinded for his treachery. Now a group of Vikings from Angers threatened the peace. They had set up camp in the city 'after ravaging various towns, raising fortresses to the ground, burning churches and monasteries and turning cultivated land into a desert'.[103] Regino of Prüm, writing early in the tenth century, noted that there were women and children also taking up residence in Angers, suggesting that some of the warriors were not just engaging in these campaigns as individuals but as part of family units. These were further signs of a change in direction towards settlement rather than just raids.

Charles, determined to bring the depredations of this group to an end, laid siege to Angers, surrounding it with earthworks. While the siege was ongoing, Charles received the gratifying news that the troublesome Rodulf had been killed in a battle further north, along with 500 of his men. Charles then brought the siege at Angers to a satisfactory conclusion. Hemmed in as they were, the leaders of the Viking force there sought terms. Some of the besieged were baptised as Christians; those who did not comply were forced to leave Francia as part of the deal that was made.

Those Vikings who remained in Francia after this deal was struck asked for permission to set up a market on an island in the Loire until February of the following year; a recognition that such locations played a prominent role in economic activities. Here we have a direct reference to the chameleon-like flexibility of the Vikings, equally adept as raiders and traders, just as much at home when acting as merchants or as warriors. There was also clearly a suppleness of conscience that allowed such men to undergo baptism as an acceptable cost to be incurred in return for useful trading concessions.

Trading remained a core part of the Viking world. One of the most remarkable of all Viking hoards ever found, the Spillings Hoard, was discovered on a farm of that name on Gotland in 1999. Some coins had been found there previously but when a random metal detector scan of the fields took place no one had the slightest idea just what lay hidden under the soil. The detectorists first of all found a small deposit of silver objects; no doubt that was exciting in its own right, but it was as nothing compared to what happened next. Shortly afterwards, they found another. This time the measurement dial on the detector registered 'overload' and then turned itself off. Realising that something big was on-site, the detectorists summoned specialists from Gotland Museum and a methodical dig was then arranged. What it uncovered was truly sensational. One hoard weighed in at 27 kg, another at 40 kg. Additional finds followed. It transpired that the 'treasure', for such in archaeological terms it was, had been buried under the floorboards of what was a warehouse or something similar.

The dating of the building proved inconclusive, anywhere between 540 and 1040. The structure appeared to be from the Viking Age, though it had been built over a former Iron Age site. The coins that were found provided the decisive dating evidence. They spanned centuries and continents. The earliest in the hoard dated back to 539 and the latest

870 (meaning that the hoard was not buried before this date) though the chest in which one hoard was found dated back to the seventh century. As remarkable as their age was, so was where these coins came from: sixty-nine different mints in fifteen different modern countries. The vast majority of the coins were Islamic dirhams: evidence of just how far-flung Viking contacts were in the ninth century. A good proportion of the items were bundled up in standard-sized packages of 200 gm, which equates to a standard unit of Viking measurement – the mark.

Gotland as a whole is a treasure trove. More items have been found in hoards here than in the rest of Scandinavia combined. It is not hard to work out why; a look at the map reveals all. The island is at the epicentre of the Baltic, the hub in the centre of the wheel of Viking trade routes in the region from east to west and north to south. Although it would be claimed by Denmark from time to time, Gotland was typically within the orbit of Sweden. However, from what we can make out of the Gotlanders and their entrepreneurial spirit, they were unlikely to have felt comfortable in being subservient to anyone.

What these hoards were actually for is unclear. In some cases, there is a strong suspicion of a votive element based on where they were interred. For example, a find of 163 mid-tenth-century coins from Central Asia, mainly from Samarkand, was buried in a much older prehistoric burial mound in Uppland, Sweden, and it is hard not to speculate that there was some spiritual rather than prosaic reasoning behind such actions. On the other hand, an alternative view is that these hoards were hidden away in times of trouble, to be reclaimed later when it was safe to do so; obviously, it never was.[104]

Clearly the coins involved in the find in Uppland had stopped being used as coinage some time before: a number had holes drilled through them as if they were being utilised as pendants rather than for practical currency exchange.[105] The large number of Islamic coins found in Sweden and Gotland resonates with our knowledge of the trading routes that had opened up from the Viking world to the Middle East, utilising great water routes such as the Volga as the way into the region.

Scandinavia was still not at peace with itself, however. By this time, whatever unification in Denmark there might have been under the rule of Horik I and II was shown to be an illusion. There were at least two kings in place, named Sigfred and Halfdan, and according to the later eleventh-century chronicler Adam of Bremen, there were a number of other minor rulers, who we might refer to as sea kings, who were renowned for launching pirate attacks on their neighbours. The process of centralisation was still very much in its infancy and there was some way yet to go before recognisable nation states in Scandinavia in the modern sense would appear.

6

England on the Brink
(876–900)

… the berserkers bellowed as the battle opened, the wolf-coats shrieked
loud and shook their weapons…

Snorri Sturluson

The end of Charles the Bald

On Christmas Day 875, Charles the Bald was crowned as Carolingian
Emperor by Pope John VIII in Rome. It was seventy-five years to the
day since Charlemagne was installed as Emperor in the same city and
the fact that this was an anniversary was assuredly not a coincidence.
But if the intention was to inspire the Franks to restore past glories, it
was ultimately a failure – despite Charles's attempts to reinforce his new-
found status by wearing clothes in the style of the Byzantine Emperor and
his ongoing strenuous efforts to reinvigorate the legacy of Charlemagne.
More infighting threatened to sap Charles's diminishing reserves – he was
in his fifties now and had lived a tough life – as he sought to expand his
empire with his main domestic opponent now his older brother, Louis the
German. Charles journeyed to Italy, the throne of which had fallen vacant
with the recent death of Louis II, son of Lothar. But it was a dangerous
move to leave Francia as a whiff of further Viking attacks was in the air
there. That said, when Charles sat in state on his return to Francia and
held his summer assembly in 876, a party of newly converted Vikings
from the Loire region was wheeled in to be ceremonially baptised, a nice
symbolic way of demonstrating that the threat the Scandinavians posed
could be dealt with by one means or another.

Showing how empty this symbolism was, however, a party of aggressive
Vikings made its way up the Seine, first appearing on 16 September 876.
Charles was distracted with ongoing internecine struggles, in the course
of which he suffered a humiliating defeat at Andernach and was forced to

flee for his life, or at least for his freedom. This left him powerless to do anything about the Northmen on the Seine, so he sent his cousin Conrad to treat with them and make the best deal possible to encourage them to go away. An event of great significance also took place in Normandy in 876 (according to the *ASC*) when a man called Rollo and his men invaded the region and, to paraphrase the chronicler, he reigned there for fifty-three years (which is clear evidence, if any is needed, that much of the *ASC* was written up, or at least revised, after the event). Rollo would later be given part of Normandy as his own fief by the king of France in · return for helping the latter resist Viking attacks.

These morale-sapping events continued in Francia into 877 when tribute again needed to be raised to buy off a Viking raiding party on the Loire.[1] The writer Adrevaldus talks of Vikings using the island of Saint-Florent-le-Vieil as a port for their ships and a refuge. They built a fort, which the writer calls a 'hut-camp', where they kept their 'crowds of prisoners in chains' and used it as a base for further raids, sometimes by ship, sometimes on horseback.[2] This sounds like a processing camp for slaves who could be shipped across the Viking world as well as a fortified base for further raids in France. To deal with this latest incursion, a further tax of 5,000 lbs of silver was collected; this time it was raised from a wider area including Burgundy, which had previously avoided such payments. Taxes were also collected from the nobility when before they had been focused on the peasantry, the laudable benefits of progressive tax measures clearly not always figuring highly in Carolingian fiscal policy.

While journeying to Italy again in 877, Charles was taken ill (according to the annalist of St Bertin he was poisoned; again revealing his anti-Semitic prejudices the annalist gleefully noted that a doctor who administered the medicine which poisoned him was Jewish) and died soon after. Charles was disembowelled in an attempt to preserve his body until it could be buried in St-Denis, but this gruesome process was in vain. When his corpse soon after started to turn, it was unceremoniously shoved in a barrel that had been smeared with pitch. This did nothing to stop the stench and, unable to bear it any longer, those carrying Charles later buried him, still in the barrel, near Lyons, though his remains were eventually moved to a place of honour at St-Denis. It was a fitting anecdote with which to end the career of a man whose aspirations ultimately proved beyond his talents. And the Viking threat to Francia was far from over.

Wessex and the lurch towards disaster

While the position of Francia vis-à-vis the Viking raiders was still a dangerous one, it did not at least match the alarming experience that Wessex, just across the Channel, was about to go through. The Viking force at Cambridge launched a renewed attack on Wessex in 876 and achieved total surprise, taking Wareham. This was a significant achievement. Wareham was in Dorset, at the very heart of Wessex. It should have been relatively well guarded as it had a long association with Saxon royalty; King Beorhtric's final resting place was there (the West Saxon king had died in 802). As a place with royal connections and a major town in the context of the times, as well as a collection point for tax tributes for the fertile local area round about it, it was again probably well stocked for the winter. If the Vikings could penetrate here and stay, then nowhere in Wessex was safe. Certainly according to Æthelweard they ravaged the greater part of the province.[3]

Alfred had had four years since the last Viking attacks on Wessex to prepare but nonetheless appears to have been caught on the hop (though there is mention of a small sea-borne raid in Wessex in 875 when Alfred managed to capture one of the Viking ships). He was about to be caught out again. He negotiated with the Vikings, which is to say he probably bought them off. They in return agreed to leave Wessex. Hostages were exchanged, and the raiders swore an oath on their own pagan version of holy relics (possibly arm rings) that they would comply with the conditions of the agreement that had been made. But rather than return north to Mercia, East Anglia or Northumbria, the raiders upped and left under cover of darkness and rode west to Exeter. The hostages they held were killed. Alfred chased after them but too late to stop them entering Exeter. However, the Vikings had in the meantime suffered a bad reverse. A fleet was sailing west to reinforce the raiding land army but was caught in a storm off Swanage and many ships were lost (120 according to the *ASC* but this seems a very high figure and probably some kind of shorthand surrogate for 'a significant number').

The loss of these ships in Swanage Bay was a major blow to the Viking forces in south-west England. The event is now marked by a promenade memorial in Swanage, erected when the Victorian era was in full swing. The Victorians played up both Alfred and the Vikings for all they were worth, and the memorial gives us a clear insight into the historical revisionism that was then at its height. The text on it says boldly that 'a great naval battle was fought with the Danes in Swanage Bay by Alfred the Great A.D. 877'. In fact, the reference in the *ASC* says nothing of the sort and the loss of these ships was attributed to 'a great storm'. To add an element of anachronistic confusion, the memorial is adorned with stone cannonballs. The Victorian claim is nonsensical in other ways; not until the 890s do we have any intimation that Alfred took large-scale measures to build up a navy of the type that would have been needed to defeat 120 Viking ships in a battle; these later measures resemble the acts of Charlemagne.[4] There is certainly a danger that those eulogising Alfred are writing of what he should have done rather than what he actually did.

The *ASC* is frustrating in its lack of detail for this period, again probably not wanting to draw attention to Alfred's inability to stop the Viking raid. Æthelweard later wrote that the raiders ravaged the greater part of the province. We can only surmise but it is very likely that contemporary monastic establishments, such as that at nearby Wimborne (just 10 miles from Wareham), suffered badly as a result of this ravishing. As the raiders moved into Devon, there are intimations that this shire also suffered significant damage. Once caught in Exeter, Guthrum's army again agreed to leave; the chronicles imply that they handed over more prominent hostages. And this time they did go; we are told by Æthelweard that they moved to Gloucester, just over the border in Mercia. Leaving at harvest time 877, they took over parts of Mercia for themselves.

This was an event of profound significance. Mercia was effectively partitioned and the first steps were being taken towards the creation of the Viking polity (in the loosest sense of the word) that became known as the Danelaw. Over time the precise boundaries of this would morph like an amoeba; and indeed some historians would even argue that it should not be defined by geographical boundaries at all but rather by other criteria such as whether or not Danish law applied to certain populations regardless of where they lived. But if the lazy shorthand can be allowed, at its greatest extent the 'Danelaw' would cover the so-called Five Boroughs of Stamford, Lincoln, Nottingham, Leicester and Derby; the South-East Midlands; much of Yorkshire; and East Anglia. That said, even here it was a process where assimilation was far more obvious than Viking domination; one of the most fascinating aspects of Viking settlement was that it was not homogenous and what happened in one part of their world was not necessarily replicated everywhere else. That may make matters much more complex but also adds to the inherent interest of these remarkably adaptable people.[5]

Rather than being a mere puppet, the surviving evidence suggests that Ceolwulf, who was then ruling Mercia, operated as a conventional king of the time; and charters show that his nobility continued to witness key documents for a long time after the so-called Viking takeover.[6] This intimates that the Vikings were content to leave matters largely undisturbed in Mercia provided, of course, that Ceolwulf proved himself to be cooperative. Allowing the Vikings to base themselves at Gloucester was presumably part of this cooperation; in any event Ceolwulf was probably powerless to resist. This part of Mercia was dangerously close to Wessex and the Vikings had no intention of giving up their attacks on it from over the border.

Shortly after Twelfth Night (6 January) 878 they descended on Chippenham; in the *ASC's* account they were now under the sole command of Guthrum.[7] Chippenham was a royal residence but was totally unprepared for the attack. This was again a sloppy state of affairs. Chippenham was close to Gloucester and yet the Viking attack achieved total surprise. This was despite the fact that Viking raiders were notoriously unreliable when it came to keeping to the terms of a treaty.[8] Perhaps it was assumed that no Viking raids would be launched in winter; but English winters were nothing to those that the raiders would have experienced in Scandinavia. Chippenham would have ample provisions to support a winter campaign. It is a useful reminder that we can get blind-sided by thinking that the Vikings were purely obsessed with lucre; they were after all made of flesh and bone and needed to eat to live, especially when on campaign in the winter, with extended supply lines to contend with.

Following this dramatic coup, Alfred fled for his life. The raiders occupied a significant chunk of Wessex and we are told that some of Alfred's Saxon subjects travelled overseas into exile. The chroniclers suggest that most of the West Saxons submitted. Alfred retreated to his royal estates to the west in Somerset. Here, after Easter 879, he found refuge on Athelney, 'the Island of Princes', set among woods and salt marshes (many of the rivers round about are tidal, almost making it a true island at certain times of the year, though more recent land reclamation disguises this). This was the ultimate place of last resort: should Alfred be taken by the raiders then his kingdom would be forfeit. So too probably would his life: the precedents set by the execution of Ælle in Northumbria and the demise of Edmund in East Anglia (if the saga stories of their deaths are true) were horrific.

Nowadays it is hard to imagine Athelney as a place of destiny. It is an inconsequential hump in the middle of flat, green fields, standing only 30 feet above the surrounding lowlands, the Somerset Levels. Some degree of imagination is required to paint a mental image of the 'island' as what it was a thousand years ago. It would then have been a true island, surrounded by the tidal waters of the rivers that criss-crossed the region and the dense, impenetrable marshland that then blanketed the area; according to Asser, it was only accessible by a flat-bottomed punt steered through the fens.[9] This would be a tough nut for any Viking army to crack.

From Athelney, Alfred organised guerrilla raids on Viking patrols: he even, hints Asser, raided his own people who had submitted to Viking authority to forage for provisions. Archaeology suggests that the site at Athelney was also used for the manufacturing of weapons for Alfred's army. It was later connected to the 'mainland' surrounding it by a narrow causeway that was linked to the nearby settlement of East Lyng, which was in turn defended by 'a fortress of formidable elegance' at its west end.[10] The site may not be much to look at now, but it was to be the launch pad for a spectacular recovery on Alfred's part.

The Viking assault on Wessex appears to have been two-pronged. While Guthrum came overland, a fleet made its way to the west. The naval assault was led by Ubba, allegedly one of the sons of Ragnar Lodbrok.[11] The events that followed suggest that Alfred was not quite as alone as the traditional accounts of his resurrection from near-oblivion might suggest. A fleet of about twenty-three Viking ships sailed across the Bristol Channel from Dỹfed in Wales where they had spent the winter. As they made landfall, they were faced by a strong West Saxon force encamped in an old hillfort known as Cynuit. Where this actually is remains a matter of speculation, but two popular candidates are Countisbury in Devon and Cannington in Somerset, then a significant royal estate.[12]

The Saxon force was led by Odda, ealdorman of Devon. The site of Cynuit, wherever it was, was in a strong position. Asser tells us that the place was not protected by anything other than hastily erected earthen ramparts. But it had strong natural defences on all sides except the east. Seeing that it would not be easy to take Cynuit by direct assault, Ubba laid siege to it and prepared to starve the defenders out. Asser suggests that what happened soon after was inspired by God; but it could just as easily have been inspired by desperation. Odda and his followers looked down from their strong position and realised that if they stayed where they were they would eventually be worn down by hunger, thirst and fatigue. They therefore resolved to go on to the attack.

They charged down the hillside in an unexpected dawn assault and fell on the Viking force when it was off its guard. It was overwhelmed and at the conclusion of the fight, 800 men lay dead.[13] Among them was Ubba. The scalp of a son of Ragnar Lodbrok was a formidable prize. It would have been a grievous blow to Viking morale and a corresponding boost to the English. So too would have been the taking of Ubba's magical raven banner. The *Annals of St Neots* explained that this had been woven by three sisters of Ubba and that whether it hung lifeless or flapped in the breeze predicted the result of impending battle. References to such a sacred banner are not unique; similar stories regarding the capture of Viking banners are mentioned in accounts from Francia in 865 when they were sent by Robert, count of Angers, to Charles the Bald. Others are mentioned as being captured at a battle on the Dyle in 891.[14] A similar banner was later carried by the Earl of Orkney at the Battle of Clontarf in 1014.

While his stay on Athelney has become a core part of Alfred's legend, his guerrilla campaign against Guthrum was short if sharp. Asser says that he moved there after Easter 878 (23 March that year) but within seven weeks he was on the offensive. While at Athelney, he had received the personal support of the thegns of Somerset – the later chronicler Æthelweard suggests that they were led by Æthelnoth, the ealdorman of

Somerset – and he moved east with them. He also, according to a later account found in the *Historia de Sancto Cuthberto,* received support from an altogether more remarkable source.

The writer here suggests that, while he was in Athelney, Alfred was visited by a stranger who asked him for food. Alfred had precious little to spare but nevertheless shared what he did have with the unknown visitor. That night, the king was visited in a vision by the same man who revealed that he was actually Saint Cuthbert. He told Alfred that he would be victorious in his campaign and that he was destined to be king of Britain, a significant exaggeration as it turned out, though it gave justification to his descendants in their attempts to fulfil such a claim. The modern reader would of course be sceptical of such a supernatural intervention. Such scepticism is reinforced by the fact that this account was written up in the tenth century when the brotherhood of Saint Cuthbert was actively engaged in building strong relationships with the royal dynasty of Wessex that was by then staking a claim to govern all of England.

Alfred summoned the *fyrds* of Somerset, Wiltshire and Hampshire to meet him at Ecgbert's Stone, which was in the region of Selwood Forest; the Victorian edifice known as Alfred's Tower, near Penselwood on the borders of Wiltshire and Dorset, marks a location that is associated with the assembly point. Here he was joined by a good body of men. This suggests several things: that there were more of his supporters remaining in the area than the chroniclers suggest, that the communications network that Alfred controlled was still working well, and that the Viking hold over the region was not as strong as it might appear to be on the surface.

By the same token, it is likely that Guthrum's fighting force was no longer at full strength. The Great Heathen Army had split at Repton, 120 ships had been lost with their men in Swanage Bay and probably some of the remaining army had stayed behind in their newly occupied lands around Gloucester. Alfred's army moved into camp at Iley Oak near Warminster. Guthrum was aware of the threat and moved his men out to meet it. The two armies met at Edington with Guthrum camped in a defensive position, possibly at an old Iron Age hillfort known as Bratton Castle; Viking forces had developed the habit of fighting behind fortifications and Anglo-Saxon tactics had not proved very adept in removing them. But here, Alfred led his men tenaciously in a long slugging match where they relied on their conventional but effective tactics of fighting in a compact shield wall. It won them the victory and it appears to have been one that resulted in many Viking lives being lost.

Edington was part of a royal estate at the time. Threatening such a place was a regular occurrence for Viking raids during the period; other examples include attacks on Wilton, Exeter, Wareham, Chippenham, Carhampton and Winchester; all places with strong associations with the ruling Anglo-Saxon dynasty. Such places were likely to be well stocked with food and wealth. In addition, an attack on such a high-profile location would represent a challenge that a king could not ignore without a substantial loss of face. Guthrum and his men escaped to a fortification, perhaps their base at Chippenham. Alfred hurried after them with his army and laid siege to it. There was no attempt at assault but instead a siege to starve them out was put in place. For Guthrum's trapped men, hunger, fear and cold soon turned to despair. Seeing no way out, after two weeks they sought terms. Asser noted exultantly that those terms were tougher than any others imposed on any Viking force so far.[15] The fact that Alfred could do so shows how decisive his victory had been. One of those terms was that Guthrum should convert to Christianity. This was to be accompanied by an extraordinary procession around some of the royal estates in Somerset, almost mimicking an Anglo-Saxon version of a Roman triumph.

Guthrum, dressed in white, the garb of a convert, was baptised soon after in the small church at Aller accompanied by thirty of his men. He was given a new Christian name – Æthelstan. In accordance with the conventions of the time, a fillet of white cloth was tied around the head of the new converts. This was taken off a week later in a ceremony at nearby Wedmore called a 'chrism loosing'. Alfred acted as Guthrum's sponsor at his baptism, which was not just a magnanimous gesture but a way of tying the Viking warlord closer to the English king. The terms made with Guthrum were in fact surprisingly generous. Looked at objectively, this might mean that the extent of Alfred's victory has been exaggerated by Asser; and maybe the whole of Guthrum's force had not taken part and been defeated at Edington. It is likely in any event that Guthrum still had significant forces available to him, and Alfred wisely saw that it was better to negotiate a workable deal with his opponent rather than drive too hard a bargain.

The making of Alfred 'the Great'

Alfred subsequently earned his title of 'the Great'. He rebuilt English learning, which had suffered greatly in recent times and was, in his view, a pale shadow of what it had been in earlier days. He lamented the damage inflicted on his country by the Vikings; he recalled the time when 'before everything was ransacked and burned, the churches throughout England stood filled with treasure and books'; a reference to the scale of the damage that the country had suffered. Now there were only a handful of literate scribes left in Anglo-Saxon England.[16] Nor was it just monks who had suffered at the hands of the raiders. Nunneries in England were devastated; at least forty-one such establishments were destroyed and there were very few remaining.[17] Nuns were almost as likely to perish as monks; when Vikings attacked the nunnery at Barking back in 870, the women inside were burned alive.[18]

In the ninth century, learning was largely the preserve of the Church: and the devastation of the latter by Viking raiders had a huge impact. There is strong circumstantial evidence for this, such as the abandonment of the sees at Whithorn and Hexham in the north and Dunwich, Elmham and Lindsey further south. In addition, the fact that the archbishops of York also took on the bishopric of Worcester to increase their income because of funding shortfalls and the moving of the see at Leicester for purposes of protection adds to this impression. These were harrowing times.[19] Despite this, some historians still maintain that the scale of Viking attacks on churches has been overstated, arguing that few archaeological discoveries have been made to provide evidence of such raids.[20] While this latter assertion is partially true (though relevant evidence recently emerged at Portmahomack), this seems dangerously like equating an absence of evidence with an evidence of absence, particularly when other sources suggests that raiding was widespread and often devastating.

Alfred transformed the system of defence in England in several ways; this was greatly needed as successful surprise attacks on towns such as Winchester, Wareham, Exeter and Chippenham suggested. After his decisive triumph over Guthrum at Edington, he designed a system of fortifications by establishing *burhs* (fortified settlements) in key places, no more than 20 miles apart, about a day's march. They could be defended against Viking attack and the local population from outlying areas could find sanctuary in them when threatened. They were also places where mints and markets could operate in a secure environment, so they had a strong commercial use too.

The relative closeness of the *burhs* to each other allowed reinforcements to arrive from nearby when a raid was underway. This would enable time to be bought and more resources to be assembled to face up to the threat in due course. It would also allow forces to assemble in relative safety, which was not always the case when the *fyrd* had gathered previously. This formed part of a wider strategy developed by Alfred. Troops were to be available at all times, some fighting on active service, some remaining at home and some on garrison duty. This was in fact a development of longstanding practices; traditionally, Anglo-Saxon kings had been able to summon men via a legal right known as the *trimoda necessitas*. This gave kings the right to call up some men to fight while others were to assist in the building and repairing of bridges or the construction of fortresses.[21]

It was not that the Anglo-Saxons were unfamiliar with fortifications. The *ASC* records the building of a fort at Bamburgh as long ago as 547 and the frontier work of Offa's Dyke, constructed in the eighth century, was further evidence that they were familiar with the skills required. There is evidence too of more general fortification building programmes in eighth century Mercia in the time of Offa, and even before. Reminders of Alfred's efforts are nevertheless widespread. For example, the twelfth-century historian William of Malmesbury wrote that there was an inscription in the Chapter House at Shaftesbury Abbey which boldly stated, 'Alfred made this town in 880'.[22] With the emergence of a strong protective shell of such improved defences, raids were to become more dangerous and less profitable for the raiders, encouraging the Vikings to look elsewhere for easier targets.

As one example, other *burhs* were created in Dorsetshire, including at Wareham, Twynham (Christchurch, then in Hampshire, now in Dorset) and Bredy, probably Bridport. Some were created in Mercia, with early examples at Worcester and Gloucester (taking advantage of the surviving remnants of Roman defences in both places) though the building programme there really only took off following Alfred's death, with his offspring Edward and Æthelflaed taking the lead. There is circumstantial evidence that it took some time for the building programme to reach Kent and this perhaps explains why when Viking raids took place in earnest in 892 this was the region that was targeted.[23] But that said, it was a very ambitious programme, effectively putting England on an ongoing war footing. A close reading of Asser's biography of Alfred suggests that not all his subjects were particularly happy at being put to work for the good of the kingdom; taxes were high, and this programme of public works came at a cost.

Ironically, Alfred may have been encouraged to build these defences because of lessons learned from Viking raiders. They had had conspicuous success when defending themselves behind fortifications at Nottingham in 868 and were strongly entrenched when attacked at Reading in 871. In Ireland they had their earth-banked encampments by the rivers, the *longphuirt*. Alfred also introduced more rigour into the *fyrd* system with his reforms demanding that groups of men be deployed systematically on a range of duties. It was a system that made the most of England's manpower and other resources to face the Viking challenge full on. It was not fully innovative; Carolingian defence models were based on similar principles.[24] But it was effective. By the close of Alfred's reign, he had at least 27,000 men available for garrison duty and probably more.[25]

This completely changed the dynamics of warfare in England from a Viking perspective. It meant that some of their military advantages were negated. There was now less chance of catching their Anglo-Saxon opponents by surprise; raids could now expect to achieve only limited penetration before a defence was organised. The character of war therefore changed and the rate of attrition that the Vikings could expect to suffer increased. It also helped the English to avoid bleeding away their strength in a series of costly pitched battles such as those that had marked the 870s.

In the aftermath of his triumph, Alfred built a monastery on Athelney to mark his seemingly near-miraculous survival. And something else remarkable happened, for we read that before long a young novice was brought up in the monastic life, a monk who was of Viking parentage – and, according to Asser, 'assuredly not the last of them to do so'. It is a shame that we do not know more about him, though it has been speculated that he later became Oda, bishop of Ramsbury, a man who later accounts say was of Danish origin and who eventually became Archbishop of Canterbury.[26]

After the defeat of the Viking army at Edington, the survivors from Guthrum's war band made their way to Cirencester, still dangerously close to Wessex, where they remained for a year. Another war band arrived from overseas around the same time. Although they made contact with Guthrum, they do not appear to have moved far from the base they established at Fulham on the Thames and they sailed away soon after, journeying to Ghent and unleashing themselves on Francia where they would remain for many years; that country was in trouble – Charles the Bald's heir, Louis the Stammerer, had lasted less than two years and the raiders smelt fresh blood.[27]

In 880, Guthrum and his men moved to East Anglia where they divided up the land between them; the third such Viking 'sharing-out' in five years after similar events in Northumbria and Mercia. This was a different form of economic exploitation or development, depending on one's point of view. It probably did not involve the mass extinction or deportation of existing Anglo-Saxon communities but a change in ownership; those from the lower levels of society found themselves with different overlords to pay taxes to. Controlling land generated longer-term rewards than plundering did and can also be contrasted with returns from trading. Bringing in taxes and developing the local economy led to a change in practice whereby control of land and the economic benefits flowing from it encouraged the growth of towns.

Certainly over the course of the next century there were profound social changes in England. With the breaking-up of large estates into smaller units there was both an increase in the agricultural use of previously unexploited land (assisted by a warmer climate) and a marked increase in the size of towns. Population followed suit; it has been suggested that the population of England doubled between the time of Alfred and the preparation of Domesday Book two centuries later from less than a million to about two million. The Viking settlements alone do not explain this increase, but the knock-on effects of their incursions and the development of smaller workable land units helped. Alongside this, monasticism went into steep decline – again probably caused in part by Viking attacks – and the fortunes of the secular classes conversely improved as a result of the vacuum that was created.[28]

There are hints that Alfred would experience occasional friction from the direction of East Anglia. Despite this, there is also powerful evidence that Guthrum adhered to some of the responsibilities he assumed as a result of his baptism; coins dated to his reign use his Christian name of Æthelstan rather than the pagan Guthrum. He ruled for ten years before dying in 890. The treaty made between Alfred and Guthrum allowed for cross-border trading and this fits in with a picture that sees Vikings being able to slip into the role of trader very easily from that of raider. Guthrum's adoption of a coinage using his name was innovative by Scandinavian standards. He appears to have used Continental coiners for his currency and although later issues are similar to those used in Alfred's Wessex, they are consistently lighter; whereas once it was argued that this was just a poor imitation of Alfred's coinage, it is now argued by some that this was a result of a deliberate monetary policy rather than any shortfall in craftsmanship.[29]

By now, Northumbria in the north of England had become an Anglo-Danish territory. After Eoforwic/Jorvik (modern York) had been taken and then held by Viking forces in 866/7, several English kings had been placed on the throne of Northumbria. However, after the death of Ecgbert II, he was replaced by Gofraid, son of Harthacnut, a man of Danish origin who had allegedly been previously captured and held as a slave in the northern part of Northumbria with the abbot of Carlisle. These details come from a later work, the *Historia de Sancto Cuthberto,* and are viewed with suspicion by some modern commentators, especially as the shade of Saint Cuthbert was allegedly behind the move.[30] Nevertheless, the community seems to have acquired land as a result of its involvement in these negotiations and it is conceivable that they presented themselves as brokers in the discussions as a way of improving their own position; extraordinary times required extraordinary measures.[31] Gofraid[32] was certainly a Christian; on his death in 895 he was entombed in York Minster.

It is notable that these two Viking kings, Gofraid and Guthrum, both adopted Christianity. It was a trend that would increasingly be emulated by aspiring Viking leaders and their peoples in the future and by the mid-tenth century, a number of officials of the English church were being appointed from the region that became known as the Danelaw.[33] Soon after Gofraid's enthronement the peripatetic existence of the relics of Cuthbert, which were carried around from pillar to post for seven years, came to an end, which was probably no coincidence. Neither is the fact that his community from this point on continued to accumulate territory at the expense of now-diminished but formerly important sites at places like Hexham and Monkwearmouth.

Francia: the war goes on

This major activity in England might at first glance suggest a reduction of fighting in Francia during the same period. Hincmar, the Archbishop of Rheims, the probable compiler for the entries concerning the last two decades covered by the *Annals of St Bertin,* died on 23 December 882 and his helpful commentary on contemporary events therefore comes to an end.[34] There are far less frequent comments about the 'Northmen' in the latter entries made in the *Annals,* but this does not mean they were any less active; possibly Hincmar felt there was nothing new to say or he had become tired, even depressed, at the ongoing depredations his countrymen were suffering. However, the relatively infrequent references Hincmar does make to the Northmen give enough data to put together a sketchy understanding of what was happening. In 880 King Louis III, 'the Younger', of Francia (yet another Louis to contend with) triumphed against one Viking force in Belgium but shortly afterwards was bested by another in Saxony. Nevertheless, there was certainly less frequency in such references, particularly considering that there was mention of Viking raids in the *Annals* for literally every year between 841 and 875.

A Frankish force was deployed to Ghent to keep an eye on the Northmen newly arrived there in 880 but it only met with limited success. Asser wrote up some important details from which the progress of the Viking force in Francia can be traced. By procuring horses, they became a mounted body, giving them manoeuvrability and flexibility. They spent the winter at Courtrai and when it was over, they crossed the Somme, getting as far as Beauvais. The following year, 881, there were attacks on the monastery of Corbie and on the *civitas* of Amiens, as well as what are described vaguely as 'other holy places'.[35] But then this force was defeated at Saucourt by the combined forces of the Carolingian rulers Louis III and Carloman II and thousands of them were lost. The event was celebrated in a German poem known as *Ludwigslied* – 'The Song of Ludwig'. This paints the triumph of Saucourt as a victory for Christians over pagans. It also portrays the Vikings as a punishment from God for the sins of the people; a very familiar presentation.

After Saucourt, the defeated Vikings sought other, easier targets. They moved into Lotharingia in the north and east of Francia. They spent the winter at Elsloo (in what is now the Netherlands) on the River Meuse. When the season for doing so arrived, they returned to raiding. They launched attacks on the Rhine and the Moselle. Some raided Aachen, during which they tethered their horses inside the king's chapel there, an act of sacrilege which might have made Charlemagne turn in his grave. The next winter (882–883) was spent at Condé on the Scheldt where there was a convent that they occupied. This approach, raiding in summer and stopping somewhere over the winter, seems to have been this group's *modus operandum*. For several more years they raided, moving from one area to another, from the Rhine to the Scheldt to the Somme and so on. They were helped by a series of disasters that removed several important figures in the various parts of the dispersed Carolingian federation; these included Louis III falling off a horse after chasing after a young woman and Carloman being fatally wounded in some horseplay with some boisterous young friends when hunting.

As a result, the Carolingian Empire was for a short time reunited under Charles the Fat, effectively the last man standing. He managed to assemble strong forces to face up to the Viking threat, though he was not always successful in his attempts to defeat them. When he moved on Asselt on the banks of the Meuse in 882 he had a large army with him, but he was not able to bring the Vikings to a decisive battle; instead he was forced to negotiate. As a result of the discussions that followed, the leader of the Viking force, Gofraid, was baptised and in return was given lands in the Netherlands.

England remained under threat. Although Alfred had greatly improved the situation, the threat from the Viking territories bordering Wessex was still considerable; and anyway some historians are sceptical about the reasons for the *ASC's* silence on the subject of raiding throughout most of the 880s, suggesting that this is not because there were none but that the mention of such would not fit with the image the chronicler wished to present of Alfred's victory over his Viking enemies.[36] Nevertheless, the *ASC* does mention that in 885, a party of raiders set up camp at Benfleet, on the north bank of the Thames. From there they would be ideally based to move downriver and unleash more havoc. Chaos duly came, this time with the help of half the force from Francia who crossed over the Channel and laid siege to Rochester.

But things had changed in England. Rochester was resilient in the face of a determined Viking assault. The defenders held out, confident that Alfred would come to their aid. When he arrived, it seemed to come as a surprise to the besieging force, which collapsed. The Vikings rushed back to their ships and sailed on to Francia, leaving behind much of their plunder and even many slaves they had brought over with them. Alfred then attacked the Vikings in East Anglia, probably in retaliation for support they had given to the incursion of the raiders from Francia. There was a sea battle at the mouth of the River Stour, a waterway dividing Suffolk and Essex, in which many Vikings were killed and their ships captured. However, it was not all going the Saxons' way. As their fleet was about to head for home, more Viking ships came up and defeated them.

The raids and problems of 885 probably precipitated Alfred's next significant action: the capture of London in the following year. London was far removed from the bustling metropolis it later became, with a population at the time estimated at around 6,000 inhabitants.[37] It was in a vitally important location and by taking it, Alfred immensely improved his own strategic position. Rather than reoccupying the abandoned settlement of Lundenwic he built up the defences of the nearby former

Roman fortress of Londinium slightly to the east and it now assumed the name of Lundenburh. Alfred issued commemorative coins to celebrate his triumph and was soon after given the title of king of all the free Anglo-Saxons. The Vikings, through their actions and the threat that they posed, were playing an unwitting but crucial part in the creation of a country called England.

This was illustrated when, after the capture of London, Alfred agreed a treaty with Guthrum. It drew a dividing line across England, to the south-west of which would be Anglo-Saxon territory ruled by Alfred and to the north-east the territories held by Vikings that would later become known as the Danelaw. There is a detailed description of this boundary, approximately along the line of Watling Street, the old Roman road, and that of the rivers Thames, Lea and Ouse. As well as boundary lines, the treaty also set scales of *wergild,* the values set on a human life, and payable in compensation to both 'Danes' and Anglo-Saxons when crimes were committed.[38] Restrictions were placed on traders crossing over from the Danelaw into Anglo-Saxon England and vice versa. Clearly, whatever else was happening, there was an acceptance that for the time being there would be two distinct spheres of influence in England, one involving Wessex and part of Mercia and the other that of the 'Danes'.

Although the deal was a success for Alfred, it also set a seal on Viking conquests in England and gave those who had settled in the Danelaw a permanent home. Of course, treaties are often made to be broken and this one would be no exception to this general rule. But it demonstrated a recognition of the *status quo* and an acceptance on the part of Alfred that the 'Danes' were here to stay. The five main towns of what was effectively now 'Danish Mercia' became known as the 'Five Boroughs' of Derby, Leicester, Lincoln, Nottingham and Stamford; all but the last remain county towns in modern England. Each of these boroughs was built around a fortress and had its own *jarl.* There were other places further south also under 'Danish' control, though not formally part of the Five Boroughs, including Northampton, Bedford, Huntingdon and Cambridge. There were also, of course, parts of Northumbria, especially Jorvik, that were under Viking control.

That said, this was not all a one-sided agreement. Guthrum, by being baptised and taking a Christian name, was showing that he wished to be regarded as a Christian ruler. While he may have originally done so under a degree of duress, he could easily have reneged on this at a later stage but we have no evidence that he ever did. Therefore, we can assume that he saw advantages in taking on the appearance of a conventional West European leader of the time. If the Vikings were changing England (and the other territories that they were involved in) then England (and elsewhere) was also changing them.

Soon after these events, Alfred sent a delegation to Northumbria in a diplomatic initiative to reach an understanding with the Viking leadership there. It was led by Æthelnoth, a trusted adviser whose links with the king may go back to the man of the same name who had supported him so valiantly in that year of destiny, 878. It was a realisation on Alfred's part that for now he would have to make do with the *status quo*, that is being recognised as ruler in the southern part of England only.[39]

Alfred continued to face occasional threats from the Vikings based in York/Jorvik. They had developed links with other potential enemies of his. One of these, Anarawd ap Rhodri, the son of the late Rhodri Mawr, was king of Gwynedd, in north Wales. At the time, Wales was divided into several kingdoms though in recent decades Gwynedd had emerged as the strongest, gobbling up several of the others such as Powys in the process. Anarawd and the Vikings of York saw a mutual benefit in uniting their forces against Alfred; Gwynedd had suffered from Mercian aggression in recent times and therefore had no reason to be well disposed towards the Anglo-Saxons. However, this was not a very profitable alliance. Anarawd's manoeuvres only succeeded in driving other Welsh kings into Alfred's arms and the alliance eventually died a natural death when the ruler of Gwynedd saw that he was getting nothing from the arrangement.

Wales was an interesting case study in the Viking Age. Evidence of Viking settlement during these years is scant; very little archaeological evidence has been found to support the idea that they set up towns or even rural communities there. Even place name indication of settlement is rare; just the occasional example survives, such as Swansea ('Sveinn's island') and Fishguard ('fish enclosure'). This mirrors the situation in Ireland, where Norse place names are almost exclusively of coastal towns in which Scandinavian settlers had established a foothold.[40]

Hæsten in Francia and England

On the Continent, other Vikings remained very active. There was a confrontation in Germany where local Saxons allied with Frisians: both were Christians and may have seen a common interest in combining against the pagan Vikings. It seems that this was a different group of Vikings than those who had been active in Francia. The evidence suggests that there were several battles in 884 and 885, over the course of which the raiders got the worst of it. Henry of Saxony was particularly notable in these.[41]

The inhabitants of the Somme basin were having a bad time of it though. They were attacked by Vikings led by the experienced Hæsten and appeared to have suffered grievously in the process; according to a contemporary annalist 'the Northmen did not desist from the slaying and taking captive of Christians, tearing down churches, razing fortifications to the ground and burning settlements. On all the streets lay corpses of clerics, of nobles and of other lay people, of women, young people, and sucklings. There was no street or place where the dead did not lie, and it was for everyone a torment and a pain to see how Christian people had been brought to the point of extermination'.[42]

It is a harrowing picture, a vision of apocalypse. It paints a landscape that reminds one of the terrifying scenes that were created by the later medieval artist Hieronymus Bosch. No one, it seems, was safe. The behaviour of these savage pagans, as implied, contrasts with the norms of Christian behaviour and as such again seeks to portray these attacks as a head-on assault on the true faith, as it is seen to be by the writer. Nevertheless, there were instances of Viking defeats too. In 890, a Breton force confronted a party of Vikings at Saint-Lô. The *ASC* explains that the Bretons won a great victory in which they forced the raiders into the River Dyle where many of them drowned; the Fulda annalist gloated that the waterway was blocked with the corpses of the dead.[43] In the very same year, another group of Vikings was bested by an army led by King Arnulf of the East Franks, supported by Saxons and Bavarians. Clearly, opposition to Viking attacks on the Continent was firming up.

Despondent at these defeats in Francia and suffering from food shortages due to famine on the Continent, in 892 a Viking army fell on south-east England again, making the short crossing over from Boulogne. It caught the Anglo-Saxons on the hop. The raiding force, said to be 250 ships strong, sailed up the Rother River and landed near the Weald, then a great forest 120 miles long and 30 wide. The only defences locally were composed of a half-finished fortress that was not provided with a proper garrison and it was quickly overwhelmed; evidence that Alfred's *burh* building programme was not yet complete and suggesting that some regions, as mentioned by Asser, were dilatory in complying with it (in fact, Kent seems to have been largely outside of the programme). Part of the army, led by the veteran Viking Hæsten, who by now had been active for decades, made its way up the Thames with eighty ships and set up camp at Milton Regis while another encampment was established at Appledore.

Hæsten deserves to be better remembered than he is. Since his semi-legendary excursion around the Mediterranean some decades earlier, he had spent much of his time in Francia. He is mentioned as being active on the Loire and Sarthe rivers in the 860s. In 882 he made a treaty with Louis III, king of Francia, and then left the immediate vicinity for a while. However, from 890 to 892 he was known to be on the Somme and in Amiens. Hæsten never seems to have shown any intention of settling down, unlike some of his contemporaries such as Guthrum. He had the *wanderlust* and adventurism that is part of the stereotypical Viking.

What happened in England following Hæsten's arrival stretched Alfred's newly developed defences to the limit. Viking assaults were launched across his kingdom over an extended period. To what extent these were coordinated is unclear, but it is likely that there was some cohesion between the attacks. The Viking armies at Milton Regis and Appledore stubbornly refused to budge. They were aided by raids from East Anglia and Northumbria on Anglo-Saxon England, despite promises made not to attack Alfred's territories and even the handing-over of hostages. The *ASC* suggests that sometimes these armies acted together and sometimes on their own. They appear to have been effective: ominously coin minting at Canterbury stopped abruptly in 892 and did not start again until 910.[44]

In response, Alfred gathered his own force and placed it between Appledore and Milton Regis so that he could keep an eye on both Viking armies. The Vikings then sent out small raiding parties on horseback, who hoped to elude Alfred's men by making their way through forests. This was a change of tactics, prodding and probing to see if a weakness in Alfred's defensive structure could be identified and exploited. A to-and-fro campaign followed in which the Anglo-Saxons chased after these small parties of raiders and tried to prevent them from causing extensive damage.

There was, however, one larger Viking break-out that succeeded in making off with a great deal of booty. Æthelweard later wrote that Hampshire and Berkshire were laid waste by raids after Easter 893.[45] The Anglo-Saxon army under Alfred's son, Edward, caught the raiders at Farnham and inflicted a major defeat in which a good deal of the plunder was recovered. What followed was a disorganised rout. The surviving raiders managed to flee across the Thames, taking up residence on an island there (Thorney Island, 'the island of the stake'). The Anglo-Saxon force attempted to starve them out but then a weakness in their organisation revealed itself. The army was only required to serve for a certain period and at this critical point many of them left before reinforcements had arrived. It seems they were also running out of provisions. The campaign had gone very well for the English so far, but there were still issues to be resolved.

Now a certain amount of coordination in Viking manoeuvres became very apparent. While Alfred was on his way to Thorney Island to complete an Anglo-Saxon victory there, ships from East Anglia and Northumbria sailed down the coast and descended on Devon. Some attacked Exeter and others sailed around Land's End and raided the north coast of the county. Alfred had no choice but to move his men westwards to face this new, dangerous threat. However, he left some men to move east, where they joined with an army from London. This combined force then marched to Benfleet where Hæsten had established fortifications. The Anglo-Saxons fell on the town and breached the defences, taking a great deal of plunder as well as women and children who would make a valuable bargaining chip. The Anglo-Saxons also seized ships, either burning them or taking them off to London and Rochester; the reference to destroying captured ships is not unique and suggests that the Viking forces were very large, and the number of vessels greatly exceeded those that might be needed by the fledgling Anglo-Saxon navy.[46] This was potentially disastrous for the Vikings as it deprived them of the means to escape back to the Continent if the campaign continued to go badly for them.

When these events took place, Hæsten was absent; he was raiding across Mercia as far as the borders of Wales and was presumably dismayed to learn that his wife and two sons had been taken. However, Alfred – who was godfather to one of the sons – returned them to Hæsten. This was perhaps a surprising move: Hæsten had previously sworn oaths to Alfred and given hostages but not long after had returned to his old raiding ways. But Alfred was very capable of making seemingly unorthodox gestures and this is one example. The information that Alfred was godfather to one of the sons – his son-in-law Æthelred had served the same function for another – comes as a bolt out of the blue as this highly significant information was not previously mentioned in the *ASC*. A very plausible reason has been presented by one modern historian, namely that baptism was the price that Alfred extracted from Hæsten in return for a large payment to get him to leave Kent alone in the first place; the region was very difficult to defend from Wessex as the Weald prevented easy reinforcement from there. Hæsten may then have reneged on a deal not to cause trouble in Mercia, launching new raids on there from Benfleet.[47]

When Alfred marched his men to Exeter, the Vikings besieging it left before a fight took place. However, this may have been part of a wider plan to distract Alfred, for despite their defeat at Benfleet, the Vikings had regrouped at Shoebury in Essex where they were joined by reinforcements from East Anglia and Northumbria. They moved up the Thames and from there to the Severn. In response to their moves, the ealdormen Æthelred, Æthelhelm and Æthelnoth (Alfred's Mercian son-in-law and the ealdormen of Wiltshire and Somerset respectively) assembled an army and chased after the Vikings.

The armies met at Buttington, near Montgomery on the Welsh borders (there were also Welsh warriors with Alfred's army, confirming that the sub-kings of Wales were starting to think that the Viking threat was more dangerous than that posed by their traditional Anglo-Saxon foes). The Vikings took refuge in a fortification and a siege followed in which hunger took its toll on those inside; they were forced to eat their horses to survive. Alfred had clearly learned his lesson from the chastening defeat of the West Saxon army when they had attacked the Viking camp at Reading two decades before and he now sought to starve the enemy out rather than attack head-on. The Vikings tried to fight their way out but in the battle that followed they were soundly beaten, though some important Anglo-Saxon figures, including several of the king's thegns, were killed. Unusually, these events seem to be mentioned in the *Annals of Ulster*, which recorded that a battle was fought in England against the Dark Foreigners and that 'countless multitudes fell'.

Those Vikings who managed to escape from Buttington fled to Chester, then in a ruinous state and long past its prime as a key legionary city in Roman Britain, where they were joined by reinforcements from East Anglia and Northumbria; evidence of yet more coordination. The Anglo-Saxons could not stop the Vikings from entering Chester, but they could capture many of their cattle and much of their corn and, starving once more, the Vikings broke out and made their way into Wales. From there, they made their way circuitously across the north of England and then down through East Anglia to Mersea Island in Essex.

While some have argued that Essex may have retained a stubbornly independent streak that made it resistant to any attempts at a West Saxon takeover,[48] this use of naval bases there by Viking fleets suggests that the area was at this time firmly under the thumb of Scandinavian-ruled East Anglia. There is evidence that Essex occasionally formed part of the sphere of influence of ealdormen of East Anglia during some parts of the later Anglo-Saxon period, as did some areas of Buckinghamshire, Bedfordshire and Hertfordshire, though this tends to date from the tenth rather than the ninth century.[49]

The Vikings had landed many punches across a wide area, but they were nowhere near producing a knock-out blow. Alfred and his armies, ably commanded by ealdormen who were up to the task, had countered every blow so far. Even when the raiders retreated from Exeter and launched a subsequent raid on Chichester, they were beaten off. Stretched Alfred's defences might be, but they were coping with the strain. Yet it was not quite all over. Perhaps there was overconfidence in the air for when a Viking fortification about 20 miles from London on the River Lea (on the border as defined by the treaty between Alfred and Guthrum) was attacked, the assault was beaten off with significant losses among the attackers. Alfred, now freed of the threat in the west, moved up and subsequently blockaded the Vikings there, building forts that would prevent the enemy from returning along the river. The Vikings were forced to abandon their ships and made their way overland to Bridgnorth where they set up another fortification. They over-wintered there in what was the third year of their extended campaign in England. However, by now they were losing their will to fight. Those Vikings who held lands in East Anglia or Northumbria made their way back there: those who did not sailed to Francia and the Seine. Despite this, raids from East Anglia and Northumbria continued to be launched from the sea on the south coast of Wessex. The Northumbrians, led by a man called Sigfred, in 893 or 894, attacked with a great fleet that ravaged the coast before making its way safely back home. It may be that this Sigfred was the same man who is mentioned as being active in Ireland around the same time though we cannot be sure (an individual with the same name was soon after king of York). If he was, then he may have been trying to take advantage of dynastic disputes among the descendants of Ivarr at about the same time; there are hints of this in some sources.[50]

In response, Alfred constructed ships, not creating exact copies of Viking ships but adapting them to his own design, longer and higher than those of his opponents. Not all the Viking forces he had to face were large. The chroniclers record a raid by six ships that fell on the Isle of Wight in 896, which provides a little colour to the outline records that have survived. Alfred's fledgling navy sailed after them. The Anglo-Saxon ships managed to catch the raiders in an estuary and captured two of their vessels, killing those on board. Three of the other Viking ships ran aground. So too, unfortunately, did some of the Anglo-Saxon fleet, suggesting that while Alfred's ships may have been powerful they were also cumbersome.

A land battle followed, in which 62 of the Anglo-Saxon force (which apparently also included Frisians) were killed along with 120 Vikings. But with the return of the tide the smaller Viking ships made their escape while the Anglo-Saxon vessels were still stuck. This suggests the possibility that Alfred's experimental fleet included ships that were simply too large to handle in comparison with the more manoeuvrable Viking vessels that opposed them. But as far as those who escaped were concerned, their luck was running out. Two ships were forced ashore by the waves; the Vikings who manned them were taken off to Winchester where they were hanged; mercy was apparently only for Viking leaders.

At about this time, Alfred received visitors from Scandinavia. One of them, Othere, told tales of the Far North which must have been particularly gripping to his audience in the royal hall. Even now, they have a capacity to keep the reader spellbound with stories of adventures from the distant past. Othere lived, as he described it, as the 'farthest north of all Norwegians'. Yet he knew that the Norwegian coast extended much further up. Inspired by nothing more than his inquisitive nature, he had decided to find out for himself what lay up there in the Great Unknown. He sailed for three days, which took him as far north, he told Alfred, as the whale hunters went. After another three days the land turned east and Othere followed it around. He was now sailing past the North Cape, the very tip of Norway.

Sailing eastwards for four days, he then saw the land sweep to the south. He was approaching the Barents Sea off the coast of Finland and then took a southward course for a further five days. Eventually he reached a point where a great river poured forth into the sea. On turning into the river, he and his crew saw that the land on its banks was cultivated and dared not go further in case they were attacked. It was the first sign of other human beings they had seen since leaving home other than the occasional fisher, hunter and fowler, who were all Sáami.

Othere told Alfred that there was also a commercial aspect to his journey. He was after walrus, which he describes as a small whale (the Dutch word for whale, *walvis,* has been suggested as the origin of the word in English). The walrus, he explained, was valuable for both its ivory and its hide, which could be transformed into strong ships' cables. However, he said that he had seen larger versions closer to home that were seven times as big. In one whaling expedition, he and his partners had killed 60 of them in two days.

He was clearly a wealthy man. He had 600 domesticated reindeer at home, a fact that has led to the rather appealing description of him by a modern historian as 'a reindeer baron from north Norway'.[51] Six of them were decoy reindeer, used to entrap their wild cousins. He had in contrast only 20 sheep and 20 pigs. What little ploughing he did was performed by horses. He also told Alfred that he and his fellow Norsemen were able to extract tributes from the Sáami. These came in the form of marten furs, reindeers, animal skins, whalebone and bird feathers (to make objects that used down; something for which Norway remains famous with small cottage industries still producing very expensive products). From some of the higher-ranking Sáami more exotic tribute such as bear and otter skins were required. This is an invaluable insight into the way that life was lived in the Far North at the time and also into the spirit of adventure among some of the Scandinavian people, which led them to the far stretches of the wild Atlantic in one direction and to the Middle East in the other.[52]

These fireside tales must have been a welcome distraction from the trials and tribulations of war for Alfred. From time to time, a confrontation would still take place but they were less frequent now. For much (though not all) of the next century after Alfred's death in 899, the Vikings in England, whether they be Danish or Norwegian in origin, would be on the back foot while one of the greatest royal dynasties that England has ever had laid the foundations of the modern country. Included among their subjects in the future would be men and women who could proudly lay claim to Viking heritage.

Alfred's greatness had been shaped by the Viking threat. In putting together a unified regional response, he helped solidify Wessex and raise it to prominence among the Anglo-Saxon parts of England. In the process, this reinforced a wider concept, that of the 'English' (though it was not new: Bede after all had written of the English peoples). It is tempting to wonder how Alfred felt when he looked back on his reign; and we have a very strong clue as to exactly how he saw it. He was involved in the translation of various classical works into English. One of them was Boethius' *Consolation of Philosophy,* a hugely influential work in medieval times. In a new translation of this sixth-century work, the king looked back to an age when 'no merchant had gazed on strand or island, and no man had heard tell of the pirate host'.[53] It was as if Alfred longed for the return of a golden age which, like all such, had probably never existed, back when the realities of Viking raids were nothing more than a dimly imagined nightmare that would never become a reality.

Alfred's reign reached a triumphant conclusion, but it is easy to forget that the ransacking and pillaging that had gone on before must have had a devastating effect. Individual stories of the impact of Viking raiding are few and far between; but they can from time to time be glimpsed. In the National Library of Sweden in Stockholm is an eighth-century Gospel Book known as the *Stockholm Codex Aureus.* It includes the Four Gospels and some lavish illustrations. However, its original contents are not the only interesting thing about it. There is a later inscription in it, probably dating from the late ninth century. It records how the manuscript had been pillaged by Vikings and had been redeemed with pure gold by Alfred, ealdorman of Surrey, and Wærburh, his wife. They did this, the ealdorman said, for the love of God and the benefit of their souls. They donated the repatriated manuscript to Christ Church, Canterbury. According to the National Library of Sweden's website, the *Codex Aureus* probably left England during the chaotic Reformation period and it may have changed hands a number of times before it ended up in Sweden. Given the destruction that occurred during Henry VIII's reign, we are fortunate to still be able to consult this document centuries later.

Other snippets of information have come down to us that hint at the suffering caused by the Viking raids during these troubled times. Bishop Denewulf of Winchester later told how an estate of his church at Beddington in Surrey had been 'stripped bare by heathen men'. Estates belonging to others, such as a woman called Eahlburgh who hailed from Kent, had been unable to pay their rents because of the 'heathen army'.[54] In our search to understand the huge events that were taking place it is easy to overlook how personally devastating they must have been to many ordinary men and women who had the misfortune to be in the way of this onslaught that overwhelmed them.

Paris besieged again

Even as the birth pains of England were being endured, the dynamics of Francia were changing dramatically. From the dizzy heights of Charlemagne's empire, Francia had gone downhill, with deep fissures in her society forced open by Viking raids exploiting internal weaknesses. As previously omnipotent central power eroded away, the status of local warlords grew. In return for their protection, men would link themselves with them, to work the land (or at least oversee those who did) and fight for them when the occasion required it. It was the beginnings of a new society; as one commentator put it, 'the Vikings were the midwives of feudalism in France'.[55] While no doubt some historians who specialise in the birth of feudalism might object to the oversimplification, the actions of the Vikings helped to redefine the countries of Western Europe.

They sought to exploit the situation, notably in yet another raid on Paris. Depressed that the city had already fallen to the Vikings on several occasions, its citizens resolved that it should not happen again. The riverway of the Seine was the weak point that a Viking ship could sail along as surely as a horse could move along a road. But if fortified bridges were used to obstruct their progress, then the defence of Paris should become more viable. When in 885 a Danish fleet, allegedly composed of 700 ships, a massive force, moved up the Seine, the Parisians were ready for them.

The battle went on for a year with the defenders heroically refusing to give way in the face of this terrifying assault. It became a trial of wills, the Verdun of its day. Both attackers and defenders were regularly reinforced by new intakes of men. Inside, Count Odo (the son of Robert, count of Anjou, killed by the Vikings two decades earlier) led a superb defence. Two bridges across the Seine blocked Viking passage past the city. A ferocious attack followed: according to Dudo of St Quentin 'they shook it with their engines and stormed it with arrows. The city resounded with clamour, the people were aroused, the bridges trembled'. The Vikings, under Sigfred and Sinric (Rollo, later ruler of Normandy, may have been there too, though not all historians are convinced of this), had siege engines – Dudo talks of 'stones hurled by slings and war-machines' – but only managed to obtain limited results from their use. In response, the defenders poured hot wax and pitch on any attackers who got too close to the walls. This caused horrific injuries, in some cases tearing off the scalps of the attackers while others threw themselves into the Seine in an attempt to soothe the pain. Battering rams were used in unsuccessful attempts to bring down the gates. The bishop of Paris, Gozlin, played a prominent and most unpriestly part in the defence and was often seen with a bow and an axe in his hands. Count Odo also fought heroically. The attacks were particularly relentless between November 885 and January 886. Then the Vikings tried using fireships against one of the bridges. While they did not succeed in bringing the bridge down immediately, they severely weakened it and in February, after a bout of bad weather, it collapsed.

The fall of the bridge left one tower hopelessly isolated on the far bank. There were only twelve men left inside it and the Vikings called on them to surrender. They defiantly refused and were soon after taken and killed. But the men defending Paris clearly had a high fighting spirit and some were determined to fight to the death. As the German army found out in 1914 outside Paris and again at Verdun in 1916, a Frank can be an implacable opponent when his sacred places are threatened. Charles the Fat at last moved up a force to attack the Viking besiegers but, rather than do so, he instead paid the Vikings. He had been told bluntly by Fulk, the Archbishop of Rheims, that Paris, with its vital strategic positioning on or near the Seine, the Marne and the Yonne, was the key to his kingdom (he described it as 'the head and key' of Neustria and Burgundy). No doubt Charles thought that, by buying the Vikings off, he had done his bit to save it. But, as has been remarked, 'this may have been the act of a statesman, but to the Franks it looked the act of a coward'.[56] The defenders of Paris were furious that, after their efforts, yet again a humiliating peace had been bought.

To compound the deed, Charles did not actually pay these Vikings to go away but instead encouraged them to fight for him. They did so, taking on powerful domestic opponents in Burgundy on his behalf. Vikings had become 'guns for hire' to be used at the behest of embattled and beleaguered kings and warlords. Sometimes they received land in return for their mercenary assistance, most famously when they were established in Normandy early in the tenth century. But by his submissive actions, Charles had sealed his own fate for he was removed from power by his own people and his death in January 888 followed two months later. He had been at one time king of all the former parts of Francia, which had in previous decades been divided among several different kings. For a short while he had been a true Carolingian Emperor, in name if not in practice. He had even been crowned as such by Pope John VIII. Now with his death the Carolingian Empire also expired. Charles's successor in the west of Francia, then known as Neustria, was the hero of the defence of Paris, Odo, who promptly handed over money to the raiders to go away. This time the tactic worked, and Paris was never again to witness an assault from Viking raiders.

In other parts of Francia though events had taken a turn for the worse for the Vikings. In 891, a battle was fought at Leuven on the River Dyle. The Franks defeated a Viking army in a reverse that was so serious that it was said by the *Annales Fuldenses* that the bodies of dead warriors blocked the flow of the river. Among the dead were two Danish kings, Sigfred and Godfrid. This defeat was followed soon after by a major famine. For those Vikings there, who had spent the best part of a decade in the region raiding and eking out a precarious living, this was enough. Their next move was to make the short crossing from the Low Countries back to England, as we have already seen. But although they came in great numbers – perhaps 4,000 strong[57] – they found a country much changed from the relatively easy touch of a few decades before. Alfred's establishment of the *burghal* system along with his reform of the *fyrds* proved its worth. The challenge facing Viking attackers was far greater now.

Hafrsfjord and Iceland

Much had been happening in Norway in the meantime. Harald Fairhair had been ruthless in building up his powerbase there. He first expanded his landholdings in the Vestfold region and then further extended his influence by persuading the powerful *jarls* of the Trøndelag to recognise him as their overlord. As part of his strategy to cement this alliance, Harald married the daughter of Håkon Grjotgardsson, the most powerful of the *jarls*, probably a marriage of convenience for both parties, which is an unromantic alternative to the saga writer's contention that Harald only sought to rule Norway to prove himself to his true love Gyda. The Trøndelag was then left largely to its own devices while Harald turned his attention elsewhere.

The greatest opposition to Harald's ambitions was always likely to come from the fiercely independent region of Vestland in south-west Norway. Many of the overseas raiders came from there so there was a large pool of warriors with battle-hardened skills available to resist him. But Harald was relentless in pursuing his goals and smashed his way through Vestland despite fierce opposition. It all came down to one decisive battle at Hafrsfjord. There, near Stavanger, the battle site is now marked by three huge swords, such as one might imagine were used by the giants of Norse mythology. These were erected by the water's edge in 1983 on a low-lying rocky outcrop on the shore of the hammer-shaped fjord, towering above modern visitors to the site.

Harald was faced by a confederation of enemies composed primarily of local kings and chiefs who wished to retain their independence from the centralised monarchy but in the battle that followed they were crushed. These events are described in the saga of King Harald, the *Heimskringla*. We read of the deaths of Erik, king of Hordaland in the Vestland region and of Súlki, king of Rogaland, another west Norwegian territory, along with his brother, the Earl Sóti. Kvotji the Wealthy, king of Agthir, barely escaped with his life to an island where he was able to defend himself. Those who could, fled. Although the fighting took place offshore, it was effectively a land battle fought on the water, with a series of boarding actions followed by vicious hand-to-hand fighting. The numbers involved are impossible to establish though the sagas suggest that this was the largest battle that Harald was ever involved in. A key part of the battle occurred when Harald, in the thick of the fight, got his ship alongside that of Thorir Longchin, one of the foremost fighters opposing him. A storming party of berserkers jumped across and in the hacking match that followed Thorir fell and his men lost heart.

Snorri Sturluson paints this as a stirring confrontation. He writes vividly of how 'the berserkers bellowed as the battle opened, the wolf-coats shrieked loud and shook their weapons'.[58] No doubt the story got better in the telling; but the strategy of sending in shock troops to take out a leader of the opposing forces has much to commend it. But behind the flowery language and purple prose, there was no hiding the fact that Harald was now, as a result of Hafrsfjord, the dominant force in southern and south-western Norway. The exact date of this significant battle is very hard to discern. Though it was once considered that it took place in around 872, most historians now believe this date is at least a decade too soon. But its results are more straightforward to interpret; the way was left open for Harald to tighten his grip on the Vestland.

For Harald, winning this victory was one thing; keeping the conquered under control longer term quite another. Rather than kowtow to the new regime, some of the more powerful men in the region sailed off to the Scottish Islands and beyond. There had been raids on the Northern Isles from Norway for decades but now, with Harald's triumph, more permanent large-scale settlement took place. And before long, rather than Vikings sailing from Norway to the British Isles to launch raids, they were launching them in the opposite direction.[59]

Harald was not the sort of man to take this lying down. He set up naval patrols to guard the shores of the Vestland from these Viking raids in reverse, launched against and not from the Scandinavian homeland. But when the patrols were not wholly successful, he decided on more drastic action, leading a fleet to devastate Shetland, Orkney and the Hebrides. In some accounts, largely dismissed by historians, he even continued southwards and reached the Isle of Man and then Ireland.[60] These lands were not conquered as a result; some had already been Norse territories for over half a century; but this gave a new impetus and shape to colonisation in the region.

As the ninth century neared its close a Norse earldom was established in Orkney by Harald, though it is very likely that settlement started there a long time before this. Its first *jarl* was Sigurd, who became infamous for the ferocity of his attacks on the Scottish mainland. Norse dominance in this part of the world appears to have been virtually total. About 99 per cent of Orkney place names are of Norse origin. Norse territory in the region also included the islands of Shetland, and Caithness and Sutherland on the north of the Scottish mainland. In these northern territories, a distinctive Norse-based language called Norn was established and was spoken, albeit increasingly infrequently, until relatively modern times.

The Vikings literally took over the land as far as can be discerned from archaeology. At Buckquoy in Orkney, Viking houses overbuilt Pictish ones. The Pictish broch of Aikerness was replaced by a Viking burial and building. This was the case in other places in Orkney too. We are fortunate that archaeological evidence of the Viking Age is stronger in Orkney and Shetland than elsewhere on the Scottish mainland or indeed further afield in places such as Wales that were also subject to the effects of Viking incursions. That said, it should be noted that the two archipelagos, though adjacent to each other, are quite different in their natural character with Orkney being far more fertile than Shetland. Orkney would become the political epicentre of the region.

Some time in the ninth century, the Hebrides had a famous Norse ruler. His name hints at his appearance: Ketill Flatnose, a man of Norwegian origin. He took control of the Hebrides, which had already been settled in parts by Scandinavians. The works known as the *Landnámabók* and the *Eyrbyggja* say that this was on the orders of Harald Fairhair in an effort to deal with émigrés who had been launching raids on Norway, while the *Laxdœla Saga* says that Ketill fled to avoid Harald's tyranny: given the much later date of this evidence we cannot be confident which, if either, of these versions is true.[61] Before long there would be a Viking chain spreading down from Shetland and Orkney in the North (only a day's sail from Trondheim according to Adam of Bremen),[62] through the Hebrides, on to the Isle of Man and down into Ireland, though it would be extremely difficult for any aspiring king of Norway to keep firm control over such an extended chain of territory. Indeed, there are accounts that say that it was not long before Ketill was falling out with Harald Fairhair.[63]

Ketill was the son of Björn 'Buna' Grimsson, whose family were among the most important early settlers of Iceland.[64] According to the *Landnámabók* Ketill had a daughter, Aud 'the Deep-Minded', who came from the Hebrides and was married to the famous king of Dublin, Óláfr the White. She had an adventurous life. After Óláfr's death she moved to Scotland where her son Thorstein the Red embarked on a war of conquest in partnership with Sigurd the Mighty, Earl of Orkney; they conquered the whole of Caithness and a large part of Argyll, Moray and Ross. There is place name evidence of this found for example at Dingwall in Easter Ross. For a time, connections between Dingwall and the site of a Viking '*thing*' were not wholly accepted; but an archaeological dig under a car park in 2012 provided compelling evidence that such was indeed the case.

When Thorstein was killed, Aud initially went to Orkney and then to Iceland.[65] Sigurd met a strange death which owed much to the supernatural. He killed Máel Brigte, the mormaer of Moray, in an ambush and cut off his head as a trophy. While riding away with it, the head bit him, the wound turned septic and Sigurd soon after died; or so the saga writers say.[66] Aud had sailed west, stopping in the Faroes before continuing on to Iceland with a body of slaves who were prisoners of war from the fighting in Scotland; she was a devout Christian, but this did not stop her from keeping a number of bondsmen; it also did not prevent some of her kinsfolk from continuing to offer sacrifices. In Iceland, Aud acquired territory, some of which she parcelled out to her retainers.

Eventually, Aud grew old and realised that she was dying. She summoned her people to a great gathering, which she announced to them was her '*arval*' or funeral feast. She died during the festivities and was buried on the shore, between the low and high water mark, saying that she did not wish to be buried in unconsecrated ground. The *Landnámabók* suggests that her people soon relapsed into paganism; though there is perhaps a risk that the writer of this work was overplaying her Christian credentials in the first place in an attempt to make her more attractive to the later generation that he was writing for. There is little doubt that Christianity was still a minority religion on the island and would remain so for quite a while. Even a century later, paganism remained strong and enthusiastic evangelists were required. One of these, Fredrik, was a Saxon bishop who was accompanied by a Viking convert, Thorvald the Far-Traveller, whose very name betrayed pagan origins. They received a frosty reception in Iceland and poems were written about them with barely concealed claims that they were involved in a homosexual relationship. So incensed was Thorvald that he killed two men who were mocking him, which might not seem to be a very good example of the Christian maxim of turning the other cheek but may ironically have made a positive impression on some contemporary observers as an example that those of the new faith were not all a pacifist-inspired pushovers.[67]

There were some interesting repercussions from this colonisation of Iceland, which opened up new vistas. One of the settlers, Jorund, sent a present of a she-bear and two white bear cubs back to Harald Fairhair, the first polar bears to be seen in Norway (as it was then; it is very likely that polar bears were present in the far north of what is modern Norway, but such extremities would then have been populated by the Sáami).[68] There is a record of one particular disastrous interaction between man and bear in Iceland. A father and son, Arngeir and Thorgils, went out in a blizzard to make sure that their sheep were all right. When they did not return, another son, Odd, went to look for them. He found them both, dead. He looked on in horror as he saw a polar bear sucking the blood from one of them. Odd killed the bear and dragged its body home with him. Then he ate it: men said that he killed the bear to avenge his father and he ate it to avenge his brother.[69]

To some men, Iceland gave a chance of a different way of life, perhaps more settled than the one they had been used to. One example was Ævarr (Ivarr) who 'went to Iceland, leaving off Viking raids' with all of his family except for a son, Vefreyd, who 'remained behind sea-roving'. Vefreyd eventually joined him, though there was almost an unfortunate accident when Ævarr fought his son because he did not recognise him when he arrived; fortunately his true identity was uncovered before any damage had been done.[70] The journey was not without its perils: the *Landnámabók* describes how Kampr-Grimr sailed from the Hebrides to Iceland but 'he was tossed about upon the sea for the whole summer' before his ship was wrecked on the coast of Iceland and other wrecks are regularly alluded to by Ari, the author.[71]

An early settler of Iceland was Uni, who the *Landnámabók* suggests was sent there by Harald Fairhair to be his man with the intention that he should become its earl. However, Ari suggests that the settlers in Iceland got wind of this scheme and would not cooperate with him. Uni was eventually killed in a domestic dispute. He had set up home with a man named Leidolf and he made himself too comfortable when he got Leidolf's daughter, Thorun, pregnant. Uni ran off but was pursued and caught by Leidolf. He was brought back but when he ran off once more soon afterwards Leidolf caught him again and this time he killed him.[72]

Harald was not the only powerful man in Norway. In the Trøndelag, Håkon Grjotgardsson continued to be a powerbroker for a time. Also influential was Ragnall Eysteinsson, the first *jarl* of Møre, the northernmost part of the Vestland. Ragnall played a role in the establishment of the earldom of Orkney and one of his sons, Einar, became its second *jarl;* it was said that all the earls (or *jarls)* of Orkney were descended from this stock. Einar has a particular claim to fame as it was said of him that he was the first man to dig turf for fuel in the region, firewood being very scarce in the island territories.[73] Ragnall is sometimes described as the father of Hrolf (Rollo), the first Viking ruler of Normandy, though this claim is contradicted in continental sources who state that Rollo's father was an unnamed Norwegian or Dane, or alternatively a man called Ketill.[74] Rollo's precise point of origin remains a matter of contention, with some writers such as Snorri Sturluson saying that he came from the west coast of Norway while others such as Dudo of St Quentin suggest that he was Danish.[75] Einar's son was a famous warrior with the sinister name of Thorfinn Skull-Splitter. Perhaps surprisingly given this title, he lived a long life and was, the *Orkneyinga Saga* recorded, ultimately to die in his bed and was buried in a mound at Hoxa on the remote island of North Ronaldsay. It seems an inappropriate end for someone who was seemingly destined for Valhalla, but it was said of Thorfinn that 'people thought him a very great man'.[76]

The Viking attacks on Scotland abated for a while, perhaps because affairs in England had distracted many of their men further south. But there was a renewal of hostilities in 889 when Domnall, son of Constantin, defeated a Viking force at *Innisibsolian,* tentatively identified as the Isle of Seil in Argyll. It has been suggested that this may be a continuation of a blood feud between the relatives of Óláfr and Constantin. Alternatively, this may have been linked to events in Dublin where Viking infighting led, according to the *Annals of Ulster,* to some elements leaving Ireland.[77] If there was such a feud, this may not have been the end of it. In 900, a Viking force possibly including elements from Orkney fell on the great northern Pictish fortress at Dunottar and in the fight that took place there Domnall was killed. Such blood feuds were a regular feature of Viking, Anglo-Saxon and Celtic contemporary politics, as is evidenced in the *Landnámabók* where several specific references to them are made. These were extremely violent times; clearly it was not just Vikings who were responsible for the violence.

7

An Uneasy Equilibrium (901–925)

...Æthelflaed, sister of the king and relict of Æthelred, ought not to be forgotten...

William of Malmesbury

Scandinavia at the beginning of the tenth century

As the tenth century began, the Scandinavian world was on the verge of dramatic change. The transition towards a form of nationhood in Norway (or at least a land under one overall king) was echoed in Denmark, where moves in that direction had been made before in the reigns of Godfrid and Horik. Alongside that, there would be a dramatic uptake by Vikings of the Christian religion. Again, such measures were not completely new. Harald Klak had been baptised three-quarters of a century before and the efforts of Ansgar, though of limited impact, did have a modicum of success in Sweden. Since then, Vikings had been encouraged, persuaded or cajoled to support Christianity in other areas such as Britain, Ireland and Francia, but now there would be a quantum leap in terms of scale.

Already during the latter years of the tenth century the trend towards Christianisation in both Scandinavia and further afield, for example among Viking communities in Britain and Ireland, accelerated. It would by no means be universally accepted, even by the end of the tenth century, and many parts of Norway and especially Sweden would stay outside the Christian fold for some time yet. And it may well be the case that, even where Christianity was nominally accepted, old pagan habits remained, as is often the case in such a conversion process. Some beliefs survived and were most likely adopted, or at least adapted, by Christianity. But the landscape in 1000 would look very different than it did in 900.

It is highly likely that one reason for this acceptance of Christianity among the Scandinavians was the political benefits it offered. It brought Vikings, and more particularly Viking leaders, into the political fold and gave them a degree of acceptance and credibility. It made it easier to rule newly converted Christian subjects and also to enter into alliances with Christian communities. It also aided the opening up of trade relationships with Christian states. In other words, conversion was good for business. In addition, Viking leaders could now hope to gain the support of the Church, a powerful and legitimising institution. This was a two-way street for the Church could also cultivate relationships with powerful Vikings, or at least protect themselves from them. This proved to be one of the most remarkable features of the later years of the Viking Age: that men who had once attacked the Church could be its benefactors and that Church leaders who once demonised the raiders would now work hand in glove with their descendants. This seemed a long way off in the year 900, even if Guthrum had ostensibly become a Christian ruler in East Anglia. The first decades of the tenth century were turbulent ones for many parts of Britain. Across the island tensions bubbled up like an overheated cauldron on the brink of boiling over. Yet again, forces of Scandinavian origin were at the heart of much of the disruption as the fortunes of all sides ebbed and flowed.

Despite the success of the many Danes who had fought and settled in England, the situation back in Denmark was far from healthy at this point. We know very little about the state of Denmark in the second half of the ninth century but, from what we can tell, there had been a marked weakening of centralised control. By about 900 some parts of the country had been taken by Swedish kings. The first of them was named Óláfr and he was followed by his sons Chnob and Gurd. The islands of Gotland and Öland were now in Swedish hands and so too were important trade lands in the south of Jutland. Swedes were also well established in the East Baltic and beyond into Russia. Although there is limited evidence of the shape taken by the Swedish government in Denmark, there are some oblique references to it in runic inscriptions around Hedeby.[1] It was however a situation that would not last and by the end of the tenth century Denmark was very much in the ascendant in the region, both in the Baltic and beyond.

Post-Alfred Wessex: a rulership divided

The death of Alfred in 899 led to a succession crisis in England. Such an occurrence became an almost inescapable part of the political landscape after the death of an Anglo-Saxon king and the Vikings were quick to try to take advantage of it. This was never better demonstrated than in the following year. Alfred had declared that his son Edward should succeed him, a measure that was confirmed soon afterwards by the *witan*. Edward had proved himself a resilient warrior in recent campaigns against the Vikings but he had a rival. When Alfred came to the throne nearly three decades before, it was as the brother of the previous king, Æthelred I.

Æthelred left a son, Æthelwold. He was a young child at the time of Alfred's succession and therefore clearly not the right king when England had a mighty Viking army on its doorstep. But with the passing of the years Æthelwold was now a grown man and felt that he was more than capable of being a king in his own right. Æthelwold was mentioned in Alfred's will but received only a few estates such as Godalming and Guildford; the lion's share went to Edward. A discontented Æthelwold made his move at Wimborne in Wessex, significantly the place where his late father had been buried after the Battle of Meretun, also seizing the nearby *burh* of Twynham (Christchurch) and claiming his right to the succession. Edward assembled an army to crush the rebellion. When it encamped at nearby Badbury Rings, Æthelwold made good his escape, allegedly after abducting a nun. He then made his way north to Northumbria: the Vikings there proclaimed him king, sensing an opportunity to divide England as a result. It is significant that the later tenth-century Wessex chronicler Æthelweard writes of dissension previously among the English in Northumbria and it may be that Æthelwold found a willing audience when he arrived there.[2]

Significantly, the twelfth-century *Annals of St Neots* described Æthelwold as 'king of the Danes' and later 'king of the pagans';[3] though there must be some doubt about this as we have coin evidence for two kings of Northumbria with very Norse names, Sigfred and Cnut, at about this time. Æthelwold later led a largely Viking army to Essex (again suggesting that this border territory might present a vulnerability for the kings of Wessex) and then moved to East Anglia where there were many men of Scandinavian descent. He was able to assemble a strong force, one which Edward knew needed to be eliminated. After a raid on Cricklade, Æthelwold's force returned across the Thames with Edward hot on his tail.

A decisive confrontation took place somewhere in the Fens at the Battle of the Holne in 902, though it has something of an accidental feel about it. Edward told his Kentish allies to return home but for whatever reason they failed to do so, despite the king sending no less than seven commands for them to withdraw. They were surrounded and attacked by Æthelwold's force. The Viking force suffered badly in the fight that followed, though so too did the Kentishmen. Among the Viking dead were Eohric, the king of East Anglia, a number of noblemen and

Æthelwold himself. The Vikings eventually held the field; but it was the archetypal Pyrrhic victory.

This campaign in which Viking forces had allegedly happily attached themselves to an Anglo-Saxon king is thought-provoking; cultural and ethnic boundaries were becoming blurred. Very probably 'Viking' armies from above Watling Street included many men of Anglo-Saxon origin who happened to live there. In later decades in the tenth century many Anglo-Saxons from Northumbria may have found themselves in 'Viking' armies while Danes from the Danelaw equally formed part of armies alongside men from Wessex. Ethnic distinctions were starting to become less clear-cut. Such events might seem extraordinary from a modern perspective when a concept of 'Englishness' has been in place for a thousand years and more. But things were rather different in the early tenth century. While it is unlikely that the people of Northumbria welcomed a Scandinavian ruling elite, neither would they have been receptive to West Saxon overlordship.

Two otherwise little-known Scandinavian rulers of Northumbria, Cnut and Sigfred, have been identified from coins as the men in power during the late ninth century and in the early years of the tenth century. What is remarkable about these is the presence of devout inscriptions on them such as *Domine Deus Omnipotens Rex* ('The Lord God Almighty is King').[4] It is unlikely that these words were chosen by enthusiastic new converts to Christianity but were probably inspired by churchmen in York who sought to protect their position by forming a potentially unholy alliance with the ruling Scandinavians in the city. In return, Viking overlords in York were seemingly prepared to accept this terminology as a way of establishing a legitimate ruling elite in the style of Anglo-Saxon and Frankish norms at the time. A peaceful co-existence between leading clerics and Scandinavian overlords is strongly intimated.

Yet there was something about this apparent conversion which suggested that it either did not take hold among all the Scandinavian rulers of Northumbria or perhaps that they were able to keep a foot in both camps in a religious sense. Some coins in the first part of the tenth century in Northumbria carry motifs that appear to be pagan; and funerary statutory from the period in the York region exhibit a fusion of styles, Scandinavian and Northumbrian, Christian and pagan, with Viking legends portrayed on them. The mention of this man Cnut is a good example of the difficulties of interpreting evidence from later sagas. A Cnut from the period is mentioned in later thirteenth- and fourteenth-century Scandinavian sagas but the lateness of this evidence might be enough to allow some modern commentators to dismiss it. It is only the random find of coins that confirm his existence: without this chance discovery historians might well doubt it. It is a salutary reminder that, however cautious we should be in allowing the later sagas as a source of evidence, we should be careful not to reject them altogether.

The Vikings ejected from Dublin

There was significant Viking activity further north in Britain during this period. In one raid Domnall, king of Alba, was killed by the *Danair* in 900. He met his end at Dunottar, as dramatic a setting as you are likely to find, marked by a later medieval castle perching precariously on the edge of sheer cliffs on the east coast of Scotland, hanging on for grim death and threatening to plunge into the waters far below at any moment. Domnall had been king for eleven years and earlier in his reign the Northmen had wasted Pictavia. Pictavia and the Picts were now, at least as far as the historical record is concerned, no more. Domnall's title as king of 'Alba' rather than Pictavia or Scotia signalled a massive change in direction for the country. His death, however, was far from the end of his country's difficulties. In fact, the pace of events in both Scotland and northern England was about to move up several gears.

The catalyst for this increased level of activity was found in Ireland. For decades the port of Dublin had been a point from which Viking forces created havoc both on the island itself and also on the other side of the Irish Sea in England, Wales and Scotland: the crossing from Ireland to Wales for example was short and later medieval voyages might be made in benign weather with favourable winds in about 6 hours.[5] Some degree of intermingling between Scandinavian and Irish had taken place and we might now talk of a Hiberno-Norse culture. But in 902 the resurgent Irish ejected the Northmen from Dublin. They were significantly helped by a series of power struggles in the port during the 890s that weakened the position of its ruling elite.

However, the situation in Dublin was not quite as black and white as it first appears to be. Archaeologists now tend towards the view that settlement in Dublin was continuous between 902, when we are told by annalists that the Vikings were ejected, and 917 when we are told they came back.[6] With respect to the latter year, it was perhaps ominous in the context of the times that the *Annals of Ulster* noted there were horrible portents and 'the heavens seemed to glow with comets; and a mass of fire appeared with thunder in the west beyond Ireland, and it went eastwards over the sea'. The most likely explanation for the Vikings' eventual return to Dublin after a fifteen-year absence was that it was only the leadership that had been ejected and not the rest of the population.[7] After all, Dublin was a wealthy and industrious port; why would Irish overlords want that to change? It is far more likely that they wished things to carry on largely unaltered, only with profits flowing to them instead of Dublin's former masters. At the same time, they would be much safer from Viking attacks launched from the settlement if they were in control there.

Those Vikings who were ejected from Dublin were unlikely to meekly go back to Scandinavia and they were shortly afterwards extremely busy in Britain. In 903, they ransacked Dunkeld and 'all of Albania' [Scotland]. As part of this process, it is likely that Pictish culture took another hammering. In the words of one historian when talking of its decline, 'the prime candidate for the cause of the cultural shift is likely to be the Viking attacks on Scotland, especially in the period from the 830s to the early 900s, provoking Gaelic migration into Pictland, disrupting established political relations, and providing a catalyst for the redistribution of land to a more Gaelic-speaking elite'. In other words, it was not only Vikings profiting from the raids, Gaelic Scots were also stepping into the vacuum they created wherever possible.[8]

But the year after, Ivarr (often assumed to be the grandson of the Ivarr who had founded a dynasty in Dublin in 851) was killed at *Strath Erren* by the forces of Constantin II, king of Alba, 'and there was a great slaughter all around him'.[9] It was a morale-boosting triumph for Constantin who was fairly new to his role and who would reign for four decades. It was ironic that he would, towards the end of his life, be on the wrong end of a catastrophic defeat, this time fighting alongside Scandinavian allies. There was always an element of unpredictability to the fortunes of war and in 904 the Vikings won a victory and killed an important Pictish leader, Aed. The exact level of importance of their victim is unclear; but as Aed is one of the last named Pictish leaders, this was in itself a significant event.

Scotland was not the only region to feel the fall-out from events in Ireland. In the same year that the Vikings were ejected from Dublin, Anglesey was attacked by a force led by Ingimundr. However, there is evidence that he did not stay there long and was thrown out. He and his men then made the short journey to the north-west of England, where he set up his base near Chester, perfectly placed to interface with Irish Sea traffic given its location on the Dee. In the meantime, Ireland was not left entirely alone and in 904 there was a raid on Ailech, the seat of the northern Uí Néill kings in Donegal. The Uí Néill had split into two rival factions, a state of affairs that the raiders may have known about and taken advantage of.

Some Vikings settled in north-west England and may have been given permission to stay by the rulers of Mercia, Æthelred and his wife Æthelflaed, the daughter of Alfred the Great. Mercia seemingly accepted being a junior partner to Wessex as the lesser of two evils as it may otherwise have been faced with extinction in the face of the Viking threat and the marriage had been part of Alfred's strategy to secure this.

It may be that Ingimundr saw the couple as a soft touch; Æthelred was now incapacitated through poor health and Æthelflaed, of course, was a woman.

In any event, the new arrivals from Ireland were given lands in the Wirral. This was a sensible move – after all, Alfred had also reached a negotiated settlement with the Vikings who attacked his kingdom – but in this case the strategy was of limited use in bringing an end to hostilities. Ingimundr and his men soon after attacked Chester. It was a major miscalculation on their part. Æthelflaed responded vigorously. While details are scant, Chester remained in Anglo-Saxon hands or, at the worst, was returned to them soon after it was captured. Some accounts suggest that the raiders were beaten off by a determined defence when the residents of Chester hurled boiling beer and beehives down on the heads of the raiders.[10] After the Viking attackers were driven off, Chester was added to the growing list of *burhs* in Mercia. Again, the substantial remains of the Roman defences formed an integral part of the fortifications erected there.

North-west England and possibly parts of what is now south-west Scotland too (we simply have insufficient evidence to be confident) remained populated by Scandinavians, if place-name evidence is indicative; though how reliable this is as evidence of actual Scandinavian settlement and how dense such settlement might have been remains a matter of disagreement between historians.[11] The Wirral, on the Mersey, was rife with such names, such as Kirby and Frankby, and it would be hard to find a village anywhere in England with a more Norse name than Thingwall. Within a few decades, this region around the Wirral may have played a part in one of the key battles in the formation of early medieval Britain.

At the same time, lands to the north in Cumbria and Galloway were populated by Vikings who came over from Ireland.[12] Settlement in Cumbria and on the nearby Isle of Man seems, if uncovered archaeology is a clue, to date to the tenth rather than the ninth century as opposed to other parts of England, Ireland and Scotland.[13] There are also indications that at around the same time Viking elements from Ireland were making their way to other places such as the Faroe Islands and the Cotentin Peninsula in Normandy.[14] However, it is not clear whether these movements came about as a result of the expulsion of an important group from Ireland or from longer-term migration patterns.

The process of 'Viking-isation' is particularly strongly evidenced in some specific areas in England. For example, there are many Norse place names in the Lake District, and in Amounderness in Lancashire, one of that county's six traditional hundreds based around Preston and the Ribble and extending over as far as the western boundaries of the Yorkshire Moors. Amounderness took its name from the Scandinavian known as Agmund (possibly the same man as Ingimundr?)[15] What is also of interest is that place names derived from a Scandinavian source in the region are usually of Hiberno-Norse rather than Danish origin. Only in the far-flung eastern part of the territory are Danish-derived place names found, suggesting that Viking influence came from the west, across the Irish Sea, in most parts of the region.[16]

One of the most remarkable Viking finds in England is the Cuerdale Hoard, which was found near Preston, Lancashire. This trove contained 7,500 coins and over 1,000 other items, the collective weight of which came to over 40 kg. There were coins from Wessex (both Alfred and Edward the Elder's reigns), from Francia, and dirhams from the Islamic world (from Cordoba to the Hindu Kush) with a spread of dates ending in around 905. In total, 59 different mints have been identified as being responsible for producing the coins, though the majority (about 5,000) were from Viking areas such as Northumbria and East Anglia, with a number being freshly minted at York. To put this in perspective, such a trove would be worth the equivalent of 6,000 sheep or 1,000 oxen at the time.[17] The hoard had a high content of material from Ireland, suggesting that it might have been brought over with those Viking leaders who had been ejected from Dublin and there has been speculation that it might even have been a war chest to finance a reconquest there. Much of the silver had signs of being 'nicked', a tell-tale sign that it had been checked for the purity of its content.[18]

Æthelflaed and her brother, Edward the Elder, formed a formidable double act. In 906, Edward entered into an agreement with the 'Danish' inhabitants of East Anglia and Northumbria in 'the Peace of Tiddingford', which merely bought Edward time. Tiddingford was near Watling Street, the border between the Danelaw and Anglo-Saxon England. It was several decades since Guthrum and Alfred had agreed the frontier between the two and in the succeeding years the precise definition of the border had probably become blurred. In addition, the arrival of new Viking forces from Ireland made it of paramount importance that those of Scandinavian origin in Northumbria did not lend them their support.

The arrangement made at Tiddingford only papered over the cracks. By 909, Edward was ravaging Lindsey, then held by 'Danes', with an army composed of men from both Wessex and Mercia. It was a great success and the holy relics of St Oswald were recovered from Bardney in Lindsey and taken back to a gilded shrine in Gloucester. After decades of fighting on the defensive, the Anglo-Saxons were now on the front foot. They were encouraged by a decline in the fortunes of Northumbria: Northumbrian coinage from this period lacks the name of any prominent individual ruling the region but has more general motifs in the form of the name of St Peter. This 'St Peter's Pence' suggests an attachment to Christianity, but also a possible vacuum of secular leadership.[19]

The next year a decisive Anglo-Saxon triumph followed. The protagonists were the same: men from Wessex and Mercia on the one side, forces from Northumbria on the other. Northumbrian forces had advanced into Mercia, probably a retaliatory strike for the aggression of the previous year, and penetrated as far as the Bristol Avon. As they returned, a chasing Anglo-Saxon army caught them as they crossed the Severn at Wednesfield ('Woden's Field') near Tettenhall on 5 August. It resulted in a crushing victory for the Anglo-Saxons where according to the *Anglo-Saxon Chronicle* many thousands of the enemy died including two Norse kings, Halfdan and Ásl, though where they were kings of is not clear.

With the benefit of hindsight, this confrontation assumed the appearance of a decisive battle and it would be a number of years before the Vikings in Northumbria could launch a serious challenge to the increasing supremacy of the Anglo-Saxons in the south of England. It would have been surprising if the Anglo-Saxon soldiers fighting in the battle had not noticed that this stunning triumph came on the anniversary of the death and martyrdom of King Oswald, struck down when fighting against a pagan enemy, and whose remains had been moved to Gloucester not long before. However, even now from some parts of the Danelaw a significant Viking threat would emerge from time to time. In 913 a Danish army from Northampton and Leicester launched a raid in the region of Hook Norton and Luton although they were driven back by the actions of local Anglo-Saxon defence forces.[20]

These references to kings who are not known from other sources gives us a tantalising hint of what may have been going on in England at the time (the later writer Æthelweard also mentions a third king at Tettenhall, called rather unoriginally Ivarr).[21] That they are otherwise unknown suggests that they were 'kings' of small regions rather than larger territories ('kinglets' we might again call them), rather like the Viking 'kings' in Ireland who governed self-contained, limited areas. The most likely scenario is that some Vikings who had been resident in England for a while joined forces with relatively recent arrivals in the north-west, not liking the increasing assertiveness of the Anglo-Saxon dynasty in the south. It is interesting that the next named Northumbrian king is a man with the very Anglo-Saxon name of Eadwulf, so presumably the Viking dynasty in Northumbria may have come to an end – but not for long.[22]

Edward's triumph was shared by his sister, the formidable Æthelflaed, soon to become sole ruler of the Mercians on the death of her husband Æthelred in 911, though he had been ill for some time before that and it is likely that she had been holding the reins of power for a while by then. She was known as *Mrycna hlaefdige,* 'the Lady of the Mercians', and she and Edward together drove forward a comprehensive building programme of more *burhs* with which to face up to the Viking threat; though the location of some of them might suggest that they were also to protect against raids from the Welsh.

The Battle of Tettenhall cemented Edward's position and from then on he normally had the advantage against the Scandinavians in England. There was still a significant threat from elsewhere, evidenced by a raid into the Severn by a Viking fleet from Brittany. This raiding fleet was led by two *jarls*, Ottar and Hroald, and had sacked the monastery at Landévennec in Brittany during the previous year. Now the fleet attacked the coast of south Wales. The bishop of Archenfeld (on the northern shores of the Severn Estuary), Cyfeiliog, was captured and ransomed for 40 pounds. The investment by Edward of significant resources in building up the defences of the south-west, on both the English and the Bristol Channel coasts, suggests that he took these threats very seriously.[23] Edward also agreed an alliance with the Welsh to face up to the Viking threat, which at one stage reached as far as Hereford. The raiders were taking advantage of a long sea corridor that included the Bristol Channel and the large Severn Estuary.

Combined English and Welsh forces successfully drove back this threat.[24] Hroald was killed in the fighting, as was a brother of Ottar. Some of the Vikings were then stranded on Steep Holm, the island in the Bristol Channel, and a number died of starvation. There was then a sea clash off the Isle of Man, this time between two Viking fleets, one led by Bárid, son of Ottar, and by a warrior called Ragnall who had previously been active in Ireland. Ragnall had the better of it – Bárid was killed – and already planned to move on to greater things. The Isle of Man now became a Norse stronghold, unsurprising as it was strategically critical in its position, perfectly placed for sea traffic between England, Wales, Scotland and Ireland; but Ragnall had set his sights still higher.

Man became a rich Viking possession. There is some debate about its origins. It has until recently been assumed that the rich Scandinavian-Gaelic culture there suggested it was a Gaelic territory before the arrival of the Norsemen. However, it has been pointed out that the Vikings may have brought Gaelic culture with them if they had previously been sojourning in Celtic territory further north. There are indeed snippets of evidence suggesting that Man had earlier been British territory, ruled by kings of Gwynedd in North Wales.[25] Some historians even suggest that based on the archaeological evidence uncovered, Viking occupation may not predate 930 – though this seems fairly unlikely given the strategic importance of Man and the fact that it was right in the line of sight for any Viking seafarers travelling to and from Ireland and the Hebrides.

There was a mixed response among the Scandinavian community in England to this assertion of authority from Edward. Many settlers of

Danish origin appeared to be happy enough to settle down and retain a degree of autonomy while recognising the English king as their nominal overlord; some more senior figures are later found witnessing Anglo-Saxon charters. But others, such as the *jarl* Thurcytel, based in Bedford, took himself off to Francia, possibly encouraged to do so by Edward. The king built up defences in Bedford (symbolically important as the last resting place of Offa), part of an accelerated programme of *burh* building which also included Buckingham and Warwick. Soon another threat emerged, this time from the north-west of England where Norsemen from Ireland had come over and settled.

By now Edward and Æthelflaed had built up a series of *burhs* stretching from Runcorn in the north-west to Maldon in the south-east; this offered protection against the Welsh as well as the Vikings in the north, though the fortresses that were established at Eddisbury and Runcorn seemed to have water-borne attackers primarily in mind as they stood guard over the Mersey estuary. One such was also established at Bridgnorth which was unsurprising as Viking forces had passed through on several occasions, most recently probably during the campaign that culminated disastrously for them at Tettenhall. These *burhs* were clearly not just defensive in nature; they represented a launchpad for offensive action against Scandinavian settlers living in the Danelaw and Northumbria. The period of an uneasy co-existence was about to come to an end as Anglo-Saxon England prepared itself to go on to the attack. Men like Thurcytel, anticipating problems, decided to move elsewhere. In 917 an offensive was launched against the Vikings further north using these bases as a starting point. The latter probably saw what was coming. The strong fortresses right on their borders were a clear statement of intent but the attempts that the Vikings in the north made to eliminate them were repulsed. When Edward built a fortress at Towcester, right on the border astride Watling Street, it was attacked by forces from the Danelaw who were beaten off after a fierce confrontation. Edward's actions had been provocative, and the Danes had responded to the provocation. The gloves were now off.

The English did indeed use these fortresses as a stepping-off point for their invasion of the north. Derby fell to them in 917 after a fierce fight in which several prominent Anglo-Saxon thegns were killed. Leicester submitted soon after. There were also Anglo-Saxon successes further south. A Danish fortress at Tempsford was attacked and taken and in the process the Danish king of East Anglia was killed. The English had the advantage in terms of a unified leadership as opposed to the less united Viking forces arrayed against them; Edward and his sister Æthelflaed were working co-operatively together and proving to be a formidable alliance. Colchester also fell; there, the attack was particularly violent and was accompanied by a great loss of life among the defending Danes with only a few men escaping over the wall. A subsequent revenge attack, launched by the survivors in combination with a new influx of Danish raiders, was beaten off after another English triumph.

By 918, it was all over, though the English suffered a grievous blow in June of that year with the death of Æthelflaed at Tamworth, occupied not long after by Edward who effectively annexed Mercia. Æthelflaed's daughter, Ælfwynn, was taken into custody, allegedly according to the twelfth-century writer Caradoc of Llancarfan because she was negotiating to marry Ragnall, a Hiberno-Norse leader who was staking a claim to York. This evidence comes from a later and single source so may not be reliable; but it is nevertheless an intriguing explanation that is offered by Caradoc.

Not long before Æthelflaed's death, she had captured Leicester, one of the Five Boroughs, apparently without a fight. She had then been offered York. It appears that by now the city was without a king – possibly he had been killed at the Battle of Tettenhall a few years earlier. York had become increasingly isolated. The northern part of Northumbria, Bernicia, was in the hands of a separate ruling dynasty and there was an increasing level of threat from the Viking settlers in north-west England.

In such circumstances, it may have seemed a sensible policy to seek the protection of the formidable Lady of the Mercians rather than rely on their own devices to survive as an independent state. But the offer was overtaken by events with the death of Æthelflaed.[26]

Shortly after the death of his sister, Edward took Nottingham, another of the Five Boroughs. Thurferth, the Viking ruler of Northampton, paid homage to Edward at about this time. Unlike Thurcytel, Thurferth chose to stay in England and was well rewarded by Edward for his decision. The Danes of East Anglia entered into some kind of alliance with Edward, whose position was strengthened another notch as a result. The power of Wessex was growing; and the threat of the Vikings gave ample justification for an increase in centralised power in England that followed as a natural consequence. It helped to give the royal dynasty legitimacy as it sought to extend its rule over all of England, a process that was by now in full swing.

The Hiberno-Norse threat

Even as the Viking threat was diminishing in the south of England, it was building up again on the other side of the Irish Sea. The danger posed by the Norsemen had not gone away as far as Ireland was concerned, despite their ejection from Dublin. There is mention of a sea battle between the Vikings and the Uí Néill off the coast of England in 913–914 (an insight into the fact that the Irish still had significant naval resources available to them despite the supposed supremacy of Viking sea power). In 914, a large fleet of Viking ships hove to at Waterford, probably under the command of that same Jarl Ottar who had come from Brittany via Wales as recorded in the *ASC*.[27] They were possibly opponents of the dynasty of Ivarr who had been expelled from Dublin, and before long they were raiding churches and secular settlements in Munster.

Now, determined to restore badly damaged Hiberno-Norse fortunes there, fleets under Ragnall (Old Norse Rögnvaldr), Sitriuc and Gofraid, famed as the 'grandsons of Ivarr' (Ua Ímair) attacked the ports that had been lost to them over a decade previously. By the end of the year, Dublin was back in Viking hands. Ragnall did not stay, however, and returned to the north of England, leaving Dublin in the possession of Sitriuc. Waterford, Dublin and Limerick in the west of Ireland now became the major Viking centres on the island, with Wexford and Cork probably holding relatively minor status at the time.[28] While these towns were, in modern terms, small, they became important bases and trading sites. It is also significant that many of them were on the borders between competing Irish kingdoms where the Vikings perhaps hoped to intervene with benefit to themselves, much as they had done so successfully previously in Francia and England.

Archaeology, particularly at Fishamble Street and Wood Quay in Dublin and Coppergate in York, suggests similarities in building styles and diet between peoples across this Viking region. They were also conscious of the need for strong defences, though the approach was different in Ireland than in England. In Dublin and Waterford defences were built from scratch and by the latter stages of the eleventh century both had stone walls (earlier defences at Dublin built in the tenth century after the Viking re-occupation seem to have been constructed of earthen ramparts topped by timber palisades).[29] In England, at York and Lincoln for example, the settlers adapted old Roman defences and built on them to create strong new fortifications.[30]

The existence of towns implies that a significant proportion of the population were by now engaged in non-agricultural activity. It suggests the development of local industries. In Dublin, evidence has been found of comb manufacture along with the making of bone and antler pins. Wood was widely worked; the Viking ships are evidence of their skills in that department. Leather products were also extensively made. Amber workshops in both York and Dublin suggest busy trade with the Baltic. Silk came in from much further afield. On the other hand, England gained a reputation for pottery and many items seem to have been exported from there to other parts of the Viking world, and Yorkshire jet was also traded widely. In other words, this was an extensive trading network with goods flowing across it on a frequent basis.

The inference from the surviving evidence, especially archaeological, is that Dublin expanded significantly after 917. This was probably helped by a significant Viking victory over the forces of Leinster near Leixlip on the Liffey, where the king of that Irish kingdom and many of his nobles were among the dead. Two years later, the high king of Ireland, Niall Glúndub, fell in battle at Dublin.[31] A rural Viking hinterland around the town, known as the *Dyflinarskiri* ('the shire of Dublin'), then developed. But the spectacular finds in Dublin and York, and the attention that they understandably attracted, create a misleading general impression. The likelihood is that such bustling and, by the standards of the time, large towns like this were the exception rather than the rule. Many Vikings would have lived in smaller settlements or even isolated farms in the same way that would have been the case in Scandinavia where places such as Hedeby, Ribe, Kaupang and Birka were also not the norm.

Dublin became the most prominent port in the Irish Sea region. While we might envisage fleets of sleek Viking longships sailing in and out of the harbour this would not be the case. Much more typical would be the stubby but extremely functional *knarrs*, vessels built for comfort and robustness rather than speed, of which a fine example can be seen in the form of a modern replica moored outside the Roskilde Viking Ship Museum. Such craft were the workhorses of Viking trade, wider, deeper and shorter than a classic Viking longship.

Ragnall returned to Britain with forces from Waterford. He was then involved in a battle with the Scots under Constantin II who were in alliance with the Anglo-Saxon Northumbrians led by Ealdred, son of Eadwulf, who seems to have been ejected as king by Ragnall's Vikings. The battle was fought at Corbridge, astride Hadrian's Wall and the confluence of major east-west and north-south road and river routes including the famous Stanegate, an old Roman road linking Corbridge and Carlisle. Ragnall and Constantin/Eadwulf fought a hard fight; in fact, some accounts say that the Scots were triumphant while others give the victory to the Vikings, so it was possibly a bloody but drawn battle in which two Viking *jarls* fell; one of them was called Ottar, who may well have been the man of the same name who had previously been involved in the raid from Brittany and had then moved on to Ireland.

But strategically the triumph was Ragnall's, for he ended up firmly in place as king of Northumbria, as evidenced by coins issued in his name shortly afterwards in York. He proceeded to claim a number of lands in the region, some of which he gave to his lieutenants, Scula and Onlafbald. The *Historia de Sancto Cuthberto* claims that Ragnall was a bitter enemy of Christianity generally and of Saint Cuthbert in particular. He was therefore given a predictably exemplary end. After issuing threats against Cuthbert and his community in the name of

Thor and Odin, he was soon after struck down dead and his soul thrust by the devil into hell.[32]

Faced with this threat from the Hiberno-Norse, an accommodation had already been entered into by the Scots, the Strathclyde Welsh and the formidable Æthelflaed before her demise. In a controversial text known as the *Fragmentary Annals of Ireland* we are told the following:

> Æthelflaed, through her own cleverness, made peace with the men of Alba [the name for Scotland at the time] and with the Britons [of Strathclyde] so that whenever the same race should come to attack her, they would rise to help her. If it were against them that they came, she would take arms with them. While this continued, the men of Alba and the Britons overcame the settlements of the Norsemen and destroyed and attacked them. The king of the Norsemen [Ragnall] came after that and sacked Strathclyde and plundered the land. But the enemy was ineffectual against Strathclyde.[33]

Strathclyde had assumed a position of some strategic significance. Its southern parts were adjacent to ancient Roman road networks and the Clyde valley provided an access route between Dublin and York. In addition, the coastal areas of Strathclyde were also crucial to mastery of the Irish Sea region, so it was understandable if certain Viking elements wished to bring the kingdom under their direct control. It was very unfortunate for the people of Strathclyde that Vikings, Picts, Scots and Anglo-Saxons all coveted their territory. The threat from the Hiberno-Norse was forcing different parts of mainland Britain to ally themselves in response. Regions which were traditionally rivals were combining against a common danger. The Norse threat was bringing about significant change.

Buoyed by their return to the island, Vikings were increasingly aggressive in Ireland. The Viking threat here was by now so serious that for once the Northern and Southern Uí Néill agreed to fight together under the leadership of Niall Glúndub, son of Aed Findlaith. The resultant battle fought to the south of Dublin was an unmitigated disaster for the Irish. Niall lost his life, as did six other Irish kings. It secured the place of the returned Vikings at Dublin and Waterford for the foreseeable future.

Strathclyde resisted the threat for the time being and there was seemingly a revival of fortunes in Cumbria at the time, based on the evidence of Brittonic place names replacing Norse ones.[34] Both Strathclyde Welsh and Norse were competing for land in areas where vacuums had been created after the disintegration of Northumbria and there is enough evidence to suggest that the Britons were sometimes getting the better of it. Anglo-Saxon residents in the region may have had little time for either party; stories of the last abbot of Heversham in

Westmoreland escaping to Northumbria in the early 900s and a farmer called Alfred who did the same thing, 'fleeing the pirates' and seeking 'the mercy of St Cuthbert and Bishop Cutheard', suggest that these were unsettling times for them in the region.[35]

Despite being unable to neutralise Strathclyde, Ragnall was however now firmly established in the north of England. Edward bided his time rather than making an impulsive and immediate response; his priority was to ensure that the areas of Danish Mercia that he had conquered were properly under control rather than over-extending himself. He had no need to respond aggressively at this stage; Ragnall soon after recognised Edward as his overlord. At the time it was a convenient arrangement given the mutual interests of both Edward and Ragnall; but it was unlikely to last.

A remarkable find made in 2007 near Harrogate in Yorkshire attests to the uncertainties of these times. The Vale of York Hoard was buried around 927–928. One of the largest yet found in England, it contains Anglo-Saxon, Viking, Frankish and Islamic coins and was buried in a Frankish box which appears to have been a church vessel. There was also metalwork from Britain, Ireland, Scandinavia and Russia revealing that someone in the York region was involved in international operations on a large scale, and it is probable that they were not the only ones. York was clearly a vibrant economic base with significant mercantile and industrial activity, evidenced by areas such as Coppergate (from *koppari,* cup maker) and Skeldergate (*skjaldari,* shield maker).

To face up to the threat posed by Ragnall in York, Edward erected a new *burh* at Bakewell in the Peak District in 920. Here an important meeting was held. What was said of it was:

> And then the king of the *Scottas* and all the people of the *Scottas* and Raegnald [Ragnall] and the sons of Eadwulf and all who live in Northumbria, both English and Danish and Northmen and others, and also the king of the Strathclyde Welsh and all the Strathclyde Welsh, chose him [Edward] as father and lord.[36]

There is much of potential significance in this brief paragraph. For a start, we read for the first time of a people called the *Scottas:* clearly something profound had been happening in Scotland. Then there was a recognition that somehow the 'Danish' and the 'Northmen' were different; a distinction was being made between what might be called the 'Vikings' in Northumbria and the English there. Most of all, there is the first reference ever to a king of England being recognised, however nominally or symbolically, as an overlord of most of what we would now call Britain (a caveat is necessary here for northern Scotland and the Western Isles effectively lay outside of the areas ruled by the kings of Alba); though some commentators believe that the *ASC*, in some respects a propagandist tool for the Anglo-Saxon dynasty, is overplaying its hand here in giving Edward lordship over the other kings of Britain.[37]

Given the context in which the meeting was held, when Ragnall was new to the throne of York and the king of Scotland had not as yet suffered any direct threat from Edward, an assumption that this is a submission to Edward as overlord of Britain is a highly dubious interpretation of the situation. Much more likely, this was a meeting at which the various parties discussed a deal whereby the *status quo* was recognised for the time being.[38] However, there was a sub-stratum of subtlety underlying this arrangement. Constantin of Scotland and his counterpart in Strathclyde are referred to as kings; no such exulted title is given to Ragnall, an important distinction (even though there is little doubt that the Viking rulers of York thought of themselves as kings and various Irish annals and other versions of the *ASC* referred to Ragnall as such). England was now divided into two distinct power blocs. The southern part, Wessex and much of Mercia (sometimes conveniently abbreviated as 'Southumbria'), was under the control of Edward. The Welsh princes acknowledged allegiance to him too. In the north of England, on the other hand, most of Northumbria was under the control of Ragnall; though that portion known as Bernicia, centred on Bamburgh, remained stubbornly independent. It perhaps deserves to be better remembered as an independent Anglo-Saxon kingdom than it actually is – it is very noticeable how few Norse place names there are north of the Tees.[39]

The people of the so-called Danelaw in the east midlands lay uncomfortably somewhere in between. They had cultural ties to their cousins in Northumbria; but by religion and even to some extent their way of life more generally they by now had a closer connection to the Anglo-Saxon dynasty in the south. For the rest of his reign Edward restricted himself to fortress building on his borders, sometimes provocatively so, such as when he ordered the Roman defences of Manchester, strictly speaking not in Mercia, to be rebuilt; but nothing more aggressive than this on his part took place.

Edward died in 924 and, by then, all the Danelaw south of the Humber had been taken by him. He had inherited the legacy of his illustrious father Alfred and taken it to the next level. His successor, Æthelstan, would carry on where he left off. By now, Viking York/Jorvik had a new king, Sitriuc, the kinsman[40] of the now-departed Ragnall who died in 921. Sitriuc had moved to England in 920, leaving Dublin in the hands of his kinsman Gofraid. Soon afterwards Gofraid launched a raid on the important ecclesiastical centre at Armagh; an event that was distinguished by the chroniclers for the way in which the prayer houses and the sick of the establishment were deliberately spared destruction. Even the pagan Vikings were subtly changing. As evidence of this, a Viking coin from York in the 920s carried an image of both St Peter and Thor (both were associated with fishing).[41]

Sitriuc's journey from Dublin to York suggests that Ragnall had been ill for a time and a ready-made replacement may have been needed.[42] Ragnall's obituary notice in the *Annals of Ulster* referred to him as being both king of the 'Fair Gaill and the Dark Gaill', the two competing factions in Ireland. Æthelstan attempted to secure his position with Ragnall's successor Sitriuc by arranging for his sister Editha to marry him at Tamworth, then an important town with longstanding royal connections in Mercia, in 925. Pillaged by Vikings in 874, Tamworth had been rejuvenated by Æthelflaed and was therefore an appropriate symbolic site on which to hold celebrations connected to such an event.

Æthelstan was an unknown quantity. He had grown up in Mercia, away from the powerhouse of Anglo-Saxon England in Winchester. The Winchester version of the *ASC* barely refers to his reign, in stark contrast to that of Alfred, and gives the distinct impression that he was not the preferred candidate to take Edward's place in some quarters; although Mercia recognised Æthelstan as Edward's successor, initially the people of Wessex did not, opting for another of Edward's sons, Ælfweard. Within weeks though Ælfweard was conveniently dead. Æthelstan therefore became king of both kingdoms. If he had grown up out of sight of the ruling elite in Winchester, it should not escape notice that he had been under the wing of the formidable Æthelflaed; time would reveal how important the significance of such an upbringing would be. Sitriuc died not long after and Æthelstan soon struck north and took York. The king of England had added a further piece to the jigsaw; but in the process he had laid the foundations for what would be an apocalyptic confrontation a decade later.

Rollo and Normandy

While in England the fortunes of the ruling Anglo-Saxon dynasty were on an upward trajectory, other parts of Europe continued to feel the sharp claws of Viking aggression, leaving deep scars and sometimes forcing elements of the population to seek safety elsewhere. Brittany in particular suffered during the first two decades of the tenth century. The writer Flodoard noted that 'the Bretons were abducted and sold, while those who escaped were driven out'.[43] As the Bretons were often at odds with the Franks as well, their position was extremely difficult. Later tradition asserted that Matuedoi, the Breton count of Poher, ended up at the court of King Æthelstan in England and that his son, Alain, became the king's godson. There are also indications that it was not just the Bretons who found a bolthole from Viking raids in England; another suggestion is that refugees from Ponthieu also made their way there, reflected in the naming of 'Pontefract' in Yorkshire.[44] It is a reminder that those seeking asylum from extreme violence are not just a twenty-first-century phenomenon.

Æthelstan also made other 'adoptions', for it was claimed that he fostered Hákon, son of the Norwegian ruler Harald Fairhair: an example of a common arrangement during the Viking Age when marriage, fosterage and godparentage were used to help develop and cement alliances.[45] Harald even sent Æthelstan a well-equipped Viking ship as a mark of his desire for friendship.[46] This was no ordinary vessel either. It was a very ostentatious craft; William of Malmesbury talks of it as having a 'gold beak and purple sail, surrounded inside with a dense rank of gilded shields'. Æthelstan was clearly an important and powerful man, it was worth developing good relations with him even if extravagant gifts were involved.

It was not just the aristocratic leadership fleeing to England from Brittany. Many Breton clerics sought and found sanctuary in Æthelstan's court, bringing with them a large number of relics which the pious king greatly appreciated. Winchester became a favourite centre and they brought with them their learning and even their music.[47] How ironic that half a millennium after Britons fled to Brittany to escape Anglo-Saxon incursions, in a mirror image of that journey they were now travelling back the other way to find safety. In this respect, it is noteworthy that a poem, possibly composed in Alfred's last years, wrote of Æthelstan, supposedly his favourite grandson, predicting a period of peace under his later rule following a victory over the demons, which presumably refers to pagan Scandinavians.[48] That was a particularly prescient prediction.

The Franks adopted a risky scheme when Normandy was entrusted to the Viking leader Hrolf, better known as Rollo. He was not new to Francia; he had been involved in the sacking of Rouen as far back as 876 and had seemingly enjoyed a good relationship with Guthrum in England too. During that attack on Rouen subterfuge came into play. The Viking attackers ran in confusion when charged by Frankish cavalry, but it was all a trick. The chasing pack fell headlong into concealed ditches that had been prepared for them and Rouen fell as a result. Rollo comes across as a larger-than-life figure in every sense of the word; it was said of him that he was so big that no horse could carry him.[49] As a result of this, he was sometimes called Rollo the 'Ganger' or 'Walker'.

A Frankish charter of 918 refers to 'Rollo and his associates' and suggests that they had been in Normandy for some time by then. Rollo's life was written up by a tenth-century historian, Dudo of St Quentin. Dudo tells us that Rollo had been forced to leave Denmark in a hurry by a hostile king. The alliance with 'Rollo and his associates' was sealed by a marriage between him and a daughter of the king of West Francia,

Charles III ('the Simple'), Gisela. Gisela did not survive for long – it has been suggested that she may even have been a child bride given to a much older man as a way of sealing a political alliance [50] – and Rollo then went back to his long-term partner, Poppa. A son from this later relationship, William 'Longsword', was ultimately declared Rollo's heir. William would lead a fascinating life, expanding the extent of Norman territories and being a committed patron of the Church, even at some stage possibly considering becoming a monk. In keeping with the complicated kaleidoscope of Viking life at this time, he would meet a violent end, murdered by the count of Flanders in 942.

Rollo was given land around the lower Seine as a royal fief, territory that would later form the core of the Duchy of Normandy; a transaction that was formalised at Saint-Clair-sur-Epte in 912. In an amusing story told by Dudo of St Quentin, Rollo was asked to kiss Charles's foot as a sign of homage but refused to do so and instructed one of his men to perform the disagreeable act instead. However, his delegate had no more liking for it and refused to bow down to do so. Instead he pulled the king's foot up towards his lips, causing Charles to lose his balance and fall over. There were predictable guffaws from the Vikings in the crowd and no doubt barely subdued outrage from the Franks there.

In return, Rollo was to help protect Charles's kingdom from further Viking attack. Ironically, this came after Charles had defeated Rollo and his men in battle in 911 but Charles realised that it was wise to be magnanimous in victory. This reflected current realities: Charles's writ ran weakly in Normandy now and the fact that he was prepared to give up the crucial city of Rouen showed just how fragile the Frankish position there was. Rollo's new powerbase was within a very short distance of Charles the Bald's much-vaunted bridge defences at Pîtres and times had certainly changed since they had been constructed.

Although more Viking raids were forestalled by the move, it did Charles little personal good for he was removed from power by his own dissatisfied nobles who, after being conditioned to think of Vikings as the enemy for the best part of a century, did not perhaps take kindly to this *volte-face*. However, Rollo did assist Charles in the battle that led to the death of the chief rebel, Robert of Neustria, near Soissons in 923. But this was insufficient to restore Charles's position – he was defeated and taken prisoner – and he would never regain power. The Carolingian Empire was by now in irreversible decline. The centralised control that Charlemagne had established was ebbing away, and the empire was fragmenting, allowing local warlords such as Rollo to increase their power.

The immediate objective in setting up Rollo in Normandy was achieved though; he was an effective barrier to further Viking attacks. Yet this came at a cost. Normandy became a constant thorn in the flesh of Frankish and, later, French kings for centuries. In the later tenth century tensions would frequently emerge. In one such example, Richard I, ruler of Normandy (it was not until the time of Richard II in 1006 that the expression 'duke' was used), was seized by King Louis IV of West Francia and held as a hostage. This move backfired on Louis who was later briefly held captive himself. The Norman dukes were fiercely independent and when they later became kings of England they caused many of their French counterparts sleepless nights. They also become renowned mercenaries and adventurers further afield too, in Italy and Sicily, in the Byzantine Empire and the wider Middle East.

Several stories told by Dudo of St Quentin suggest that there was still something of the ruthless Viking in Rollo. He introduced tough laws across his territories, one of which concerned the protection of farmers' property. When a farmer's wife alleged that some of their property had been stolen overnight, several suspects were tortured before it emerged that she had made up the allegation and her husband had known of this. Both of them were hanged as an example to others not to try to pervert the course of justice.

Rollo and his successors consolidated and then enhanced their position in Normandy, using it as a base for further expansion. The neighbouring Channel Islands were annexed and divided up. Within a century, during the time of the most famous of Norman dukes, William – later king of England – properties on the islands were being distributed to his henchmen and to various elements of the Church.[51] But the establishment of a Viking territory in Normandy fundamentally changed the occupiers too. They adopted Frankish practices and economics. There was also a profound spiritual impact; by the end of the century Duke Richard I, Rollo's grandson, was supporting monasteries such as Mont St Michel and financing the construction of major building projects there.

Many of Rollo's men appear to have been Danish even if he himself may have been Norwegian. Detailed investigation by J. Adigard des Gautries[52] suggests that some had previously settled in the north of England. There were other men in Rollo's army who came from Ireland or Scotland, probably originally of Norwegian origin. However, these studies suggest that they had few women with them, a problem they presumably had to deal with by local intermarrying. They point to a significant degree of fluidity across the region and the fact that a number of Vikings were still very happy to roam in search of profit and opportunity.

The granting of Normandy to Rollo made permanent what was already largely a *fait accompli*. He subsequently accepted baptism as the price for this recognition but the later chronicler Adémar of Chabannes suggested that he came to regret this and as a way of re-ingratiating himself with the old Norse gods ordered the sacrifice of 100 Christian captives.

A churchman, Hervé, noted in a letter to the pope that a number of Viking converts had later relapsed into paganism. The pontiff in response showed considerable discretion and suggested that Hervé should react tactfully given the newness of the apostates to the dictates of Christianity. That said, William of Jumièges, the eleventh-century Norman chronicler, wrote that Rollo eventually 'died in Christ'.

Although Rollo granted lands to his followers, he made it clear that they held them directly from him; in other words, there were things that they would be expected to do in return and if they did not meet expectations then those lands would be forfeit. Historians assume that the Normans succeeded so well because they integrated fully into French society; for example, they quickly started to speak French rather than Norse. But I am not so sure. Their future actions as first raiders and then conquerors of Sicily, as mercenaries for hire in the Byzantine Empire and the takeover of England have enough resonance with the actions of their Scandinavian forebears to suggest that a spark from their origins kept the embers of Vikingness alive in them.

Ibn Fadlān and the Rūs

One of the best-known pieces of evidence we have for the activity of the Vikings on the other side of Europe in the land of the Rūs comes from an Arab ambassador, Ibn Fadlān. He was part of a delegation sent by the Caliph al-Muqtadir in Baghdad to the Bulgars on the Volga. Traditionally, this was a nomadic group of tribes who now sought help in building a fort and a mosque as well as instruction in the Muslim religion; their chief also wanted to forge an alliance against his traditional Khazar enemies. In 921/2, Ibn Fadlān met with a group of Rūs merchants on the Volga, who probably came from Kiev, and while he was there he witnessed something extraordinary, namely the funeral of a chieftain. These events are normally interpreted as being a representation of conventional Scandinavian rituals, though a caveat is needed as there might also be an influence from Slavic customs that gave them a particular local flavour.[53]

The ceremony that Ibn Fadlān witnessed lasted for several days and was marked by sacrifices of animals and slaves. A volunteer was requested, a slave girl who would willingly die and take her place next to their dead lord. For several days this volunteer was waited on hand and foot before the act of sacrifice was carried out. As the climax of the ceremony approached, she was raised in the air three times; the first time she said she could see her father and mother, the second time her dead relatives and following the third elevation she said that she could see her Master sitting in paradise, which was green and beautiful. She was then led to the funeral ship. Two bracelets that she was wearing were taken off and handed to the old woman who was to perform the sacrifice, a witch-like hag known as 'The Angel of Death'. Two anklets were also removed and handed to the serving girls who had attended her during the previous few days who were the daughters of the 'Angel'.

The victim was given a cup of alcoholic *nabid* to drink and sang a song in honour and perhaps trepidation of her approaching death. She was taken into the pavilion on the deck of the ship where six men entered and had sex with her. Finally, they strangled her while the Angel thrust a dagger between her ribs. While this horrific ritual was being played out, the men surrounding the pavilion beat an intoxicating rhythm out on their shields, a sound mostly drowning the cries of terror emanating from inside the pavilion from the sacrificial victim. Animals were slaughtered and thrown onto the ship; a dog was cut in half, two horses were chopped to pieces, two cows were slain, as were a cockerel and a hen. This was a gruesome coterie of death. Archaeological evidence from elsewhere also attests to the use of sacrifices in burials, giving indirect credence to these events; for example, a tenth-century burial of a man at Lejre, Zealand, who was interred with grave goods was accompanied by a decapitated male who had been tied up.[54] Lejre is associated with a great pagan temple and human sacrifice, though nowadays it tends to be less remembered for these purposes than Uppsala in Sweden.[55]

The sacrifice that Ibn Fadlān witnessed was followed by a cremation of the chieftain with his funeral ship. The dead man was dressed in splendid clothes; trousers, socks, boots, a tunic, a caftan and a cap. Food such as meat, bread and onions was laid out for him on the ship and alcoholic drink, fruit and basil were placed near him before the vessel was set ablaze. The dead man's nearest male relative approached the vessel naked, carrying a torch which he threw on board. A violent wind blew up and the heat of the fire intensified as everything went up in flames. These scenes made a vivid impression both on contemporaries and on later readers; the thirteenth-century historian al-Watwat noted that the Rūs burned their dead.

Ibn Fadlān, a man with an enquiring mind, asked for the reasoning behind the cremation (a practice which was frowned upon both by Islam and Christianity) and it was explained to him that this was necessary for the chieftain to go directly to the Hereafter. Indeed, the Rūs laughed at the ignorance of Muslim practices whereby a family would bury the person they love the most in the earth to be eaten up by worms and insects. To them, it seemed logical that the quick action of the fire would send the dead person to paradise far more quickly. After the flames had done their work, a funeral mound was raised over what was left as a permanent marker of the grave site of the departed.

These traders were heavily into slaving; the region they were operating in was essentially a link point between Europe and Asia; not only slaves would pass through there but also furs – such as those of beavers, sable and mink – for onward shipment to places as far off as India and China. When a new Viking slaving/trading party arrived, they would go ashore with supplies of bread, milk, onions, meat and *nabid*. They would set up pagan idols by the shore which they would bow down to and ask for their blessing on the coming trading venture. Clearly, Christianity was a long way from taking root among this particular group of adventurers.[56]

They set up camp on the river banks in large buildings, which held up to twenty people. Ibn Fadlān commented specifically on the presence of many beautiful slave girls there being taken for sale. If a Viking wished to satisfy his lust, he would have no compunction in doing so while others looked on. If a merchant arrived to conduct business, he would sometimes have to wait until the Norseman had finished the act he was currently engaged in.

These tales are a stark reminder of how awful the life of a slave was; they had no more rights than cattle and their owners were able to do whatever they wanted, whenever they wanted to do it. Yet occasionally amidst these dreadful tales of slavery a slightly brighter story emerges. One of them concerned an Irishman named Moriuht. His wife was captured in a raid. He found out that she had been taken to Northumbria but when he next got word of her in Bamburgh she had already been transported to the Continent. He eventually caught up with her in Rouen where he managed to gain the support of the bishop and his wife was freed. They then decided to stay and build a life in Rouen together.[57] However, such stories were exceptions to the rule. Human misery was far more likely to be the outcome for those caught in the crossfire of raiding and slaving activities.

Ibn Fadlān was impressed by the northern visitors. He described the Rūs as 'perfect physical specimens, tall as date palms, blond and ruddy'. He noted that they were well armed, each of them carrying an axe, a sword and a knife that they kept with them at all times. Their swords were grooved in a similar style to Frankish weapons. He saw women there too. They wore a box of iron, silver, copper or gold round their necks. The metal with which it was constructed was a sign of the wealth possessed by the box's owner. They also wore neck rings of gold and silver and necklaces on which green glass beads were strung. This is another indication that Viking expeditions were certainly not male-only adventures.

Ibn Fadlān wrote about what he found concerning the habits and personal hygiene of the Rūs in terms of horrified fascination and barely concealed disgust. These people, he said, did not wash after urinating or defecating, neither would they clean themselves up after having sex. Each morning a bowl of water would be passed around a group of them and they would spit in it and clear the phlegm from their noses into it; they would then pass the water on to their neighbour so that they could wash with the same filthy liquid.

Ibn Fadlān also referred to a practice among the merchants of making offerings before a raised pole that was erected next to their trading place. They would sacrifice animals to their gods, leaving some of the butchered meat behind them while feasting on the remainder. In the morning, the meat that they had left for the gods had almost invariably been devoured, by their gods, so they said (though the sceptical ambassador thought that it was more likely to have been eaten by packs of wild dogs). Another tenth-century Arab traveller, al-Tartushi (also known as Abraham ben Jacob), noted the sacrifice of animals while visiting Hedeby, adding that the animals involved included oxen, rams, goats and pigs. It would be fair to say that these Scandinavians did not make an overwhelmingly positive impression on their visitors from more sophisticated lands. One such, the Persian geographer Ibn Rustah, described how among them 'treachery is endemic, and a poor man may be envied by a comrade, who will not hesitate to kill him and rob him'.

8

Nation-building (926–950)

A great, lamentable and horrible battle
The Annals of Ulster on the Battle of Brunanburh

The conception of Viking nations: Scandinavia and Iceland

The emergence of King Gorm 'the Old' in Denmark marked the beginning of the nation as we now perceive it, though its overall shape would alter greatly in the centuries that followed, particularly as regions like Skåne changed hands. Since the days of Godfrid over a century before, Denmark had drifted back into obscurity, the events and deeds that took place during these times being largely unknown to us. Probably it again became a region of petty fiefdoms where, from time to time, one man would emerge from the shadows to lord it over others for a while, though without permanent effect.

With more certainty we can say that by the beginning of the tenth century the Swedes were providing kings for Denmark. Gorm and his lesser-known father, Hardegon-Hardaknut, before him, gradually took power from the Swedes who had recently dominated the peninsula. This dynasty's point of origin was at Jelling in Jutland, a place of historic resonance even to modern Danes. They laid the foundations for a significant northern nation to emerge from the obscurity of the post-Godfrid period.

Adam of Bremen provides evidence that Gorm was the power in the land by around 935. Gorm and his father apparently came from the north of Jutland and also held some lands in Norway (though at some stage, according to the *Tale of Ragnar's Sons,* the latter were lost).[1] But of Gorm himself we know very little. We can presume he was a ruthless and ambitious man who furthermore was a fierce protector of pagan tradition. He certainly gained an unfortunate reputation for being less wise than his forebears, both in the sagas and in the writings of the waspish Adam of Bremen.[2] However, a note of caution is necessary as pro-Christian commentators would not have been impressed by Gorm's staunch adherence to paganism and this potentially made them biased against him.

Adam wrote his work, the *History of the Archbishops of Hamburg-Bremen,* in the second half of the eleventh century. He had access to some quality informants, including Sveinn Estrithsson, then king of Denmark. Adam is our main source of information on Scandinavian history during the Viking Age, but he had his own axe to grind. He was irritated that Scandinavian churches had sought to be free of subservience to his own archbishopric of Hamburg-Bremen, which he naturally thought should not be the case. In this he was fighting a losing battle; during the twelfth century the churches of Denmark, Norway and Sweden were all recognised as independent entities.

Gorm became king when approximately forty years of age. He united a region that had previously been very fragmented, though it has been suggested that his rule only extended over Jutland. The sagas suggest he had two sons, Cnut and Harald. Cnut was killed while involved in an expedition in England, or so says the *Jómsvíkings Saga*: so great was Gorm's grief that soon after he died. Supernatural forces are present in the story of Gorm's death: he had said that, if his beloved Cnut was killed, the person who broke the news would also die in very short order. The person who indirectly informed him, his wife Thyra, spoke of her son's death in the form of a riddle: when Gorm correctly interpreted it, he himself died.[3]

A singular society was developing by this time in Iceland which, due to its isolation, was able to assert a large degree of autonomy despite the efforts of several kings of Norway such as Harald Fairhair and, later, Óláfr Tryggvason, to acquire it as essentially an earldom under their direct control. In 930, a representative assembly, the *Althing*, was set up. It was an assembly for the whole island: previously there had just been the local '*things*'. It was originally dominated by the thirty-two *godi* or local chieftains. The *Althing* met annually in June in a great cleft in the rocks about 45 kilometres to the south-east of Reykjavik. Every free man could attend and listen to the discussions chaired by a speaker, the *Lögsögumaor,* who sat on a large rock. It was perhaps a throwback to the old ways of doing things in Norway before Harald Fairhair had established himself as king over all.

The *Landnámabók* is a source of a great deal of information on Iceland. It is full of genealogies and information concerning the settlement of the island, with fascinating reference to where the settlers came from; not just people from Norway but Svartkel from Caithness and Kalman from the Hebrides for example. We also get glimpses into family tragedies; Kalman and his two sons were drowned in separate incidents, in Kalman's case while visiting his sweetheart.[4] Through it all a sense of awe occasionally comes through, such as when the settlers saw the volcanic crater of Eldborg in the west of Iceland for the first time.[5]

There are many references in it to petty disputes (and, in more extreme cases, murders) and a generous smattering of references to skirmishes among rival groups. Horse rustling is also mentioned on occasion; horse stock in Iceland developed in its own sturdy direction and in modern times the resident breed is tightly protected against foreign interlopers that might undermine the purity of the bloodline of those that remain. The *Landnámabók* is a good example of a historical record written up some time after the events that it describes but which nevertheless should not be dismissed out of hand. Much of the information it contains is entirely believable. If we ignore the occasional references to mermen, shape-shifting wizards and spell-chanting witches, it is everything it claims to be; a book of settlement giving us snippets of information about the adventurous settlers who set up home on this remote and harsh, if beautiful, island and the tough, often epic, lives they led.[6] Even when blaming wizards and witches, the writer seems to be sometimes looking for explanations for natural events that actually occurred such as landslips, which, given Iceland's volcanic nature are hardly unusual events.[7]

Assemblies similar to the *Althing* were typically held in prominent places across the Viking world. They were often associated with places such as burial mounds, boundaries and topographical features that stood apart as sacred sites; something resonated deep inside those attending, perhaps connected to a process of honouring ancestry or the gods. In the early days at least, local justice was more often served by means of these assemblies rather than the development and approval of new legislation.[8] As is almost inevitable when a relatively large group of people gather on a regular basis, commerce was not far behind. Markets developed alongside such assembly sites with traders sensing the chance to make a living out of the events held there.

Despite its remoteness, Iceland was part of a joined-up Viking world. Communication may not have been quick, but it was possible and it did take place. When the father of a man called Thord who lived in Orkney died in Iceland, his son heard of it and sailed there to claim his inheritance. There are also stories in the *Landnámabók* of Vikings from Sweden who went to Ireland raiding and fostered children in the Hebrides before ultimately settling in Iceland.[9]

Anyone who has travelled to some of the remoter parts of the Viking world will be struck by the stunning and sometimes otherworldly landscapes that typify them; remote but strangely beautiful while at the same time carrying an element of underlying threat, giving a strong reminder of the essential weakness of humanity in the face of nature. What might be described as ceremonial landscapes evolved in many places, containing a great hall where the chieftain held court, with burial mounds dotted around and *nausts* or boathouses silently denoting the connection between Vikings and the sea. It is a noticeable feature of such sites that they would be used, re-used and re-invented throughout the Viking period.

The hall itself was of monumental significance; burning it was seen as an act personally aimed at the credentials of the chieftain who had previously held court there. It would almost invariably be raised on an elevated platform, either natural or manmade, and as such was an unmistakable symbol of power. Halls long pre-date the Viking Age in Scandinavia and their broad architectural form changes little over the centuries. Surprisingly perhaps, there is less evidence of halls being burned down in the Viking era than before, suggesting that the increasing strength of centralised monarchies was a powerful deterrents to such acts.[10] Later on, churches emerged, the stave churches built of wood taking full advantage of Viking skills in carpentry. Even these sacred buildings (of which unfortunately only later examples survive) seem to have formed part of the natural landscape; anything further removed from the later great medieval stone-built cathedrals is hard to imagine.

In Norway, the long reign of Harald Fairhair came to an end probably in about 933. He had transferred his centre of power from the region of the Oslofjord to Vestland where he developed a royal estate at Avaldsnes, on an island in a fjord on the western coast. It was an area that had historical significance: the oldest ship burial yet found in Scandinavia, dating to around 700, has been found here. Harald fathered many sons; in the various records discussing this, nine is the lowest number recorded, and some records go up to as many as twenty.[11] Of this large brood however, only two need concern us; one the extraordinary character known as Erik Bloodaxe and the other his half-brother, Hákon 'The Good'.

Erik Bloodaxe was a formidable figure who did not suffer fools gladly. His word was law, and his law was often savage. A great poet, Egil Skalagrimsson, fell out with Erik and it was decreed that he should die. But he was given a chance to save himself if he wrote a work that impressed Erik so much that he thought his life was worth preserving. The result, appropriately called *Head-Ransom,* did the trick, and Egil's life was spared. The poem survives and includes some typical war poetry of the Viking Age, of how the 'cranes of battle [ravens] flew over piles of carrion; the mouths of the wound-gull [again, ravens] did not want for blood; the ravenous one [this time, a wolf] tore the wound, and the wave of the spear-point roared on the raven's head-prow'.[12] Such animalistic symbols closely reflect those used in the Anglo-Saxon epic *Beowulf* where ravens, eagles and wolves are also referred to as creatures of death.

Hákon was much younger than Erik and was fostered by King Æthelstan in England. Given the alleged unruliness of the sons of Harald Fairhair and their generally self-serving natures it would be a reasonable assumption that this was for his own protection. But in the war between Hákon and Erik that followed it would be the former who emerged triumphant and the latter who found himself seeking a kingdom. Erik Bloodaxe appeared to be in a much stronger position when the conflict began. He was the son of Harald and Ragnhild, the daughter of King Erik of Jutland. Erik Bloodaxe's Danish connection was further strengthened by his marriage to Gunnhild, daughter of Gorm the Old. But perhaps these Danish connections worked against him in the eyes of some of his would-be subjects in Norway. When Hákon arrived in Trondheim, Erik departed rather than fight – suggesting that he felt his position to be surprisingly weak. Instead he sailed west to seek out a new career for himself. His story was far from over.

The road to Brunanburh

Æthelstan's support was presumably very useful to Hákon in the war the latter fought to become ruler of Norway. The English king had become very powerful and was a player on the European stage. However, although Æthelstan appeared to be the supreme and unchallenged ruler in England, he would find his position under threat. An alliance of Vikings from Dublin, under Óláfr Gofraidsson, Scots under their king, Constantin, and warriors from the Strathclyde 'Welsh', under Owain, invaded the north of England in 937. These events had been a decade in the making since the time that Æthelstan had seized control in York.

Sitriuc, king of York, died in 927. His marriage to Æthelstan's sister was brief; according to the later chronicler Roger of Wendover, it was also unconsummated, and the bride rejected (though it has been suggested that this is unlikely as Æthelstan would quickly have intervened if this had been the case).[13] The abandoned wife, Editha, became the abbess of Polesworth Abbey and would subsequently be made a saint. This rejection may explain the course of events soon after Sitriuc's demise. Sitriuc had been replaced by Gofraid who came over from Dublin. By this time, York and Dublin were seemingly being ruled as part of an extended Viking kingdom with York the senior of the two.

Gofraid left his sons in charge in Dublin to take up the reins in York but he struggled to cement his control there and Æthelstan was quick to take advantage and sent an army. Overwhelmed by Æthelstan's attack, Gofraid fled to Scotland.

On 12 July 927, Æthelstan was recognised as overlord by all the kings of Britain at Eamont Bridge in Cumbria (some accounts have the meeting a few miles away at Dacre: it is not impossible that events took place at both as there was an important contemporary church on the site of a very old monastery at Dacre, which claimed connections to St Cuthbert). It was significant that the meeting place was on the very frontiers of Æthelstan's kingdom, close to the borders of Strathclyde. As part of this sequence of events, Æthelstan also razed the Viking fortress in York to the ground so that it could not be used as a rallying point for potential opponents in the future. It seems that an amicable agreement was made between Æthelstan and Gofraid who returned to Ireland; but William of Malmesbury notably described Gofraid as a pirate who was more at home on the water than he was on the land.

The impressive group that met at Eamont Bridge and/or Dacre included Constantin of Scotland, the kings of Wales and the Strathclyde Welsh,[14] and Ealdred of Bamburgh, a quasi-autonomous part of Northumbria in Bernicia. Significantly there was no independent Viking quasi-king left in Britain to take part in the ceremony: indeed, the signatories to the deal were required to renounce their *deofelgeld*, which may be translated as either 'idolatry' or 'devil tribute', probably a reference to alliances with Viking leaders. Æthelstan now took to calling himself *'monarchus totius Brittaniae* ('king of all Britain') on his coinage. The agreement was a potential blow for the Vikings, who in theory would now find it more difficult to make alliances with the peoples of Northern Britain. It also undermined Constantin and the various Welsh representatives present who were effectively recognising Anglo-Saxon supremacy.

Just a few years into his reign, Æthelstan was already showing himself to be a man with imperial pretensions; but in the process he initiated a chain reaction as opposition grew from those who had no wish to be dominated by an Anglo-Saxon king. What happened in Northumbria during the years that immediately followed is unclear, though it may possibly have been ruled by Ealdred of Bamburgh as a client of Æthelstan. However, Æthelstan was quick to take control of the minting of coins at York and he held court there on occasion as ways of reinforcing his rule over Northumbria. He also did so by building relationships with Wulfstan, the archbishop of York, and by venerating the cult of St Cuthbert, then based at Chester-le-Street where the saint's mortal remains currently rested.

In 934 Æthelstan launched a punitive expedition into Scotland – for which the support of the Northumbrians would be vitally important – which was unprecedented in terms of the depth it penetrated into the country. It was a two-pronged assault with a land army reaching as far as Dunottar and a fleet that sailed all the way up to Caithness; this latter expedition may have been a warning shot to the earls of Orkney to stay out of Anglo-Saxon affairs. At the end of it, Constantin remained as king but was forced to accept Æthelstan as his overlord once more. Indeed, at the end of the year he appears as a witness on charters issued in the south of England so he had clearly been brought back from Scotland for a time, in circumstances that amounted to something of a humiliation. Although he probably returned home in the interim, the next year (935) Constantin appears as a witness to a charter issued in Cirencester, this time with Owain, king of Strathclyde, also present. Constantin was not present when the Christmas festivities were held that year at Dorchester in Dorset although Owain of Strathclyde was. This suggests that Constantin was, soon after Æthelstan's campaign, managing to re-assert a degree of independence. Owain also stopped witnessing charters shortly afterwards, suggesting that he had managed to do the same.

At about this time, there were rumours of a plot against Æthelstan. Not long before, his brother Eadwine had died in controversial circumstances; one version of his end is that he was put to sea in a leaky boat on Æthelstan's orders, a sentence that in Irish law was meted out as punishment for the homicide (or attempted homicide) of a brother. It is possible that in the now-existing uncertain climate the Scots had taken the opportunity to cause problems for Æthelstan in the aftermath of Eadwine's demise. This explanation is necessary to understand the formation of the unlikely alliance that was evolving in Britain. The Scandinavian element in Britain and Ireland would soon be involved in it too. They retained ambitions in England, in Northumbria in particular, and their ejection from York by Æthelstan in 927 still rankled.

The dispossessed Gofraid had died in 934. His son, Óláfr Gofraidsson (in other versions known as Amlaib or in Old English Anlaf), took up his claim to govern Northumbria. Both Scots and Strathclyde 'Welsh' at some point entered into discussions with him, neither of them wishing to have a powerful English neighbour breathing down their necks. Óláfr brought a Viking contingent over from Dublin with him. In some ways this was an unlikely alliance: Strathclyde Welsh, Scots and Vikings had often been at each other's throats. Now they had come together to face a common threat: a classic case of 'my enemy's enemy is my friend'. Later sources even suggest that Constantin had given his daughter as a bride to Óláfr;[15] Constantin's grandson, who appears in the royal records of the later tenth century, was indeed called Óláfr.

Óláfr Gofraidsson had enjoyed much greater success than Gofraid: the latter had a chequered war record. Óláfr had recently won a great victory over a rival Viking force based in Limerick in the west of Ireland and had triumphantly taken their king back to Dublin as his prisoner. He had defeated the kings of Brega, Irish rulers in the region around Dublin, in 935. He then pillaged the sacred site of Clonmacnoise, a place of great symbolic significance that was sponsored by the Irish kings of Mede and Connacht. The year 937 may even have seen the high point of Viking fortunes in Ireland.[16] However, York was a great prize, in some ways more lucrative even than Ireland, and Óláfr was not prepared to let it go without a fight.

Limerick had become an important base in the west of Ireland, though it is unclear whether or not there had been a permanent settlement there since the first indication of a Viking presence locally in about 845. This appears to be a different group than the descendants of Ivarr in Dublin. The death of Ragnall in 921 gave the Vikings in Limerick an impetus to declare their independence from those on the east coast of Ireland. There are several raids recorded on Lough Ree in 922, 924 and 932, which were presumably launched from there. Although a long way inland, the Lough was on the Shannon River which flows out into the Atlantic at Limerick so it was ideally placed for raids upriver in the traditional Viking fashion and several churches fell prey to these. There is archaeological evidence of a *longphort* being constructed at Ballaghkeeran Little on Lough Ree. Hoards of silver and gold found in the vicinity also suggest trading activity. Coins from the later reign of King Edgar of England, dated to 970, are particularly intriguing as he was credited with providing peace and stability to his country; if this is true, then these coins presumably were not obtained through raiding activity but by other more peaceful means.[17]

Gofraid had taken hostages from the south of Ireland in 924 but an attack by him on Limerick in the same year was repulsed with heavy losses. This smouldering contention between at least two rival Viking camps forms the backdrop to activity further afield in Britain. Further conflict between the two followed but Gofraid was distracted by activities in York in 927, which took him away from Irish affairs for a while. The confrontation between Limerick on the one hand and Dublin and Waterford on the other spread across Ireland and pulled in indigenous Gaelic kings and kingdoms in a sometimes bewildering state of affairs when alliances were made and broken with regularity. Not until 937 did Dublin finally get the upper hand when Gofraid defeated and captured the memorably named king of Limerick, Óláfr Scabbyhead, and destroyed his ships.

When Óláfr Gofraidsson joined his confederates from Scotland and Strathclyde in 937, contemporary commentators, even from the Anglo-Saxon side, give the impression that Æthelstan was caught unawares. Totally triumphant three years before in his Scottish campaign, he felt over-secure in his position. The invasion of the north of England – for such it was – that followed could not have come at a worse time. The crops were ripe for picking (which suggests a date somewhen in September) and now there was a risk that they would remain unharvested or, worse still, used to feed the enemy. Óláfr, having won a decisive victory over rival forces in Limerick, was now free to further his ambitions on the other side of the Irish Sea.

The twelfth-century writer, William of Malmesbury, suggests that Óláfr received a strongly positive reception in the north, parts of which, after all, had been in the Viking sphere of influence for most of the previous six decades.[18] William also wrote how now,

>...there returned that plague and hateful ruin of Europe. Now the fierce savagery of the North couches on our land, now the pirate Óláfr, deserting the sea, camps in the fields, breathing forbidden and savage threats. At the will of the king of the Scots, the northern land lends a quiet assent to the raving fury; and now they swell with pride, now frighten the air with words. The natives give way, the whole region yields to the proud.[19]

The chronicler is maybe using some licence here, exaggerating the seriousness of the situation for effect, but this sounds like a country on the verge of a meltdown.

Æthelstan marched his men up to face what he knew would be a moment of destiny. Arrayed against him was a formidable force, including powerful Norse elements and a strong Celtic alliance determined to push the alien Anglo-Saxon occupiers of lands that were traditionally theirs back across the sea to to where they had come from centuries before. The position of the Strathclyders in this fight is unclear; contemporary accounts do not mention them, but some written not long after suggest that they were there and fighting alongside the Vikings and the Scots, which makes a strong degree of strategic sense given their desire to preserve their independence in the face of Æthelstan's imperial ambitions.

The battle that followed at Brunanburh was ferocious in its intensity. Although medieval historians are notoriously unreliable with their numbers, the accounts that survive suggest that by contemporary standards the armies involved were very large; *Egil's Saga* describes Æthelstan playing for time when he heard how big the army arrayed against him was so that he could muster a large force of his own. It was a long, hard slugging match. At the end of it, the coalition arrayed against Æthelstan was shattered. Among the dead were five minor kings and seven Viking *jarls* who had fought alongside Óláfr. Constantin's son was also killed. The surviving Norsemen, broken in spirit, their hopes and dreams shattered in the violent and cataclysmic slaughter, took themselves off to Dublin to lick their wounds. The Strathclyders were badly cut up too and it is possible that their king, Owain, was among the dead; certainly local legend asserts that the so-called Giant's Grave in St Andrews Churchyard, Penrith, Cumbria, marks his burial place and that he died in 937.

The combined forces of Æthelstan's enemies were sent packing. Some of the Vikings escaped back across the sea though they needed far fewer ships to do so. Constantin was again forced to do homage for his kingdom to Æthelstan, who claimed not just to be king of England but also emperor, *basileus*, the contemporary Byzantine term, of Britain. By providing the Anglo-Saxons with a common enemy, the Vikings were playing a critical role in helping to give birth to a country called England. But to others in Britain the Vikings were natural allies. Many saw the Anglo-Saxons as the foe and the Vikings as part of the solution. The poet of the Welsh work, the *Armes Prydein*, hoped that:

There will be reconciliation between Cymry and the men of Dublin,
The Irish of Ireland and Anglesea [sic] and Scotland.
The men of Cornwall and of Strathclyde will be welcome among us...
The men of the north in the place of honour...
The stewards of Cirencester [the Anglo-Saxon tax collectors] will shed
    bitter tears...
As an end to their taxes they will know death.[20]

The poetry of the *ASC* is saga-like in its comments on the battle in contrast to its often laconic style. After the battle, the black raven, the white-tailed eagle, the hungry hawk and the grey wolf scoured the field for carrion; and they ate well. The Norsemen departed the field dejectedly, making their way under a cloud of shame across the sea back to Dublin. The *Annals of Ulster* called it 'a great, lamentable and horrible battle', though there was probably little lamentation on the part of the victors, even though their losses also appear to have been heavy.[21] Half a century later, Æthelweard, a chronicler from Wessex, would say that his people still referred to the campaign as 'the great battle'.[22]

Other writers too would adopt saga-like description in their accounts of the battle and its aftermath. The twelfth-century chronicler Henry of Huntingdon described the carnage:

> Then the dark raven with horned beak,
> And the livid toad, the eagle and the kite,
> The hound and wolf in mottled hue,
> Were long refreshed by these delicacies.[23]

As the writer in the *ASC* exultantly noted, 'never until now in this island, as books and scholars of old inform us, was there greater slaughter of an army with the sword's edge, since the Angles and Saxons put ashore from the east, attacked the Britons over the wide seas, proud forgers of war conquered the Welsh, and fame-eager warriors won them a homeland'.[24] If this seems to be over the top, it should be remembered that the Anglo-Saxon chroniclers were normally to the point in their approach and were trying to emphasise the epic nature of the victory.

There were warriors who might be called Vikings on both sides at Brunanburh. This is intimated from a discussion of the battle that appeared three centuries after it was fought when the famous *Egil's Saga* was produced in Iceland. Although the battle was called *Vinheior* in the saga, the details – while wrong in some respects – are close enough to convince us that it is Brunanburh that is being alluded to in it. It describes how Óláfr had been raiding in the north of England, forcing Æthelstan to respond; a likely enough scenario. Æthelstan, needing every available warrior to meet the threat posed to him by the formidable alliance in the north, recruited Viking mercenaries including Egil and his brother Thorolf.

Where the verbatim accuracy of the saga must come into question is in the way that it extols the heroism and – that much valued Viking quality – the cunning of Egil, who becomes the hero of the battle and indeed is primarily responsible for Æthelstan's victory. Yet due to underhand tactics, his brother Thorolf is killed in the battle, that bitter-sweet departure for Valhalla being another much-employed saga technique. Egil buried his brother with dignity before going to Æthelstan for his reward; it was all very well to lament a departed brother who had died a hero but one could not afford to take one's eye off the prize altogether. Thorolf at least had died a heroic death, as required by the storyline, after cutting down Hring, a prominent Strathclyde general. It was, in saga terms, a 'good end', appropriate to a great warrior. Inspired by Egil, the mercenary contingent continued to attack their Strathclyde opponents ferociously, bringing down another important figure called Adils in the process.

Another mercenary who fought loyally for Æthelstan at Brunanburh was a man called Turketyl; and it is interesting to note that in Malmesbury, one of the king's favourite places and where he was eventually buried, there was once a Turketyl's Bridge, perhaps named in honour of this Viking warrior who fought for the English.[25] While the *ASC* does not mention the mercenaries involved in the battle, this is not in the least bit surprising. The scribes who wrote up the battle wanted nothing to detract from this as a crushing Anglo-Saxon victory. However, the hiring of mercenaries to support Æthelstan's forces made sense. Such tactics were employed on other occasions in the Viking era and the king certainly had the financial resources to make it a viable policy. In addition, he was faced by a massive coalition, his worst nightmare when so many of his opponents had joined together, and possibly he felt that exceptional measures were needed.

Unsurprisingly many legends grew up around Brunanburh. One of them has Óláfr Gofraidsson entering Æthelstan's camp disguised as a minstrel (much as Alfred had supposedly done before the Battle of Edington). In this guise he succeeded in finding out where the English king's tent was. Æthelstan however saw through the ruse and exchanged his tent for that of the bishop of Sherborne. When Viking forces launched a surprise attack in the night, it was therefore the unfortunate bishop rather than the king who was on the wrong end of it.[26] The fighting was clearly hard and apparently lasted all day; among the dead were two grandsons of Alfred, Ælfwine and Æthelwine.

The exact location of this decisive confrontation is not known. However, modern historians have tended to lean towards Bromborough on the Wirral as the most likely spot. There is strong circumstantial evidence to support this. This area was ideal for Vikings coming across from Ireland and had been populated by many of Scandinavian descent since the beginning of the tenth century when many of them had fled from Ireland. It was also accessible by road from Strathclyde and Scotland further north.[27]

But not everyone agrees: and some criticise modern scholars for relying solely on tenuous place-name evidence while suggesting other possible sites for the battle further north in Lancashire or somewhere in Yorkshire. Their case is strengthened by slightly later accounts from writers such as Symeon of Durham and Florence of Worcester who state that the Viking fleet made its way up the Humber on the eastern coast. While this might seem counter-intuitive, it was by no means impossible and would make sense if York was an early target for the combined force.[28]

The remarkable nature of Æthelstan's reign in England is attested by the fact that it made an impression on Scandinavian as well as English praise poets. Egil wrote after the triumph of the English armies at Brunanburh and did so at the king's court, where he was well received and generously rewarded. Egil in return praised the king, saying that 'the highest path of the reindeer [possibly Scotland] now lies in the power of the brave Æthelstan'.[29] An early charter of Æthelstan's reign refers to him as *Anglosaxonum Denorumque gloriossisimus rex* – 'most glorious king of the Anglo-Saxons and Danes' – emphasising that he saw himself as a king of both peoples.[30] To some of the chroniclers, the triumph of Brunanburh was the greatest victory ever won, not just by him but by any other Anglo-Saxon king.

Æthelstan has had a raw deal from history. He has been sometimes ignored, perhaps unsurprisingly when, just over a century later, usurpers from Normandy seized the throne from his successors – history is usually written by the victors and praising the virtues of an Anglo-Saxon monarch was not in their script. However, the twefth-century chronicler William of Malmesbury wrote a lot about the king, probably influenced by the fact that Æthelstan was a generous sponsor of his abbey and was buried there; William had even seen his remains with his fair hair. Despite their largely ignored status, there is reason to argue that the dynasty of Alfred, Edward and Æthelstan, not to mention the redoubtable Æthelflaed, was one of the greatest in English history, both before and after the Norman Conquest in 1066.[31]

Many countries have a creation myth: examples that resonate to this day include Serbia which was, according to nationalist interpretations of history, forged on the fields of the bitter defeat at Kosovo in 1389; or Turkey where the capture of Byzantine Constantinople in 1453 is still seen as a formative moment in the country's history. Of course, this vastly overstates the case: Turkey and Serbia both have long histories before these events. The creation myth is not so much about when the nation came into being but concerns an event that makes the country what it is, or at least what it is seen to be. Such in its way was the case with Brunanburh, now in general terms largely unremembered by any save enthusiastic historians of the period, probably because Anglo-Saxon England did not outlive 1066 except in a vastly changed and virtually unrecognisable form. But at the time it was something that was a celebrated part of Anglo-Saxon history and a critical moment in it that helped to shape the kingdom.

The part played by 'Vikings' in the formation of England should not be understated. For over half a century they had had a massive impact on the formation of England (and Scotland, Wales and Ireland too). The Anglo-Saxons had been forced to unite against this common enemy, to put aside their differences, recognising that this was the only way to survive. In the process an English nation – ironically one with a strong element of Scandinavian blood coursing through its veins – had been formed. It was indeed a long, unlikely but spectacular journey from Athelney to Brunanburh.

Æthelstan was personally unlucky in that he did not live long to enjoy the fruits of his triumph. After his death, his dynasty then went into decline for a little while before its fortunes flew like a phoenix under the short but notable rule of Edgar; though he may have been spared too much Viking attention because King Harald Bluetooth had domestic distractions to occupy him. Edgar indeed was criticised by some near-contemporary commentators for his protection of 'foreigners'; and charters from the early part of his rule when he was king of Mercia only show a marked mix of Anglo-Saxon and Danish names among the witnesses.[32] But then the situation declined alarmingly, leaving the door open for a Viking opportunist called Sveinn Forkbeard to walk through and exploit it. While an English nation had been formed, it still had a twisting, tortuous route to follow before it reached its ultimate state.

The impermanence of the impact of even a great king like Æthelstan became clear soon after his death in 939; arguably 'there was no major change to the political map of Britain'.[33] There was no doubting Æthelstan's personal qualities; the neutral *Annals of Ulster* noted in his obituary that he was the 'pillar of dignity of the western world'. But his impact had been temporary in nature. This was shown within months of his death. Óláfr (Amlaib/Anlaf) Gofraidsson soon returned to England to successfully stake his claim to be king of York.

Before long, he was raiding the midlands of England. He reclaimed Leicester, Derby, Nottingham and Lincoln and then turned north to bring the northern, stubbornly independent part of Northumbria under his control but died before he could do so, though he did raid Lindisfarne again, an act of doubtful political intelligence on his part. He was joined by his cousin, Óláfr Cuarán, who succeeded as ruler in York on his death in 941.

This turn of events followed Óláfr Gofraidsson's pillaging of the monastery at Tyninghame in East Lothian. There lay the remains of a revered Northumbrian saint, Balthere (also known as Baldred). Within days, Óláfr was dead, allegedly slain by the vengeful spirit of the saint, emphasising that in some ways the conflict still remained one between Christianity and paganism.

The 'Danes' become 'English'

For a short while, it was as if Æthelstan had never existed in parts of England. The new king Edmund was inexperienced but would grow into the task. It was not long before he won back the lands in the Danelaw that had recently been lost to the Vikings from York. It was an event celebrated in the *ASC* where we read that 'for a long hard time had the Danes been forcibly subdued in bondage to the heathens, till king Edmund, Edward's son, protector of warriors, released them again by his valour'. The remarkable feature of this statement is that it postulated that the 'Danes' in England were being persecuted not by the English but by other Scandinavians, suggesting that they now had more in common with their Anglo-Saxon neighbours than with Norse warriors from the north of England and Ireland. It was as if the Danes of the Danelaw were becoming English.

That said, Danish areas retained to an extent their own distinctive practices in England. Administratively they were divided up into *wapentakes* – literally the taking of weapons in Old Norse – something similar to the Anglo-Saxon hundreds.[34] Regular assemblies were held where freemen could express their views: they were called *things* as was also the case in Iceland and there are place name reminders of their existence: Dingwall and Tinwald in Scotland for example, Tingwall in Shetland and Orkney, Thingwall in Lancashire, Tynwald on the Isle of Man (still the name of the Man parliament, who ceremonially meet on Tynwald Hill on 5 July, 'Tynwald Day').[35]

The recovery in England vis-à-vis the Scandinavian north was not an overnight one by the Anglo-Saxons. For a time, Edmund left York to its own devices. But in 943, the Viking ruler of York, Óláfr Cuarán, accepted baptism with Edmund as his baptismal sponsor; a sure sign of subordination and one which had been used before, both in England (for example, Alfred and Guthrum) and also on the Continent (for example with Charlemagne and Louis the Pious). It benefitted Edmund significantly as it gave him a kind of supremacy over Óláfr.[36] Óláfr later renounced his conversion for a while but by the time of his death four decades later, he would be firmly back in the Christian fold. This would be in line with what increasingly happened to Viking rulers who saw the benefits of their alliance with the Church; 'ruler and religion united ... the church supported the kings and the king's power increased as he claimed to be chosen by God'.[37]

The situation in England shortly thereafter is unfortunately rather vague. Several other Viking rulers of York are known: one, called Sitriuc, from a single coin recovery, and another named Ragnall. How they came to be there is not known; they may have done so in coordination with Óláfr or they may have effectively usurped his position. However, it did not last for the next thing we know for certain is that Edmund had taken over York for himself. This expulsion of men who were named as 'traitors' (presumably they had broken some commitment to Edmund) was apparently facilitated by Wulfstan, archbishop of York, evidently a man of remarkable flexibility of conscience given his actions during these years. The *Annals of Clonmacnoise* record that a Viking ruler in York, presumably Ragnall, was killed at about this time. A recorded attack by the Anglo-Saxons on Strathclyde in 945 may suggest Anglo-Saxon efforts to destroy alliances with Vikings; granting the land to Mael Colaim I, king of Alba, afterwards suggests attempts on the part of Edmund to build new ones.

By 945 Óláfr was back in Dublin, where he succeeded in ousting the current Norse ruler, Blácaire, the cousin of the late Ragnall. He then entered into an alliance with one of the Irish kings of nearby Brega, Congalach of Knowth, who had recently usurped the high kingship of Tara. Strange bedfellows, perhaps; but the picture is clear enough again – that any interpretation of Viking and contemporary politics based on simplistic views of nationalism or even faith is way off the mark. In these times, as in most others, it was expediency rather than principle that was the defining factor in political alliances.

Dublin had changed in character since its early days. When it was first founded by the Norsemen, it had essentially been a garrison. It had now become something far more. It was a trading settlement, essentially an *emporium* in Ireland where goods freely flowed in and out. (It is interesting that the stem of the word *emporium* is the Ancient Greek 'poros', meaning journey.) While no doubt the Vikings exploited the local Celtic population, recently suggestions have been made that this was a two-way street whereby native Irish rulers also made the most of the ability to buy in exotic goods from further afield through Dublin; trade as much as warfare may have been the way of things in Ireland for some of the time.[38]

On the death of Edmund of England in 946, he was succeeded by his brother Eadred; the third son of Edward the Elder to become king of England with two other disputed candidates to add to that total too. It is a salutary reminder that contemporary kingship at the time –not just in Anglo-Saxon circles – was inherited through a blood connection to the previous monarch which often varied from the simple father to son (or daughter) inheritance that later became the case. Edmund had a son but he was too young to rule effectively so he did not succeed to the throne. It was a pragmatic solution that had echoes in Norse practice too. It was perhaps wise in the short term, but it made for complicated succession disputes when disenfranchised wannabe kings subsequently decided to assert their claims through assertive/aggressive action as Æthelwold had previously done after the death of Alfred.

This was the case now in York where the inhabitants found themselves caught up in just a Scandinavian succession dispute. Northumbria was now in a very uncertain position. In a charter issued in the first year of the new English king's reign, it is specifically mentioned separately from 'the kingdoms of the Anglo-Saxons'. One of Eadred's first acts was to proceed to Yorkshire and receive homage from the leading Northumbrians, evidently after a period of uncertainty after the death of Edmund when the people of the city may have tried to throw off Anglo-Saxon rule. However, this did not mean very much for soon afterwards there is mention of a Viking called 'Erik' as the ruler of York (the largely ignored *Life of St Cathróe* suggests that he was even king there before the death of Edmund). In later Icelandic sagas he is named as Erik Bloodaxe; they described him as 'a big man and handsome, strong and valiant, a great warrior and victorious in battle, very impetuous in disposition, cruel, unfriendly and silent'. The lateness of this evidence has led some modern historians to reject this connection and suggest that this 'Erik' may be a different character than Erik Bloodaxe.[39] Certainly, 'Erik' felt secure enough to issue coins in his name; these were struck by Rathulf who had minted currency for the English king, Eadred.

Erik's place as the ruler of York was clearly based on a takeover of some sort as Eadred responded with fury. In a ferocious expedition launched in 948, Ripon Minster was burned. This was a very unchristian act for an English king to undertake, but there is a very clear explanation for it. Ripon was the jewel in the crown of the possessions then held by the archbishop of York at the time, Wulfstan. The most logical reason for this violent attack was that Wulfstan had supported the usurpation of Erik and was now suffering the consequences. Eadred's fierce reaction to these events generated the desired response. The Northumbrians ejected Erik and submitted to Eadred. But this allegiance was only skin-deep as by 949, Óláfr Cuarán had been ejected from Dublin by Blácaire (who had himself been thrown out of the port a few years previously) and returned to York to resume his rulership there. The merry-go-round of Hiberno-Norse politics continued to impact on the affairs of northern England.

Tenth-century Vikings in Scotland and Ireland

There was still much Viking activity in other parts of Britain and Ireland. Viking settlements now straddled the western Scottish islands. Some left little impression on the wider historical landscape in all but indirect ways which are now not easy to spot. But in the Outer Hebrides on the conjoined islands of Lewis and Harris there is widespread linguistic evidence for their presence: on Lewis for example 99 out of the 126 villages have Norse names and another 9 have Norse elements in theirs; a remarkably high percentage.[40]

Yet confirmatory archaeological evidence of their presence in the Outer Hebrides is in comparatively short supply. There is some but nothing like the amount we might expect: at Drimore on South Uist for example, a solitary homestead has been unearthed, which is one of the few echoes of Viking colonisation in the region. It is a humble dwelling with very shallow foundations, suggesting that a turf-walled structure once stood here. On nearby North Uist a larger settlement was found at the Udal; the archaeology there suggests Viking residency as far back as the ninth century while the discovery of a Harald Hardrada coin on the site suggests that it was occupied for at least two centuries.

Barvas on Lewis reveals more evidence of everyday existence, a routine lifestyle that was as far removed from the epics of the sagas as it was possible to be. Pottery there was in abundance, demonstrating Scandinavian antecedents. Animal bones provide mundane but important evidence of how these people lived: mainly on a diet of sheep and cattle but also of goats, pigs and red deer. The evidence suggests regular culling; many beef animals were killed when very young, suggesting that their mothers were being primarily kept for dairy production while the sheep were only marginally luckier, perhaps living for two summers before being butchered. Fish too were popular: cod, ling and saithe from further out, plaice, turbot and flounder from shallower waters. Barley, oats and flax were also grown by the settlers.[41]

Yet even here there were some more exotic objects. A spectacular find among the otherworldly landscape of the Storr in the north of Skye contained 111 coins (perhaps a magic number as it turns up on other occasions?). They were a mixed bag of Anglo-Saxon and Arabic examples, showing that the locals were benefitting from an international trading/raiding network. They seem to have been buried around 935. However, it is argued that these were not the panicked burial of a man in imminent danger but rather a ritual offering to some deity.[42]

The exact nature of the Viking colonisation of the Western Isles is something of a puzzle. While the almost total dominance of Viking place names in islands such as Lewis may suggest that the local population were extirpated, the survival of Gaelic in the region argues against such an extreme outcome. Other tantalising evidence for assimilation rather than extermination was found in a grave at Bhaltos on the island where a woman had been buried with both Viking and Celtic jewellery as grave goods. Perhaps we will never know for sure whether the Vikings wiped out the local Pictish inhabitants of the region or rather merely merged with them.

The historians Andrew Jennings and Arne Kruse have suggested that a distinction should be made between what they call the outer and inner zones of Viking occupation on the west coast of Scotland. The outer zone consists of the islands of Islay (where the Viking element became particularly dominant, leading to suggestions that the islands may have become a launchpad for raids on Ireland), Coll, Tiree and the Outer Hebrides, the western part of Mull and Skye. Here they suggest that the Vikings made little effort to integrate with the pre-existing local population. The inner zone consists of the mainland part of Dál Riata, Arran, Bute and the eastern part of Mull. There, evidence of Gaelic survival is stronger, and the Vikings seem to have integrated and learned the local language; in other words, they became far more assimilated.[43] Evidence from Viking grave sites is supportive of this argument. There are a number of such in Islay and its neighbours, Colonsay, Oronsay, Tiree and Eigg. There are far fewer to the east and Jura, Kintyre and Bute have no known Viking burials while there are few on Arran. Further, the islands in the west include female remains while those to the east that have been found include a lower proportion of women. It has been suggested that this higher proportion of female burials in the west may intimate either the local economic significance of women and girls or a strong adherence to Scandinavian roots (female displays of 'homeland' culture are sometimes a feature of a diasporic environment) or perhaps both.[44]

If this argument is valid, then Viking development varied in different parts of western Scotland. While on the mainland and the adjacent islands there was a significant degree of assimilation, on the more westerly islands a distinctive Scandinavian-rooted culture was in place. Over time this latter area developed into a distinctive region, which became known as the Kingdom of the Isles, though exactly when is unclear; at times it included the Isle of Man and the Hebrides as well as parts of Argyll and Galloway in mainland Scotland. While dates going back to the ninth century have been argued for these developments, it has been noted that contemporary evidence suggests that a tenth-century date is more likely. While the Vikings were certainly active in the area in the ninth century, it seems that at that particular time the region remained politically fragmented.[45] Indeed, the very foundation of the Kingdom of the Isles became a battleground for nationalist historians in later times; Scottish claims that their foundation can be dated back to Cináed McAlpin have been countered by Norwegian assertions that they were established by the Norwegian king, Harald Fairhair. Irish chronicles start to mention the *Innis Gall* – 'the islands of the foreigners' – from about 940.[46]

On occasion the Hebrides attracted attention from further afield given their position as part of the wider Irish Sea region. In 941, the overking of the northern Uí Néill, Muirchertach, son of the late high king Niall Glúndub, attacked the islands showing that the Vikings by now did not have control of the seas in this area to themselves. The Hebrides may have been allied to the dynasty of Ivarr's descendants in Dublin who now found themselves part of the wider field of activity regarding Viking warfare and its fall-out.

The war with Muirchertach, one of the most renowned Irish warriors of the tenth century and a persistent enemy of the Vikings, went on for several years and ended with his death in 943 at the hands of the Dubliners at the Battle of Áth Fhirdiach (he had been captured by them and ransomed a few years before). However, this was very much a period of ebb and flow for the Viking settlement of Dublin, which was thoroughly sacked by the Irish in 944; several annal accounts describe how 400 Vikings were killed and the fortress there was burned. One account, that of the *Annals of the Four Masters*, claimed that the whole population was taken into slavery apart from those who managed to make their way to sanctuary on Dalkey Island but this may be an exaggeration. The year after, Muirchertach's son, Domnall Ua Néill, wiped out a party of Vikings on Lough Neagh, taking advantage of unusually wintry conditions to lead his men across the ice. He also destroyed their ships that had been trapped there.

The men of Waterford were also involved in these wars, again often in alliance with Gaelic kings. A human tragedy illuminates the otherwise sometimes featureless one-line accounts of battles and conflicts. The abbot of Killeigh in County Offaly was taken prisoner on one of the campaigns and was incarcerated on Dalkey Island near Dublin. Presumably he was being held for ransom but we can also assume that his captivity was not particularly pleasant. In 939, he was drowned while trying to escape, a reminder that the events of these traumatic and turbulent times had some devastating personal consequences that are all too easy to overlook.

Soon after, Óláfr Cuarán returned from his unsuccessful venture in York and seized control of Dublin from a Viking rival. Of this rival little is known. He was Blákári the son of Gofraid, who had led the Viking force which had defeated Muirchertach (presumably the same man as 'Blácaire' who was mentioned earlier). This marked an important change in direction for the dynasty of Ivarr as control now moved from the bloodline of Gofraid to that of Sitriuc, an example of what one historian remarked as being a dynastic situation where its members 'began as families and developed into large cousinhoods of military competitors'.[47] Not only were the Vikings in Ireland fighting Irish kings and rivals from Limerick, now even the line of Ivarr was splitting into two and were at odds with each other: it was from among Sitriuc's descendants that the later Viking kings of Dublin would emerge. Óláfr in particular would show himself to be a born survivor and would rule in Dublin until 980.

Dublin continued to thrive and there is every indication that business continued to boom, both with the indigenous Irish kings and their people and further afield. But from time to time events would occur that would remind everyone of the duality of the Vikings, both merchants and warriors, traders and raiders (to which we should also add as an additional layer of complexity, settlers too). So for example in 942 there were 'heathen' raiders attacking the monastic sites at Kildare and

Clonmacnoise in Leinster and Meath. In 950, what appears to have been a particularly vicious attack on Slane occurred when many of the monastery's treasures were destroyed and some of the monks were burned alive when they sought refuge in a round tower, a famous and distinctive example of contemporary Irish architecture. The following year Kells was ransacked and 3,000 captives were taken, along with many cattle and horses. The message was that you took the Vikings for granted at your peril; and it was one that was still being delivered, particularly in Ireland, with disturbing regularity.

9

Harald Bluetooth (951–975)

We have heard of the thriving of the throne of Denmark, how the folk-
kings flourished in former days...

Beowulf

The end of Erik Bloodaxe(?)

The somewhat bewildering sequence of events in York continued to
evolve. Óláfr Cuarán was driven out in 952 and replaced by 'Erik,
Harald's son', a description that would be consistent with the lineage
of Erik Bloodaxe though Harald is a common enough Scandinavian
name and this evidence on its own is not conclusive.[1] Along with a
reference in the *Annals of Ulster* for the same year that mentions a
victory for the Gaills over the men of Alba, the Britons and the Saxons,
one suggestion is that this might have been a hostile takeover on this
Erik's part. On this occasion the Scots and Strathclyde 'Welsh' had
allied themselves with the Anglo-Saxons in contrast to their position
not long before at Brunanburh.

All of this is somewhat speculative in terms of spelling out Erik's
story. Another great imponderable in all this is the role of the enigmatic
Archbishop Wulfstan, who stopped witnessing charters at Eadred's
court from 951 onwards and was arrested in the following year for
accusations which had 'often been made to the king against him'.[2] He
had been prominent in Northumbrian affairs for several decades and
appears to have been something of a wheeler-dealer there. The frequent
regime changes in York during his time as archbishop are unlikely to be
a coincidence.

After his arrest, Wulfstan appears as a charter witness, but only in one
case (in 953) and the last we hear of him in 956 is when he is exercising
his episcopal authority in Dorchester, 200 miles to the south. He died

that year in a Mercian monastery. The fact that the accusations against him reached their head in 952, the same year that Erik took over in York, is suggestive of double-dealing on his part, though exactly what form this took is impossible to be sure of. But there is a very strong whiff here that this is a case of a Christian archbishop collaborating with pagan Scandinavian confederates.

Erik Bloodaxe (if indeed it was he) endured a difficult relationship with his subjects in York. He was driven out of the city again in 954. After his ousting, he was killed in a skirmish at Stainmore, on the border between Northumbria and Cumbrian Strathclyde, on the road from York to the Irish Sea coast. Stainmore is a remote setting in the Pennines, an ideal spot for an ambush, and it is tempting to think that this isolated pass through the fells is where Erik met his end, a suitably romantic and atmospheric setting for such a character to make his exit – though there are alternatives offered by some saga writers for the end of the man called Erik Bloodaxe, such as death in Spain. The *Orkneyinga Saga* has an end involving something more than a skirmish for Erik, saying he fell in battle alongside six other kings, including one called Guthorm, after 'the English were killed in large numbers'.[3] One is almost tempted to hope that the scene of Erik's entry into Valhalla as described by the *Eiríksmál* is true; it has him being greeted by Odin with the words 'Hail to you Erik, be welcome here and come into the hall, gallant king!'

Erik was the last Scandinavian king of York. From now on, Northumbria became more firmly assimilated into the rest of England (though never completely so), a situation which became apparent with King Eadred's quick appointment of Oslac, the reeve of Bamburgh, to take over the administration of the city. Oscytel, who came from the Danelaw and was probably of Danish blood, was appointed archbishop in 956. From then on Northumbria remained in the main assimilated within England – not always a state of affairs that the Northumbrians felt comfortable with. For many of them, the West Saxon or the Mercian may have been the enemy more than the Scandinavian was. In many ways, the passing of King Erik, 'Bloodaxe' or not, marked the end of the Viking Age in Northumbria. When a Scandinavian next ruled it, it was in a very different time and world, over half a century later. Nevertheless, the fear of Viking attack remained real for Anglo-Saxon England; in the 950s Eadred left £1,600 in his will to his bishops with the injunction that it should be used to resist 'a heathen army should they need'.

Relationships between Vikings and England further south are unclear at this time. There are snippets of information hinting at some of the initiatives that were taking place; a man with the Scandinavian-sounding name of Siferth was witnessing a charter in Eadred's reign in 955. Later, in 962, a king of the same name – so quite possibly the same man – committed suicide in Wimborne; this much we know, giving us a tantalising glimpse of something dramatic going on but not providing us with the detail to understand more of what sounds like a fascinating state of affairs. Who this Siferth was, and why he committed suicide, we do not know. Neither are we clear about why he was then buried in what was a royal church at Wimborne, particularly as the fact that he committed suicide would normally preclude him from being buried in consecrated ground.

It has been suggested that an increase in hoards found in the Isle of Man from about this time may be linked to a group of political exiles arriving from York; there are also contingents of 'Deirans' noted in the armies of Richard of Normandy in 962.[4] Man certainly made a convenient and relatively safe bolthole for Viking émigrés from Northumbria. It was at a crossroads of major shipping routes from east to west and north to south; an ideal position for both raiding and trading. A burial at Ballateare on the island gives a very revealing insight into Viking ritual practices on the island. The main burial was of a young man lying with his weapons. Interred unceremoniously was a young woman, without any grave goods, apparently killed by a sword blow to the back of the head: seemingly a case of ritual sacrifice to sanctify the burial. At Balladoole, a Viking ship burial apparently desecrated a previous Christian burial, suggesting that the Viking occupation of Man may not have been an altogether peaceful or friendly one. This impression is supported by the fact that there are very few examples of obviously Viking burials in mainland England, where perhaps assimilation and integration was more necessary if the Scandinavian settlers were to thrive, compared to the relative abundance of such on Man.[5]

Now back in Ireland, Óláfr Cuarán allied himself with the Irish kings of north Leinster and they defeated and killed Congalach, king of the south Uí Néill. This brought time and breathing space for Dublin and a period of relative tranquillity followed, which was much needed. There were still threats emerging it is true, not least from the rival descendants of the bloodline of Gofraid who had been displaced in Dublin; but Óláfr managed to hold onto his position for several decades to come, even though during one of the battles against his rivals he was wounded by an arrow in the thigh. In some of these conflicts, it appears that the rival bloodline was receiving support from Viking elements in the Hebrides but Óláfr Cuarán emerged, politically if not physically, unscathed.

Harald Bluetooth and the Christianisation of Denmark

The main focus of the next stage in the Viking story takes us back to Denmark. Gorm the Old died in about 958; his wife Thyra predeceased him by a few years. In the inscription that Gorm ordered to be carved on a memorial stone for Thyra, we come across something very significant. It states boldly that 'King Gorm made this memorial to his wife Thyra, the glory of Denmark'. It is the first time that an entity called 'Denmark' had been recorded in the country, though the Anglo-Saxon version of it, *Danemearc,* is used in the translation of the late Roman historian Orosius made for King Alfred in the twilight years of his reign.

Thyra was regarded as a remarkable woman in her own right and legend credits her with the responsibility for building the earthwork known as the Danevirke, though archaeology suggests that it had been there for a good few centuries before her arrival. She was, according to later saga writers, a woman with the gift of prophecy, especially skilled in the interpretation of dreams, and someone of exceptional beauty. The story of the reasons behind her marriage in the *Jómsvíkings Saga* is decked out with all sorts of mystical overtones.[6] In reality, it had probably much more to do with pragmatic politics as her father, Klak-Harald, was earl of Holstein, in a strategically critical position on the southern borders of Denmark.

The royal mausoleum at Jelling was furnished with two great burial mounds. The North Mound at one stage contained a burial but when excavated in the nineteenth century it was found to be empty. The South Mound betrayed no sign of ever having been 'lived in' at all. Nowadays, a white church sits between the two mounds; either a confident interloper forcing them apart or, alternatively, one overshadowed and in danger of being crushed between them as if they were two towering animate objects bearing down on it.

The North Mound probably originally contained the body of Gorm, who had ordered its construction, but his remains were moved to the new church that was built on the orders of his son and successor, Harald 'Bluetooth' (also known as Harald Gormsson). Shortly after he became king, Harald was visited by a Christian missionary, Bishop Poppo; we know frustratingly little about Poppo but the actions which he employed to convert Harald to the Christian faith became well known.[7] The South Barrow was constructed on the orders of Harald 'Bluetooth' Gormsson and is a cenotaph rather than a grave. While this may seem unusual it was not unique; there are several other examples of such cenotaphs to be found in Scandinavia.[8]

In the late twentieth century, restoration work at Jelling revealed much about the site. The latest church, still standing there now, was built in about 1100, making it the oldest known such edifice in Denmark. Digging on the site however suggested that there were three previous buildings there before the stone church was erected. They were all made of wood and had all burned down. Most intriguingly the double grave of a man and a woman was found, which could conceivably be the remains of Gorm and Thyra. The remains seemed to be as old as the first church and indeed that building may well have been constructed around them.

Gorm was a convinced pagan but after his death and with the emergence of a new, young king, Poppo saw an opportunity. He journeyed to Harald's court in an attempt to convince him of the merits of Christianity (his mission took place in around 960). He employed a good old-fashioned Christian tactic to do so: a miracle. He had his hand encased in a red-hot iron glove but when he removed it his skin was unsinged and he himself completely unharmed. That did the trick. Harald became a devout Christian and an enthusiastic supporter of the religion in Denmark. Not everyone in his country however was as convinced by the Christian faith as he was; and in reality it is probable that Harald adopted Christianity as a political move, both to build his own centralised power and to ingratiate himself with his powerful neighbour to the south, Emperor Otto I. Certainly, it was said that it was on Otto's insistence that Harald was baptised along with his wife Gunnhild and his son Sveinn Otto (better known as 'Forkbeard').[9]

The concept of a king meant something different in Viking society than it does in the modern world. Now we associate a king or queen with a country. However, in the Viking world a king was a ruler over a smaller group of people, perhaps something we would now call a clan. Such a ruler would not only lead his folk in war, he would also be an arbitrator in matters concerning the law and could equally fulfil a function as some form of priest leading his followers in rituals including sacrifices. This meant that in the past a number of kings could be around at the same time: for example, when Erik Bloodaxe was killed in 954 there were supposedly six kings with him.[10] Now Harald was about to claim the whole territory of Denmark for himself, much as his namesake, Fairhair, had attempted to do in Norway earlier.

Not long before (in 948) Otto had threatened to intervene in Denmark to impose Christianity in the country. He unilaterally designated three bishops to different towns in Denmark: at Hedeby, Ribe and Åarhus. The fact that Denmark was an independent nation state did not enter the equation, as it had not when Charlemagne forcibly converted the continental Saxons nearly two centuries before; and as would also be the case when a militant Christendom launched the Crusades two centuries later. But in this case, Harald neatly removed the *raison d'être* for intervention by adopting Christianity. Otto recognised this formally, as can be seen in later charter evidence.[11]

Here we have a fine example of the creation myth, a defining moment that brings forth a nation, in this case Denmark. There had been previous kings of Denmark dating back to Godfrid at the beginning of the ninth century and possibly even before that. Harald's own father, Gorm, played a critical role in the formation of the country he inherited. Yet it is Harald who now generally receives the kudos for the foundation of Denmark. Certainly, he contributed significantly to the birth of an assertive nation state that would have dramatic repercussions, both close to home in Scandinavia and also further afield, in the British Isles especially; but his adoption of Christianity probably added to the lustre he was assigned by later historians.

His reputation contrasts with that of his father. Gorm, probably because of his pagan beliefs, is dismissed as 'a savage worm' by the eleventh-century writer Adam of Bremen on whom we rely for much of our information about these times (*Vurm* probably being a pun on Gorm). Adam accuses him of trying to destroy Christianity in Denmark, driving priests out of the country and torturing many of them to death.[12] Harald was to take things to the other extreme. Adam does not paint a flattering picture of Denmark as a whole; he writes of a people who would as happily raid each other as they would foreigners and willingly sell their own compatriots into slavery. They were, however, a people with great personal pride, who would, according to Adam, rather be beheaded than flogged; it was important that, whatever punishment they were condemned to for any alleged crimes, that they took it cheerfully, looking it full in the face. Weeping was expressly frowned upon. There was also, he said, 'very much gold in Zealand, accumulated by the plundering of pirates'.[13]

Putting aside its religious significance, Harald's conversion was a moment of great political importance. Vikings had become Christians before, even in Scandinavia, though it was typically overseas that Vikings had converted *en masse*. Now the new faith was being invited in. It does not matter that it was quite possibly because of political expediency, for this time it would take root in the North, even though it was a stop-start, long-term process in many regions. It was an act that eventually brought Denmark, and the rest of Scandinavia, into the 'league of nations', no longer 'other' but part of the mainstream.

Any rapprochement with Otto certainly made political sense from Harald's perspective. Otto was far too powerful a neighbour to take on; and Harald had many ambitions in the north to pursue and he would welcome a quiet life on his southern border. Harald's later marriage in 965 to a princess of the Wends, a people on the Baltic coast in the region that now includes the eastern part of Germany and Poland, is a strong hint of where his political priorities lay. There were stories of Danish involvement in a raid into Sweden which got as far as Uppsala before being beaten in battle. The vague accounts we have suggest that Danish involvement in the fight was not very distinguished and that those there as support to a Swedish claimant to the throne, Styrbjorn Starki, did not do a very good job. The outcome of the battle left the current holder of the Swedish crown triumphant and he was ever after known as 'Erik the Victorious' (Segersäll).

Harald left evidence of his own beliefs in a remarkable way. At Jelling he had a figure carved on a large piece of stone that had probably been deposited there when a glacier retreated thousands of years before. This was an amazing rendition of the Crucifixion, all spirals and twirls (surely linked to the image of Odin in the 'World Tree'), a fusion of Christian symbolism and pagan naturalism; a carving so famous to Danes that it has become known as 'Denmark's Birth Certificate', one which adorns the current version of the Danish passport. The impression of pagan antecedents behind the design of the stone is reinforced by the carving on the reverse side: a snake curled around an animal in a sinister embrace. Excavations in 2006 revealed the existence of a massive ship-shaped edifice at Jelling at one time, reinforcing the Viking heritage of the site.

The memorial stones that Harald caused to be erected at Jelling were in honour of his parents. A runic inscription tells us that 'King Haraldur had this memorial made for Gormur his father and Thyra his mother: that Haraldur won all Denmark'. It goes on to say that he also won Norway and made her people Christian. This is more controversial: generations of Danish kings claimed to govern Norway but not always convincingly. That he won Denmark for himself is harder to argue against. He seems to have been the unrivalled claimant as king of Denmark when Gorm died, in itself a rather rare situation. However, he was soon facing external threats.

Early on in his reign Hákon the Good, king of Norway, launched raids on Denmark. Jutland, Zealand and the Danish territories in Sweden all felt the bite of this attack. Harald was in addition under pressure from German lands in the south. But these were all challenges from outside of Denmark. It was not until much later in his reign that he faced serious challenges from within: and then it came from a source rather close to home. Despite being brought up at the court of Æthelstan, who was regarded as a Christian paragon, Hákon soon re-adopted the old pagan religion when he returned from England. He quickly realised that there was little appetite for the new religion in Norway and pragmatically turned his back on it. Churches he had ordered to be constructed were burned down and priests he had put in place were slaughtered. He was also a pragmatist in other ways, forming a good relationship with Jarl Sigurd in the Trøndelag – a region which could have caused him a good deal of grief – and he set up two of his nephews as sub-kings in the east of Norway.

Hákon won a reputation for being a man who respected the laws and customs of Norway, earning him the respect of his people. He also constructed defences to protect against raids from Denmark and raised naval levies to form a fleet to resist Danish attack. Harald had a claim to Norway through his sister Gunnhild, the widow of Erik Bloodaxe. In the sagas she is portrayed as an eager assistant of evil warlocks, whom she later murdered so that she could marry Erik. In these tales, she was given a reputation for being rather too generous with her favours. All of this is unproveable and, more to the point, largely unbelievable. But the suggestion that, after the death of Erik, she returned to her brother to seek help in advancing the interests of her son, Harald Greycloak, in Norway seems plausible.

Several attacks on Norway were subsequently beaten off. But then, tragedy struck. In 961, battle was joined at Fitjar in Hordaland in the south-west of Norway. The invading forces were led by three of the sons of Erik Bloodaxe, named Harald Greycloak, Gamle Eriksson and Sigurd Sleva. In the battle that followed, the forces of Hákon were victorious, but the cost of victory was enormous. It was another Pyrrhic triumph. Hákon was mortally wounded (allegedly shot by an arrow from a child's bow) and Norway was open to the sons of the Bloodaxe. Eventually it was Harald Greycloak who assumed the highest position in Norway, though his direct rule was limited to the west of the country with the prime territory around the Vik kept under direct Danish rule.

Despite rising to the top of the pile, Harald Greycloak's reign was not a success. He was adventurous enough and explored into the Far North even more than his predecessors had done. He also defeated his immediate opposition in the south and west of Norway. But his close association with Harald Bluetooth did him few favours in the eyes of his erstwhile subjects. He might have been forgiven even that, but his active adoption of Christianity posed greater problems. This was especially so when he took tough measures to stamp out paganism in Norway, which contrasted with the conciliatory methods of the late King Hákon in a way which many Norwegians did not appreciate.

When harsh weather conditions followed, affecting both crops and livestock alike, the grumbling grew. But it was not in the end the Norwegians who brought him down. It was not even in Norway that he met his sudden end but at the entrance of the Limfjord in Denmark. Harald Bluetooth grew tired of Greycloak and developed more cordial relations with the jarls of Hladir in Trøndelag, the present incumbent being Jarl Hákon. Hákon had fallen out with Harald Greycloak and fled Norway with ten ships with which he returned to launch raids on the region. The *Jómsvíkings Saga* says that he went to Denmark where he allied himself to Harald Bluetooth.[14]

Harald Greycloak was killed at Hals in 974 in what has all the hallmarks of an ambush. In any crime scene, a good investigating officer will look at motive as a strong indicator to ascertain who might be a suspect. Given the fact that Norway was now split up between Hákon Sigurdsson, the jarl of Hladir, and Harald Bluetooth, one does not have far to look. Hákon was to hold the lands he was given with Harald Bluetooth as his ostensible overlord, so the king of Denmark was certainly the prime beneficiary from the demise of his former protégé. Hákon accepted Christianity as the price of his reward. However, he ignored this condition when he returned to Norway.[15] He also promised Harald an annual tribute of twenty falcons and agreed to provide military support when asked to do so.

This turn of events ignited a family feud. Gunnhild and her surviving sons took themselves off to Orkney, ideally placed to cause problems by raiding along the Norwegian coast. Hákon did very well out of the deal and was probably helped no end by his determined allegiance to the old gods, and the return of good harvests and better weather also aided his cause. The holy places that Harald Greycloak had destroyed were restored to their former condition and the practice of sacrifice was reintroduced.

Quite what the life of the inhabitants of the Viking diaspora was like is a matter of speculation. The *Orkneyinga Saga* gives some interesting detail on the way of life on Orkney and while many historians would rightly advocate caution in taking the words of the saga writers at face value, there is an element of believability in their words concerning this. The writer, an Icelander writing after the event as per usual, describes the life of a twelfth-century resident of Orkney, a nobleman called Svein Asleifarson. Svein spent winter at home in his hall at Gairsay on Orkney, allegedly the biggest one in the territory. He would look after the sowing of the seed in the spring. Then in summer he would go off plundering in the Hebrides and Ireland, his 'spring trip' as he called it. Then it was home again to reap the grain before his 'autumn trip', when he went off raiding once more.[16] One suspects that this was a way of life for many other 'Vikings' across Britain, Ireland and Scandinavia for centuries before that.

In 965, an Arab traveller from Cordoba, Al-Tartushi, visited Hedeby. What he found clearly shocked him. Archaeology reveals a cramped settlement with people living on top of each other; the inhabitants would do well to pass the age of forty. While Hedeby had its own mint, one of the earliest known in the Viking world, and had plenty of craftsmen's workshops and traders' warehouses, it clearly had another side which did not impress the Arab visitor one little bit. That said, the fact that Cordoba was at the time one of the most magnificent cities in the world cannot have helped when he started to draw comparisons with life back home.

He wrote of a festival where the Viking gods were honoured in a drunken, riotous celebration. Animals were slaughtered as honorary sacrifices and hung on poles outside houses. Oxen, rams, goats and boars were among the victims. Infanticide was still practised, sometimes by throwing an unwanted child into the sea; and this at a time when infant mortality was very high, with approximately 25–30 per cent of the discovered graves in cemeteries being those of children. Al-Tartushi wrote that the staple of the Viking diet was fish, which was in plentiful supply. He disparaged the quality of the local singing; 'it is like a growl coming out of their throats, like the barking of dogs, only much more beastly'. He was also deeply shocked when he noted how easily women divorced their husbands; not to mention that both sexes frequently used eye make-up to enhance their appearance.[17]

Another Islamic observer of the time was Ahmad ibn Rustah, a Persian who visited Novgorod in the land of the Rūs. He told a revealing story of how a Viking father would present a newborn son with a sword. Throwing it down he would say 'I shall not leave you with any property; you will have only what you can provide with this weapon'. It is a revealing insight into the martial nature of Viking society and how contemporaries perceived it. Ibn Rustah also noted that the Rūs had wizards who would decide what should be sacrificed, animal or human. Their decision was final; when the offering had been selected, the animal or person was led away to be hanged without any prevarication.

Relationships between the Islamic and Viking worlds were about to become more difficult for practical, logistical reasons. As the tenth century drew towards its close, something happened to interrupt the steady flow of Kufic silver from the eastern Islamic world until it became no more than a trickle. This led to the terminal decline of Birka and also to the need to draw virtually incessant tribute from Western Europe in the early part of the eleventh century. Certainly, something happened that led to a sea change in the Viking world during this period; and the wider world was to feel the impact of this at the edge of a sword.[18]

Wales and Ireland in the latter part of the tenth century

While Scandinavian interventions in England had eased off in the reign of King Edgar (959–975), there were bursts of Viking activity in the surrounding region. Two Viking brothers raided Anglesey (Mon) in successive years, 971 and 972, possibly trying to take advantage of chaos in Gwynedd following the death of Rhodri ad Idwal in 968. Their names were, according to a later record, Mark (highly unlikely and a probable Christian scribe's insertion at a later date in a garbled attempt to write down an unfamiliar Norse name) and Gothfrith; the 'Mark' in this partnership is normally referred to as 'Maccus'.[19] A likely target was the abbey of Penmon, making this something of an old-fashioned Viking raid.

Anglesey is sometimes overlooked in the story of the Vikings in the British Isles. They set up a fortified port at Holyhead in the tenth century and in the eleventh, settlers from Dublin established a colony at Moel-y-don Ferry.[20] A raid was recorded there as early as 853.[21]

Other recent finds at Llanbedrgoch on the island reveal evidence of a Viking trading and manufacturing site. The island had several major attractions. It was in a prime strategic spot, a hub point between Chester and Dublin, adjacent to the Isle of Man and proximate to the north-south waterway that ran up and down the Irish Sea linking the Continent at one end and the western and northern islands of Scotland at the other. It was also very fertile. For a time, it formed part of Gwynedd, often the strongest of the Welsh kingdoms, but it was also an attraction for the Anglo-Saxons too. It provided a focal point for Viking attentions in Wales, though later on south Wales also became of interest due to their activity in the south of England and the early development of Bristol.

The brothers are termed rather vaguely 'sons of Harald'. Given the dateline this could mean Harald Bluetooth, king of Denmark, or the former King Harald of Norway, making them brothers of Erik Bloodaxe. Most likely, however, in terms of geographical proximity if nothing else, they were sons of a Harald who had been active in Ireland in the region of Limerick, though he had been killed in 940.[22] After the raids on Anglesey, the brothers turned their attentions elsewhere. It is probably no coincidence that soon after the raids took place, King Edgar of England sent his fleet on a high-profile journey up the Welsh coast as a warning to the raiders to stay out of what he regarded as his backyard. This was in keeping with his overall policy of aggressive peacekeeping, which included sending a fleet to circumnavigate Britain on a regular basis as a way of reminding everyone who was in overall control. Possession of Anglesey enabled Vikings to directly threaten Chester, by now the second port in England after London. Edgar's efforts merely diverted their attention elsewhere.

The next we hear of Maccus and Gothfrith is in Ireland. They plundered the monastic complex at Scattery Island ('Inis Cathaig'), at the mouth of the Shannon in the west, sacred to the memory of the fifth-century saint, Senan, who had lived in the area. They were supported in the raid by other Vikings known as 'the lawmen of the Isles'; so here we see the extended area of the Irish Sea as a chessboard around which men like Maccus and Gothfrith moved their pieces. In fact, the area extended beyond the strict confines of the Irish Sea and into the Western Isles off Scotland and on occasion beyond to Orkney and Shetland. This reference to 'the lawmen of the Isles' is only the second that has been found in surviving records; the earlier one is to another raid on Ireland in 962. It has been suggested that the name refers to the Scandinavians inhabiting the western isles off the coast of Scotland and that the unusual title intimates that the social organisation of those who had taken up residence there was a loosely grouped confederation rather than being subject to the overlordship of one overall king.[23]

The raid was successful and resulted in the capture of the Viking king of Limerick, Imar (Ivarr). There were further raids such as that on Rechru (possibly Lambay, the island off the coast of Dublin),[24] where Ferdal, the head of the resident Columban establishment, was killed; despite the adoption of Christianity in some parts of the Viking world old habits again proved stubbornly resistant to change. In another raid on Scattery in 977, King Ivarr, who clearly had arranged a deal for his freedom, was killed by an emerging Irish warlord named Brian Boru. This effectively brought the ruling Viking dynasty in Limerick to an end.[25] From this point onwards, the town and its resources, including its fighting men, appear to have been under the power of Brian who also built a relationship with Waterford.

Brian was the overking of the Dál Cais, a group in the north-west of Munster. He became a great figure in Irish history and his exploits assumed legendary status. He and his predecessors allied themselves with the Vikings in Limerick and also from time to time played off one group in Dublin against the other in Waterford. By so doing, they significantly weakened Viking power in Ireland. There had been a major confrontation near the important religious site of Cashel in 967 when the Dál Cais bested the Vikings in battle at Solchóid and then sacked Limerick. However, a Viking counter-attack killed the vice king of the Dál Cais and there were violent raids into Irish territory shortly afterwards. The king of the Dál Cais, at that time Mathgamain, worked out his differences with the Vikings in Limerick and the two groups were soon working in tandem with each other, though this alliance occasionally broke down as seems to have happened in 972 when Limerick was sacked by the men of Munster.

The 960s had seen another bout of fighting between Vikings from Dublin, allied with Irish forces, taking on other indigenous kings in Ireland. Leinster was a particular hotspot, the main rivalry being with Domnall ua Néill, king of both the northern and the southern Uí Néill. This was a gruelling campaign in which both sides struggled to gain a decisive advantage. One victim of these campaigns was the important religious establishment at Kells, plundered in 969 and 970. Rather than anti-Christian actions, these events should be seen as largely politically motivated as Kells was closely linked with the Uí Néill.

Again, not just military measures were taken here. The marriage of Óláfr's daughter to Domnall son of Congalach overking of Brega, a kingdom to the north of Dublin, was an obvious alliance-building measure. The Uí Néill threat remained very real and an attack on Brega in 970 saw important church sites at Monasterboice, Dunleer, Louth and Drumiskin attacked; this time the churches were being defended by Viking forces.[26] A decisive battle was fought at Kilmona with the Dublin forces triumphant and Domnall ua Néill was forced onto the back foot as a result. Above all of these developments in Ireland though loomed the giant shadow of Brian Boru, who increasingly came to dominate affairs in succeeding years.

Denmark and England: changes afoot

Although his reign had seen much progress in terms of advancing his own interests, in 972–3 Harald Bluetooth paid homage to the Emperor Otto at Quedlinburg. This was probably not something he enjoyed very much and his allegiance was only skin-deep. When, just a few months after the meeting, Otto died and was replaced by his son, Otto II, Harald was quick to raid his territory. This was soon shown to be a major miscalculation. Otto II assembled a large army and broke through the Danevirke. Harald called on Hákon in Norway for help. It was duly given. However, our sources (this time German in origin) suggest a one-sided campaign in which Otto's men stream-rollered their way through Jutland. A peace deal was brokered, with Harald having been put firmly back in his place. Hedeby was lost to Denmark for a time, though the Danes seized it back again in 983.

While Harald's fortunes had taken a knock, he was at least still around to try to pick up the pieces. The same could not be said for Edgar, king of England, who died in 975. His reign had been a tranquil one and he was called 'the Peaceable', a name which owed much to the absence of Scandinavian raids during his reign. However, there was still Scandinavian influence at play; there are references in his law code (later adopted by the Scandinavian ruler of England, Cnut the Great) stating that elements of 'Danish' law were to be recognised in parts of the country. The only criticism that contemporaries could find to make of Edgar's reign was a suggestion that he loved foreigners too much, perhaps a clue that not everybody liked his tolerance of non-Anglo-Saxons and to undercurrents of cultural antagonism that were to be spectacularly played out in the reign of his son and eventual successor, Æthelred.[27]

Two years before his death, one of the most celebrated events of the Anglo-Saxon age took place at Chester where Edgar met up with kings from around Britain including those from Strathclyde, Alba and Wales. Edgar was ceremonially rowed up the River Dee, an event that was celebrated by the Anglo-Saxon chroniclers as one of huge symbolic resonance. In their eyes, he was being recognised as overlord of the whole island. It was probably no such thing. More likely this was some kind of official meeting where improving relationships between the various regions of Britain was on the agenda. There is evidence, albeit from a source written several centuries after the event, that several familiar Viking names were present. John of Worcester included 'Maccus, king of very many islands' as one of the attendees. He also mentioned 'Giferth', possibly a garbled version of Gofraid. Perhaps they were there to explore the possibilities of an alliance against Óláfr Cúarán in Dublin. Certainly, for a time Maccus and Gofraid turned their attentions back to Ireland.[28]

There was peaceful trade between Anglo-Saxon and Scandinavian in England during these years. One example is that traders from Dublin were known to frequent Cambridge, far to the east in Edgar's England.[29] Perhaps in those heady days the people of England thought that Viking raids were a thing of the past. If so, they were to be shockingly proven wrong. Edgar died at a young age, still in his thirties when he expired. There then followed, as was so often the case in the early medieval period, a vicious succession dispute which ate away at the fabric of England.

At the end of it all, several larger than life characters emerged. On the English side there was King Æthelred II, better known as 'the Unready' (though not as far as we can tell until the twelfth century) and his son Edmund, later called 'Ironside'. On the other side, another father-and-son duo led an attack on England that was so fierce that eventually the kingdom was overrun. The time of Sveinn Forkbeard and, several decades later, his son Cnut, was at hand. What some have called the Second Viking Age was about to begin. Its repercussions would be profound and frightening for those exposed to them.

10

Conflict and Adventure
(976–1000)

Eager the fleet-men stood, the crowding raiders, ravening for battle...
From 'The Battle of Maldon'

The end of the 'Babylonian captivity'

In 980, a climactic battle was fought at Tara in Ireland, marking a sea change in Scandinavian fortunes. War between Óláfr Cuarán and the Uí Néill had been ongoing for several decades and now Máel Sechnaill, Óláfr's stepson, emerged as the new king of the latter. Any thoughts that this might be the beginning of better relations could not have been more wrong, for Óláfr led a force against Máel Sechnaill at Tara, possibly even on the occasion of his inauguration.

Óláfr recruited men from the Viking islands off Scotland as a way of boosting his forces, but the battle at Tara was an overwhelming triumph for Máel Sechnaill and his Ulster Ulaid allies. Óláfr's son Ragnall was one of the many Viking casualties, though the long-time Viking king was not himself present – he was an ageing man by now. The cost of defeat was exorbitant for the Vikings. One phrase in the terse commentary on the battle in the *Annals of Ulster* stands out: 'and the power of the Gaill was ejected from Ireland'. What another work, the *Annals of Tigernach*, described as the 'Babylonian captivity' of Ireland was coming to a close.

Yet how absolute this 'Babylonian captivity' actually was is a matter of debate. The Vikings never established a strong foothold in the interior of Ireland and both Irish and Scandinavian had benefitted from trading activities involving them. Nor were the Vikings unbeatable in times of war. Statistical analysis is interesting here: it has been calculated that 25 battles took place between the Irish and the Vikings of Dublin between 917, when Dublin was re-established as a Viking base, and 1014 when the Battle of Clontarf was fought. The Irish won 15 of them and also, between 936 and 1013, launched 13 assaults on Dublin, many of them successful.[1] This suggests that the Irish had the wherewithal to eject the Vikings if they wished to do so; the fact that they did not suggests that they valued the benefits they enjoyed from the trading that was facilitated by the presence of Vikings, given their access to an international mercantile network.

At about this time, Máel Sechnaill sent ambassadors to a 'Danish' Viking camp. What they saw there horrified them. The 'Danes' were cooking and their spits were thrust into the sides of dead 'Norwegians'. The ambassadors graphically noted that 'the fire was burning their bodies, so that they belched forth from their stomachs the flesh and fat which they had eaten the night before'. On the ambassadors remarking on the savagery of this conduct, the 'Danes' look quizzically askance and replied that the 'Norwegians' would undoubtedly have done the same to them.[2]

And what of Óláfr? His end could not be more ironic or poignant. There would be no heroic death in battle and a welcome into Valhalla for him. Instead the *Annals of Tigernach* give us the following remarkable conclusion: 'Óláfr son of Sitriuc, high king of the Gaill of Dublin, went to Iona in repentance and in pilgrimage and afterwards died there'.[3] It is an extraordinary picture, the veteran Viking warrior, one-time king of Northumbria and Dublin, living out his last days at this sacred Christian site. The times certainly were a-changin'. As one modern historian has described it, 'the aged king, perhaps aware of his declining health, vested his final efforts not in shoring up the troubled fortunes of Dublin, but in seeking salvation in the life that may follow'.[4] One can almost imagine the spirit of Columba (whom Óláfr apparently much admired) watching over his deathbed, looking on with a warm smile as he glowed in his ultimate triumph over the pagans who had so often harassed and killed his followers.

The same modern commentator also opined that while on the one hand Óláfr's reign saw the highpoint of Viking fortunes in Ireland, by its very nature as an apogee it witnessed the start of a decline from which no full recovery was ever made.[5] The ongoing attrition, both with Irish rivals and competing dynastic elements from within the Viking world, had taken its toll, as had Óláfr's ambition, which had encouraged him to focus not just on Ireland but also on lands on the other side of the Irish Sea.

However, the involvement of the Viking element in Ireland was not yet over. After the death of Ivarr of Limerick and the ejection of Óláfr, Imar (Ivarr) of Waterford attempted to pick up the mantle of leadership of the Hiberno-Norse faction. He sacked Kildare in 982 but was defeated in battle by Máel Sechnaill the following year. During this period, Irish kings took advantage of disputes between the Viking leaderships of

Waterford and Dublin, and allied with them opportunistically. The star of Máel Sechnaill soared high in the heavens; but it was later to be outshone – and not by a Viking. In the west of Ireland, a man of modest dynastic antecedents, Brian Boru, was showing himself to be a man of very immodest ambitions.

This situation may have led to another significant development in 984, when the two brothers, Maccus and Gothfrith, sons of Harald, journeyed to Waterford with the aim of forging an alliance with Ivarr. It is generally believed that the Harald who is mentioned was a king of Limerick, though an alternative view that has been suggested in recent times is that he was Harald of Bayeux, a Danish Viking active in Francia in the 940s and 950s.[6] The brothers had been busy in the interim with attacks on North Wales in 980 and on St David's two years later. Hostages were exchanged in Waterford to cement the deal between Ivarr and the siblings. At one stage an attack on Dublin was considered but came to nothing.

There is an intriguing entry in the *Annals of Ulster* when the word *Danair* was applied to a new wave of raiders. The Irish chronicles had not previously used this term in their records, so it may be that this was a fresh injection from Denmark (or perhaps it was just a change in the style of referencing used by later chroniclers; we have noted previously the interchangeability of the terms used for 'Vikings' which may sometimes misleadingly suggest that they came from specific geographical regions when this was not in fact the case). They did not receive a warm welcome. Arriving in Dál Riata with three ships, seventy of them were killed and some of the others sold as slaves. While we are short on additional details, this was either a diplomatic mission gone wrong, a hostile raid that was beaten off, or an accidental landing brought about by bad weather which was not well received.

An entry in the *Annals* for the year 986 is probably related: nothing less than a raid on Iona, the first for over a century. The fact that this took place on Christmas Night can only have added to the horror felt on the part of the victims. Again, the timing of a raid launched on the occasion of an important Christian festival is unlikely to have been accidental. At the end of it all, the abbot and fifteen of the elders lay dead; a return to the bad old days of Viking raiding. It was a reminder that whatever steps forward had been made by Christian missionaries in Scandinavia, there was still a long way to go before it could truly be said that paganism in the region and among the Viking diaspora had been completely replaced. However, again the aim of the attack might have been political rather than religious: the fact that Óláfr Cuarán had chosen to see out his days there suggests that the community was well disposed towards the kings of Dublin.

In 987, Gothfrith joined the *Danari* in their ongoing activities. There was a fierce battle on the Isle of Man where a thousand men lay dead on the field at its conclusion. A raid on Anglesey followed, in which 2,000 slaves were taken away as booty; the Welsh prince Maredudd led the survivors away to safety on the mainland in Ceredigion and Dyfed but it had been a chastening defeat. Two years later, he paid a tribute of a penny for each of his men to the so-called 'black army' in Anglesey, which may be a ransom payment for some of the more important of them taken captive earlier. There was another Viking attack on Anglesey which created havoc, destroying the corn stocks on the island and leading to famine as a result. The Vikings in this instance may have been allied to one Welsh party in a bitter civil war to decide who was to rule Gwynedd; the other party was led by Maredudd. Certainly, the *Brut y Tywysogion* for the year 991 refers to Maredudd hiring those 'pagans' who were willing to join him when he devastated Glamorgan in a campaign brought about in response to Saxon incursions from the east.

Viking attacks on south Wales took place in 988 and were wide-ranging in nature. A number of sites are recorded as being plundered, including St David's and St Dogmael's, Llanbadarn Fawr in Cardiganshire, and Llanilltud Fawr and Llancarfan in Glamorgan. However, it did not all go the way of this new alliance of Vikings. In 988, 360 of those responsible for the raid on Iona two years before were killed and the following year Gothfrith was slain in Ireland. No doubt some observers regarded this as divine retribution for the outrage committed in Iona. Gothfrith's obituary calls him 'king of the Innse Gail', or 'Lord of the Isles'. This was the first time that such a phrase has been linked with an individual in the surviving records.[7] It lived on into more recent historical times, until the last MacDonald holder of the title forfeited his estates to the king of Scotland in 1493.

Vikings returned to attack south Wales during the last decade of the tenth century. Cornwall, Devon and south Wales were raided in 997 and St David's was ransacked in 999, leading to the death of Bishop Morgenau in the process. Dyfed was attacked again in 1001. The seaways into and out of Bristol may have been a prime attraction for these raids around Wales as the port's importance developed; the ongoing attacks on an increasingly vulnerable Wessex may also have played a part. Significant coin hoards found in south Wales that can be dated to this period may also intimate Viking incursions in the region. The accumulated evidence has led one commentator to describe this time as 'a particularly brutal period in the history of Viking activity in Wales'. There are records of famine, the taking of captives and the paying of tribute, which suggest that this was a horrific time for the people of south Wales in particular.[8]

'Silkbeard'

The best known of the later Viking kings of Dublin was the splendidly named Sitriuc Silkbeard who assumed the role in 989. He was the son of Óláfr Cuarán, the first Christian Viking ruler of Dublin, and Gormlaith, daughter of the king of Leinster; in other words, he was the product of a political marriage alliance and to all intents and purposes was part-Viking, part-Irish. His emergence coincided closely with that of Brian Boru. To add a layer of complexity to this intermarrying, the widowed Gormlaith, Sitriuc's mother, later moved on to another husband, none other than Brian himself. Viking-local intermarriage was a common feature across their world, making a nonsense of twentieth-century Nazi stereotypes that claimed them for propaganda purposes based on their 'racial purity'. Gormlaith's second husband was Máel Sechnaill II whom she seems to have divorced before moving on to Brian. In recognition of her marital history, a poem in the *Book of Leinster* said of her that 'three leaps did Gormlaith perform which no other woman will do to Doomsday; a leap into Dublin, a leap into Tara, a leap into Cashel, the plain with the mound that surpasses all'.[9] Gormlaith was later caricatured in Icelandic sagas as a particularly evil woman, a classic motif often employed in such tales and by no means a reliable representation of her true self.

Sitriuc reigned, with interruptions, for forty-seven years and it was in some ways a remarkable time. He introduced coinage to Dublin in 997 and later journeyed to Rome as a pilgrim; on his return he founded a cathedral in Dublin. For the next century following this, the archbishop of Dublin would be installed at Canterbury. Sitriuc was not just a Hiberno-Norse ruler, he also felt comfortable in an Anglo-Saxon environment (though in later years, the term 'Anglo-Danish' might sometimes be a more appropriate one for the residents of England).

Sitriuc's accession gives a striking insight into the precarious nature of Hiberno-Norse politics. After his father's defeat at Tara in 980, he was succeeded by Sitriuc's brother, Glún Iairn. That situation did not last long: the new king was murdered, while in a drunken stupor, by one of his servants. Sitriuc was chosen to take his place and began a regal career that was significant both for its longevity and also for some of the events that took place during it.

He was however evicted from Dublin in 994 by the rival Viking dynasty from Waterford, led by Imar (Ivarr) who then put his son Ragnall in as ruler. Ragnall launched a raid on a church at Downpatrick, which had been sponsored by Máel Sechnaill. This was a very unwise move on his part as Máel Sechnaill launched a successful raid on Dublin in retaliation. During the raid on the town, the Irish king captured a sacred pagan relic known as the Ring of Thor. Ragnall was subsequently killed by warriors from Leinster and Sitriuc was re-installed, seemingly having been on good terms with Máel Sechnaill. There were clearly close links between Sitriuc and England, for he started copying the coins of the current English king, Æthelred II, with a version so fine that it may well have been made by English moneyers; though interestingly the image of Sitriuc on it shows a clean-shaven man, which is not what we might expect given his nickname, 'Silkbeard' unless it was so fine that it was hard to see it.

England: renewed hostilities

During the last two decades of the tenth century, Viking raids on England broke out again. This reversion to the bad old days was linked to a less stable political situation in the country. With the passing of time, the reign of Edgar the Peaceable became a distant memory, a Golden Age that soon faded. He was replaced by his teenage son, Edward, but some opposed his succession. In 978, Edward was assassinated at Corfe Castle, with the connivance – if not the active involvement – of his stepmother Elfrida. Her son Æthelred assumed the throne, though still only a child. A new phase in the Viking intervention in England was about to begin with a dramatic denouement at journey's end; what some modern historians have called 'the Second Viking Age' was beginning.[10]

References to raids in the *ASC* suggest that they may have restarted as far back as the short reign of King Edward and there is a charter reference in his reign that suggests a need to build coastal defences in the west of England, an area that was ideally located for raids from Viking bases in Ireland.[11] Taking advantage of sudden downturns in political fortunes was a Viking trademark and again suggests that the raiders had access to an effective information network. They were certainly quick to take advantage of any hints of internal weakness, and succession disputes were a particular favourite.

The new English king, Æthelred II, was later called the 'Unready' by his critics.[12] His reign ended in disaster, but it is easy to overlook the fact that he ruled for nearly four decades, something that would have been unlikely to have happened if he was as totally bad a ruler as negative chroniclers assert he was. His caricature as an inept, even useless, ruler is too black and white an assessment. It is worth noting that the Norse *skald* Gunnlaug Serpent-Tongue wrote of Æthelred as a 'good ruler' (*godr hofdingi*). Gunnlaug had visited London and seen the English court up close so was in a good position to judge.[13] Having said this, he probably expected a nice reward in return for his praise.

There were several raids during the 980s and the *ASC* mentions attacks on Southampton, Portland, Thanet and Watchet. Chester also suffered a heavy raid in 980; based on its geographical location, this may have been launched by those same Vikings active in the Irish Sea area who had been attacking Wales, including a raid on St David's. Gothfrith (who had Welsh allies who were struggling to gain supremacy) is known to have been actively raiding at around this time and may also have been responsible for other raids in the west, for example that on Dorset noted in 982.

Even London was burned in one of the raids. However, these seem to have been hit-and-run in nature and in only one case, the attack at Watchet, was there a major confrontation. These attacks are not all mentioned in every version of the *ASC*: for example, the Winchester version does not mention the attack on Southampton, even though it was just down the road from the city. A possible leader of the 'Danes' (sic) who had become active in Britain was Óláfr Tryggvason who was to figure prominently in Viking affairs generally and in those of Norway specifically; later Scandinavian sources suggest this is the case.[14]

Negative near-contemporary commentators on Æthelred may have had their own agenda. The scribe who wrote the Abingdon version of the *ASC* goes into much greater detail on these raids early in Æthelred's reign than the other contemporary chroniclers did, suggesting that he had an axe to grind. The fact that he wrote his account several decades later when England had been through an apocalyptic meltdown probably prejudiced his account, as he was writing with the benefit of very bitter hindsight.[15]

Unfortunately for the English, there was much to attract a would-be raider. England was not only vulnerable and politically divided after the assassination of the previous king, she was also full of rich monasteries that had been given a new lease of life after a great reforming movement in Edgar's reign. Not only was a great deal of religious reform introduced (such as the replacement of secular clerks by monks in many of the great religious institutions of the realm) but many gifts followed, increasing their wealth and hence their attractiveness to raiders.

There was the occasional reverse for the Vikings along the way, sometimes allegedly with supernatural help. When raiders fell on Malmesbury Abbey, the monks got wind of the impending attack and took their portable wealth to safety. However, the shrine of St Aldhelm was too big to move and had to be left to its fate. When a sacrilegious Viking tried to hack off a jewel from it, he was struck unconscious by the saint. The raiders, suitably warned to respect Aldhelm, left the Abbey alone – or so we are told.[16]

The location of these early raids is significant. They were nearly all on the west coast of England, and geographically this suggests that they were being launched from across the Irish Sea from bases such as

Dublin. That said, there was another source of threat, this time from the south and Viking bases in Normandy. The brokering of a peace deal between England and Normandy in 991 under the auspices of Pope John XV gives credence to the possibility of attack from this direction. The treaty optimistically talked of a peace that 'should remain ever unshaken'; this 'peace for our time' statement proved as illusory as Neville Chamberlain's hopeful claims after Munich a millennium later. These raids were perturbing, but the situation was about to get a whole lot worse as they developed into something far more serious.

The fall of Harald Bluetooth

To understand the emergence of this new and greater threat, we need to return to Scandinavia. Here events were taking place that threatened chaos in the region but which also had repercussions for the wider world. The kingdoms of Denmark and England were on a collision course, though there would be many a fork in the road before one crashed into the other; and Norwegian affairs also played their part. The emergence of Sveinn Forkbeard, son of Harald Bluetooth, was to bring about a remarkable upsurge in the danger posed by the Viking threat.

Harald built a strong centralised state in Denmark the robustness of which was evidenced by some of the public works constructed during his reign. One of the most impressive was a bridge, some 700 metres long, built as an approach to Jelling.[17] From as far back as the time of the Pharaohs, large projects were a projection of State power and, while the bridge might have been on a much smaller scale than the pyramids, it served in the same way as a reminder of the strength of royal influence. The increase of centralised power was the primary aspiration of the rulers of the age, most famously seen in the actions of Charlemagne in Francia but also in those of Anglo-Saxon rulers like Alfred and Æthelstan. Scandinavian rulers such as Harald Bluetooth or his Norwegian namesake of the Fairhair variety, and his grandson Cnut later, sought to emulate this model of kingship. Public building schemes served to emphasise and reinforce this power.

In the latter years of his reign in Denmark, Harald Bluetooth lost some of his spark. It did not help that his son, Sveinn, was a remarkably energetic and ambitious man in his own right. He was for a time prepared to be an instrument for his father's policies; but from early on there must have been a doubt about how long he would be prepared to play second fiddle, given the extent of his aspirations.

In 983 Otto II, the Holy Roman Emperor, suffered a disastrous defeat at the other end of Europe, in Calabria, in the south-western part of the Italian peninsula, which distracted his attention. Taking advantage of the geopolitical situation the Danes launched an attack on Slesvig, the German name for Hedeby. It had fallen to the Holy Roman Empire in 974 and clearly Harald thought this was the right time to recover it. The attack was launched and met with success. Harald backed up this move with wider political initiatives. Sveinn, now in his early twenties, was married to a Wendish princess with the Polish name of Świętosława. As the daughter of the aggressive King Mieszko she was a prize catch and had previously been married to King Erik the Victorious of Sweden. Little is known about her, apart from the fact that the marriage produced three sons named Óláfr, Cnut and Harald.

The marital alliance proved its worth. While the Danes attacked Hedeby, Mieszko launched raids on the Empire, attacking Brandenburg and burning Hamburg. The success of these initiatives seemed initially to cement Harald's position in Denmark but in the longer term it had entirely the opposite effect. All it did was bolster Sveinn's already considerable self-confidence as he had been prominent in the successful campaign. Within a few years, he launched a bid for the throne. Harald was forced to flee to Slavic territories on the Baltic coast, the home of his allies, and he soon after died.

Several circular fortresses were constructed during these years, the most famous at Trelleborg, though several others were built in the same style (Aggersborg was three times as big and there were other camps at Fyrkat and Nonnebakken). Neatly laid out with a gate for each cardinal point on the compass, these give the appearance of well-laid-out barracks, though possibly ones that were meant for short-term use, perhaps as an assembly point for an army, rather than for long-term occupation. They were built from a common template, an architectural masterplan used at several different sites. This suggests a strong, centralising hand on the tiller. That said, the development of such circular defences was nothing new in the Viking world; similar designs have been found at earlier sites in the Baltic Åland Islands for example.[18]

It was argued in the past that they were probably gathering points for the Viking invasion armies that were formed to attack England early in the eleventh century but the evidence for this is not conclusive. Dendrochronology now suggests that their construction predates these major assaults – in 1010 and the years that followed – by several decades, to around 980–991. Their strong defensive focus also argues against such a purpose: the English were in no position to launch a pre-emptive assault against Denmark so why were such strongly defended sites needed?[19]

A possible reason for the construction of Trelleborg and the other camps in Denmark was that they were to protect armies against assaults from fellow Danes. Certainly, Harald's reign ended in a vicious civil war with his son, Sveinn; these were turbulent years when brother fought brother and father was arrayed against son. How this had come about is a moot point. Harald had been an aggressive Christianiser and this may have alienated some of his people. Sveinn would, in the view of some, prove ambivalent on the point of religion, as if playing a double game. While supporting Christianity on occasion, he could also allegedly be a defender of the old religion.

Here there is good cause to reflect on the source of some of our information on Sveinn. Much of what we know comes from the later eleventh-century writer Adam of Bremen, who was caustic in his assessment of him; but Adam was very much a writer with an axe to grind. He was not impressed that the archbishopric of Hamburg-Bremen, which was his spiritual home, did not have ascendancy in religious terms in Denmark during the time that he wrote and this was hardly likely to make him objective when giving his views on Sveinn, who would recruit bishops from England rather than Hamburg-Bremen. Probably motivated by this, Adam unambiguously painted the war between Sveinn and Harald as a battle between the old religion and the new.[20]

There are contrary views on Sveinn's Christianity stating that he was an enthusiastic believer, though these come from the equally unreliable *Encomium Emmae Reginae*, a work written in praise of Emma, queen of England, wife of two later kings, Æthelred II and Cnut. The fact that Sveinn was ultimately buried in a church suggests that stories of his paganism have been much overplayed; but this does not mean that he was not a formidable and ruthless opponent for those who got on the wrong side of him. And it is by no means unlikely that like many other Scandinavians of his time, Sveinn could be ambivalent about his faith and retained elements of pagan beliefs (or at least customs) in his practices. Certainly in Denmark evidence of eleventh-century pagan burial rites has been found coexisting alongside Christian churches,[21] something that is perhaps not so surprising when one considers that similar ambivalence characterised aspects of Roman society when Christianity was first adopted as the state religion in the fourth century.

The sagas also have their part to play in the story of Sveinn. The *Jómsvikings Saga* says that Sveinn was born out of wedlock to a serving woman, Saumæsa, and that Harald subsequently refused to recognise him.[22] This sounds suspiciously like a piece of poetic licence as the hint of bastardy is a classic motif employed in folktales to introduce an element of intrigue into a plotline. It is noticeable too that the anonymous writer of this saga has little good to say about the bloodline of Gorm the Old or Harald Bluetooth (who is given particularly negative treatment). Sveinn is painted in this particular version of events as a brigand and a robber, preying on largely defenceless Danes.

The landholding class in Denmark may well have resented the increased centralised control they experienced as Harald's power grew, primarily at their expense. They may also have seen something promising in the character of Sveinn that appealed to their adventurous spirit; Sveinn would launch a new period of Viking raiding to the west that offered magnificent opportunities for profit and sometimes more, such as the prospect of settling in new lands with the opportunity of improving one's wealth and status. All this helped to make him an attractive alternative to Harald.

The writer of the *Encomium Emmae Reginae* gives a very human explanation for this conflict between father and son. He suggests that Sveinn was fired by ambition, and his desire to become king was fired by his perception of Harald Bluetooth as an ageing and increasingly irrelevant ruler. Harald in contrast watched with envy as he saw the exploits and achievements of his son, and it was good old-fashioned jealousy that inspired him to fight back. These are very plausible human motivations, which may well have led to this fatal conflict between two strong-willed men.[23]

The opposing forces of Harald and Sveinn moved against each other. An action was fought, possibly off the island of Bornholm. According to the *Jómsvikings Saga* Harald was assassinated, shot by an arrow fired by a famous (but quasi-mythical) Viking called Palnatoki, the legendary founder of the Jómsvikings. Palnatoki was supposed to have crept up on Harald when he was was unguarded (Palnatoki's prowess with a bow has definite similarities to the story of William Tell; the later Danish writer Saxo Grammaticus relates a story of how he was forced to shoot an arrow from his son's head).

Whether this is true or not – this is a dramatic end perhaps more in keeping with the requirements of an imaginative saga than a strict history – the fact is that Harald died at about this time and his place in Denmark was taken up by Sveinn Forkbeard. It is more widely held that Harald died in exile rather than being assassinated in the way that the *Jómsvikings Saga* describes it. Adam of Bremen wrote that he was wounded in battle, escaped by sea and died of his wounds among the Slavs shortly afterwards. His remains were brought home to Denmark and interred in Roskilde where his tomb is still. Adam asserts that this became a site of pilgrimage and miracles were witnessed there such as the blind having their sight restored.[24]

The Jómsvikings, Sveinn Forkbeard and Óláfr Tryggvason

The Jómsvikings were a famous group of warriors who allegedly operated in the Baltic as the tenth century neared its close, but they may never have existed at all. It is grudgingly accepted by a number of historians that if their base, Jómsborg, was real then it was probably equated with Wolin at the mouth of the Oder. Certainly, some of the men associated with them were real enough; evocative characters such as Thorkell the Tall and Sveinn Forkbeard. Their story is told in the *Jómsvikings Saga,* written up several hundred years afterwards by an anonymous Icelander. The saga has aptly been described as 'a historical novel rather than a history'.[25] While some of the main characters are known historical figures, the actions attributed to them are sometimes wrapped in fantasy; for example, the suggestion that one of their number, Búi, ended his days as a dragon, with a very Tolkienesque characteristic of brooding over his gold. This is entirely consistent with the netherworld described by the *Prose Edda*, a mythical land populated with giants, dwarves, elves and monsters with names that would be familiar to any Tolkien aficionado such as Gandalf, Durin, Glóin, Kili and Oakenshield.

The Jómsvikings were, in the sagas, a close-knit brotherhood, bound in loyalty to each other and sworn to avenge the death of members of their group. No man was to flee from battle unless his compatriots did so. Women were debarred from entering their base and they were dedicated to the arts of war, being men in their prime between the ages of eighteen and fifty. No warrior was to be away from base for more than three days. Kinship played no part in recruiting for the Jómsvikings; merit as demonstrated by military prowess was the prime requirement.

They were committed to annual summer raids. They met at the start of the raiding season to discuss which targets to attack during the forthcoming campaigns. In one such gathering, Sveinn Forkbeard met up with the Jómsvikings and there followed a heavy drinking session when he and they sought to outdo each other with their boasts of what they would achieve in the upcoming season. Sveinn said he would raid England and enrich himself significantly in the process. Other Jómsvikings in response said that they would conquer the lands of Earl Hákon in Norway. Having sobered up the next morning, they may have doubted the wisdom of the commitment that they had taken on but nevertheless felt honour-bound to go through with it.

The saga gives interesting details of the campaign that followed. While accepting that these need to be interpreted with caution, one commentator has suggested that the geographical information that is included suggests that the saga writer was certainly familiar with Norway. The Jómsvikings first crossed to the Vik, in the region of Oslofjord. They then raided a town called Tønsberg in the south of Norway, causing a great deal of death and destruction as a result. However, survivors of the raid (the saga suggested an official in the town called Geirmund the White) escaped and got word to Hákon, who was able to prepare himself to meet the Jómsvikings in battle. He sent the war arrow (a token that was sent from farm to farm to summon the men there to battle; it is mentioned in other sagas too) so that he could assemble a force strong enough to meet the threat.

The two fleets met at Hjörungavágr – near modern Ålesund, now an impressive town with fascinating art deco architecture and a frequent stopping-off point for cruise ships. The Jómsvikings had something rather different in mind back then (the date is normally interpreted as being around 986). However, they were unprepared for the large fleet that Hákon had waiting for them. He had been able to assign different parts of it to take on specific elements of the Jómsviking force.

What was effectively a land battle fought at sea ensued; close-quarter contact with arrows, spears, swords and axes being used as one side tried to board the other's ships. It was a disaster for the Jómsvikings who were badly battered; only a few of them survived and they were taken captive. The seventy who were left alive were sentenced to be beheaded. They were roped together and made light of their fate, joking as one after the other was released from the rope only to be told to face the axe and death full in the face. They did so with determination and without a hint of fear.

One of the first victims was an adolescent of eighteen years of age. He had long flowing hair and asked that someone of noble birth from among his executioners should hold his hair away from his face so that it might avoid the spurting blood. One did so but just as the axe was falling, the young Jómsviking jerked his head back and the axe fell on the arms of the man holding his hair, cutting both off at the elbow. Rather than angering the executioners, they admired his cunning and offered to spare his life. He accepted but only on condition that his comrades were spared too, which they were.

One remarkable figure who emerged on the Norwegian scene, Óláfr Tryggvason, was the son of a former sub-king in the Oslofjord area, Tryggvi Óláfrsson. Tryggvi fell victim to the warring sons of Erik Bloodaxe. Then began something that seems like, and may in part actually be, a fairy tale. In one version of the tale Óláfr's mother, Astrid, had not even given birth to him when these events took place. Heavily pregnant, she found refuge on a small island in a lake where Óláfr was born. Other versions of the tale rather destroy this romantic illusion by saying that Óláfr was three years old when Tryggvi met his violent end. There then followed a dramatic escape across eastern Norway and Sweden. Continuing the fairy-tale-like backdrop to the early life of Óláfr Tryggvason, Astrid was chased by Gunnhild, the widow of Erik Bloodaxe, but mother and son managed to escape. Astrid had a brother, Sigurd, who had found fame and fortune in the far-off regions of Russia and it was to him that they headed for protection. This was a wise plan but, unfortunately, it went wrong. As they were crossing the Baltic, their vessel was taken by pirates from Estonia and they were sold into slavery. It was not until six years later that Óláfr was released, bought in a slave market by his uncle and taken back to Novgorod. While there and walking through the slave market, he saw a man he recognised. He was a slaver who had butchered Óláfr's foster father when he was captured, thinking that he was too old to be of any use to anybody. Recognising the man responsible for this callous act, the adolescent Óláfr picked up a nearby axe and smashed in his skull with it.

Óláfr's career as a Viking began when he was eighteen years of age. He was involved in an attack on Bornholm and then moved to the land of the Wends. There he met a princess, Geira, who subsequently became his wife. When she died a few years later, he returned to his piratical activities. His main sphere of involvement was around Britain and Ireland. He seems to have been involved in Viking activity from the north of Scotland right down to the Scilly Isles. In one version, it is claimed that he became convinced of the merits of Christianity when involved in conversation with a hermit in the Scillies, after which he became a fierce defender of his adopted religion, not hesitating to use violence to convert people to the faith.[26] Óláfr took another wife from Dublin, Gytha, the daughter of Óláfr (Amlaib) Cuarán, one-time king of Dublin and therefore the sister of Sitriuc Silkbeard. The couple lived together in Dublin until 995 and Óláfr's eventual return to Norway (the year in which Sitriuc raided the monastic establishment at Downpatrick). They had a son, Tryggvi, who eventually died in battle against Sveinn, the son of Cnut, decades later.

During this last decade of the tenth century Dublin started minting its own coins; there are suggestions that this development may be linked with a raid on Watchet in the west of England which had its own mint and therefore, by definition, dies for producing coins.[27] Dies for minting coins from Bath and Lydford were also used in Dublin and it is highly likely that they had all been taken from England during raids there.

Maldon and Danegeld

Óláfr's time in Britain and Ireland was seminal for him. He was probably involved in the great set-piece epic at Maldon, accounts of which have been preserved in a remarkable remnant of a work of Anglo-Saxon poetry, *The Battle of Maldon*.[28] Some caveats are necessary as to its historicity. Although a superb example of the Anglo-Saxon art of poetry, it is not written as a historical account and it is also incomplete though it appears that the bulk of the work has survived, certainly enough to weave a coherent story together.

The story that can be reconstructed from the poem, as well as from entries elsewhere such as those in the *ASC,* is clear enough. In 991, a raiding party made its way from Folkestone in Kent and up along the coast of East Anglia. The *ASC* says that it was led by a man called Anlaf (Óláfr) and this has led to speculation that it was headed by Óláfr Tryggvason, the later king of Norway, a reasonable enough supposition. This was a large raid in comparison to those of the 980s and its main objective seems to have been the extortion of money. The local ealdorman, Byrhtnoth, a veteran with decades of experience to call upon, summoned the local *fyrd* to face up to the raiders.

Byrhtnoth got his men together by the *burh* at Maldon on the Essex coast. The Viking fleet anchored offshore at Northey Island, a typical tactic on their part as it protected their ships from direct assault. Between the two forces was a narrow causeway that could only be crossed at low tide. It was so narrow that just a few warriors could hold back a much larger force; three brave Saxons, Wulfstan, Ælfhere and Maccus, were singled out for particular admiration for the part that they played in blocking the crossing. The Viking force was unable to cross because of their actions. That said, it should be noted that the heroic defence of a narrow strip of land was a classic storyline going back as far as Horatius defending the bridge in the time of Ancient Rome. A similar motif would later be employed in saga accounts of the Battle of Stamford Bridge in 1066, so possibly this element of the story is employing a degree of poetic licence.

An envoy was sent by the Vikings to ask the blocking force to move so that they could come over and have a fair fight. Byrhtnoth acquiesced; to some, even the poet who wrote the *Battle of Maldon,* it seemed rash; 'then the earl was overswayed by his heart's arrogance to allow overmuch land to that loath nation'. Byrhtnoth has frequently been criticised for his decision, but it has been pointed out that if looked at from a certain angle, it was one that made sense. He was confident of victory, otherwise he would not have taken on the fight. But he may also have reasoned that it was better to attack the Viking fleet when he was in position rather than let it sail off and cause devastation unopposed elsewhere.[29] In any event, he opted to take on the Vikings.

There followed a tough slugging match, like two heavyweight fighters standing toe to toe. If the poem is to be believed, Byrhtnoth and his men initially held the upper hand. But then Byrhtnoth fell in single combat and the course of the battle quickly swung the other way. Some of the Anglo-Saxon army preferred to fight to the death and fall beside their lord but others, less committed, decided to run for it, and so the battle was lost and won with the Vikings holding the field and the opposing army either fled or dead.

There is much in the *Battle of Maldon* that resonates with artistic licence: heroism and glory, self-sacrifice and laughing in the face of death. But against this, there are baser human elements too that might hint at reality. Not only is there cowardice, even treason, but the villains are named: 'Odda's kin were first away,' we are told, then 'Godric turned, betrayed the lord who had made him a gift of many good horses' and 'with him his brothers both ran, Godwine and Godwiy, who had no gust for fighting'. This disunity in battle seems to reflect the disunity in the wider country at the time.[30]

In response to the reverse at Maldon, Æthelred assembled a fleet at London in 992. But as well as adopting martial measures, the king also took monetary ones. In 991, Æthelred made his first payment of what later became known as 'Danegeld', though it was not so called at the time, the name used being *gafol*. It was not the first time that money had been used in an attempt to make the Vikings go away; it was adopted as a tactic in Carolingian France some time earlier and even Alfred had recourse to it when under pressure. Nevertheless, in 994, Æthelred was forced to pay over £16,000 for the privilege of being left alone by Sveinn and his fellow Vikings.

Sveinn Forkbeard continued to make a major nuisance of himself. It is possible that he was a king in search of a kingdom: Adam of Bremen says that Denmark had been taken from him – 'abandoned by God and vainly trusting in his idols' – by King Erik the Victorious of Sweden after a series of naval battles.[31] Erik was, according to Adam, a fierce pagan but was converted to Christianity while in Denmark and was baptised, though he later relapsed into paganism.[32]

It was not only Æthelred who was under pressure; in 995 Sveinn raided the Norse territories on the Isle of Man. These were now definitively Scandinavian, so Sveinn was attacking other Vikings. An extraordinary amalgam of local and Scandinavian traditions had emerged on the island. Over thirty carved stones survive as evidence of this period and one of the most marked features of what happened there was the emergence of a style of memorial that brought together Norse inscriptions with Celtic crosses. Cross slabs decorated in Borre style with plaited knots, plant designs and ribbon-like bodies are similar to ninth- and tenth-century examples from Scandinavia. Celtic names were also recorded alongside Scandinavian ones, suggesting that a strong degree of assimilation was taking place.[33]

One of the first beneficiaries of England's largesse was Óláfr Tryggvason who was encouraged to leave the country well alone in the future and concentrate his efforts on conquering Norway for himself instead. Much as Æthelred has been criticised for his incompetence by later historians, this was a wise move. It would not only keep Óláfr away, but it also increased the odds that his increasingly bitter rival Sveinn Forkbeard would be forced to face up to his adversary's attempts to claim Norway for himself, and this is precisely what happened. To encourage him further, Æthelred stood sponsor for Óláfr at his baptism at Andover.[34] A treaty was agreed in which Óláfr vowed that 'he would never come back to England in hostility'[35] – a pledge he subsequently lived up to. The former pagan would spend the rest of his days in Scandinavia where he proved himself to be a staunch defender of Christianity. This fits in well with perceptions that a treaty made between two Christians was more likely to hold than one made between Christian and pagan; it would be naïve to think that this always worked, but it perhaps increased the chances of peace between the parties involved.

Æthelred and Óláfr Tryggvason agreed that 'foreign' ships should have safe passage in English waters and that this would be reciprocated when English ships were encountered by Vikings away from home territory.[36] This has an element of wishful thinking about it, in that it implies there was one overall leader of the Viking forces then operating over a wide geographical area and this cannot be the case.

The problem for Æthelred was the regularity with which he was forced to hand over large sums of money in the future and the fact that his policy ultimately failed in its aim of enticing the Vikings to cease their raids. On the contrary, like many blackmailers, once they had been paid off once, they simply came back for more; a tendency noted in the famous poem penned later by that doyen of the Victorian and Edwardian era, Rudyard Kipling. Kipling opined that the proper response to a demand for Danegeld was as follows:

We never pay anyone Danegeld
No matter how trifling the cost
For the end of that game is oppression and shame
And the nation that plays it is lost!

It is significant that Kipling wrote these words as a citizen of a worldwide empire, then at something close to the height of its imperial power.[37] It might have been more difficult for him to take such a hard-line 'purist' view had he been in Æthelred's position at the close of the tenth century and beginning of the eleventh.

Allied to the payments of *gafol*, Æthelred also raised taxes to fund his own army; the tax was known as the *heregeld*. So the people of England were taxed to the hilt for one reason or another yet found themselves living with no more security as a result. It was hardly likely to make for a contented population. Such is the case for taxpayers, who are being squeezed until the pips squeak, in any generation.

There is an alternative explanation for this payment of *gafol* and that is that it was not tribute at all. Rather, it was money paid over to buy the support of Óláfr and his men, essentially hiring them as mercenaries.[38] The argument is not wholly convincing as there is no evidence that Óláfr's men fought for Æthelred after the treaty was made and Óláfr certainly appears soon afterwards in Norway, so this would seem to be a case of paying him to go away. But it is certainly true that in other cases there is evidence of employing Vikings as mercenaries so Danegeld should not always be seen as a simple case of handing over protection money.

Nevertheless, images of Æthelred's uselessness have been overplayed, at least until his final years when he was ageing and ill. A large raid by Æthelred on Strathclyde in 1000 may have been a violent response to cooperation between the people of that region and Scandinavian raiders (certainly as far as the twelfth-century writer Henry of Huntingdon was concerned); an attack by Æthelred's navy on the Isle of Man, by now a thoroughly Norse island, even more so – a rare example of Æthelred taking the fight to the Vikings in their own backyard.

There are some intriguing examples of artistic fusion taking place in remoter parts of Britain during this period. Among the more unusual monuments of the period were the hogback grave markers that were a feature of the north of England and southern Scotland (Govan in Glasgow and Penrith in Cumbria have particularly fine examples). As the tenth century neared its close and a new millennium dawned, some of these grave markers exhibited signs of mixed Anglo-Saxon, Celtic and Scandinavian influence. A Norse influence is very apparent in the famous Gosforth Cross (there are also several hogback markers by the church there), which has a design that looks similar to the smaller Thorwald's Cross on the Isle of Man. It has references to Loki and Thor alongside Christian symbols (including the Crucifixion), a real hedging of bets and an example of 'live and let live' as opposed to religious fanaticism.[39]

The hogback markers typically have ridge-shaped tops and resemble an abstract version of an animal, hence their name. But their curved ridges give another impression: that of a Scandinavian-style house, complete in many cases with shingles on the 'roof'. Stylistically, they show a mix of influences; Anglo-Saxon, Celtic and Norse. But while the Norse influence is in many cases irrefutable, it is striking that there are no such monuments back in Scandinavia. A unique culture was created in the north-west of England and the south-west of Scotland. Money was also flowing into parts of Britain from Viking territories elsewhere. A shipwreck found in Bearreraig Bay, Skye, was carrying late tenth-century Anglo-Saxon coins and others from further afield, namely Samarkand. It is an insight into just how extensive the Viking sphere of influence was. While southern parts of England may have stayed aloof from this general trend, other areas were markedly affected by it.

The new millennium famously brought people out onto the streets in fear as many were terrified that the year 1000 would bring something awful to the Christian world. Historians have argued that the effects of the coming of the millennium have been overplayed. However, in more recent times there has been a slight rebalancing as some have argued that for some inhabitants of the world back then it was indeed a time of awful and awe-inspiring significance.[40] Any objective reading of the works of contemporary writers such as Wulfstan, the archbishop of York, and the homilist Ælfric of Cerne and Eynsham, cannot fail to elicit a response from the reader that these men feared that something dreadful was abroad in the world. The Vikings had raided England in 997, 998 and 999, though not yet on the scale of those at the beginning of the decade. They were but an ominous shadow of what was to come.

Within the next decade or so in England, thoughts of the apocalypse were for some never far away. Again, it seemed as if God was angry; and the Vikings, even though many of them were now becoming Christians in name, seemed to be His avengers. It was an impression that continued over time. The author of *The Life of King Edward*, writing some decades later, described how 'God's wrath of justice had swept away by the oppression of the Danes what had displeased him among the people'. In a world that was dominated by religion, the Vikings certainly seemed to have a purpose, even if it was not one that many would have enthusiastically embraced.[41]

The Christianisation of Norway

After leaving England, Óláfr returned to Norway transiting via Orkney, where he convinced Earl Sigurd to become a Christian through the persuasive argument that he would kill his three-year-old son if he did not do so. Although the strongman in Norway was still Hákon Sigurdsson in the Trøndelag, he could not summon up sufficient support when faced by the newly successful – and wealthy – pretender. Óláfr's men were riding on the crest of a wave. They had met with great success in England, their spirits were high and their fighting skills well honed. Hákon fled but, according to one tradition, died soon after when his throat was cut by a disloyal servant while he was hiding in a pigsty. Óláfr was declared king in Trondheim. Other regions, including territories in the Oslofjord area which had been under recent Danish overlordship, also declared for him.

He then set to work converting his new subjects to Christianity. Óláfr was a well-travelled man, fully aware of the advantages that Christianity could bring in a practical sense. He could see what happened when a king and the Church worked together for mutual benefit. It allowed a more fully developed sense of centralised control to be followed with

Conflict and Adventure (976–1000)

each institution, the secular and the spiritual, supporting each other. Óláfr became a zealous supporter of Christianity, though the later writer Adam of Bremen suggested that his conversion was far from total. Adam suggested that Óláfr was skilled in divination, for which he used animal parts as his props, and he bestowed on Óláfr the nickname 'Crowbone' because of this practice. As we have noted, Adam had no time for Óláfr, who preferred to use churchmen from England rather than those from Hamburg-Bremen so it is not difficult to guess the reasons for his cynicism. This conveniently, and one might think unfairly, ignores Óláfr's overt Christian actions such as the building of what is said by the sagas to be the first church in Norway over an old pagan temple at Moster.

However, Óláfr's aggressive enforcement of Christianity met with widespread resistance. The most stubborn opposition came from the Trøndelag though Óláfr allegedly even pushed further north into the wilds of Hålogaland, 'the Land of High Fire', which refers to the Northern Lights that can be seen in the region. It was known for its strident paganism and a fierce fight ensued between the local inhabitants and Óláfr. Unfortunately for Óláfr, there was a formidable alliance building against him. Sveinn Forkbeard was determined to recover the lost Danish territories in Norway, having already recovered his crown in Denmark following the death of Erik the Victorious who had, according to Adam of Bremen, seized it from him.[42] Earl Erik, the son of the late Jarl Hákon, was determined to regain the place he had lost by his father's removal from power and the Swedish king, Óláfr Skötkonung – the first known to rule over both the Svear and the Goths and also to mint his own coins for his Swedish kingdom – was also keen to get in on the act and extend his influence.

Snorri Sturluson adds story-telling flair to the otherwise straightforward tale of the lust for power and dominance being fought out in Norway. He tells us that Tyri, Sveinn's sister, had married Óláfr Tryggvason having previously been pressured into marrying the much older King Boleslaw of the Wends. She fled from Boleslaw and the marriage, which she found to be every bit as unsatisfactory as she had always feared it would be; some accounts suggest that she went on a hunger strike and Boleslaw sent her back to Sveinn. After her later marriage to Óláfr she bore a strong grudge against her brother Sveinn who had forced her into the union with Boleslaw. Sveinn had also allegedly refused to hand over any dowry for her to Óláfr, having previously done so for her failed marriage to Boleslaw.

Snorri also introduces us to Sigrid the Haughty, a classic fairy tale villainess. She had, he says, been involved in marriage discussions with Óláfr but was a confirmed pagan. When she refused to convert to Christianity on the orders of her would-be husband, he struck her. She had then married Sveinn and began working on him in a scheme to

259

dethrone Óláfr. Given the recent Danish claims to be rulers of Norway plus Sveinn's own personality, it is unlikely that he needed much persuasion even if these details are correct.

The web is further tangled in Snorri's story when Óláfr was persuaded by Tyri to enter an alliance with Boleslaw, her former husband. Quite why she should have had any reason to do so after having run away from him is not clear. These romantic and contorted events may or may not be true; but the unavoidable fact was that a decisive confrontation now loomed in which each constituent part of Scandinavia – Denmark, Sweden and Norway – was involved.

Óláfr set out to protect his territories in his great longship *The Long Serpent*, surrounded by his retainers such as Thorstein Ox-Foot, Thrond Squint-Eye, Lodvir the Long, Ketill the Tall, Griotgard the Quick and Bersi the Strong; his ship, with thirty-four rowing benches, was exceptionally large for the time. He made first of all for Boleslaw. Although this was ostensibly to recover property that had been left behind when Tyri left him, the two men got on well and an understanding of sorts was reached.

The precise details are confused but Óláfr subsequently sailed straight into an ambush. What followed, which became known as the Battle of Svold, may have been fought in one of several places; in the narrow strait of the Øresund between Sweden and Denmark, near an island off Copenhagen, or the island of Svold, off Rügen, which is on the Baltic coast of modern Germany. Adam of Bremen places the battle off Elsinore, famous for its setting as the home of the Shakespearian tragic hero Hamlet, Prince of Denmark; he noted that it was 'a covert well known to pirates'.[43]

Like all Viking sea battles, the fight that followed was again a land action on the sea. Warriors sought to board their enemy's ships and take them. There was much close quarter, hand-to-hand fighting but the advantage lay with Sveinn and his confederates who had a much larger force with them. Eventually, Óláfr's own longship was boarded in a fierce assault led by Earl Erik from his ship, *The Iron Beard*. Óláfr fought bravely but he was eventually overcome. His exact end is a matter of debate. In one version, rather than be captured he threw himself into the sea and in his heavy armour he sank straight to the bottom. In another account, he managed to escape and ended his days many years later as a pilgrim in faraway Jerusalem, which seems a most unlikely end for such a determined warrior.

In Snorri's words,

I wot not whether he who stilled the raven's hunger
Should of me be praised as of the living or of the dead,
Since of a truth his men tell either tale.

Whatever the precise details, Óláfr Tryggvason was removed from Norway for good. Adam of Bremen questioned his attachment to Christianity and suggested that he took part in occult rituals; but all other sources suggest that he was a strong believer in the new religion.[44] It was a moment pregnant with significance, one that was exploited to the full by the saga writers who wrote of it. During the battle, Óláfr had at his side Einar Thambarskelvir, a renowned poet and a mighty archer. A freak arrowshot hit Einar's bow and shattered it with a great clatter. Óláfr, alarmed, turned to Einar and asked what broke with such a noise. The response was to the point and, as this was saga written after the event rather than being a work of history, precisely accurate: 'Norway, King, from your hands'.

The victors carved up Norway between them. Sveinn – who was now, according to Adam, a Christian who wiped out 'idolatrous rites' in his newly acquired territories – took land in the Oslofjord and assumed nominal overlordship over much of Óláfr's former lands too, while the Swede Óláfr Skötkonung was given territory in the south-east of the country and the eastern part of the province in which Trondheim was situated. Jarl Erik assumed the position formerly held by his late father, Hákon. It seemed as if Norway was being partitioned with foreign powers taking for themselves a large part of the prize. But in hindsight it was only to be a temporary halt along the road towards the building of a Norwegian state.

Óláfr's fierce (and in this case the word should be taken literally) insistence that his subjects should adopt Christianity did not only have an impact in Norway. In Iceland too, Christianity was officially adopted as the formal religion in 1000 when the lawspeaker, Thorgeir Thorkelsson, declared it so, though not without some interesting insights into previous pagan practices:

> Then it was made law that all people should be Christian and those be baptised who were still unbaptised in this land; but as to exposure of children the old law should stand and also as to eating of horseflesh. People might sacrifice to heathen gods secretly, if they wished, but under penalty of outlawry if this was proved by witnesses. But a few winters later this heathendom was abolished like the rest.[45]

This two-stage adoption of Christianity is suggestive. It implies that at first the *Althing*, the Icelandic parliament, was not confident that it could completely eliminate the people's adherence to the old religion but as time passed its confidence grew and it made all adherence to pagan practices illegal. As a result of this move, both the *godi* and the church grew in power, and the political infrastructure of Iceland began to change significantly. That said, there is a suggestion that the conversion process in Iceland had started quite early with a grandson of Björn Grimsson establishing a church dedicated to St Columba on the island.[46]

The Christianisation of Iceland had been a long time in the making. Óláfr had already sent over Bishop Fredrik and Thorvald the Far-Traveller as we saw earlier but their attempts had come to nothing. Next, he delegated an Icelander, Stefnir, to take up the challenge. When the gentle arts of persuasion were unsuccessful he tried the Carolingian approach, that is, conversion through the use of violence. But Stefnir failed to realise that he was not in Norway, let alone Carolingian Francia, and was in no position to enforce the religion on the Icelandic people without their cooperation. Stefnir was brought to account by his own family, charged with blasphemy and forced to leave the country. It could perhaps have been worse for him, but it was an interesting example of how important compliance with the law was in Iceland.

The third attempt was made by another Saxon, Thangbrand, on behalf of Óláfr, and he also turned to violence in an attempt to enforce his will. This only resulted in him being outlawed as well. Storms prevented him from leaving; or, as one of the poets, a woman called Steinun, put it:

Christ was not watching, when
The wave-raven drank at the prows.

Eventually, the weather changed for the better and Thangbrand managed to get back to Óláfr, who was predictably furious at another rejection and planned sterner measures. However, delegates from Iceland who had accepted Christianity journeyed across the North Atlantic to see him and, leaving hostages behind them, then returned home to put their case before their countrymen, arguing that they were more likely to be listened to than a Saxon foreigner. Fierce argument and counterargument followed at the *Althing*. The Lawgiver, Thorgeir, after a long private deliberation where he sought a conclusion to this seemingly insoluble problem, gave his judgement in favour of Christianity even though he was himself a pagan. He had perhaps seen the way that the tide was flowing and had his own auguries of the future, and even if he did not like what he saw, he knew in his heart that change was inevitable. If there was an element of compromise in his judgement, it was still heavily weighted towards the new religion.[47]

Greenland: frontier country

'Only the man who makes far journeys and has travelled extensively ... can truly be self-possessed'. So said the *Hávamál,* Viking Age poetry imaginatively attributed to Odin. Such words could have been a leitmotif for the intrepid explorers who reached out to the far side of the unrevealed Atlantic. In about 980, an adventurer called Erik fled from Iceland. He was a man who was habitually in hot water. It ran in the family; his father Thorvald had been exiled from Norway when he was involved in an unlawful killing. The *Landnámabók* says that Erik took part in several bouts of fighting in Iceland, so he presumably had a fiery and violent temper too, but we must remember that he was living in a land of marginal quality where life was a struggle, which helped to breed men like him. Frontier territories have never been lands for shrinking violets.

Erik was a man of proud heritage, a great-grandson of a Norwegian *hersir* who was brother to Naddod, the early explorer of Iceland.[48] While in Iceland, Erik heard accounts concerning Gunnbjörn Ulf-Krakason who had half a century earlier discovered a land to the west. Now forced to leave Iceland too, Erik found this land for himself. He called it 'Greenland', a description for which he would nowadays probably be penalised under any Trades Descriptions Act, though as the global climate was then in the Medieval Warm Period this attribution perhaps was not so ridiculous as it now seems.[49] But one factor that was definitely working in Erik's favour was that, as the first settler in Greenland, he would have the pick of the land there.

The narrowest crossing from Iceland to Greenland was a four-day voyage, we are told by the *Landnámabók* (it has even been suggested that on a clear day when the atmospherics are right Greenland can be seen from Iceland).[50] After having spent three years exploring the territory to find the spot that would make the best site on which to settle, Erik set up a farm at Brattahlid ('Steep Slope'), which was ultimately named the Eastern Settlement (which confusingly is at the southern tip of the island). Even at Brattahlid, in a settlement which can never have been large, the pollen count reveals the chopping down of trees (probably of small size) while it also shows that some attempts were made to grow grain in the form of rye.[51]

Another base grew up to the north of the so-called Eastern Settlement, equally confusingly called the Western Settlement. Although they had a good stock of wildlife around them, including seals, walrus and whales, the settlements were always on the margins of viability with perhaps no more than 3,000 settlers living there even at Viking Greenland's peak.[52] That said, a book published in 1986 noted that 300 separate farm settlements had been so far uncovered across the island, a figure that is only going to increase over time.[53]

The first houses were hastily erected; this was no place to be living out in the open despite the deceptive charms of meadows festooned with flowers and the few months in which flora and fauna flourished in the tantalising but too brief summer window. Some houses had watercourses, such as streams, flowing underfloor through the middle of the building, allowing easy access to running water as well as a convenient means of removing human waste, an approach also occasionally known in Iceland and Norway. These residences were simply longhouses but over time they would be added to and evolve into more complex structures such as multi-roomed passage houses. Archaeology intimates concessions to the Greenlandic climate, harsh even compared to Iceland: walls were thicker, rooms smaller and fireplaces spread far more liberally around the buildings. With only a few hours of daylight in the winter months, this was truly living on the edge.

Winter shelter was needed for the livestock too, though there is evidence that there was enough produced to have a small dairy surplus which could be exported so that items that were not available in Greenland could be exchanged in return. Bog iron allowed for some small amounts of metal to be produced locally, though the process of obtaining it was difficult and wearisome, but walrus ivory and whalebone was used as an alternative when possible. At least easily carved soapstone deposits, widely employed in Norway for use as cooking dishes but unavailable in Iceland, existed on the island and could be exploited. Runic inscriptions even reveal the names of some of these otherwise anonymous pioneers: Thor, Bardr, Björk.

Due to the time that the island was discovered, Christianity came early to Greenland. Erik the Red's wife, Thjódhild, was a Christian and built a small oratory near her house; she was descended from the family of an Irish king a few generations back; after her conversion she subsequently abstained from sex, much to Erik's displeasure.[54] The marginality of Greenland can be gauged from the size of the building called Thjodhild's Church that was constructed with turf walls at Brattahlid. The building was tiny, measuring about 2 metres by 3.75 metres.

However, there were still adherents of the old faith too and the sagas record stories of soothsayers. Eventually the new faith emerged triumphant and a bishopric was established for the scattered settlements of the island based at Gardar, not too far from Brattahlid. The remains of a bishop were later unearthed at Gardar; he had been buried with his crozier, which has carvings scoured out of walrus ivory, and this bears mute testimony to the presence and power of Christianity in Greenland. The discovery of this *in situ* in the grave was an incredible find for archaeologists and provided overwhelming evidence of the occupation of the incumbent skeleton.

The first years in Greenland were harsh. A ship carrying Thorbjorn Vifilsson, whose daughter Gudrid played an important part in the settlement story in the west, was becalmed on a journey there from Iceland and a number of those aboard died. They eventually arrived in Greenland after nearly being swamped when the weather changed. But their troubles were not over, for hunting was lean and some of those who went out searching for food did not return. As it inevitably does from time to time, the supernatural intervened in the saga stories. The lot of the settlers was only improved by the actions of a seeress, Thorbjorg, who wove her magic during rituals in which she was aided, however unwillingly, by the very Christian Gudrid. This story is a nice metaphor for the coexistence of the old and new religions especially on the frontiers of Viking society.[55]

Greenland is something of a twilight zone in the sagas, its remoteness and harshness no doubt adding to its sinister, otherworldly ambience. Dark spirits are never far away in this ethereal realm.

In *Erik the Red's Saga* there is an account of a woman called Sigrid who lived on the island with her husband at a time when the island was plagued by a vicious epidemic. One night she was about to go outside when she stopped on the threshold in a state of alarm. Gudrid, who was visiting with her husband Thorstein, asked the woman why she had stopped and shivered so.

The response came that she had seen a party of the dead standing outside the hut, among whom were included both Sigrid and Thorstein, both then very much alive. The farmer's wife duly died but that was not the end of the tale, for soon after the farmer called out in a state of alarm that his dead wife was trying to climb into bed with him. The terrified man drove an axe deep into her breast, presumably bringing an end to her nocturnal visitations.

Life in Greenland was always harsh and existence there was always likely to be attended with a higher level of risk and danger than anywhere else. It was remote and exposed to the elements, a long way from mainstream Scandinavian culture. Viking society would not survive there unscathed in the long term; but the fact that it survived at all given the challenges to be faced is something of a minor miracle.

On to Vinland

Greenland was not the limit of Viking discovery. When Bjarni Herjólfsson returned to Iceland after a trip 'back home' to Norway in around 985, he discovered that his parents had in his absence upped and left with Erik the Red. His predicament was that he could not find anyone to sail with who had journeyed westwards from Iceland before, so it was a leap of faith when he sailed forth to find his parents in Greenland. Here there is an interesting insight into the peripatetic lifestyle of some Viking Age residents of the outlying territories like Iceland and Greenland, sailing backwards and forwards to and from Norway, maintaining the most fragile of lifelines between the different territories. For Bjarni, that lifestyle was about to involve him in an epic adventure – though not quite as epic as it could have been.

Within three days of setting out for Greenland, catastrophe threatened. First of all, they lost sight of the land. Then the wind failed. Finally, a thick cloak of mist blanketed their vision so that they were effectively sailing blind. They had no clue where they were and sailed hither and thither for many days, hoping against hope that the fogs would lift and they would miraculously catch sight at last of their intended destination. Then the mists finally rolled away and they could see land. But as they looked more closely, they were baffled. Although Bjarni had never seen Greenland for himself, those who had told him that it was home to enormous glaciers. There were no such objects here. Instead, the land that they could see was carpeted with thick and seemingly impenetrable forests cloaking the sides of low hills.

Bjarni did not land and instead turned his ship around to head back in what he thought was the general direction of Greenland. He sailed along the coast and was often in sight of land but did not put ashore, even though some of his men wanted to do so to collect timber and water. As a result, he missed the chance of becoming the first European to set foot in America. There are two sagas that describe the discovery of Vinland – the *Greenlanders' Saga* and *Erik the Red's Saga* – and the first of these suggests that Bjarni was much criticised for not landing and trying to find out more about the unknown country.

From this, we might conclude that Bjarni lacked that 'X factor' level of adventurism that marked out some of the Viking explorers. On the other hand, that would be rather a superficial judgement when it is remembered that Bjarni was a man who sailed to and fro across the wild North Atlantic in a flimsy ship that was very much at the mercy of the elements, which is more than sufficient adventure for most people. In any event, Bjarni decided that enough was enough and set up a permanent home in Greenland; his sailing days were over.

But now that the discovery was out, albeit one made only at a distance and without any landing to investigate further, it was only a matter of time before someone with an adventurous streak set out for themselves to see what Bjarni had not. It was left to Leif Eriksson, the son of Erik the Red, to lead the expedition that would find those forested lands again and investigate them; he acquired Bjarni's ship from him, presumably as its pedigree was well-proven having survived the previous expedition. Leif tried to persuade Erik to lead the expedition, though his father responded that he was now too old to accompany him (he subsequently changed his mind but fell off his horse when journeying to join up with the expedition and so never made it).

Leif was, according to *Erik the Red's Saga,* an example of the wandering Viking adventurer who had a foot in many camps but no real roots anywhere. He had journeyed extensively around the north and at one time was in Norway whose king, Óláfr Tryggvason, asked him to try to convert the people of Greenland to Christianity when he found out that Leif was planning to journey there. This particular account of the discovery of Vinland has Leif blown off course when journeying to Greenland and being amazed to discover a country that was rich in wild wheat and vines. What Leif finds is a region where even the winters are surprisingly clement compared to what he was used to; solar measurements showed it to be to the south of Greenland. Three names emerged to go with these lands; territories called *Helluland, Markland* and *Vinland;* the last two named after some of their geographical characteristics as 'forest land' and 'wine land' respectively[56] while the first of them has been rather ponderously translated as 'slab-stone land' and may be Baffin Island.[57]

After over-wintering in temporary accommodation Leif's party returned to Greenland with a healthy supply of timber which would have been much appreciated. It had been a good trip, for which its leader earned the nickname 'Leif the Lucky' as he rescued some stranded sailors on his way back, which was deemed to be a portent of good fortune for him; one wonders who these rescued men were as they were also clearly early travellers around the region of the North American eastern seaboard.

A little while later an expedition led by Leif's brother, Thorvald, set out for Leif's property. He settled there for several years, exploring the region which was well-forested with a coast that was liberally sprinkled with beaches of white sand. Thorvald and his party explored both by land and by sea and at one stage his ship was driven ashore by bad weather and damaged, forcing them to spend some time undertaking repairs. However, the land already had a resident population. Coming across a party of nine of them, all but one of the native tribesmen was killed. The survivor however brought back a large force with him in a 'vast number of hide-covered boats' and a fierce battle followed. In this, Thorvald was struck by an arrow under the armpit and mortally wounded. Revealing his religious affiliations, he was given a Christian burial at Krossanes, the 'Headland of Crosses'.

This tragic end laid the path for the next unsuccessful venture, an expedition led by Leif Eriksson's older brother, Thorstein. He journeyed with a crew of twenty-five but the weather was atrocious and they never got close to land. They eventually returned to the Western Settlement in Greenland where Thorstein died during the following winter. He was buried at Brattahlid after being struck down in an epidemic, which took many others with him, such as the farmer's wife Sigrid who was discussed earlier. Picking up the supernatural theme, when Thorstein died, as the deceased woman had seen in her terrifying premonitory vision, he came back to Gudrid and told her he wished to be buried in consecrated ground. He also said that Gardi, the first to die in the epidemic, should be exhumed and burned as he was its cause, a classic remedy in medieval tales of vampirism.[58]

Thorstein then told Gudrid to marry again (but not to a Greenlander) before expiring one final time. She married a wealthy merchant by the name of Thorfinn Thordarson (the son of Thord Horse-head), better known as Karlsefni. He had come across from Iceland to trade with Erik the Red in the company of another trader, Snorri Thorbrandsson. They spent a convivial winter season at Brattahlid and enjoyed a particularly fine Yule feast marked with splendid storytelling and many hours of board games, though the highlight was the wedding ceremony in which Karlsefni married Gudrid (the Old Norse name for Yule was *Jól:* Jólnir was an alternative name for Odin).

Karlsefni was ambitious and his ambitions now took a different direction as he sailed west with the intention of settling in Vinland, as opposed to previous missions there, which had been probing expeditions. With him went sixty men, five women (including Gudrid) and an assortment of livestock.[59] Leif Eriksson offered to lend him the buildings he had constructed there but would not give them to him permanently. They found plentiful food to eat on arrival due to the timely beaching of a whale. Thereafter they discovered good supplies of game, fish and grapes and cut down large stocks of timber.

During the following spring the settlement was visited by a group of indigenes whom the Vikings called *skrælings*. The exact identity of these indigenes is impossible to verify, given the uncertainty around the location of these encounters. The term *skrælings* appears to be a generic word, similar to the Greek 'barbarian' (which is how *skræling* is translated in modern Icelandic), someone of another culture. It had strong pejorative overtones and one suggestion is that the word originally comes from the Old Norse *skrækja*, which means someone who bawls, yells or shouts; in other words, someone who is speaking in a language that is totally undecipherable to the hearer. Certainly, the Inuit who were present in Greenland several hundred years later were also called *skrælings* by the Greenlanders and the two groups often came to blows; but these were not the same people that the Vikings met in Vinland in the early eleventh century.

Although initially friendly trading took place, the presence of the *skrælings* put Karlsefni on his guard – he refused absolutely to trade weapons with them for the supplies that they had but they were delighted with the dairy products they received instead – and he took the precaution of erecting a stockade around the settlement. It was presumably here that Gudrid gave birth to a boy called Snorri, the first child of European descent to be born in North America. There was then a fight with the *skraelings* which broke out after one of them was caught stealing a weapon and was killed. The attack was beaten off, but the settlers shortly afterwards decided to cut their losses and returned to Greenland with large stocks of grapevines, berries and animal skins. They had by now started to argue among themselves; there were not enough women to go around, which was a major oversight if a settlement was planned, and those who were without a partner sought to win them off others who were more fortunate.

The last expedition described in the sagas is regarded with some suspicion by historians.[60] The main character in this was a particularly nasty villainess called Freydis, the illegitimate daughter of Erik the Red, who is almost too bad to be true; she had also been present in Karlsefni's expedition when she had used the unusual expedient of baring her breasts to scare off attacking indigene warriors. She dominated her weakling husband Thorvard whom she allegedly only married for his money. They were joined on their journey by a party of Icelandic adventurers. While in Vinland, Freydis arranged the murder of the Icelandic party and, when her menfolk refused to kill the women that were with it, she did it herself. The expedition petered out and, when news of Freydis's wicked acts got out on its return to Greenland, she found herself cold-shouldered by everyone.

The very names of the women involved here encourage a cautious interpretation. Gudrid, the first European woman to bring forth a child in America, is associated through her name to the Christian God. This image is reinforced when we are told that, late in life when a widow, she went on pilgrimage and lived out her days as an anchoress, a female hermit. Freydis on the other hand is linked to the pagan god Frey/Freyr and her evil acts are vicariously linked to paganism. This is not a story of ordinary folk, a Norse version of the *Little House on the Prairie*, but of a battle between different religions, different gods, and different world views.

Finding out much about Vinland is difficult, an extreme example of looking through a glass darkly. There are only fleeting glimpses of it in the historical-legendary record, as if seen through a thick mist which only lifts briefly from time to time. This is not just the case for the modern observer, but it also appears to have been a problem back in the medieval period. There are twelfth-century Icelandic records which talk about the delightfully named Bishop Erik *Upsi* (Codfish) Gnúptson who decided to try to re-find Vinland, which had clearly by now been lost. Erik duly sailed off into the west and was never seen again.

Beyond the references in the sagas, there was not much other evidence available to later archaeologists for any Viking settlements in North America. In more recent times, various items that emerged and were claimed to be Viking were widely regarded as forgeries. But then a massive breakthrough occurred in 1960. Two Norwegian archaeologists, husband and wife Helge and Anne Stine Ingstad, discovered a Viking site in Newfoundland at L'Anse aux Meadows (on the northern tip of the island). Despite its name, suggestive of rolling green fields, L'Anse aux Meadows probably means Jellyfish Bay. The initial finds at the site were of mundane items such as spindle whorls and a ring-headed pin which closely mirrors the design of similar items from Hiberno-Norse Ireland. As digging continued, it emerged that the buildings that had been erected there were of Norse design. They were in every sense humble, constructed of sod placed over wooden posts; a building style that was widely used in Greenland and Iceland. At the maximum, the settlement would have held no more than 160 people. Radiocarbon dating places it as being inhabited between 990 and 1050. Nearby deposits of bog iron, small lumps from which smiths could extract workable material, would have provided invaluable if limited local resources.

However, L'Anse aux Meadows did not last long as a Viking settlement; the humble structures built there probably collapsed after about a dozen years and were never rebuilt. There were outbreaks of violence with the locals and although game was plentiful at certain times of the year – remains found included those of caribou, lynx, marten, fox, birds and fish, bear, seal, whale and walrus– in the harsh winters it may have been hard to find. At the end of the day, there was simply an insufficient critical mass of human beings available to fully exploit the opportunity that had been revealed. This point should be borne in mind when considering the possibility of wider Viking settlement in North America. Greenland was at the edge of the world and in some ways the hypothetical Vinland was beyond it. There were few potential settlers to go around and numerically massively superior and potentially hostile indigenes to face.[61] Neither did the Vikings enjoy a huge superiority in weaponry to compensate as, for example, was enjoyed by sixteenth-century Conquistadores in Central and South America. Viking incursions to North America were always a longshot, though the possibility of probing expeditions of a trading nature over an extended period after these early expeditions should not be excluded given their general attitude to risk.

Ships' rivets have been found at L'Anse aux Meadows, suggesting that this might have been a staging post between Greenland and somewhere on the North American mainland. The buildings there seem to include significant areas for storage suggesting the same, as does the position of the camp helpfully on the route between Greenland and the lands beyond Newfoundland. On the other hand, the presence of butternuts there suggests contacts with the mainland as they are naturally found there but not in Newfoundland.

A second site discovered at Point Rosee at the extreme south-west tip of Newfoundland in 2015 also shows initial signs of being a Norse settlement. But investigations there have not as yet come up with any conclusive, undisputed evidence of a Viking presence and have not so far revealed any 'smoking gun'. The main evidence is that iron smelting took place on the site and some archaeologists think that this should be attributed to Viking activity: others are not so sure. Further, the site is not a conducive one for any Viking. The seaborne approaches to the Point are strewn with rocks and offer no easy landing place. Nor is there any fresh water nearby.

This is one area where we must hope that future archaeological discoveries will uncover more definitive evidence and help us to understand more about how far the Vikings penetrated the North American continent; for the evidence that exists at the moment is vague and very little can be said about Norse incursions onto the mainland with any confidence. A considerable amount of ink has been expended over the origins of the word *Vinland* in particular. It has been suggested that the word for 'wine' and 'meadow' are very similar in Old Norse and may have been conflated but strong counterarguments have been made against this. If it is accepted that the origin of *Vinland* is indeed the Old Norse name for 'wine', then the presence of grapes is naturally intimated. This is highly unlikely to have been Newfoundland; grapes on the other hand are found on the American mainland between northern Maine and southern New Brunswick in the north and the Hudson River in the south. Perhaps this is the most likely area to look for Viking incursions into North America though this would be equivalent to looking for a very small needle in a rather large haystack.[62]

However, that has not prevented some educated estimates being made with Prince Edward Island and the southern shores of the Gulf of St Lawrence finding favour with some. This is partly because of the presence of wild grapes there. Salmon is also found there; the fish is mentioned in the sagas but, based on archaeological evidence, would not have been found further south at the time as the climate was not favourable for them then.[63] This is one area we will have to watch and hope that more persuasive information emerges.

II

The North Sea Empire (1001–1025)

Broken were oaths, the words and pledges, all the powerful agreements
that had passed between them.

From *The Sibyl's Prophecy*[1]

Ireland and Britain at the dawn of the new millennium

As the new millennium arrived and, contrary to the fears of some, the
world did not come to an apocalyptic end, there were nevertheless
significant changes happening. Not the least of these was in Ireland
where Brian Boru took Dublin on New Years' Day 1000. Sitriuc
'Silkbeard' had been involved in an uprising against Brian, which also
included his maternal uncle, Máel Mórda. Sitriuc was not present
at the climactic battle after which Dublin fell but his brother Aralt
(Harald) was, and lost his life. The confrontation, which took place
at Glenn Máma in the foothills of the Wicklow Mountains, was a
catastrophic defeat for the Dubliners. Sitriuc's role was to defend
Dublin but he was unable to do so and the town fell. After his triumph,
Brian burned the nearby wood of Tomar, which was sacred to the
Vikings. This suggests that there were still many vestiges of paganism
remaining among them.

However, Brian knew a good thing when he saw it. While he allowed
his men to help themselves to Dublin's wealth, he prevented them from
burning it. As a valuable trading centre, it was worth far more intact than
devastated. Sitriuc was forced to accept the situation and, making the
most of an unsatisfactory state of affairs, accepted Brian's triumph and
became his man. The deal was sealed when Sitriuc became Brian's son-in-
law, marrying his daughter Sláine. Brian's rise had been stellar; he had a
well-honed tool at his disposal in the shape of his army with his warriors
from Munster supplemented by mercenaries. He had frequently raided

across the borders of his great Irish rival, Máel Sechnaill, sometimes in alliance with Viking forces. Eventually, he and Brian agreed to divide Ireland between them. The two men had even joined forces to advance on Dublin, compelling the inhabitants to hand over hostages as surety for their good behaviour in the future.

Shortly after this, forces from Dublin took part in a raid with the men of Leinster on Tara. Máel Sechnaill, the target of this raid (his alliance with the king of the Dál Cais had clearly broken down), came to terms with Brian who then sought to bring the rest of the Uí Néill under his rule, again with the help of contingents from Dublin. Brian was a man of vast ambition and great drive but at the same time was prepared to build alliances as much as win military victories in his bid to become the supreme ruler in Ireland. It was not until 1011 however that his triumph appeared complete, and even then his grip on power was not total.

Across the Irish Sea, Æthelred II began the new century with the Viking threat to his country being significant but as yet far from terminal. There had been frequent attacks, growing in both scale and regularity, during the previous two decades but these had diminished in recent years probably owing to distractions back in Scandinavia. However, the turn of the century saw the scale of the Viking threat escalate once more as new raids were launched, which, over the course of succeeding years, increased in intensity.

Æthelred strengthened his position by his marriage to Emma, daughter of Duke Richard of Normandy; he was two decades older than her and had possibly ten children already from previous relationships, but in the context of the times this was neither particularly unusual nor was it problematic. Given Normandy's connections with the Vikings and the fact that the latter frequently found shelter there when raiding England, this was an important political move, but in the longer term it created unforeseen complications.

The target of subsequent Viking raids is relevant. There was an attack in 1001 on the estate in Sussex known as Æthelingadene. Here the clue is in the name, for an Ætheling, loosely translated, was a royal prince and the name was therefore linked to a place with strong royal connections.[2] Exeter was a town with links to the ruling dynasty having been granted by the king to his new wife Emma. The Viking raid on it which occurred in 1003 met with complete success and an important royal town was sacked (it had also been attacked in 1001 with other towns in the west of England). Wilton was also raided; another place with royal connections as it was the site of a nunnery closely connected to St Edith, Æthelred's half-sister. The targeting of attacks on royal estates was a regular Viking tactic that served several purposes. Firstly, such places were well stocked with potential plunder. Secondly, such raids also served a strong symbolic purpose emphasising the impunity with which such raids could be launched, and the powerlessness of the monarch to do anything about them. Such specifically targeted attacks can hardly have been coincidental. Wilton was renowned as a particularly rich establishment – the late abbess Edith had been notorious for her sumptuous dress even after she had taken the veil – and this would have added to its specific attractions.

In response, Æthelred launched violent actions which were ultimately totally counterproductive. These culminated in the so-called St Brice's Day Massacre (Brice being a fifth-century saint from Tours). On 13 November 1002, Æthelred, according to Roger of Wendover, advised by a military commander called Huna who told him that there was a plot afoot to remove him, launched dawn raids on all the Danes in England. Some caveats are needed with regard to this broad statement; it is inconceivable for example that all the Danes in the Danelaw were subject to the atrocities that followed. It is more likely that they were targeted on groups of Danes south of Watling Street, the dividing line between the loosely defined Danelaw and Anglo-Saxon England proper.

There is powerful evidence of large-scale atrocities against groups of Danes. The discovery in 2008 of the butchered remains of men of Scandinavian origin at St Frideswide's Church in Oxford revealed that they were tied up, hamstrung and then burned, though possibly the latter was a *post-mortem* act. This brutal event may well have been linked to the St Brice's Day Massacre. Subsequent research has come up with the suggestion that the victims were a group of professional warriors of Danish origin. Whoever they were, there are several things that the evidence points to, such as that they were of Scandinavian origin and they were executed around the end of the tenth or the beginning of the eleventh century. That these men were slaughtered as part of an organised massacre in 1002 has strong supporting evidence in a remarkable contemporary document. In a charter issued in 1004, which discussed the rebuilding of St Frideswide's, Æthelred gave his reasons for ordering a massacre to be carried out. In a phrase that has not lost the capacity to disturb, it was said that the Danes in England had been 'sprouting like cockles [poisonous weeds – a biblical term found in the book of Job] among the wheat' and must therefore be cut down. The charter went on to state that the draconian action had been sanctioned by the king's councillors and was 'a most just extermination'. William of Jumièges informs us that some survivors from the massacre made their way back to Denmark with the dark tidings; Sveinn Forkbeard's reaction was predictably violent.

The charter gives vivid details of what happened during the massacre, specifically in relation to the events that occurred at St Frideswide's, and here we have a potentially decisive link with those skeletons as an explanation of an event that took place on the very spot where they were found. The scribe described how the Danes present in Oxford in 1002 broke down the bolted doors of the church, hoping to find sanctuary inside. However, a mob chased them and tried to force them out of the church. When they could not do so, they set the building alight. The church was consumed by the flames.

A recent addition to the evidence for massacres at about this time in England was made in 2009 when a group of over fifty decapitated skeletons was uncovered during the construction of a bypass near the Dorset Ridgeway close to Weymouth. The victims were probably of Scandinavian origin according to scientific isotope research, emanating from a wide area in the north. Possible points of origin included Norway, the north of Iceland, the Baltic States, Belarus and Russia. The cosmopolitan nature of these points of origin reinforces the point that raiding parties could be drawn from a wide geographical region. It is conceivable that this was part of a raiding party; fifty individuals equates well to an average-sized Viking ship's crew and a prominent hilltop location in full sight of the sea would seem the perfect place symbolically to execute a pirate war band. Radiocarbon dating suggests that these individuals met their end somewhen between 970 and 1025. They could therefore have been killed as part of the pogrom launched on St Brice's Day 1002. The method of their killing was different though from that in Oxford; these men were not butchered during an outbreak of mob fury but as part of an organised execution. They could possibly have been executed after a raid that went wrong during that period. It is even conceivable that they were mercenaries fighting for the English who were killed by Vikings. But it would be premature to rule them out as victims of the 1002 massacre; there are other instances of links between mob violence and organised public execution, as witnessed for example in France during the Reign of Terror in 1793/4.

Although a few older men, possibly fifty or over, were identified among the Ridgeway victims, the majority of those killed were adolescents or young men. Skeletal development showed greater upper rather than lower body development, consistent with engagement in a repetitive physical activity such as rowing. Evidence of pathological wear and tear on the body reinforces this perception. One individual's dental remains suggests that he had had his teeth filed; this practice is not widely evidenced in Britain, but examples have been found in Sweden and Denmark.[3] It is hard to see much purpose for such ornamentation other than to add to the aggressive appearance of the person on which the cosmetic dental shaping had been performed.

The men had been executed in an inexpert fashion; a hint perhaps that despite the apparently organised nature of the killings, there were amateur executioners at work here. There was evidence of multiple blows on some of the skeletons rather than a clean strike; the killing seemingly took place in a frenzied atmosphere. A few skeletons showed defensive injuries as if arms or hands had been raised in a futile attempt by the victim to protect himself from the blows. The men, when dead, had been dumped in a shallow grave which appears to have been the remains of an old chalk quarry. They were thrown in without respect or care. All in all, it is a gruesome reminder of the harshness of the times and what a captured raider might expect at the hands of his captors.

The Vikings soon returned with a vengeance, with forces that appear to have been quite international. The future King Cnut and his father, Sveinn Forkbeard, and grandfather, Harald Bluetooth, had Baltic connections beyond Denmark. Cnut's mother was the daughter of King Mieszko I of the Piast dynasty in Poland. Nor was it just the royal bloodline that had a wider Baltic connection. Recent excavations in Denmark of a cemetery from Harald's time reveal a number of graves that contain remains from individuals from the eastern Baltic.[4]

There may have been good reasons for Æthelred to be angry at the actions of some Danes, not least with a man called Pallig (who he had appointed his ealdorman in Devon) who had aided and abetted attacks into Anglo-Saxon England, even though the English king had been generous with gifts of 'manors, gold and silver' to him. But the massacre was wholly unsuccessful in inhibiting Viking attacks and whatever justifications Æthelred offered it was an act of arrant rashness, even stupidity; rather than deter Viking raids, it had precisely the opposite effect. Pallig was, according to some accounts, married to the sister of Sveinn Forkbeard and she was among those summarily executed; in the more graphic descriptions that survive she was first forced to watch her son done to death by being run through with spears. Sveinn was not a man who would take such matters, if true, lying down and when retribution came it would be vigorous and devastating. Æthelred's actions in unleashing the violence that manifested itself so horrifically on Saint Brice's Day 1002 was perhaps one of his greatest mistakes; and that is no mean claim to fame.

England and the lurch to catastrophe

Æthelred's marriage to Emma of Normandy in 1002 was to have massive consequences for the entire history of Western Europe. The marriage of a king of England to a foreigner was very unusual at the time. It was undoubtedly the product of geopolitical considerations. Very possibly some Viking attacks on England had been launched from

Normandy and the marriage alliance was a sensible way of trying to reduce if not eliminate the threat coming from there. There are even some accounts that Æthelred may have launched a pre-emptive strike on the Duchy in 1000, though according to one chronicler, the late eleventh-century Norman writer William de Jumièges, they did not achieve much.[5]

Emma was a remarkable personality who was a player on the English stage for the next five decades. As wife to Æthelred she was mother to a later Anglo-Saxon king, Edward the Confessor. When, as Æthelred's widow, she later married Cnut of Denmark she had other children including Harthacnut who would become (briefly) king of Denmark and England. Through her bloodline, later Norman claims to England would be based – with dramatic consequences on the field of Hastings in 1066.

The later Norman writer Orderic Vitalis suggested that Emma brought many of her adherents over from Normandy with her and as a result they formed an influential clique in England. The Normans were therefore introduced into English power politics with well-known catastrophic results just over half a century later.[6] Yet the arrangement probably suited both parties well at the time; the death of the formidable Duke Richard I in 996, after he had ruled for over forty years, left Normandy as well as England in search of potentially useful allies. Richard's wife Gunnor survived him for twenty-five years and continued to play a high-profile role in political affairs, suggesting that she was a woman who is somewhat unfairly overlooked by history.

Emma is an important figure in the history of both England and the Vikings. She brought several power blocs – Anglo-Saxon England, Normandy and Viking Scandinavia – further into each other's orbit. It did not appear to matter at the time that Æthelred, as mentioned, already had a wife and a number of children;[7] this was perhaps best explained by the fact that previous relationships were not regarded as formal marriages but rather a form of concubinage; Cnut of Denmark would do something similar a few years later. But the fact that no English king had married a foreign princess for seventy years suggested both that the plan was innovative but was also brought about by difficult circumstances.

The English were still capable of putting up a fight though. When the 'Danes' attacked Norwich in 1004 the man in command of local English forces, Ulfcytel Snilling (a very Scandinavian name), led a fierce response. Ulfcytel moved on the Viking ships beached at Thetford and only narrowly failed to win a victory. This was a very wise strategic move on Ulfcytel's part; the Vikings were reliant on their ships and their whole campaign plan often revolved around them; deprive them of their fleet and the Vikings would be robbed of their mobility and means of escape if needed. The Anglo-Saxon chroniclers made it clear that only Ulfcytel's inability to muster together his full force in time prevented him from winning a decisive triumph. It was a symptom of England's greatest malady, her inability to move fast enough when faced by a threat from highly mobile raiders.

There were major changes afoot by now in Denmark. Some of the older Danish towns such as Ribe, Hedeby and Åarhus had gone into terminal decline. New settlements had developed, or would soon develop, to take their place such as Viborg, Lund in Skåne and Roskilde in Zeeland. They were all noticeably far away from the German border and correspondingly from the danger of being threatened from there; they were also all in a position to dominate key parts of the Baltic region. In the battle for regional supremacy, first against his own father, then against Óláfr Tryggvason, Sveinn had emerged triumphant and was determined to use his accumulated power to optimal effect. England was next on the menu.

Major raids on England now became an almost annual event. A great fleet (*micla flota*) caused serious damage in the south of England in 1006. With wearying predictability this was bought off with the virtual certainty that the raiders, or their compatriots, would be back again for more in the near future. It was effectively a large-scale protection racket. The need for Viking fleets to find new sources of profit had become acute. The fall of the Sāmānid dynasty in the previous year created chaos in Khazar territories far to the east and a consequent drying-up of supplies of silver appears to have had a dramatic impact on hoards of the precious metal back in Scandinavia and new sources of wealth needed to be exploited in compensation.

With the benefit of hindsight, 1006 appears to be a seminal year. The time was ripe for a major Viking assault: the archbishop of Canterbury, a highly influential figure, had just died; there was trouble in Mercia where a new rising power, ealdorman Eadric Streona, was coming to prominence and threatening to sow chaos in his wake; and in Northumbria ealdorman Ælfhelm had been murdered and his sons blinded at the instigation of the said Eadric.[8]

The Viking raid of 1006 was deliberately provocative. Recent historians have looked more deeply into warfare in the Viking Age and concluded that there was an element of ritual in it. While the argument may on occasion be overstated what happened now backs up the theory. There was an old burial mound far inland at *Cwichhelm's hlaew* (also known as Cuckhamsley barrow or Scutchamer Knob). It was associated with a seventh-century king of Wessex, Cwichelm. It was said that any raiding party that had the temerity to strike this far into the heart of Wessex (it was at the time in Berkshire, though has since 'moved' to Oxfordshire due to local authority boundary changes) would never make it back unscathed to the coast. A Viking raiding party now resolved to test the validity of the theory. Not only did they make it to the barrow, but they returned triumphantly to the coast without any opposition, marching boldly past the walls of Winchester, the major town of Wessex, in the process. No one sought to block their way or bring them to task. Æthelred was far away at the time, ensconced in Shropshire and celebrating Christmas with his new-found advisor, Eadric Streona. He cannot be blamed for not having advanced intelligence concerning this insult to his honour and to that of Wessex, but it had the unfortunate result of making him look wrong-footed and incompetent. From this moment on it was all downhill for him. The raiders took up residence on the Isle of Wight, a handy base from which to launch more attacks on Wessex as and when they chose. The raids not only had a material impact, they struck hard at something else: morale. The Vikings were employing terror as a weapon of war, a classic strategy in much of medieval warfare; and they were particularly good at it.

Æthelred was nevertheless still able to assemble large armies when he had time to do so with, in theory at least, 30,000 men he could call up.[9] But this was all too often a notional number and even when a sizeable force was assembled it did not usually fight with vigour or unity. And even though defensive measures had been developed over the decades such as the establishment of military roads, the *herepaths,* and a well-attested network of beacons by which one place could warn another that trouble was on its way, the raids increased in intensity until they transmuted into an all-out attempt at conquest.

As the intensity of Viking attacks increased, Æthelred tried to strengthen his hand. When he raised money, it was not only to encourage his Viking enemies to go away, it was also to strengthen his own military resources, so there were large taxes raised to do so. Between 1008 and 1013 several measures were taken to raise taxes to equip a fleet of 200 ships (the *ASC* states that each 300 hides of land were responsible for providing one ship) and to provide armour for over 20,000 troops. From this we can assume that such resources were urgently needed and that matters had gone into steep decline since the halcyon days of Edgar the Peaceable when a great armada had sailed around the coasts of not just England but the whole of Britain in what seems to have been a largely successful attempt to deter Viking attacks.

Since Edgar's perceived golden age, matters had taken a sharp turn for the worse. The *burhs* that had been established in Alfred's reign were now decaying. Rebuilding works were needed to restore them to their former strength, such as those undertaken in Æthelred's reign at Wareham in Dorset. The seriousness of the Viking threat was reinforced by the decision to move some of the mints across the country to places of safety, as a result of which old hillforts like South Cadbury in Somerset and Cissbury in Sussex were brought back into use.[10] From some perspectives, these were very sensible moves. But from others they looked like signs of weakness and even panic.

The problem was not so much in Æthelred's ideas but in the execution of them. The great fleet that Æthelred assembled achieved nothing, not because of any efforts on the part of the Vikings but because the English ended up fighting each other; the enemy within was in many ways more powerful and effective than that without. England was now bitterly divided and for this Æthelred, as its king, must take ultimate responsibility. His sponsorship of Eadric Streona as one prominent example would expose deep fault lines within the ruling English establishment.

In 1008, the country turned to God for help. An extraordinary Whitsuntide convention of the leading figures of England at Enham in Hampshire issued a law code for the nation, which included a strict diet of prayer and penance in an attempt to be restored to the good graces of the Almighty. It must have been a remarkable gathering; the lambs in the field a reminder of the Lamb of God – 'Enham' means 'the place of the lambs'[11] – while the discussions were led by a fire-and-brimstone preacher in the form of the formidable Wulfstan, archbishop of York. A new coin was issued to mark the occasion; a Lamb of God on one side and a dove on the other; very unusually there was no portrait of the king on it.[12]

These pleas for divine intervention were of limited use. Another larger-than-life Viking character was about to get involved in the form of Thorkell 'The Tall'. He is first mentioned in the *ASC* when he landed at Sandwich in 1009. Though mentions of him in works such as the *Jómsvikings Saga* are historically contentious, he was probably associated with the rulers of the rich and fertile land of Skåne, now in south-west Sweden, then part of Denmark.[13] It was wealthy enough to employ *skalds,* poets, at its court which was a sign of relative affluence, financed probably by both the agricultural produce of the region and the tolls it could extract from passing merchants through the narrowest points of the Baltic.

The writer of the *ASC* told of 'an immense raiding army' arriving with Thorkell. Sandwich seems to have been a major weak spot in the English defences given the number of times that a Viking force found egress into the country from there; the port was protected by a shingle bank that made any counter-attack from the English fleet difficult. The later works of John of Worcester add further detail, describing how a large fleet of Danes led by two men called Hemming and Eilaf joined up with Thorkell.[14] There were also some Norwegians with this large force, according to actions attributed to them written up in various relevant praise poems.[15] The writer of the *Encomium* suggests that Thorkell's reasons for attacking England were in response to the killing of his brother there, though the timings given by the scribe are suspect with regard to this course of events as it appears that Hemming died after 1009.[16]

Canterbury was attacked and a ship base for the Viking fleet was set up on the Isle of Wight, a regular anchorage for the marauders during these years given its perfect position proximate to the English coast but safe from counter-attack. This was followed by moves on London and Oxford. The army over-wintered in England, establishing a base (unfortunately the exact location is unspecified) somewhere on the Thames, clearly ready to return to the fray when the time was right in the New Year.

The next move in 1010 – a year when the chronicler lamented that 'no shire would help the next' – was on East Anglia where a furious battle was fought at Ringmere on 5 May. The later Icelandic poet Sigvat Thordarson wrote how 'all the race of Aella [sic] stood arrayed at Ringmere Heath'. The allusion to the former king of Northumbria who had in some accounts been blood-eagled by the Vikings was a reminder of the dominance (in the poet's eyes) of Viking forces over those of the Anglo-Saxons and how this latest Viking victory fitted into a long historical context which, by this stage, was reaching the endgame. It was a crushing triumph for Thorkell and among the dead was Æthelstan, the son-in-law of King Æthelred. Raids on the other side of southern England in Wiltshire suggest the Viking army could now move across the region with virtual impunity, hence the chronicler's bitter commentary. Æthelred contained Thorkell in East Anglia for a while but eventually his army had been in the field for so long that his soldiers drifted back to their homes. Apologists for Æthelred suggest that this was a normal and inevitable part of campaigning at the time, but it contrasts rather unfavourably with the ability of Alfred at the end of the ninth century to keep armies in the field.[17]

The scene was set for one of the darkest acts of the Viking era in England. In 1011, Canterbury was attacked and taken, allegedly with the help of an English traitor inside the gates (named as Ælfmar, abbot of St Augustine's); a frequent motif in the writings of Anglo-Saxon chroniclers. This followed a siege that had lasted for three weeks. They looted and pillaged until sated and then returned to their ships with Ælfheah, the archbishop of Canterbury, as a hostage. Among those taking part in these very unchristian activities was a man called Óláfr Haraldsson who would later become the foremost Viking Christian saint; this was indeed an age of contradictions. A tribute was agreed, effectively another chunk of protection money. The English council assembled in London, which remained in their hands throughout this period, with the Viking force moored on the Thames, either at Southwark or

Greenwich. A thick cloud of tension lay heavy over the river as the two parties prepared to exchange money and hostages. And then the tension ratcheted up several notches.

A personal ransom for the archbishop was suddenly required. There are several versions extant of what happened next. In the more heroic of them, Ælfheah defiantly refused to countenance such a bargain. In the slightly more prosaic version, the archbishop was unable to raise the money. What followed next seared itself into Anglo-Saxon consciousness, and quite possibly into that of the Vikings too. Ælfheah's captors assembled and engaged in a drunken carousal where large stocks of wine that had been seized were freely passed around. The archbishop was dragged in to be abused. Things quickly turned violent. Cattle bones started to fly around, flung with force at the defenceless prelate. He collapsed to the floor and was finished off with a blow from the butt of an axe, supposedly from a Viking who had only just converted to the Christian faith. The near-contemporary writer Thietmar of Merseburg suggests that Thorkell tried to intervene and stop the murder from taking place; however, as he also confuses the victim Ælfheah with the prominent English tenth-century churchman Dunstan in his account we should perhaps take this version of events with a generous pinch of salt.[18]

On the following morning there was palpable shock at what had happened even among those who were responsible for the archbishop's death. His body was taken with dignity to nearby London for burial, which can only have occurred if the Viking force there had allowed it to happen. It should be remembered that in recent decades parts of both Denmark and Norway had ostensibly become Christian and there were members of the army who were adherents to the faith. In the cold light of day, what had happened appeared appalling even to them. A decade later, the then-king of England, Cnut, would have the archbishop's remains transferred with all due pomp and ceremony from St Paul's in London to Canterbury, an act of contrition and penance for the murder (although more cynically it was also a way for him to humiliate London, as he didn't have much time for the Londoners). The example of the martyred archbishop continued to inspire veneration for centuries; 250 years later, his successor Thomas Becket, after delivering his final sermon at Christmas 1170, foresaw his own martyrdom and referred in an aside to one of his men to Ælfheah, who he would soon be emulating; in fact, the chroniclers of Becket's death suggest that one of his very last thoughts, just before the final fatal blow killed him, was of his murdered predecessor.[19]

Sveinn triumphant

Even the *ASC*, whose authors must have been in danger of being anaesthetised by this apparently endless catalogue of disaster, exhibits disbelief at this turn of events. The butchering of Ælfheah had dramatic and immediate results. Thorkell 'the Tall' soon after switched sides. Along with forty-five ships and their men, he joined forces with King Æthelred. Possibly even Thorkell had been revolted by the murder of the archbishop; alternatively, perhaps good old-fashioned opportunism was the prime motivation. The receipt of a massive payment of £48,000 from the English, the biggest yet, was presumably a very persuasive argument. At any rate, it was a great coup for Æthelred, who gained a further useful ally in the shape of the future king of Norway, Óláfr Haraldsson, shortly after. Óláfr joined forces with him after a raid into Iberia, probably meeting Æthelred in Rouen; by then, the English king was in exile.

The alliance between Æthelred and Thorkell did not deter further attacks on England and the end soon drew nigh. Sveinn descended on the country again in 1013 and this time he scented that the time was right to finish things off. Some contemporary chroniclers suggest that this whole expedition took on the nature of a national enterprise. Large numbers of men, they say, were recruited from across Denmark and it was a vast armada that set sail for England.[20] The scene was set for a remarkable confrontation. There are hints – and they are not much more than that – that Thorkell and Sveinn did not always see eye to eye; one gets a strong impression that they were rather too similar to each other for comfort. Now men who had been with Thorkell a year or so before were conceivably on the verge of fighting against him. Sveinn's armada again initially descended on Sandwich but on this occasion, it did not stay there. Instead it sailed north to the Humber and set up camp at Gainsborough. This was inside the area that was later named the 'Danelaw' and it is notable that while in the region Sveinn and his men were meticulously well behaved. The Danelaw quickly submitted to him and, in the far north, Earl Uhtred of Bamburgh did so too.

But the moment Sveinn's force crossed the old Roman road, Watling Street, the gloves came off. The Anglo-Saxon territories to the south received much harsher treatment. London still stubbornly held out. Sveinn moved on it but some of his men were drowned trying to cross the Thames. He moved west where both Oxford and Winchester were forced to hand over hostages, fording the Thames at Wallingford, a crucial crossing point (William the Conqueror would also cross here after Hastings in 1066). Sveinn then moved to Bath where he received the submission of many of the leading Anglo-Saxons from the west of England. The location was probably no coincidence; Bath was associated with the faded glories of the Roman Empire and there, just a few decades earlier, Edgar had been ostentatiously recrowned when at the peak of his powers. Sveinn was making a clear statement of his ambitions.

London finally capitulated soon after. It was a hammer blow. It was the foremost trading *emporium* in England and probably now its largest town. With less than 10,000 inhabitants it was dwarfed by the great cities of the East such as Constantinople and Baghdad but its importance to England could not be understated. Anglo-Saxon England seemed to be on the brink of extinction. When Alfred the Great had been at a similar low ebb, he took up residence in Athelney from where he plotted and executed a successful counter-attack. King Æthelred's response was to take himself off to Normandy, a safe haven indeed but far away from England. The later writer William of Jumièges suggested that Duke Richard was by now doing very brisk trade with the Vikings even while Æthelred sought refuge with him and although this is a single-source account, it does have a veneer of believability. It was an indictment of the English king's state of mind, fuelled by his own personal exhaustion and loss of self-belief after over two decades of consistent battling against the Viking threat. Sveinn Forkbeard was now *de facto* king of England.

However, fate was about to intervene. When it seemed that England was at last his, without warning, Sveinn died. His death came suddenly on 3 February 1014; in some accounts, it was said that he was killed by the avenging spirit of St Edmund whose abbey he had been mistreating.[21] Sveinn was never formally elected king although there is some suggestion that the *witan,* the Anglo-Saxon council, was due to meet him in York and formalise his claim to the throne within two weeks of his death.[22] Sveinn's son Cnut was with him when he expired and seems to have assumed that stepping into his late father's shoes was a mere formality. It was a major miscalculation. The *witan* invited Æthelred back, although with conditions. The exiled king accepted these and returned.

Sveinn certainly divided opinion among contemporary commentators. The acerbic comments of Adam of Bremen have already been noted, and similarly negative remarks emerged from the quill of Thietmar of Merseburg. The latter says that 'Sven [sic] lived for a long time, a burden on his own people and his contemporaries, an impious man among the pious'. He also noted that Sveinn was responsible for many deaths during his lifetime. The writer of the *Encomium,* on the other hand, is largely positive about him and his actions, suggesting that when he was on his deathbed he summoned Cnut to him and adjured him to be a just and Christian king when he succeeded to his throne. Even at the time this fierce man was able to generate both positive and negative responses.[23]

Little is known of Cnut's life before his appearance in this invasion of England. The evidence we have suggests that he was still a young man, possibly not even out of his late teens. There are glimpses of his family life and his mother was a daughter of Boleslaw I, king of the Piast dynasty in Poland, though she fades out of the picture later in his life. Cnut had a brother, probably older than him, named Harald who was left behind in Denmark presumably so that he could keep an eye on things in Sveinn's absence. There were also sisters, one of whom (Estrith) would play an important role in future Scandinavian succession politics. There may well have been an older half-sister called Gytha. Other more shadowy and less definite siblings also lurk in the background.[24]

Cnut entered into a relationship with Ælfgifu, daughter of Ælfhelm, former ealdorman of Northumbria who had been killed on the orders of Eadric Streona a few years previously. It was a political 'marriage' and its exact status is uncertain, for a few years later Cnut would take another wife while Ælfgifu was still very much alive. This might seem an unusual state of affairs but was not so rare in practice. It was quite common for kings and nobles to take a wife early on in their lives before later marrying a more senior wife: there was even a name for this practice of an initial semi-official marriage, *more danico* – 'in the Danish way'. Despite this suggestive name, it was not just Vikings or 'Danes' who engaged in the practice; King Edgar was in a similar situation and was not alone in Anglo-Saxon circles in this respect. There is a danger that such a relationship is taken out of context when looked at through modern eyes. Although it has been suggested that these 'unofficial wives' were concubines, this in the view of some commentators does them an injustice. Ælfgifu was an important woman in her own right, well connected to a family that played a significant role in Mercian and Northumbrian affairs. Allegations of concubinage on her part come from the probably scurrilous gossip of the writer of a biography of Cnut's second wife who made the suggestion in his work, the *Encomium Emmae Reginae;* it has rightly been suggested that 'as a rule of thumb it is perhaps good practice when one wants to understand a man's first wife to take all comments from the second wife (or produced for her) with a pinch of salt'.[25] However, it is significant that Ælfgifu's family had apparently fallen out of favour at Æthelred's court during recent times and an alliance with Cnut therefore seemed like an excellent opportunity to restore their fortunes. Before being too judgmental, it is worth remembering that Charlemagne, a supposed role model for Christian rulers, had four wives (two of whom admittedly died) and at least four concubines, so views about marital morality were clearly different then than they are now.

Cnut seemed unaware that his assumption of power was not a given; Sveinn's powerbase in England was in the northern half of the country, in the Danelaw and the Scandinavian part of Northumbria around York especially. The Anglo-Saxon ealdormen and nobles in the south might be more reluctant to throw in their lot with the Danish forces. Æthelred had in the interim got together an army and marched on Cnut's camp at Gainsborough after moving on London; Snorri Sturluson suggests that Óláfr Haraldsson (sometimes called Óláfr the Stout) was prominent in this attack and in one incident his men tore down the defences on London Bridge, allegedly leading to the creation of that famous nursery rhyme, 'London Bridge is falling down'.

Cnut was completely unprepared when the attack came (the *Encomium* suggests that he was also heavily outnumbered).[26] He managed to escape with his life but many of his men were not so fortunate. It was a bruising and painful experience for the young and inexperienced would-be king. He was forced to flee back to Denmark, where his brother Harald had assumed the kingship, having been left effectively as Sveinn's regent when their father had launched the attack on England.

As he was scurrying away from England, Cnut made one last savage gesture. He held hostages who were put ashore at Sandwich minus their hands, ears and noses: a permanent reminder to those who saw them in the future of what awaited those who went against the might of the Danes (a fate that Adam of Bremen tells us was also inflicted by Viking raiders of the period who fell on Saxony).[27] The outlook for hostages at this time was sometimes grim. *Hemmings Cartulary,* a record of contemporary charters, records the fate of one such, Æthelwine, nephew of Earl Leofric, who had both his hands removed when a captive of the Danes.[28]

After taking these violent actions, Cnut returned to Denmark. He suggested to Harald that they should divide Denmark between them, but this was something his brother was not prepared to do. Therefore, in the short term, England was the only available option if Cnut wished to have a kingdom of his own to rule, though some sources suggest that Harald was happy enough to supply him with men and other practical support for his planned invasion.[29]

Despite this seemingly miraculous release from Sveinn and then Cnut, there were some who nevertheless saw 1014 as one of the lowest points in English history. Wulfstan, the archbishop of York, offered an assessment of the Viking invasions of England that echoed that of Alcuin after the sack of Lindisfarne in 793, though he was even more outspoken. His *Sermon of the Wolf to the English* (the 'wolf' element was a pun on his name) started by asserting that 1014 was a year when the Danes were persecuting the people of England to the greatest extent. He saw an apocalypse as being imminent: 'Beloved Men, realize what is true; this world is in haste and the end approaches; and therefore in the world things go from bad to worse, and so it must of necessity deteriorate greatly on account of the people's sin before the coming of Antichrist, and indeed it will then be dreadful and terrible far and wide throughout the world'. The archbishop would not have been a cheerful companion at the dinner table; yet perhaps it is not surprising in an age when success in battle was linked to the will of God/the gods that the archbishop feared that his flock was in danger of losing belief.

In Wulfstan's view, again like that of Alcuin, the people of England had brought the Viking scourge upon themselves through their sinfulness and for turning their backs upon God: 'with great deserts we have merited the miseries with oppress us'. He bemoaned the fact that slaves fled their masters and joined Viking forces (and then, worst of all, turned their former master into a slave), that one 'pirate' often put ten of the English to flight, that Englishmen watched powerlessly while their wives or daughters were subject to multiple rape, that a handful of slavers could march their prisoners unmolested through hundreds of onlookers. His anger comes across loud and clear: 'But all the insult which we often suffer we repay with honouring those who insult us; we pay them continually and they humiliate us daily; they ravage and they burn, plunder and rob and carry on board, and lo, what else is there in all these events except God's anger clear and visible over this people'.[30] Once more mirroring Alcuin before him, he reminded his readers of the dire prognostications of Gildas, the Jeremiah of the British, half a millennium before; the ancient prophet's bitter, harrowing words seemed as apposite as they had ever done. Wulfstan was clearly apoplectic at the failure of the English to resist the Viking menace; and it therefore comes as a surprise to find him just a few years later as the trusted adviser of a Viking king.

Clontarf

In Ireland, the pot was boiling up again. Resistance to the ambitions of Brian Boru were evident among the Cenél Eógain from the north of the island. These tensions erupted into open hostility in 1012 after just a couple of years of Brian's overlordship. This was no surprise as their leader, Flaithbertach, had been his foremost opponent in the first place and had delayed Brian's remarkable achievement in being able to claim rule over all of Ireland for over half a decade. Máel Sechnaill was sent to bring him back under control but ultimately failed to do so. Flaithbertach then showed his contempt for Brian's rule by breaking the holy relic of St Patrick's staff at Armagh; Brian had attempted to increase his influence by forging links with the monastery there, which was Ireland's foremost religious site, so this was a defiant gesture not just against the church but also against the would-be overking himself.

By 1013, Sitriuc in Dublin was seemingly also keen to free himself of Brian's rule and was perhaps encouraged to do so by the overwhelming success of Sveinn Forkbeard over the water in England. Sitriuc even launched a raid on Cork, though his force was defeated in battle there and his brother was among those killed. Brian moved towards Dublin and spent the rest of the year hovering close to it in an effort to intimidate Sitriuc back to obedience, but it did not have the desired effect. The year after, sensing a showdown, Sitriuc sought out alliances. Sensing that a decisive campaign loomed, he risked the winter seas to search for allies further afield and seemingly found them, in the form of Sigurd Hlodvisson the Stout, jarl of Orkney, and Brodir, a leading Viking figure from the Isle of Man; *Njal's Saga* suggests that he offered Ireland to both of them as their prize for defeating Brian. He also had a long-term Irish ally in the shape of Mael Mórda, overking of Leinster.

Sigurd's mother, Eithne, was an Irishwoman from Leinster; this again shows how interconnected the Irish Sea region was, including its extended 'outposts' in Orkney. Sigurd won himself a reputation as a very effective jarl, a position he had held since 985. The *Heimskringla* describes him as a powerful man and a great warrior. He took over Orkney when he emerged triumphant in a struggle with other local Viking leaders and he extended his power in Caithness on the north of mainland Scotland. He brought together under his own rule a region that had, until then, been very fragmented. *Njal's Saga* mentions a conflict with the Hebrides and the Kingdom of the Isles, which were under different leadership. The *Orkneyinga Saga* mentions annual summer expeditions when Sigurd would raid the Hebrides, Scotland and Ireland – so he clearly had an adventurous and aggressive streak.

The sagas claim that Sigurd was forced to become a Christian by Óláfr Tryggvason when he was held as a prisoner on the island of Ronaldsay. This may be true, and it seems from his later actions that his conversion was entirely a matter of convenience rather than conviction. After Óláfr's death he seemingly gave his allegiance to Mael Coluim, the king of Alba, and married his daughter. Given Sigurd's interests in holding land on the mainland, and Mael Coluim's need for strong allies, it was an arrangement that suited both men well.

Sitriuc was fortunate to find allies in the shape of men like Sigurd and Brodir. Possibly such men were inspired by the exploits of Sveinn Forkbeard in England and wished to emulate his success in Ireland where much of the island remained unconquered. In some ways though their timing was off; Sveinn's sudden and unexpected death early in 1014 when on the verge of his ultimate triumph and the subsequent decline in the fortunes of Cnut (equally sudden and unexpected) had forced the Vikings in England to regroup; otherwise it is possible that they too might have become involved in the looming campaign.

The Scandinavian fleets had assembled in Dublin by the week of Good Friday, 23 April in 1014. The town was bustling with their men and those of the army of Leinster (though not all of them apparently as only warriors from the region close to Dublin were there), along with Sitriuc's Dubliners. Brian was probably aware of the support Sitriuc had canvassed from across the seas at this time and he ensured that the defences of important sites near Limerick were fortified so he was possibly unsure from where any attack might come. Despite this uncertainty, Brian ordered his army to march towards Dublin. Included in their number were Hiberno-Norse elements from Munster so there would be 'Viking' elements on both sides in the imminent war.[31]

On Holy Thursday, Brian's army had encamped at Clontarf, close to Dublin, having pillaged outlying Hiberno-Norse settlements outside the town. Clontarf is on a small plain close to Dublin and there is a modern suburb bearing the name. Máel Sechnaill joined Brian but for reasons that were probably opportunistic, neither he nor his men took any part in the imminent battle. As time moved on during the following morning, it became clear that a battle was highly likely. The forces from Dublin made the short journey out of the town to face up to Brian. Brian delegated command to his capable son Murchad and retired behind the lines, allegedly to pray though as always one must be a little suspicious of the reliability of some possibly hagiographical accounts. However, as Brian was now about seventy-three years old, there were practical reasons to explain why he might not fight in the battle, though *Njal's Saga* claimed that he did not want to fight on a Friday as it was a holy day.

There was a clash of fighting styles at Clontarf even though there were Irish and Viking elements fighting on both sides. Brian's force had a significant advantage in terms of numbers, but his opponents were better armed with better armour. The Irish warriors relied heavily on spears (for which there were twelve different words in their language) though their leaders would carry swords. They did not typically wear metal armour, even in terms of helmets, relying instead on boiled, hardened leather for protection. In contrast their Viking opponents, at least the better equipped ones, wore mail shirts and metal helmets. A carving on an elk horn found at Sigtuna near Uppsala shows a warrior wearing a conical helmet and a well-trimmed beard and moustache giving an insight into what the best-dressed Viking liked to look like.

In the absence of reliable historical information, we have to look for clues in various sagas to try and determine the course of events, especially *Njal's Saga* and the *Orkneyinga Saga*. They claim that Brian's opponents fought under the raven banner of Sigurd of Orkney, a type of standard that is referred to in other accounts of Viking battles such as that at Ashingdon in England in 1016; similar banners existed well into Christian times and it is recorded that one was used in the reign of King Sverri of Norway who ruled from 1184 to 1202.[32] However, according to some Viking sagas it was an unfortunate man who received the honour of carrying such a banner; although it will bring victory to the man that it is carried before, it will bring death to the one who carries it. Sigurd's had been woven by his mother, a renowned sorceress, and it carried such a curse.[33]

The battle that followed lasted for most of the day. Saga accounts suggest that it began with single combat between elite warriors from either side. The battle itself is likely to have been a classic Viking-Irish encounter, Brian's men throwing their spears and pushing forwards, their opponents' shield wall standing against them. Probably the main commanders of either side were targeted and their men fought to protect them. As men fell they were replaced by those in the ranks behind in a blood-soaked battle of attrition, no doubt as the various sagas state accompanied by the hacking off of limbs and heads, to the cacophony of steel striking on shields and armour, the war cries of the warriors and the groans of the wounded. Those who fell lay where they were, trampled underfoot, the numbers of dead rising on both sides in a bloody heaving scrummage.

Slowly the greater numbers of Brian's army gained the ascendancy. Sigurd fell, allegedly pierced by an Irish spear; his fate was no doubt determined the moment that he carried the magical raven banner into battle because no one else would. *Thorstein's Saga* suggests that he died shortly after he had been advised to retreat to his nearby ships; however, an unusually high tide had floated them off. A massacre of defeated Viking warriors on the beach followed. But Sigurd was not the only victim. Murchad was in the thick of the fighting and was mortally wounded; he died the day after. The fighting around him was particularly fierce and many of his noble retainers fell too. Brian's Viking opponents and the men of Leinster who were with them resolved to go down fighting and, seeing no escape from their predicament, determined to meet a glorious end. Perhaps, even in these days when the Christian God was gaining the upper hand, the lure of Valhalla still exerted a siren-like pull.

At the culmination of the battle, with victory for the forces of Brian Boru secure, there was an unexpected twist. Brian, who according to the hagiographic *Cogadh Gaedhel re Gallaibh*, had uttered 50 psalms, 50 prayers and 50 paters ('our fathers') during the course of the battle, was taken by surprise. He was on the periphery of the battlefield and largely unprotected; his bodyguard had apparently lost their discipline and rushed off to participate in what was now obviously the imminent triumph. It is also possible that Brian had earlier thrown them in as a reserve if the outcome of the battle had at one stage appeared to be in the balance.

The sagas claim that Brodir, the Viking leader from Man, was lurking nearby in some trees when he saw that Brian was undefended. Brodir had only a few men with him but these were enough to overwhelm Brian and the small number of personal servants who remained with him. Brian was struck on the head and killed, though only – according to the *Cogadh Gaedhel* – after he had hacked at Brodir with his sword, cutting off his left leg at the knee and his right at the foot. Perhaps a warrior's death was required in the interests of Brian's legend – after all, it was Good Friday, the anniversary of the death of Christ, and an appropriate day on which a man who would later be eulogised as a paragon of kingly Christian virtue should be sacrificed, playing the part of a martyr. The Viking killers of Brian also duly played their part, as required by these later story tellers, as the villainous murderers of the paragon. Brodir was captured soon after and executed; considering the injuries he had supposedly suffered, it was perhaps not difficult to catch him.

Brian was the foremost warlord of his time. He was not though the unifier of Ireland in the way that later story tellers (and more recent Irish nationalists) would say he was, for Ireland was in no position to be unified at the time. Unlike England, she had few towns (and those that were there, were Viking settlements, even though they had become part of a more integrated Hiberno-Norse culture). The Vikings were convenient villains for nationalists in a number of countries to help in 'explaining or excusing the rise of modern nation states'.[34] It is an assessment that would fit equally well with their activities in England vis-à-vis leaders such as Alfred the Great.

It became a point of pride for Irish clans to claim a part in the victory of Clontarf. Centuries later, in 1856, an Irish historian, John O'Donovan, wrote up an account of the history of the O'Kellys of Uí Maine which told how one of their ancestors, Teige Mor, had taken part in the great battle at Clontarf and had been killed. As he fell, a dog came out of the sea and stood guard over his body to protect it from the 'Danes'. O'Donovan also wrote how there were still many other traditions current even in the nineteenth century of many men from Connacht falling in the battle.[35]

Myth and legend are often more powerful than fact when preserving or, more precisely, developing a reputation. The role of Sitriuc is a case in point. In some versions of Sitriuc's role in the battle, he was

an observer on the sidelines, watching from the walls of his town.
Other accounts, such as those in the *Orkneyinga Saga* and *Njal's Saga*,
give him an inglorious role, fleeing the battle when all was lost. One
explanation, suggested by Howard B. Clarke, was that Sitriuc's actual
role was pragmatic. He theorises that Sitriuc stayed in Dublin, not out
of fear or cowardice, but due to the realisation that someone would
have to defend the town if the battle was lost. This has an air of truth
about it; an astute commander would not see warfare as a matter
of glory and honour but as a strategic real-life chess game. It was
important to ensure that, even if a battle was lost, a war was not. [36] The
later Irish work, the *Cogadh Gaedhel re Gallaibh,* claims that Sitriuc
was watching on with his wife Sláine, daughter of Brian Boru who,
seeing which way the battle was going, remarked that 'the foreigners
are being driven back into the sea, their natural inheritance'. Perhaps
understandably, Sitriuc struck her.

The aftermath of Clontarf was described further in literary works.
The writer of *Njal's Saga* told of the web of man, which sounds very
poetic, even philosophical. But then we are told:

The warp is made
Of human entrails;
Human heads
Are used as weights;
The heddle-rods
Are blood-wet spears;
The shafts are iron-bound,
And arrows are the shuttles.
With swords we shall weave
This web of battle.

It is terrible now
To look around.
As a blood-red cloud
Darkens the sky.
The heavens are stained
With the blood of men,
As the Valkyries
Sing their song. [37]

War in this writer's view of it is a mixture of gore and glory, of battle
and blood, of heroes and horror. This is the saga writer's perspective
on conflict, certainly not a view derived from intimately involved
participation. Clontarf, like other set-piece battles of the Viking Age,

was a close-up melee, a trial of brute strength and animal will, where the action is contained within the few yards around each combatant, pushing and shoving, hacking and stabbing at those within his immediate reach. Once one opponent is brought down, then it is on to the next, to repeat again and again until the battle is won or he is himself overwhelmed. There would be little of tactics once close-quarters conflict was launched, it would be every man for himself. It was a Darwinian affair, decided by the survival of the fittest, brute strength, stamina and ultimately overwhelming exhaustion.

Estimates of the numbers involved in contemporary battles are notoriously unreliable; when medieval chroniclers made such estimates, they were sometimes so high as to be frankly incredible. A modern historian, G.A. Hayes-McCoy, estimated that about 5,000 men took part at Clontarf when both sides are added together, and this does not appear to be unreasonable.[38] However, the various accounts of the battle are highly consistent in stating that both armies suffered heavy losses and this seems to have been a particularly savage confrontation. The losses on the part of Brian's army were certainly devastating; they included Brian himself, his son Murchad and his grandson Turlough. Other prominent figures killed included Brian's nephew Conaing and one of his grand-nephews; these were possibly members of his personal bodyguard and fell alongside him. Five Munster sub-kings died, as did two from Connacht. A leading Scottish noble, Domnall, son of the *mormaer* of Mar, also perished. In the aftermath of the battle, Brian and Murchad among other leading figures were taken to Armagh for burial where a wake was held for twelve successive nights in the high king's memory. Losses on the losing side were also severe, particularly in terms of leading personalities. There were Sigurd and Brodir; Óláfr, son of Lagmann, probably from the Hebrides, also fell. Sitriuc's brother, Dubgall, perished, as did his nephew Gilla Ciaráin. King Máel Mórda of Leinster was killed as was another Leinster sub-king, Domnall of Fortuatha Laigen.

The only real winner of the Battle of Clontarf was Máel Sechnaill who, ironically, was not actually there. The Dál Cais went into almost immediate decline and Máel Sechnaill had reinstated himself as high king within a few years. He was supported in his efforts by Flaithbertach. Máel Sechnaill died in 1022, allegedly as a result of drinking too much mead; a sharp irony this, an indirect victim of Viking culture perhaps. On his death, Ireland split once more into competing factions; later attributions of Irish unity to Brian Boru would have seemed laughable to contemporaries.

Despite this, Clontarf became one of those battles that assumed a huge symbolic significance in more recent times and was seen by later Irish nationalists as a defining moment in the fight for independence, a victory given an almost solemn resonance by the death late on in the battle of the high king Brian Boru. So iconic an event did Clontarf become that it was used as a rallying point by Irish Nationalists in the nineteenth century, leading to the British government proscribing rallies that were planned in commemoration of it.[39]

There was a marked deterioration in the fortunes of Orkney as a result of the death of Sigurd, who seems to have been the firm hand that kept the dispersed islands and adjacent mainland territories together. The jarldom was split between his four sons, and the kings of Norway started to interfere with affairs there. The *Orkneyinga Saga* also suggests that serious famine followed. Eventually Sigurd's youngest son, Thorfinn, would emerge as the sole ruler of Orkney but a war then followed between him and his nephew, Rognvald (Ragnall) Brusason, who had the active support of King Magnus the Good of Norway.

Some of the elements of 'colour' concerning the Battle of Clontarf can be attributed to the sagas and this links to a significant point. The role of the sagas in Viking history is a complex one. Historians in the past regarded them as being based on fact, the argument being that while they were written down centuries later they were based on oral tradition. Of course, the weakness of this argument is that, while it may be true, we cannot be sure that it is. Further, some of the references in the sagas are so outlandish – references to dragons, supernatural creatures, etc. – that they are clearly not accurate; consequently, there must be a suspicion about everything else.

As a result, there has been something of a counter-reaction. The approach of recent historians has been in some cases to dismiss the sagas altogether unless there is definitive corroborative evidence from elsewhere to confirm the detail. Given the paucity of documentary evidence (though archaeological finds are helping to close the gap) this does seem like a counsel of despair. Surely it is better to note some of the details that we glimpse in the sagas that may be true and not dismiss them out of hand; in the process other research can be undertaken which may, or of course may not, corroborate these details?

A good example is found in *Njal's Saga* when it refers to a man called Arnljot, described as Sigurd's 'man in charge' of the island of Stroma, the last island between Orkney and mainland Scotland. In this snippet of information, we get some insight into how Orkney was governed at the time. To ignore such evidence as being at least a possibility seems a trifle odd given how few alternative contemporary references we have to refer to. The later Irish work, the *Cogadh Gaedhel re Gallaibh*, while not being contemporary and also being hagiographical in its tone, mentions that the last Viking killed at Clontarf was a man called Arnaill Scot and it has been suggested that this may be the same man as Arnljot; a ray of light in an otherwise rather grey landscape. Should we automatically completely write off such details from problematic sources? I think not, unless there is good reason to doubt them.[40]

One significant feature of the impact of Clontarf is how widely it was reported. Not only does it receive many mentions in Irish accounts and later Icelandic sagas such as *Njal's Saga* but also in the Welsh chronicle, the *Brut y Tywysogíon* ('The Chronicle of the Princes'). Clontarf was also written up in a chronicle prepared by Adémar of Chabannes from Francia so clearly it was seen as a very significant event outside of Ireland itself.

Whatever the reality of the impact of Clontarf, Sitriuc Silkbeard was now seriously weakened. Dublin was burned in 1015 by the forces of Máel Sechnaill II. But Sitriuc was not yet beaten for good and he raided Kells in 1019, taking a number of prisoners as a result. But in succeeding years Dublin was forced to exchange hostages to keep on the right side of powerful Irish warlords involved in a battle for supremacy on the island. For the Irish, the ongoing existence of a thriving trading centre was very welcome, especially if it also gave them access to tribute as well as Viking warriors and sea power.

The power of the Vikings in Dublin was by now clearly in sharp decline. While Clontarf on its own might not have been a decisive reverse, it was not the only one and the cumulative effect of defeats there and at Tara in 980 were taking their toll. Viking-descended elements continued to play their part in Ireland far into the future but no longer as a dominant force. Sitriuc hung on for a while and continued to provide evidence of his propensity to swap sides when the winds of change suggested that it was in his interests to do so. Mael Mórda's son, Bran, was captured by him and blinded in 1018; it did not seem to matter that Bran's father had died fighting on Sitriuc's side at Clontarf and that Bran was Sitriuc's nephew. But Sitriuc's army was defeated by Augaire, king of Leinster, in 1021 at the Battle of Delgany, an outcome that may have encouraged him to seek support from England which, by then, was under a Danish king.

Clontarf signified in many ways the end of the dynasty of Ivarr, a remarkable and hugely influential group that dramatically influenced the development of England, Ireland, Scotland and Wales. It was an unusual quasi-empire that he had spawned several centuries before, one that was essentially maritime rather than land-based as in some ways the future realm of Cnut would be. And like that later empire, its widespread range would prove an Achilles heel. It enabled land-based neighbours to pick away at its fabric bit by bit, eventually bringing it down. But it had an incredible run and its impact over Britain and Ireland should not be overlooked.

The return of Cnut

Events now moved towards a dramatic conclusion in England. In 1015 Cnut was back, coming with 200 ships to the 'mouth of the Frome' in Dorset – that is, Poole Harbour.[41] Shortly before, according to the writer of the *Encomium*, Thorkell returned to Denmark with nine ships seeking an audience with Cnut. This was granted and Thorkell explained to Cnut that he wished to support him in his bid to regain the Crown of England. Fences between the two men were patched up, for the time being at least. Shortly afterwards Cnut returned to the offensive. His was a bold and calculated move, an arrow aimed at the heart of Wessex itself, the core heartlands of the Anglo-Saxon kingdom. Æthelred was now old and ailing, and less able than ever to face up to the threat, so it fell to his son, Edmund 'Ironside', to lead the defence of the realm.

The *Encomium* waxes lyrical about the force that descended on England. It describes how 'in this great expedition there was present no slave, no man freed from slavery, no lowborn man, no man weakened by age; for all were noble, all strong with the might of mature age, all sufficiently fit for any type of fighting, all of such great fleetness that they scorned the speed of horsemen'.[42] They stopped first of all at Sandwich, a familiar egress point by now, but here they found a defensive force ready to meet them. They therefore returned to their ships and sailed west along the south coast of England to Wessex.

There are some intriguing later references to suggest that Cnut may have had help from further afield in his endeavours. William of Jumièges wrote that Cnut sought assistance from Óláfr of the Northmen and Lagmann of Sweden in his quest. It has been suggested that Óláfr of the Northmen was Óláfr Haraldsson, which is confusing as he and Cnut were territorially at odds with each other (Óláfr was the incumbent ruler in Norway, which Cnut later claimed for himself). Lagmann's association with Sweden may be a mistranslation, the Latin for Hebrides being similar to the name for Sweden. There is no Lagmann of Sweden noted from this period but the Norse word for 'lawman' is similar and was being used in the Hebrides at about this time, so perhaps Cnut was getting help from further afield in his efforts. There was also a Lagmann, son of Óláfr, from the Hebrides fighting at Clontarf in 1014.[43] Certainly, Hebridean Viking warriors would achieve a particularly fearsome reputation for their toughness and vigour in battle and become prized as mercenaries.[44] The presence of *lagmain* or a 'lawman' is usually associated with the Vikings in the

Hebrides. However, it seems very unlikely that they were in practice narrowly limited to just one region. There is evidence of lawmen in other Viking settlement areas such as in the Danelaw in England or in Iceland. They seem to have been drawn from families of high social standing and were very respected members of the community who wielded a significant amount of power.[45]

Thorkell was at Cnut's side – though the *Encomium* disingenuously suggests that he had always secretly sided with the young king and had stayed behind in England as a way of facilitating his later access to it.[46] It is possible that with the death of King Æthelred, Thorkell considered that he was no longer bound to support the ruling Anglo-Saxon dynasty in England.

Another supporter of Cnut was Erik Hákonarson, the earl of Lade in the region of Trondheim. His family was very powerful in the north of Norway and were long-term allies of Cnut and his ancestors; his father Hákon had been a staunch supporter of Sveinn Forkbeard – there are suggestions that at some stage father and son had had a falling-out though good relations were later restored. Erik was also Cnut's brother-in-law, being married to his half-sister Gytha, and he subsequently earned a reputation with the saga writers for Viking activities, especially in the Baltic region. He had fought alongside Sveinn Forkbeard at the Battle of Svold where Óláfr Tryggvason was defeated. Erik was given lands in Norway following Sveinn's victory, though he possibly also recognised the authority of Óláfr, king of Sweden. He came with Cnut to England but, as a result, his possessions in Norway were dangerously exposed and ultimately lost to Óláfr Haraldsson, the current ruler there.

The English forces, led by Edmund Ironside, son of a now fading King Æthelred, were disunited, which made Cnut's task easier. Edmund and Æthelred did not see eye to eye and it was difficult to coordinate the English armies as they should have been. There was always major uncertainty about the loyalties of some of the Anglo-Saxon leadership, especially Eadric Streona. Edmund entered into an alliance with Uhtred, the lord of Bamburgh, and the two men moved on the west of Mercia together, attacking Eadric head-on. Cnut bypassed them and moved up to Northumbria, forcing Uhtred to break away and scurry back. There he tried to make his peace with Cnut, who was not convinced of his sincerity and had him executed. His place as effective ealdorman of Northumbria was promptly taken by Erik of Lade.

Soon afterwards, Æthelred died; Adam of Bremen noted that 'this was a just judgement of God; for he had befouled the sceptre with blood for thirty-eight years after his brother died a martyr'.[47] Predictably, there was a succession dispute in the aftermath of his demise. The Anglo-Saxon nobles in London plumped for Edmund to take his place, while another group in Southampton opted for Cnut. This illustrated the major tensions among the Anglo-Saxon leadership, which were to reveal themselves in the form of treasonous actions in a series of battles that were about to come.

A titanic contest followed Cnut's invasion, reaching its climax in 1016. Five times Edmund assembled a national army. Cnut and his men laid siege to London. It proved a tough nut to crack. London Bridge provided a formidable defensive barrier, which acted as an obstacle to any Viking ships attempting to sail downriver. To counteract this problem, Cnut ordered his men to dig a ditch around the river defences along which his ships could be manhandled. Edmund then ordered an earthen wall to be erected opposite the fortifications protecting London. There was therefore no easy way out for the citizens, although inside the walls there were a number of market gardens which would be useful in providing food while the siege was underway. However, it proved very difficult to bring in grain from outside the city, as a result of which bread could not be made. Before long London's citizens were starting to suffer from food shortages. Edmund, however, was able to escape from the city before the siege was fully laid and he reached the west of England where he raised an army to fight back against the Vikings. Battles were then fought across the length and breadth of southern England at Penselwood, Sherston and Otford and neither side won a decisive advantage. There was another at Brentford on the western approaches to London on an old Roman road there; Edmund's army was victorious, but a number of English warriors were drowned when they over-enthusiastically pursued the fleeing Scandinavian force.

Cnut had recruited a strong army in his attempt to conquer England. There is some interesting evidence that it was not exclusively Danish. Two sons commemorated their father Ulf of Borresta with a monument back in Sweden carrying a runic inscription that tells us that he had received three separate payments ('gelds') for his services in England, one from Tosti, one from Thorkell and one from Cnut.[48] Another runic inscription, this time from Aust-Agder in south-east Norway, reinforces the point. It says that the man it commemorates 'met his death in the army when Cnut attacked England'.[49] So we have here several examples of men from Cnut's armies coming from both Norway and Sweden as well as Denmark and possibly the Hebrides. This emphasises that these campaigns were attractive to mercenaries rather than solely national enterprises launched in support of a king. Indeed, there is a strong impression that at the time there were many such opportunists active around England like so many vultures scenting blood having witnessed what might be the death throes of the ruling Anglo-Saxon dynasty in the country.

Neither side managed to win a decisive advantage in the battle for England until the crucial contest loomed at Ashingdon in Essex. Alongside Edmund was Eadric Streona and it is no surprise to read from the *ASC* that the latter fled from the field at a key moment. This has happened so often, according to the chronicler of the Abingdon version, that one is increasingly suspicious that Eadric is being caricatured as a pantomime villain. With Eadric went men from the *Magonsaete,* from a region in the west of Mercia. Perhaps this tipped the battle decisively Cnut's way, for in the end he emerged triumphant. There was a long roll call of significant Anglo-Saxon dead including the bishop of Dorchester and the abbot of Ramsay (there was again no difficulty with prelates being involved in battle), the ealdormen Ælfric of Hampshire and Godwine of Lindsey, and the redoubtable Ulfcytel.

The Scandinavian armies appear to have been on a massive scale compared to previous ventures, and it is worth considering the range of weaponry and equipment available to the warriors that composed them. The bow appears to have been used by the Vikings and their Anglo-Saxon counterparts. It is referred to in both Anglo-Saxon poetry and Viking sagas. Arrowheads have been found in some graves, although they could have been used for hunting as well as fighting. There is some evidence too of a pointed arrow, rather like the later medieval bodkin, that could have been used for piercing armour. There are also grave finds of women with bows.[50]

Spears were relatively easy and cheap to make and were unsurprisingly much more common than swords. There is evidence that some weapons had spearheads that were very streamlined, as if they were made for throwing like javelins. However, others were heavier and would have been best used as a thrusting spear, held in the hand. The spear could be deployed easily as part of a large mass of men employed in a tactical formation, especially in a shield wall, which was a prominent battle tactic of the day.

The Vikings were particularly known for their fearsome axes. A range of surviving examples shows that there were several different types in use. Some were small enough to be used one-handed but other larger specimens must have required both hands to use them. They would have had a staggering impact when striking a man or even a horse. They also became part of the Anglo-Saxon armoury as well, but this may have been because they were later used in English armies after Cnut became king.

The sword was a particularly prized weapon. It is mentioned frequently in saga accounts and in legal documents such as wills. In previous centuries, swords had often been pattern-welded by hammering and twisting several bars together. They were much valued and travelled far afield; the Ballinderry Sword, a famous example from the ninth century that was found in Ireland in 1932, was crafted in the Rhineland by a craftsman called Ulfberht. Such pattern-welded swords still appear in the later Viking period, though they were less common by the time the eleventh century arrived. By now, it was more usual to have a single blade, often decorated with inlay. The extra work expended on it reinforced the value of the sword as a status symbol as well as a practical weapon. Several typologies have been developed to categorise Viking swords. One, the Oakeshott typology, divides them into five categories across the Viking period. By the mid-tenth to mid-eleventh centuries Type 4 swords had arrived, typically shorter than those of previous centuries with blade lengths between 63 and 76 cm long. They would give a longer cut than an axe blade would, but it would have been difficult to achieve the same level of forceful impact that was generated by the axe's blow. Later Viking and Anglo-Saxon swords are often well-balanced weapons but would have been easier to use as a cutting rather than a thrusting weapon. They were, at this stage in their development, designed to be used as one-handed weapons. Interestingly they also seem to have been used as the weapon of choice for execution, as shown by the remains uncovered at Ridgeway Hill where the victims were most likely beheaded with swords rather than axes. An account of an execution of Jómsvíkings also describes executions that were carried out by the sword.

Shields appear to have been in common use during the period, though only a few near-complete survivals have been found. The use of perishable materials such as wood and leather in their construction is a significant reason for this. The giveaway to the existence of shields however is often the metal boss which was included in the shield as a way of protecting the hand. These have been found in significant numbers as they were buried in graves and survive better than the leather or wood from which the shield itself was made. Thirty-two shields were found with the Gokstad ship. Although it has been surmised that these might not have been typical as they were grave goods, a shield found near the Viking encampment at Trelleborg is similar and therefore the Gokstad shields may be more representative than was once thought. They were made of wooden planks; small holes round the edge may suggest either a leather rim or a leather covering across the whole shield. Lime wood was a popular material from which to make shields, though it appears that they were relatively fragile and expendable in practice.[51] Typical Viking shields of the period were round. While they would give protection against spear-thrusts or arrows, they would only have been of limited use against powerful blows from swords or axes.

In terms of helmets, there are surprisingly few examples of these found through archaeological excavations. There may be several reasons for this. Possibly such items were not routinely buried. It is also feasible that helmets were made of perishable leather rather than metal. A third possibility is that they were not available to every warrior. Surviving examples do however suggest that the 'spectacle' style helmet found from Vendel times and at Sutton Hoo remained in use to some extent. However, pictorial evidence far more routinely portrays Viking warriors wearing conical helmets, like those worn by the participants at Hastings. These protected the upper skull area but were of little use elsewhere apart from the nose guard.

In terms of body armour, mail shirts ('byrnies') were commonly used. These usually protected the body from the neck to the knees though a few examples went lower. They were made of thousands of small links joined together either through riveting or welding. Making one of these shirts must have taken an extraordinary amount of time. They would have been of limited utility in certain situations though. They might stop a direct cut or thrust but in terms of the trauma of a heavy blow could not always prevent fractured bones or internal injuries.

It is highly unlikely that this range of equipment was available to all warriors, given its cost. There is evidence from the Anglo-Saxon side that there were shortages. In 1008 King Æthelred II of England issued an order that an enormous number of byrnies should be acquired to arm his warriors. This clearly implies that there was an insufficient number available at the time. It is also possible, though less certain, that the byrnies were required because their Viking opponents were better equipped in comparison.[52]

Viking armies used several main tactical formations. One was similar to that used by the Anglo-Saxons, the shield wall or *skjaldborg* where the warriors would overlap their shields. Typically, the men would be formed in several ranks. It was a tactic that could be used either defensively or offensively, in the latter seemingly something like a phalanx with spearmen prominent. An alternative was the 'swine array' or *svinfylka*. In this formation, the ranks were arrayed like a Christmas tree with two men in the front rank, three in the second, five in the third and so on. It acted like a wedge being thrust into the ranks of the Vikings' opponents in an attempt to punch a hole in their formation and then widen the gap made as a result.[53]

Cnut, king of England

England was split up between Edmund and Cnut after Ashingdon with much of the country going to the Danish victor though Wessex stayed in Edmund's hands. Hostages were exchanged, and the English were forced to hand over tribute in recognition of the fact that the Vikings had come out on top in the recent conflict. It is tempting to wonder how long this arrangement might have lasted if Edmund had not conveniently died within a few weeks of this deal being brokered. Various nasty ends are given by different chroniclers, ranging from the unlikely sounding demise of being impaled by a sword through the rectum while sitting on the lavatory to the rather more conventional method of poisoning given by Adam of Bremen. Whatever the reality, Cnut now had England to himself.

Following his conquest, Cnut was quick to adopt and adapt the laws of England, though pointedly these were largely those of the late, great Edgar rather than the discredited Æthelred. He was well aware of the disunity that had brought the last Anglo-Saxon king down, as shown by one of his pronouncements:

> Concerning the man who deserts his lord. And the man who through
> cowardice, deserts his lords or his comrades on a military expedition,
> either by sea or by land, shall lose all that he possesses and his own life,
> and the lord shall take back the property and the land which he had
> given him.[54]

One of Cnut's first acts was to divide England into four earldoms over which he placed lieutenants to guard his interests. His choices were interesting. East Anglia went to Thorkell, while Mercia went to Eadric Streona, the ealdorman there before the Viking invasion. Eadric had changed sides in the recent conflict with bewildering frequency but now Cnut gave him a key role, perhaps hoping to retain some continuity in a potentially troublesome region. It was an experiment that did not survive the test of time; within the year Eadric was dead, having been brutally removed on Cnut's orders; the fact that the untrustworthy ealdorman had been implicated in the deaths of several members of the family of Cnut's wife may have done him no favours.

The young children of the late Edmund Ironside were sent to the court of Óláfr Skötkonung in Sweden, allegedly with orders to dispose of them. These orders shocked the Swedish king and he arranged for them to be discretely transferred to the court of the king of Hungary, where they and their descendants continued to have an influence on British affairs for another half-century.

Northumbria went to Erik of Lade (Hladir). Erik was a trusted lieutenant and long-time supporter of Cnut. He had previously ruled in the Trøndelag on Cnut's behalf and was now given his reward in England. It was from a personal perspective just as well, for Norway would soon be lost to Cnut when the country was taken from him by Óláfr Haraldsson and Erik lost his lands there in the process too. Giving Erik Northumbria showed canny political acumen, as did the handing over of some of the power in western Mercia of the executed Eadric Streona to the earl's son, Hákon. Erik disappears from view after 1023, according to some accounts dying of blood loss after an operation, which was always a risky business given the primitive surgical conditions of the time. Other parts of Eadric's former lands were given to two more Scandinavians, Hrani and Eilaf. Charter evidence shows Hrani as being active in the region for several decades after this whereas Eilaf was to fall out of favour with Cnut within a few years.

That left Wessex, the traditional powerhouse of England, and Cnut took this for himself rather than assign responsibility for it to anyone else. His strategy in Wessex was to put in place trusted confidantes at the local level. In Dorset, charters granted lands to a group of such men with distinctive Scandinavian names: Ork, Bovi, Agemund for example. They would be there for the long term; Ork would be very much in evidence nearly four decades later.[55] They worked closely together from what we can make out, frequently appearing as each other's witnesses when grants were being made to them.

Both Ork and Bovi were described as Cnut's *huscarls,* a name anglicised as housecarl. The name was originally applied to a manservant in Old Swedish but developed to have a more specific and significant connotation as a high-status retainer, often to a king. Housecarls were in part the king's bodyguard but also had specific administrative functions. We can be doubly confident that Ork was not of English origin by statements in a surviving diploma that he had been named 'after the fashion of his own people', clearly implying that he was not of local origin.[56]

There is evidence of Scandinavian landholders in Devon too, including one with the unmistakably distinctive name 'Viking' who was also recorded as being a moneyer at Lydford (probably the same man, though it is possible that two different men with the same name are being referred to here). The position that such men held, influential at a local level, suggests a deliberate policy on Cnut's part to develop groups which would look after his own interests in the western shires of England.

Scandinavian landowners were also given lands in East Anglia. Thorkell of Harringworth was one such (not to be confused with Thorkell the Tall who he postdates in terms of his longevity, he appears in *Domesday Book* unimaginatively named Thorkell *Danus,* 'the Dane'). Another Thorkell later appears in the region, mentioned with his wife, Æthelgyth, who appears from her name to be of English origin so some intermarrying between groups of different ethnic origin is suggested here.[57]

Cnut slowly got the affairs of England in order. There is good evidence of a number of Scandinavians receiving lands in the country after Cnut's accession but also that some Anglo-Saxons who held influence beforehand continued to retain it after the event; this applied both to secular notables as well as churchmen. But this was not the whole picture; Edmund Ironside's young heirs were in danger of their life and only escaped through good fortune. Other Anglo-Saxon nobles did not long survive the change of government such as two prominent men from the West Country, Æthelweard, probably the son of a famous figure, Æthelmær the Stout (though Æthelmær is a very common Anglo-Saxon name for noblemen), and Beorhtric, son of Ælfheah who governed Devon, who were both executed. Cnut certainly had a ruthless streak that he did not hesitate to exercise when the occasion demanded it.

While the freedom from Viking raids that Cnut brought was surely welcome, it came at a significant cost. The last payment of 'Danegeld', raised to pay off portions of Cnut's army of mercenaries, was the largest yet; £72,000 from the country (an amount so large it pretty much equated to the full amount of the national wealth created in that year) and a further £10,500 specifically from London. English taxpayers groaned under the strain, but it was a measure that largely worked. There may have been a few subsequent attempts at raids on England from Viking free spirits who had no wish to be subservient to any king but the amount of damage these caused was limited. These expensive measures to pay off Cnut's Viking mercenaries is a reminder that he did not have a national Danish army behind him. Indeed, it was probably a continuation of the situation with Viking war bands for time immemorial, albeit on a grander scale. This meant that 'essentially warriors were recruited and maintained by informal, highly personalised means. They joined with, and fought for, leaders whose military prowess might guarantee material and political gain'.[58]

In 1017 Cnut married Emma, widow of the late Æthelred II. Cnut, as we have seen, was already in a relationship with another woman, Ælfgifu of Northampton, with whom he already had several sons; Harold 'Harefoot' and Sveinn, would later play a part in royal affairs. The decision to marry Emma, already a queen of England, helped to further cement relations between that country and Denmark. Less opportunely it also entangled English with Norman affairs with ultimately catastrophic results for Anglo-Saxon England in 1066.

The *Encomium* implies that the marriage between Cnut and Emma was entered into voluntarily by the bride. The writer suggests that she made her way over from Normandy and was pleased to be joined in matrimony to the new king of England. Other accounts, such as those found in the *ASC*, suggest an alternative situation. They imply that Emma was taken prisoner and that her marriage to Cnut was essentially a matter in which she had little say. Such pressurised marital arrangements were far from unique, and it is possible that Emma was forced to become Cnut's wife whether she wished to or not. Thietmar of Merseburg gives a confusing account which lends some support to the latter theory. He suggests that Emma was trapped in London by the Danish army, which he says was led by both Cnut and his brother Harald, and that there was no obvious means of escape. Cnut offered her her freedom if she paid over a massive tribute and also gave him her two sons, Edward and Alfred, for execution. These demands understandably disturbed her greatly; but she appeared to have little option but to comply. However, her two sons escaped by boat and reached freedom. This hardly appears to be a happy basis on which to build a married life.[59]

There are indirect hints that the match did not meet with the approval of Emma's family back in Normandy. A book written at the time by Emma's brother, Robert, the archbishop of Rouen, has a satirical account of how a queen, Semiramis, after her death began a supernatural and distasteful affair with a bull. It has been suggested that the queen is an alternative representation of Emma and the bull is Cnut. This would suggest if it is true that some of Emma's family were outraged at her marriage to the new king of England.[60]

Emma had Danish blood flowing through her veins via her mother, Gunnor, at one time the mistress of Richard I, ruler of Normandy, and later his wife. The contemporary chronicler Dudo stated unequivocally that Gunnor was 'from the noblest house of the Danes' and if this is correct she was clearly of high status.[61] However, there is evidence that this is an exaggeration of her real background and that she was more probably of humbler Danish settler stock in Normandy.[62] Nevertheless, Emma would prove to be a significant if not always successful political player in her own right.

Cnut was very keen to emphasise his credentials as a king of England –after all he only held the title through right of conquest – and sought to reinforce this by establishing his main base in Winchester, traditionally linked with the old line of Anglo-Saxon monarchs, even though London was by now rising significantly in importance in economic and political terms and a sizeable Viking garrison had been installed close by, probably at Southwark. It would be anachronistic to call Winchester his capital for such a concept did not really exist at the time; kings were peripatetic and travelled around their territories to be seen by the people and perform administrative and legal functions. But Cnut marked London down as hostile territory given its previous strong support for the old regime. Even the Church there suffered as he gave strong support to a local rival, the then insignificant monastic establishment at Westminster.[63]

Cnut also made generous gifts in Winchester to his wife Emma on the occasion of their marriage, which might have also taken place there (though we do not know this for sure). There is evidence of higher than normal Danish activity in the city during Cnut's reign through the presence of many humble items in the archaeological record such as combs in the Danish fashion (some Scandinavian craftsmen were renowned as skilled comb makers and took great pride in the fact; one example found in Lincoln has an inscription which proudly stated that 'Thorfast made a good comb'). Other references hint at the development of *skaldic* poetry in the Norse fashion in Winchester.[64]

Emma was no meek cipher in this set-up. She took an active role in the government of England. She was an ambitious, self-motivated woman who had little compunction in leaving her children, Edward, Alfred and Godgifu, in Normandy for several decades while she took on her repeat role as queen of England. In contrast to the norm with Anglo-Saxon queens she appears regularly as a signatory to charters, high up the list of those who were witnesses, sometimes next in the pecking order after the king himself. And, although Cnut had children from a previous relationship with Ælfgifu of Northampton, Sveinn and Harold Harefoot, Emma insisted that those born from her marriage to him should take precedence in the line of succession. This created a future problem that would come back to haunt the players in this particular play with a plotline that would do Shakespeare justice.

Cnut issued his own legal code, substantially modelled on that of Edgar, adopting it at a great conference held at Oxford in 1018. It had some important clauses in it. One attempted to prevent the selling of slaves from England to heathens, especially those abroad. Despite this, it appears likely that the trade continued. One story told by William of Malmesbury states that Cnut's sister-in-law Gytha, the wife of Godwine, a rising star in the English firmament, procured English slaves for sale outside the country with a particular focus on pregnant women.[65]

Cnut was able to secure his position in England partly because a number of important Englishmen such as Godwine changed sides; *The Life of King Edward* says that Godwine's marriage was in part a reward for services he had given to Cnut during a campaign in Denmark early in his reign.[66] The importance of Godwine and other Englishmen's position can be inferred from the listing of their names on charters issued during Cnut's reign and in a number of cases seem to be those of men who were also acting in the same capacity during Æthelred's reign. It was shocking, even at the time, that some of them were prominent Anglo-Saxons who had already proved disloyal during the battles fought by Edmund Ironside while he had been alive.[67]

Establishing an Anglo-Danish Empire

Establishing stability in England was critically important to the next development in Cnut's career. When Harald, Cnut's brother and the ruling king of Denmark, died in 1019 it meant that Cnut could leave England for a while and concentrate on establishing himself as his replacement, an ambition he successfully achieved. Cnut told his English subjects that the reason for his absence in Denmark was to ensure that no more Viking raids came from there; in reality, it is more likely that he went there to take the country for himself. For much of the next decade he spent significant amounts of time on the Continent. This was only possible because he had established a viable administration to run England in his absence.

Not least among Cnut's strategies were his vigorous attempts to build relationships with the English Church. He inherited two archbishops from his predecessor, Lyfing of Canterbury and Wulfstan of York. He seems to have got on well with both of them and early on made gifts, perhaps to curry favour with them as much as for the good of his spiritual health.[68] It is widely believed that it was Wulfstan who was behind two legal codes issued by Cnut, in 1018 and 1020. The preamble to one of them encourages the people of England to 'love King Cnut with due loyalty'. This perhaps sounds an unremarkable statement until it is remembered that this is a Christian archbishop writing on behalf of a man who some would argue was a Viking king. Neither was Wulfstan the first archbishop to reach an accommodation with Scandinavian conquerors; as far back as 872, when there was an anti-Viking revolt in York the incumbent archbishop, Wulfhere, had fled the city, conceivably because he was rather too closely associated with the enemy. This is a reminder of just how complex the Viking world could be.

It was not all plain sailing back in England while Cnut was away from her shores. There was a falling-out with Thorkell who was exiled to Denmark in 1021. Although there is very limited evidence to explain why this happened, what there is suggests that Thorkell had been creating problems in Cnut's absence from England and that his wife, whose precise identity is unclear, was also implicated in some way. It seems strange that Thorkell now went to Denmark, a place far away from Cnut in England where it appeared much easier for him to stir up trouble. Two years later Cnut was forced to journey back to Denmark, possibly because Thorkell was again proving problematic. It is significant that he took with him forces from England, apparently including Earl Godwine. Earl Erik became the leading figure in Thorkell's absence, though this situation did not continue for very long due to his death a few years later.[69]

There were other signs that Cnut was not yet fully secure in his position in England. In 1020, Æthelweard, the ealdorman of the western part of Wessex (which seems to have been split into two for administrative purposes at the time), was declared an outlaw and disappears from view thereafter, either dead or in exile. That suggests a decisive move on Cnut's part, perhaps responding to a fit of pique from the ealdorman who may have been unhappy at the way in which some of Cnut's Scandinavian supporters were being given generous grants of land in Dorset.

Cnut came up with a masterstroke when he appointed the Anglo-Saxon, Godwine, to take over in Wessex and become in effect his deputy in England in the longer term, a decision that he had no reason to look back on with regret. He also advanced the interests of Scandinavians and one of them, Thored, commenced a career in England that was to last for the next three decades; he appears frequently in charters throughout this period (there may perhaps have been two men with the same name involved) and snippets of information about him exist but his impact on longer-term history was limited.[70] Alongside men who were of Anglo-Saxon stock such as Odda and Ælfgar Mæw, who had acted the part of double agents in the fight against Edmund Ironside, this was a council that managed to carefully strike a balance between indigenous and Scandinavian interests.

Ælfgar is an interesting figure and perhaps can stand as a surrogate example for all those indigenous leaders who facilitated the task of the Scandinavians, whether as raiders or conquerors, by their cooperation, whether that be in England, wider Britain, Ireland or Francia. He came from an important family and his father, Æthelweard, had played an integral part in establishing the fortunes of two Benedictine monastic establishments at Cranborne in Dorset and Tewkesbury in Gloucestershire; indeed, the two would remain sister houses for another 600 years until that later destroyer of the monasteries, Henry VIII, came along and brought the existence of both to a shuddering halt. It was even suggested by the later *Tewkesbury Chronicle* that Ælfgar was descended from the bloodline of the early tenth-century English king, Edward the Elder.[71]

Ælfgar succeeded to the family fortune on his father's death. He appears as a witness to charters during the reign of Æthelred II, showing that he remained in favour during his reign. He took part, ostensibly supporting Edmund Ironside, in the battles against Cnut; and here we have the first sign of a problem. After the Battle of Sherston, reports emerged that at the crucial moment in the fight he switched sides.[72] He was not alone in this change of allegiance; John of Worcester suggests there were men from both Hampshire and Wiltshire fighting for the 'Danish' side there. Edmund was far from commanding universal respect among his own people. The evidence that Ælfgar was what we would now call a 'collaborator' at Sherston is not perhaps decisive; what appears to be so is the fact that Ælfgar later appears as a witness on charters issued during Cnut's reign. His career continued after the regime change and in many ways his position seems to have improved. His son, Beorhtric, was a major player in later politics though his position collapsed after the Norman Conquest; *Domesday Book* quoted him as being the wealthiest thegn in the kingdom below the rank of earl. Men like Ælfgar Mæw appear to have done rather well out of Cnut's triumph.

It has been suggested that this was not morally acceptable even at the time and that Wulfstan, the archbishop of York, had been particularly scathing in his criticism of such turncoats.[73] Wulfstan was a formidable figure, yet he is an unfortunate witness against the evils of collaboration for he too made the transition from being a major figure in Æthelred's government to being one in that of Cnut. He might have argued that the ends justified the means and that he was able to significantly shape Cnut's rule, for the new king's law codes owe much to him. But the fact remains that he also transferred his allegiance. Men of position across the western world appear to have had a very flexible conscience when their own interests were involved, and this was something that prominent Scandinavians such as Cnut and even those Vikings who were active in the ninth century in Britain, Ireland or Francia were able to adroitly exploit.

In Britain, Cnut looked outside the borders of England to strengthen his position. Anglo-Saxon monarchs such as Æthelstan and Edgar had received the homage of kings from Scotland and Cnut sought to emulate them. The Burgundian chronicler Ralph Glaber, writing as a virtually contemporary recorder, stated that Cnut and the king of the Scots, Mael Coluim ('Malcolm') fought for some time but were brought to the peace table by Duke Richard ('the Fearless') of Normandy, the brother of Cnut's wife Emma. The dukes of Normandy showed a remarkable talent for being able to run with both the hare and the hounds. Over the years they had given the Vikings sanctuary while at the same time not being completely unsupportive to the English royal family. It was a remarkable exercise in being able to walk along a very thin tightrope without actually falling off it.

Cnut stood as godfather for Malcolm's son at his baptism ceremony. This must have taken place before 1026 if Ralph's account is correct for that was the year in which Duke Richard died. Cnut's sister, Estrith (whose Christian name was Margaret), was offered as a bride for one of the Norman dynasty (which one is a matter of some contention, though it was probably Duke Robert I, whose son William was destined to play a critical part in future English history). But this marriage never took place and she was instead wedded to Ulf, a Danish nobleman who for a time served with Cnut in England.

There is circumstantial evidence that Sitriuc Silkbeard and Cnut entered into an agreement. Sveinn Forkbeard had been active in the Irish

Sea for a time and there had been close connections between Dublin and York in the past. Now Sitriuc needed allies: even with Brian Boru dead after Clontarf, Sitriuc's position in Ireland remained insecure. Entering into an alliance of some form with Cnut, possibly even recognising him as his nominal overlord, made a lot of political sense. Coinage provides some of the circumstantial evidence for connections between Cnut and Sitriuc. A Hiberno-Norse coin of Sitriuc's reign, boldly carrying the legend 'Sitriuc, king of the Irish', seems to be modelled on Cnut's quatrefoil silver penny. It has been suggested that the coin was minted in Chester.[74] Eleventh-century kings were very jealous of their moneyers and would not have turned a blind eye to one of them minting coins for another king. Control of the coinage was a very direct way of controlling the economy; every so often, the existing coinage would be called in and replaced by a new version. Taxes would be levied as part of the process and kings would therefore be able to top up their coffers as a result. Three different pennies were issued during Cnut's reign as one example of how this money-making enterprise actually worked. A king would therefore be very jealous of protecting his rights to issue and control coinage. It is very likely therefore that, if the moneyer in Chester was minting coins on behalf of Sitriuc, then he was doing so with Cnut's express approval.

Cnut's ambitions went far beyond England. In Denmark, he was reunited with Thorkell. There seems to have been a reconciliation at some stage and Thorkell was even appointed as his regent in the country and the two men exchanged sons in a fostering arrangement that gave some hint of an improved relationship between them. However, Thorkell disappears from the record soon after, a situation that causes one to fear for him and his ongoing survival prospects. One work, the *Translatio Sancti Ælfegi*, suggests that he met his end at the hands of a mob in Denmark, though the extent, if any, of Cnut's involvement in this violent conclusion is not mentioned.

Nevertheless, Denmark posed a conundrum for Cnut. He could not be in two places at once and had been away in England for the past few years. Perhaps in an effort to strengthen his position there, his sister Estrith had been married to Jarl Ulf who was an important figure in Denmark. On the face of it, it was a sound political move; but it was an arrangement that would not survive the passage of time. Harthacnut, Cnut's young son, also took up residence in Denmark as a way of providing a token presence to govern on his behalf. Harthacnut was far too young to rule in his own right but he was an important symbolic figurehead to help cement Cnut's position in the country.

Cnut wanted to add Norway to his territories and may also have had problems with the independent spirit of the inhabitants of Skåne. From what we can tell, Skåne was often a source of tension for the kings of

Denmark. At one time, there was an important settlement in the region at a place called Uppåkra where some stunning archaeological finds have been uncovered.[75] Skåne went into steep decline during the reigns of Sveinn and Cnut and an alternative settlement developed nearby at Lund, possibly a royal alternative to the traditional main town of the *jarls* of Skåne whose independent spirit could no longer be tolerated.

As it happened Cnut was about to face a major challenge that focussed his attentions on Scandinavia for a while. He had made many enemies there just by virtue of his success and ambition. Those in the region who felt threatened by Cnut's rise to power were about to fight back. The North Sea Empire, extended over a wide range of territory, was proving difficult to sustain; and the situation was not about to improve.

12

Emperors, Saints and Legends (1026–1050)

...by God's gracious mercy there came for the English, who had suffered so long under the yoke of the barbarians, the jubilee of their redemption...

The Life of King Edward

The Battle of Holy River

Two figures in particular played a shadowy part in the events of the next few years. They would demonstrate that those we might call 'collaborators' were not just a problem for the enemies of the Vikings. One of them, Ulf, was Cnut's brother-in-law. He is recorded as witnessing a charter in England in 1022 so was present in the country then but he seems to have returned to Denmark soon after. When Cnut's young son Harthacnut was sent to Denmark to become its titular ruler, the experienced Ulf was the one who was designated to hold actual power until the boy came of age. Cnut presumably thought that his brother-in-law would be a reliable ally allowing him to concentrate his attentions elsewhere. It was an enormous error of judgement.

Another individual in whom Cnut unwisely put his trust was a man named Eilaf. There was someone of that name that Cnut gave lands to in Mercia; the Welsh *Annales Cambriae* record him as leading a raid along the south coast of Wales in 1022 or 1023. By 1024, he disappeared from the English record and resurfaced back in Denmark. This may have been a move on Cnut's part to appoint another experienced, reliable ally there. If so, again, this was a mistake.

The danger to Cnut was greater because he did not just have internal opponents to concern him. Norway was ruled by Óláfr Haraldsson who knew that Cnut desired his lands and it would only be a matter of time before he tried to take them. Óláfr had consolidated power in Norway over the previous decade while Sveinn Forkbeard and Cnut had been focusing their attentions elsewhere. He was an advocate of Christianity, in the imposition of which he was supported by an English bishop called Grimkel, but many in Norway opposed his religious views, which threatened his position there.

To the east, the Swedish king, Anund Jakob, was also nervous. He was the son of Óláfr ('Olof') Skötkonung who had been a successful ruler and an ally of Sveinn and Cnut for a time, having initially been concerned by the ambitions of the former Norwegian king, Óláfr Tryggvason. Now, however, the pendulum had swung the other way; Óláfr Haraldsson had formed an alliance with the late Óláfr Skötkonung (who died in 1022) by marrying his daughter Astrid. Adam of Bremen suggests that the Swedes and the Norwegians were generally on good terms with each other, perhaps brought together by what they saw as a common threat coming from the direction of an ambitious and expansionist Denmark.[1]

The combined forces of Óláfr and Anund descended on Denmark, focusing their attentions on Skåne. On hearing the news, Cnut, who was then in England, quickly assembled a fleet and sailed for Denmark where he joined up with his allies in the country. The combined Norwegian and Swedish fleet made its way east across the Baltic and Cnut gave chase. He caught up with them either in Skåne or in Uppland in Sweden. A battle followed at what was called Helgeå ('Holy River'). The chronicles sometimes fail to provide a clear explanation of events and the accounts they give as to this specific battle are as confusing as any. It is not even clear who won it so perhaps the most logical conclusion is that it was particularly hard-fought and both sides retreated to lick their wounds. The *ASC* took a particular interest in this battle, with the 'E' (Peterborough) version of the Chronicle suggesting that a number of English soldiers lost their lives fighting in Cnut's army.

This was one of those events in which what happened next was more important than the battle itself. A later work, *The Older Saga of St Olaf*, suggests that Cnut got his fleet to blockade the narrow Øresund, which certainly is a plausible reason to explain subsequent events. The Swedes, on the right side of the blockade, so to speak, could simply return home. The Norwegians could not. Eventually the truth dawned on the trapped Norwegians that the only way to extricate themselves was to march back home overland. This was difficult at the best of times but now assumed nightmare proportions as winter was approaching and those who were with the Norwegian fleet had not expected to be in this position, so were ill-equipped for the conditions. As was to be the case in Napoleon's Retreat from Moscow, the losses among the retreating Norwegians were probably horrendous.[2]

Cnut returned to Denmark and took his revenge on those who he felt had let him down in the recent conflict. The major victim was his brother-in-law Ulf, who died shortly afterwards. The circumstances of his death are rooted in controversy for it appears that Ulf was killed inside the walls of Roskilde Cathedral. Some accounts suggest that this followed on from the disputed result of a board game that Cnut and Ulf had played (though this may be a *topos* as board games play a part in other events of the period, for example they are mentioned in Irish accounts of the Vikings leading up to the Battle of Clontarf).[3] Cnut made reparations to his sister Estrith by giving funds towards the building of her favourite church at Roskilde, but such compensation cannot disguise the ruthlessness with which he protected his interests when he felt them to be threatened. Estrith's marriage was marked by tragedy in more ways than one; a son, Harald, was later murdered in Germany on the way back from Rome in a spat over a breach of protocol.[4] Being a member of Cnut's family clearly did not guarantee an easy life.

The Rome visit

Cnut's visit to Rome in 1027 marked a coming of age, both for himself and for Scandinavia generally. It served several purposes. Attendance at the coronation of the new Holy Roman Emperor, Conrad II, was an important symbolic moment, sealing an alliance between him and Cnut. In Germany, Conrad now had space to deal with the troublesome tribes to the east while Cnut was free to sort out unfinished business in Scandinavia. Pending his return, Cnut wrote to his subjects in England with justifiable pride of how he had been received with honour and showered with valuable gifts. This was the political side of the agenda.

Being welcomed by Pope John XIX gave Cnut something else; acceptance. It meant that he was formally recognised as a Christian king and that he and his kingdoms joined the mainstream of nations; Denmark especially, was no longer outside the pale but firmly integrated within it. This served a strong political purpose too. It allowed Church and State to support each other to mutual benefit. A strong king furthered the cause of the Church and helped to build its power, especially in lands that were relatively new to Christianity. By the same token, the Church gave a king legitimacy and, by focussing on the sacred nature of his crowning and appointment as a monarch, emphasised the solemn covenant between him and his people, which could not be broken without seriously threatening the spiritual well-being of those who chose to do so. Cnut played the part of the pious pilgrim well. He was liberal with his gifts to the churches and monastic establishments he passed on his way to Rome, weeping tears of emotion as he ostentatiously did so.

This convenient alliance of mutual interests was not a new idea – it has been said of another great European ruler of times past that 'power politics supposedly blessed by sacramental agency is the emperor Constantine's fateful legacy' – and the concept of 'sacral kingship' was one that Cnut fully understood and sought to benefit from.[5] There was nothing idealistic about this; in some ways it was something of an unholy alliance. Both parties to the bargain understood that they were putting themselves in a mutually supportive arrangement whereby they could obtain and exploit power over others. It is interesting that the decline of Carolingian Francia coincided with the weakening of links between the Church and State within it; on the other hand, the link remained strong in Ottonian Germany which was a supreme irony as this was a region whose hub was Saxony, the precise spot where Charlemagne had launched his brutal campaign of forced conversion a century or so earlier. Cnut and other Danish rulers such as Harald Bluetooth who strengthened relationships between themselves and the Church had the Ottonian example close to hand to emulate.

That Christianity played a key role in building national identities in Europe and shaping them around this alliance between Church and State (or more pertinently king) is a widely held view. As one commentator remarked 'conversion was ... the single most important element in the fabrication of identities right across Europe'.[6] Scandinavia might have come late to the game, but the important point is that come to the game it did. Such conversions played a catastrophic part in encouraging many parts of Europe to march down the road that led to Jerusalem and the Crusades, a sequence of events that was only just over half a century into the future. The role of Scandinavian crusaders in these later expeditions is sometimes overlooked.

These events in Rome played to Cnut's imperial pretensions, which seem to have been inspired by his interaction with the leading powers of Europe who were in the city. The fight for Norway was still unfinished and taking it would add to his status. It is noteworthy that after returning from Rome he had an imperial crown made in the style of Conrad's. This was seemingly an age when to be a king on its own was no longer enough. Earlier in the century, Brian Boru had styled himself emperor of Ireland; and in the previous century Æthelstan had called himself the *basileus* of Britain, a Byzantine imperial term. Cnut did not want to be left out. Significantly, when on his way back from Rome he wrote to his subjects in England referring to himself as the king of England, Denmark, Norway and part of Sweden – a somewhat clunky description perhaps, but one that carries with it unmistakable pretensions to imperial power and status. The achievements and elevated status of Charlemagne had set a benchmark that others desired to emulate. Perhaps this pretension was also reflected in Cnut's shipbuilding exploits. The largest longship yet discovered was excavated at the dockyard at Roskilde, Denmark, in 1996–7. It had thirty-nine or forty pairs of oars, a truly titanic vessel by Viking standards. Unimaginatively now named *Roskilde 6* (one wonders what the makers of the *Long Serpent* would make of this insipid title?), it was built in around 1025, when Cnut was approaching the height of his powers. As its timbers have been identified as coming from southern Norway, an equally intriguing possibility might be that it was made for Óláfr Haraldsson, Cnut's main opponent, and might therefore have been captured from him and taken back to Denmark.

Rome had achieved predominance as the foremost site of Christian pilgrimage, especially as Jerusalem had been in Islamic hands for centuries, so for Cnut, and many other contemporary European rulers, it had iconic status. Although there were still instances of pilgrimages to the Holy Land itself, they were dangerous to make and only two decades before, Christians there had been persecuted by the Fatimid caliph al-Hakim. Rome was an altogether more achievable, if still not easy or danger-free, ambition for pilgrims. There was a Saxon quarter there on the banks of the Tiber, not far from St Peter's, and it is likely that Cnut took up residence there where more than one Anglo-Saxon king had spent the twilight years of their lives after giving up the trappings of earthly glory. The Church of Santa Spirito in Sassia marks the site of the old Anglo-Saxon *schola* (hostel) first erected there in the eighth century though it is now home to a rather unassuming and externally plain (by Roman standards) sixteenth-century church.

Conrad's coronation took place in Old St Peter's. The glorious Renaissance art of the building we see today is very different from the vision that would have met Cnut's eyes. Old St Peter's was erected as a basilica in the fourth century. It did not apparently change much between then and the sixteenth century when Michelangelo weaved his magic on it but then the rebuild was total.[7] There are other old churches in Rome, such as that of Santa Sabina, where one can still get a sense of what it would have been like for Cnut to stand in such a building for the first time; a long way indeed from the wooden stave churches of his native Scandinavia. He would have seen a series of antique columns, neatly organised and referring back to the magnificent classical heritage of the greatest city of Antiquity, one that had inspired more recent leaders such as Charlemagne with their own imperial vision. And he would be standing, almost literally, on the mortal remains of Peter, founder of the Church of Rome, apostle of Christ and early martyr.

There was also a personal spiritual element to Cnut's visit to Rome. Although the city was much diminished from its imperial heyday and its population was just a fraction of what it had been then, the development of Christianity had, in some ways, given it a new lease of life. For this was the eternal resting place of the great Christian saints Peter and Paul, not to mention many other martyrs, and since the sixth century the pilgrim trade to the city had been growing rapidly. Hostels (*scholae*) for visiting pilgrims had developed and north Europeans were particularly enthusiastic visitors. These *scholae* were crammed around St Peter's, the spiritual epicentre of Western Christendom in which Cnut clearly aspired to be a leading player. His journey to Rome reads like a classic pilgrim's progress with frequent stops at important monasteries *en route* and spontaneous outbursts of religious emotion. Perhaps those who wrote up the accounts of the journey were using formulaic motifs to express Cnut's conventional Christian piety; but it is possible that the king saw this as part of his own personal spiritual journey. Certainly he wrote after his visit of how he would 'amend my life from now on in all things'. He even ostentatiously informed his officials to avoid inequitable tax collection on his behalf 'for I have no need that money should be amassed by me by unjust exaction', a very atypical comment from a Viking ruler.

Cnut became a strong champion of the Church. In England he and Emma became patrons of some of the leading religious establishments. Best known was their support of the Old Minster in Winchester but other places received assistance such as Abingdon, Shaftesbury and Sherborne. While Cnut no doubt obtained political advantage for his support of Christianity, he also comes across as a man of genuine religious conviction and his journey to Rome as, to an extent, a real pilgrimage. Another way in which he showed his Christian credentials was by translating relics of English saints to new locations; Ælfheah, the murdered archbishop of Canterbury, from St Paul's in London to Canterbury Cathedral, Saint Mildreth from Thanet to St Augustine's Abbey in Canterbury and St Wystan from Repton to Evesham.

The archbishop of Canterbury for most of his reign was Æthelnoth who replaced the incumbent Lyfing when he died in 1020; Cnut was particularly generous in his grants to the archbishop in Kent during his reign. The cleric was an aggressive champion of the English version of the faith too, for the overwhelming power of the Papacy had not yet fully developed and it was by no means unusual for the clerisy of one country to find themselves in competition with those of another. Such was the case in Cnut's reign where priests from England were sent to Denmark, much to the chagrin of supporters of the archbishops of Hamburg-Bremen who saw it as being on their patch.

However, there was seemingly a good deal of ambiguity concerning religion to contend with, especially from some of his Scandinavian subjects. Earlier in his reign, Cnut had issued a set of laws – drafted by Wulfstan, his fiery archbishop of York – containing injunctions against witchcraft, divination, the worship of idols and heathen sacrifice.[8] Such caveats were not unique to England. In Ireland, where conversions to Christianity among the Hiberno-Norse community were certainly taking place, there was a grove of trees outside Dublin which was deemed to be sacred to Thor; this was attacked and destroyed on several occasions by Irish kings.[9] A number of Cnut's leading supporters were seemingly still of pagan persuasion, the earls of Lade as one example being renowned for their fierce attachment to the old ways.

It is possible, though not likely, that Cnut visited Rome more than once. One version of the *ASC* notes that he was in Rome in 1031. This might be a case of an error by the scribe; or possibly there were two visits. Certainly, Cnut seems to have spent much less time in England between 1027 and 1031, in large part presumably because he was occupied with the planned conquest of Norway and needed to be close at hand to supervise it, as well as needing to ensure that Denmark was now firmly under his control again. In the meantime, the government of England was left in the hands of his council and in particular his trusted lieutenant, Earl Godwine.

The imperial coronation was the culmination of a process that had been in train for a while. The Holy Roman Emperor was a position that had essentially evolved from the former Carolingian Emperors though he was based in Germany (the east of Francia, as it formerly was), but the incumbent was elected and did not merely inherit a right to the imperial throne. Conrad had been one of several potential candidates. A possible alternative, Duke William V of Aquitaine, received precious gifts from Cnut. There are few obvious reasons why Cnut should have done this: Aquitaine was a long way from his main sphere of interest. The most logical reason Cnut might choose to make friendly overtures towards him was he was a rival to Conrad and, at that time, that suited Cnut's interests.[10]

Conrad, based in Germany, was very definitely in Cnut's sphere of influence. His lands abutted Denmark, but they were also adjacent to those of the Poles, who had been particularly aggressive in the past two decades or so. Eventually, Conrad came out on top in the election and Cnut was forced to accept this. But the Anglo-Danish king had made clear that he was not a man to be ignored and Conrad decided to build an alliance with him. The Poles on his eastern border were the more dangerous threat and Cnut also welcomed friendly relations as it freed him to resolve the problem of Norway. A peace agreement between Conrad and Cnut served mutual interests. It was the start of a longer-term process that included, a decade later, the marriage of Cnut's daughter Gunnhild to Henry, Conrad's son, though Cnut would not be around to see it eventually take place.

Cnut the Great

Cnut had a complex, multi-faceted character. While he could play the part of warrior as required of a Viking leader, he also understood the importance of diplomacy, crucial given the wide extent of the territories he ruled. Cnut's achievement in managing to hold together this extended empire, though not without its challenges and occasional hiccups, was exceptional; he was fully deserving of the epithet 'great', every bit as much as Alfred. Ironically, the main testament to his greatness was how quickly his empire evaporated after his death.

After the Battle of Holy River, Cnut had unfinished business to attend to in Norway. Óláfr's pre-emptive strike had backfired on him and he cannot have been surprised when Cnut prepared to add Norway to his expanding empire. Yet Cnut's approach this time was not so much a military as a political one. Óláfr had many subjects in Norway who were not well disposed towards him. These included the supporters of the earls of Lade who had never taken to Óláfr and his Christianising tendencies. To exploit these tensions, when Cnut eventually led a fleet towards Norway it included among its numbers Hákon, son of the now-deceased Erik of Lade, the long-time supporter of Sveinn Forkbeard and Cnut. Other prominent opponents of Óláfr included a leading Norwegian figure, Kálfr Árnason. He was recorded as being at Cnut's court and seems to have been promised substantial benefits if he helped Cnut conquer Norway. The end result was that when Cnut sent a fleet of fifty ships to Norway,[11] with his ship decked out in gold to emphasise his magnificence and power, resistance to him quickly evaporated.

Óláfr survived but his kingdom was gone. He escaped to fight another day. Cnut rewarded those who had helped him add Norway to his dominions and some of those Norwegians who had left while Óláfr was at the helm now returned. Cnut triumphed, partly because of his own generosity and political acumen and partly due to the weaknesses of Óláfr who had failed to retain the loyalty of his people. The catastrophic aftermath of the Battle of Holy River had destroyed his reputation; for a Viking ruler to be associated with a disaster like this was a personal catastrophe. It seems to have been a bloodless coup on Cnut's part. Snorri Sturluson later wrote that 'everyone he got to know and who seemed to him to be a man of some mettle and inclined to attach himself to him, got his handfuls of money'. Bribery could be as effective as warfare.

The *ASC* states that after Cnut eventually returned to England from Rome after sorting out his Scandinavian affairs, he journeyed north to Scotland to take the homage of Malcolm and two sub-kings, Maelbaethe (possibly 'Macbeth' of Shakespeare fame though not everybody agrees with this identification)[12] and Echmarcach, son of Ragnall. We are told that the king of Scotland 'surrendered' to Cnut. This was presumably a symbolic ceremony as the *Chronicles* suggest that it made little difference in practice as Malcolm 'became his man but observed it little time'.[13] But it was another example of re-asserting old rights from the great days of Anglo-Saxon monarchs such as Æthelstan and Edgar who had allegedly received similar declarations of homage from the other rulers of Britain.

Echmarcach is something of a forgotten figure in accounts of the Viking Age but there are suggestions that he was a leading figure of his time. He was twice king of Dublin, from 1036 to 1038 and 1046 to 1052. When he was finally ejected from Dublin in 1052 by the Irish king, Diarmait of Leinster, he may then have been involved in raids on Anglesey and eventually ended up on the Isle of Man. However, accounts that he finally died in Wales are often disputed by historians, given evidence that he breathed his last in Rome in 1065.[14] Echmarcach is also recorded as being the king of the 'Rhinns of Galloway', Galloway being a region where Viking presence and even ownership has often been posited but written records to confirm this are sadly absent; even the borders of the territory are very unclear. However, the very name Galloway suggests a Scandinavian presence; it probably derives from the phrase *Gallgoidil* (foreigners-Gaels), suggesting that the inhabitants were of joint Norse-Gaelic origin.

Archaeological evidence of Viking presence in Galloway is limited but includes several Viking-style graves. There was a thriving trading centre at Whithorn, a site that was very important for its religious connotations and historical links with St Ninian, and some of the buildings found there suggest architectural connections to Dublin and Waterford. Although not much is known for certain about Viking Galloway, it has been suggested that a ruling Viking elite moved in there in the late tenth/early eleventh century. This is a period when the emergence of Brian Boru in Ireland was limiting opportunities there and forcing Vikings from the island to look further afield for new challenges.[15] Galloway was conveniently close at hand for such men.

Cnut possibly wanted to ensure that Mael Coluim's ambitions did not run away with him. Over a decade before, the king of Alba won an important victory over the Northumbrians at the Battle of Carham.[16] After Cnut's triumph in England, the northern part of Northumbria, Bernicia, stayed largely independent though the Danish part of the region, Deira and York in particular, formed an integral part of Cnut's kingdom. Given this, Cnut perhaps did not mind too much that the quasi-independent Bernicia had been taught a painful lesson by the Scots at Carham. But ten years on, it was time to vigorously assert his right to rule over all of Northumbria and ensure that the Scots knew their place.

It seems probable that the still-independent kingdom of Strathclyde was subject to some firm discipline on Cnut's part too. Strathclyde has few written records for this period and there are only scant mentions of affairs there in English or Scottish chronicles. Therefore, we have to make the most of any fleeting reference we come across. One such is found in the *Annals of Tigernach*. For the year 1030, there is the following small but significant entry: 'Ravaging of the Britons by the English and the Foreigners of Dublin'.[17] With some informed speculation, a bit of flesh can be added to these meagre bones. The 'Britons' were probably the people of Strathclyde while the 'English' are presumably those who were now subject to Cnut, most likely those from Northumbria, close to the borders. The 'Foreigners of Dublin' are clearly the Scandinavians from that place so there now seemed to be some sort of alliance between them and Cnut. The raids may have been devastating – 'ravaged' is a very descriptive word although it is frequently used in chronicles of the time – and it might help to explain why an independent Strathclyde did not survive beyond the eleventh century. Surrounded by powerful and assertive neighbours on all sides, the life was being crushed out of the British kingdom. In political terms, this was a Darwinian conflict, one that Strathclyde was evidently losing.

It has been plausibly suggested that this was a time when Hiberno-Norse contingents were active in Anglesey, again in alliance with the English with their Danish king, Cnut. Given the difficult position of the Hiberno-Norse in Dublin after Clontarf, widening horizons to take in Wales as a bolthole in times of trouble in Ireland was a wise move. It also allowed Viking ships to protect trade routes between Chester and Dublin. It appears that Sitriuc's son, Godfrey, was killed in Wales in 1036, and that Sitriuc abdicated in the same year and disappeared from view, again quite possibly in Wales.[18] Just a few years before, in around 1033, there was a Sitriuc witnessing several of Cnut's charters in England. Although it is possible there was another man of this name at Cnut's court, it is tempting to think that this is evidence of links between Sitriuc Silkbeard and Cnut.[19] The existence of a trading outpost from the men of Dublin in London at around this time has also been suggested in recent years.[20]

Even a resolute Viking leader like Sitriuc was now seeing the benefits of adopting Christianity. He journeyed to Rome in 1028, in the company of the king of Brega. Returning, he founded a cathedral in the heart of Dublin. But in 1031 a raid on Ardbraccan, near Kells, left 200 people dead, burned alive in their church, while a similar number were taken away as fodder for the slave markets. However, the ageing Sitriuc's days were numbered. In a dispute with the ruling dynasty of Waterford, its king, Ragnall, was murdered while visiting Dublin in 1035. Soon after, Sitriuc was forced to abdicate, possibly having bitten off more than he could chew, and was then exiled in Wales where he died in 1042. He had been driven out of Dublin by another Hiberno-Norse figure, Echmarcach son of Ragnall, making another appearance; his father was the former king of Waterford who had been killed by Sitriuc's men.

Sitriuc has been described as 'for the most part a small-time operator in [an] unstable environment. From time to time he engaged in disputes with his near neighbours north and south. His kingdom was smaller territorially than is sometimes supposed and its military capacity quite limited'. The latter part of this statement is given credence by his need to recruit Viking forces from elsewhere in the Clontarf campaign. In some ways, he was a throwback to the past, raiding and pillaging even against Christian targets (though it should be pointed out that indigenous Irish sub-kings were doing so too) and the contrast with the imperial pretensions of Cnut could not be more marked. In this relationship Sitriuc was very much the junior partner. But in other ways Sitriuc was definitely part of a new age. His adoption of Christianity is one obvious example of this. In Ireland, some of the Vikings appear to have come to this pass quite late, compared to some of their contemporaries; evidence of pagan totems still in use in Ireland have been found that can be dated to the early eleventh century. Because his military resources were relatively weak, Sitriuc looked further afield for allies to maintain his position; to the islands off the north of Scotland, to the Isle of Man and probably it would seem to England (not just during Cnut's reign but also before that with Æthelred II). He adopted English-style coinage and despite losing Dublin on several occasions usually came bouncing back until old age caught up with him. In short, Sitriuc was first and foremost a survivor.[21]

That Dublin stayed wealthy despite the outcome of Clontarf is evidenced by the size of the massive ransom that was paid for the release of Óláfr, Sitriuc's son, in 1029. This included 1,200 cows, 120 Welsh horses (evidence of cross-Irish Sea trading and raiding), 60 ounces of gold and 60 of pure silver. Also handed over was an iconic weapon known as the 'sword of Carlus', possibly a relic from Viking campaigns in Carolingian Francia in earlier times. Óláfr was later killed in 1034 in England while on pilgrimage to Rome, though exactly why is not clear.

The death of a king and the birth of a saint

Matters in Scandinavia were about to change direction. In approximately the year 1015, Queen Asta Gurbrabsdatter gave birth to a boy. She was the wife of Sigurd Sow, ruler of the petty kingdom of Ringerike in Norway. This was her second marriage, having previously been the wife of King Harald of Vestfold. Shortly afterwards, in 1016, a son from that relationship became King Óláfr of Norway. His newly arrived half-brother was named Harald. He would become a king in his own right: as Harald Hardrada he would become one of the most famous Vikings of all.

After Cnut's move on Norway, Óláfr and those who escaped with him stopped at Akergarn in Gotland. Historians dispute the exact date of Óláfr's visit there and some suggest that its impact has been exaggerated).[22] The local ruler, Ormika, made him a present of twelve yearling rams. In return, Óláfr gave Ormika some drinking vessels and a battle axe. He also spent the time on his hands in a productive way by converting Ormika to Christianity – or so the saga writers say.[23] Ormika built an oratory at Akergarn, though it would be some time before the Gotlanders on a large scale allowed themselves to be persuaded of the merits of the new religion. Óláfr eventually moved on from Gotland to Novgorod.

Other Gotlanders were tempted to dabble with Christianity. One of them, a merchant called Botair of Akebäck, built the first church on the island, which was promptly burned down by pagans who had no intention of blithely letting the old religion be overturned. But Botair was persistent and built a second church. When his opponents threatened to mete out the same fate that had overtaken the first, Botair showed himself ready to become a martyr for his faith. He stood on top of the church and said that, if the building went up in flames, then so too would he. Fortunately for Botair he had a father-in-law who was both sympathetic and powerful. He intervened and persuaded Botair's angry opponents to let the building stand. The sympathetic father-in-law, Likkair Snielli, was later converted himself and took Christianity to another part of the island, which appeared to have been divided into three for administrative purposes, a standard Viking bureaucratic tactic (as with the 'Ridings' in Yorkshire, from the Scandinavian 'thridding', a third).

The religion was gaining a foothold in Gotland, if tenuous at first. The grip of Christianity would later be strengthened by Scandinavian bishops doing good works while on their way on pilgrimage to Jerusalem, which in that part of the world often took them through Russia via a stopover in Gotland.[24] The Gotlanders eventually came under the sway of Swedish bishops and, in the process, of Swedish kings also. They were then required to send eight longships to the aid of the Swedish king should he campaign, although significantly only against non-Christian opponents. They could, however, pay a fine in lieu of this service. They did not have to provide these if too short a notice period was given, or if the winds were contrary at the time that they were summonsed. With our current limited understanding of the position of Gotland during the Viking period, we cannot be sure just how integrated it was with other regional powers such as Sweden; but there is enough evidence to suggest that whatever integration there was was far from complete and that the Gotlanders remained to some extent stubbornly autonomous.

Óláfr Haraldsson later returned to Norway in a defiant attempt to recover his lost lands, this time in the company of Harald Hardrada, his half-brother. He may have been encouraged by the sudden death of Earl Hákon, whose ancestors had for long been supporters of both Sveinn Forkbeard and Cnut, thereby leaving a vacuum. But Óláfr had no real support. He was met by a hotchpotch army at Stiklestad (the saga writers say that this force was composed of 'farmers'), about 50 miles north of Trondheim. The details are garbled but the end was clear; Óláfr lost his life. The *ASC* says Óláfr was killed by his own people, while Florence of Worcester says he died in an ambush. Adam of Bremen even suggests he was not killed in battle at all, but by poison on the orders of Cnut.[25]

It had been a bitter conflict between Cnut and Óláfr. Adam of Bremen gives a very black-and-white analysis of its causes, which fails to convince. He says that between the two men 'there was continual war and it did not cease all the days of their lives, the Danes struggling for dominion, the Norwegians in truth fighting for their freedom.' The fact Óláfr was killed in a battle against other Norwegians suggests this does not capture the whole truth, which was subtler than that suggested by an explanation of a battle between nations.[26] Adam suggests, by way of justification, that a rebellion was led against Óláfr by nobles whose wives had been imprisoned for sorcery.[27] He eulogises Óláfr as a just Christian ruler who rooted out the magicians who had formerly been in Norway, saying the country was full of such men. He suggests that Óláfr was supported in his task by missionaries from England though the names he gives for some of them – Siegfried, Rudolf and Bernhard for example – suggest that these men were just as likely to be of Germanic origin. They also preached in Sweden and in the islands beyond Norway.

Christianity was by now also making inroads in Sweden where King Óláfr Skötkonung (possibly the half-brother of Cnut through a shared mother) had considered taking steps to destroy the great pagan site at Uppsala. For the time being, a compromise was brokered whereby individuals would be able to choose for themselves which particular god to adopt, possibly reflecting opposition from the Svear element among his people who were more opposed to the change. There were still those prepared to take tough action to defend the old gods; when an English missionary, Wolfred, smashed an image of Thor with an axe he was quickly 'pierced with a thousand spears' before his body was thrown into a swamp.[28] An intriguing hypothesis made in recent times suggests that Christian evangelists from Western Europe found themselves in opposition not just to paganism but also to Greek Orthodox influences that had returned to Sweden with ex-Varangians who had been required to adopt the faith when being recruited to the Guard.[29]

The demise of Óláfr Haraldsson might seem to mark the end of his career but it was only the beginning; he proved to be far more successful in death than he ever was in life. The young church in Norway needed a saint to help establish its credentials, a counterbalance to the saintly kings of other countries. Óláfr, in many ways a typical Viking but one who had also assumed the mantle of a Christian ruler, proved a compelling candidate for the role. His tomb at Trondheim soon became linked with miracles; the king was well down the road to canonisation.

This metamorphosis from failed king to saint is hard to understand but one could do worse than refer to the incisive words of T. S. Eliot in *Murder in the Cathedral* when writing on the death of Thomas Becket:

> When king is dead, there's another king,
> And one more king is another reign.
> King is forgotten, when another shall come:
> Saint and martyr rule from the tomb.

Óláfr was an attractive heavenly patron for Christianised Viking warriors. In the context of the times, this was a useful quality. Anglo-Saxon England was almost overrun with kings who were also saints. Some were famous such as King/Saint Edmund, King Edward the Martyr and, most of all, Edward the Confessor. There were also a number of minor kings in the Anglo-Saxon period in England who were made into saints of no more than local or regional significance. Óláfr served a similar purpose for Vikings, a helpful symbol for the Church to increase its power and influence among these new converts.

The tactic succeeded in attracting new recruits to the Christian cause. One was Óláfr's nephew Guthorm who had a base at Dublin from where he launched raids across the Irish Sea on Anglesey. He got into a dispute with a fellow raider, possibly Echmarcach, son of Ragnald (though again there is no unanimity concerning this conclusion)[30] who claimed a share of the booty. They came to blows and, with battle imminent, Guthorm promised to make a gift to Óláfr in return for his support. The battle was duly won by Guthorm and a silver cross was presented by him to Óláfr's church in Nidaros. Other accounts tell of Óláfr being adopted as a patron by mercenaries in faraway Constantinople.[31]

There is one more colourful account to refer to that is important in setting the scene for the arrival of an epic Viking warrior, in some ways the last of his breed. The battle that finally brought Óláfr's traumatic reign to an end took place in the summer of 1030 under the shadow of an eclipse. Harald, Óláfr's half-brother, was at his side when the climactic battle was fought to its bitter conclusion. In *King Óláfr's Saga,* we read that Óláfr thought Harald was too young to fight though, given the fact that he was then around fifteen years of age, this seems to be stretching a point. Harald furiously insisted that he should take part.

Later, Harald Sigurdsson (as he should properly be called) rose to prominence and earned the name Hardrada – 'The Ruthless' or 'The Severe'. It is notable that this nickname was not a contemporary one and it would not be until the thirteenth century that he was so called. Harald fought at Stiklestad and was wounded but managed to make good his escape. Óláfr did not but, as sometimes happens, his death was the making of him, for he became a Christian hero, a martyr for the cause in which he believed. For him it was redemption of sorts; a failure in life, he would soon be triumphant in death. Within a generation, the missal of the Anglo-Saxon bishop of Exeter Leofric would contain a reference to the mass for 'St Olaf's Day', quite a turnaround in fortunes.

And so Óláfr entered the pantheon of Christian saints. His body was later exhumed with the permission of Bishop Grimkel and found to be uncorrupted (a classic *topos* of the time; English saints such as Cuthbert and King Edmund of East Anglia were linked to such signs, along with many other less well-known saints). Óláfr was duly sanctified; Sigvat Thordarson who was first responsible for eulogising him, wrote of his sanctification within only a decade of his death. He was portrayed as a martyr-king even though there is no evidence that he died as a result of defending his faith as opposed to his own self-interest. He had his own hagiography, the *Acta sancti Olavi regis et martyris*, normally attributed to Archbishop Eysteinn of Nidaros who was active in the second-half of the twelfth century. Within decades of his demise, churches in his honour were being erected across the Viking world, for example in York and London where such buildings still remain active and over in Ireland where parishes of St Óláfr developed in Dublin and Waterford. His memory would also be preserved in several of the sagas produced by Snorri Sturluson. By as early a date as 1050, even the *ASC* would be describing Óláfr as 'holy'. Today he is the patron saint of Norway; a failed Norwegian king who despite his initial failure has achieved a kind of immortality.

Cnut: the last years

Óláfr's demise seemingly left Norway for Cnut to enjoy. As he matured as a king there was little sign of trouble from either England or Denmark. In England, two earls emerged as the most senior figures in Cnut's regime.[32] Godwine completely owed his position to Cnut. Godwine came from a reputable family but they had fallen out of favour in Æthelred's reign and the restoration of their position was entirely due to Cnut's actions. Godwine therefore was likely to be loyal to Cnut and was a very reliable lieutenant for him. The other prominent earl in England during the latter part of Cnut's reign was Leofwine of Mercia. Leofwine had been a councillor to King Æthelred. He proved himself a survivor when many of his contemporaries, such as Eadric Streona and others, had fallen by the wayside in spectacular fashion. With their example before him, he too had to watch his step with Cnut and Leofwine was for this reason likely to be a loyal supporter too. A third prominent earl emerged in England later in Cnut's reign. This was Siward who became earl of Northumbria stepping into the shoes that were left empty when Hákon, son of the late Erik of Lade, died in unclear circumstances (though most likely drowned).

Siward seems to have come over from Scandinavia. It has been suggested that he may have been part of Cnut's 'extended family'.[33] Siward demonstrated one great quality above all others: longevity. He held his position as earl of Northumbria for several decades, long after Cnut's direct line of succession in England died out. This was an interesting trinity at the helm of English government at the highest level after the king: the Anglo-Saxon newcomer, the Anglo-Saxon old hand and the Scandinavian. Perhaps on occasion this created tension, and perhaps Cnut wanted it to – it kept all of them on their guard.

There was then a second level of government in England, again reflecting a balance of Anglo-Saxon and Scandinavian interests. In the former camp, men like Odda and Ælfgar Mæw continued to witness charters throughout the 1030s. Another man with the distinctive name of Ordgar also did so; his name was uncommon and was probably linked to a very prominent Anglo-Saxon family on the borders of Devon and Cornwall from whose stock a former English queen, Elfrida, had come. Other men, of Scandinavian descent, appeared such as Osgot Clapa and Tovi the Proud. Again, there seems to have been an equilibrium in play here, a form of power sharing.

There are unmistakable signs that Scandinavian life entered the mainstream of the Anglo-Saxon kingdom. This can be seen in the praise poems that were written for Cnut later in his reign, at a time when he was mainly resident in England, as these were written for personal hearing, so it is most likely that they were performed before him at his court. It can also be seen in evidence of Scandinavian artistic motifs discovered at Winchester, for example a frieze that shows the story of Sigmund and the wolf, which appears in the *Vǫlsunga Saga*.

Any personal satisfaction that Cnut felt at the conquest of Norway was short lived. After Stiklestad, Cnut despatched his teenage son Sveinn to be his man there. With Sveinn went his mother, and Cnut's first 'partner', Ælfgifu of Northampton, along with Harald Thorkelsson who, it has been suggested, may have been the son of Thorkell the Tall.[34] One problem they faced was Óláfr, which may seem ironic as he was now dead; but he now became a symbolic figurehead for opposition to what was after all a dynasty of foreign origin. What brought matters to a head was the imposition of new laws which were seen as repressive – one element, which stated that the word of a Dane was equivalent to that of ten Norwegians, was particularly inflammatory and foolish – and here perhaps something should be placed at Cnut's feet which rarely is done: a misjudgement. It is inconceivable that new laws would have been imposed without Cnut's approval, and more likely at his active insistence. But in pushing them through, Cnut drove his newly acquired Norwegian subjects to reject his rule. Perhaps he had been misled by his success in driving through harsh conditions when he became king of England – where he had imposed a record 'Danegeld' payment on his new subjects – and did not appreciate that the conditions were essentially different in Norway.

There was another problem too: nature. In Norway, the harvests failed – and that was deemed to be the fault of the new regime. People looked back nostalgically – as they still often do after a régime change which does not especially benefit them – to the rule of Ólàfr as some kind of golden age when the harvest never failed, and the weather was always just as it should be, or at least that is how they remembered it. The poet Sigvat Thordarson told how 'different it was when Olav [sic] the warrior, ruled the land, then everyone could enjoy stacks of dried corn'. Now the people had to eat food normally reserved for animals: 'Ælfgifu's time long will the young man remember, when they at home ate ox's food, and like the goats, ate rind'.[35]

Cnut was to emulate the Anglo-Saxon kings in one way that he would have preferred to have avoided: a premature death when still far removed from old age; the same fate that had befallen kings such as Æthelstan and Edgar and even, to an extent, Alfred. Cnut died in November 1035 at Shaftesbury, suitably enough the location of a nunnery with close connections to the royal family of Wessex and England. Though his date of birth cannot be confirmed with certainty, the most likely scenario is that he was barely forty years old at the time of his death. Within months his legacy and his empire began to unravel. Bad luck attended Cnut's dynasty; his daughter Gunnhild married Emperor Conrad II, a fabulous prize for the family, but the arrangement did not long survive due to the premature death of the bride.

Cnut's reign in some ways marked the high-water mark of the Viking Age but in others presaged the beginning of its end. He had built a reputation and a status as a mainstream European king rather than a raider from the periphery. He desired nothing more than to be accepted as a part of the ongoing business of the league of nations and a very highly regarded part at that. His ambitions were imperial in nature and he succeeded in laying the foundations of a North Sea Empire but it did not survive him. At the same time there were still elements of the Viking about him; he appears to have loved the poetry and storytelling of the *skalds*. In other ways, Cnut became quintessentially English. He enthusiastically sponsored the shrines of former Anglo-Saxon monarchs and helped protect their memory, whether by adopting the laws of Edgar the Peaceable or making gifts at the shrine of the assassinated King Edward 'the Martyr'. He even made gifts at the tomb of Edmund Ironside, whom he came to call his 'brother' in later life, in so doing emphasising his legitimacy and connection to the Anglo-Saxon royal bloodline. Just how great Cnut's success was in pacifying England and generally increasing her security can be evidenced by the fact that at the start of his reign he kept together a standing fleet of 40 ships but by its end it had fallen to 16. In the far more turbulent days that would follow in the reign of his son and ultimate successor Harthacnut, it would rise again to 60.[36]

Cnut was buried in the Old Minster at Winchester and was ultimately joined by a select group of others such as his wife Emma, his son Harthacnut and his nephew Björn, who was murdered by his cousin Sveinn in Devon in 1049 (the remains of Edmund Ironside were also translated there at some time, possibly during Cnut's reign). This meant a small royal mausoleum was established which emulated, probably consciously, that of Alfred the Great and his immediate family in the nearby New Minster.[37] Such symbolic gestures were not unique at the time; the early Carolingian kings had chosen to be buried at St Denis near Paris where the Merovingians from whom they had usurped the throne had also been interred, giving their line a sense of continuity and legitimacy.

Cnut left two surviving sons from different mothers. It was bad enough to have to cope with competing brothers but two rival widows made the situation infinitely more complicated. One son, Harold Harefoot, child of Cnut's first partner, Ælfgifu of Northampton, acceded to power in England while the other, Harthacnut, became king in Denmark. It was not an amicable arrangement: Harthacnut, whose formidable mother Emma was still on the scene, wanted England for himself and the power struggle that followed was almost as much about the two competing mothers as it was the ambitions of their sons. But Harthacnut was in no position to push the point at first, being preoccupied in Denmark where his position was under threat from the direction of Norway and Magnus, the son of Óláfr Haraldsson, who had taken up power there in 1035 even though he was still a child at the time.

At one stage, a compromise deal was considered by which Harold would have England north of the Thames while Harthacnut was to have the territories to the south of it. But this suggestion came to nothing; Harold wanted the lot and the ongoing absence of his brother played into his hands. In desperation, Emma – effectively abandoned in England – ordered her two natural sons from her first marriage with Æthelred to return from Normandy (the writer of the *Encomium* suggests that the letter which she allegedly sent to them was actually a forgery composed by Harold Harefoot).[38] It was a disastrous move, as one of them, Alfred, was captured by Earl Godwine who was keen to ingratiate himself with the new regime. Alfred was brutally blinded at Ely and subsequently died of his wounds. Emma went into exile in Flanders – perhaps significantly she did not return to her native Normandy, which was at the time politically unstable and where she may not have been welcome – hoping against hope for an upturn in her fortunes; the *ASC* describes with an atypical poetic flourish how she was 'driven out without any mercy to face the raging winter'. But when Harold died in 1040 after a short and undistinguished reign, Harthacnut was quick to move in and take the throne of England for himself, having by now secured his position in Denmark. Harthacnut had been waiting for his moment, in command of a fleet about to invade England. A vision came to him in his dreams telling him that his brother Harold would shortly afterwards die and leave the throne of England to him; God was assuredly on his side. Saintly emissaries visiting would-be kings in the night: how the Viking world was changing!

Harthacnut's reign was even shorter than that of his half-brother whom he detested; one of his first acts on returning to England was to have Harold's corpse disinterred and thrown in a nearby marsh. But Harthacnut died in 1042, collapsing at a wedding feast for Tovi the Proud in a drunken stupor and never coming around. He was only in his mid-twenties and was an unpopular monarch due to the high levels of taxation that he levied. He had reigned for only two years; all that the chronicler of the *ASC* could find to say about him was that 'he never accomplished anything kingly for as long as he ruled'. There appears to have been a raid on the north-west of England by the men of Thorfinn, earl of Orkney, during his reign which was beaten off. Thorfinn decided to try again and this time with a large army, including men from Scotland and Ireland, he won a decisive victory and stayed in England for a little time thereafter.

The writer of the *Orkneyinga Saga* waxed lyrical about these events. He wrote how:

Against England the Earl
Urged his banner;
Oft his war-band
Blooded the hawk-beak:
Fire shrank the halls
As the folk ran, flame
Ravaged, some reared
Reeking skyward.
Through forts the famed one
Went fearless to the fight-throng.
Many a horn howling, but
High his banner.
Nothing weakens the warriors
Of the wolf-lord; war
Dawn then, steel dazzled,
Wolves dined on the dead.[39]

At around the same time Sveinn Estrithsson was ejected from Denmark by a resurgent Magnus and arrived in England, only to find his brother dead. The throne now went to Edward, son of the late and largely unlamented Æthelred II and Emma. Edward allegedly reached an agreement with Sveinn that the latter should be his heir; Sveinn then returned to Denmark to try to win back his throne there.[40] The Anglo-Saxon bloodline had been restored and the experiment of a Danish dynasty in England was to a large extent over, though influences from it would continue to have an impact. The situation was building up towards an apocalyptic conclusion in 1066.

In the interim, there were ongoing interactions between English and Danish affairs. In 1047 and 1048, Sveinn Estrithsson, then king of Denmark, sought help from England in the form of military resources to face the threat from Norway though it seems unlikely that this led to very much in terms of tangible results. Osgot Clapa, the long-time supporter of Cnut, was exiled in 1046 and took to raiding the Sussex coast, though he apparently returned to England before his death in 1054. Scandinavians like Ork continued to hold land in England and moneyers with the very English names of Leofwine, Ælfnoth and Ælfweard were minting coins in Scandinavia for several generations to come.

Harald Hardrada and the growth of a legend

Another key participant in the events of 1066, Harald Hardrada, enjoyed an extraordinary range of adventures. In the hands of Snorri Sturluson, Harald's career is that of the perfect warrior. Snorri's saga begins with one battle, Stiklestad, and ends with another, Stamford Bridge; two defeats neatly bookending the tale. It is a salutary reminder that Viking leaders were expected to taste defeat as well as triumph and, to anachronistically paraphrase Rudyard Kipling, treat those two impostors just the same. The pagan roots of Viking lore have death in battle as a prime prerequisite for entering Valhalla and while a man might die in a winning cause, he was perhaps equally likely to perish in a losing one. A number of characteristics come through in Snorri Sturluson's portrait of Harald in *King Harald's Saga*. These have been characterised as including resourcefulness, ambition, cunning, ruthlessness, leadership, single-mindedness and a seemingly inexhaustible capacity for double-dealing.[41] How much some or all of these attributes were accurate in their detail we shall never know; but the end result of the writing was to shape a character and a personality that bestrides the Viking landscape like a colossus.

A story told by Snorri Sturluson in *King Óláfr's Saga* gives us an interesting insight into Harald's early years, or at least the tales that grew up around them. The story goes that King Óláfr was hosting a feast.

Two of his young relatives, Guthorm and Halfdan, were brought in. Óláfr sat them both on his knee and pulled faces at them, at which they began to cry. But when Harald was brought in and given the same treatment, he scowled back at the king. When Óláfr began to pull Harald's hair, the child in response tugged at the king's long moustache. Óláfr looked at him and said 'you are going to be vengeful one day, kinsman'.[42] It has the feel of a classic folk tale, forged in a way beloved of contemporary writers to play up the significance of their hero, much as the boy Alexander is told by his father Philip in the ancient classics that continued to inspire the medieval world that his kingdom is not big enough for the two of them.

Harald gained a reputation for fighting bravely at Stiklestad.[43] He was led away wounded from the battlefield by Rognvald Brusason who found him shelter and a safe haven for recuperation in an isolated farmhouse. Then he was escorted east across the Kjolen Mountains and led by mountain pass and remote forest track to Sweden and safety. There he met other refugees from Norway. They joined forces and sailed east to Russia and the court of King Jaroslav, known as the Lawgiver or the Wise. At the time, Jaroslav was joint ruler with his brother Mstislav; from 1036 to 1054 he would be sole ruler. During his reign a bishopric would be established in Novgorod and his son Vladimir was installed as ruler there. The new arrivals were well received; as swords and axes for hire they could be a useful addition to Jaroslav's forces. Harald was made joint leader of his defence force along with Eilif, son of Earl Ragnall Ulfsson.

Harald was soon involved in aggressive action against some of Jaroslav's neighbours. In 1030–1031 he took part in ferocious raids in Poland. He then turned his attention to Estonia and parts of Finland. These were traditional targets of Viking raids and perhaps Harald felt that he was destined for something on an altogether grander scale for he was soon looking further afield. Harald and many of his men left and went on an expedition to 'Greece', eventually finding themselves at the court in Constantinople. One can imagine that first distant glimpse of the magical city, Miklagard, the greatest metropolis in the western world. It takes just a little exercise of the imagination to picture the moment when 'the great prince saw ahead the copper roofs of Byzantium; His swan-breasted ships swept towards the tall-towered city'.[44]

Byzantium was at the time under joint rule, with the Empress Zoë and her husband Michael IV Catalactus on the throne. Zoë had been married before to the Emperor Romanus Argyros but that marriage ended abruptly when she had him strangled in his bath. The empress was something of a late developer; about fifty years old when married for the first time, she proceeded to accumulate three husbands in the next two decades. Zoë liked what she saw in Harald and he was quickly put in command of one of her ships. He was accompanied by his own men and found himself as the unofficial head of the Varangian Guard, the mercenary bodyguard that became so famous in Byzantium.[45]

The word 'Varangian' was given by the Greeks to those of Viking origin who settled in and around Kievan Rūs and derives from the Old Norse *væringi,* which means 'faith companion'. The Varangians had by now become an important player in Byzantine politics. As far back as 874, an agreement between the then emperor, Basil I, and the Rūs required the provision of men from among the Varangians and soon after there are records of them fighting as mercenaries, for example in expeditions against Crete in the early tenth century. Later that century, they were deployed as far apart as Italy and Syria. Vladimir I, the ruler of Kiev, in 971 sent a contingent of 6,000 men to help Basil II, the emperor of Byzantium, though he used this as an opportunity to transfer the unrulier (and perhaps more pertinently in this case unpaid) men in his kingdom somewhere else.

They were formally established as a bodyguard by Basil in 988. Basil was a man with a very sensible distrust of Byzantine politics (in Byzantine history an emperor dying in his bed was the exception rather than the rule; they were often removed from the scene by internal rivals). Basil earned a reputation for ferocity for his extreme violence against his Bulgar neighbours, for which he earned the sobriquet of 'Basil the Bulgar-Slayer'. Ironically, Basil felt that he could rely more on Viking mercenaries than he could his own people and as a policy this was well regarded and emulated by later emperors. Initially the Varangians in the Guard could trace their ancestry back to the east of Scandinavia but eventually recruitment took place further afield. The *Laxdæla Saga* mentions that the Icelander Bolli Bollason, born around 1006, was the first known Icelander or Norwegian in the Varangian Guard. *Njal's Saga* refers to another Icelander, Kolskegg, who also joined. References to Scandinavian warriors joining the Guard continue well into the twelfth century and the Crusader historian Villehardouin mentions 'Danes' in it during the catastrophic sack of Constantinople by the Fourth Crusade in 1204.

Harald Hardrada played the part of the hired hand perfectly: a mighty warrior but one whose loyalty was generally reliable, high maintenance certainly but as a rule trustworthy. Another ironic turn of events would occur within a few decades of Harald's appointment; after the catastrophic defeat of the Anglo-Saxon army at Hastings in 1066, many exiles from England would find refuge as part of the Varangian Guard which, over time, came to be dominated by Anglo-Saxons rather than Vikings. That said, there is also evidence that a number of these later arrivals were referred to as being of Scandinavian origin, so perhaps they should be termed as Anglo-Danish rather than Anglo-Saxon. These later recruits continued to be renowned for the mighty battle axes that they used, another possible indication that there was more continuity with previous 'Viking' Varangians than might at first appear.

Harald quickly found himself at odds with the leader of the Byzantine army on campaign, Georgios Maniakes, allegedly a kinsman of the empress though there is no substantiating evidence surviving to support the claims of the saga writer. There was a petty dispute over who should camp where and Georgios and Harald almost came to blows over it. A duel was narrowly avoided but Harald won the right to choose his campsite through trickery, displaying Loki-like skills that would serve him well over the years.

As the campaign developed, it was noticeable that when Harald and his men were at the heart of the battle, it was inevitably won, whereas when they were not, the results were less favourable. Georgios and Harald soon fell out again and the young Viking and his men went their own way, fighting a successful campaign in what the saga writer calls Africa but was probably the western part of Asia Minor.[46] Then they were off to Sicily, in some ways the crucible of the Mediterranean world at that time. There was a battlefield frontline, where the Byzantine Empire had some claim to rule but had recently been supplanted by Muslim forces. A third element also entered the equation, Norman warriors who would eventually win the island for themselves though only after a long and gruelling campaign.

Harald led his force against several towns on the island. In his first siege, he was unable to break through the stout walls, so he took to trickery. He noticed that some of the small birds inside the town were flying over to nearby woods in a desperate search for food. He had some of them caught and released with an added sinister burden to carry – fir shavings that were set alight. When they flew back to their nests in the town, the thatched roofs of the buildings round about burst into flames. Their town ablaze, the previously mocking residents were forced to surrender.

Such devilish deviousness sounds unlikely to be true. Most likely such details come from the fertile imagination of a master saga teller at the height of his powers, shaping a verbal concoction of his own design. Yet perhaps it still tells us something: a Viking leader was expected to provide a combination of crafty stratagem and ruthless cruelty in the pursuit of victory.

In another episode, Harald was taken ill. His illness was so bad that he died from it. His grief-stricken followers begged that his body should be allowed Christian burial inside the town that they were attacking. This was duly granted, and his coffin was carried through the gates. It was heavy and was laid down by its bearers, right by the gate, which could not now be shut. Suddenly, Harald – very much alive – leapt out and he and his followers burst through the jammed-open gates and thoroughly plundered the town, causing much loss of life in the process.[47]

Harald fought bravely and successfully and won himself great wealth. That which he did not need for immediate expenses, he sent back to Novgorod and the court of King Jaroslav. He returned to Constantinople after several years of hard campaigning during which, according to the poet Thjodolf, he fought eighteen battles. At some stage Harald journeyed to Jerusalem, possibly as the leader of a military escort guarding a party that had been allowed by its Muslim owners to restore the dilapidated Church of the Holy Sepulchre, the holiest church in Christendom and the site of Christ's tomb.[48] While he was there, he undertook many of the actions conventionally associated with a pilgrim, such as bathing in the Jordan and making offerings at 'the grave of our Lord' and other sacred sites – or at least so we are told by Snorri Sturluson, who was keen to show Harald in a suitably Christian light.

When Harald returned to Constantinople, he heard that his nephew, Magnus Óláfrsson, was now king of both Norway and Denmark. Magnus had become ruler of Norway in 1035 when his supporters ousted King Sveinn, the son of the legendary Cnut who had proved completely unsuccessful as a ruler. After the death of another of Cnut's sons, Harthacnut, in 1042 he also became king of Denmark having driven Sveinn Estrithsson (Cnut's nephew) out. Hearing of this, Harald wished to return home to stake a claim of his own. However, the Empress Zoë was livid when she heard of this. He had apparently already asked for the hand in marriage of her niece, Maria. This request had been turned down, reputedly because Zoë wished to marry Harald herself, though this was not the story that was publicly told. Harald therefore found himself in hot water, more pertinently in a prison cell. And here the divine intervened, in the form of his late brother, St Óláfr. A distinguished woman from the city helped him break out; she had been visited by the shade of Óláfr who had once healed her and now instructed her to repay the debt she owed by assisting in Harald's escape. Returning to the environs of the palace, where the Varangian Guard was based, Harald was greeted enthusiastically by his men. In response to the actions of the co-emperor who had ordered Harald's imprisonment they now blinded him or, as the poet Thjodolf more eloquently if brutally put it, 'the warrior who fed the wolves ripped out both the eyes of the emperor of Byzantium'.[49]

It has been suggested that this rather fanciful chain of events obscures a more prosaic tale. The emperor, Michael V Calaphates (not his successor Constantine Monomachus as described in error by the saga writer), was indeed overthrown and blinded at this time but more because of a palace coup than the supernatural intervention of St Óláfr. That said, it might well have been the case that Harald had been released in the chaos that ensued and subsequently led the party of Varangians that broke into the monastery where Michael had taken refuge and put out his eyes.[50] The Empress Zoë remained in power despite the brutal deposition of her co-emperor. Harald managed to make good his escape with two ships, breaking the chain that ran across the Golden Horn though the vessel with him came to grief in the process with the loss of many men. He then made his way back to Novgorod and the court of King Jaroslav where he was greeted with enthusiasm. Harald now owned vast wealth; convention allowed that when a Byzantine emperor was deposed the Varangians could help themselves to his stores of treasure as palace plunder and no doubt Harald had not been slow to avail himself of the recent opportunities given to him in this respect.

Harald not only found a warm welcome in Novgorod but also a wife, Elisif, Jaroslav's daughter. Jaroslav 'the Wise' was an extraordinary man in his own right; one of his other daughters was married to Andrew, the future king of Hungary, and another to King Henry I of France. Harald stayed in Novgorod for several years, but something was clearly gnawing away at him for he started to show signs of restlessness. Novgorod was only a stepping stone on the way back to Scandinavia. He journeyed to Sweden where he met and joined forces with Sveinn Estrithsson. Sveinn had been made earl of Denmark by Magnus, who successfully staked a claim to be king of that country. However, Sveinn wanted more than this and subsequently staked his own claim for the leading role. Three battles between the two men followed; in each of them Sveinn was the loser. Now an alliance with Harald seemed to offer him a chance of success.

Swearing to support each other loyally, Harald and Sveinn led an army on the short crossing to Denmark where, 'on the flat Danish islands, maiden hearts were trembling'. The army plundered extensively in both Zealand and Fyn (Funen). Many Danes fell to the raiders' axes and many others ran into the forests to hide. Women were dragged off into slavery, the metal chains tied so tightly around them that they were biting into their flesh. Magnus naturally reacted to these events. He gathered together a large Norwegian army and a climactic confrontation loomed. As the poet put it, 'death-dealing King Magnus will sail his vessels southwards while Harald's ocean-dragons are pointing to the north'.[51] But Magnus's advisors did not want to see him and Harald at each other's throats and secret negotiations between the two men began. As part of the deal, Magnus offered to share Norway with Harald and, while such a power-sharing arrangement may appear unusual, there were other similar instances in contemporary politics. In any event, a peace was brokered and, for the time, being stability returned to the region.

The remarkable tales of Harald Hardrada dominate these years, overshadowing the story of an incredible adventure led by Ingvar the Far-Travelled. He led an expedition into distant Serkland, between the Black and Caspian Seas. It was an epic challenge and it ended in disaster, at the end of which only one man lived to tell the tale. A runestone described the expedition as one that was inspired by gold and in the process much food was provided for the hungry eagles who soared over the fields of battle for carrion; though other accounts suggest that Ingvar was more of an explorer who was seeking to discover the source of several rivers and that many of the deaths suffered by the expedition were attributable to disease or through shipwreck on the way back. At least twenty-six runestones are known to have been erected in what may have been a throwback to a classic Viking raid of old or alternatively more like the activities of a New Age explorer.

King Harald

Soon after, Harald and Magnus met and greeted each other warmly. We are told that Magnus fulfilled his part of the bargain and duly gave Harald half of Norway, though he made it clear that he would continue to claim precedence as the senior of the two men in the country, and that Denmark was his alone. Harald responded by halving his vast treasure trove with Magnus; the latter was desperately short of resources and all he had in the way of gold was the bracelet that he was wearing, which had been bequeathed to him by his late father, Saint Óláfr. Both men therefore brought something to the table. The joyous reconciliation did not last long, as might be expected when an ambitious man like Harald was involved. Although they journeyed together to Trondheim, they kept separate courts and within the year trouble was brewing.

Sveinn, in the meantime, had made his way back to Denmark, which he continued to claim for himself. He perhaps hoped that Magnus and Harald would fall out and it must have irked the latter that his nephew continued to claim precedence over him in Norway. There was one incident when Magnus and Harald almost came to blows in a petty quarrel about who should moor their ships where. It was, the saga writer admitted, a delicate situation, so finely poised that just a slight miscalculation could lead to the relationship between the two men coming to grief. But it was Magnus who came to grief first. He and Harald had patched up their differences and moved together on Denmark. Their campaign was successful and Sveinn was forced to flee. Magnus then became ruler of Denmark. But shortly afterwards, following a vision in which he was visited by his father, Saint Óláfr, it became clear that he was dying.

He bequeathed Denmark to Sveinn and Norway to Harald. But as might be expected from the ambitious Harald, one kingdom was not enough, and he asserted his claim to Denmark as well as Norway. Not everyone sided with him. Einar Paunch-Shaker, a powerful magnate from the north of Norway, for one, averred that he would not support Harald's claims in Denmark. Many of the Norwegian warriors present agreed and drifted back to Norway. Very likely they had little wish, as Einar had said, to fight 'foreign wars'. Harald, seeing well enough which way the wind was blowing, realised that at this stage it was best to hang on to what he held and he returned to Norway. At least his claim to be king there was uncontested.

Magnus was buried with due pomp in St Clement's Church at Trondheim, where his father lay. During life, Magnus had gone out of his way to show respect to Óláfr's sacred relics, going so far as to ensure that the nails and the hair of the cadaverous remains were trimmed annually and keeping the keys to the shrine himself.[52] Now it was time for the saga writers to pen an obituary for Magnus. One said that he was a man of medium build with fair complexion and hair. The writer noted that he was well spoken and quick thinking, noble minded and exceptionally generous, a great and courageous warrior. He was very popular and widely respected by friend and foe alike.[53]

Sveinn heard the news of Magnus's demise when he was in Skåne. With the Norwegian army returned home, Denmark was open to him and he went back there, vowing never to leave it again as long as he lived. He attracted many supporters and the people of Denmark accepted him as their king. Magnus's half-brother Thorir was one of those who joined him; Thorir was well received by Sveinn and stayed at his side for some time. But Harald had only postponed his efforts to conquer Denmark, not abandoned them altogether. Magnus had died on 24 October 1047 and the following spring Harald assembled a large army and moved on Denmark. They pillaged Jutland, though thinking that they would later raid more widely afield; 'next year our cold-blooded anchor will drop in warmer oceans; thus I read the future; we will cast our anchor deeper'.[54] They reached deep into the country: the church at Åarhus was burned and that at Schleswig raided.[55]

There was a great chieftain in Denmark by the name of Thorkell Geysa. His daughters had mocked Harald the previous year, making anchors out of cheese and saying that these would be enough to tether his ships. Now they were laden in chains and taken off into captivity; 'today these very maidens can see the iron anchors holding his warships; and none is laughing now'.[56] They later raised an exorbitant ransom. In the meantime, Harald plundered much of Denmark but he did not fully conquer it. He returned to Norway in the autumn with unfinished business to attend to. He was back the next year, and again 'the ravens fed on corpses'.[57] But Sveinn was not meekly hanging back and letting Harald do as he would without resistance. He assembled his own force to face up to the threat and it looked as if a decisive battle was imminent:

> The battle-hardy farmers
> Of Trøndelag will be meeting
> The warlike king of Denmark
> On the ship-strewn ocean.
> God alone will decree now
> Which king will rob the other
> Of life and all his lands;
> Sveinn cares little for broken pledges.
>
> Often Harald of Norway
> He launched his bristling vessels;
> Now he sails in anger
> South across the ocean;
> While King Sveinn's sea-dragons,
> Gold-mouthed, brightly-painted,
> A host of deadly warships,
> Are straining to sail northward.[58]

Seeing that Sveinn had a strong force with him, Harald split his own into two. The peasant levy with him was sent back home, while he kept the cream of his men by his side. Landing on Jutland he was too strong for Sveinn to face him. The plundering that followed was again brutal, turning into 'one year of evil memory'. The important Danish town of Hedeby was taken and burned. Soon after, there was a major sea battle at Nisa where Harald was again triumphant, but Sveinn survived and lived to fight another day. Despite determined efforts, Harald was unable to land a knock-out blow; Sveinn was down but not out. At the end of the conflict for Denmark, Sveinn Estrithsson was confirmed as the country's king. It was a remarkable outcome, for he had done so by virtue of being the last man standing. Thus, a king who lost nearly every major battle that he ever fought remained as king, to reign in Denmark for another three decades.

Harald returned to Norway to oversee the completion of St Óláfr's church at Trondheim. On the spot where the building was erected, the body of the late King Óláfr had briefly lain. Magnus had founded a royal residence nearby, but the church was unfinished at the time of his death. Harald also erected a church, St Mary's, nearby on a spot where Saint Óláfr had been interred during the first winter after his death. He also ordered a new royal hall to be constructed and another church was erected during his reign in Trondheim dedicated to St Gregory. The number of Christian foundations established during the period of his rule shows just how much the Viking world had changed since the times when paganism was the norm, just a century or two before.

Harald was renowned for his autocratic rule which, according to Snorri Sturluson, became more marked as time went by. His demeanour discouraged any dissent or debate, but it also led to friction. One particularly serious disagreement occurred when Einar Paunch-Shaker, chief man among the farmers in Trøndelag in the centre of Norway, found himself in opposition to Harald. Einar had a great knowledge of the law and used this to argue the case for protecting the interests of the farmers against those of the king. While this endeared him to the farming community it had, as might be expected, the reverse effect on Harald. Harald was incensed, so much so that Einar took to ensuring that he had a strong escort of men whenever he journeyed around and when he was at home he always had a vigilant group of bodyguards at hand. On one occasion he journeyed to Trondheim in the company of 500 men. As Harald watched, he reasoned that Einar would not be content until he had seized the throne for himself. He was said to have composed a poem on the subject, including the following lines:

> Einar of the flailing sword
> Will drive me from this country
> Unless I first persuade him
> To kiss my thin-lipped axe.[59]

There soon followed a very serious incident. An associate of Einar's was charged with being a thief but when he was brought into the court to answer the charge, Einar entered it with a body of armed men and stole him away. This brought matters to a head. Eventually both parties were prevailed upon to affect a reconciliation but when Einar entered the presence of Harald and left his men outside at the request of the king, he walked straight into a trap. He was pounced on by a group of Harald's men hiding in the shadows and hacked to death. While this brought an end to the immediate threat of rebellion, there was widespread resentment at Harald's underhand tactics and he was subsequently despised for it.

Another important figure in the affairs of Norway at the time was a man named Finn Árnason. Finn had fought against King Óláfr at Stiklestad and in some accounts his brother, Kalf, had struck the fatal blow that brought him down. Kalf had then fallen out with King Magnus and went into exile. In return for reconciling Harald to the farmers of Trøndelag, Finn insisted that his price would be the homecoming of Kalf to Norway, terms to which Harald agreed.

The friction between different Viking and Scandinavian groups continued to reveal itself over a wide area. There was a battle involving Thorfinn, the son of Sigurd the Stout, jarl of Orkney, and his nephew Rognvald (Ragnall), which took place at Roberry on the Pentland Firth in the 1040s. It was a sea fight. Jarl Thorfinn had 60 ships on his side, most of them small though his own vessel was a large and well-fitted-out longship. He also enlisted men from the Hebrides and Scotland to support him.

His adversary Rognvald had 30 large ships, a number of them Norwegian. These were sizeable fleets in the context of the times. This was part of an ongoing war in Orkney in which Magnus the Good had taken the part of Thorfinn's nephew, Rognvald, and had supplied troops to assist him. The outcome of the fight was in the balance until Kalf, who was there with 6 large ships but had stayed on the sidelines, 'like a cat in a cave', came in on the side of Thorfinn and tipped the battle his way. Kalf was given the governorship of the Hebrides as a reward for his assistance at the vital moment.

The story was far from over. Rognvald escaped to Norway but returned to Orkney in the depths of winter, hoping to catch Thorfinn off his guard. He almost did so. His men surrounded Thorfinn's house while he was drinking. They set fire to it but the earl managed to break out through a wooden partition wall, with his wife. In the darkness of the night, they managed to escape and were rowed over to Caithness in a small boat. No one knew of Thorfinn's escape or survival and it was assumed that he had been consumed in the flames that had eaten up the farmstead Rognvald and his men had attacked.

The uneasy situation had been several decades in the making. Thorfinn, the grandson of Malcolm, king of Scotland, was a child when his grandfather gave him Caithness and Sutherland and granted the title of earl. He grew into a tall, strong man but it was said that he was 'someone who everyone can see was going to turn out greedy'. He was also described as an 'ugly-looking man with a black head of hair, sharp features, a big nose and bushy eyebrows, a forceful man, greedy for fame and fortune'. He had two brothers who could not have been more different in character from each other. One, Einar, earned a reputation as a bully and someone who would insist on raiding in the summer even though there was not a lot of loot available. The other, Brusi, was content with his lot and enjoyed good relationships with the farmers who were his tenants. The two men shared out Orkney between them although Einar had the lion's share. But Orkney was in a difficult location, adjacent to routes to the west and many men, both Norwegians and Danes, often came ashore there and raided.

Many important figures had defected from Orkney to Thorfinn on the Scottish mainland, discontent with their lot on the islands. Thorfinn had claimed a one-third share of the islands when he came of age. This was something which was his as of right, but Einar was unwilling to go along with the suggestion. However, an uneasy peace was brokered, and Einar continued to spend his summers raiding in Ireland, Scotland and Wales. Nevertheless, problems soon emerged in Orkney between Einar and the representatives of his brother Thorfinn who sent envoys over to King Óláfr in Norway in an attempt to resolve the problem

Soon afterwards, Einar was killed at Sandwick on Orkney by Thorkell the Fosterer, Thorfinn's envoy, at a supposed reconciliation feast that got out of hand. It was not long before the two surviving brothers, Brusi and Thorfinn, were at odds with each other about the government of Orkney. Back in Norway, King Óláfr had sensed an opportunity to further his own interests through his intervention in the dispute, persuading both men to recognise him as overlord. Despite this, tension between Brusi and Thorfinn continued. When Brusi died, his son Rognvald (who had been left as a hostage with Óláfr) took his part in the dispute and the uncertain environment continued for several decades thereafter. Rognvald had been a staunch ally of Óláfr and had fought on his side at Stiklestad, rescuing the badly wounded Harald Hardrada from the field of battle.

The conflict with Thorfinn only finally ended when Rognvald, described as 'one of the handsomest of men, with a fine head of golden hair, smooth as silk', was taken by surprise on the Orkney island of Papa Stronsay and killed. The attack was the reverse of that which had been made on Thorfinn. This time it was Thorfinn who surprised, surrounded and attacked Rognvald and set fire to the property in which he was based. Rognvald managed to escape but was betrayed while hiding on a nearby beach when his pet dog barked and revealed his location.

Thorfinn had also proved a formidable force in mainland Scotland. Moray and Ross appeared to have been part of a frontier zone, perhaps one where the border moved around with some frequency. He came face to face with the leading Scottish power in the immediate region, Karl Hundason ('son of a bitch': he may be the same person as the infamous Macbeth), who was defeated by a Norse force at Tarbat Ness, just north of the Moray Firth, in 1035. Following his triumph there, Thorfinn pushed deep into Scotland, creating chaos, burning hamlets and farms, and killing everyone they met, forcing many to seek sanctuary in the woods.

Thorfinn lived to a ripe old age, forsaking piracy in his later years and devoting himself to the good government of his territories.In keeping with contemporary convention, he made his way on pilgrimage to Rome to give thanks for his achievements, receiving absolution for his sins from the Pope, and was no longer challenged from Norway after the death of Magnus. When he died in 1058, he was buried at Christchurch, Birsay, the church that he himself had ordered to be built.

But the underlying dynamics were not good and within a few years of his death Orkney fell apart.[60]

Harald Hardrada's remarkable story undoubtedly has been improved in the telling by Snorri Sturluson yet, at its core, there appears to be a kernel of truth. He was a larger than life character, a mighty warrior and a formidable leader. Snorri Sturluson attributed many Christian acts to him but in many ways he was the archetypal Viking. In Scandinavia, and across the wider Viking world, life in many places went on as it had done for decades. Yet time was running out. Europe was on the cusp of epochal change and the Vikings were by now living on borrowed time.

13

Harald Hardrada and the End of an Age (1051–1066)

... the thunderbolt of the north, a pestilence to all...
Adam of Bremen on Harald Hardrada

The reinstatement of the Anglo-Saxon dynasty

After the death of Cnut and his sons, first Harold Harefoot, then Harthacnut, the rule of England reverted to the Anglo-Saxon dynasty through King Edward, later known as 'The Confessor'. The hagiographical writer of *The Life of King Edward* saw these events as a restoration to God's favour after the punishment of the English people's grievous sins during the Danish 'oppression'.[1] However, the Danish element in the Anglo-Danish ruling class remained strong and exercised significant power, and Edward, who had spent several decades in exile, also introduced a Norman element into English society. The Danes were by now increasingly assimilated into this. For example, in the north, Earl Siward stayed powerful and influential but very much within the tent as far as power politics in the country was concerned. Vikings, in Britain at least, were becoming mainstreamed.

One of Siward's major achievements was to remove the infamous Macbeth from power in Scotland in 1054. He may also have been responsible for taking a chunk out of the kingdom of Strathclyde in the form of lands that were south of the River Solway. In effect, he probably added what is now Cumbria to England where it remains to this day. Soon after, we find a reference to a man called Gospatric making a grant in the region to Thorfynn mac Thore. Gospatric is a Strathclyde name, whereas Thorfynn is distinctly Scandinavian although the 'mac' reveals a Scottish connection, a sign of how cosmopolitan north-west England had by now become.[2] It was the same too at the other end of England where Cnut's appointees in the region, such as Ork in Dorset, continue to appear as charter witnesses several decades after the late king's death.

The Viking world was changing rapidly, and in the process some of their power was dissipating. Instead, nation states like Norway and Denmark were assuming increased importance. Christianity was fundamentally changing the political structure of the Viking world and political dynamics were mutating as a result.

In 1052 the last Viking ruler was ejected from Dublin by the Irish when Diarmit ejected Echmarcach (who possibly withdrew to the Isle of Man). But the victors realised that it was foolish not to maintain friendly relations with Scandinavia, given the economic advantages that could be gained from such a relationship and Viking trade continued to be important. Irish troops would be involved in later Viking incursions into England in 1058 and 1066, the former part of an attempt by Magnus, son of Harald Hardrada, along with men from the Hebrides and Orkney, the latter involving his father. Following the capture of the city 'the Irish kept the ties – military, economic and cultural – with the outside world that came with the capture of Dublin'.[3]

At about the same time that a Viking ruling elite was replaced in Dublin, archaeological evidence suggests there was significant urban development going on at other Viking centres in Ireland such as Waterford, Wexford and Cork. The reasons for this are as yet not understood, so any history of the Vikings must inevitably remain a work in progress; and some of the sites such as Cork have not revealed much evidence of significant urbanisation until later in the century when what might be regarded as the Viking era had come to an end. But any analysis who suggests that one culture, the Viking culture, was thrown out and replaced by another that was Irish seems to be way wide of the mark. Rather a process of ongoing assimilation seems far more likely when people of different origins learned to live alongside each other, accept their cultural differences and generally get along. It is likely that they intermarried, and a fusion of cultures was the result. This is also suggested by art forms, across many areas, fusing local and Scandinavian patterns, designs and techniques to produce locally distinctive end results.

Viking involvement in England in 1058 took the shape of a force led by Magnus Haraldsson with men from Dublin, Orkney and the Hebrides. They were supporting the efforts of Ælfgar, earl of Mercia, who had been outlawed and now sought to win his lost lands back again. They were allied to the great Welsh leader, Gruffydd ap Llewelyn. The details concerning the end result are unclear, other than that Ælfgar was reinstated. Gruffydd himself was a famous figure and succeeded in uniting much of Wales under his rule, if never securely.

He was eventually forced to flee after getting on the wrong side of King Edward the Confessor and his right-hand man, Harold Godwinesson. Gruffydd was ultimately murdered in mysterious circumstances; all we know with reasonable certainty is that he was killed by one of his own people. It has often been assumed that Gruffydd met his end in Wales, but a theory has emerged that he may have been killed in exile in Dublin. The suggestion is that links between Wales and Viking Dublin were strong at the time and certainly there is evidence of the marriage of a leading Welshman, Cynan ap Iago, to Ragnhild, the granddaughter of the famous Sitriuc Silkbeard.[4]

As king of Norway, Harald Hardrada earned a favourable reputation with the Icelanders. He sent help to them when there was a severe famine in 1056. He also allowed those on the island who could find the means to escape from the harsh conditions to take up residence in Norway. This allowed the country, desperately exposed to extreme weather and shortages due to its precarious environment, to eventually recover. It did not work for everybody though. One of those mentioned in Snorri's saga of Harald's life was Halldor Snorrason, who was famed for his good looks and huge physical strength, but who was also dour and taciturn. This man of few words took success and failure in his stride with equanimity, but he was also outspoken, a quality that Harald did not warm to. In the end, Halldor went back to Iceland, taking up farming at Hjardarholt, which had been founded by the delightfully named Óláfr the Peacock.

1066: The Year of Three Battles

The Viking world was reaching a tipping point. This brings us to the events of 1066, that critical year for England and her neighbours. On 6 January 1066, Harold Godwinesson was made king of England, an act that was bound to invite trouble, not least from the direction of Normandy where Duke William reckoned he had a superior claim to the throne. But it also drew the attention of Harald Hardrada, another man who reasoned that his own claim to England outranked that of Godwinesson.

Godwinesson had a lot going for him. At the age of forty-four, he was a good age to be king; no longer in the bloom of youth perhaps but an experienced warrior from the leading family of England. He could even claim a distant relationship through marriage to Cnut the Great. His father was Anglo-Saxon, his mother Danish, so he was well placed to act as a unifying influence. Unfortunately for Harold, he had problems close to home to deal with. His brother Tostig had ruled Northumbria for a time but had been forced out under a cloud, allegedly for being a harsh and unjust ruler, though subtler political manoeuvrings may have played their part. Now in exile, Tostig looked around for allies. After having been rebuffed by William of Normandy, Tostig formed an alliance with Harald Hardrada. Harald had a claim to the English crown through previous agreements between Harthacnut and Magnus the Good. But they were indirect and – more importantly – unenforceable without further action. In addition, the English crown could not be handed on from one king to another as if it were some disposable piece of real estate to be passed down the generations on a whim. The English crown was awarded by election through the governing council known as the Witanagemot and it was they who had offered the crown to Harold Godwinesson.

None of this would have concerned Harald Hardrada, a man who seems to have lived for war. Adam of Bremen wrote of him that 'after he came into his fatherland, he never ceased from warfare; he was the thunderbolt of the north, a pestilence to all...'[5] His sweep of military activity since returning to Norway had been vast; the Danish islands had felt the sting of his sword, as had Orkney, the lands of the Slavs and even, according to Adam, Iceland (though no other source mentions this). Adam also paints Harald as an old-fashioned, unreformed pagan wedded to the magic arts.

To Harald, might equalled right, and whatever excuses he offered to justify his claims to the English crown, they were window-dressing only. A fleet set out for England in which Harald Hardrada would be the senior partner compared to the disenfranchised Tostig. Tostig made his way to Scotland, where he was on good terms with King Malcolm, and waited to meet up with Harald. Harald made his way over, stopping at Shetland and Orkney *en route* and recruited there. He left one of his two wives and his daughters on Orkney before sailing south. It has been estimated that the combined forces of Harald and Tostig now consisted of about 300 ships and at least 9,000 men, possibly more.[6]

On 8 September 1066, the longships arrived at Tynemouth. After consolidating their position, they set out for the most important target in the region: York. The Anglo-Saxon defence was in the hands of two ealdormen, Edwin of Mercia and Morcar of Northumbria, young and largely untried war leaders. They moved their armies up to Fulford on the outskirts of York to block the invasion army's further advance. A confrontation loomed. On the right flank of the English was the River Ouse, on their left, swampland, a position that prevented them from being outflanked.

Hardrada experienced delays in assembling his troops. Sensing this, the Anglo-Saxon forces attacked and pushed Hardrada's army back. But his men counter-attacked and forced a gap in the English line. They fought fiercely beneath Hardrada's banner, the Land Waster, a white silk standard with Odin's black raven portrayed on it, wings spread wide, surveying the battlefield looking for the blood and gore of the fallen on which to sate itself. The late arrival of some of Hardrada's men gave him a sudden and unexpected injection of fresh energy at the vital moment. While the weaker troops on his right flank struggled to hold their own, his veteran warriors on the left began to push the English troops back.

Now it was the turn of the English to feel the heat. They were slowly but inexorably pushed back. In a head-on battle such as this, the advantage lay with the army with the greater numbers if, in other ways, they were well matched. Hardrada held that advantage. The English, now on the back foot, were forced back into the marshy ground and became bogged down. The battle moved decisively against them. Unable to retreat, many of them were bludgeoned down in the marshes. It was said that there were so many dead that the Viking force ultimately advanced through the marshes without getting their feet wet along a pathway formed of dead English bodies. This left the gates of York open. Rather than let the triumphant army inside the citizens negotiated a settlement – a wise move given the propensity for pillage that Viking forces had demonstrated in the past and the fact that Hardrada's men had already thoroughly ransacked Scarborough earlier in the campaign. It was agreed that 100 hostages would be given to recognise York's submission. Hardrada and his men retreated to Stamford Bridge, a few miles off, to recuperate after their exertions at Fulford.

The Battle of Fulford was fought on 20 September. Far to the south, Harold Godwinesson, who had been waiting in vain for an invasion fleet from Normandy to materialise, burst into action when he heard of the news of Hardrada's onslaught. He could not possibly get there in time to intervene in the events at Fulford, but he was determined to face up to Hardrada's threat as soon as possible. It was vital that he did so, for of all the regions incorporated into Anglo-Saxon England, Northumbria had proved the most volatile and its associations with troublesome Norwegian/Hiberno-Norse Vikings just a century or so before gave ample evidence of the dangers that could spread from there should Harold Godwinesson not respond with vigour and energy.

Hardrada was blissfully unaware of Harold's energetic response, which saw him arrive at Tadcaster on 24 September 1066. The time taken to cover a distance of more than 200 miles from London to Yorkshire was incredible, perhaps four or five days at a time when 20 miles a day would have been a good marching pace. While Hardrada's men were busy processing hostages at Stamford Bridge, on the River Derwent, they were so relaxed that many of them were not even dressed in armour, which they had left on their ships that were a good distance off. It was unseasonably hot, and it was understandable that they wanted to cool off; but it was a rash move that they came to regret. They must have been amazed when over the horizon a large Anglo-Saxon force materialised, intent on giving battle. Harold Godwinesson had marched through York and was up for a fight. He had, according to the later writings of Snorri Sturluson, taken the precaution of doing everything he could to ensure that no inhabitant of York could escape from the city and run to Hardrada to tell him that an English attack was imminent. Now, here was the English army, 'and their glittering weapons sparkled like a field of broken ice'.

There was a formal exchange before the battle in which a message from Harold Godwinesson was delivered to his errant brother Tostig offering him back the earldom of Northumbria if he would change sides. Understandably, Tostig refused, the die had been cast long before. Defiantly, Tostig told the messenger that this was all too late: Harold had humiliated him not long before, so his change of heart now meant little to him. The messenger then turned to Hardrada, who was interested to know if there was any deal available for him. The answer came, boldly defiant: for Hardrada, there would be just 7 feet of land in which he would be buried, or as much more as he needed given the fact that he was unusually tall.

Battle was joined, and it was brutal. The English force initially gained the upper hand against their unarmoured opponents. Part of the Viking army on the west bank of the Derwent was overwhelmed. However, the English faced a difficult obstacle when they reached a bridge that led across to the eastern bank. According to the *ASC* a lone Scandinavian barred the way across. For a while, no one could pass him. But then an Anglo-Saxon warrior floated upstream in a barrel and, when he was underneath a gap in the bridge above which stood the defiant Viking, he thrust upwards with his spear and killed him. The way this story is told is rather surprising; it is recorded in a later version of the *ASC* but Snorri the saga writer does not mention the epic feat of the defiant soldier holding the bridge until struck down, one rather expects the references to be the other way around.[7]

The main battle then commenced against a shield wall organised by Harald Hardrada. It was set up in a semi-circular formation with the Land Waster banner at its centre. If the account about the brave, lone Viking was true, his actions would have bought time. A brutal battle followed. For a while, the fighting was hot, but as time went on, the Anglo-Saxons gained the upper hand as was probable given the lack of armour among the Viking warriors.

The decisive moment came when, with the day drawing in and twilight not far off, Hardrada fell with an arrow in his windpipe: he would be claiming that 7 feet or so of English ground after all. It was an ending that sounds suspiciously similar to the demise of Harold Godwinesson at Hastings just a few weeks later. Tostig too died soon after, his body so cut up that it was said that he could only be identified by a tell-tale wart between his shoulders.

The late arrival of Viking reinforcements from Riccall made no difference other than to add to the roll call of Viking dead. They were led by Hardrada's brother-in-law Eystein Orri. He and his men were slaughtered in the fight that followed. At the end of the Battle of Stamford Bridge, Harold Godwinesson was triumphant. Harald Hardrada, on the other hand, was dead and according to some historians so too died the Viking Age.[8] Hardrada had arrived in England with a fleet of 300 ships. Only 24 of them were needed to take the survivors away.

Yet for Godwinesson fortune proved a fickle mistress. Just three days later, on 28 September, hundreds of Norman ships landed at Pevensey. Harold was now faced with his own appointment with destiny at Hastings on 14 October following another brutal forced march with his depleted army to the other end of England. Stamford Bridge played a pivotal role in William of Normandy's ultimate triumph by diverting English forces away from the south coast where they might successfully have opposed his landing.

The Danes had not yet given up on England though. During the decisive battle at Hastings, there were, according to William of Poitiers, many Danish warriors fighting for the English, or one might more accurately say Anglo-Danish, for king Harold.[9]

The Normans themselves were only a few steps removed from Vikings; or as one recent historian called them 'Frenchified descendants of earlier generations of Vikings who had settled in Normandy'.[10] Hastings was not the first time that men of Scandinavian origins had fought each other, of course; Normans and Varangians had come to blows at Bari in 1009. The Normans had changed much, admittedly; it is ironic to read that some of them were afraid to cross the Channel to reach England when their cousins had sailed halfway across the world. But in the build-up to the battle at Hastings they pillaged the surrounding countryside, a move made all the more significant as these included lands held personally by King Harold. Attacking royal estates was, as we have seen, a standard Viking tactic.

On the other hand, the changes that had been made in the past half-century to the Viking world were epitomised by Hastings in other ways. Harold Godwinesson was himself of part-Danish stock as his mother, Gytha Thorkelsdóttir, was the sister of that same Ulf who had been killed in Roskilde Cathedral on the orders of Cnut. William of Poitiers even stated that Sveinn Estrithsson, Cnut's nephew and now the king of Denmark, sent Danish troops to fight alongside Harold at Hastings against their distant Norman cousins (William duke of Normandy had also, according to the same chronicler, sent a delegation to Sveinn asking unsuccessfully for his support).[11]

The world was certainly much changed; indeed, more than one world came to an end in that apocalyptic year when the fortunes of both Anglo-Saxons and Vikings, for many years bitter opponents and latterly on occasion unlikely allies, irretrievably declined. For Britain and Ireland, for Scandinavia, and indeed for other far-flung outposts of Christendom, nothing would ever be quite the same again. Towns in the south of England surrendered precipitously to William: Dover, Canterbury and Winchester, though London was more stubborn in its resistance. It is as if the townsfolk of such places were reminded of how settlements had been thoroughly sacked in previous wars against the Vikings, some within living memory, and they were reluctant to experience a repeat (William's brutal pillaging of Romney in Kent after Hastings would surely have been a powerful reminder).

The fading of the Viking Age

While these dramatic events were taking place, in other parts of the Viking world there were also signs that the end times were approaching. Hedeby suffered a disastrous raid from Slavic attackers in 1066 and had also been violently assaulted by Harald Hardrada in 1050. The town now fell into terminal decline and a nearby settlement at Slesvig grew up to take its place. Yet history rarely deals in convenient 'full stops' when one period definitively ends and another begins. The Vikings did not die; they morphed into something else. Where once there were warlords and sea kings, now there were emerging nations in the form of Denmark, Sweden and Norway and, further afield, Iceland and the Faroes. And then there was Normandy, not a kingdom itself but perhaps more influential than all of them. The impact of these developing states on the wider international scene would be profound.

The process of Christianisation was an ongoing one in Scandinavia, even now. Adam of Bremen informs us that Bishop Egino was appointed to the see of Dalby in Skåne, an event that seems to have taken place in about 1061. Egino became well known for converting stubborn adherents to the older pagan religion in Sweden and on the island of Bornholm to the new one. He was an eloquent and moving speaker; after listening to him many pagan adherents would break up their old idols and gave up their possessions to the Church. With the money so obtained, church buildings were erected and captives, of whom there were many in the region, were ransomed.[12] Yet the mere fact that men like Egino had to undertake such proselytising missions shows that Christianity was still not firmly established everywhere in the Viking world.

But its triumph was probably inevitable by now. Scandinavia was just catching up with the position that much of Western Europe had arrived at long before; for the second-half of the first millennium AD was one in which Christianisation and militarisation were the prime features of contemporary society in the region and the two very often marched hand in hand to some effect.[13]

But even Adam of Bremen, writing in the second-half of the eleventh century, said that 'until now [Sweden and Norway are] nearly unknown to these parts' so they remained beyond the boundaries of the known world. The little he did know had been told to him by his informant, King Sveinn Estrithsson. He told Adam that Norway could barely be crossed in a month and Sweden in two. Both lands were he told Adam mountainous as he had discovered when he had campaigned there for a dozen years. As he warmed to his theme, Adam threw in details concerning the Far North that were positively fantastical in terms of content; of Amazons and Cyclops, of peoples who hopped around on one leg (he does not explain why), of cannibals. In these remote lands, Adam tells us that conditions were so harsh that some of the women grew beards.

More salacious details were related by Adam, particularly concerning the Swedes. They did not have a lot of time for material wealth but they took great pride in their ferocious sexual appetites. Men might have two or three wives at one time; rich men might have more. Any sons born of such unions (Adam is gender-specific on this point) were considered as legitimate. However, sexual violence against a woman was a capital offence if she was someone else's wife or a virgin. The Swedes took pride in treating travellers with generosity, even competing with one another to entertain strangers. Adam's words suggest that even now, converting the Swedes to Christianity was an uphill battle. However, some of the Christian preachers who had been active had some rather pagan-sounding powers; one of them, Bishop Adalward the elder, was much respected by the Swedes (or more specifically the Goths) for his ability to control the weather and cause it to rain when it was needed.

The Swedes were surprisingly democratic. The people took decisions that were subsequently ratified by their kings. The king could decide not to adopt a particular course of action recommended by the people, though they might then only accept this decision reluctantly. In battle they called on their multitude of gods to aid them, but they were coming to accept that the Christian God was the strongest of all. That said, one of the better-known elements of Adam's account concerns the pagan temple at Uppsala. He wrote that this was decked out in gold and there were statues there of the three greatest Norse gods, Odin,

Thor and Frikko (Freyr). Everyone was required to attend the temple once every nine years when a great festival was held. Gifts were offered and sacrifices made, including (as Adam sniffily noted) by Christians who had previously been converted. Nine heads of different animals were offered as blood sacrifices, including those of nine men. Their decapitated bodies were hung in sacred groves, those of men dangling alongside dogs and horses. Adam said that these facts had been related to him by a seventy-two-year-old Christian.[14]

Given the visceral ritual violence of these ceremonies it is unsurprising to find that the devotees of the old religion still proved stubbornly resistant to change, as evidenced when later on in the eleventh century an English bishop named Eskil was stoned to death for smashing up a pagan idol.[15] Not until 1090 did King Inge of Sweden have the confidence to demolish the temple at Uppsala. Inge had initially refused to undertake the pagan sacrifices required to sanctify him as king and his brother-in-law Sveinn was enthroned instead. He willingly took part in the ceremony in which a horse was slaughtered, cut up and then eaten, earning him the name Sveinn the Sacrificer. Inge had later got rid of Sveinn by burning down the house in which he had taken up residence and had, at last, become king in his stead.

Adam contrasted Norway with Sweden as far as the process of Christianisation was concerned. Whereas poverty had formerly forced the Norwegians to engage in piratical raids, they now accepted their condition with more equanimity due to the widespread adoption of Christianity, something Adam infers was partly due to the saintly example of Óláfr Haraldsson. They were extraordinarily generous in their gifts to the Church, to such an extent that Adam felt they were being shamelessly exploited by avaricious churchmen. He also proudly noted that 'Holy Mother Church is enjoying prosperous increase in all the provinces of Norway'. Their devotion to Christianity did not prevent Adam from continuing to refer to them as 'barbarians'.[16]

Despite Adam's gripes, Scandinavia was changing in ways that, one would think, Adam should surely have accepted made it less barbaric from his perspective. By 1060 Skåne had two bishoprics and the rest of Denmark had seven. Norway and Sweden had three each. What would have made him less happy was that the region was stubbornly independent in ecclesiastical matters and was increasingly resistant to being subservient to the archbishopric of Hamburg-Bremen, a point of view that was guaranteed to make him seethe. He would have been even less happy if he could see into the future and foretell that Lund would become responsible for the administration of the whole Scandinavian see by 1104; Hamburg-Bremen had by then lost its fight for regional ecclesiastical dominance. It was a sign of a still-evolving world; Lund was a relatively recent creation, established by Cnut the Great who hoped it would grow to emulate London in terms of its mercantile importance. It did not ultimately succeed in doing so, though it became important enough in its own right; but it was a sign of confidence and ambition nevertheless. The archbishopric of Hamburg-Bremen was one of those to suffer in the fallout that emerged from this transformation towards a brave new medieval world. As always, there were winners and losers from such moments of historical transition, and the precise identity of such were sometimes unexpected.

Epilogue

Viking Twilight

The sun grows black, the earth sinks into the sea. The bright stars vanish from the heavens.

The Prose Edda

The world reshaped

Despite William of Normandy's triumph at Hastings, England did not fall meekly into his lap. There was ongoing resistance and the north of the country, always somewhat detached from the rest, was more problematic than most. The ongoing threat of an invasion from Sveinn Estrithsson was a major headache for William, particularly if coordinated with the support of the Scottish king and dissatisfied elements inside England. It is worth reminding ourselves that it was not just Anglo-Saxons who had lost out in England after Hastings, for the country had become Anglo-Danish in many areas. For example, when we read that around Lincoln lands were confiscated that were held by men with the very Scandinavian names of Toki and Ulf, it is a reminder that England was much changed.[1]

The aftermath of the Norman Conquest and the vigour and rapaciousness with which William exploited England contrasted with the more nuanced way in which Cnut had ruled the country. When the *Domesday Book* survey was completed in 1086 only 8 per cent of land in England was owned by the same people who had held it in 1066; although admittedly some formerly significant landowners, among the most important and powerful men in the country, had breathed their last on the field of Hastings, this was not the only explanation.[2] By 1086, there were only three Englishmen holding baronial estates south of the Tees and all of them were what might be termed 'collaborators' with the Norman regime.[3]

The family of Harold Godwinesson had naturally enough lost out in the aftermath of Hastings. Harold had been married twice and left a number of children. One of the sons of the late king, also called Harold, accompanied Magnus 'Bare-Legs' Óláfrsson of Norway when he led an expedition to Ireland at the end of the century. Some of his sons joined the court of Sveinn Estrithsson in Denmark while others went to Ireland. Sveinn had a claim on England that could be traced back to the days of Harthacnut and Magnus 'The Good' when an agreement had been reached that, whichever one of them died first, the other would inherit all three kingdoms: England, Denmark and Norway. It was based on this claim that Harald Hardrada had launched his bid for England in 1066 and now Sveinn had inherited it. Of course, it was one thing to make such a claim, quite another to enforce it and William the Conqueror was unlikely to meekly accept it. Nevertheless, given its existence as a potential reason to support those who had counterclaims to William, it provided convenient justification for renewed attacks on England from Denmark.

In 1068, Godwine – another son of Harold Godwinesson – launched an attack on the West Country of England from Ireland. While he won a victory against the Normans there, it was not decisive and he suffered significant losses. It was more of a raid than a campaign of reconquest, very likely involving the hiring of mercenaries, some of them almost certainly of Hiberno-Norse stock given the point of origin of the raiding fleet. It seems to have been an old-fashioned style Viking raid. Another attempt was made on England in 1069. Again, the target was the south and west coast of England and men from Dublin were involved. But the question was now becoming how much were these Hiberno-Norse raiders Hibernian and how much Norse? The question was becoming both irrelevant and impossible to answer. The inhabitants of places like Dublin were intermarrying and assimilating and had already become a hybrid people. Their rulers were now of Irish stock even if some of them had names that still sounded Norse, such as Godfrey Óláfrsson who was ruling in Dublin in 1072.

The 1069 raids on England were potentially serious, including contingents from Wales, Ireland, Scotland and Denmark, but they were not well coordinated and came unstuck in the face of the Conqueror's castle-building programme. The threat these raids posed though, allied to much disturbance in the northern part of England, helps to explain the violence of William's response in the 'Harrying of the North'. This event, a brutal set of reprisals against the northerners for having the temerity to revolt, was catastrophic from the perspective of northern England with *Domesday Book*, prepared several decades later, suggesting that large tracts of the countryside between York and Durham even then remained wasteland. The 'Harrying of the North' was probably as destructive (if not more so) as any Viking war in England had ever been. Yet the image of Viking terror has lingered on more through the centuries than the acts of William the Conqueror have done. Perhaps this was because William invaded England with explicit papal blessing, even fighting under a papal banner at Hastings, whereas Vikings were perceived as pagans directly attacking Christendom (even when they had in some cases long since converted to Christianity).

In hindsight, the Danish raids that took place in 1069–1070 were a missed opportunity for those who sought to overturn the Norman Conquest. William was very unpopular in the north and there was much resentment against his rule from a part of England that had always been stubbornly autonomous and contained significant Anglo-Danish elements. However, the Danish fleet that arrived off Yorkshire did little during its stay; and the force it carried suffered greatly from an abnormally harsh English winter. It moved to East Anglia in 1070 and Peterborough Abbey was sacked, though on this occasion treasures were stolen but no monks were killed; some were taken away, possibly as hostages though they may have gone of their own volition (a new Norman abbot had just been imposed on them).

Sveinn Estrithsson did not even join the force until 1070 and seems to have been persuaded to go away easily enough; he was by now more interested in enhancing his wealth than conquering a kingdom. While there was much anti-Norman sentiment in England, resistance was centred around Edgar the Ætheling, who was of the Anglo-Saxon bloodline rather than an Anglo-Danish alternative to the Conqueror (he was descended from the children of Edmund Ironside who had found refuge in Hungary after Cnut's orders to the king of Sweden to dispose of them half a century before; but did not have the same leadership qualities as his illustrious ancestor). The Danish armies assiduously avoided open battle with William, perhaps perturbed by his military reputation, and eventually left. Those English who had revolted were left to pick up the pieces and deal with the horrific aftermath of William's subsequent oppression and scorched-earth policy. Unfortunately for the cause of Anglo-Saxon England, Edgar was no Alfred and this time there would be no last-minute recovery.

The Danes abandoned them to their fate, although some of the Anglo-Danish were determined to fight on, probably driven to do so out of desperation and feeling that there was very little to lose. Among those fighting alongside the famed English resistance leader Hereward 'The Wake' were men such as Thorkell of Harringworth[4], a major landholder in England, the equivalent of a Norman 'baron', and Siward of Maldon; both men with names that betrayed a Scandinavian heritage not far in the past. Another was Waltheof, son of the late Earl Siward of Northumbria, who had come over from Scandinavia during Cnut the Great's reign in England and had achieved fame and fortune. Waltheof's mother was of the Northumbrian house of Bamburgh's bloodline and this family relationship serves as a good example of intermarriage and integration between Scandinavian and Anglo-Saxon. These attempts to unseat William eventually fizzled out. Godwinesson's children faded into obscurity, although a daughter, with the very Scandinavian name of Gytha, married King Vladimir II of Novgorod and they had children who married into the royal houses of Norway and Denmark. One of them would marry first King Sigurd the Crusader of Norway and, after he died, King Erik Eriksson of Denmark.

Further Scandinavian interventions in England followed. An attack in 1075 involving forces from Denmark, meant to coincide with revolts from across the country known as the Rising of the Earls, petered out. However, York Minster was pillaged in a throwback to an older Viking era (the Minster had also suffered during the 1069–1070 campaign). Some members of the Anglo-Saxon/Anglo-Danish elite who had survived the traumas of the years since 1066 were permanently removed from the scene in the reprisals that followed. A final intervention threatened in 1083, led by King Cnut IV of Denmark ('The Holy'). Cnut assembled a sizeable fleet, large enough to cause William the Conqueror to halt campaigning in France to face up to the threat. But the sudden death of Pope Gregory VII created ripples on the Continent and the Holy Roman Emperor, Henry IV, threatened Denmark from Germany and the impetus behind Cnut's planned attack was completely lost. Cnut's campaign, and with it in some ways the Viking Age, faded out with a whimper. Nevertheless, some prominent Anglo-Saxons who could not bear the Norman yoke lived out their lives in exile in Denmark, often churchmen such as Æthelsige, prior of St Augustine's, Canterbury, or Ælfwold, abbot of St Benet's, Holme.[5]

These Scandinavian interventions post-1066 can be summarised as being half-hearted or poorly coordinated, and often both. Europe was becoming increasingly cosmopolitan and distinctions between Anglo-Saxon, Anglo-Dane, Norman, Scandinavian et al were becoming increasingly indistinct. Ethnic definitions outside Scandinavia (and even to some extent inside it, for example, where Anglo-Saxons of English origin had assumed a place in local society) were becoming blurred. Over time bloodlines mixed and ethnic distinctions became increasingly irrelevant. Assimilation and integration followed, not always smoothly but usually inevitably. The last vestiges of paganism were evaporating and men from Scandinavia were soon to be found in significant numbers fighting for Christendom in that extended period of holy warfare known as the Crusades.

Viking legend: villain or hero?

Yet even as the Vikings were beginning to fade into history, they were emerging more sharply in legend. This was true not only in their own region but in others too. Just as in England the Viking 'bogeyman' became a core part of the story of Alfred the Great, much the same occurred in Ireland, and it happened quite quickly too. In the reign of the Irish King Muirchertach Uda Briain (1086–1119), a work called *Cocad Gaedhel re Gallaibh* ('War of the Irish against the Vikings') appeared. It reworked older material from the late tenth century but included additional detail of its own. It added a great deal of gloss to the career of Brian Boru, who had been killed in battle against the Vikings (or at least against an army with many 'Vikings' in it) at Clontarf on Good Friday, 1014. Despite the fact that the forces opposing Brian contained not only Vikings from Ireland, the Hebrides and Orkney but also Gaelic warriors from Leinster, his foe became a 'pagan' army in this account. It has been noted of the Vikings – and to me it seems that this statement is entirely justified – that 'as their military threat receded, their literary villainy increased'.[6]

In the *Cocad Gaedhel re Gallaibh*, Brian Boru is linked with great figures from the Bible and Antiquity: men like Alexander the Great, the kings Solomon and David, and the prophet Moses. He becomes unashamedly a champion of Christendom as well as a throwback to the great heroes of the classical world, the necessary heroic Christian warrior who is a counterpart to the alien heathen menace. He is the Irish equivalent of Alfred, perfect, irreproachable, almost too good to be true (as, indeed, in this account he is).[7] His Viking opponents are the antithesis of him: the perfect foil, the pantomime villains who provide the ideal contrast. So completely do they fit this bill that they are represented by serpents and monsters living in lakes, pools and caves: otherworldly beings, creatures of the night, altogether too bad to be true.[8]

Towards the end of the eleventh century, Magnus Barelegs became king of Norway; 'that violent man who ruled for a lurid decade' as he was once described.[9] He intervened in the affairs of Britain and Ireland and, in one such case in 1098, was recognised as overlord of the Scottish Isles. However, when his men raided Iona during that year he stopped them from sacking the monastery. He stood outside the little chapel known as Columba's Shrine, locked the door and instructed his men not to violate this precious sanctuary. In its own way this action symbolised perfectly the transition which had taken place in the Viking world in his times.[10]

His next intervention in 1103 was less successful. Uniting with the Irish high king in Ulster, he was killed in an ambush in County Down. His death was a gruesome one according to the *Hiemskringla;* he was wounded by a spear that passed through both thighs and was then struck on the neck with an axe, which killed him. Yet these attacks were no longer Viking raids; they were essentially overseas wars fought by an emergent nation state in Norway on behalf of her king. Further, in Ireland these were not wars of conquest; Magnus was fighting as an ally of an Irish high king, Muirchertach Ua Briain. Magnus had attempted to secure the Isle of Man and Anglesey for himself and in the process came into direct confrontation with the Norman conquerors of England. At the Battle of the Menai Straits in 1098 Magnus found himself faced by the forces of the earls of Chester and Shrewsbury, his help having been sought by a Welsh warlord, Gruffudd ap Cynan, who needed allies to beat off the Norman threat. The Normans had only captured Anglesey a few days before when the Norwegian fleet appeared. There was an exchange between the two forces, as a result of which one of the English earls was killed. Deprived of one of their key leaders the Norman army retreated to England and Gruffudd was reinstated. However, with the death of Magnus in 1103 violent Norwegian inputs to English affairs came to a halt. Of course, Viking influence did not stop at once, as if a tap had been turned off. There is, for example, ongoing evidence of Norse influence on language in north-west England into the 1100s.[11]

The Viking world was now gone though, and Scandinavian nation states were establishing themselves, a new iteration of life emerging from the chrysalis of the old. Even remote Greenland now paid homage to the Christian God. In 1126 the population there received the Christian bishop, Arnald, they had requested (quite what he thought of taking himself off to the far-distant *úbygdir* – 'unpeopled tracts' – of the vast island with its savage environment we can only speculate). Membership of the Christian church required the payment of tithes, which were made in the form of unusual objects such as walrus and narwhal tusks, furs and hawks and the occasional polar bear cub.[12] Ancestor veneration however appears to have remained important even into Christian times; three bishops are said to have proudly claimed descent from Karlsefni and Gudrid, those early settlers of Greenland and, for a short space, Vinland.

The Greenlanders came to realise the problems of living independently of others when their available resources were limited and eventually in 1261 they accepted the nominal suzerainty of King Hákon the Old of Norway. It only bought them borrowed time. The settlements there were always out on a limb and, with Europe decimated by the Black Death in 1348–9, the situation rapidly approached catastrophic proportions and the island's last bishop in residence, Alf, died in 1377. The inhabitants had received a visit from a ship from Bergen from time to time but, when the designated vessel sank *en route* in 1369, no further trips were made. They were already acutely aware that they were in trouble; by 1351, the residents of the Eastern Settlement had received no word from those of the Western for a while and Eskimo hunters were known to be in the area. When a brave man called Ivar Bardarson sailed up the coast to find out what was going on he found neither settlers nor Inuit; but the settlers' livestock were running wild. Economic realities also impinged as they always do; the *King's Mirror* noted that many things had to be imported – particularly iron and timber – and, because of the great distance that merchant traders had to travel (not to mention the risk factor), they could be prohibitively expensive.

The last few years were terrible for the Greenlanders. The weather got progressively colder and stock started to die off; the relative balminess of the Medieval Warm Period was being replaced by the harshness of the Little Ice Age. The absence of clergy on the island meant that the residents were living in a perpetual state of sin; not a problem for a modern secular society but disastrous for a medieval religious one. Antagonistic Eskimos probed further into Greenland, adding to the sense of challenge and danger facing the settlers. In one raid, eighteen settlers were killed and two young boys carried off into slavery; a harrowing example of role reversal. Even later Basque whalers have been blamed for the ultimate demise of the tiny and exposed Norse settlements as they sailed to Labrador to seek out their leviathan prey.

The settlements clung on like limpets, but their grasp grew progressively weaker although it was a long, lingering death. Inuit hunters, hunger, cold, as well as economic and ecological factors have all been suggested as the cause of the ultimate demise of the Greenland settlements but in truth no one really knows why they faded into history. It is an end that remains cloaked in mystery. There is an intriguing but suspect report of a visitor from Iceland seeing a dead Norseman on the beach in 1540 but the likelihood is that by around 1500 all the settlers had either died or left. In its own way, the obliteration of the Norse settlements of Greenland stood as an analogy for the fading away of the Viking Age.

The great sagas

Even though the Viking world had to all intents and purposes physically ceased to exist, it lived on elsewhere – in the deepest recesses of the imagination. Much of what we know of the Vikings, or at least much of what we think we know, comes from the contentious source of later Viking sagas, mainly written in Iceland. There is a danger, of course, that the lateness of the writing, not to mention that the writers were exposed to a Christian view of the world, significantly distorts the underlying reality, and the tendency of people in any era who write up oral traditions to suitably 'adapt' them to the writer's own cultural context has been noted.[13] To make sense of these literally epic works, the rationale behind their creation needs to be appreciated for to the writers, to all intents and purposes, 'history and literature among the Icelanders were one'.[14] In this merging of two different disciplines, boundaries become blurred, the line between what was and what should have been is lost and instead what emerges is a fusion of reality and fantasy, of actuality based on a dream as surely as is a Turner masterpiece.

The greatest exponent of the craft of saga writing was Snorri Sturluson. He was born in 1179 at Hvamm in the west of Iceland. He came from a powerful family; he was descended from Snorri the Priest who died in 1031 and whose son Halldor Snorrason had fought alongside Harald Hardrada at Stamford Bridge, having earlier accompanied him to Sicily. On his mother's side, Snorri Sturluson's ancestors included Egil, the star of *Egil's Saga*. Snorri would enjoy a career as a landowner, a politician and a lawyer; in other words, he was a multi-faceted high flyer.

In 1181 he was sent to Oddi, the centre of culture in Iceland at the time. There he served (and was effectively apprenticed at) the court of Jon Loptsson, the most sophisticated of the Icelandic chieftains of his day. At Loptsson's court Snorri was brought up on a diet of Norwegian history and culture; history seen through the prism of people with a proud traditional heritage. This history and culture continued to live through the poets who kept them alive through their oral renditions in the halls that throbbed to the hum of music and the warming flicker of the fire's flames on cold, wintry nights when no sane man or woman would be abroad.

When Loptsson died in 1197, Snorri was old enough to start chasing his own dreams and ambitions. He made a good marriage that brought him wealth and a chance to secure his future. He moved to Borgarfjord in the west of Iceland, a place that was already known for its learning even before Snorri arrived on the scene. It would be home for the rest of his life. Soon other trappings of success arrived: power, wealth, lands. Snorri was a dab hand at building alliances that almost invariably saw his position improved as a result. He was not just interested in these trappings though; he was also developing his skills as a poet, then a dying art. His was the kind of poetry that echoed back to the great days of the Scandinavian court poets, now long in the past, a past for which Snorri seemingly hankered. He also became a prominent official, being elected the *Althing's* law-speaker, the highest official in contemporary Iceland, in 1215 and again in 1222 (the speakers were elected for three-year terms).

Snorri visited Norway in 1218, when he spent time at the court of King Hákon Hákonsson. The king had a not altogether healthy interest in Iceland, which he ultimately annexed. Snorri also visited Sweden during this period, which was one of great personal success. He was well received and given premier treatment by King Hákon and seems to have been a man of great charisma. His timing was fortuitous. Hákon was preparing plans to send a naval expedition to Iceland in an attempt to add it to his empire. Snorri was naturally opposed to this and did his best to talk the king out of the idea. All his interventions could do though was to push back the date of Hákon's interference to a point some years into the future. It bought Iceland time but only succeeded in delaying the inevitable.

Iceland was on the cusp of implosion, a demise fuelled by the petty self-serving attitudes of the island's competing great men. Wonderful writer though he may have been, sad to say, Snorri was one such man. When he later returned to Iceland, Snorri became embroiled in a series of feuds. The infighting represented the death throes of the republic. The island nation, with limited natural resources, was already largely depleted by the overenthusiastic, short-termist practices of the over-large population. It was adrift like a rudderless boat in the middle of a mighty ocean, a nation whose past was already greater than its future. Even by Adam of Bremen's time, it was noted that the people of Iceland were dependent on their cattle for just about everything including clothes; there were no crops and wood supplies were meagre. There were no towns and the inhabitants were quite content to share their houses with their livestock.[15]

A later anonymous writer from around the end of the twelfth century whose words were appended to a manuscript of Adam of Bremen's works provides some disturbing details. He wrote of how Iceland was so harsh that 'they dare not leave their underground hollows in the wintertime. For if they go out, they are burned by the cold, which is so extreme that like lepers they lose their colour as the swelling gradually spreads. Also, if they happen to wipe their noses, the whole nose pulls off with the mucus itself and, having come off, they throw it away'. The nose-less inhabitants of Iceland must have come as a shock to the unsuspecting visitor though this is one story that has surely been improved in the telling.[16]

It was a period of Icelandic history known as 'the Sturlung Age', 'one of flagrant lawlessness, of pledges broken and honour cynically ignored, of pitched battles between chieftains and their inconsistent supporters, of cruelty and treachery and arson, murders and blood-feuds'.[17] Iceland disintegrated; and there, waiting patiently for the Icelanders to pull each other apart, like a wolf outside the sheepfold, was King Hákon of Norway. His plan was a simple one; to be the last man standing, to step in and take over when every leading man in Iceland had collapsed in a state of exhaustion.

The political infrastructure of Iceland had now changed out of all recognition from what had existed two or three centuries before. Power had concentrated in the hands of an ever-smaller group of men until six families of the *godi* had emerged as the dominant oligarchy on the island. As ever, power corrupts and absolute power corrupts absolutely; and these six families plotted and fought against each other in an age that was increasingly characterised by violence, intrigue and murder across the island. Only two main power blocs were left at the end, the Oddi and the Sturlungar who were closer to the ruling royal dynasty in Norway.

Snorri's situation deteriorated; he was not safe in Iceland, so he took himself off to Norway again. But now he was no longer a favourite of Hákon and instead found refuge with Duke Skuli, a fierce rival of the Norwegian king, a dangerous ally to have. Snorri had returned to Iceland by 1239; Hákon had put an injunction on all Icelanders leaving Norway and returning home but Snorri ignored this and went nevertheless. In the interim, Snorri's power and influence back on the island had gone forever. Once back in Iceland, he was a marked man. Hákon sent word that Snorri should return to Norway or be killed if he refused to go. On the night of 23 September 1241, a large group of men appeared outside Snorri's house at Reykholt. The house was, surprisingly given the tension in the air, unguarded. There was a wooden fence around it but, with no sentries manning it, this was a small enough obstacle for the raiders to negotiate. They skipped over it with ease and broke into the house.

Snorri was asleep in his bedchamber but was awake soon enough. He realised what was happening and formulated a spur of the moment escape plan, making his way down into the cellars, hoping to evade his attackers. It was not to be. Five of them made their way down and hammered the life out of the defenceless Snorri. It was a shocking and brutal end to a life of remarkable literary fecundity, though perhaps a dramatic conclusion that fitted well enough with his turbulent career and which even he as the victim might accept as a violent finale well suited to one of his saga heroes. It presaged the demise of Iceland itself as an independent state, a situation which was formalised when in 1262 the *Althing* recognised Norwegian supremacy and the experiment of the Icelandic Commonwealth ended.

Snorri's epitaph was monumental, not in the form of a mighty mausoleum but in one of the most remarkable works of history/saga ever penned. This was his *Heimskringla* ('The Orb of the World'), a history of Scandinavia from prehistory to 1177. It is a history on a grand scale, unlike any of the other sagas, broader in sweep and coverage, a vast *opus* worthy of a Bede or a Herodotus. Whereas other sagas are mainly the stories and histories of individuals or families, Snorri gives us the story of his peoples as a whole. Of course, some modern historians cannot desist from taking a swipe at it for its unreliability and it is true that this is saga, not history. In saga, the literature is more important than the facts; Snorri is writing to entertain as well as to inform. As one commentator wisely wrote, 'he wanted to illuminate the past, not merely to report it'.[18] It is as a work of literature, not history, that it should primarily be judged. But to completely disregard what it tells us of the latter seems short-sighted given the dearth of other sources for the period to rely upon.

Snorri was only the latest, if the greatest, of a steady stream of Icelandic saga writers. He acknowledged his debt to an earlier author, Ari Thorgilsson the Wise (1067–1148). Snorri describes Ari's work as being 'altogether remarkable'. Ari was a man, Snorri said, with the sharpest of memories and, as a confidant of great men, had access to a vast store of intellectual treasure. He was also blessed with a long life and this enabled Ari to put together what was, for Snorri, an altogether credible chain of events. Ari took great pride in his reputation for accuracy and informed his readers unreservedly that if they found something that appeared to them to be more reliable than his own work, then they should accept it without a qualm.

Snorri also acknowledged the debt he owed to another great Icelandic saga writer, Karl, abbot of the Benedictine monastery of Thingeyrar. Karl was a great friend of Sverrir, king of Norway, and wrote a *Life* on this subject. It was so compelling in Snorri's eyes that he ended his *Heimskringla* in 1177 as the period after this was covered by Karl's work and could not, he thought, be surpassed. When he wrote *Heimskringla* Snorri was not making everything up; he was drawing on a range of existing sources. These may have been subject to inaccuracies or exaggeration in the originals and this should introduce a healthy degree of caution in their interpretation. There are other useful insights he gives us too; he tells us what was expected of a Viking ruler. Such a man should have a prominent lineage, be marked by wisdom and insight, and should demonstrate both boldness and success in battle. These were a difficult-to-achieve set of criteria.[19]

Snorri had access to some oral traditions that had not previously been written down. Particularly useful in this respect was Jon Loptsson who had a remarkable first-hand insight into what was for him relatively recent Norwegian history. Again there may have been bias plus the danger that what was not initially written down becomes a distorted image over time. But these inputs, however imaginative they might have been, are a fertile source of additional information.

As elsewhere in Europe at the time, historical works on Iceland were often produced by monks (Snorri being an obvious major exception) and two men in particular were the focus of the attention of such authors. Óláfr Tryggvason was one; he was after all king of Norway when Iceland came into the Christian fold in 1000 and was likely to be singled out for this reason alone. Óláfr Haraldsson, Saint Óláfr of Norway, was the other, in keeping with his exulted status in Scandinavia. But historical accuracy could not always be relied upon, as even the saga writers acknowledged. One of them, Karason the Learned, a close friend of Snorri, wrote as an introduction to his own work that 'you can accept from this composed saga whatever you think most likely, for in old sagas many things are confused. This is only to be expected where oral tradition alone supplies the material'.[20] And such works, we might add, were often unashamedly hero-worshipping in nature, another good reason that should make us suspect the objectivity of what is written. Sorting the wheat from the chaff in such circumstances can be very difficult and introduces another layer of subjectivity, that of the interpreting historian.

Two traditions emerged in Viking poetry, *Eddic* and *skaldic*. *Skaldic* poetry was constructed in such a way as to make it easier to remember. Snorri specifically argues that *skaldic* lines are subject to little corruption, even though they might represent traditions that are centuries old. Again this does not mean that they are to be regarded as detailed renditions of actual history, rather they are detailed renditions of remembered mythology which is something quite different. The *skalds* were highly valued men, much sought after by kings, earls and other important people. Fierce competition for their services could arise; to have a renowned praise teller in your court was a mark of distinction. They were often peripatetic; the late thirteenth-century saga of Gunnlaug, who was a famous Icelandic *skald* in his own right, mentions him being in Dublin, where Sitriuc Silkbeard is the object of his praise, as well as visiting London, Orkney, Sweden and Norway.[21]

Snorri Sturluson does his best to protect the great poets of the Viking period against accusations of misleading their audience. He says that no court poet would dare tell a story about a king that was blatantly untrue as everyone would know this to be the case and what would follow would be more a form of mockery than of praise. One commentator suggested that 'a Court-Poet, in effect, could over-praise, but he could not lie'.[22] Yet it is debatable whether or not in the end there is much of a difference. Once a truth is stretched over time it becomes ever more elastic until at the conclusion of a game of 'Chinese Whispers' the reality is obscured beneath a heavy historical mist that conceals what actually happened.

Often a saga writer's view of an individual or a series of events was shaped by where they came from in Scandinavia. For example, Harald Hardrada was painted heroically in Snorri's saga of which the Norwegian king is the hero; Harald was generally good to Iceland, possibly because he had bigger fish to fry elsewhere. The Norwegian writer Theodoricus, writing in about 1180, also sees Harald as a praiseworthy figure. But Adam of Bremen, whose main source of information was King Sveinn Estrithsson of Denmark, a bitter rival of Harald's, paints him as an evil figure and some later writers even accused him of killing his half-brother St Óláfr, the worst of all possible accusations in Scandinavian Christendom given the latter's status in the eyes of many hagiographers.[23]

Ultimately the saga writers were concerned first and last with the actions of their main characters and not the events that they were involved in, or only in so far as they said something about the respective protagonists. The sagas are really heroic biographies, telling of the epic actions of the men (and women) involved in them in ways that inform the reader about their essential character, personality and motivations. They are not histories at all, they are soap operas in verse, penned with a heroically minded audience in view. The great historical events of the age are background landscape details of limited relevance to Snorri's wider story, that of the great hero at the epicentre of whatever particular saga he is writing at the time.

This goes too for the stories the saga writers told of Viking religion. Much of what we know of the Norse pantheon is derived from these sagas. It has been said that these religious stories 'are the product of the high imagination of a sophisticated literary civilisation of the twelfth and thirteenth centuries. They represent the triumph of antiquarian reconstruction. As such our *Tales from Asgarth* tell us much of the fine achievements of Icelandic civilisation; they only reflect dimly, and sometimes distort grossly, the gods of the Viking Age'.[24]

The sagas come in different guises. In keeping with that foible of humanity that insists on allocating labels, different names distinguish these guises. For example, there are *konungasögur,* 'king's sagas', or *fornaldarsögur,* 'sagas of old times'; *Islendingasögur,* 'Icelandic sagas' which tell the island's early Viking history; or *riddarasögur,* 'knightly sagas' complete with Iceland's own version of chivalric storytelling including wizards and dragons.

Now modern scholars have had time to further reflect on the labelling process, they have decided it is unwise to insist too much on strict categorisation and that some sagas may have elements of more than one 'type' present in them. Of course, distinguishing fact from fiction may not always be as easy as it is when the writer talks about dragons and wizards; and the difficulty is compounded when one realises that those who wrote up the sagas were not only capable of adding their own factoids to a given storyline but on occasion were positively encouraged to do so.[25]

While the Icelandic saga writers are now the most internationally recognisable, there were other contemporary authors from elsewhere. Probably the best-known was the Dane Saxo Grammaticus ('the learned') who wrote a 'Danish History' (the *Gesta Danorum)* which was heavily based on mythology. Ubiquitous semi-mythological figures such as Ragnar Lodbrok make an appearance, this time with the story that he gained the hand of his wife by taking on and eliminating giant adders that she had hand-reared which had got out of control. The supernatural form of these snakes is emphasised by the information that they were given an ox carcass to feed on daily; it can confidently said no currently existing species of adder would be capable of doing such a thing.[26]

Yet rank and file Vikings added to the legend in their own way, long after the classic Viking Age had passed. On one bitterly cold January evening on Orkney in 1154 (the saga writer even gives us the date; thirteen days after Christmas), a party of men of Norse descent were fighting their way through a blizzard. Caught out in the open, they sought refuge in an extraordinary place. Nearby was the Neolithic burial mound of Maeshowe, even then 4,000 years old. They broke into its inner chamber for sanctuary and a party quickly started. In the course of it, allegedly two of the men went mad. We are told this in the *Orkneyinga Saga.*

Yet it was not just a saga writer who told the story; the men themselves did. On the stone walls of this sacred place they carved one of the richest rune collections that has come down to us; and what a story they relay. There were thirty-three runic carvings in all. One spoke with salacious relish of the charms of Ingigerth, a local woman. Another suggested that the tomb even pre-dated the time of Ragnar Lodbrok. A further inscription was laconic but easy to interpret: 'Thorni bedded. Helgi carved.' All very Viking one might think; a drunken orgy in a pagan monument. All except for one inscription. This referred simply to the men as 'Jerusalem travellers'. These men of Viking descent were, it seems, not just old-style Vikings, not even old-style Vikings, they were Crusaders. It was an incredible change of direction in the story of a group whose ancestors had sacked Lindisfarne and Iona.[27]

The post-Viking age

Following the passing of the Viking age, Scandinavian influence lived on in various parts of Britain, in Scotland in particular. Yet this no longer had the characteristics of the Vikings of old, rather it involved the ongoing interest of a new nation state, Norway, in affairs there. In 1263,

Hákon of Norway, moved on the west coast of Scotland to reinforce his endangered authority there, assembling his forces in Orkney before advancing further. He moored off the Little and Great Cumbrae islands in the lower Firth of Clyde. Chroniclers did their best to talk up the Battle of Largs that then took place on 2 October as a bloodthirsty affair and a fitting end to Viking involvement in Scotland. In fact, it was nothing of the sort. As one writer remarked, 'the Battle of Largs is an epic conflict of Scottish legend, wherein single corpses are counted as tens, and a ragged seashore skirmish is transformed into a struggle of giants'. The reality, he goes on to say, is that 'the weather, which wins more battles then generals admit, won this engagement before it was truly begun'. Contrary winds drove the Norwegian fleet aground and a brief engagement on the beach followed before the Norwegians disengaged.[28]

There was nothing particularly dramatic or saga-like about the end to this phase of Scottish history; but the Battle of Largs marked the closing of a chapter for the Vikings and their descendants in Scotland. Scandinavian involvement in Scotland went out with a whimper rather than a bang. A few decades later the Western Isles were ceded to Scotland by the Treaty of Perth in 1266, although the inhabitants of those distant places maintained a stubborn autonomy from the government in Edinburgh for centuries. Not until 1472 though did Orkney and Shetland transfer ownership from the King of Norway to his counterpart in Scotland.

In 1645, a Papal delegate by the name of Giovanni Battista Rinuccini visited Ireland. He took with him a potted history of the country, which had been prepared for him by way of a briefing. This told him unambiguously that Christianity had been virtually wiped out by the Viking incursions and when the English king, Henry II, conquered Ireland with papal support it was with the express purpose of bringing the true faith back to the fore again. This was a gross exaggeration and a significant distortion of the truth; and many an Irishman would not look fondly on the incursions of Henry II that ushered in nearly 750 years of English rule. But the image of the pagan invaders had clearly by now taken strong root. It was easy to be fixated on the threat from pagan Vikings when some places were attacked so frequently; for example, there are mentions of eleven raids on St David's in the south-west of Wales between 967 and 1051.[29]

Contemporary writers had emphasised the pagan nature of the attackers; references in the various accounts often talk of 'pagans', 'heathens' or 'gentiles'. As such the perception was created that these were specific attacks on Christendom, a theme taken up by later writers such as the author of the *Cogadh Gaedhel re Gallaibh*, an almost unashamed work of Christian propaganda.

It is highly unlikely that the religious attachment of the institutions raided was of much concern to the majority of the attackers though there may have been some zealots who abjured Christianity such as the raiders who smashed the cross slab at Portmahomack into several hundred pieces or the raiders of the lonely rock of Skellig Michael. Primarily such institutions were sources of wealth that offered significant numbers of potential slaves, the men, women and children working the lands round about. These was the raiders' prime motivation.

With the rise of nationalism in the nineteenth century matters developed further. British writers looked back to a part-Viking heritage which had helped to form their national character. Writing in 1841, the Anglo-Irish George Darley wrote of the Viking king Anlaf [Óláfr] who had fought at Brunanburh in the following terms:

> Anlaf's ... picturesque retinue – the sea-kings or prince-pirates of Scandinavia – gave occasion to sketch that people also, from whom we, as part Danish, have derived, perhaps, much of our enterprising character, as well as the daring and wild sublimity which distinguishes our poetic genius.[30]

This was a period which saw a concentration on the emergence and importance of nation states. Scandinavia was not exempt from this trend. Denmark was a prime example of this, seeking redemption in the aftermath of crushing defeat against the Prussian juggernaut in 1864 when Schleswig-Holstein, historically normally a part of Denmark, was lost. The Dane Johannes Steenstrup made great play of Danish involvement in the Viking colonisation of Europe and in the process claimed Rollo of Normandy as one of his own countrymen. The Norwegians and Swedes were not slow onto the bandwagon either.[31]

The year 1892 saw the quatercentenary of the rediscovery of the Americas by Europeans in the shape of Christopher Columbus. As a reminder that he was not the first man from Europe to set foot there, a copy of the Gokstad ship set sail for America in the following year. It was skippered by Captain Magnus Andersen who was full of praise for the vessel, saying that with the wind in support the ship sailed at speeds of up to 11 knots, a very respectable rate of progress and one which on occasion left the modern American clipper ship accompanying it far behind. A more recent journey made in a replica Viking *knarr* (merchant vessel) called the *Saga Siglar* in 1984 survived 70-knot winds and 45-foot waves on the way from Norway to Boston via Greenland, Labrador and Nova Scotia, though the crew had to use bailers to make it through as no doubt the original Viking seafarers had to do on occasion.[32]

The Vikings in the New World were appropriated in all kinds of inaccurate ways. The so-called Kensington Stone was found in Minnesota in 1898. It was helpfully dated by part of the inscription to

1362 and told of a party of Scandinavian traders who had undertaken a ten-day journey across land from their ships which they had sailed across from Vinland. It is a fascinating piece of 'evidence' for post-Viking Age Scandinavians in Vinland and of their visits deep into the heart of North America, except for the fact that runologists and historians have picked huge holes in its authenticity.[33]

Neither was this the first example of 'wishful thinking' concerning Vikings in America. Benedict Arnold, Governor of Rhode Island in 1675 (not to be confused with the American general of the War of Independence who infamously defected to the British) noted a tower in his region which two centuries later was claimed to be of twelfth-century vintage by a Swedish expert, Oscar Montelius. In reality, the Newport Tower probably dated back to no more than three decades before Arnold first wrote about it.

Other items of highly dubious 'evidence' emerged to populate ancient America with a hungry horde of expansionist Scandinavians of Viking heritage. They all paled into insignificance compared to the so-called Vinland Map which appeared in 1965. It portrayed Greenland in surprisingly good detail and made mention by name of Leif Eriksson and Bjarni Herjólfsson. It also showed the specific locations of Vinland, Markland and Helluland. It was a major discovery; that is until scientific investigation showed that the ink with which it had been produced could not be dated back before the First World War. It was subsequently shown to probably be a product of the overactive imagination of a Yugoslav professor of history, Luka Jelič. It was slightly disconcerting during the research for this book to watch a reputable BBC documentary from 1966 in which some prominent historians from the time questioned the authenticity of L'Anse aux Meadows as a Viking site but accepted the Vinland Map as a genuine document; a necessary reminder to historians and archaeologists never to be overconfident about their interpretation of the truth.

The Vikings came to be regarded as some kind of 'noble savage'. In nineteenth-century Britain, they had a role in the works of Sir Walter Scott and were a popular subject for pre-Raphaelite artists. Twentieth-century historians have on occasion more subtly picked up the theme, suggesting that accounts of their horrors have been vastly overplayed; but not everyone agrees. To quote the words of a prominent Viking historian, Alfred P. Smyth, those who insist that they have had 'a bad press [from] narrow-minded monkish chroniclers who enjoyed a monopoly on reporting, do so in face of a formidable body of evidence centring on the ninth and tenth centuries which testifies to a relentless catalogue of treachery and cruelty ranging from Ireland and Spain in the West, to the banks of the Volga in the East'.[34]

In recent times, Bernard Cornwell in his books on Uhtred of Bebbanborough drew heavily on the complications of having both

Anglo-Saxon and Viking influences on an individual's life. This idea was also mined successfully at around the turn of the nineteenth/ twentieth centuries. The writer Charles Whistler wrote a number of books exploiting the theme, such as *King Óláfr's Kinsman* (1897), *King Alfred's Viking* (1899), *Havelock the Dane* (1900) and *A Son of Odin* (1914). In 1925, Captain W. H. Milligan's work *Helgi the High-Born: A Story of the Days of Athelstan* was run as a series in *The Boy's Own Paper*.[35]

The historiography of the Vikings has also evolved. Following the work of Peter Sawyer in 1969, the history of the Vikings in England specifically was divided into two 'Viking Ages'. Sawyer saw the first of these as an age when the Vikings were seeking out land to settle, while the second was a quest for wealth, particularly in the form of tribute. In some ways, this appears over-simplistic and even to an extent confusing. In the so-called Early Viking Age, Vikings were certainly seeking out wealth as well as land. They were also receiving tribute on occasions. In the second 'Late' Viking Age they certainly conquered land in which to settle, in the case of England, in a political sense, all of it.

Despite these criticisms, the general thinking behind Sawyer's analysis has been widely accepted and extended to include all regions of the Viking-affected world, so that the period before 950 is seen as one that was 'the classic period of Viking activity as it is normally conceived' while the Late Viking Age (*c* 950 to 1100) is one that 'was characterized by various forms of acculturation abroad and by progressive developments in the homelands evinced by state formation, town growth, mintage, and conversion to Christianity'.[36]

The Vikings continue to live on and their mythology continues to evolve. Every so often, it is given a new lease of life, when a Hollywood epic is released or a major TV series is launched. There is nothing new in this. The Up Helly Aa festival held in Shetland every January celebrates a past that is now long gone; but it dates back only to the late nineteenth century. As in so many other cases, the past is now a long-forgotten country; or at least one that is very dubiously remembered in terms of historical accuracy. No matter; mythology in itself is a way in which history lives on, even if that mythology is relatively recent in its development.

That the Vikings played their part in shaping local legends is irrefutable. As a concluding example, there is in West Dorset a small hamlet, Whitchurch Canonicorum. The church there houses a medieval shrine, one of only two to survive the destructiveness of Henry VIII with its saint's relics intact.[37] The remains are those of a Saxon holy woman, Wite. Legend asserts that she was killed by Viking raiders in an attack on the hermitage where she lived her saintly life. There is precious little evidence to back up this story and there are other versions of the tale which make no mention of Vikings; it is probably part of a 'tendency [for the Vikings] to turn up in English folklore as all-purpose adversaries'.[38] As ever, the truth is tantalisingly unclear but that is not the point. The Vikings continue to inhabit the imagination, a terrifying manifestation of the 'other' and how it threatens us. It is such little glimpses, as we see in the stories of Saint Wite, Up Helly Aa and others, which will help to ensure the survival of their memory, however distorted a picture it gives, far into the future.

The Vikings in Perspective

This book has attempted to tell the history of the Vikings seen not just through the eyes of others but also through their own. It would be remiss to finish it without a final conclusion. Were they really the 'evil from the North' as referred to by contemporary chroniclers when seen through the prism of the Old Testament prophet Jeremiah or were they more than this? The answer to both questions is in my view 'yes'.

There is no doubt that they were a terrifying phenomenon to those on the receiving end of their unwelcome attentions. Their ability to strike without warning and escape again before local defences could be organised was something that distinguished them from other groups, even if other men of piratical persuasion were also active at the time. What also distinguished them from many other groups was that no target was sacrosanct, however holy its reputation. This to Christian eyes was undoubtedly shocking. There is plenty of evidence to back up these perceptions of terror: through chronicles, through sagas which often seem to have a germ in reality, through archaeology such as the sites at Portmahomack with its slaughtered monks or Ballateare with its sacrificial slave burial, through museum examples such as the slave chain in Dublin to quote some selective illustrations.

Yet did the terror become any less great when the Vikings adopted Christianity? In this case, the answer is, in the main, 'no'. They remained violent and unpredictable. While they possibly burned down churches less often, there were still occasions when such places did not escape destruction at their hands. Their faith was adaptable, a cloak that could be taken off when the occasion demanded. Cnut the Great, a generous benefactor of the Church, ordered his brother-in-law to be murdered on hallowed ground. He was not alone in this; later monarchs like Henry II of England and Robert the Bruce of Scotland were also implicated in similar outrages. And this is perhaps a useful reminder that these were violent times with many violent men around, Christian and non-Christian alike.

As the Vikings turned to conquest as opposed to just raiding they became if anything even more formidable opponents. Sweyn

Forkbeard's conquest of England was a hugely destructive campaign which unleashed terrible consequences for some of those caught up in it. Rollo created a Norman polity that became the scourge of Europe from Ireland to Sicily and even beyond to the Middle East. Norwegian and Danish contingents would take part in the Crusades. As Viking violence became more organised and centrally controlled, it also in some ways became more deadly.

Yet the Vikings were not alone in committing outrages. The latter years of what we might call the classic Viking Age also spawned the Crusading movement which unleashed unspeakable atrocities against Jews in Western Europe and against Muslims who were slaughtered in their thousands in Antioch and Jerusalem. The Vikings were in some ways just a particularly terrifying illustration of these violent times given their ability to raid from out of the blue.

So if the terrifying accounts of the Vikings are backed up by appropriate and relevant evidence, at the same time so are those committed by contemporary Christian warriors. It is debatable whether the end result of a brutal murder is justified any more by saying that it is an Act of God than it would be if it was claimed to be one inspired by Odin or Thor. We need to take into account the violent backdrop of these formative years in the history of Europe before being too harsh in our own judgements as to just how evil the Vikings were.

Maps

SCOTLAND IN THE VIKING AGE

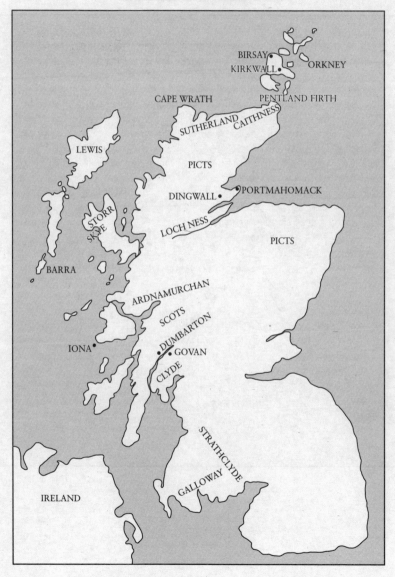

IRELAND IN THE VIKING AGE

ENGLAND AND WALES IN THE VIKING AGE

SCANDINAVIA IN THE VIKING AGE

EUROPE IN THE VIKING AGE

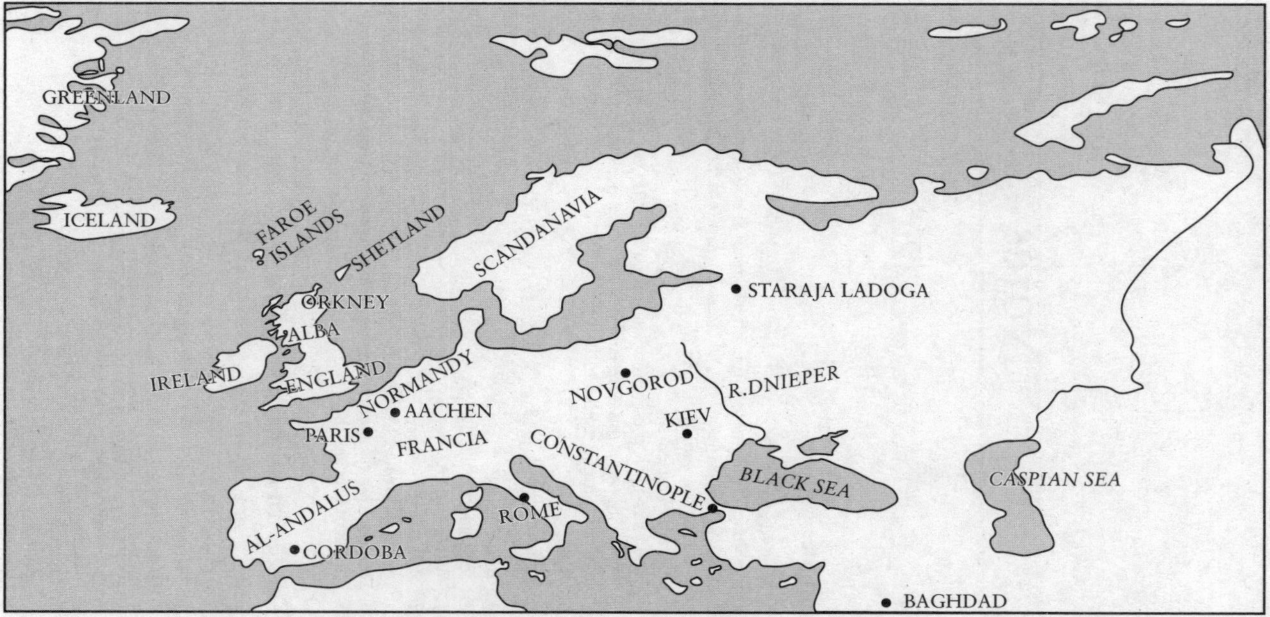

GREENLAND

ICELAND

FAROE ISLANDS

SHETLAND

ORKNEY

ALBA

IRELAND

ENGLAND

NORMANDY

PARIS

AACHEN

FRANCIA

AL-ANDALUS

CORDOBA

ROME

SCANDINAVIA

STARAJA LADOGA

NOVGOROD

R. DNIEPER

KIEV

CONSTANTINOPLE

BLACK SEA

CASPIAN SEA

BAGHDAD

Notes

Prologue

1. Randsborg 2
2. *See* Jones 77 footnote 1, Carroll, Harrison and Williams 6 and Richards 10
3. Jesse Byock, professor of Old Norse Literature at the University of California, Los Angeles, quoted in Gabriel
4. Adam of Bremen 20
5. That has been the contention until recent times. However, alternative explanations for this differentiation have been posited recently. These will be explored later in the book.
6. Wahlgren 34
7. E.g. Downham xv
8. In Jones 62
9. Woolf 50–51
10. *See* Jones 83
11. Wahlgren 150
12. Parker 140
13. Adam of Bremen 191
14. Figures from the National Survey and Cadastre of Denmark 2003
15. Adam of Bremen 187

1 The Dawn of the Viking Age

1. Jones 24
2. Wilson 17
3. Nelson 12
4. Jones 29
5. Ibid 30
6. *Prose Edda* xxii
7. Magnusson 7
8. Jones 3
9. Zaluckyj 42
10. Randsborg 1

11. Adams 59
12. Magnusson 15
13. Quotes in Magnusson 26–27
14. Magnusson 12
15. Peers 26. William of Malmesbury tells us, however, that they were variant branches of the family tree, being descended from different sons of Woden.
16. Zaluckyj 48
17. Hilts January 2015
18. *Prose Edda* 93
19. It is not clear if Snorri wrote the whole of the *Prose Edda* or just part of it. See *Prose Edda* xii.
20. *Skald* is the Old Norse word for 'poet'.
21. *Prose Edda* 6
22. Ferguson 21–22
23. Zaluckyj 51–52
24. *Prose Edda* 39
25. *Landnámabók* 154, Helgi later settled in Iceland and was surprised when, after releasing two pigs into the wild there, he came back two years later to find a herd of 70: ibid 155
26. Bolton *Cnut the Great* 38, Æthelweard 26
27. Carroll, Harrison and Williams 59
28. Randsborg 25. Ferguson 369, Richards 126 notes about 2,500 examples from Sweden, 220 from Denmark, a handful from Norway and none at all in Iceland.
29. Wahlgren 52
30. Fuglesang in Clarke and Johnson 38
31. The basis of this was the Frostathing Law; *see* Jones 148. It is one of the oldest Norse laws known, most famously for its assertion that 'with law shall our land be built, and not desolated by lawlessness', a maxim that some modern countries might do well to follow.
32. Jones 150
33. Article by Sarah Zielinski, Smithsonian.com July 8 2015
34. Price etc. Uppsala assumed great symbolical importance and became associated with the royal dynasties that later emerged in Sweden, especially from the early ninth century onwards.
35. There were two such horns found in Jutland, one in 1639, the other in 1734. They were both stolen from the Royal Treasury in Denmark in 1802 and melted down for their bullion value. The runes on the Horns revealed that they were made by Hlewagistir, son of Holti. *See* Wahlgren 46–47.
36. Zaluckyj 26, Young 26–27.
37. *Guta Saga* vii. This is a short but valuable work – the analysis and introduction to the modern translation of the text is comfortably longer than the saga itself. For its oral origins, see xvi
38. *The Saga of Ragnar Lodbrok and his Sons* 19. Viking poets had a stock of various names to call beasts such as ravens, wolves, horses as well as various other objects.
39. Hill *Anglo-Saxons* 41
40. Peers 30
41. Downham 11
42. McGettigan 32, quoting from the *Annals of the Four Masters*
43. Ferguson 72
44. Loyn 41

45. To the Vikings, Germany – especially the northern part – was 'Saxland' after the Saxons who lived there.

46. Ganz *Einhard and Notker*... 23

47. H.B. Clarke in Keen 58

48. Ganz *Einhard and Notker*... xi

49. *Alcuin of York* 42

50. There are a few surviving references where Irene calls herself Emperor in official documents; though in the interests of balance it is only right to point out that there are many more when she calls herself 'Empress'.

2 The Great Suffering

1. Both January and June are given as dates for the attack on Lindisfarne. As the Vikings are known for their summer raiding the June date seems more likely.

2. Ferguson 56

3. *Alcuin of York*, 18. Reading Alcuin's letters to Æthelred, he clearly did not have a lot of respect for his kingly qualities or way of life. When reading letters that begin with phrases such as 'it is because I remember your tender affection...' or similar, then one learns to recognise that a telling-off will follow on not long after. The allusion to incest needs to be seen in context. This period in history saw a stricter interpretation of the degrees of relationship within which marriage was allowed, so some which would previously have been acceptable were now prohibited such as those between cousins (there had also been instances of sons marrying their stepmothers). The laws were tightened by Charlemagne, to whom Alcuin was a close and trusted adviser.

4. Ferguson 43

5. *Alcuin of York*, 36

6. Ibid 52

7. Smyth 81

8. *See* Woolf 359 for a summary of current thinking on the *Historia*

9. Dales 53

10. *Alcuin of York* 66

11. Hadley 16

12. *Ibn Fadlān* 17

13. Woolf 43–44

14. It is a typically laconic comment from the writer of the *Annals,* but this was largely representative of chronicle writing of the time. In contrast it is something of a light relief to read the *ASC's* occasional references to ominous omens, fiery portents and the terrifying appearance of comets: sadly, these are not that common.

15. Woolf 45

16. Loyn 47

17. Suggestions have also been made that this was on the Isle of Man, though these are now largely discounted. *See* Griffiths 25

18. In Newman 19

19. Carroll, Harrison and Williams 130

20. In a number of hikes up Snowdon in North Wales I once saw Ireland across the sea from the top, though on every other occasion I was there the summit was shrouded in mist.

21. The two monasteries are referred to as a dual foundation in a way that might suggest they were actually physically adjacent. In fact, there was a 7-mile gap between Monkwearmouth – on the Wear – and Jarrow on the Tyne.

22. *Alcuin of York* 40
23. *See* Woolf 69, footnote 2. Hartness later became Hartlepool – *see* Adams 10
24. *Alcuin of York* 54
25. Ibid 44–45
26. William of Malmesbury 40
27. *See* Lavelle and Roffey 10
28. Woolf 52 and William of Malmesbury 8
29. *See* Ferguson 44
30. Zaluckyj 67
31. Hill *Viking Wars* 95
32. In a charter to Christchurch, Canterbury, dated 792: *see* Adams 23. In another translation, the words are as follows: that men of the Archbishop of Canterbury's estates were to provide 'army service against the heathen of the seas with their roving fleets'.
33. *See* Lavelle and Roffey, 2
34. Adams 65
35. Eamonn P. Kelly in Clarke and Johnson 55
36. Introduction to Ganz *Einhard and Notker* xi
37. Wahlgren 149
38. David Talbot Rice in the Preface to Wilson, 8
39. Magnusson 68
40. Ganz *Einhard and Notker…* 105
41. *See* Derek Gore in Lavelle and Roffey 58–59
42. *See* Williams 123
43. Ganz *Einhard and Notker* 30–31

3 The Shadow of Terror

1. Loyn 33
2. Adams 89 states that in the pre-Viking Age no coins were minted in Britain north of York though some circulated in what is now Scotland as bullion
3. Loyn 34
4. *Annals of Ulster*
5. Meehan 10
6. Ibid 10
7. Slightly different dates are given in various annals
8. *Refer to* Clarke and Johnson 13. Given its proximity to the coast, this appears very plausible.
9. Loyn 42
10. *See* Carver
11. Woolf 58–59
12. Purcell in Clarke and Johnson 52
13. Ibid 54
14. Adams 83
15. In Clarke and Johnson 219
16. Griffiths 26–27
17. Stenton 246
18. The debates for and against the demolition of the ninth-century church by Viking attacks are well summarised in Hadley Chapter 5
19. Hill *Viking Wars* 8
20. Zaluckyj 241

21. Magnusson 91.
22. Ringstedt 127
23. Harrison 32. The later writer John of Wallingford described the Vikings' bathing habits and noted, perhaps with an element of surprise, that they changed their clothes quite regularly; *see* O'Brien 50.
24. Ringstedt 143
25. *Prose Edda* 8
26. Wilson 106
27. *See Ibn Fadlān* 250 (Appendix 2)
28. Adams 28 (footnote) suggests that there twelve places called Tarbert or Tarbat in Scotland and two in Ireland.
29. Ganz *Einhard and Notker ...* 10
30. Randsborg 14
31. Williams 129
32. *See* article by Sindbæk.
33. Jones 168
34. *See* Ganz, *Einhard and Notker...* 104
35. Ibid 30. Einhard records that the elephant was the only such example in the possession of Harun al-Rashid, which emphasises its rarity value.
36. Ibid 28
37. Ibid 31
38. *See* Hadley 32 for comment on the later treaty made between Alfred of Wessex and the Danish leader Guthrum as a similar example of an event which drew the Vikings into the mainstream of English affairs.
39. Adam of Bremen 21

4 Breakout

1. *See* Nelson 78, who says that these events took place at Ingelheim as does Parker 14 and 47. However, Adam of Bremen 21 specifically places these events at Mainz.
2. Smyth 82–86
3. *Alcuin of York* 73
4. *See* Zaluckyj 44
5. Adam of Bremen 22
6. Fuglesang in Clarke and Johnson 40
7. Adam of Bremen 51
8. Ibid 26
9. Ibid 105
10. *See* Einhard 16
11. Williams 300
12. *Einhard and Notker...* 113
13. Derek Gore in Lavelle and Roffey 58, quoting D. Hill, *An Atlas of Anglo-Saxon England*
14. What the term *longphort* specifically means is not completely clear; it could either be 'ship-harbour' or 'ship-fort'. *See* Gareth Williams in Clarke and Johnson 94
15. Emer Purcell in Clarke and Johnson 41–43
16. Linzi Simpson in Clarke and Johnson 128
17. Griffiths 120, quoting work by Linzi Simpson and others
18. *Annals of St Bertin* 35. Horik soon followed his complaint up with another delegation of envoys to Louis, this time claiming compensation.
19. Derek Gore in Lavelle and Roffey 58

Notes

20. The letter is quoted at length in the *Annals of St Bertin* under the year 839.
21. Quite why he was called this remains a bone of contention. Some argue that it is because he simply lacked hair. Others say that the reference is in fact an ironic one because he was liberally endowed with it. A subtler interpretation is that the name came about because he was originally landless, being by far the youngest sibling, while his brothers were well provided with territory.
22. The *Annals of Fulda* for 852 note the death of 'Harald the Northman' who 'became suspect to the leading men of the northern regions and the warders of the Danish March as of doubtful loyalty and a potential traitor and was therefore killed by them'.
23. Nelson 137
24. Adam of Bremen 38 though probably referring to events that happened later and conflating them.
25. Magnusson 71; Jones, 211, reckons that they were men who had by now established a base in Ireland from which they could launch further assaults such as this one. There is some confusion about the year of this raid with some accounts giving it as 842, others 843.
26. As per the *Annals of St Bertin* for 843. Actions such as the killing of bishops during church services have become a part of the standard stereotype for the excesses of the Vikings and accounts of such events should be treated cautiously.
27. *See* Williams in Clarke and Johnson 127
28. Nelson 5
29. *Ragnar Lodbrok* 8. See also Ferguson 142
30. Nelson 141
31. Ibid 151
32. For example, when trading with the Venetians who paid for goods in local currency. *See* Williams 271
33. Persuasively argued in Nelson 24–25. The same author, 31, suggests that by the 860s perhaps 'tens of millions' of coins were in circulation in Francia. It appears likely that a shortage of coins at around this time led to Charles the Bald opening more mints.
34. Williams in Clarke and Johnson 107
35. Carroll, Harrison and Williams 102
36. Ibid 22
37. *See* Nelson 152
38. In Magnusson 72
39. In Jones 215
40. The figure of 600 ships is regarded by some prominent historians as being implausible and seems a very high number. *See* footnote 3 in *Annals of St Bertin*, 61. *See also* Adam of Bremen 26 and footnote 63.
41. Williams 300
42. Nelson 20
43. The Moors were more than capable of launching piratical attacks of their own. Reports of such on Francia during this period are referred to in the *Annals of St Bertin*.
44. In *Ibn Fadlæn* 204
45. *See* for example Kennedy in *Muslim Spain and Portugal: A Political History of Al-Andalus,* Routledge, 2011
46. Precisely where this was is a matter for debate. It has been traditionally suggested that it was just to the north of the Forth, but Alex Woolf has recently argued it was further north around Moray and Ross. *See* Downham 139, Evans 8.

47. Woolf 66–67
48. Ibid 13
49. Carroll, Harrison and Williams 80
50. Griffiths 122
51. The story is summarised in Newman 52
52. *See* for example Donnchadh Ó Corrain in Clarke and Johnson 486–487
53. *See* Clarke and Johnson 9
54. H.B. Clarke in Keen 54
55. *See* map in Griffiths 29
56. Williams in Clarke and Johnson 123
57. Jones 194
58. Ibid 190
59. *See* Harris et al for further information. *See* Marianne Hem Eriksen in Eriksen et al Chapter 6 for the importance of rings of various types.

5 The Great Heathen Army

1. *See* Williams in Clarke and Johnson 104. The 860s and 870s saw a particularly marked increase in the 'bullion economy': ibid 114.
2. Jones 193, Wahlgren 151
3. Asser 68, Æthelweard 32
4. Smyth 9
5. Thanet is named in the *Anglo-Saxon Chronicle* as the place where they overwintered. Asser 68 names it as Sheppey but may well be mistaken as the *ASC* puts them here in 855. Æthelweard 31 also names it as Thanet; but betrays a limited knowledge of his own country by saying that it was 'situated not far from Britain' which suggests he thought that it was entirely separate from it.
6. Asser 69
7. Woolf 70
8. Ibid 107
9. Downham 15
10. Ibid 15 and introduction, xv–xx. These arguments were developed by the late Professor Alfred Smyth and taken on by David Dumville.
11. Adam of Bremen 37
12. *Ragnar Lodbrok* 12
13. Williams in Clarke and Johnson 120–121
14. Downham 204
15. Adams 87–89
16. Woolf 101
17. *See* footnote 9 in *Annals of St Bertin* p73 for a brief summary of the respective arguments
18. Woolf 53
19. Adam of Bremen 21
20. *Annals of St Bertin* for 853
21. Adams 97
22. Norton 63
23. Simpson in Clarke and Johnson 138
24. Purcell in Clarke and Johnson 53
25. Downham 22
26. *See* Woolf 26 for a discussion on the role of kings in Pictland at a similar time in history.

27. *See Annals of St Bertin* for 857
28. Nelson 38
29. *Annals of St Bertin* for 858
30. Nelson 160
31. Ibid 35
32. Ibid 188
33. *See* Benjamin Pohl: *Dudo of St Quentin's Historia Normannorum – Tradition, Invention and Memory,* University of York, 2015, p136
34. *Landnámabók* 105
35. Ibid 107
36. Ibid 144
37. Ibid 19
38. Wilson 116
39. Carroll, Harrison and Williams 127
40. *Landnámabók* 35–36
41. Ferguson 162
42. *Landnámabók* 29 has some detailed direction finding for the route from Norway to Iceland. Wahlgren 150 points out that seven days is rather slow time in absolute terms, the sedate rate of progress being due to unhelpful current and wind direction though if the conditions were right there are records of the trip taking only four days. The journey the other way from Iceland to Svalbard/Spitzbergen was on the other hand regularly made in only four days.
43. Wilson 78
44. The '*things*' are listed in *Landnámabók* 22. For courtyard sites *see* Olsen in Eriksen et al Chapter 4.
45. Jones 250
46. Wahlgren 34. While the whole *Chronicle* was once attributed to Nestor, modern scholars now believe it to be a composite collection.
47. *See* Nelson 199
48. Asser 74
49. *Annals of St Bertin* for the year 863
50. Ibid 129
51. Asser gives the year as 864, the *ASC* as 865
52. Æthelweard 35. Note that there are no contemporary references to Ubba who only appears in accounts that were written sometime after the event.
53. Woolf 72
54. The name of 'the Great Heathen Army' was recorded in the 'B' (Abingdon) version of the *ASC* for 867.
55. Randsborg 127 says that evidence of lances and stirrups that can be dated to the tenth century have been found in graves in Denmark but none from the previous century. This suggests that over time perhaps cavalry did come into use to a limited extent among Viking forces.
56. *Ragnar Lodbrok* 30
57. Asser 76
58. The *Historia de Sancto Cuthberto* 51 says that the leader of this Viking army was Ubba.
59. Ibid 85
60. Hadley, 11
61. *See* Woolf 74–76
62. *Orkneyinga Saga* 30
63. Smyth 24

64. Abbo in Arnold 15: 'suffering as a noble martyr like Sebastian'
65. Downham 66
66. *Ragnar Lodbrok* 70
67. Bartlett 109–110
68. Foot 109. For the connection between Edmund's later status and the death of Sveinn, *see* e.g. Young 101
69. Adams 107, Young 72–73
70. Hadley 11–12
71. Clarkson *Strathclyde* 45
72. Which strictly speaking means that any reference to 'Strathclyde' before these events is an anachronism. The name first appears in the *Annals of Ulster,* in 872.
73. Hill *Viking Wars* 38
74. Asser 78
75. The 'place of slaughter' or mælstow is the name routinely given by the *ASC* to battlefields.
76. Asser 80
77. Ibid 79. The Saxon succession process did not require that sons should be the heir apparent, merely that the successor should be an Atheling, 'throne-worthy' or in other words a member of the royal bloodline.
78. It is only mentioned in the *ASC*. This is an example of a number of question marks in Asser's account. His work often verges on hagiography regarding Alfred. So major are some of the inconsistencies that several leading historians have concluded that his work is a later forgery. This is one significant contention of Smyth's *Alfred the Great*.
79. Hill *Anglo-Saxons* 12. Hill *Viking Wars* suggests that the battle may have been fought at Marten, near the Iron Age hillfort of Walbury Camp, 20 miles north of Wilton; 49.
80. Smyth 38
81. Ibid 81
82. *See* Nelson 145
83. Æthelweard's account is particularly useful as it contains information not found elsewhere but as it is 'only' a century later than some of the events that he describes there is a decent chance that he had access to other information that has been subsequently lost.
84. Zaluckyj 244. Æthelweard 40
85. Sawyer, *Anglo-Saxon Charters, etc.* Downham 70
86. The suggestion of the numbers present comes from Richards 23. A number of the *longphuirt* in Ireland have similar 'D-shaped' characteristics. There are similar examples in Scandinavia, though interestingly many of them based on current knowledge seem to post-date the sites in Ireland; *see* Kelly in Clarke and Johnson 57. Dublin provides an interesting variation as the *longphort* there was constructed on the intersection of the Liffey and Poddle, which means it had water on three sides and only one landward side. The two rivers met in a place that was known as the 'black pool': in Irish 'Dubh Linn'.
87. The process of classifying different types of Viking-era swords was developed by Jan Peterson in 1920, hence the name given to the generic categorisation system of Viking sword types.
88. *See* Biddle and Kjølbye-Biddle
89. Discussed in the BBC archaeological TV programme *Digging for Britain* in 2017
90. Downham 23

91. Ibid 67; Smyth 61
92. *Ragnar Lodbrok* 70
93. *See* Brian Hodkinson in Clarke and Johnson 183
94. Woolf 124 See also Adams 88
95. Marshall 41
96. Adams 123
97. A styca is a copper alloy coin specifically connected with Northumbria. Silver pennies were the norm in Wessex and Mercia. Hacksilver was the most common item found in many of the main Viking sites in England and Ireland. *See* Williams in Clarke and Johnson 109
98. Williams in Clarke and Johnson 99
99. *Historia de Sancto Cuthberto* 53
100. Woolf 113
101. *Historia de Sancto Cuthberto* 59
102. South 3
103. *Annals of St Bertin* for 873
104. *See* e.g. Jones, footnote 2 242–243
105. *See Irish Archaeology* at http://irisharchaeology.ie/2016/11/hoard-of-islamic-silver-coins-found-in-sweden/

6 England on the Brink

1. *Annals of St Bertin* 200
2. *See* Purcell in Clarke and Johnson 48
3. Hinton 54, Æthelweard 41
4. Einhard 30
5. Zaluckyj 245. For detailed consideration of the Danelaw *see* Lesley Abrams, Chapter 10 in Higham and Hill
6. Smyth 54–55
7. In contrast to the *ASC*, Asser suggests that the Viking raid was launched from Exeter, suggesting that they had not left there at all. For a possible explanation concerning a missing entry from the *ASC see* p83 of Asser, footnote 94. A surprise raid from Gloucester makes more sense than one from Exeter given the former's proximity to Chippenham; from Gloucester to Chippenham is about 30 miles; from Exeter it is nearer 90. In this instance, Asser's account seems plain wrong.
8. Smyth 72
9. Asser 103
10. Ibid 103
11. The *ASC* does not mention Ubba by name; however, several slightly later sources do. It is equally unclear whether the said Ubba was actually one of the sons of Ragnar, along with the infamous Ivarr the Boneless, as the suggestions that he was only emerge some time after the event.
12. Horspool 66 suggests Countisbury; Hill *Viking Wars* 70 Cannington. A site in Somerset makes more practical sense if Ubba's attack was coordinated with that of Guthrum's force.
13. So says the *ASC*: Asser says 1,200
14. Smyth 79.
15. Asser 85
16. From his translation of *Gregory's Pastoral Care,* in Asser 125
17. Norton 91

18. Ibid
19. Ibid 75
20. Carroll, Harrison and Williams 23
21. Clarkson Æthelflaed 46
22. Hill *Anglo-Saxons* 89. William's words were given credence by the discovery of a fragment of an inscription in 1902 which, though not fully complete, suggests that it quoted the same.
23. Hill *Anglo-Saxons* 90
24. Ibid 43
25. Ibid 46
26. *See* Asser 103 and footnote 233. It has been argued since that this identification is incorrect; but it would be nice to know more about this young man whose life had spanned cultural boundaries. Oda is discussed in Ferguson 227–229 who theorises that he was of Danish heritage, based on later accounts.
27. There is some divergence of opinion here. The *ASC* implies that the two forces, those of Guthrum and the new arrivals at Fulham, did not combine. Asser suggests that they did. *See* Smyth 87.
28. Williams in Clarke and Johnson 104. *See* also Richards 70.
29. Hadley 34
30. The arguments are summarised in Downham 76. *See also Historia de Sancto Cuthberto* 53
31. *Historia de Sancto Cuthberto* 59
32. Also called Guthfrith in some accounts
33. Downham 78
34. The *Annals* were not written at, or for, the Benedictine abbey of St Bertin, which is in Saint-Omer. They get their name from the fact that the sole surviving complete copy of the work was preserved there.
35. *Annals of St Bertin* 222. The term *civitas* was applied to the see of a bishop – see Introduction to the *Annals*, 18
36. Smyth 110
37. Adams footnote 45, quoting Cowie and Blackmore (2012). Adams considers the estimate to probably be on the high side.
38. The use of the word 'Danes' when there appear to have been men from elsewhere in continental Europe in the Viking army (*see* Hadley 32) is a reminder that this is a generic categorisation for those who were with the Great Army rather a nationalistic designation.
39. The chronicler Æthelweard mentions a peace treaty but gives no details of what was included in it.
40. Carroll, Harrison and Williams 52
41. *See* Asser, footnote 253
42. Smyth 129
43. Ibid, especially Chapter IV which discusses possible reasons for this in some detail.
44. Adams 205 footnote
45. Smyth 122
46. Ibid 134
47. Ibid 125. He also suggests it is possible that the reason that Alfred stood godfather for Hæsten's sons rather than the veteran Viking leader may be because the latter had already been baptised in Francia earlier on in his career.
48. Hadley 35
49. Bolton *The Empire of Cnut...* 60–61
50. *See* Downham 73

51. Loe et al 13
52. For a discussion of Othere and his intrepid adventures, *see* Jones 158–162
53. Smyth 577
54. Ibid 40
55. Magnusson 78
56. Jones 225
57. Keynes and Lapidge in the Introduction to Asser 40
58. *Heimskringla*. 'Wolf-coats' is another name for berserkers.
59. These events are described in the *Orkneyinga Saga*
60. Jones 90
61. *See* e.g. *Landnámabók* 38
62. Adam of Bremen 216
63. *Landnámabók* 70
64. Ibid 37
65. Hudson 15. These events are discussed in Erik the Red's Saga in *The Vinland Saga*. More detail on them is given in the *Orkneyinga Saga* 27
66. *Orkneyinga Saga* 27
67. Ferguson 298
68. The polar bear reference is from *Landnámabók* 133. Polar bears are not resident in modern Iceland, but an occasional interloper will occasionally drift over from eastern Greenland on the ice. They are invariably euthanised in Iceland nowadays as they are hungry when they arrive and a danger to humans and livestock.
69. *Landnámabók* 172
70. Ibid 139
71. Ibid 167
72. Ibid 181
73. *Orkneyinga Saga* 29. Carver *Portmahomack – Monastery of the Picts* 158 points out that the claim is nonsensical as evidence from the monastery showed the monks there to have burnt turf as fuel 200 years earlier
74. Probably not the Ketill Flatnose referred to earlier. Ketill was a fairly common Viking name.
75. O'Brien 16
76. *Orkneyinga Saga* 33
77. Downham 76

7 An Uneasy Equilibrium

1. Jones 112
2. In Asser 191
3. In Hill *Anglo-Saxons* 103
4. Coins of Æthelwold have also been found that were minted in York.
5. *See* Hudson 22
6. E.g. Griffiths 21
7. See Kelly in Clarke and Johnson 90
8. *Chronicles of the Kings of Alba* in Wolff 127. *See also* Evans 107
9. *Annals of Ulster* for 904, in Wolff 127
10. Hudson 25
11. A short summary of these differences of opinion can be found in Hadley 2–7
12. Clarkson *Strathclyde* 58
13. Carroll, Harrison and Williams 53

14. Downham 84
15. Clarkson *Strathclyde* 63, 80
16. Ibid 64
17. Carroll, Harrison and Williams 109. There was a recorded raid on Abaskun on the eastern Caspian in 910 and another in the region of Baku, modern Azerbaijan, in about 912 so possibly coins from these raids also made their way back to Scandinavia and eventually Western Europe. For more details on the Cuerdale Hoard *see* James Graham-Campbell in High and Hill 220–223
18. Richards 16
19. Ibid 86
20. Zaluckyj 250
21. These names match those of Viking leaders named in the 870s. Unless we assume they are simply mistakes, these may have been men related to the same dynasty: *see* Downham 87 quoting a suggestion by David Dumville.
22. Æthelweard mentions that the ruler of Mercia, Æthelred, also ruled Northumbria so maybe this invasion by Northumbrian forces was an effort to reject his rule there. Æthelred died in the following year.
23. Derek Gore in Labelle and Roffey 64–65
24. Clarkson *Strathclyde* 59
25. Downham 180
26. Clarkson *Æthelflaed* 145
27. Downham 31
28. Carroll, Harrison and Williams 89
29. Simpson in Clarke and Johnson 134
30. Carroll, Harrison and Williams 95
31. This grand title had more symbolic than actual importance. At the time ownership of it alternated between the Southern and Northern Uí Néill. It has been described as being at the time 'a weak institution'. *See* McGettigan 29.
32. *Historia de Sancto Cuthberto* 61–63. The same source states that there were two battles of Corbridge. However, some feel that this is a mistake by the scribe and that one battle has been confusingly reported, ibid 107.
33. Clarkson *Strathclyde* 60
34. Ibid 60–61
35. Ibid 67
36. As quoted in Woolf 146. Woolf also discusses the possible nature and reasons for these acts of symbolic submission
37. Clarkson *Strathclyde* 72
38. Clarkson *Æthelflaed* 161. Richards 33 suggests that there are about 850 place names ending in the Scandinavian '-by' in England with by far the heaviest concentration in the Danelaw: 220 in Lincolnshire and 210 in Yorkshire, especially around the Vale of York.
39. Adams 102
40. It is not clear whether Sitriuc was Ragnall's brother or cousin. *See* Livingston 9.
41. Carroll, Harrison and Williams 83
42. Wolff 148
43. Foot 53
44. *See* footnote 8, 217 Hill: *The Age of Athelstan*...
45. Downham 7. Many examples of these alliance-building tools can be found throughout this book.
46. Foot 92
47. Ibid 103

48. Ibid 111. Scholarly opinion now suggests that the poem was written on Æthelstan's later accession to the throne, which in many ways makes more logical sense
49. *Orkneyinga Saga* 26
50. Ferguson 187
51. Alderney official guide, 25
52. *Les noms de personnes scandinavies en Normandie de 911 à 1066. See* footnote 1, Jones 230
53. *See* Signe Horn Fuglesang in Clarke and Johnson 28
54. Randsborg 134
55. Ferguson 28
56. Jones 164–165, *Ibn Fadlān* 46–55
57. Hudson 31

8 Nation-building

1. *Ragnar Lodbrok* 70
2. E.g. in the *Tale of Ragnar's Sons, Ragnar Lodbrok* 70
3. *Jómsvíkings Saga* 39–41. The saga is hopelessly out in its dating here. It says that Cnut was killed in a raid during the reign of Æthelstan, who died in 939: Gorm died around 958. The details given in the *Sagas of Ragnar Lodbrok,* 70–71 are very similar: both mention a battle being fought near Scarborough and the submission of many of those living in Yorkshire to the raiders. They both mention Cnut being killed in a surprise attack when the raiding army was relaxing, bathing and without their armour.
4. *Landnámabók* 53
5. Ibid
6. The Reverend T. Ellwood, the nineteenth-century translator of the *Landnámabók,* noted a number of similarities between the lore of Iceland and that of his native region, Cumbria.
7. *See Landnámabók* 137 for reference to such an event.
8. Griffiths 65
9. *Landnámabók* 160
10. Eriksen et al, 21
11. Jones 93
12. In Carroll, Harrison and Williams 33
13. Woolf 151
14. Probably the king of Strathclyde. Some contemporary accounts mention an Owain of Gwent being there but no man of that name is known from other records. On the other hand, there was an Owain of Strathclyde and convincing arguments have been made for his involvement rather than 'Owain of Gwent'. *See* Downham 165.
15. Clarkson *Strathclyde* 83
16. *See* e.g. Livingston 12
17. Kelly in Clarke and Johnson 70. Kelly presents multiple examples of possible *longphuirt* in Ireland.
18. Not everyone agrees that the reception was so positive. *See* Livingston 15.
19. *See* Zaluckyj 264
20. Hill *The Age of Athelstan...* 57. That said, there is little evidence that the Welsh of modern Wales were part of the anti-Anglo-Saxon alliance at Brunanburh.
21. Foot 170

22. Livingston 20 and 49
23. Ibid 63
24. In Jones 238. Alex Woolf's personal translation of this passage ends with the memorable phrase how 'nobles eager for glory got a country' – *see* Woolf 173
25. Hill *The Age of Athelstan* ... 37
26. Hill *Anglo-Saxons* 84
27. *See* Livingston 18–20. However, the circumstantial nature of the evidence should be noted. There is no 'smoking gun' e.g. in the form of archaeology to enable us to state with confidence where the battle was. For more detailed discussion of the location of Brunanburh, *see* the essay by Paul Cavill, 327–349 in Livingston.
28. Clarkson *Strathclyde* 92–100. Michael Wood, in his BBC series *King Alfred and the Anglo-Saxons,* suggested somewhere off the Great North Road in Yorkshire. *See also* Hill, *The Age of Athelstan...* Chapter 7.
29. Foot 115
30. Ibid 116
31. An example of how these Anglo-Saxon monarchs are overlooked can be found in the numbering system applied to English kings. 'Edward I' is the name normally given to the king of England from 1272–1307, ignoring the fact that there were three Anglo-Saxon 'King Edwards' before him.
32. *See* Lesley Abrams, *Edgar and the Men of the Danelaw,* in Scragg, Chapter 8.
33. Woolf 174.
34. Such are particularly noticeable in Derbyshire, Nottinghamshire and much of Yorkshire. Hundreds remained in Durham, east Yorkshire and East Anglia. *See* Hadley 89–90.
35. Carroll, Harrison and Williams 123
36. Downham 111
37. McGettigan 44
38. Hudson 26
39. *See Erik Bloodaxe – Axed?* by Clare Downham in *Medieval Scandinavia* 14 (2004), 51–78. *See also* Downham 115–120 and Michael Wood 164.
40. Armit 188
41. Ibid 188–193
42. Ibid 194
43. Summarised by Clare Downham in Clarke and Johnson 192
44. Ibid 194–5
45. Ibid 196
46. Downham 183
47. Christiansen 60

9 Harald Bluetooth

1. Text 'E' of the *ASC*. This version derives from Peterborough and has more information on events in the north of England than others. Some historians think that the several mentions of 'Erik' during these years might mean that there is more than one Erik involved; *see* Downham, *Erik Blood-Axe – Axed?*
2. *ASC* Version D. He also stopped witnessing charters between 936 and 941, suggesting that he may have been involved with a faction opposed to the West Saxon dynasty during this period: *see* Hadley 51.
3. *Orkneyinga Saga* 33

4. *See* Downham 122. Deira was an ancient Celtic kingdom that survived in the region of York until the seventh century. The name was not commonly used in the tenth century, which creates suspicion about the reliability of the reference. However, place name evidence from Normandy at around this time also hints at the possible arrival of political Viking exiles from England.
5. Carroll, Harrison and Williams 127. *See also* Richards 105.
6. *Jómsvíkings Saga* 30–35
7. Adam of Bremen, 79, suggests that Poppo was an envoy sent to the Swedish king Erik the Victorious rather than Harald Bluetooth.
8. *See* Jones 117, footnote 1
9. Adam of Bremen 56
10. Carroll, Harrison and Williams 114
11. Lavelle Æthelred 60
12. Adam of Bremen 49
13. Ibid 190. The translation specifically refers to these people as 'Vikings' though Adam notes that in his language they were called Ascomanni.
14. *Jómsvíkings Saga* 42
15. Ibid 43
16. McGettigan 82–83
17. Magnusson 65. *See also* Jones 177. The statistic on infant mortality comes from Eriksen 97, quoting Gräslund, 1980.
18. Jones 7
19. The name suggests Gaelic ancestry too (mac being Gaelic for 'son') so perhaps there was some intermarrying taking place. Maccus is also the name of a character in the recent *Pirates of the Caribbean* films. This would seem very appropriate given the career of the original Viking holder of the name.
20. Hudson 25, 78
21. The *Brut y Tywysogíon* records a raid on 'Mona' in this year.
22. Woolf 207
23. Ibid 213
24. Considered the most likely location for Rechru though Rathlin Island has also been suggested: *see* Adams 24.
25. Downham 55
26. Ibid 50
27. Ibid 124
28. Clarkson *Strathclyde* 122
29. Hudson 30

10 Conflict and Adventure

1. Clarke and Johnson 24
2. Smyth 77 quoting some edited annals assembled by J. O'Donovan (1860).
3. Wolff 214–215
4. Downham 52
5. Ibid 53
6. Downham 186
7. Wolff 218
8. Downham 228
9. In McGettigan 46
10. E.g. Lavelle and Roffey 123 following Sawyer in 'The Two Viking Ages of Britain' in *Medieval Scandinavia* 2 (1969)

11. Lavelle and Roffey 124
12. The actual appellation is Æthelred Unraed, a clever pun around his name: a literal translation would be 'noble counsel, no counsel', a critique by those who felt he had been poorly advised; particularly the 'C' (Abingdon) version of the ASC.
13. Lavelle: Æthelred 10
14. Wolff 218
15. Lavelle: Æthelred 52–53
16. Norton 176
17. Lavelle Æthelred 61
18. Harrison 17
19. Lavelle Æthelred 63
20. Adam of Bremen 72
21. Bolton *Cnut the Great* 39
22. *Jómsvikings Saga* 51 and after
23. *Encomium* li
24. Adam of Bremen 72. Although Harald's tomb remains in Roskilde Cathedral, his remains have been lost: when excavated, it was found to be empty. The current brick-built cathedral long post-dates Harald's time.
25. Hollander 14
26. *Orkneyinga Saga* 37
27. Hudson 117
28. The evidence is inconclusive. Although the Winchester version of the ASC says that he was at Maldon, the famous poem on the subject is silent on the point. But one is inclined to be led by the greater likelihood of historical accuracy in the ASC than in a praise poem.
29. *See* Lavelle Æthelstan 72
30. The surviving portion of the poem can be found in full in Alexander.
31. Adam of Bremen 75
32. Ibid 80–81
33. Carroll, Harrison and Williams 63
34. Not all historians think that Óláfr was baptised at Andover: some suggest that he was only confirmed there after his baptism elsewhere: *see* Lavelle and Roffey 128.
35. ASC for 993/4
36. Jones 163; Eriksen et al 22
37. *See* Lavelle Æthelred 75
38. Niels Lund, quoted in Lavelle Æthelred 76
39. Clarkson *Strathclyde* 127–129
40. *See* e.g. Lavelle Æthelred 97–101
41. *The Life of King Edward* 5. The biblical basis of this quote is from *Hebrews* 1:8. *Adam* of Bremen 81
42. Adam of Bremen 81
43. Ibid 82
44. Ibid
45. In Wilson 132
46. *Landnámabók* 39
47. *See* Ferguson 302–306
48. Wahlgren 75
49. Adam of Bremen 218 suggests that the island got its name from the fact that the people were green from the salt water.

50. Wahlgren 76
51. Ibid 26
52. Wilson 81
53. Wahlgren 15
54. *The Vinland Saga* 35
55. Ibid 31–33
56. Vinland was referred to by Adam of Bremen. He suggested that it took its name from the wild vines producing excellent wine (Adam of Bremen 219). This is an implausible characteristic for Newfoundland. which is often regarded as being synonymous with Vinland.
57. Introduction to *The Vinland Sagas* xv. *See also* Ferguson 293.
58. Some time before the sagas were written up, the chronicler William of Newburgh was active. In an account he wrote of a revenant visitation at Melrose Abbey, the body of the cause of supernatural attacks was exhumed and burned.
59. So we are told by *The Greenlanders' Saga*. However, *Erik the Red's Saga* states that there were three ships with 140 men in total.
60. Wahlgren 93
61. Although accurate estimates of the population in Greenland in 1000 are impossible to make, a figure of about 2,000–2,500 settlers has been proposed; *see* Wahlgren 153. This left very few spare settlers to go round for expansion into North America.
62. Wahlgren discusses the location of Vinland; *see* Chapters 8 and 9 in particular.
63. Introduction to *The Vinland Sagas* 35

11 The North Sea Empire

1. *Poetic Edda* 52
2. Æthelings included not only the sons of a ruling monarch but also other members of his family such as brothers, uncles, etc.
3. For further evidence of Scandinavian teeth filing *see* Loe et al 213.
4. Quoted in Ibid, 10
5. Lavelle Æthelred 103
6. Norton 70
7. Ibid 171
8. Lavelle Æthelred 117
9. Hill *Anglo-Saxons* 36
10. Lavelle Æthelred 152
11. Ibid 154 quoting M. K. Lawson. *See also* Ferguson 345–346.
12. *See* Bartlett 89
13. Bolton *Cnut the Great* 60
14. The works of John of Worcester were once ascribed to another cleric called Florence. Recently many historians have suggested that Florence's role has been significantly overstated to the detriment of John's part as an author.
15. *See* Ann Williams in Lavelle and Roffey 145. Her chapter in this work entitled *Thorkell the Tall and the Bubble Reputation: The Vicissitudes of Fame* is an excellent discussion and summary of Thorkell's career
16. *Encomium* 11
17. Lavelle Æthelred 160
18. Thietmar 337
19. Urry 82, 130

20. *Encomium* 13
21. A thirteenth-century manuscript shows Edmund running Sveinn through with a spear
22. Bolton *The Empire of Cnut* 11
23. Thietmar 333, *Encomium* 15
24. *See* Bolton *Cnut the Great* 33 for a summary.
25. Ibid 68
26. *Encomium* 15
27. Adam of Bremen 76. He shortly afterwards describes how a Saxon knight called 'Heriward' trapped the Viking army by leading them into a swamp which sounds very similar to the actions of Hereward the Wake in England a few years before Adam wrote – was he getting his countries and events mixed up?
28. Hill *Anglo-Saxons* 38. John of Worcester suggests that the hostages 'merely' had their nostrils slit.
29. *Encomium* 19
30. In Whitelock 855–859
31. McGettigan 90–91
32. Bartlett 154
33. *Orkneyinga Saga* 36–37
34. Griffiths 13
35. McGettigan 25
36. *See* Clarke and Johnson 256
37. In Magnusson 16
38. Quoted in McGettigan 98
39. Clarke and Johnson 15 Note 111
40. Details from McGettigan 105–107
41. Adam of Bremen, 91, gives the incredible figure of 'a thousand large ships for this invasion fleet'. He, more plausibly, noted that it was a three-day voyage from Denmark to England.
42. *Encomium* 21
43. Downham 133
44. Ibid 190
45. Ibid 185
46. *Encomium* 17
47. Adam of Bremen 91
48. Wilson 74
49. Quoted in Loe et al 12
50. Wahlgren 48
51. H.B. Clark in Keen 44
52. For further information *see* Gareth Williams in Loe et al 214–224
53. Harrison 12–13
54. In Hill *Anglo-Saxons* 43
55. For further information, *see* Ann Williams in Lavelle and Roffey Chapter 11; *A Place in the Country: Orc of Abbotsbury and Tole of Tolpuddle, Dorset.*
56. Ibid 159
57. Bolton *The Empire of Cnut...* 67
58. H.B. Clarke in Keen 42
59. Thietmar 335–336
60. O'Brien 104
61. Ibid 19

62. O'Brien 20
63. Bolton *The Empire of Cnut* ... 87
64. Lavelle and Roffey 18. *Eddic* poetry was anonymous while *skaldic* was written by known *skalds*. *Skaldic* poetry tended to have more complex metre and more intricate word choices. In practice there was a great deal of overlap between the two. See *Prose Edda* x.
65. Hudson 31
66. *The Life of King Edward* 6
67. Bolton *Cnut the Great* 87
68. *See* especially Bolton *The Empire of Cnut...* Chapter 4 for a discussion of Cnut's relations with the English Church.
69. This is the opinion of Simon Keynes in Rumble 84.
70. *See* Bolton *The Empire of Cnut* 15–19
71. Bolton *Cnut the Great* 87
72. These were mentioned in the later works of 'Florence' of Worcester. Ælfgar had clearly already developed a reputation for double-dealing by the time that the cleric of Worcester wrote, though this may be because his son, Beorhtric, had fallen out of favour with William the Conqueror, which would not have helped the family's standing. *See* also Bartlett 148 and Bolton *Cnut the Great* 86.
73. Bolton *Cnut the Great* 87
74. *See* Hudson 50
75. Bolton *Cnut the Great* 64

12 Emperors, Saints and Legends

1. Adam of Bremen 211
2. Bartlett 218
3. McGettigan 88
4. Adam of Bremen 109
5. Williams xiii
6. Ibid 369
7. Webb 8–10
8. Wulfstan had been the first man to write of the *Dena lagu,* which translates as 'the law of the Danes' though it is more often referred to as the 'Danelaw' in modern times: *see* Hadley 71.
9. Hudson 150
10. Bolton *Cnut the Great* 163–167
11. Under the *ASC* 'E' version for 1028
12. The identity of both Maalbaethe and Echmarcach form a significant part of the discussion in Chapter 3 of Hudson.
13. Woolf 246
14. Hudson 74–75
15. Downham 175
16. The chroniclers are contradictory in their dates; some say that Carham was fought in 1016, others in 1018. They also disagree over who the leader of the Northumbrian force was; either Earl Uhtred, who the *Anglo-Saxon Chronicles* say died in 1016; or his successor Eadwulf Cudel ('Cuttlefish'). *See* Clarkson *Strathclyde* 135–137
17. Clarkson *Strathclyde* 144
18. Hudson 55

19. Ibid 57
20. *See* Clarke in Clarke and Johnson 262–3
21. Ibid 266–267
22. *Guta Saga* xxxviii. Akergarn was later called St Olofsholm.
23. Ibid 9
24. Ibid 11. The saga is in effect mainly a short history of the Christianisation of Gotland.
25. Adam of Bremen 97
26. Ibid 94
27. Ibid 96
28. Ibid 98
29. See Ferguson 374
30. Hudson, 75–76, argues compellingly that it was a subsequent ruler of Dublin, Murchad, who was Guthorm's opponent. Murchad was the son of the man who ejected Echmarcach from Dublin, the king of Leinster, Diarmait.
31. *See* Chapter 4 Hudson
32. With the arrival of a Scandinavian king and to some extent Scandinavian systems, those who had previously been called ealdormen increasingly came to be 'earls', a derivative of the Scandinavian 'jarl'.
33. Bolton *Cnut the Great* 175
34. Ibid 186
35. Ferguson 358
36. Hill *Anglo-Saxons* 73
37. *See* Martin Biddle and Birthe Kjølbye-Biddle: *Danish Royal Burials in Winchester: Cnut and his Family,* Chapter 12 in Lavelle and Roffey for more detailed discussion.
38. *Encomium* 41–43
39. *Orkneyinga Saga* 61–62. The saga is confusing around the chronology of these events. It says they happened during the reign of Harthacnut but also that at the time he was still in Denmark. Perhaps the events described may have happened during the short reign of Harold Harefoot?
40. Adam of Bremen 108
41. Introduction to *King Harald's Saga* 33
42. Ibid 30
43. A reputation shaped by the later Icelandic saga writer Thjodolf Arnorsson whose words were quoted by Snorri Sturluson. *See King Harald's Saga* 46
44. Ibid 48
45. A portrait of Zoë can still be seen in Hagia Sofia in the shape of a magnificent mosaic of her which is one of the treasures of this stunning building. The mosaic represents something of a potted history of Zoë's marital adventures; each time a husband died, his image next to her in the mosaic was replaced by the latest spouse.
46. *King Harald's Saga* 51 *see* especially footnote 2
47. Ibid 52–58. The story of the ruse involving Harald's funeral appeared recently in a TV series, *Vikings* (Octagon Films and Take 5 Productions) though here it is Ragnar Lodbrok who acts out the trick. Viking legends continue to develop.
48. *See* footnote 2 in *King Harald's Saga* 58
49. *King Harald's Saga* 62
50. Ibid footnote 1

51. Ibid 68
52. Ibid 74. This rather macabre practice was not unique for the times; similar treatment was given to the remains of St Edmund in England.
53. Ibid 78
54. Ibid 79
55. Adam of Bremen 124
56. *King Harald's Saga* 79
57. Ibid
58. Ibid 80
59. Ibid 92
60. For reasons of space, this account is only a summary of these turbulent years in Orkney. More details can be found in the *Orkneyinga Saga* 40–76.

13 Harald Hardrada and the End of an Age

1. *The Life of King Edward* 7
2. Clarkson *Strathclyde* 155: it is a good theory which, although it cannot be conclusively proved, fits well with the limited surviving evidence.
3. Hudson 80
4. Ibid 95
5. Adam of Bremen 128
6. Wood 149: the writer estimates that the force may have consisted of as many as 12,000 men.
7. Ibid 155
8. Ibid 157
9. Hill *Anglo-Saxons* 47
10. Clarke and Johnson 20
11. Wood 178 and 133
12. Adam of Bremen 192
13. Williams 13
14. Adam of Bremen 203–208
15. Ferguson 376. The town of Eskilstuna in Sweden still commemorates his memory.
16. Adam of Bremen 211–215

Epilogue

1. Rex 41–42
2. Wood 204–205
3. Rex 43
4. Not to be confused with a contemporary, Thorkell of Arden, Sheriff of Warwickshire, who successfully made the transition to being a supporter of the new Norman regime: Rex 231
5. Ibid 70 for these and other examples.
6. Hudson 136
7. Academics have argued that the work was influenced specifically by writings such as those of Asser on Alfred. Ibid 134
8. Ibid 132
9. Introduction to *King Harald's Saga* 16.

10. Marshall 44
11. Clarkson *Strathclyde* 64
12. Wahlgren 148
13. *See* introduction to *The Vinland Sagas* xvi
14. Wahlgren 71
15. Adam of Bremen 217
16. Ibid 228–229
17. Introduction to *King Harald's Saga* 18
18. Ibid 13
19. Bartlett 136
20. In introduction to *King Harald's Saga* 23
21. Carroll, Harrison and Williams 65
22. Introduction to *King Harald's Saga* 25
23. Introduction to *King Harald's Saga*, 29
24. Loyn 13
25. For more detail on saga 'types', *see* e.g. Waggoner xi–xv.
26. Saxo Grammaticus 255
27. *Orkneyinga Saga* 188, Pickering and Foster, 18–23
28. Prebble 56
29. Griffiths 45
30. In Livingston 394
31. Ferguson 5
32. The replica *knörr* was modelled on that found in Roskilde Fjord in 1962 and was under the command of the well-named Ragnar Thorseth.
33. For a brief summary of its inaccuracies, *see* Wahlgren 100–104
34. Smyth 77
35. See Livingston 404–405
36. Clarke and Johnson 21
37. In fact, it has been conjectured that the 'Danes' and Normans combined only caused a tenth as much material damage to the monasteries as Henry VIII did. *See* Gneuss 10
38. Young 132

Bibliography

Primary sources

Alexander, Michael (translated): *Beowulf,* Penguin Books Ltd., Harmondsworth etc., 1973

Alexander, Michael (translated): *The Earliest English Poems,* Penguin Books Ltd., Harmondsworth etc., 1970 reprint

Allott, Stephen: *Alcuin of York – his life and letters,* Williams Sessions Ltd., York, 1987 reprint

Arnold, Thomas (edited): *Memorials of St Edmund's Abbey,* Her Majesty's Stationery Office, London, 1890

Barlow, Frank (edited): *The Life of King Edward the Confessor,* Thomas Nelson and Sons Ltd., London et al, 1962

Byock, Jesse L (translated): *Snorri Sturluson – The Prose Edda,* Penguin, London et al, 2005

Campbell, A (edited): *The Chronicle of Æthelweard,* Thomas Nelson and Sons Ltd., London et al, 1962

Campbell, Alistair (translated): *Encomium Emmae Reginae,* Cambridge University Press, London, 1998

Cross, Samuel and Sherbowizt-Wetzor, Olgerd (translated and edited): *The Russian Primary Chronicle,* Medieval Academy of America, Cambridge, Massachusetts, 1953

Elton, Oliver (translated): *Saxo Grammaticus – The Danish History,* Bravo Ebooks (originally published 1905, reprint undated)

Elwood, Rev. T. (translated): *Landnámabók – Viking Settlers and Their Customs in Iceland,* Huginn and Muninn Publishing, Port Townsend, 2016

Forester, Thomas (translated): *The Chronicle of Florence of Worcester with the Two Continuations,* Henry G Bohn, London, 1854

Ganz, David: *Einhard and Notker the Stammerer – Two Lives of Charlemagne,* Penguin, London, 2008

Giles, J. A.: *Williams of Malmesbury's Chronicle of the Kings of England,* Henry G Bohn, London, 1847 (reprinted 2012 Forgotten Books)

Greenway, Diana (translated): *Henry of Huntingdon – The History of the English People 1000–1154,* Oxford University Press, Oxford, 2009 edition

Hennessy, William Mac: *Annals of Ulster – Otherwise Annals of Senat; A Chronicle of Irish Affirs* [sic] *From AD 431 to AD 1540, Volume 1,* Forgotten Books, London, undated – originally published HMSO 1887

Hollander, Lee M. (translated): *The Saga of the Jómsvíkings,* University of Texas Press, Austin, 1955

Ithel, The Rev. John Williams ab: *Brut y Tywysogíon; or The Chronicle of the Princes,* Green, Longman and Roberts, London, 1860

Keynes, Simon and Lapidge, Michael (translated): *Alfred the Great – Asser's Life of King Alfred and Other Contemporary Sources,* Penguin, London etc. 2004

Kunz, Keneva (translated): *The Vinland Sagas – The Saga of the Greenlanders and Erik the Red's Saga,* Penguin, London et al, 2008

Lunde, Paul and Stone, Caroline: *Ibn Fadlän and the Land of Darkness – Arab Travellers in the Far North,* Penguin, London etc., 2012

Magnusson, Magnus and Pálsson, Hermann (translated): *King Harald's Saga – Harald Hardrada of Norway (from Snorri Sturluson's Heimskringla),* Penguin, Harmondsworth, 1976

Magnusson, Magnus and Pálsson, Hermann (translated): *Njal's Saga,* Penguin, London et al, 1987

Nelson, Janet L. (translated and annotated): *The Annals of St-Bertin,* Manchester University Press, Manchester and New York, 1991

Pálsson, Hermann and Edwards, Paul: *Orkneyinga Saga – The History of the Earls of Orkney,* Penguin, London et al, 1978

Peel, Christine (edited): *Guta Saga – The History of the Gotlanders,* Viking Society for Northern Research Text Series, University College London, 1999

Reuter, Timothy (translated and annotated) *The Annals of Fulda – Ninth-Century Histories Volume II,* Manchester University Press, Manchester, 1992

Scholz, Bernhard Walter: *Carolingian Chronicles,* University of Michigan, 1970

South, Ted Johnson (edited): *Historia de Sancto Cuthberto,* DS Brewer, Cambridge, 2002

Stokes, Whitley: *The Annals of Tigernach,* Librairie Emile Bouillon, Paris, 1896

Sturlason, Snorre [sic][translated S. Laing]: *Heimskringla – The Norse Sagas,* Edinburgh, 1844 (modern undated reprint)

Swanton, Michael (translated and edited): *The Anglo-Saxon Chronicles,* Phoenix Press, London, 2003

Tschau, Francis J. (translated): *Adam of Bremen – History of the Archbishops of Hamburg-Bremen,* Columbia University Press, New York, 2002

Van Houts, Elisabeth M.C. (edited and translated): *The Gesta Normannorum Ducum of William of Jumièges, Orderic Vitalis and Robert of Torigni, Volume 1,* Oxford Medieval Texts, Clarendon Press, Oxford, 2003 reprint

Waggoner, Ben (translated): *The Sagas of Ragnar Lodbrok,* New Haven, 2009

Warner, David A. (translated and annotated): *Ottonian Germany – The Chronicon of Thietmar of Merseburg,* Manchester University press, Manchester and New York, 2001

Whitelock, Dorothy (edited): *English Historical Documents c500–1042,* Eyre & Spottiswoode, London, 1955

Secondary sources

Adams, Max: Ælfred's Britain – War and Peace in the Viking Age, Head of Zeus Ltd., London, 2017

Armit, Ian: *The Archaeology of Skye and the Western Isles,* Edinburgh University Press, Edinburgh, 2005

Bibliography

Balbirnie, Cameron: *The Vikings at Home* in *The Story of Vikings and Anglo-Saxons – Migrations, invasions and the battle for Britain,* BBC

Barlow, Frank: *The Godwins,* Routledge, Abingdon, 2003

Bartlett, W.B.: *King Cnut and the Viking Conquest of England 1016,* Amberley, Stroud, 2016

Berend, Norma: *Christianity and the Rise of Christian Monarchy: Scandinavia, Central Europe and Rūs' c.900–1200,* Cambridge University Press, Cambridge, 2007

Biddle, Martin and Kjølbye-Biddle, Birthe; *Repton and the Vikings* in *Antiquity,* 66, 1992

Bolton, Timothy: *Cnut the Great,* Yale University Press, New Haven, 2017

Bolton, Timothy: *The Empire of Cnut the Great,* Brill, Leiden, 2009

Brøndsted, Johannes: *The Vikings,* Penguin, London et al, 1980

Carroll, Jayne; Harrison, Stephen H.; and Williams, Gareth: *The Vikings in Britain and Ireland,* The British Museum Press, London, 2014

Carver, Martin (2004): *An Iona of the East: the early medieval monastery at Portmahomack, Tarbat Ness.* Medieval Archaeology. See White Rose reprints: http:// eprints.whiterose.ac.uk/1830/

Carver, Martin: *Portmahomack – Monastery of the Picts,* Edinburgh University Press, 2016

Carver, Martin: *Tarbat's Pictish Sculptors,* University of Aberdeen, 2016

Christiansen, Eric; *The Norsemen in the Viking Age,* Oxford, 2002

Clarke, Howard B. and Johnson, Ruth: *The Vikings in Ireland and Beyond – Before and After the Battle of Clontarf,* Four Courts Press, Portland, 2015

Clarkson, Tim: *Æthelflaed – The Lady of the Mercians,* Birlinn, Edinburgh, 2018

Clarkson, Tim: *Strathclyde and the Anglo-Saxons in the Viking Age,* Birlinn, Edinburgh, 2016 reprint

Dales, Douglas: *Alcuin – His Life and Legacy,* James Clarke & Co, Cambridge, 2012

Downham, Clare; *Viking Kings of Britain and Ireland – The Dynasty of Ivarr to A.D. 1014,* Dunedin Academic Press, Edinburgh, 2012 edition

Eriksen, Marianne Hem; Pedersen Unn; Rundberget, Bernt; Axelsen, Irmelin; Berg, Heidi Lund (edited): *Viking Worlds – Things, Spaces and Movement,* Oxbow Books, Oxford and Philadelphia, 2015

Evans, Nicholas: *A Historical Introduction to the Northern Picts,* University of Aberdeen, 2014

Ferguson, Robert: *The Hammer and the Cross,* Penguin, London et al, 2010

Foot, Sarah: *Æthelstan – The First King of England,* Yale University Press, New Haven and London, 2011

Fossier, Robert (edited), Sondheimer, Janet (translated): *The Cambridge Illustrated History of the Middle Ages Volume 1, 350–950,* Cambridge University Press, Cambridge et al, 1989

Gabriel, Judith: *Among the Norse Tribes – The Remarkable World of ibn Fadlan,* in *Aramco World,* Volume 50, Number 6 (November/December 1999)

Gneuss, Helmut: *Ælfric of Eynsham – His Life, Times and Writings,* Old English Newsletter Subsidia 34, West Michigan University, 2009

Griffiths, David: *Vikings of the Irish Sea,* The History Press, Stroud, 2010

Hadley, D.M. *The Vikings in England – Settlement, Society and Culture,* Manchester University Press, Manchester, 2006

Harris, Oliver; Cobb, Hannah; Gray, Helena; Richardson, Phil and others; *Ardnamurchan Transitions Project, Season Six, 2011: Archaeological Excavations Data Structure Report*

Harrison, Mark: *Viking Hersir 793–1066 AD,* Osprey, Oxford, 2008 edition

Higham, N.J. and Hill, D.H. (edited): *Edward the Elder 899–924*, Routledge, London and New York, 2001

Hill, Paul: *The Age of Athelstan – Britain's Forgotten History*, The History Press, Stroud, 2004

Hill, Paul: *The Anglo-Saxons at War 780–1066*, Pen & Sword, Barnsley, 2014

Hill, Paul: *The Viking Wars of Alfred the Great*, Pen & Sword, Barnsley, 2008

Hilts, Carly: 'A prey to pagan people'? *– The Viking impact on Britain and Ireland*, *Current Archaeology*, January 2015

Hindley, Geoffrey: *A Brief History of the Anglo-Saxons*, Robinson, 2006

Hinton, David: *Discover Dorset – Saxons and Vikings*, The Dovecote Press, Wimborne, 1998

Hudson, Benjamin: *Irish Sea Studies 900–1200*, Four Courts Press, Portland, 2006

Jones, Gwyn: *A History of the Vikings*, Book Club Associates London, 1973

Keen, Maurice: *Medieval Warfare – A History*, Oxford University Press, BCA, 1999

Laing, Lloyd and Jennifer: *The Picts and the Scots*, Sutton Publishing, Stroud, 2004

Lavelle, Ryan: *Aethelred II King of the English*, The History Press, Stroud, 2008 edition

Lavelle, Ryan and Roffey, Simon (edited): *Danes in Wessex – The Scandinavian Impact on Southern England c.800–c.1100*, Oxbow Books, Oxford, 2016

Lavelle, Ryan: *Fortifications in Wessex c.800–1066*, Osprey, Oxford, 2003

Livingston, Michael (edited): *The Battle of Brunanburh – A Casebook*, University of Exeter Press, Exeter, 2011

Loe, Louis; Boyle, Angela; Webb, Helen and Score, David: *Given to the Ground – A Viking Age Mass Grave on Ridgeway Hill, Weymouth*, Dorset Natural History and Archaeological Society Monograph Series: No. 22, 2014

Loyn, H.R: *The Vikings in Britain*, B.T. Batsford Ltd., London, 1977

Magnusson, Magnus: *The Vikings*, The History Press, Stroud, 2016 (first published in 1980)

Marshall, Rosalind K.: *Columba's Iona – A New History*, Sandstone Press Ltd., Dingwall, 2013

McGettigan, Darren: *The Battle of Clontarf – Good Friday 1014*, Four Courts Press, Dublin, 2013

Meehan, Bernard: *The Book of Kells – An Illustrated Introduction to the Manuscript in Trinity College Dublin*, Thames & Hudson, London, 2015 edition

Nelson, Janet L.: *Charles the Bald*, Routledge, London and New York, 1992

Newman, Roger Chatterton: *Brian Boru – King of Ireland*, Mercier Press, Cork, 2011

Norton, Elizabeth: *Elfrida – The First Crowned Queen of England*, Amberley, Stroud, 2014

O'Brien, Harriet: *Queen Emma and the Vikings*, Bloomsbury, London, 2006

Oliver, Neil: *Vikings – A History*, Weidenfeld and Nicolson, London, 2012

Parker, Philip: *The Northmen's Fury – A History of the Viking World*, Vintage, London, 2015

Peers, Chris: *Offa and the Mercian Wars*, Pen and Sword Military, Barnsley, 2017

Pickering, Rachel and Foster, Sally: *Maeshowe and the Heart of Neolithic Orkney*, Historic Scotland, 2018

Prebble, John: *The Lion in the North*, Book Club Associates, London 1971

Price T. Douglas; Peets, Jüri; Allmäe, Raili; Maldre, Liina and Oras, Ester: *Isotopic Provenancing of the Salme ship burials in Pre-Viking Age Estonia* In. Antiquity (2016), Vol 90, pp. 1022 – 1037

Randsborg, Klavs: *The Viking Age in Denmark – The Formation of a State*, Duckworth, London, 1980

Rex, Peter: *The English Resistance – The Underground War Against the Normans*, Amberley, Stroud, 2014

Bibliography

Richards, Julian D.: *Viking Age England*, Batsford, London, 1994

Ringstedt, Nils: *The Birka Chamber-Graves: Economic and Social Aspects – A Quantitative Analysis*, in *Current Swedish Archaeology, Volume 5, 1997*

Roesdahl, Else: *The Vikings*, Penguin, London et al, 1998

Rumble, Alexander R.: *The Reign of Cnut – King of England, Denmark and Norway*, Leicester University Press, London and New York, 1999

Sawyer, Peter: *The Oxford Illustrated History of the Vikings*, Oxford University Press, Oxford, 2001

Scragg, Donald (edited): *Edgar – King of the English 959–975*, Boydell Press, Woodbridge, 2008

Sindbæk, Soren M.: *A northern emporium – Unearthing the beginning of the Viking age in Ribe, World Archaeology*, volume 90, August/September 2018

Sjovold, Thorleif: *The Viking Ships in Oslo*, Universitetets Oldsaksamling, 2016

Smyth, Alfred P: *Alfred the Great*, Oxford University Press, Oxford, 1995

States of Alderney Recreation and Tourism Committee: *Alderney Channel Islands – An Official Guide*, 1980, 5th edition

Stenton, Sir Frank: *Anglo Saxon England*, Oxford University Press, Oxford et al, 1988 edition

Urry, William: *Thomas Becket – His Last Days*, Sutton Publishing, Stroud, 1999

Wahlgren, Erik: *The Vikings and America*, Thames and Hudson, London, 2000

Webb, Matilda: *The Churches and Catacombs of Early Christian Rome*, Sussex Academic Press, Eastbourne, 2010

Williams, Hywel: *Emperor of the West – Charlemagne and the Carolingian Empire*, Quercus, London, 2010

Wilson, David: *The Viking and their Origins – Scandinavia in the First Millennium*, Thames & Hudson, London, 1970

Woolf, Alex: *From Pictland to Alba 789–1070*, Edinburgh University Press, Edinburgh, 2007

Wood, Harriet Harvey: *Edward the Elder and the Making of England*, Sharpe Books, 2018

Wood, Harriet Harvey: *The Battle of Hastings – The Fall of Anglo-Saxon England*, Atlantic Books, London, 2008

Wood, Michael: *In Search of the Dark Ages*, Book Club Associates, 1981

Young, Francis: *Edmund – In Search of England's Lost King*, Tauris, London and New York, 2018

Zaluckyj, Sarah: *Mercia – The Anglo-Saxon Kingdom of Central England*, Logaston Press, Woonton, 2013

Index

Index

Hastings, Battle of 283, 301, 333, 349, 350, 351, 355, 356, 357
Hávamál, Viking poem 262
Hayes-McCoy, GA, historian 293
Head-Ransom, poem 208
Heahmund, bishop of Sherborne 139, 140
Heath Wood, Ingleby, England 143
Hebrides, Scotland 54, 111, 175, 178, 189, 207, 228, 234, 288, 293, 296, 297, 298, 341, 345, 359
- 9th Century Viking rule in 176
- 10th Century Viking activity in 221–223
Hedda Stone, Peterborough 134
Hedeby, Denmark 11, 60, 61, 72, 82, 84, 92, 96, 100, 142, 181, 193, 204, 230, 234, 238, 248, 278, 339, 351
- defences of 77
- developed by King Godfrid 75–76
Heimdallr, Norse god 32, 34
Heimskringla 30, 31, 106, 174, 288, 364, 365
Hel, daughter of Loki 32
Helgi the Lean 32
Helgö, Sweden 11, 23, 71, 77
Helluland 267
Hemming, king of Denmark 78
Hemming, Viking 280
Hemming's Cartulary 286
Henry I, king of France 336
Henry II, king of England 369, 373
Henry IV, Holy Roman Emperor 358
Henry of Huntingdon, chronicler 215, 257
Henry of Saxony, Frankish ruler 164
Henry VIII, king of England 50, 171, 308, 372
Henry, son of Conrad II 318
Hercules 30
Hereberht, ealdorman of Kent 99
Hereford, England 189
heregeld 256
herepaths 279
Hereward 'the Wake' 357
Herodotus, Greek historian 365
hersirs 24, 35
Hertfordshire 168
Hervé, cleric 201
Heversham, England 194
Hexham, England 157, 160

Hiberno-Norse 67, 184, 187, 221, 241, 244, 270, 289, 291, 310, 317, 321, 348, 356
- development of threat in Ireland in early 10th Century 191–194
Hieronymus Bosch, late medieval artist 165
Higbald, bishop of Lindisfarne 50, 52
Hincmar, archbishop of Rheims 118, 140, 160, 161
Hindu Kush 187
Hingston Down, Battle of 88
Historia de Sancto Cuthberto 131, 132, 145, 155, 160, 193
Historia Regum Anglorum 52, 53
History of the Archbishops of Hamburg-Bremen 206
History of the Miracles and Translations of St Philibert 95
Hitler, Adolf 56
Hittites 18
Hjardarholt, Iceland 346
Hjörungavágr, Norway 252
hnefatafl 37
Hod, Norse god 32
Holne, Battle of the 182
Holy River (Helgeå), Battle of 313, 319
Holy Sepulchre, Jerusalem 335
Holyhead, Anglesey 235
Hook Norton, England 188
Horatius, Roman hero 254
Hordaland, Norway 12, 58, 122, 174, 233
Horik I, king of Denmark 79, 87, 88, 89, 94, 95, 96, 116, 117, 148, 180
Horik II, king of Denmark 117, 148
Horn, Iceland 124
Hostage Stone 66
Howth, Ireland 68
Hoxa, North Ronaldsay 178
Hoxne, Battle of 134
Hrafnaflóki; see Flóki Vilgerdarson
Hrani, Viking landholder in Mercia 303
Hring, Strathclyde general 215
Hroald, Viking *jarl* 189
Hrolf; see Rollo
Hrólfr Kraki, early Danish king 78
Hudson, river 271
Huginn and Muninn, Odin's ravens 27
Humber, river 132, 133, 196, 216, 283
Huntingdon, England 163
huscarls 303

Index

Index

Stavanger, Norway 174

Steenstrup, Johannes, Danish
historian 370

Steep Holm, Bristol Channel 56, 189

Stefnir, Icelandic settler 262

Stenton, Frank, historian 70

Stiklestad, Battle of 323, 325, 327, 331,
332, 340, 342

Stockholm Codex Aureus 171

Stockholm, Sweden 23, 25, 37, 38, 71,
75, 171

Stolpe, Hjalmar, archaeologist 71

Storr, Skye 222

Stour, river 162

Strabo, Walafrid, cleric 19, 68, 84

Straits of Gibraltar; see also Pillars of
Hercules 121

Stranraer, Scotland 56

Strath Erin, battle at 185

Strathclyde/Strathclyde Britons
('Welsh') 45, 112, 136, 143, 144, 194,
195, 196, 209, 210, 211, 214, 215,
216, 220, 226, 227, 238, 257, 321, 344

- and Cnut 320

- in pre-Viking Age 44

Stroma, Scottish island 294

Sturlung Age 363

Sturlungar, Icelandic power bloc 364

Sturluson, Snorri, saga writer 27, 30, 31,
38, 106, 175, 178, 259, 286, 319, 326,
331, 335, 340, 343, 349, 366

- life of 362–365

Suffolk, England 162

Súlki, king of Rogaland 174

Sussex, England 273, 280, 331

Sutherland, Scotland 175, 341

Sutton Hoo, England 38, 39, 42, 301

Svartkel, Viking from Caithness 207

Svear; see Swedes

Svein Asleifarson, nobleman 234

Sveinn Estrithsson, king of Denmark 206,
331, 335, 336, 337, 338, 339, 350,
351, 353, 355, 356, 357, 367

Sveinn Forkbeard, king of Denmark 78,
94, 135, 218, 230, 239, 245, 251, 274,
276, 278, 288, 297, 311, 313, 319, 323

- and England in 990s 255–256

- campaign against Harald
Bluetooth 247–250

- campaign against Óláfr
Tryggvason 259–261

- conquest of England 283–284

- death of 286

- views on his Christianity 249

Sveinn the Sacrificer 353

Sveinn, killer of Björn 329

Sveinn, son of Cnut 253, 304, 306, 309,
327, 335

Sverri, king of Norway 290

Sverrir, king of Norway 365

svinfylka, 'swine array' formation 301

Svold, Battle of 260

Swanage, England 151, 155

Swansea, Wales 164

Sweden 10, 11, 12, 13, 15, 17, 19, 20, 24,
25, 35, 38, 58, 67, 73, 125, 148, 180,
206, 207, 231, 275, 298, 315, 336,
351, 366

- Christianisation of 324, 353

- early Irish finds in 22

- early links with Estonia 37

- geography of 14

- links with Gotland 39–40

Swedes/Swedish 11, 14, 19, 21, 30, 38,
40, 42, 83, 125, 181, 205, 231, 259,
302, 303, 313, 323, 352, 370

- pre Viking Age activity of in Latvia 39

Świętosława, Wendish princess 248

sword of Carlus 322

Swordle Bay, Scotland 105

Symeon of Durham, chronicler 52, 53,
133, 216

Tacitus, Roman historian 19, 28

Tadcaster, England 348

Tajikistan 113

Tale of Ragnar's Sons 111, 135, 143, 205

Tamar, river 88

Tamworth, England 191, 197

Tanngnoist, goat 29

Tanngrisnir, goat 29

Tanum, Bohuslän, Sweden 18

Tara, Ireland 43, 220, 244, 273, 295

- Viking attack on 240

Tarbat Ness, Scotland 342

Tarbat Peninsula, Scotland 66, 67

Tarbert 74

Teige Mor 291

Temhnen, anchorite 86

Tempsford, England 190

Tettenhall, Battle of 188, 189, 191

Tewkesbury Chronicles 308

Tewkesbury, England 308

Thames, river 137, 138, 159, 162, 163,
165, 166, 167, 182, 281, 283, 329

Index